WebSphere® Application Server Bible

WebSphere® Application Server Bible

Bryon Kataoka, David Ramirez, and Alan Sit

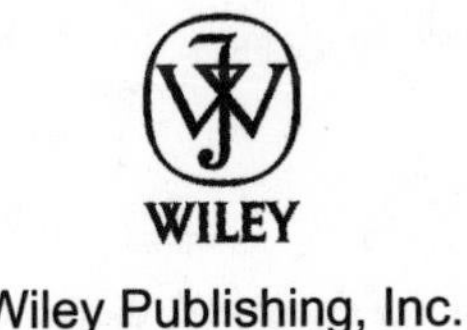

Wiley Publishing, Inc.

WebSphere® Application Server Bible

Published by
Wiley Publishing, Inc.
10475 Crosspoint Boulevard
Indianapolis, IN 46256
www.wiley.com

Published simultaneously in Canada

ISBN: 0-7645-4896-4

Manufactured in the United States of America.

10 9 8 7 6 5 4 3 2 1

1B/ST/QX/QS/IN

For general information on our other products and services or to obtain technical support, please contact our Customer Care Department within the U.S. at (800) 762-2974, outside the U.S. at (317) 572-3993 or fax (317) 572-4002.

Wiley also publishes its books in a variety of electronic formats. Some content that appears in print may not be available in electronic books.

Library of Congress Control Number: 2001094149

About the Authors

Bryon Kataoka is a principal at Commerce Solutions (`www.commercesolutions.com`). He has numerous IBM certifications and is a Sun-certified Java programmer. He has contributed to multiple VisualAge for Java books and has been a speaker at technical conferences. Bryon helps chair the Northern California/SF WebSphere and Web services users groups. When he is not working, he is making wine, golfing, skiing, or spending time with his family. You can reach him at `bkataoka@commercesolutions.com`.

David Ramirez is a lead solutions developer at Commerce Solutions. He is certified in WebSphere Application Server, WebSphere Studio, DB2 7.1 and VisualAge for Java. David has a B.S. degree in Business Administration with a Management Information Systems option. David also contributes to Commerce Solution's training program and is a mentor/lead developer on most of his assignments. He has also submitted papers for publication. You can reach David at `dramirez@commercesolutions.com`.

Alan Sit is a solutions consultant at Commerce Solutions. He has a B.S. degree in Business Administration with an emphasis in Computer Information Systems. Alan also has a number of IBM certifications including, WebSphere Application Server, WebSphere Studio and VisualAge for Java. A big baseball fan, he enjoys going to the ballpark with his friends whenever he can manage. You can reach Alan at `asit@commercesolutions.com`.

About the Contributors

Gary Chappell is a Java developer with a West Coast-based insurance company. His background includes an MIS degree from the University of Arizona. Gary has been working with Java for the past five years and WebSphere for three years. He is actively involved in the migration effort from WebSphere 3.5.x to 4.x.

Brian Hanson is currently a lead developer for a healthcare organization where his major responsibilities are J2EE application architecture and enterprise security. Brian has designed and developed applications in Java for Web architectures, pervasive devices, XML/XSL, security, and several other J2EE-based technologies. He has B.S. degree in Business Administration with an MIS minor from San Jose State University.

Marcey Rhyne is a Sun-certified programmer for the Java 2 platform and graduate of the University of California at Berkeley. She has developed front-end and middleware software for insurance and utility companies and her own clients. A veteran of the U.S. Coast Guard, Marcey has written research papers used in testimony relating to statistical adjustment of the U.S. Census. She was originally tempted into a career as a programmer in order to make a living in the San Francisco Bay area. These days, Marcey lives in Bend, Oregon, with her best friend, Brian, and their son, Grip, an Australian Cattle Dog.

Credits

Executive Editor
Chris Webb

Senior Project Editor
Jodi Jensen

Development/Copy Editor
Sydney Jones

Technical Editors
Dale Nilsson
Marcey Rhyne

Editorial Manager
Mary Beth Wakefield

Vice President and Executive Group Publisher
Richard Swadley

Vice President and Executive Publisher
Bob Ipsen

Vice President and Publisher
Joseph B. Wikert

Executive Editorial Director
Mary Bednarek

Project Coordinator
Ryan Steffen

Supervisor of Graphics and Design
Shelley Lea

Graphics Specialists
Kelly Hardesty
Rashell Smith

Proofreading
Mary Lagu

Indexing
Johnna VanHoose Dinse
Tom Dinse

Preface

WebSphere Application Server 4.0 represents a monumental step in the right direction for WebSphere 3.*x* users. Since its introduction, WebSphere has been known more for its servlet engine than for its ability to deliver on the J2EE specification. All of that disappeared with WebSphere Application Server 4.0. WebSphere is now Java-certified for J2EE specification v1.2. Since WebSphere 4.0's release in June 2001, WebSphere has gained significant market share and is running neck to neck with BEA WebLogic Server.

WebSphere Application Server 4.0 didn't just stop with J2EE compliance. It goes the extra mile by supporting additional open standards and technologies. Perhaps one of the most exciting technologies included in WebSphere Application Server 4.0 is the capability to develop, publish, and deploy Web services applications, including Universal Description Discovery and Integration (UDDI); Simple Object Access Protocol (SOAP); Web services Description Language (WSDL); and enhanced integration of leading XML technologies.

And version 4 doesn't sacrifice features for performance. You will find improved capabilities for managing high-volume transactions, faster transaction performance, and improved connectivity. The software also ships with some technology previews that, through open standards (J2C), connect and interoperate with some of the leading applications from SAP, PeopleSoft, and IBM's CICS and IMS.

With WebSphere Application Server 4.0, you now have a platform that performs well, is based on open standards, continues to provide for new technologies such as Web services, and offers interoperability with leading applications.

Who Should Read This Book

This book is targeted at administrators, developers, change coordinators, and architects. In J2EE-speak that encompasses the roles of application component provider, application assembler, deployer, and administrator. These are the people who develop enterprise components (EJB, servlets, JavaServer Pages), assemble and configure them, and manage the environments.

WebSphere Application Server Bible shows you how to create, manage, and configure enterprise applications. You explore the user interfaces, the new application tooling, the helpful wizards, and common coding practices that enhance your knowledge and understanding of what it takes to deliver a Web-based enterprise application.

Developers interested in learning how WebSphere Studio Application Developer can increase productivity in creating applications that utilize servlets, JavaServer Pages (JSP), and Enterprise JavaBeans (EJB) will find it all in this book.

If you're a novice or occasional developer, this book also includes chapters on servlets, JavaServer Pages, Enterprise JavaBeans, XML and XSLT, as well as a Web services chapter that covers SOAP, UDDI, and WSDL.

If you are interested in WebSphere certification, you will find information and tips about how to best administer WebSphere as well as learn how to use WebSphere Studio Application Developer.

As an administrator new to WebSphere, you learn the techniques of WebSphere Application Server configuration, deployment, tuning, and troubleshooting. You also learn about some additional tooling that makes remote administration easier with less hassle. Administrators with a WebSphere 3.*x* background learn how the changes in version 4 can make their lives easier.

Hardware and Software Requirements

Version 4.0 of the WebSphere Application Server can be installed on a number of platforms — Win2000, Linux, Solaris, AIX, HP/UX, to name a few. This book is based on a Windows 2000 installation. As with any application server, there are requirements for database connectivity as well as a Web server component. Because WebSphere Application Server Advanced Edition (AE) comes with a Web server — IBM HTTP Server — and a supporting database — IBM DB2 Universal Database — this book walks you through the installation of those components.

Here are the minimum hardware requirements for installing WebSphere Application Server 4.0.3 Advanced Edition (AE):

- *Processor speed:* 500 Mhz pentium
- *Disk capacity:*
  - 200MB disk space for WebSphere Application Server
  - 350MB disk space for IBM DB2 Enterprise Edition
  - 50MB disk space for IBM HTTP Server
  - 135MB disk space for TEMP directory
- *Memory:* More than 128MB RAM
- *Operating System:* Microsoft Windows 2000 Server, Service Pack 1, 128 encryption; Microsoft Windows 2000 Server, Service Pack 1 or Service Pack 2; or Microsoft Windows NT Server Pack 6a
- *WebSphere Product:* IBM WebSphere Application Server V4.0.3, Advanced Edition (AE) or Single Server Edition (ASSE)
- *DB2 Product:* IBM DB2 Universal Database V7.2.1, Enterprise Edition for Windows
- *Web Server Product:* IBM HTTP Server 1.3.19
- *Java Developer Kit:* JDK 1.3 with JDBC 2.0

The AlmostFreeCruise samples and code segments used as examples throughout the book can be found on this book's companion Web site at www.wiley.com/extras. Other samples used in the book are included with WebSphere Application Server. (See the "Companion Web Site" section that follows.)

How This Book Is Organized

Part I, "Planning and Installation," introduces WebSphere and Web Services. After an overview of the product and how the Web works, it goes through the installation steps for various platforms. The discussion then moves to introducing the planning steps necessary to set up a development environment. It shows how to install WSAD, WSSD, and supporting tools.

Part II, "Application Development," is all about development. The flows of the chapters is based on iterative steps to help you prepare and organize, get an understanding of the toolsets, introduce the tool/components, see some code, and try testing/deploying. It starts with servlets, moves to JSP, EJBs, and, finally, ends with XSM/XSLT and Web services.

Part III, "Systems Administration," takes you into the realm of system administration. Although some developers might be familiar with these processes, a system administrator's primary role is to handle these tasks. This part covers the configuration of the Application server and its subparts, along with some troubleshooting in terms of setup problems.

Part IV, "Managing WebSphere," brings the book to a close with a discussion of how to manage the WebSphere Application Server. In this part, we try to ensure that you have a comprehensive understanding of the WebSphere Application Server components and the impact of various topologies. We discuss workload management and failover and the tools that monitor and support them.

Companion Web Site

This book offers a companion Web site from which you can get code examples and the sample applications used in the book, including the AlmostFreeCruise sample application. Each development chapter provides a starting point and a finished product, so you can skip ahead and look at code if you wish.

All the code resides in a single WinZip file that you can download by going to www.wiley.com/extras and selecting the WebSphere Application Server Bible link. After you download the file, named Was4Bible.zip, you can open it and extract the contents by double-clicking it if you have WinZip on your system. If you don't currently have WinZip, you can download an evaluation version from www.winzip.com.

When extracting the files, be sure to use WinZip's default options (confirm that the Use Folder Names option is checked) and extract the (2.8MB) `Was4Bible.zip` file to a drive on your system that has about 3.02MB of available space. The extraction process creates a folder called WAS4Bible. As long as the Use Folder Names option is checked in the Extract dialog box, an entire folder structure is created within the WAS4Bible folder. You see folders arranged by chapter number, and some of those chapter folders contain subfolders.

The text in the book provides you with directions about how to work with the sample files provided in `Was4Bible.zip`, but some folders also contain a `readme.txt` file. You can open these `readme.txt` files using NotePad. Just be sure to turn on Notepad's Word Wrap feature by selecting Format⇨Word Wrap (or select Edit⇨Word Wrap if you're using an older version of NotePad) from the menu to ensure that you can view all the text.

Additional install programs are available for the Web services toolkit and UDDI. The WebSphere 4.0.3 service pack and InfoCenter are also available for download.

Conventions

Here are some conventions that we use throughout to help you use the book more efficiently:

- **Bold** text indicates user input — something that you should type.
- A special `monofont` typeface is used throughout the book to indicate code, a configuration keyword, a filename or pathname, or an Internet address.
- **`Bold monofont`** text is used occasionally in code listings to point out particular parts of the code discussed in the surrounding text. In addition, we use bold monofont to highlight the placement of keywords or characters within the listing.

Another convention used throughout the book is the installation reference or environment name for the various components. The table that follows shows those references.

Component	*Default install folder*	*Install reference*
WebSphere	C:\WebSphere\AppServer	`<was_home>`
WebSphere HTTP plug-in	C:\WebSphere\AppServer	`<plugin_home>`
DB2 client DB2 server	C:\Program Files\SQLLIB	`<db2_home>`
IBM HTTP Server	C:\Program Files\IBM HTTP Server	`<http_home>`

Navigating This Book

If you're completely new to WebSphere Application Server, start at the beginning and work your way through to the end. Each chapter assumes that you're familiar with the contents of the chapters that precede it. Developers can skip the first three chapters, but we recommend that you read Chapter 4, which covers installation.

Beginning through advanced J2EE developers should be sure to read Chapters 6 through 14. They begin with some analysis and design and quickly move into the introduction of WebSphere Studio Application Developer (WSAD) and more advanced J2EE topics. If you are a developer interested in WebSphere administration, you should at least browse Parts III and IV.

Administrators should read Parts I, III, and IV in their entirety. They should begin with Part I, but Parts III and IV can be read as individual chapters when particular information is required.

Icons appear in the text throughout the book to indicate important or especially helpful items. Here's a list of the icons and their functions:

> **NOTE:** This icon provides additional or critical information and technical data on the current topic.

> **TIP:** This icon points you to useful techniques and helpful hints.

> **CROSS REFERENCE:** This handy icon points you to some place where you can find more information about a particular topic.

> **ON THE WEB:** The On the Web icon tells you to check out this book's companion Web site for related code or sample files or points you to another location on the Web for additional information.

Further Information

You can learn about Commerce Solutions Inc. and/or contact the authors by visiting:

`www.commercesolutions.com` (Commerce Solutions Inc.)

Send e-mail to `WASBible@commercesolutions.com` for comments or inquiries related to the book.

Acknowledgments

When the three of us first decided to take on this endeavor, we anticipated that it would take a lot of dedication and commitment to be successful. Little did we know that it would also require so many other folks with a similar level of dedication and commitment.

First we would like to thank Chris Webb from Wiley for having the confidence in our expertise and writing skills and Jodi Jensen for being the guiding light for so many of us. We also don't want to forget Sydney Jones, whose helpful comments and suggestions make this book easier to read.

We also want to send our appreciation to the technical editors. What good is a technical book if it's not technically sound? We send our many thanks to Dale Nilsson and Marcey Rhyne for their diligence. We know you worked as long and hard as the three of us.

We also want to acknowledge Brian Hanson for his contribution to the security chapter (Chapter 23), Gary Chappell for his excellent work with the WebSphere Control Program (Chapter 27), and Marcey Rhyne (again) for her wonderful effort on the XML chapter (Chapter 18). You are true professionals who have embraced the spirit of writing.

Last, but certainly not least, we thank Steve Pieper from Commerce Solutions Inc. for keeping the “balls in the air” as we all dedicated our extra time to the book, and “the Hot Pepper Media Girls” (Marcia Peterson, Andrea Hamilton, and Peta Scarbrough) for their outstanding Web design and sense of humor.

What would a writer be without the support of his family? For that reason, I would like to dedicate this book to my family (my wife, Cheryl, my daughters, Natalia and Bailey, and my sons, Taylor and Josh). Their constant encouragement helped motivate and inspire me. Perhaps Robert Frost said it best in the "The Road Not Taken": "Two roads diverged in a wood, and I — I took the one less traveled by, and that has made all the difference."

—Bryon Kataoka

A special thanks to my beautiful wife and amazing son for their patience during some busy deadlines. Thank you Jennifer and John David. I couldn't have done this without your love and support.

—David Ramirez

I would like to dedicate this book to my family, Hannah, and my dear friends and colleagues. I could not have done it without all your support and guidance.

—Alan Sit

Contents

Preface vii
Acknowledgments xii

Part I: Planning and Installation 1

Chapter 1: Introducing WebSphere Application Server 3

WebSphere Application Server Overview 3
Understanding Web application architecture 6
Introducing the new features in WebSphere Application Server 4.0 7
Understanding WebSphere's J2EE certification 9
Understanding the differences between WebSphere Application Server versions 3.5.3 and 4.0 9
Understanding WebSphere Application Server 4.0 packaging 10
Advanced Edition Single Server (AEs) 10
Advanced Edition (AE) 11
Advanced Edition Developer-Only (AEd) 13
Understanding WebSphere Development Tools 13
Using VisualAge for Java 14
Using WebSphere Studio Classic 14
Introducing WebSphere Studio Application Developer (WSAD) 15
Introducing WebSphere Studio Site Developer (WSSD) 16
Understanding Supporting Products 17
IBM HTTP Server 1.3.19 17
Introducing DB2 Universal Database 7.2 18
Introducing Tivioli Policy Director (Web Seal) 18
Understanding J2EE components 18
Introducing Apache Simple Object Access Protocol (SOAP) 2.1 20
Introducing Web Services Definition Language (WSDL) 1.1 20
Introducing Universal Discovery and Description Integration (UDDI) 20
Summary 20

Chapter 2: Websphere Application Architecture 23

Understanding the WebSphere Application Server Architecture 24
Understanding WebSphere domains 24
Introducing the Administrative Server 27
Understanding nodes 28
Learning about HTTP server and plug-ins 29
Understanding virtual hosts 31

Understanding Java virtual machines....33
Getting to know enterprise applications....33
Understanding EJB modules....34
Understanding Web modules....35
Understanding application server's organization....35
Default server....35
EJB container....36
Web container....36
Understanding resources....37
Understanding server groups and clones....38
Understanding topology selection....39
Choosing a topology that supports your goals....41
Understanding WebSphere Application Server Administration....44
Understanding the administrative repository....45
Understanding the WebSphere Administrative Console....45
Understanding admin.config....48
Understanding the WebSphere Directory Tree....49
Summary....50

Chapter 3: Introducing Web Services....51

Understanding the Benefits of Using Web Services....52
Who benefits from using Web services?....52
How can enterprises benefit from using Web services?....54
Understanding the Web Services Architecture....55
Exploring the Web Services Model....57
Understanding the components of Web services....58
Understanding operations performed by Web services....59
Understanding Web services implementations....59
Understanding WSDL....59
Understanding SOAP....60
Understanding UDDI....62
Understanding XML's role in the Web services model....64
Understanding other Web services initiatives....65
Understanding WSFL....65
Understanding WSXL....65
Understanding HTTPr....65
Supporting Web Services with WebSphere 4.0....65
Using Apache SOAP 2.2 on WebSphere....66
Generating WSDL files on WebSphere....68
Using UDDI on WebSphere....68
Introducing Web Services Tooling....69
Understanding IBM Web Services Toolkit....69
Understanding WebSphere Studio Application Developer....69

Introducing the Web Services Development Process 70
Understanding the development lifecycle 70
Introducing the development-process wizards 72
Introducing debugging 73
Introducing deployment tools 74
Understanding what occurs at execution time 74
Summary 75

Chapter 4: Installing WebSphere Application Server 4.01 77
Preparing for the Installation on Win2000/NT Platforms 78
Evaluating system requirements 79
Hardware 80
Software 80
Creating authorized userids 81
Userid creation 81
Userid characteristics 82
Remembering the Readme file 83
Introducing FixPak 4.0.3 84
Preinstall checklist 86
Choosing a supported Web server 87
Identifying ports to use 88
Updating the host filenames 89
Choosing the location of the WebSphere administration repository 89
Installing databases other than DB2 90
Modifying port addresses for security concerns 91
Planning for directory services (LDAP) 91
Migrating from an earlier WebSphere version 92
Preparing for a common migration 93
Migrating from version 3.x to 4.0 94
Installing IBM HTTP Server 1.3.19 95
Performing the installation 95
Verifying IBM HTTP Server installation 96
Preparing to configure the Web server 97
Setting up a Web server administration account 98
Using key directives 99
Setting up virtual hosting 100
Setting up the document root 101
Setting up aliases 101
HTTP error codes 102
Installing DB2 7.2 102
Understanding databases for the Administration repository 103
Installing the DB2 Administration database 103
Installing a DB2 remote client 105

Setting up for JDBC 1.1 or JDBC 2.0 106
Preparing for session persistence 107
Verifying the DB2 7.1 installation 108
Installing WebSphere Application Server 108
Verifying a Successful Installation 112
Checking the installation logs 112
Reviewing admin.config 114
Starting the Administrative Server 115
Starting the default server 117
Regenerating plug-ins 118
Troubleshooting Installation Problems 118
Loading the full InfoCenter 119
Taking the InfoCenter for a test drive 120
Running Sample Applications 120
Running Snoop servlet 122
Exploring the Silent Install 123
Summary 125

Chapter 5: Preparing a Development Environment 127

Introducing WebSphere's Development Tools 128
Understanding Installation Permissions 128
Choosing a Version of JDK 130
Preparing to Install WebSphere Studio Application Developer 131
Installing WebSphere Studio Application Developer 133
Installing from the installation CD 133
Installing from the installation CD in silent mode 135
Installing from the WebSphere Studio Application from developer image files 135
Migrating from other versions of WebSphere Studio Application Developer 136
Verifying the install 137
Understanding JDK Java 1.3 139
Creating the Cruise database and tables 139
Understanding the Team Repository 139
Installing CVS 140
Installing CVSNT 141
Setting up WSAD for use with CVSNT 144
Installing a Different Version of the JDK 147
Introducing Distributed Debugger 147
Understanding Roles and Responsibilities 148
Understanding CVS 150
Planning Testing Environments 151
Summary 152

Part II: Application Development 153

Chapter 6: Web Application Analysis and Design................................. 155

Understanding the Web-Development Process.. 155
Understanding roles and responsibilities.. 156
Introducing the IBM e-business application framework 156
Client-Side Processing versus Server-Side Processing 158
Understanding Remote Presentation 159
Understanding Distributed Logic Objects.. 160
Implementing RPCs 160
Implementing messaging 163
Reviewing Transaction-Processing Models.. 163
Understanding Remote/Distributed Data-Management Solutions.. 164
Reviewing Useful Web-Development Approaches.. 165
Understanding the Model View Controller (MVC) pattern 165
Layering applications.. 166
Defining and standardizing services.. 167
Facilitating communication with design patterns.. 167
Refactoring 168
Unit testing with JUnit 169
Understanding Web Application Programming Models 171
Implementing client/server versus n-tier development.. 171
Implementing single servlet versus multiple servlets 171
Planning your Web-application topology.. 172
Determining the target JVM.. 173
Naming your Application server.. 173
Selecting a virtual host 174
Determining the number of nodes to use.. 174
Determining your servlet engine parameters.. 174
Determining the type of EJB container to use.. 174
Introducing AlmostFreeCruise 175
Summary.. 176

Chapter 7: Working with WSAD and WSSD 177

Introducing WSSD and WSAD.. 177
Comparing WSSD and WSAD.. 178
Overview of Functions, Features, Wizards and Tools.. 180
Understanding the workspace.. 180
Understanding projects.. 182
Understanding the workbench 183
Understanding views.. 187
Understanding perspectives 188
Using the J2EE perspective.. 189

Using the Web perspective 191
Using the Java perspective 191
Introducting infopop 192
Understanding editors 192
Customizing the workbench perspectives 196
Using fast view 198
Introducing Web Development with WSAD 199
Creating and working with Web projects and perspectives 199
Using proof-of-concept wizards 203
Using Web application wizards that create Web resources from database queries and JavaBeans 203
Building projects in WSAD 215
Performing an HTTP/FTP import 217
Importing ZIP/JAR/WAR/EAR files into WSAD 219
Developing JSP and HTML pages in WebSphere Studio Page Designer 224
Editing support for cascading style sheets (CSS) 229
Creating servlets 229
Deploying with WebSphere Studio Application Developer 231
Using FTP to transfer files to a server 232
Introducing Java Development Features 232
Using the Java editor 233
Understanding Java elements 233
Specifying alternative JREs 234
Summary 236

Chapter 8: Testing with WSAD 237

Setting Up the Test Environment 238
Managing your server objects with the Server perspective 239
Creating a server project 241
Creating server instances and configurations 241
Creating the server instance 243
Creating the server configuration 244
Modifying the server configuration 246
Configuring the server instance 249
Setting a server configuration to an instance 250
Adding a project to a server configuration for testing 250
Adding a data source to a server configuration 251
Testing the application on the test environment 253
Debugging the application 255
Summary 258

Chapter 9: Java Servlet Development... 259
Comparing Servlets with CGI Programs.. 260
Understanding Servlets.. 262
Understanding the servlet process flow.. 262
Introducing the Java Servlet API... 263
Understanding the servlet lifecycle.. 264
Examining basic servlet examples... 265
Looking at the obligatory Hello World.. 265
Looking at a simple counter servlet... 267
Looking at a simple HTTP servlet... 268
Understanding the GenericServlet interface... 270
Understanding the HttpServlet interface.. 271
Using the HttpServletRequest and HttpServletResponse protocols............................. 272
Using HttpServletRequest.. 272
HttpServletResponse.. 276
Summary.. 279

Chapter 10: More Servlet APIs.. 281
Reviewing Controller Issues... 282
Using the ServletContext.. 282
Using the RequestDispatcher.. 284
Forwarding versus Response Redirection... 286
Understanding Cache Complications... 288
Using Precondition Processing... 289
Using Post-Condition Processing.. 289
Understanding Servlet Interaction Techniques.. 290
Enabling servlet collaboration... 290
Using servlet chaining and filtering... 291
Understanding Cookies... 292
Using the Servlet Cookie API... 292
Creating cookies... 293
Reading and specifying cookie attributes... 293
Placing cookies in the response headers.. 294
Reading cookies from the client.. 294
Using CookieCounterServlet.. 294
Summary.. 297

Chapter 11: Understanding Session Management....................................299

Introducing Session Management....................................300
Using the Cookie API to handle session tracking....................................300
Using hidden fields to handle session tracking....................................301
Using URL rewriting to handle session tracking....................................301
Using the HttpSession object for session management....................................302
Accessing sessions and state data....................................303
Running Snoop servlet....................................303
Accessing sessions and using application data....................................306
Running the Hit Count servlet....................................307
Using the HttpSessionBindingListener interface....................................310
Using com.ibm.WebSphere.servlet.session.IBMSession....................................311
Understanding Large-Scale Session Management....................................312
Using persistent sessions....................................312
Using multirow access....................................313
Understanding overflows....................................313
Using WAS Session Manager....................................314
Setting Session Support in the Sample Application....................................319
Summary....................................321

Chapter 12: Developing JavaServer Pages....................................323

Understanding Web Application Models....................................325
Developing JSPs with the WSAD Development Environment....................................328
Coding the obligatory Hello World....................................328
Running the simple JSP....................................330
Creating Dynamic Content in JSPs....................................333
Understanding JSP syntax....................................333
Using directives....................................334
Using declarations....................................335
Using scriptlets....................................336
Using comments....................................336
Using expressions....................................337
Using JSP scripting....................................337
Accessing implicit objects....................................337
Understanding JSP Interactions....................................338
Invoking a JSP by URL....................................338
Calling a servlet from a JSP....................................338
Calling a JSP from a servlet....................................340
Invoking a JSP from a JSP....................................340

Understanding JSP Tags and Tag Libraries 341
Developing JSP Custom Actions 343
Defining tag handlers 344
Using tag library descriptors 345
Understanding Differences between JSP Specification .92, 1.0, and 1.1 347
Understanding changes between JSP V.92 and JSP V1.0 347
Understanding changes between 1.0 and 1.1 347
Adding JSPs to the Almost Free Cruise Application 348
Summary 352

Chapter 13: Introducing Enterprise JavaBeans 353

Understanding Enterprise JavaBeans 353
Understanding the Reasons for Using Enterprise JavaBeans 354
Introducing EJB Architecture 356
Introducing CORBA 357
Understanding RMI 358
Understanding the Object-Persistence Dilemma 359
Understanding the Bean Container Contract 360
Understanding the Characteristics of Enterprise JavaBeans 360
Introducing Enterprise JavaBeans 361
Understanding containers 364
Understanding services 365
Persistence 365
Transactions 365
Security 365
Naming 366
Developing Enterprise JavaBean clients 366
Understanding Entity Beans 368
Understanding the lifecycle of the entity bean 369
Describing container-managed persistence 369
Describing bean-managed persistence 369
Understanding object-to-relational mapping 370
Starting from top down 370
Meeting in the middle 370
Starting from bottom up 370
Understanding Session Beans 371
Using the stateless session bean 371
Understanding the lifecycle of a stateless session bean 371
Understanding the stateful session bean 372
Understanding the lifecycle of a stateful session bean 372
Summary 373

Chapter 14: Developing Enterprise JavaBeans with WSAD 375

Preparing for the Tutorial 376
 Creating a WebSphere Studio Application Developer workspace 376
 Creating the necessary database and tables 377
Creating an EJB 378
 Mapping EJB-RDB 379
 Creating your first CMP entity bean 380
 Using the EJB Extension editor 380
 Setting up the server instance 384
 Setting up the data sources 385
Running the Test Client 387
Creating an EJB Session Bean 392
Adding a Custom Finder 394
Creating Access Beans 397
Updating the Session Bean 399
Integrating the Beans: The Home Stretch 401
Summary 405

Chapter 15: Additional CMP and Transaction Processing 407

Using the EJB-RDB Mapping Tool 408
 Understanding types of mapping 408
  Bottom-up mapping 409
  Top-down mapping 409
  Meet-in-the-middle mapping 409
 Implementing top-down mapping 409
 Creating a top-down bean 410
 Understanding the meet-in-the-middle process 413
 Defining EJB relationships 414
 Creating relationships 415
  Establishing the relationship 416
Understanding Transaction-Management Basics 417
 Understanding ACID properties 418
 Understanding transactions 419
  Understanding the two-phase commit 419
 Understanding transaction architecture 420
  Understanding JTS 420
  Understanding JTA 420

Using Transactions 420
Introducing EJB transaction services 421
Understanding transactional attributes 421
Understanding isolation and locking 422
Setting Transactions in AlmostFreeCruise 423
Summary 425

Chapter 16: Deployment Descriptors and EJB Security Overview 427

Understanding Application Assembly 427
Understanding J2EE compliance 428
Introducing the Anatomy of an EJB Deployment Descriptor 429
Understanding the document header 431
Understanding the body 432
Understanding enterprise-beans 432
Referencing other beans 435
Making environmental entries 435
Resourcing references 436
Using assembly-descriptor 437
Overviewing Security 438
Understanding EJB security 439
Declaring security-role 439
Describing method-permissions 439
Handling overloaded methods 441
Adding EJB Security Descriptors 442
Using the Application Assembly Tool (AAT) 445
Summary 445

Chapter 17: EJB Best Practices 447

Introducing Design Approaches/Strategies 448
Proactive design practices 448
Avoiding design problems 449
Things to consider in the design process 450
Improving Java Performance 450
Java proactive practices 451
Avoiding Java problems 452
Things to consider in Java 452
Enhancing EJB Development 453
Proactive EJB development practices 453
Avoiding problems in EJB development 454
Things to consider during EJB development 455

Optimizing the Web Module 456
Proactive Web-module practices 456
Avoiding problems in Web modules 456
Things to consider with Web modules 458
Summary 458

Chapter 18: Using XML/XSLT in WebSphere 459
Introducing XML 459
Understanding the need for XML 461
Understanding the advantages of using XML 462
Introducing the family of XML technologies 464
Introducing XSLT 467
Understanding the benefits of using XSLT 467
Performing an XSLT transformation using XPath 468
Putting the pieces together 471
Developing an XML Application Using WSAD 471
Introducing XML development tools 471
Using stylesheets 472
Summary 480

Chapter 19: Developing Web Services 481
Exploring Web Services 481
Understanding the components of Web services 482
Understanding the role of the service broker 482
Understanding the role of the service requestor 483
Understanding the role of the service provider 483
Understanding how Web services operate 483
Understanding the development strategies of Web services 484
Installing the IBM Web Services Tools 484
Understanding the tools 485
Installing the SOAP examples on WebSphere Application Server (AE) 485
Installing the IBM Web Services ToolKit 489
Preparing to install a Private UDDI 491
Installing the IBM WebSphere UDDI registry 491
Verifying the installation 493
Understanding the Apache SOAP ToolKit 495
Introducing AXIS: The next generation 496
Administering SOAP 496

Understanding the development lifecycle 499
Understanding the SOAP envelope 500
Using SOAP over HTTP 501
Understanding SOAP encoding 501
Using SOAP and remote procedure calls 501
Understanding client coding 502
Understanding service coding 504
Using WSDL to Describe Your Web Service 505
Separating interface and implementation 506
Defining data types 507
Defining messages, portTypes, operations, and bindings 508
Defining ports 509
Introducing tooling to make your life easier 509
Publishing, Finding, and Binding Your Services 511
Understanding UDDI 511
Getting information from UDDI 513
Making sense of UDDI 515
Understanding tModels 516
Creating UDDI Service Descriptions 517
Understanding Web Services Inspection Language 518
Using WebSphere Studio Application Developer to Create a Web Services Component 520
Creating a Web Service Project 520
Updating the EAR file with SOAPEAREnabler 522
Developing the SOAP client 524
TCPTunneling 526
Using WSDL tooling 528
Running WSAD to generate the WSDL 528
Running the AddressBookSample demo 534
Summary 538

Part III: Systems Administration 539

Chapter 20: Configuring WebSphere Application Environments 541

Reviewing WebSphere Architecture 542
Understanding the Administrative Server 542
Using the Administrative Console 543
Starting and stopping nodes 544
Creating application servers 544
Starting and stopping application servers 545
Starting and stopping enterprise applications 546
Using the Regen WebSphere plug-in 546

Exporting and Importing XML configurations....546
Checking out deployment descriptors....547
Command History....548
Running wizards....549
Configuring the Web Server Components....549
Configuring the Web server plug-in....549
Regenerating the plug-in....552
Installing the plug-in....553
Configuring virtual hosts....553
Understanding the transport options....555
Internal transport (the embedded HTTP server)....555
Non-SSL transport....556
Configuring Resources....557
Setting up JDBC connection pools....558
Creating a JDBC provider....559
Creating a data source....560
Enabling JavaMail....561
Understanding URL providers....564
Setting up JMS....565
Understanding JMS providers....565
Setting up JMS MQ Support....566
Introducing J2C....571
Understanding Resource Adapter Archive (RAR)....573
Setting up J2C....573
Configuring J2C resource adapters....574
Configuring J2C connection factories....574
Summary....575

Chapter 21: Configuring Session Management....577

Understanding HTTP Session Management....578
Understanding sessions....579
Using Cookies for session management....579
Using URL rewriting for session management....580
Using SSL tracking for session management....580
Introducing Workload Management....580
Understanding clustering....581
Understanding server affinity....581
Setting Up Session Management....582
Persisting sessions....583
Understanding overflows....585
Setting up persistence sessions....587
Enabling single/multirow support....592

Configuring persistence manually ... 592
Setting up manual updates ... 593
Setting up time-based writes to the session database ... 593
Understanding Session Security ... 594
Squeezing Out Performance ... 594
Managing memory ... 595
Managing Session cache size ... 595
Reducing I/O ... 595
Configuring the session database connection pool ... 596
Adding application server clones ... 596
Reducing session object size ... 596
Cleaning up unneeded sessions ... 596
Doing the math ... 597
Changing session timeout intervals ... 597
Using multirow persistent session management ... 597
Summary ... 598

Chapter 22: Using WebSphere's Application Packaging ... 599
Understanding J2EE Packaging and Deployment ... 600
Understanding J2EE roles ... 603
Understanding deployment descriptors ... 603
Understanding WebSphere J2EE compliance ... 605
Using WebSphere deployment tooling ... 606
Understanding IBM bindings ... 606
Understanding IBM extensions ... 607
Understanding more about IBM extensions ... 607
EJB caching ... 607
Using the FileServing servlet ... 608
Using the Invoker servlet ... 608
Using the Application Assembly Tool (AAT) ... 609
Using the Application Wizard ... 611
Using the EJB Module Wizard ... 611
Using the Web Module Wizard ... 612
Using the Application Client Wizard ... 612
Exploring enterprise applications ... 612
Understanding EJB modules ... 614
Understanding Web modules ... 617
Understanding application client modules ... 619
Exploring other AAT options ... 619
Generating code (EJBDeploy) ... 619
Performing a verification check ... 620
Using EARExpander ... 620

Creating Your Own J2EE Application 621
Running an example application assembly 621
Summary 624

Chapter 23: Configuring Security 625

Introducing Key Security-Related Definitions 625
Understanding Security in WebSphere Application Server and J2EE 626
Understanding Java authentication and authorization service 627
Understanding authentication and authorization 627
Securing a sample in WSAD 628
Developing security in WSAD 629
Creating the sample pages 631
Creating login.jsp 632
Creating logout.jsp 633
Creating error.jsp, error403.jsp, and secure.jsp 633
Adding the XML Descriptors 633
Testing what you have done so far 640
Adding Servlet Security 641
Adding EJB Security 641
Moving Beyond Role-Based Security: Programmatic Security 642
Understanding programmtic security in servlets 643
Understanding programmtic security in EJBs 644
Using the Application Assembly Tool 645
Using an LDAP User Repository 647
Understanding How Security Works 652
Summary 654

Part IV: Managing WebSphere 655

Chapter 24: Workload Management and Optimization 657

Understanding Scaling and Workload Management 657
Understanding server groups and clones 660
Understanding types of workload management 660
Understanding Web server load management 661
Understanding servlet workload management 662
Understanding EJB workload management 663
Understanding how EJB workload management works 663
Understanding session beans 664
Understanding entity beans 664
Understanding work-management selection policy 664
Setting Up Server Groups 665

Creating Clones 666
Understanding vertical cloning 667
Understanding horizontal cloning 668
Creating a Vertical Clone for AlmostFreeCruise 670
Creating Horizontal Clones 675
Manually configuring the DB2 client 676
Helping WebSphere find the shared repository 677
Creating the horizontal clone on the secondary node 679
Installing JDBC drivers on secondary nodes 681
Understanding the WebSphere 4.0 Optimizations 681
Understanding IBM WebSphere Edge Server 683
Understanding dynamic caching 683
Using WebSphere Edge Server's dynamic caching proxy server 684
Understanding how dynamic caching works in WebSphere 685
Enabling dynamic caching for WebSphere 686
Using WebSphere Edge Server's external cache 688
Understanding Optimization Methodology 688
Understanding Optimization Issues 689
Optimizing from the outside in 690
Optimizing HTTP server settings 690
Optimizing the database 691
Tuning buffer pools 691
Tuning database logs 692
Tuning database indexes 692
Determining optimal location 692
Tuning the session persistence database 692
Using prepared-statement caching 692
Tuning connection pooling 692
Tuning the JVM 693
Starting Java Virtual Machine Profiler Interface 694
Optimizing the Application Server 695
Setting Web container maximum thread size 695
Setting the URL invocation cache 695
Deploying parameters for Web applications 696
Optimizing the EJB container 696
Setting pass-by-value versus pass-by-reference (NoLocalCopies) 697
Introducing Introscope 697
Introducing Panorama 699
Summary 701

Chapter 25: Using the Resource Analyzer....................703

Introducing the Resource Analyzer....................703
- Understanding tracking....................705
- Understanding performance data organization....................705

Starting the Resource Analyzer....................706
- Starting from the Administrative Console....................706
- Starting from the Start Programs menu....................706
- Starting from the command prompt....................707

Understanding the Resource Analyzer Console....................707
- Using the Resource Selection pane....................708
- Using the Data Monitoring pane....................708
- Understanding instrumentation levels....................709

Running an Example....................710
- Logging and replaying data....................713

Summary....................714

Chapter 26: Troubleshooting WebSphere....................715

Determining Problems....................716
- Introducing logs....................716
  - Understanding installation logs....................718
  - Understanding Administrative Server logs....................719
  - Understanding application server logs....................720
  - Understanding IBM HTTP Server Logs....................722
  - Understanding plug-in logs....................722
- Understanding the Administrative Console....................723
- Understanding Log Analyzer....................724
- Understanding Distributed Debugger and Object-Level Trace....................724
- Using traces....................724
- Understanding JNDI namespace....................725

Troubleshooting: First Steps....................726
- Revisiting WebSphere topology....................726
- Understanding problem categories....................728

Using Troublingshooting Tools....................728
- Configuring console messages....................729
- Deciphering error pop-up windows....................730
- Reviewing log files....................730
- Performing educated prognostication....................734

Running traces ... 735
Setting up an Application server trace ... 736
Tracing the Admininstrative server ... 739
Formatting trace specifications strings ... 740
Tracing Administrative Server startup ... 741
Using Log Analyzer ... 742
Summary ... 744

Chapter 27: Using the WebSphere Control Program ... 747

Introducing WebSphere Control Program (wscp) ... 748
Understanding the Administrative Console and wscp ... 748
Understanding the benefits of using wscp ... 749
Understanding the limitations of using wscp ... 749
Understanding supported object types ... 749
Understanding Tcl ... 750
Launching wscp ... 752
Understanding the basic syntax ... 753
Referring to objects ... 754
Using the command shell ... 754
Executing wscp scripts ... 754
Invoking the wscp properties file ... 754
Connecting to remote nodes ... 755
Accessing online help ... 755
Getting help for objects ... 756
Getting a list of objects ... 757
Understanding error and status handling ... 758
Writing and using wscp scripts ... 758
Creating a wscp script ... 759
Running a wscp script ... 759
Using the WscpCommand interface ... 762
Using WscpCommand Constructors ... 763
Using WscpCommand public methods ... 763
Using qualified names ... 764
Migrating scripts from version 3.5.x to version 4.0 ... 766
Discontinued objects ... 766
Renamed objects ... 766
Same name, new syntax ... 767
New objects ... 767
Summary ... 768

Chapter 28: Managing WebSphere with XMLConfig 769
Introducing XMLConfig 770
Determining when to use XMLConfig 770
Understanding the role of XMLConfig.. 771
Introducing XML basics 772
Understanding the structure of Document Type Definition (DTD)........................ 772
Using objects, actions, and names in XML.. 775
Understanding XMLConfig Basics.. 777
Running XMLConfig.. 777
Exporting information 781
Performing a full export.. 781
Performing a partial export.. 781
Importing information 782
Creating resources.. 783
Updating a resource 784
Deleting a resource.. 784
Backing up and restoring the administrative repository.............................. 785
Starting and stopping Application servers 785
Management Activities.. 786
Performing substitutions.. 786
Making configuration changes 787
Adding application servers 787
Updating JDBC drivers.. 789
Updating data sources 789
Changing Vhosts 790
Deploying domains.. 790
Implementing server groups and cloning.. 791
Regenerating the HTTP Server plug-in.. 792
Summary.. 792

Index 793

Part I

Planning and Installation

Chapter 1
Introducing WebSphere Application Server

Chapter 2
Websphere Application Architecture

Chapter 3
Introducing Web Services

Chapter 4
Installing WebSphere Application Server 4.01

Chapter 5
Preparing a Development Environment

Chapter 1
Introducing WebSphere Application Server

In This Chapter

- Introducing WebSphere
- Understanding the WebSphere family of products
- Understanding WebSphere J2EE compliance
- Understanding the flavors of WebSphere Application Server

WebSphere 4.0 is the latest release of WebSphere Application Server. It represents a major enhancement that brings WebSphere in line with its competitors and, in some cases, enables WebSphere to surpass the competition. Perhaps the most important feature to you is WebSphere's Java 2 Enterprise Edition (J2EE) certification. Attaining this status is important, because it provides a new set of standards that promotes portability and scalability. You can now utilize some of the benefits of Java 1.3, Enterprise JavaBeans (EJB) 1.1, Servlet 2.2, and JavaServer Pages (JSP) 1.1. You can now be comfortable knowing that you are writing J2EE-compliant applications that work with other J2EE compliant platforms.

In addition to the J2EE certification, you can take advantage of some of the new tooling that supports WebSphere 4.0. You will enjoy the new Administrative Console, which is far superior to previous versions, and you will find new features — the embedded HTTP Server, expanded security, and Web services — useful.

Not to be outdone, WebSphere 4.0 also offers some technical previews that continue to promote WebSphere as the application server for today and tomorrow. Already, IBM has announced that it has achieved J2EE certification for J2EE 1.3. Couple the certification with the Java Messaging Server (JMS) messaging and J2EE Connection Architecture (J2C) enterprise connectivity, and you can see that WebSphere is a platform that you can trust with your e-business applications.

WebSphere Application Server Overview

IBM is delivering a number of WebSphere products. WebSphere is more than an application server, it's a family of products, and that distinction can lead to some confusion. So, when someone says "WebSphere," is he referring to *WebSphere Application Server* or *WebSphere*

Commerce Suite? WebSphere is a product brand name; so many IBM products are preceded by the WebSphere brand.

WebSphere is a comprehensive set of integrated software developed for e-business solutions. This set includes plugable solutions — e-commerce, Customer Relation Management (CRM), Supply Chain Management (SCM) — that make existing custom applications extensible. The foundation of the WebSphere family is WebSphere Application Server. It provides a flexible, portable foundation based on open standards. To take advantage of the functionality, IBM has delivered a set of foundation extensions. The extensions fall into four categories:

- Development
- Applications
- Deployment/management tooling
- Integration

The tooling and products that are part of the WebSphere family are shown in Figure 1-1.

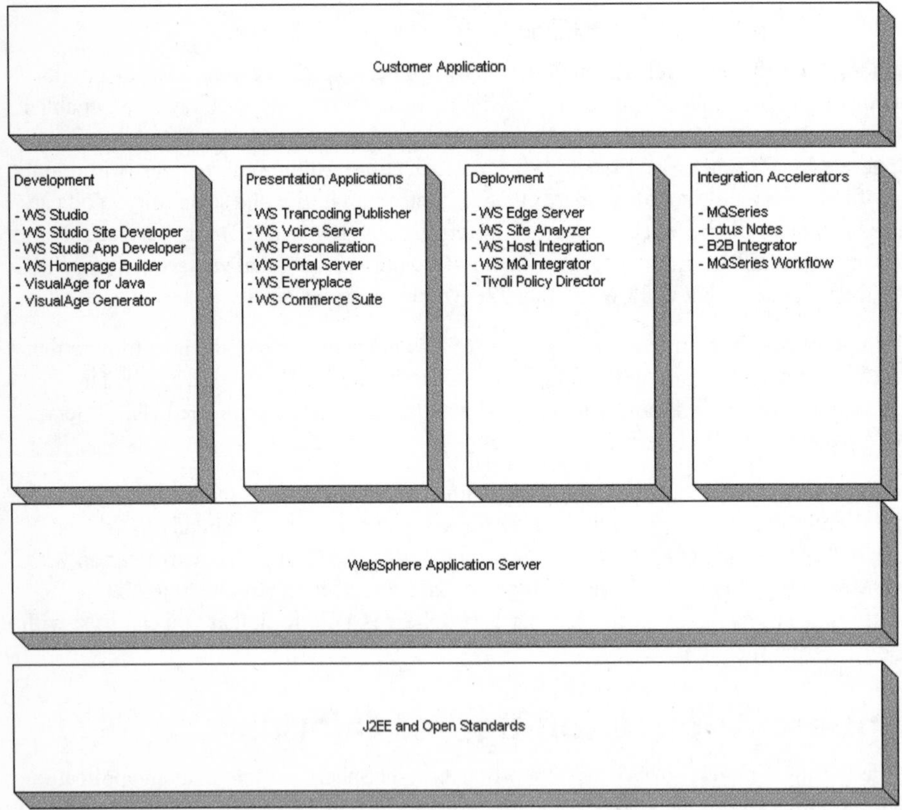

Figure 1-1: The WebSphere suite of tools provides the capability to build, test ,and deploy e-business applications.

The tools shown in Figure 1-1 provide you the capability to develop, manage, and extend Web-based applications to provide better content and coverage over a wide variety of platforms and environments. As you read further, you learn more about these products and their capabilities.

The WebSphere product family includes specialized product add-ons that extend your e-business capabilities into new markets. But that's not all. IBM also provides management tools that can help improve scalability and usability. Table 1-1 provides a short description of the available products.

Table 1-1: WebSphere Product Descriptions

Product	***Description***
WebSphere Portal Server (WPS)	WPS is a single point of entry to multiple applications and other data sources. It accomplishes the following: Aggregation: Combining data from multiple sources into one comprehensive presence Personalization: Enabling users to select individual portlets that contains specific data Presentation: Providing the capability to render pages on multiple devices, such as HTML and WML
WebSphere Transcoding Publisher	WebSphere Transcoding Publisher is a server-based software that dynamically translates Web content and applications into multiple markup languages, such as HTML to VoiceXML, HTML to Palm, HTML to WML, XML to several formats using XSLT, and image transcoding.
WebSphere Commerce Suite (WCS)	WebSphere Commerce Suite is an e-commerce suite of products ranging from merchandising to Dutch auctions. It enables store administrators to manage operations including orders, payments, and fulfillments.
WebSphere Voice Server	WebSphere Voice Server is a VoiceXML-enabled server.
WebSphere Personalization	WebSphere Personalization enables you to personalize the content of a Web site, intranet, or extranet so that it's customized to the individual user.
WebSphere Everyplace (WES)	WebSphere Everyplace Suite is a solution for pervasive e-business that connects any device to any data, anywhere, anytime. It is used for extending e-business to mobile users.

Table 1-1 *(Continued)*

Product	***Description***
WebSphere Edge Server	WebSphere Edge Server is a product that addresses problems that Web sites have with regard to response time, scalability, and reliability. Under the umbrella of WebSphere Edge Server are a number of technologies: Web Traffic Express (WTE): A caching proxy server Network Dispatcher: Provides the capability to load-balance Together these tools provide monitoring for load balancing, reverse proxy caching, forward proxy caching, filtering and blocking of Web content, and content-based routing.

Understanding Web application architecture

Figure 1-2 shows a simplified Web architecture. Understanding the flow of a Web application helps you understand the role that WebSphere plays in its success and yours. WebSphere Application Server 4.0 is the application server. Application servers extend a Web server's capabilities to handle Web application requests, typically using Java technology. The application server is J2EE compliant and contains the J2EE Web container and EJB container.

In a Web application, HTTP requests are posted from various browsers. The HTTP request is sent to the Web server for processing. The Web server, utilizing a WebSphere plug-in, forwards the request to the Web container for processing if the particular requested resource is not located on the Web server. The Web container may access Enterprise JavaBeans (EJB) in the EJB container to perform business logic and handle persistence, or invoke a servlet to deliver dynamic content to the user.

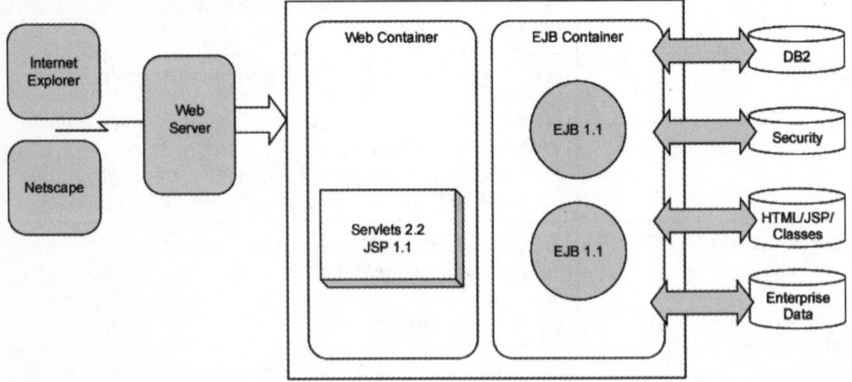

Figure 1-2: Web applications flow from a browser to the Web server and over to the WebSphere Application Server.

As you look at Figure 1-2 you are probably saying there is a lot more to the Web architecture than this high-level graphic. You're absolutely right. The figure does not show some of WebSphere's powerful features, such as workload management, scalability, security, and performance improvements. As you read more about WebSphere, these new features and improvements are discussed.

Introducing the new features in WebSphere Application Server 4.0

WebSphere Application Server (WAS) version 4.0 provides a rich environment complete with a set of application services, including capabilities for transaction management, security, clustering, availability, connectivity, and scalability.

WebSphere Application Server supplies interoperability by embracing new open standards, such as Simple Object Access Protocol (SOAP), and by providing preview implementations of J2EE Connector Architecture (JCA), thereby allowing integration with a number of Enterprise Resource Planning (ERP) and transaction environments. Now that you know WebSphere version 4.0 is new and improved, look at some of the key improvements:

- *J2EE 1.2 compliance:* Compliance with J2EE 1.2 opens up a new world for WebSphere. By achieving this high standard, you are assured that your applications can be written to a specification that allows portability and flexibility. You can also be guaranteed that future releases are backward compatible, providing you the option to update your applications to new features within your timeframe.
- *New packaging of WebSphere editions:* Anyone who has previously tried to figure out the various editions of WebSphere 3.x knows that each edition was built differently. These included a standard edition, an advanced edition, and an enterprise edition. This led to confusion about which products to install and which migration path to take. WebSphere version 4.0 is neatly packaged into three flavors: Advanced Edition (AE), Advanced Single Server Edition (AEs), and AEd (Developers Edition), all built on top of the same core.
- *Preview of Java 2 Connectors (JCA):* Continuing to lead the pack, WebSphere provides its users the ability to install future J2EE specifications in a preview form. The Java Connection Architecture (JCA), which will be part of J2EE 1.3, has been bundled with WebSphere as J2C. With J2C, you can connect to other applications, such as CICS, IMS, and ERP systems. This topic is covered in Chapter 20.
- *Incorporation of Web services:* Web services are becoming the next wave of new open standards technology led by IBM and Microsoft. WebSphere is continuing to lead the application server market by providing Web services capabilities, such as SOAP, WSDL, and UDDI. Web services are introduced in Chapter 3 and further detailed in Chapter 19.
- *Modification to the Web server plug-in:* The old plug-in processing utilized a transport mechanism called Open Servlet Engine (OSE). OSE is no longer supported, and in its place is a new HTTP transport built around a new internal HTTP server embedded within the WebSphere Application Server. Not only is it faster than OSE, the new

plug-in allows Secure Socket Layer (SSL) configuration to improve security. The plug-in configuration is now contained in a single XML file versus the three file updates required in the prior edition. This topic is covered in depth in Chapter 20.

- *Embedded HTTP Server:* Previously mentioned, the embedded HTTP server provides improved security and the capability to interact directly with WebSphere without the need for an external Web server.
- *Performance enhancements:* WebSphere has improved performance through the use of caching and improved connection pooling, as well as improvements in garbage collection, EJB deployment, and extensive use of Dynacache. Performance is also improved with the introduction of the embedded HTTP Server.
- *Improved security:* WebSphere 4.0 has adopted the security model described in the Java 2 Enterprise Edition (J2EE) specification. In the specification, there are techniques describing creating, assembling, deploying, and securing enterprise applications. Some security holes, such as unsecured text-based passwords, have now been encrypted.
- *New Administration Console:* A new easy-to-use Administrative Console has been provided to make administration easier.
- *Other tools:* Application Assembly Tool (AAT), EJBDeploy, and EARExpander are discussed in Chapter 22. The Resource Analyzer is covered in Chapter 25, and the Log Analyzer is covered in Chapter 26.
- *Expanded platform support:* WebSphere platform support includes Windows 2000, AIX, Linux, HP-UX, and Solaris.
- *Expanded database support:* WebSphere now includes support for the Merant SequeLink, Microsoft SQLServer, Oracle, Informix, and DB2.
- *Migration aids:* Migration aids are provided to assist migrations from WebSphere versions 3.02 and 3.5, as well as migration from the Single Server Edition to the Advanced Edition.
- *Enterprise Extensions:* Enterprise Extensions provides implementation of enterprise services. Some examples of enterprise services are interoperability with Active X/COM programming model, the IBM C++ CORBA server, and various CORBA (Object Request Brokers) ORBs.

NOTE: WebSphere Enterprise Extensions is a separate product requiring WebSphere Application Server (AE) as a base. It has value above and beyond J2EE capabilities. Enterprise services primarily focus on integrating existing environments to solve complex implementations with an enterprise.

Enterprise services are broken into two areas: enterprise operations/deployment and business process/application integration.

A discussion of Enterprise Extensions is beyond the scope of this book. Please visit the IBM site at `www.ibm.com/software/webservers/appserv` for more information.

Understanding WebSphere's J2EE certification

The major improvement in WebSphere Application Server 4.0 is its J2EE certification. In the past, WebSphere Application Server did not satisfy all the requirements to be J2EE certified. Although you can be compliant in a majority of the requirements, you cannot be certified unless your product's containers satisfy all the required services and extensions.

Because J2EE is a cohesive collection of the Java Enterprise-oriented APIs, having your application running on a certified J2EE container means you are ready for future releases. With any change to the specifications, you are guaranteed that all versions of the services integrate and work well.

WebSphere Application Server is a market leader in new technology. As new specifications, such as J2EE 1.3, become available, WebSphere is available as an enabler for your next killer application.

Understanding the differences between WebSphere Application Server versions 3.5.3 and 4.0

In addition to the J2EE enhancements, WebSphere administration now sports a new look and feel. It is much easier to navigate around the new Administrative Console.

Deployment has been streamlined with the use of the J2EE specification utilizing Enterprise Archives (EAR). An Application Assembly Tool is provided so you can create or edit J2EE EAR files from J2EE modules. You can also create or edit Web modules in the form of Web archive files (WAR), servlets, JavaServer Pages (JSP), EJB modules (EJB JAR files), and application clients.

The HTTP plug-in is now based in XML, and a new HTTP Server is embedded in the Web container. The embedded HTTP Server replaces the 3.5.x OSE transport. The embedded HTTP Server also allows SSL between the HTTP Server and the Web container, thereby adding another important layer of security. And speaking of security, if you are familiar with version 3.5.x, you know that passwords are stored in plain ASCII and, thus, can be a security risk. In version 4.0, passwords are encrypted. Packaging is another major change in both pricing and installation. The following section discusses packaging changes.

Understanding WebSphere Application Server 4.0 packaging

WebSphere version 4.0 is now packaged in three editions, all of which utilize the same core functionality. This functionality creates a foundation in which you can test and deploy, knowing your application is running on the same code base. An added benefit to running with the same core is that when IBM upgrades are provided; they can be applied to all versions of the product. Another benefit is the ability to synchronize with the development platform. In previous versions of the development tool (VisualAge for Java), the WebSphere Test Environment was incompatible with WebSphere Application Server.

The three WebSphere version 4.0 editions are discussed in this section: Advanced Edition Single Server (AEs), Advanced Edition (AE), and Advanced Edition for development only option (AEd).

Advanced Edition Single Server (AEs)

In WebSphere versions prior to version 4.0, WebSphere had the Standard Edition version. This version supported servlets and JavaServer Pages, but did not have support for EJBs. With the new IBM strategy of supporting the core product in all versions, the notion of the standard edition has been replaced with the WebSphere Advanced Single Server Edition (AEs). The single-server version is for organizations that do not have the requirements for scalability, clustering, and 24 by 7 operations. Targeted as a departmental server, AEs provides full J2EE support. That is one of the major differences between the old Standard edition and Advanced Single Server edition.

The Advanced Version Single Server Edition (AEs) supports the following:

- Single machine, single processor used as a departmental server. Without the need for vertical scalability, the single-server edition requires only a single machine.
- J2EE 1.2 for full support of servlets, JavaServer Pages (JSP), EJBs, and other J2EE components.
- Web services for providing service-oriented applications.
- HTTP/HTTPS support for plug-in transport.
- Roles-based security in compliance with J2EE.
- Browser-based administration for easier-to-use configuration.
- Datasource support for DB2 and Oracle to provide access to the two widely regarded database solutons.

Figure 1-3 shows the browser version of the Administrative Console available only in AEs. The Administrative Console for AEs provides you with a user interface to configure WebSphere Single Server. The interface works with a series of XML configuration files that provide the necessary parameters to configure the operations and other resources supporting applications during runtime.

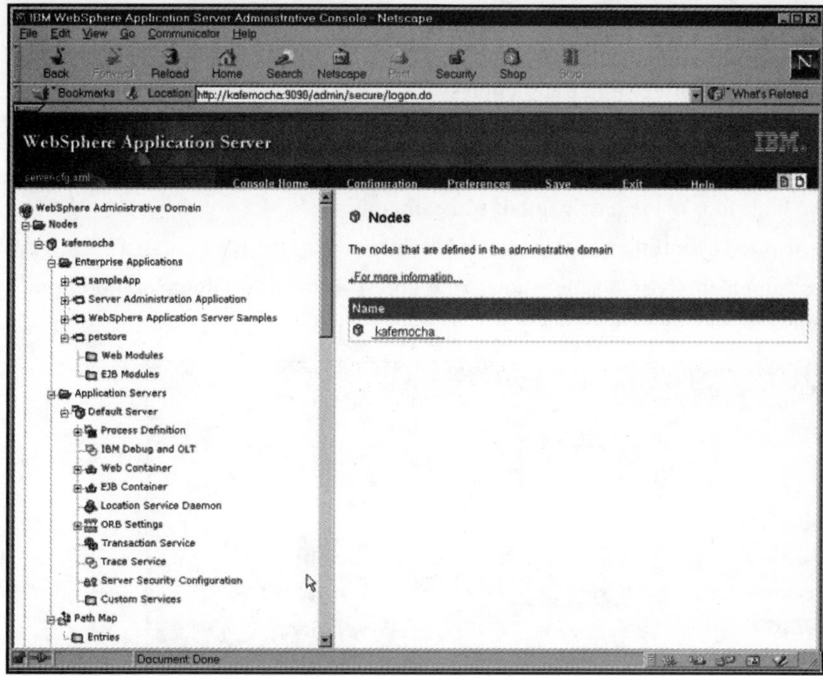

Figure 1-3: The Administrative Console for WebSphere AEs is browser-based.

Advanced Edition (AE)

The Advanced Edition (AE) is the big daddy of the other version 4.0 editions. It is fully compliant with J2EE and is the predominant choice as the application server within an organization because Advanced Edition (AE) provides multiple/distributed server support. WebSphere AE is intended for production deployment on systems that require a scalable, reliable infrastructure. AE supports the following:

- Multiple application server processes for improved performance
- Support for multiple machines providing the capability to cluster machines for improved performance and failover
- Workload management (WLM) to provide improved performance, scalability and failover support
- Transactional and expanded database support to connect to your favorite database servers (Merant, Microsoft SQLServer, Oracle, Sybase, Informix, and DB2)
- Expanded security options fully compliant with J2EE

- J2EE Future enhancements:
  - J2EE connection architecture (technology preview of future features) that allows connectivity to your existing transaction systems and ERP systems
  - Java Messaging Services (JMS/XA) interface to MQSeries (technology preview of future features)
- Migration tools to take the hassle out of some migrations
- Web services to support the service-oriented architecture of the future
- A remote Administrative Console (shown in Figure 1-4) to allow administration from any machine capable of connecting to the WebSphere domain

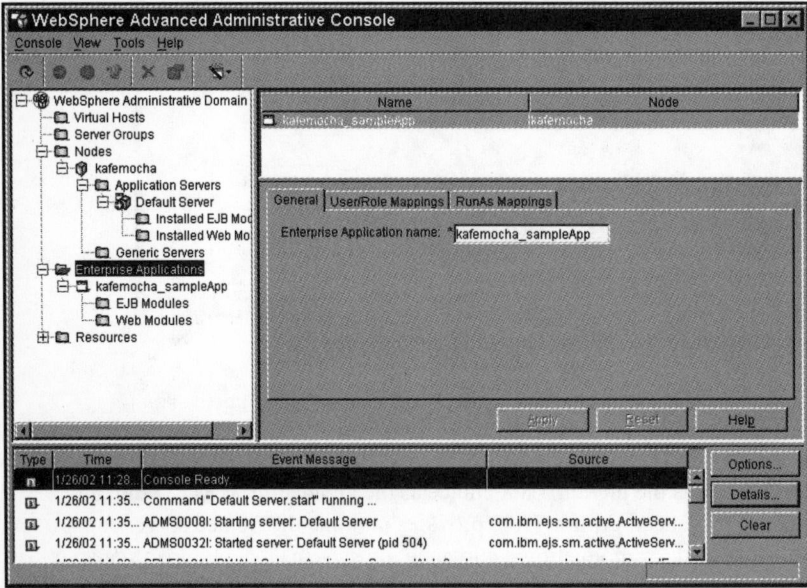

Figure 1-4: The new Administrative Console in WebSphere Advanced Edition (AE) provides a better user interface than previous editions and makes configuration and deployment tasks easier.

The new Administrative Console complies with the J2EE specifications for enterprise application deployment. Enterprise Archive (EAR) files are installed on the server as enterprise applications. These applications contain the necessary configurations and executables to run a J2EE-compliant application. Whereas the older versions of WebSphere's Administrative Console supported more of the development activities, such as assigning aliases to servlets, the new Administrative Console's primary responsibility is deployment.

From the console, you can set up configurations that support various data sources, connectors, and vertical and horizontal scaling. Features, such as workload management, are simplified by setting up application templates as server groups. You learn more about the configuration side of the Administrative Console beginning in Part III, "Systems Administration." Your first introduction to the Administrative Console is in Chapter 4.

Advanced Edition Developer-Only (AEd)

The Advanced Edition Developer-Only (AEd) has the same functionality as AEs, but has a development-only license. Because you are already familiar with the capabilities of AEs, there is no need to repeat the information. It might be helpful, however, to know the differences between the AE version and the AEs/AEd versions. Table 1-2 shows the differences between the editions.

Table 1-2: Edition Differences

Feature	*AEs/AEd*	*AE*
Full J2EE compliance	Yes	Yes
Web services support	Yes	Yes
Expanded DB support	Yes	Yes
Built-in Web server	Yes	Yes
Web-based Administrative Console	Yes	No
Security	Local	Local, LDAP, Custom
Integration with Enterprise Edition	No	Yes
Application-level WLM	No	Yes
Clustering and cloning	No	Yes
IIOP-based Administrative Console	No	Yes
Multinode administration	No	Yes
Merant JDBC drivers included	No	Yes
J2C supported	No	Yes

Understanding WebSphere Development Tools

One of the key differences between WebSphere Application Server and its competitors is that WebSphere has superior development tools. Several tools integrate with WebSphere Application Server. This section discusses tools from previous versions — VisualAge for Java, WebSphere Studio — and introduces WebSphere Studio Application Developer and WebSphere Studio Site Developer, the latest tools in WebSphere's arsenal.

Using VisualAge for Java

Since the introduction of WebSphere Application Server, IBM has had VisualAge for Java as a premier development Integrated Development Environment (IDE). VisualAge for Java is a repository-based IDE that not only supports Java development, but also provides incremental compilation, change management using the Envy repository, and guided wizards to expedite development.

VisualAge for Java is a team-based IDE for creating enterprise Java applications and components, such as JavaBeans, servlets, applets, and Enterprise JavaBeans (EJB).

The following list includes some of the key features of VisualAge:

- An incremental Java compiler that significantly reduces compilation times
- A local or shared repository that performs change-management and version-control activities
- A Visual Composition Editor to create Java swing and AWT applications and/or applets
- Code wizards to take the effort out of creating EJBs by hand. Just follow the prompts and fill in the blanks, and you're ready to go.
- A Servlet Builder Wizard to again prompt the developer through some simple steps to generate a working servlet.
- WebSphere test environment (not AEd) that enables you to test your J2EE applications within the IDE.
- Connectivity to middleware and host systems using add-on features that come with the product.
- An integrated debugger that enables you to set breakpoints, step into code, and inspect objects.

VisualAge for Java comes in two editions: Professional and Enterprise. The Professional Edition is a base edition supporting some J2EE components (servlets and JSPs). The Enterprise Edition adds Enterprise JavaBeans and more database and middleware support.

Using WebSphere Studio Classic

WebSphere Studio is a suite of tools that assists teams in developing and publishing Web-based applications. Studio can be team-based if its repository is installed on a shared server. WebSphere Studio has the following capabilities:

- Page designer for developing HTML pages
- Applet designer for visually creating an applet
- WebArt designer for designing headers, banners, and buttons
- Animated GIF designer for creating GIF files
- Integration with VisualAge for Java
- Wizards for generation of servlets

WebSphere Studio is designed for the Web developer. It has integration capabilities with the code Java developers create, as well as integration to external change-management systems.

> **NOTE**: Using VisualAge and WebSphere Studio together has some inherit problems. WebSphere Studio is fine for developing and publishing Web pages, JavaServer Pages (JSP), and other Web resources. VisualAge for Java is great for creating and deploying servlets, EJBs, and Java class files.
>
> The problem that exists between the products is that both need deployment, but there is some cross over; so coordination becomes a problem. For example, to deploy an enterprise application, VisualAge developers must deploy the EJBs and class files; whereas WebSphere Studio folks need to deploy the HTML and other Web resources.
>
> WebSphere Application Server 4.0's additional tooling helps you overcome this problem by providing the Application Assembly Tool (AAT) that can be used in conjunction with VisualAge for Java 4.0 and WebSphere Studio 4. AAT takes the Web Archive files (WAR) created by WebSphere Studio Classic and the EJB Java archive (JAR) from VisualAge for Java and (with some additional information from the deployer) creates the Enterprise Archive (EAR).

Introducing WebSphere Studio Application Developer (WSAD)

Figure 1-5 shows a screenshot of the WebSphere Studio Application Developer (WSAD). WebSphere Studio Application developer is a by-product of the open-source project code name Eclipse. Eclipse is an open-source development framework that provides the development community with a robust and flexible development tool. Eclipse is based on open standards and provides plug-and-play capabilities to third-party tools. The Eclipse platform is designed and built to meet the following basic requirements:

- Supports the construction of a variety of tools for application development
- Supports an unrestricted set of tool providers, including independent software vendors
- Supports tools to manipulate arbitrary content types
- Facilitates seamless integration of tools within and across different content types and tool providers
- Supports both GUI and non-GUI-based application-development environments
- Runs on a wide range of operating systems, including Windows and Linux
- Capitalizes on the popularity of the Java programming language for writing tools

WSAD is built upon Eclipse. WSAD provides many of the functions and features that VisualAge for Java provides, but it has some added benefits because it actually utilizes WebSphere Application Server Developer-Only (AEd) as its version of the WebSphere test environment.

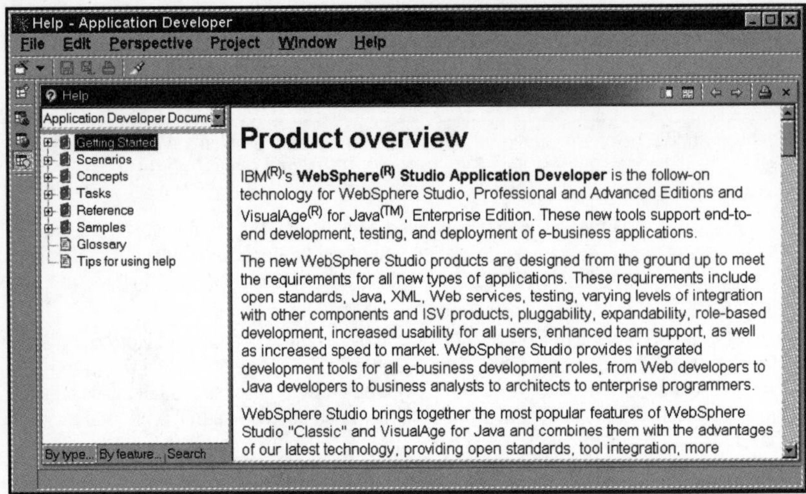

Figure 1-5: Included with WebSphere Studio Application Developer are editors for Java, EJB, HTML, and XML, as well as specific development perspectives that help organize your workspace.

You learn much more about WebSphere Studio Application Developer in the chapters to come.

CROSS-REFERENCE: Chapter 7 is devoted to the installation and use of WebSphere Studio Application Developer and WebSphere Studio Site Developer (WSSD).

Introducing WebSphere Studio Site Developer (WSSD)

Another product built on top of the Eclipse standards is the WebSphere Studio Site Developer (WSSD). WSSD is really not a tool that you will be using along with this book, but there are a few points worth mentioning. Figure 1-6 shows a screen shot of the WSSD.

Notice that Figures 1-5 and 1-6 have the same look and feel. If you were to open the Web perspective in WebSphere Studio Application Developer, you would see a screen almost identical to that in Figure 1-6. What you may not know is that WSSD is actually delivered with WSAD. So you are really getting two tools for the price of one. This is all possible because of the Eclipse framework and its plug-and-play components. You can build and add on features as desired.

You do not utilize WSSD in the book, but many of the features of WSSD are shown in the Web perspective of WSAD. For more information on Eclipse, visit `www.eclipse.org`. To learn more about WSSD visit `www.ibm.com/software/ad/studiositedev`.

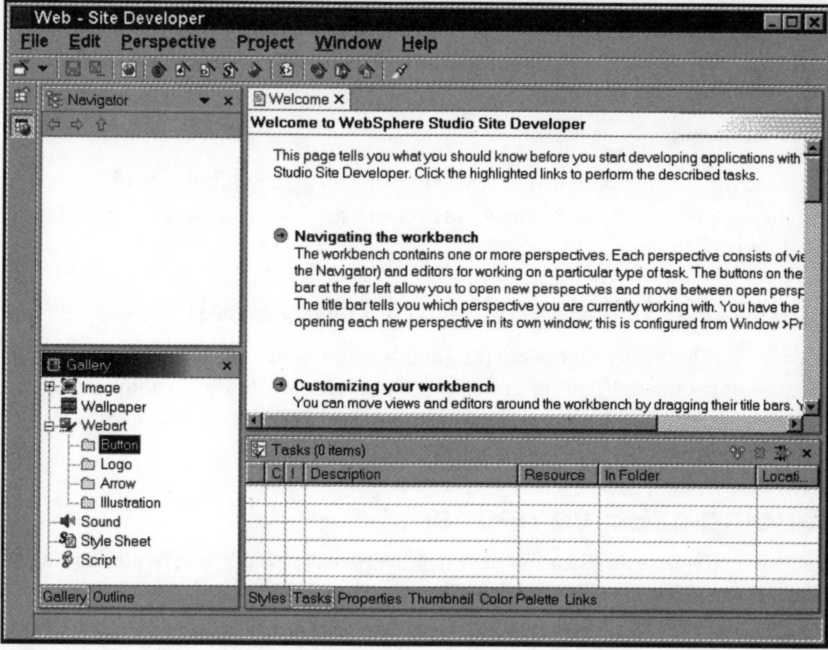

Figure 1-6: WebSphere Studio Site Developer looks very similar to WebSphere Studio Application Developer because the two products, although having different target audiences, are built upon the same framework.

Understanding Supporting Products

In this section, you learn about which products work with WebSphere Application Server and how they interact.

IBM HTTP Server 1.3.19

IBM HTTP Server is a Web server based up the popular Apache server. IBM has enhanced the Apache server to provide the following:

- Browser-based administration
- Support for Secured Sockets Layer (SSL)
- A Fast Response Cache Accelerator (FRCA)
- Shared LDAP access via a plug-in
- Simple Network Management Protocol (SNMP) to enable system monitoring

You are not required to install the IBM HTTP Server with WebSphere. You can choose Microsoft IIS, Netscape IPlanet, Apache, or Domino.

CROSS-REFERENCE: You install the IBM HTTP Server in Chapter 4.

Introducing DB2 Universal Database 7.2

DB2 provides the persistence mechanism to maintain configuration settings for WebSphere Application Server. DB2 provides the relational database-management features necessary to store and retrieve information.

Although DB2 is the product that you install if you're working along with this book, WebSphere Application Server supports many other databases. The supported databases are DB2, Oracle, Informix, Sybase, and SQL Server.

Introducing Tivioli Policy Director (Web Seal)

Policy Director provides authentication, network security, and policy management for complete protection of resources. You set these security policies centrally, so administration is simplified. Web Seal authenticates users and provides a single Web sign on. Web Seal supports up to four levels of integration to maximize security.

Understanding J2EE components

J2EE is the core of WebSphere Application Server. In version 1.2.1, J2EE provides a robust Java environment from which to build. Figure 1-7 shows the J2EE components found in WebSphere.

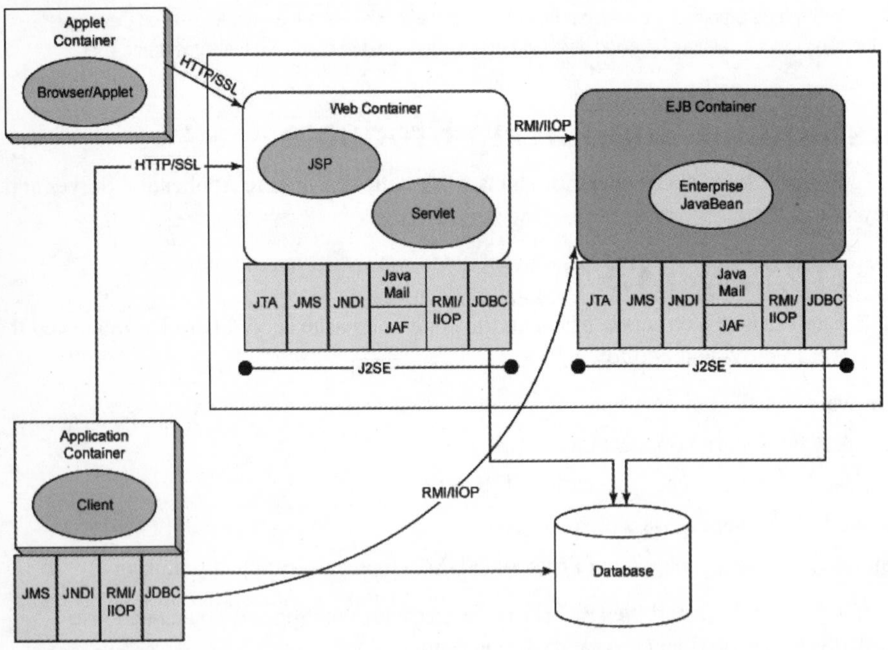

Figure 1-7: WebSphere supports four types of containers, as per the J2EE specification.

Figure 1-7 demonstrates the interactions among the different containers. The J2EE specification divides the enterprise into four containers. The Applet and Application containers represent users accessing the enterprise. The Web container is responsible for the HTML, JSP, and servlet processing. The EJB container supports business logic and data persistence.

Table 1-3 describes J2EE services and APIs for which WebSphere Application Server is certified.

Table 1-3: J2EE Services and APIs

J2EE Service/API	*Description*
EJB 1.1	Enterprise JavaBean Specification 1.1 is at the heart of J2EE. It specifies a server-side component for deploying business content.
JSP 1.1	Java Server Pages version 1.1 allows insertion of Java code with HTML pages, providing a dynamic generation of business content.
Servlets 2.2	Servlet version 2.2 is a replacement for CGI-like programs that execute on the server side.
JNDI 1.2	Java Naming and Directory Interface version 1.2 provides a standard way to interface to directory services.
JDBC 2.0	Java Database Connectivity 2.0 extends the JDBC API to include new items, such as connection pooling using datasources.
RMI-IIOP 1.0	(RMI) Remote Method Invocation over Internet Inter-Orb Protocol (IIOP) enables interoperability over the Internet, using CORBA-like interaction.
JMS 1.0	Java Message Service provides the capability to utilize asynchronous messaging between enterprise environments.
JTA 1.0	Java Transaction API defines interfaces between transaction managers and the parties involved in a distributed-transaction system.
JavaMail 1.1	JavaMail 1.1 is an API that provides a platform-independent and protocol-independent framework to build mail services.
XML	XML, the Extensible Markup Language, is the preferred technology in information-transfer scenarios because of its capability to easily encode, process, and generate information.
JAF 1.0	JavaBeans Activation Framework 1.0 enables developers, using Java, to take data, encapsulate it, discover methods available, and instantiate the appropriate operations.

Introducing Apache Simple Object Access Protocol (SOAP) 2.1

WebSphere Application Server now supports Web services. A *Web service* is an interface that describes a collection of operations that are network-accessible through XML messaging. One of the key enablers is Apache Simple Object Access Protocol (SOAP). You can create SOAP implementation of your Java classes, EJBs, and stored procedures.

Introducing Web Services Definition Language (WSDL) 1.1

Web Services Definition Language (WSDL) is the means of describing what a Web service can do, where it resides, and how it is invoked. You install a product called the Web Services Toolkit in Chapter 19. You learn more about WSDL in that chapter.

Introducing Universal Discovery and Description Integration (UDDI)

Universal Discovery and Description Integration (UDDI) is what service providers need to advertise their services. UDDI provides a directory similar to the telephone book. The directory provides white pages for businesses, yellow pages for organizations, and green pages to define how businesses communicate electronically. WebSphere supports the deployment of a UDDI registry.

CROSS-REFERENCE: Chapters 3 and 19 are devoted to Web services.

Summary

WebSphere Application Server version 4.0 is a major step in the right direction for IBM. Adhering to the J2EE 1.2 specification has made WebSphere a premier application server.

WebSphere now comes packaged very differently than in past releases of WebSphere. There are now three flavors, two of which you can purchase as separate products (AE/AEs). The third (AEd) is actually a free copy provided as the WebSphere test environment for WebSphere Studio Application Developer.

If you are in need of only a departmental server, you might consider purchasing the WebSphere Application Single Server Edition. This edition contains the same core infrastructure as all WebSphere Application Server editions, but it is without some of the administrative capabilities of the full version (AE). With Single Server Edition, you can still create servlets, Java Server Pages (JSP), and Enterprise JavaBeans (EJB).

You administer the Single Server Edition through a Web browser interface. Working in tandem with XML configuration files, this interface makes it much easier to configure and then edit files.

WebSphere Application Server Advanced Edition (AE) is the flagship product. With it, you get additional tools, such as the Application Assembly Tool (AAT), that help you prepare your J2EE deployment. AE gives you the capability to create multiple application servers on a single machine or many machines. This capability provides you with the ability to manage performance and improve scalability. You also get improved fail-over support by having multiple machines.

WebSphere also supports many operating systems and database management systems. You can run WebSphere on Windows 2000/NT, Linux, Solaris, AIX, and other IBM platforms, such as the AS400. AE supports DB2, Oracle, Sybase, Microsoft SQL Server, and Informix as database engines for its Administrative Server.

For the developer, WebSphere Studio Application Developer was briefly mentioned in this summary. WebSphere Studio Application Developer is the new platform for development of J2EE applications. Based on the open-source project Eclipse, WebSphere Studio Application Developer provides the combined capabilities of VisualAge for Java and WebSphere Studio Classic. WebSphere Studio Application Developer comes installed with the third flavor of WebSphere Application Server. Known as the WebSphere Test Environment, this version (AEd) operates the same way the Single Server Edition (AEs) does.

The chapter wrapped up with a discussion on the support products that make up the WebSphere domain, including databases, Web servers, and security servers. For the rest of the book, all examples use DB2 as the database and IBM HTTP Server as the Web server. The chapter ended with a discussion on J2EE components and the introduction of the next wave of future — Web services.

Chapter 2
WebSphere Application Architecture

In This Chapter

- Understanding WebSphere application architecture
- Introducing WebSphere plug-ins
- Introducing the Administrative Server
- Introducing the Administrative Console

In Chapter 1, you learned that WebSphere is a collection of products working together to provide a foundation of proven technologies for your e-business infrastructure. In this chapter, you begin learning about how the WebSphere foundation is layered to provide the building blocks for a comprehensive, portable, and reliable infrastructure.

You may want to think of WebSphere as business opportunity. As with any business venture, you want to see how it can make you successful, so you ask questions. Who are the customers? How do they interact? Is there room to grow? How do you handle peak seasons? What is the best way to organize so that you can balance cost while increasing your performance?

With respect to WebSphere, you are introduced to the concept of a WebSphere domain. That is the starting place when you think about configuring WebSphere. It all begins with the Administrative Server. You might want to think of the Administrative Server as the center of the WebSphere universe. As you learn more about the Administrative Server, you learn more about how WebSphere interacts with the Web server and administrative repository, which is a database.

You learn about some of the internals of the Administrative Server. After you have an understanding of the Administrative Server, you are then introduced to the Administrative Console. You learn how it works, what components you need to configure, and how J2EE fits into the overall design.

This chapter provides your first introduction to server groups and clones. The way you define server groups and distribute clones dictates how your topology is designed.

After you examine the WebSphere domain and what it's made of, you should be able to diagram the complete WebSphere architecture. You can use this information to formulate your business plan, allocate resources, and impress friends, peers, and management with your overall knowledge.

Although this chapter talks a lot about configuration, it doesn't discuss the details of WebSphere configuration. You learn about configuring WebSphere in Chapter 20.

> **NOTE**: To simplify the process of identifying the installation root of WebSphere, from this point on the installation root is denoted as `<was_home>`.

Understanding the WebSphere Application Server Architecture

One of the goals in this chapter is to ensure that you have a clear understanding of the landscape of the WebSphere Application Server environment. Figure 2-1 shows the various components that make up the WebSphere environment. It represents a topology with an IBM HTTP Server running on the same hardware as the application server. This topology is similar to the default installation of WebSphere. If you so choose, the default installation will install all needed components on the same machine.

> **CROSS-REFERENCE:** You learn more about the installation options in Chapter 4.

During the discussion of the components, refer frequently to Figure 2-1. Figure 2-1, showing a WebSphere domain, is an excellent starting point.

Understanding WebSphere domains

A WebSphere domain is a group of one or more application servers grouped together by a shared WebSphere repository. The following points describe some of the components and services shown in Figure 2-1:

- Web browser
- IBM HTTP server (Web server) that has the WebSphere plug-in installed
- Administrative Server containing an application server running in its own Java Virtual Machine (JVM)
- The embedded HTTP server (port 9080) that communicates with the plug-in or directly to a browser.

- A J2EE Web container supporting servlets and JavaServer Pages (JSP)
- A J2EE Enterprise JavaBean (EJB) container handling session and entity EJBs
- Various application-specific databases for storing application data
- Administrative Server providing security services and JNDI lookup
- Administrative Console for managing and configuring WebSphere domains
- Administrative repository for storing configuration information
- XMLConfig and WebSphere Control Program (WSCP) for providing command-line configuration capabilities
- DrAdmin, which provides a service for enabling and disabling tracing.

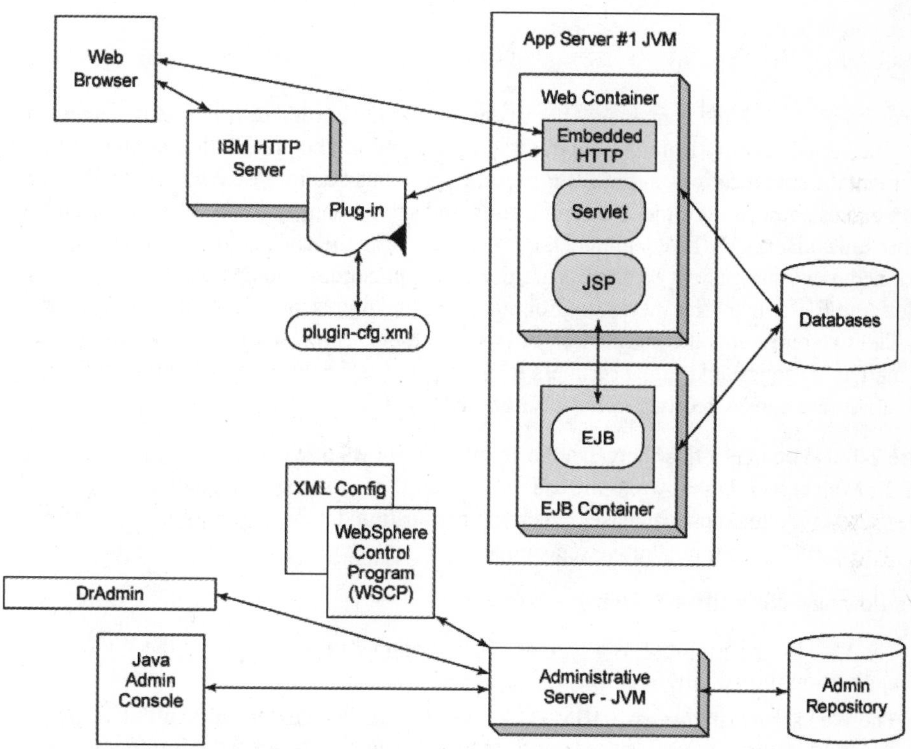

Figure 2-1: In a WebSphere domain, the administrative repository contains the configuration of all applications servers and components for WebSphere domain.

NOTE: DrAdmin is used as a last-resort debugging facility. It should be used only in situations in which
—The Administrative Console appears blank.
—The Administrative Server is not responding (is in a wait state).
—You have to dump the thread stacks in a server.
—Input to the Administrative Console is not being accepted.

The WebSphere domain shown in Figure 2-1 shows the J2EE containers specified in the Java 2 Enterprise Edition (J2EE) specification. There are four different types of containers defined in the specification. The Web container and EJB container are two of the containers. The other two are client-side containers: applet containers and application containers (not shown in Figure 2-1). Containers provide runtime support for the following application components:

- Lifecycle management
- Deployment
- Security

By providing support, the containers effectively remove the burden of lifecycle management, deployment, and security from the programmer. The vendor who creates the container must implement the specifications in the J2EE specs. In previous versions of WebSphere, the Web container was comprised of the Web application and servlet engine. There was a separate Enterprise JavaBeans (EJB) container. J2EE 1.2 introduces the concept of client containers. As mentioned previously, client containers are tier-one applications and applets that can access servlets and EJBs. In a three-tiered environment, tier one represents the level closest to the user. Tier two represents the middle tier, or business logic server. In this tier, you can process information or request additional business logic or data from a third tier. Client/server applications are considered two-tiered environments.

Figure 2-1 also depicts a flow between the services. It shows how a user can request a service from the Web server. Unknown to the user, a great deal of processing is going on: HTTP requests, resource lookups, databases accessing application databases, logging, and database activity to the shared administrative repository.

The following steps walk you through the flow:

1. The Web browser represents a type of client container that is accessing the Web application through the Web server.
2. The Web server (in this case, IBM HTTP Server) has been extended to utilize a plug-in. The plug-in uses an XML-based configuration file that provides the information necessary to determine how transportation is applied.
3. Through the plug-in, communication is established — via Hypertext Transport Protocol (HTTP) or Secured Hypertext Transport Protocol (HTTPS) — to a new embedded HTTP server located within the Web container of the application server.

4. Routing is then performed to send the request to the appropriate resource, in this case, a JSP page or servlet. If the resource requested is a static HTML page on the Web server, it's handled by the Web server.

TIP: Only Web resources defined on the application server (servlets and JSP pages) are processed by the embedded HTTP server.

5. The servlet has access to the EJB container and/or external database engines, such as DB2 or Oracle. Within the EJB container, access to the database is through container-managed persistence (CMP) or bean-managed persistence (BMP). From within the Web container, you achieve access to external relational databases by using Java Database Connectivity (JDBC).

CROSS-REFERENCE: You can learn more about container-managed persistence (CMP) or bean-managed persistence (BMP) in Chapter 13

Now that you are familiar with the flow of requests, discussions of the Administrative Server, the WebSphere plug-in, and the Administrative Console follow.

Introducing the Administrative Server

The Administrative Server (also referred as the *admin server*) provides the services you use to manage and control the administrative resources in the administrative repository. Figure 2-2 shows the Administrative Server and its components.

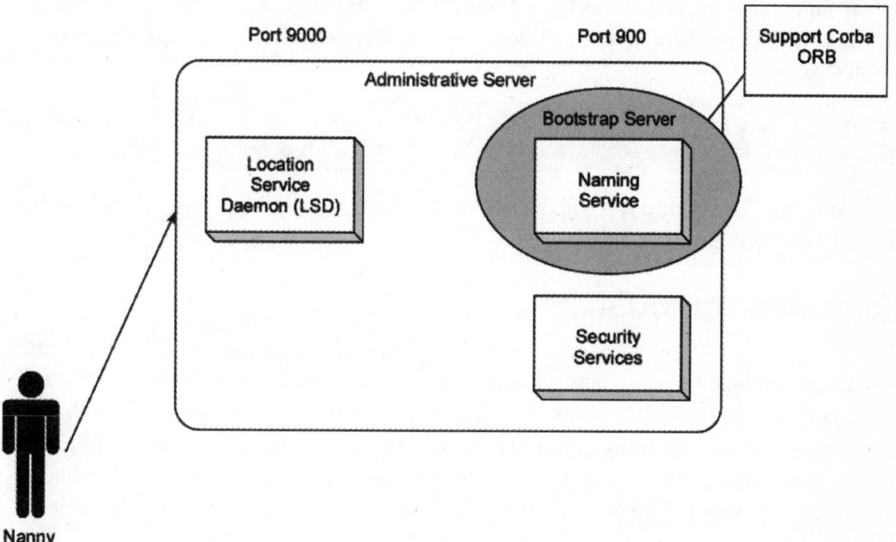

Figure 2-2: The Administrative Server provides access to important services: Java Native Directory Interface (JNDI) services through the Location Service Daemon (LSD) on port 9000 and the Bootstrap Server (port 900) where the Administrative Console connects.

The Administrative Server provides container support for Web modules and EJB modules. In fact, the Administrative Server is implemented as an EJB. That's what you might call "eating your own dog food" — your product is so good that you use it yourself. J2EE not only makes it easier for you to deliver enterprise applications; it also makes it easier for IBM to do so.

The Administrative Server also provides transaction updates to configuration changes through an Administrative Console. As you begin managing multiple machines and multiple domains, you may want to use a more command-line–driven process to help automate some of the work. You're in luck. The Administrative Server has command-line interfaces that allow most configuration updates. Those interfaces can be accessed with XMLConfig and the WebSphere Control Program (WSCP) command-line services.

Java Native Directory Interface (JNDI) naming and security are also managed by the Administrative Server. The bootstrap server is needed by the naming service. It's really the Object Request Broker (ORB) that listens for administrative requests. Remember that the Administrative Server is an EJB, and EJBs are accessed by way of the Internet InterORB Protocol (IIOP). By default, it listens to port 900.

Also within the Administrative Server is the Location Service Daemon (LSD). It is used for persistent object references. The LSD acts as the JNDI server, finding where objects live. The default port for the LSD is port 9000.

The final service provided by the Administrative Server is Security Services. Security Services manage the authentication and authorization within the WebSphere environment. No one can gain access to the WebSphere domain without being authenticated. You learn more about security in Chapter 23.

NOTE: You may have heard references to *nanny*. The nanny process exists only on Unix systems. Its primary function is to act as a watchdog to ensure that the Administrative Server is functioning.

In the sections that follow, you learn about the various services you can configure within the Administrative Console.

Understanding nodes

A node, by any other name, is a machine. A *node*, in WebSphere terminology, is a machine that contains an application server and an Administrative Server. Although only one node is necessary, you can have multiple nodes sharing a single administrative repository. In that situation, you are actually defining a WebSphere domain. During installation of WebSphere, you choose an administrative repository for your node. At that point, you determine whether this particular node is part of an existing WebSphere domain or whether you are creating a new domain.

TIP: A node is a physical machine with an Administrative Server installed to manage resources.

Learning about HTTP server and plug-ins

If you refer to Figure 2-1 again, you see the browser accessing an HTTP server that has an application plug-in installed. In the WebSphere world, a plug-in isn't a device that you plug into the wall socket to make the room smell fresh and flowery. A plug-in enables communication between the HTTP server and WebSphere Application Server. Figure 2-3 shows the plug-in architecture.

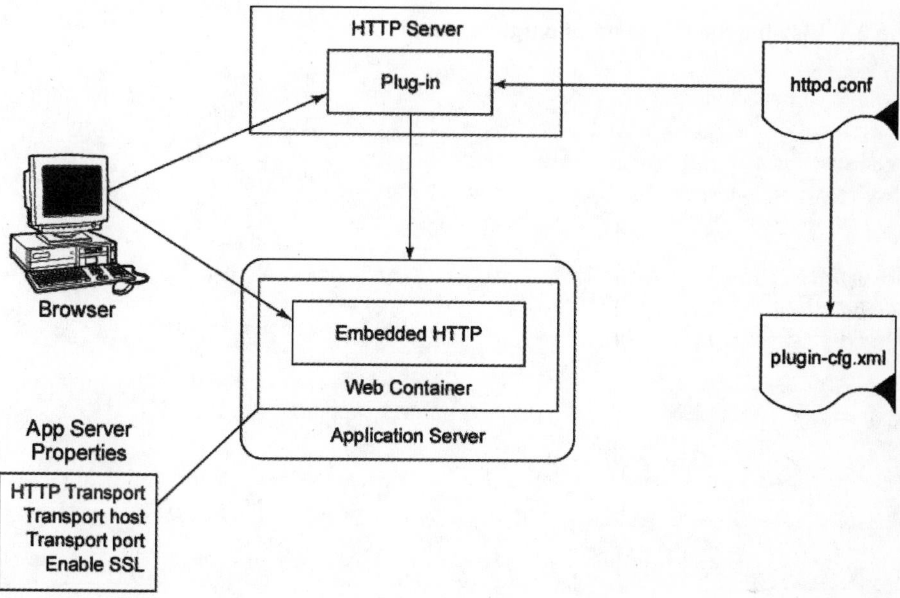

Figure 2-3: The HTTP plug-in architecture enables the most popular Web servers to communicate with the WebSphere Application Server.

In Figure 2-3, you see that the browser sends a request to the HTTP server, and the request is interpreted by the plug-in to determine where to route the request. If the request is for servlet processing, the request needs to be sent to the Web container. If the request is for static Web pages, the request is normally handled by a document residing on the HTTP server.

NOTE: You could conceivably place all your Web pages within the Web container, but for performance reasons you should not.

Figure 2-3 also shows another HTTP server — the Embedded HTTP server. The Embedded HTTP server is new with WebSphere 4.0. It replaces the Open Servlet Engine (OSE) that was utilized in versions 3.5. OSE was confusing to implement and configure and was not as fast as the new HTTP 1.1 protocol used with the Embedded HTTP server. The Embedded HTTP server is automatically installed and configured when you install WebSphere 4.0.

Communication between the plug-in and WebSphere is through HTTP 1.1. By utilizing HTTP 1.1, you gain an additional level of security, because you can configure Secure Sockets Layer (SSL) between your HTTP server and the Embedded HTTP server.

Also new with version 4.0 is the way the configuration is saved. The configuration information is contained in an XML file called `plugin-cfg.xml`. You update this file with the Administrative Console or through an editor. Figure 2-3 shows how the `httpd.conf` file references the `plugin-cfg.xml` file to determine which resources are available. Listing 2-1 shows the contents of the `plugin-cfg` file.

Listing 2-1: Viewing the Contents of plugin-cfg.xml

```
<?xml version="1.0"?>
<Config>
 <Log LogLevel="Error" Name="d:\Websphere\AppServer\logs\native.log"/>
 <VirtualHostGroup Name="default_host">
  <VirtualHost Name="*:80"/>
  <VirtualHost Name="*:9080"/>
 </VirtualHostGroup>
 <ServerGroup Name="kafemocha/Default Server">
  <Server CloneID="tgldj162" Name="Default Server">
   <Transport Hostname="kafemocha" Port="9080" Protocol="http"/>
  </Server>
 </ServerGroup>
 <UriGroup Name="kafemocha_sampleApp/default_app_URIs">
  <Uri Name="/servlet/snoop/*"/>
  <Uri Name="/servlet/snoop"/>
  <Uri Name="/servlet/snoop2/*"/>
  <Uri Name="/servlet/snoop2"/>
  <Uri Name="/servlet/hello"/>
  <Uri Name="/ErrorReporter"/>
  <Uri Name="*.jsp"/>
  <Uri Name="*.jsv"/>
  <Uri Name="*.jsw"/>
  <Uri Name="j_security_check"/>
  <Uri Name="/servlet/*"/>
 </UriGroup>
 <UriGroup Name="kafemocha_sampleApp/examples_URIs">
  <Uri Name="/webapp/examples"/>
 </UriGroup>
 <Route ServerGroup="kafemocha/Default Server"
   UriGroup="kafemocha_sampleApp/default_app_URIs"
VirtualHostGroup="default_host"/>
 <Route ServerGroup="kafemocha/Default Server"
   UriGroup="kafemocha_sampleApp/examples_URIs"
VirtualHostGroup="default_host"/>
</Config>
```

The virtual host and transport elements refer to port 9080, the port for the Embedded HTTP server. Because it's an HTTP server, you can point your browser to `http://localhost:9080/servlet/SnoopServlet` and access the server. You wouldn't want to access this HTTP server in a production environment; but as a debugging tool, it comes in handy.

> **TIP**: The `plugin-cfg.xml file` can be found in `<was_home>/config`.

Listing 2-1 uses `ServerGroup`, `URIGroup`, and `VirtualHosts`. The configurations in the plug-in file are your responsibility. When a change affects transport properties such as host, ports, protocols, and SSL, you need to regenerate the plug-in.

The following steps walk you through plug-in processing:

1. The plug-in determines the server group by comparing the incoming URI and host name and locates a match in the `plugin-cfg.xml` file.
2. If cloning is present, specialized algorithms are utilized to determine the best way to load balance and process the request.
3. If encryption is designated in the configuration parameters, the plug-in sends the request to the embedded HTTP server encrypted (using SSL).
4. Otherwise the plug-in sends the request on to the server, and the plug-in awaits a response from the server.

A lot of coordination occurs between the HTTP server plug-in and the application server. It is important to remember that the plug-in must match the parameters specified in the WebSphere configuration (host names, ports, protocols); if they don't, errors can occur or your results may vary.

> **NOTE**: The WebSphere Administrative Console does inform you of possible changes that require a regeneration of the plug-in. The information shows up as a message in the console.

Understanding virtual hosts

The term *virtual host* refers to the capability to maintain more than one server on one machine, differentiated by apparent host names. Take, for example, companies that host multiple Web domains on a single server, such as an ISP. The ISP will want to host multiple URLs, such as `www.commercesolutions.com` and `www.commercesolutions.info` without requiring the user to know any extra path information. You can be even more creative by creating virtual hosts that point to the same location. Wouldn't it be great if you could type `www.commercesolutions.com` or `commercesolutions.com` and achieve the same result?

With virtual hosting, you can independently configure and administer applications on a single machine. The benefit of virtual hosts is that they are configurable. They don't have to be associated with a particular machine. You can move the configuration to a completely different machine, and the virtual host works as configured.

Virtual hosts have logical names and a list of one or more aliases. An *alias* is a TCP/IP name and port number used to access a resource. The following list includes the default ports and aliases:

- 80 is the standard port address most external HTTP servers use. (Note: Port 80 is not secure.)
- 443 is the secure external HTTPS (SSL) port.
- 9080 is the unsecured embedded HTTP port.
- 9443 is the secure embedded HTTPS port.

Figure 2-4 shows the WebSphere Administrative Console with the default host alias for WebSphere's default_host. Because installation is not covered until Chapter 4, you can't see this screen on your own machine.

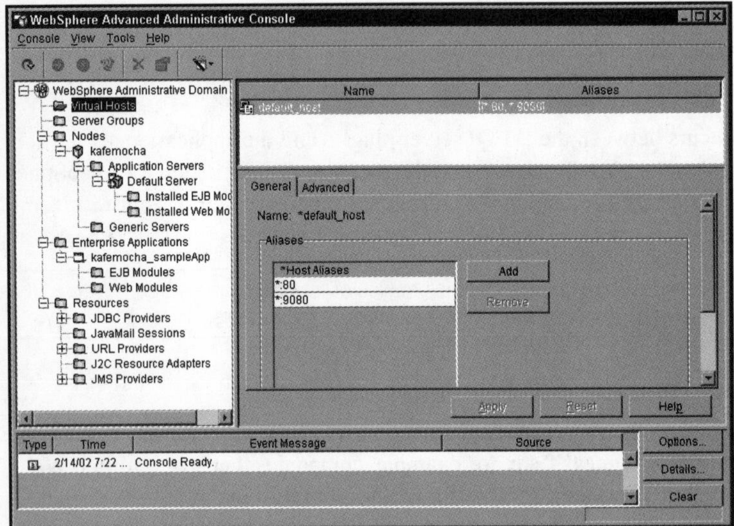

Figure 2-4: Virtual hosting is a powerful feature of WebSphere application server. This is a wonderful feature for someone who wants to maximize utilization of a machine by having many hosts.

You should note that one virtual host cannot share data with resources associated with another virtual host. That holds true even if the virtual hosts are on the same machine.

Understanding Java virtual machines

Version 4.0 of IBM WebSphere Application Server runs its own instance of the Java Development Kit (JDK) — version Java 1.3.0, which is distributed with WebSphere and is installed with the product. You may be wondering whether the WebSphere-installed version conflicts with other installed versions of the JDK. The answer is no. Because WebSphere installs its own JDK, a consistent environment is ensured.

> **TIP**: The environment variable that points to the WebSphere installed JDK is `<JDK_Home>`.

So how many Java Virtual Machines (JVMs) are running when you have WebSphere running? Each application server has its own JVM. You also have a separate JVM when you launch the Administrative Console.

The number of JVMs differs in WebSphere Application Server Advanced Single Server Edition (AEs). Although you haven't learned much about AEs, the primary difference is that with AEs you don't use the Administrative Console. Instead you use a browser-based administration facility that updates Extensible Markup Language (XML) configurations files instead of using DB2 tables.

You need to be concerned about having too many JVMs running on your machine. Table 2-1 provides some guidelines for the minimum requirements needed to support multiple-application servers.

Table 2-1: Application Server Support Guidelines for WebSphere

Components	***Rule of thumb***
Number of nodes per repository	8 nodes or fewer per repository
Number of CPUs	Greater than or equal to 1 CPU per application server
Memory on WinNT/2000	Greater than or equal to 512 megabytes per CPU minimum
Memory on UNIX	Greater than or equal to 768 megabytes per CPU minimum

Getting to know enterprise applications

An *enterprise application* is a J2EE application that is deployed on WebSphere. To be an enterprise application, it must conform to J2EE specification, meaning that it must consist of at least one EJB, Web, or application-client module. Figure 2-5 shows the Enterprise Application node selected in the WebSphere Administrative Console.

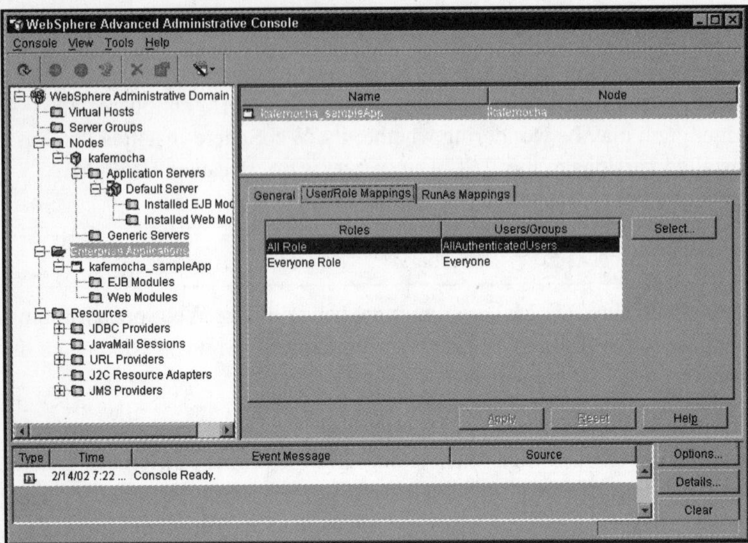

Figure 2-5: Installing enterprise applications is new with WebSphere. You now install Enterprise Archives (EAR) that expand the EAR file into the InstalledApps folder.

In Figure 2-5 the `kafemocha sampleApp` is under the Enterprise Applications node. The details about how resources are configured do not appear. The resources that comprise an enterprise application are contained in an Enterprise Archive (EAR) file, which also contains Java archives (JAR) and Web archives (WAR) files, as well as deployment descriptors.

You cannot change the resources in the JAR and WAR files. What you can change is the name of the enterprise application as referenced by the Administrative Console and security information, such as user/role mappings and RunAs mappings. You configure these mapping to match the security roles of your user directory with the roles identified within your application. This is one of the powerful features of J2EE 1.2 — role-based security.

Understanding EJB modules

EJB modules are deployable units of EJBs contained in a single module. EJB modules can be used individually or combined with other EJB or Web modules to create an enterprise application. (See the following section, "Web modules," for more information.). Each EJB module is declared in a deployment descriptor. The descriptor describes how the beans are used at runtime. EJB modules are packaged in Java Archives (JAR) files. The JAR files are then packaged in an EAR file in preparation for deployment

NOTE: In previous versions of WebSphere, each enterprise bean had its own deployment descriptor. Version 4.0 uses one deployment descriptor for all EJBs in the module.

EJB modules are constructed prior to deployment. After you deploy them with WebSphere Application Server, the Administrative Console enables you to change only the default data source for the EJB container and data sources for any beans not being used with the default datasource for the container.

> **TIP**: Within the Administrative Console, you can start and stop the EJB modules. Doing this refreshes the EJB modules from disk.

Understanding Web modules

Web modules are made up of servlets, JSPs, HTML, and images. Web modules are assembled into a Web Archive (WAR) file prior to deployment. A Web archive is implemented in the same fashion as a Java archive. Web archives also have deployment descriptors that define their runtime parameters. The Web modules are then optionally combined with EJB modules to create the Enterprise Archive's (EAR) deployment descriptors. All this is performed prior to deployment.

After you deploy Web modules, you can modify only certain information from the Administrative Console. For example, you can modify the context root. The context root is combined with a servlet mapping to compose the fully qualified URL. Imagine you have a context root named `/cruise` and a servlet alias of `shipdetails`. The combination of the two would result in the following:

```
http://host:port/cruise/shipdetails
```

Invoking this URL would call the shipdetail servlet to run within the `/cruise` application. Another item you might change is the logical name of the enterprise application.

Understanding application server's organization

All the individual components mentioned in the previous sections are contained in the application server. The application server, per the J2EE specifications, provides the runtime environment (containers) for Web modules and EJB modules.

Working in conjunction with the Web server, the application server's primary function is to return the results of client requests. You can define multiple applications servers per node with each application server running in its own Java Virtual Machine (JVM). Please refer to the section, "Understanding Java virtual machines," for more information.

Default server

When you install WebSphere Application Server 4.0, you have automatically installed a default application server. The `default_server` is automatically configured with a Web module and an EJB module.

> **CROSS-REFERENCE:** You run some of the default servlets in Chapter 4.

EJB container

Your EJB modules, when deployed, are managed by the EJB container that is a part of the application server. The EJB containers provide services to the EJB. They are responsible for the lifecycle of the bean; therefore they create, manage, and destroy beans.

The container is responsible for providing persistence services as well as security services. These services are specified at deployment. Figure 2-6 shows the Administrative Console with the Default Server node selected.

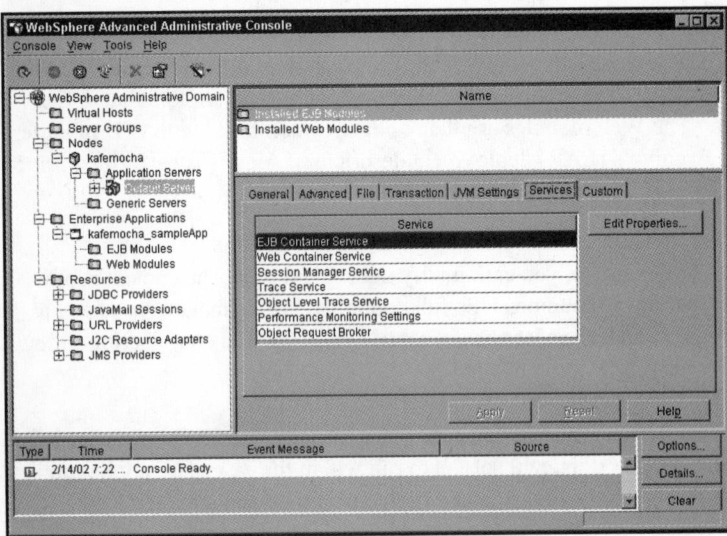

Figure 2-6: The Administrative Console enables you to configure the J2EE containers. Simply select the application server and switch to the Service tab and all services are available for editing.

The Services tab in Figure 2-6 shows the types of services provided by the application server. You can edit the properties of the EJB container service to change various performance parameters, such as cache size and cache clean-up interval, as well as to change the default datasource.

Web container

The Web container is responsible for handling requests for Web resources, including servlets and JSP files. The Web container manages the request/response interaction, loading and unloading of servlets, and other servlet performance-related tasks.

Figure 2-6 shows the Web Container Service selection on the Services tab where you can update properties of the Web container. Some of the properties you can change are as follows:

- HTTP transports that specify port numbers and queuing parameters
- Servlet caching to improve performance

Understanding resources

WebSphere Application Server supports several J2EE service-based Application Programming Interfaces (API). The following Java APIs provide communication mechanisms that enable interoperability with various Independent Software Vendors (ISV):

- Java Database Connectivity (JDBC) providers supply vendor-independent database connectivity. JDBC 2.0 is the current level of the specification.
- Datasources enable you to define and configure specific connections to a relational database that supplies a JDBC provider library. Datasources provide support for pooling connections.
- JNDI is an API that provides naming and directory functionality.
- A J2C resource adapter represents a library that supports connections from an application to a nonrelational back-end system. By using resource archives, you configure and connect to Executive Information System (EIS) services through WebSphere.
- A URL provider implements the functionality for a particular URL protocol, such as HTTP, or FTP. The default URL provider that comes with WebSphere supports HTTP, FTP, File, and Mailto. You can add new URL providers.
- The Java Messaging Services (JMS) providers APIs provide for reliable interfacing to asychronous messaging.
- The JavaMail API allows an application to send e-mail messages. WebSphere supports Simple Mail Transport Protocol (SMTP) and Internet Message Access Protocol (IMAP) protocols. You can add new JavaMail providers.

Figure 2-7 shows where in the Administrative Console you add or update resources.

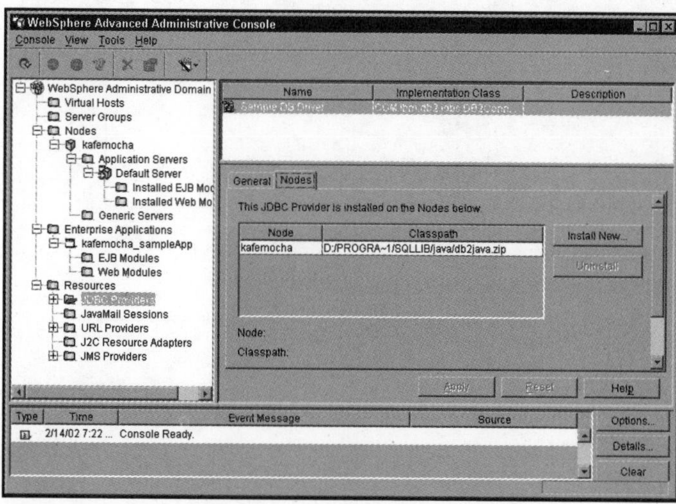

Figure 2-7: The Administrative Console lists JDBC providers.

Understanding server groups and clones

A *server group* is a template or model for creating similar (nearly identical) copies of an application server and its contents. A *clone* is an exact copy of a configured/functional application server that is managed by the server group.

Server groups and clones can be used for workload management. With server groups and clones, you can set up vertical and horizontal scaling, establish multiple servers on one node, create multiple servers on multiple nodes, or a combination.

Server groups are not Java Virtual Machines (JVMs). They are more of a convenience for managing workload. They present a logical representation of a server. Changes that occur to a server group automatically propagate to the other clones in the group. Figure 2-8 shows a graphic of a horizontally cloned domain.

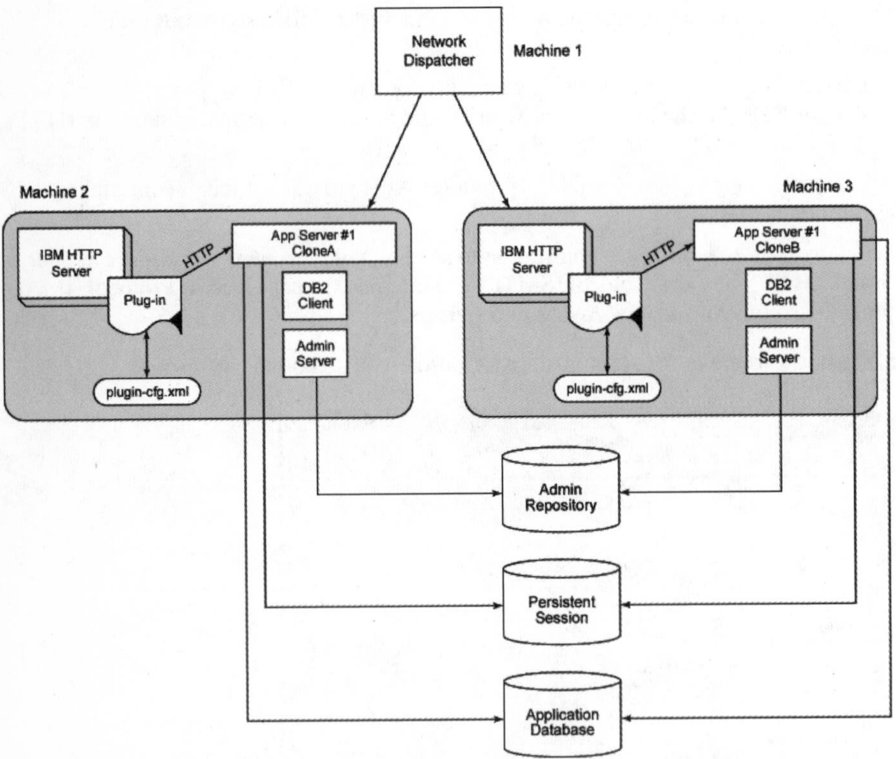

Figure 2-8: Horizontal cloning provides you with the capability of distributing the load among several systems.

In Figure 2-8, a network dispatcher (Machine 1) manages sending requests to two different nodes, each supporting the same implementation of an application server. The configuration was set up using a server group. The server group is made up of Machine 2 and Machine 3. Each machine runs a clone of Application Server 1. The configurations are nearly identical. They utilize the same administrative repository, application databases, and persistent sessions. This makes the job of the administrator easier because he needs to update only the server group to replicate changes to all the clones.

> **TIP**: Horizontal cloning is exceptionally good if you want to distribute load between a number of smaller-sized machines

An understanding of server groups and cloning prepares you for the next section, "Topology selection." Architecting an environment depends on many factors. Based on service-level agreements, you might need a system that can support hundreds or thousands of users. You might also want the ability to change application code in a controlled manner, and you definitely need the ability to bring servers up and down within your domain.

Understanding topology selection

As you develop your e-business landscape, you must determine which topology is appropriate. The goals to strive for when it comes to selecting the right topology are presented in the following list, in no particular order

- *Scalability:* For growing your systems with your business
- *Availability:* For ensuring you lose no customers due to downtime
- *Load balancing:* To keep performance snappy
- *Maintenance:* To ensure 24 by 7 availability as you update software
- *Security:* For keeping your assets safe and uncompromised

First, review the classic three-tiered architecture. Figure 2-9 shows a three-tiered server architecture with tiers one and two representing the WebSphere Presentation tier and WebSphere EJB tier, respectively. Tiers described in this context don't necessarily have to be on separate machines.

Tier one contains the dynamic presentations using JSP and servlets. Tier one contains application servers that manage Web resources. One application server has a vertical clone. A vertical clone is an additional running copy of an application server on the same node. The vertical clone improves performance and availability on the same node. Horizontal cloning is similar in that it adds additional running copies. The difference is that it is spread on other machines, thereby reducing the chance of failure by having another machine to handle the load.

The application server has access to enterprise information through JDBC and data sources. You should assume that the application database is really another node that is accessed through a relation database client, such as DB2 client.

Application Server #1 in tier two also has access to another application server that contains EJB components, which are accessed by Remote Method Invocation (RMI) over Internet Inter-ORB Protocol (IIOP). The third tier is still part of the WebSphere Administrative domain. This tier is where you store your application data. Conceivably, all three of the tiers can reside on a single node.

The entity bean, within tier two, might also have access to the enterprise information (not shown in Figure 2-9). Access to this information can be through calls to JMS that access existing legacy transactions or additional JDBC calls to distributed databases. Therefore, a third tier could be your enterprise database server.

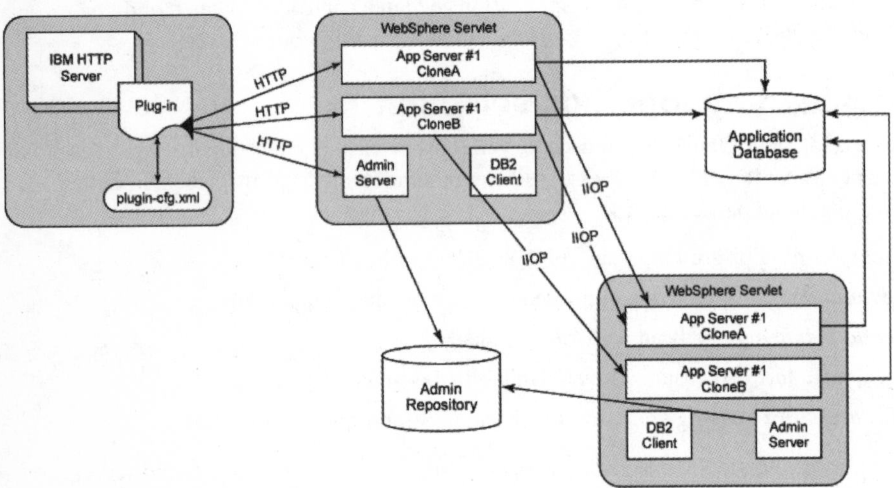

Figure 2-9: Tiering provides some separating between the components. By distributing the work you can achieve better performance and reduce the opportunity for failover.

The topology in Figure 2-9 has some interesting pros and cons. The first node communicating with tier one uses HTTP as the transport protocol, so inserting a firewall in between is possible. That is a good thing. The use of clones could also provide some performance improvements depending upon the load. The second tier allows the flexibility to look up other parties' EJBs that are distributed throughout your network. This is good, but it could also result in a performance issue because of network latency. You could possibly improve performance by merging tiers one and two and allowing JVM optimization. If performance is all you are looking for, merging is beneficial.

Security concerns provide reasons for separating the third tier from the others. You could introduce a second firewall between tiers two and three for additional protection. With two firewalls and EJB security, not to mention SSL added to communication between the HTTP Server one and tier one, you have reasonable security.

As you can tell from this simple example, quite a few factors go into your decision about the correct topology. The following section outlines those decision-making factors.

Choosing a topology that supports your goals

The preceding section reviews a single topology, and that simple example posed many interesting alternatives. When constructing your architecture, you have the basic topology alternatives:

- *Performance-based:* When having optimal response times is important
- *Availability-based:* Ensures that your application is always available (24/7)
- *Security-based:* Ensures that you are secure from evil doers throughout your network
- *Source code maintenance-based:* Ensures that you can upgrade software properly without bringing down the environment
- *Maximum throughput-based:* Enables you to take additional hits without failure

The following list includes some of the topology options that you have:

- *Single machine:* Puts everything on one machine
- *Remote Web server:* Separates the Web server on a machine of its own
- *Separate database server:* Separates the database server to a machine of its own
- *Separate Web/EJB container:* Places the Web containers and EJB containers on individual machines
- *Vertical clones:* Creates additional JVMs per machine
- *Horizontal clones:* Duplicates the applications servers onto other machines within the same domain
- *Single domain:* Runs all applications servers under one WebSphere domain
- *Multiple domains:* Runs multiple WebSphere domains

Figure 2-10 refers to the strengths and weaknesses of the topologies that separate the components. Figure 2-11 shows the strengths and weaknesses of configuration options.

Single Machine

Strengths	Weaknesses
Least expensive Easy to maintain	Competing resources Limited resources impact throughout
Opportunities	**Threats**
Development or test environments	Limited security Single point of failure

Remote Web Server

Strengths	Weaknesses
Separation of load Can tune separately	Additional complexity Plug-in has to be copied to Web server
Opportunities	**Threats**
Can introduce firewalls to increase security	Potential network traffic issues

Separate DB Server

Strengths	Weaknesses
Separation of load Can tune DB	Competing resources Limited resources impact throughout
Opportunities	**Threats**
Use of firewall Can utilize existing DB expertise Can use existing DB procedures	Potential network overhead Single point of failure

Separate Web/EJB

Strengths	Weaknesses
Separation of load	JVM optimization not utilized More admin efforts
Opportunities	**Threats**
Development or test environments	Potential network overhead Single point of failure

Figure 2-10: This list of topologies shows the strengths and weaknesses of component separation.

Vertical Cloning

Strengths	Weaknesses
Improved throughput on large machines Easy to maintain failover support	Limited by available resources

Opportunities	Threats
Can combine with other topologies for even better performance	Single point of failure Memory/CPU overhead of too many clones

Horizontal Cloning

Strengths	Weaknesses
Distribution of load failover support More nodes=more processors	Additional complexity More $$ for hardware

Opportunities	Threats
Can add more nodes if needed Cost effective	Requires session persistence, which increases network traffic

Single Domain

Strengths	Weaknesses
Easiest to maintain Only 1 DB	No software isolation between organizations

Opportunities	Threats
Can move to multiple domains	Complete outage possible

Multiple Domains

Strengths	Weaknesses
Reduced possibility of total outage	Less interprocess communication may impact performance Admin overhead More DBs

Opportunities	Threats
	Too complex of an environment

Figure 2-11: Strengths and weaknesses of administrative configurations.

You have to weigh the pros and cons of each of these topologies.

CROSS-REFERENCE: Workload management is covered in greater detail in Chapter 24.

Understanding WebSphere Application Server Administration

As you have already learned in this chapter, WebSphere is comprised of a number of components all working together in a symphony of technical instruments. The conductor that orchestrates the symphony is the Administrative Server.

The Administrative Server provides the services used to control administrative resources and perform administrative tasks that affect the repository. Figure 2-12 shows the administrative domain.

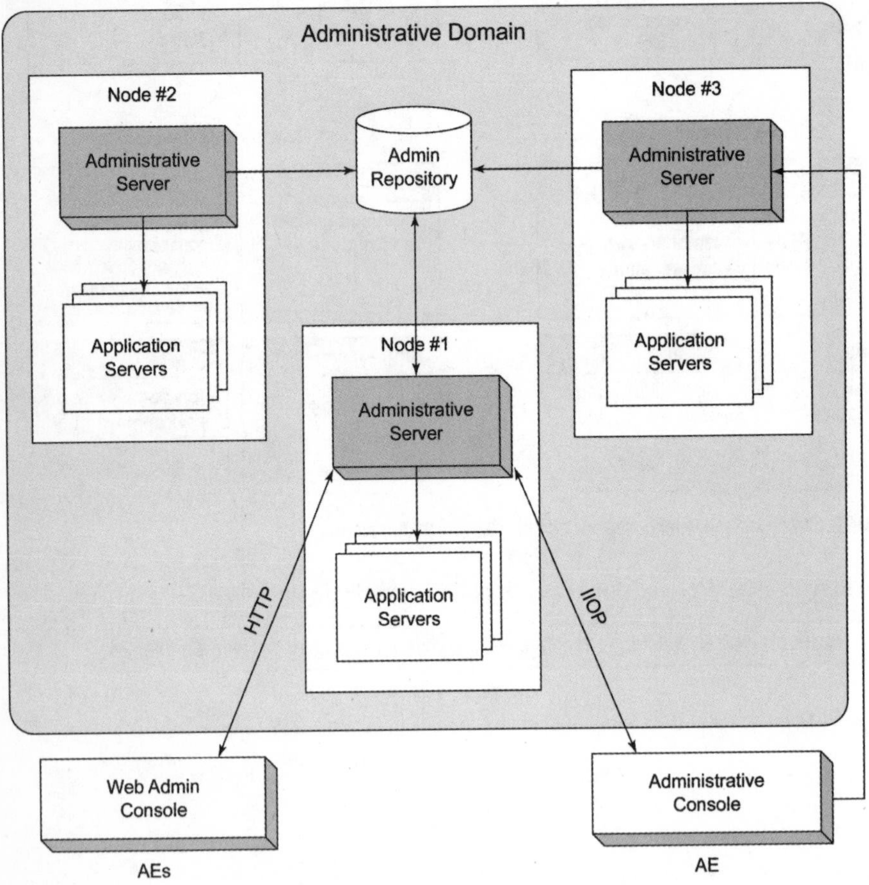

Figure 2-12: Within a WebSphere administrative domain, you can configure and manage multiple nodes from a single repository.

Every WebSphere node contains an Administrative Server, as shown in Figure 2-12. An Administrative Server requires an administrative repository to maintain the configurations of each WebSphere Administrative Server.

A WebSphere domain is comprised of one or many WebSphere Administrative Servers all sharing the same external repository. Figure 2-12 shows a WebSphere domain consisting of three nodes.

Understanding the administrative repository

WebSphere Administrative Server saves all of its configuration information in a database repository. The repository can be one of many supported relational databases:

- DB2
- Oracle
- MS SQLServer
- Informix
- SyBase

When you install WebSphere, the default database name is WAS40. The repository is configured immediately after the installation and is populated with the default server information.

> **NOTE**: WebSphere Application Server Advanced Single Server edition (AEs) does not utilize a relational database, but instead uses an XML file: `server-cfg.xml`.

Understanding the WebSphere Administrative Console

Figure 2-13 shows the Administrative Console. The Administrative Console is the control center for creating, starting and stopping, and configuring application servers.

The Administrative Console works with the administrative repository to capture and store configuration information. The Administrative Console is a Java application that can be started by using the `adminclient.bat` file and supplying the node name and port number, as shown here:

```
<WAS_HOME>/bin/adminclient <host name> <port#>
```

You can also launch the Administrative Console from a remote workstation by using the `adminclient.bat` file. The default port number is 900.

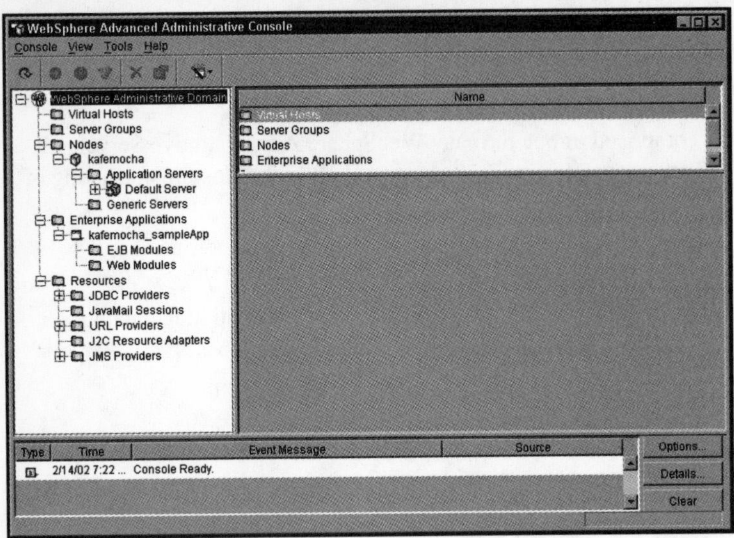

Figure 2-13: The Administrative Console is the best place to perform configurations because you can use any machine on your network to access the Administrative Console through port 900.

The program can also be launched by selecting Start⇨Programs⇨IBM WebSphere⇨ Application Server 4.0⇨Administrator's Console.

In the Single Server Edition of WebSphere Application Server (AEs) `adminclient` does not exist. Instead, you utilize a browser-based console to update the administrative repository. Figure 2-14 shows an example of the browser-based Administrative Console.

If you were using the Single Server edition, you would start the Administrative Console using the following URL.

```
http://localhost:9090/admin
```

Working with the administrative repository makes configuration easier. You have seen the different implementations of the user interface based on the version of WebSphere you have installed. There are actually two other methods you can use to configure WebSphere. You can use the WebSphere Control Program (WSCP) or XMLConfig to configure WebSphere from a command line.

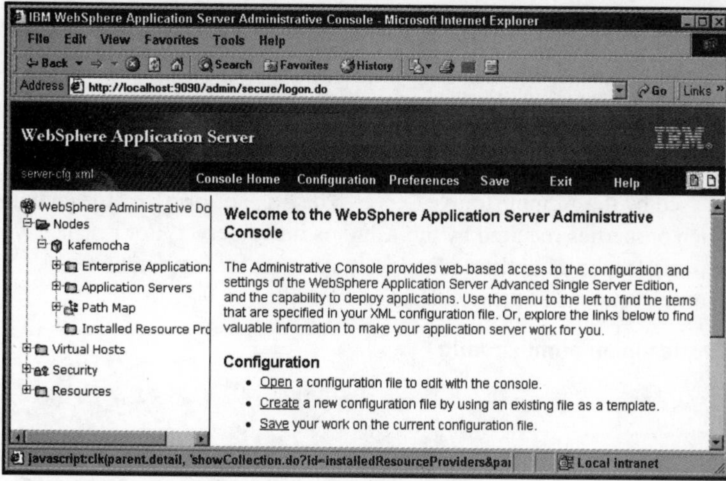

Figure 2-14: In the Single Server version of WebSphere 4.0 the Administrative Console is Web-based, and information is stored in XML files versus in a relational database.

Figure 2-15 shows the four ways in which you can update a WebSphere Administrative Server.

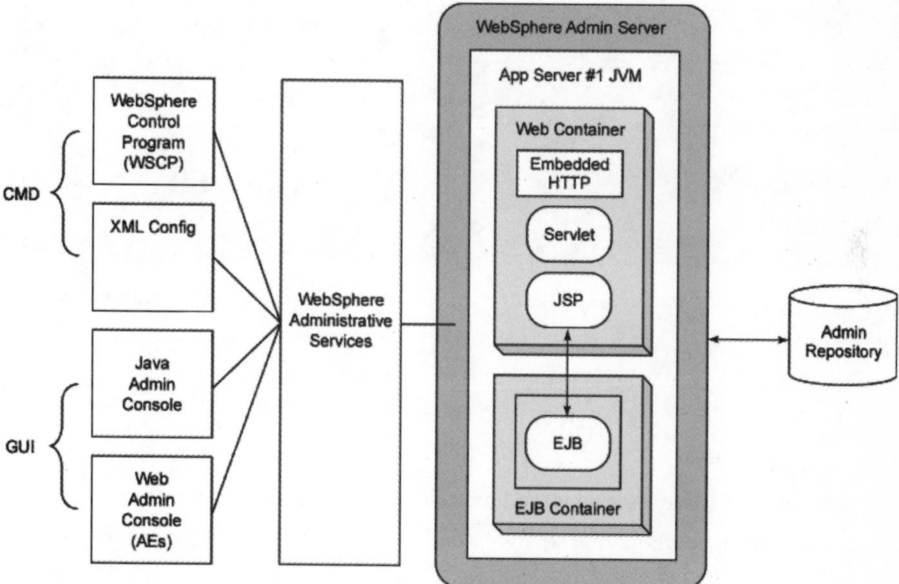

Figure 2-15: WebSphere administration can be controlled by using a graphical user interface or through the use of command-line programs.

CROSS-REFERENCE: The use of all these interfaces (GUI and command line) is discussed in Part III: System Administration.

Understanding admin.config

One piece of the pie that deserves some attention is the `admin.config` file. The `admin.config` file is used by the Administrative Server. The `admin.config` file contains the necessary configuration properties required by the Administrative Server. For instance, you can pass in the database name for the administrative repository or set tracing parameters. Listing 2-2 shows some of the contents of the `admin.config` file.

Listing 2-2: Example Entries in an admin.config File

```
com.ibm.ejs.sm.adminServer.earFile=d:/WebSphere/AppServer/config/admin.e
ar
com.ibm.ejs.sm.adminserver.classpath=d:/WebSphere/AppServer/properties;d
:/WebSphere/AppServer/lib/bootstrap.jar
...
# Trace settings
#com.ibm.ejs.sm.adminServer.traceString=com.ibm.ejs.*=all=enabled
#com.ibm.ejs.sm.adminServer.traceOutput=d:/WebSphere/AppServer/logs/admi
n.trace

# Repository database settings
com.ibm.ejs.sm.adminServer.dbdataSourceClassName=COM.ibm.db2.jdbc.DB2Con
nectionPoolDataSource
com.ibm.ejs.sm.adminServer.dbserverName=
com.ibm.ejs.sm.adminServer.dbportNumber=
com.ibm.ejs.sm.adminServer.dbdatabaseName=was40
com.ibm.ejs.sm.adminServer.dbuser=db2admin
com.ibm.ejs.sm.adminServer.dbpassword={ xor} Oz1tPjsyNjE=
com.ibm.ejs.sm.adminServer.dbdisable2Phase=true
...
```

`Admin.config` is found in `<WAS_HOME>/bin`. You can modify the Administrative Server behaviors as follows:

- Set the WebSphere JVM class path
- Set the server root to WebSphere
- Set trace parameters
- Update database name, username, and password
- Restart the initial configuration settings

Understanding the WebSphere Directory Tree

Now that you know about many of the components within the WebSphere realm, you need to learn about where the files are located. You install WebSphere in Chapter 4. When you complete the installation, a directory tree, such as the one shown in Figure 2-16, is implemented.

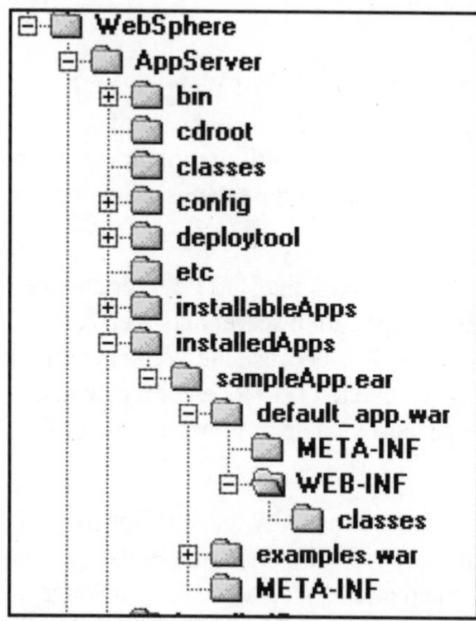

Figure 2-16: When you install WebSphere, it builds a folder tree with self-explanatory names.

Take note of the following important folders:

- *WebSphere\Appserver:* Known as `<was_home>`
- *bin:* Location of the WebSphere batch files (`adminclient` and `adminserver`) and support files, such as `admin.config`
- *config:* Contains configuration files, such as `plugin-cfg.xml`
- *installableApps:* Contains EAR files for enterprise applications ready for installation; note that these EAR file are still compressed
- *installedApps:* Contains deployed enterprise applications; note that the subfolders in this directory are uncompressed EAR files
  - *WAR (default-app.war):* Web module resources (HTML, images, and so on)
  - *META-INF:* Manifest file from WAR
  - *WEB-INF:* Class files supporting Web module and the `web.xml` deployment descriptor

- *META-INF:* Contains the `application.xml` deployment descriptor
- *java:* Contains version 1.3 of the JDK
- *lib:* Contains all the supporting Java Archives (`.jar`)
- *logs:* Contains the WebSphere log file directory
- *properties:* Contains property files used by WebSphere

Summary

The key to understanding WebSphere is to be able to describe the parts of WebSphere. It all begins with what is called the WebSphere domain. A WebSphere domain consists of machinery and a data store called the administrative repository. As configuration information is collected and placed in the administrative repository the relationships established constitute the WebSphere domain.

The first part of the WebSphere domain is the relationship between the HTTP server and the application server. The transport mechanism between the application server and Web server is HTTP. The reason these two components can exchange HTTP is because the Web container in WebSphere now sports an embedded HTTP server. The embedded HTTP server replaced the old Open Servlet Engine (OSE) that was used as the transport vehicle in previous versions of WebSphere.

The two HTTP servers really do not exchange information. It is actually the WebSphere plug-in that is part of the Web server that performs the routing. The WebSphere plug-in is the determining factor as to whether a Web resource is located on the Web server or it belongs to the application server. When you configure an application server on WebSphere, you designate a context that identifies its unique Uniform Resource Identifier (URI) to WebSphere. This information is stored in the administrative repository.

Information, such as the transport mechanism, is stored in the repository through the Administrative Console. The Administrative Console is a graphical user interface (GUI) that enables the administrator to configure the components of a WebSphere domain.

With the Administrative Console, you can create server groups and clones for performance and load balancing, Virtual hosts to maximize host names and aliases, enterprise applications (comprised of Web modules and EJB modules) and supporting resources, such as datasource, JDBC drivers, Java Messaging Services (JMS), and Java Connection Architecture (JCA).

The Administrative Console is the GUI way to configure WebSphere. A command-line alternative is using XMLConfig and/or WebSphere Control Program (WSCP). Whichever way you choose, you have the flexibility to configure scalable, reliable, and secure enterprise applications.

Chapter 3
Introducing Web Services

In This Chapter

- Understanding key roles in Web services
- Understanding the benefits of Web services
- Understanding the Web services architecture
- Introducing Web service development

You can't read a magazine or go to a conference where there isn't at least one article or session on Web services. Web services is a hot topic. The Gartner Group predicts that by 2004 Web services will be the dominant form of application deployment.

Further predictions are that, by 2005, application development projects will be split as follows:

- 40% Java
- 40% MS .Net
- 20% Legacy

So what is the big deal about Web services and how do you use WebSphere to take advantage of Web services? This chapter elaborates on the promise of Web services and provides you with background information about the architecture, components, and tooling and deployment considerations. Chapter 19 discusses installing the tools and provides actual coding examples.

Web services are self-contained modular business applications that have open, Internet-oriented, standard-based interfaces. In addition to being able to locate and utilize them within your own applications, you can also create and publish them to meet your business-to-business (B2B) and Business-to-Consumer (B2C) goals.

Web services promote loose-coupling, distributed services that collaboratively provide business processes. By utilizing standards-based technology, Web services promote agility in development, interoperability, improved integration time, and overall lower cost of ownership.

Understanding the Benefits of Using Web Services

Web services have the potential to deliver many benefits to businesses. Not only can an organization extend its business to other partners, but it can also improve internal interaction between divisions and departments. Web services provide the following benefits to businesses:

- *Interoperability:* Heterogeneous environments from various development environments (J2EE, CORBA, .Net) can be integrated into business applications.
- *Reuse:* Developers can locate existing Web services provided by third parties and incorporate these into their solution.
- *Ubiquitous:* Web services make applications that have been developed in various languages and platforms visible. In the future, Web service tools will be available on most development platforms to make it easier to extend applications to Web services.
- *Platform sensitivity*: No longer do B2B and Enterprise Application Integration (EAI) have problems with differing information interfaces. After Web services proliferate, Independent Software Vendors (ISV) will develop software packages that expose the services based on the Web services standards.
- *Return on Investment (ROI):* Existing applications that are no longer categorized as revenue drivers are revived by wrapping the service and extending its customer reach.
- *Business agility:* Developers can respond quickly to business partnership initiatives to resolve business-growth and expansion issues.
- *Leverage :* Investments made in the Internet/intranet infrastructure can be leveraged to provide new ways of providing services to internal and external customers.

Depending on your enterprise, you might find one or many of the benefits that meet your needs.

Who benefits from using Web services?

Well . . . everyone. Who wouldn't benefit from a lower-cost alternative to e-business? If you can build it cheaper, deploy it faster, and open up more opportunities for profit, why not?

Although you can view the use of Web services as a technical enabler, bringing products to market faster means lower costs to your customers and better service.

Businesses are looking to move from the Internet version of service (a Single-Service Architecture) to a Service-Oriented Architecture (SOA). SOAs primarily focus on how services are described and organized, so they can support dynamic, automated discovery. Businesses that have adopted the Service-Oriented Architecture will become brokers of services or actual providers of services. Figure 3-1 shows a view of how a service broker attains knowledge about a service provider who provides some specialized parts.

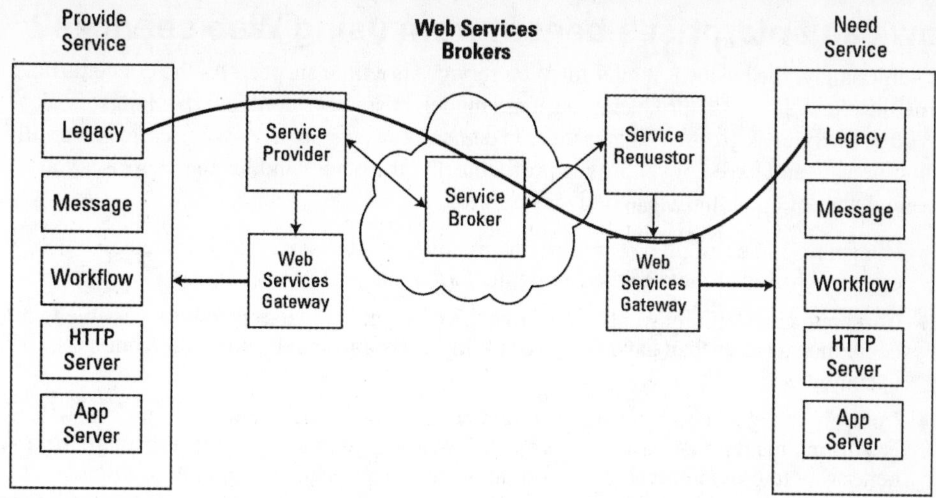

Figure 3-1: A Service broker provides the service that allows one entity (for example, PC maker) to do business with another entity (such as a storage provider).

In Figure 3-1, a business needs a part or service and wants to find a partner or company that can satisfy its particular service need. The business, unaware of all the providers in cyberspace, chooses to go through a broker.

Today's world is still primarily filled individuals looking up information on the Web. Individuals download information, link to different sites, and sometimes order goods and services online. However, Web content is becoming more dynamic, presenting combinations of information before your eyes. People are presented with advertisements they don't want to see, but overall they are demanding to see more and to customize their experiences to ones they can control.

Evidence of this trend is apparent in portals, which are becoming more personalized. Users have more options about what they can see. It's not out of the ordinary to see local weather, a list of stocks, and the day's top stories all on one page. If there is one thing that companies learned during the dot.com implosion, it is that they better have something people want if they are going to return a profit.

So whether it is B2B, online auctions, e-marketplaces, or local news, the presentation of information needs to change dynamically, and the ability to discover, deliver, and bind with additional services is required. And that is what Web services are all about.

So who is going to use Web services? Businesses will create services, and other businesses will become brokers of those services.

How can enterprises benefit from using Web services?

Not surprisingly, the business model for Web services is a little suspect. As the dot.coms have learned, without a revenue-producing business model, businesses don't survive long. Providing a service is great as long as there is demand for your service. Web services are still in their infancy and have not yet proven profitable. On the other hand, in an enterprise, you have a number of opportunities to deliver services:

- Human resources might require certain employee-related sevices; for instance, employees need to manage their retirement accounts.
- Corporate clients might want to organize their customer databases to be accessible to all departments rather than have copies or multiple systems that perform the same operations.
- Company mergers and acquisitions might need to combine systems and services, which is a difficult and time-consuming project. Providing gateways into services might be a better way to provide necessary information and functionality.
- Many corporations can benefit from utilizing standards-based languages and protocols.

Opportunities to use Web services abound in business-to-business (B2B) relationships. As shown in Figure 3-2, exposing your enterprise assets as a service can improve partnerships, reduce workload costs, and provide better integration. Using Web services is far better than using a traditional Enterprise Application Integration (EAI).

From a business perspective, you have more opportunities to use Web services in the corporate sector than in a consumer environment. The benefits are tangible and the utilization of Web services is controlled. The bottom line is that the following compelling reasons drive organizations toward using Web services:

- *Cost avoidance:* Renting a service is cheaper than building one.
- *Complexity management:* Building software on proven parts is safer than building new software.
- *Interoperability:* Systems are too vast and complex for one organization to do it all, so you must rely on others to do part of it.

Now that you understand some of the business motivations, take a look at how the Web services architecture is constructed.

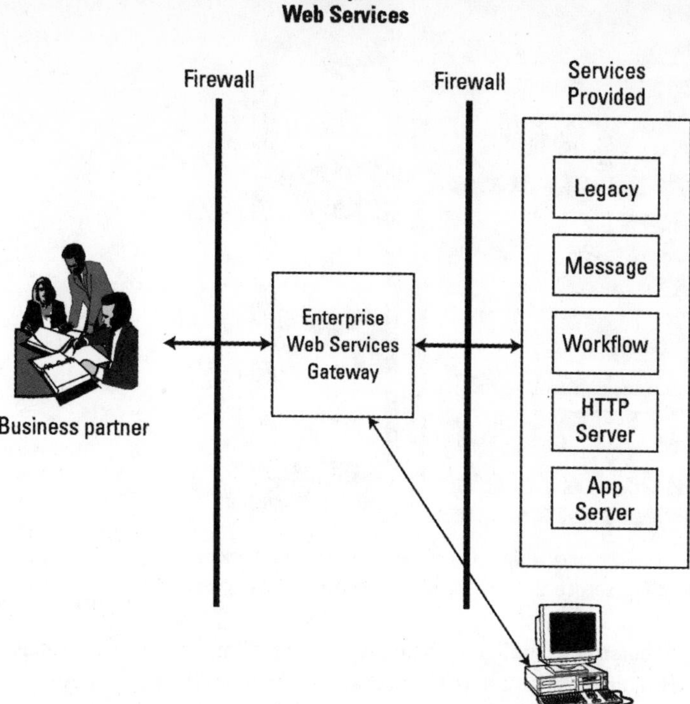

Figure 3-2: Incorporating Web services within the enterprise offers a standards-based solution for integrating disparate systems.

Understanding the Web Services Architecture

The Web services architecture is built on a number of protocols, all of which can work independently; but together, they provide a more robust implementation. Figure 3-3 shows a Web services stack. The implementing protocols are identified on the left. The upper layers build on the capabilities of the underlying infrastructure.

Starting from the bottom, HTTP is the foundation that makes Web services work. The network provides the means through which Web services can be made publicly available to service brokers and requestors. Because of its ubiquity, HTTP is the *de facto* standard for the Internet. Of course, this isn't the only way you can communicate; other methods are SMTP and FTP.

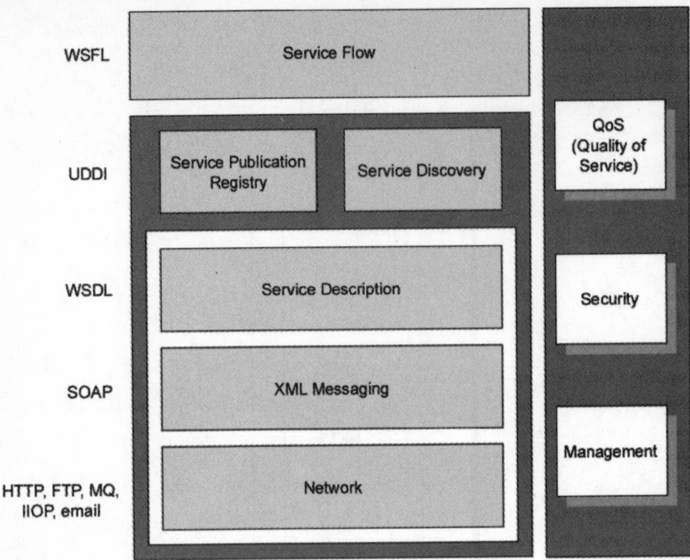

Figure 3-3: Web services are often described using an architectural stack. The stack represents how Web services apply additional protocols and service layers on top of the underlying infrastructure.

From an intranet viewpoint, enterprise applications utilize additional infrastructures, such as Common Object Request Broker Architecture (CORBA) and MQSeries (IBM's messaging product), to provide similar transport mechanisms.

One level up is Extensible Markup Language (XML) messaging. XML is the *de facto* standard for data/message interpretation. Simple Object Access Protocol (SOAP) utilizes the power of XML and is the chosen standard for XML messaging. Its document-centric messaging and remote procedure calls, using XML, make it the protocol of choice. Some additional factors important to developers are that it is simple and it defines standard encoding of operations or functions.

To make any Web Service interoperable, you need an XML-based service description. Web Services Description Language (WSDL) is the *de facto* standard for this type. WSDL defines the interface and mechanics of the service interaction.

In the stack, the first three levels (starting from the bottom) represent the minimum to qualify as a Web service. That means a Web service is a network-accessible service made accessible by SOAP and described by a service-description layer (WSDL).

So how do people utilize your service? First they need to know about it. As a simple example, suppose that your service provides the local weather for San Francisco. The simplest method is to send your description file (WSDL) to the requestor that provides the description of the service that provides the weather. This form of publication is great as long as you are aware that the weather service exists. Using this method certainly can be used in a B2B arrangement, but it leaves the discovery of the weather service up to the requestor.

The best publication method is to register the service with UDDI. Following is a list of some of the categories of Universal Description, Discovery, and Integration (UDDI) registries:

- Public UDDI
- Private UDDI
    - Internal enterprise
    - Portals
    - Partners

After discovering the descriptions, the application developer can cache them locally for use at design time or dynamically bind them to the service at runtime.

You need to consider Quality of Service (QoS). *QoS* determines the service's usability and utility, both of which influence the popularity of the service. Quality of Service falls into these categories:

- *Availability*: Availability means having the service readily available for consumption. A service cannot be fully utilized if it's not available.
- *Accessibility:* Accessibility means having the service accessible to one or many requestors, which includes ensuring that the service is scalable to handle peak loads or changes in the popularity of the service.
- *Performance*: Performance means providing decent turnaround of service requests (response times). Considerations, such as network latency, are very important.
- *Integrity*: Integrity refers to the quality aspect of transactions. Units of work need to conform to the basic principles of transactional processing; if a transaction doesn't complete, all changes are rolled back.
- *Regulatory*: Regulatory means adhering to published standards, including standards such as SOAP, WSDL and UDDI.
- *Security:* Security addresses authentication, authorization, encryption and other means to secure information and confidentiality.

Figure 3-3 shows those particular requirements being considered throughout all the layers. Now that you have a background about the architecture, you are ready to dive more deeply into the Web services model.

Exploring the Web Services Model

The Web service model shows the components discussed in the previous section. (See Figure 3-4.) The components have roles similar to the roles of service provider; service requestor, and service broker. Each role performs certain operations.

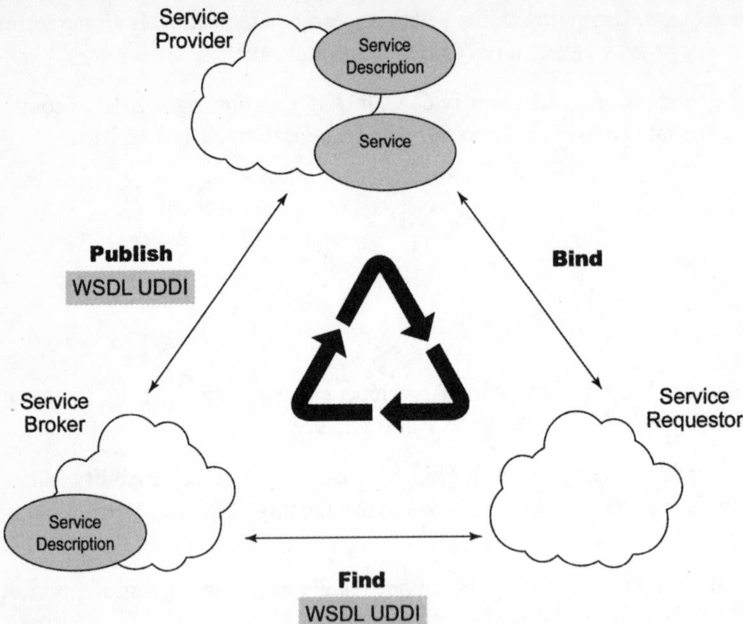

Figure 3-4: A Web service is often shown with a triangular shape showing the interaction between requestors, providers, and brokers of Web service. The provider publishes the service to brokers in the form of a service description; requestors locate the service at the broker and utilize the service descriptions to bind and run the service located at the provider.

Understanding the components of Web services

Service providers (see the top of the triangle in Figure 3-4) deploy Web services. The functions provided by the Web service are described using the Web Services Description Language (WSDL). The same service providers publish deployed services on the Web through brokers or partnerships.

A service broker helps service providers and service requestors locate each other. A service requestor uses the UDDI API to ask the service broker about the services it needs. When the service broker returns the search results, the service requestor can use those results to bind to a particular service. The diagram in Figure 3-4 shows the roles of the provider, requestor, and broker as follows:

- The *service broker* (also known as *service registry*) is responsible for making the Web service interface and implementation access information available to any potential service requestor. This usually is implemented via UDDI.

- The *service requestor* locates entries in the service registry using various find operations and then binds to the service provider in order to invoke one of its Web services. You might say that they are discovered and invoked by service requestors. The service requestor includes both the business that requires a particular function to be satisfied and the tools necessary for discovering and invoking a service.
- *Service providers* implement and publish Web services. The service provider creates a Web service and publishes its interface and access information to the service registry. From a business perspective, the service provider owns the service. You might also consider the provider as the platform that gives access to the service.

Understanding operations performed by Web services

So now you know what Web services are, but just what do they do? In the Web services model, each component has responsibilities for various operations. The operations are publish, bind, and find:

- Publish involves service providers promoting their services to a registry (a.k.a. publishing) or removing entries from the registry (unpublishing). In a situation in which a service provider utilizes a service broker, the service provider contacts the service broker to publish or unpublish a service.
- Bind takes place between the service requestor and the service provider. In the bind operation, the service requestor invokes or initiates an interaction with the service at runtime using the binding details in the service description to find, contact, and invoke the service.
- Service requestors and service brokers, in tandem, perform the find operation. Find operations entail searching for a service directly or searching a registry for a type of service desired.

Understanding Web services implementations

The Web services architecture is implemented (or built upon) using WSDL, Object SOAP, and UDDI. The combination of these three open standards allows Web services applications to interact dynamically on the Web. Look at them individually to see how each of them contributes to the Web services architecture.

Understanding WSDL

Web Services Description Language (WSDL) is an XML-based specification. It is used for describing implementation information of a Web services so that it can be integrated at a programming level. It provides a technical blueprint of a Web service's interface, including end points (URL), port assignments, signatures, and interaction requirements. Figure 3-5 shows how to utilize WSDL in a Web service.

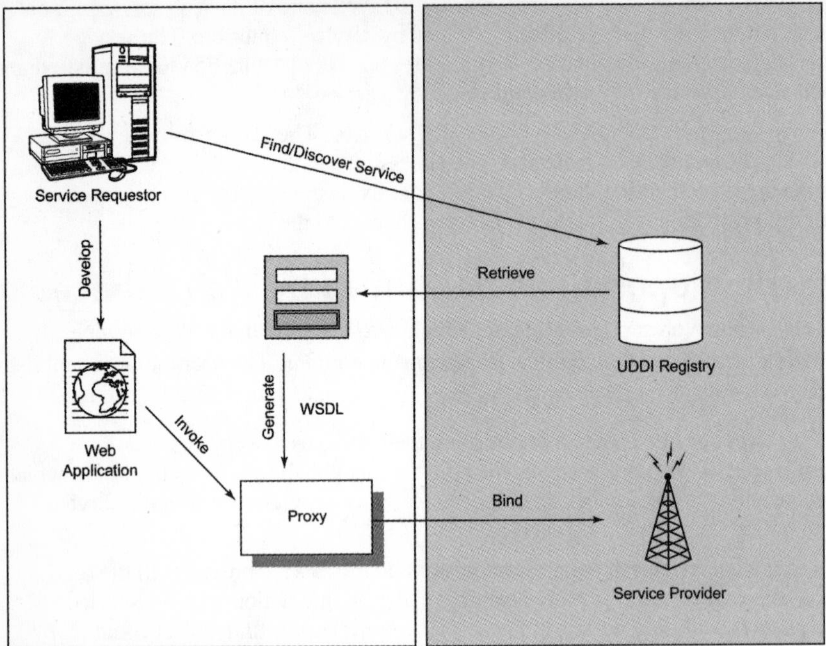

Figure 3-5: When a Web service requestor needs to interact with a published service, the requestor utilizes the WSDL descriptions, possibly obtained from a UDDI registry, to develop the necessary interfaces to access the Web service.

WSDL defines the following features:

- Binding (SOAP)
- Endpoints (URL)
- Messages defining the service
- Data types (using XML schema)
- Type of operation

To be compliant, servers must support these interfaces.

Understanding SOAP

Simple Object Access Protocol (SOAP) is a simple, lightweight XML-based mechanism for exchanging structured data between network applications. SOAP consists of three parts: an envelope that defines a framework for describing what is in a message, a set of encoding rules for expressing instances of application-defined data types, and a convention for representing Remote Procedure Calls (RPCs) and responses. SOAP has the following characteristics:

- SOAP uses simple request and response messages.
- All SOAP messages are written in XML.
- SOAP is transport-protocol independent. HTTP is one of the supported transports, but FTP, SMTP, or MQ are other transports that can be satisfied with SOAP.
- SOAP is operating-system–independent and not bound to any programming language or component technology.

NOTE: With SOAP there are no calls by reference. A SOAP client does not hold any stateful references to remote objects.

SOAP focuses on message content; therefore, it is open to interact with any service provider or requestor without knowing any of the details about how it is implemented or on which platform it is implemented. SOAP completely hides the end points. Therefore, SOAP can communicate with any program, regardless of implementation; as long as SOAP can read the message and respond to it, everything works. Figure 3-6 shows the flow of a SOAP message.

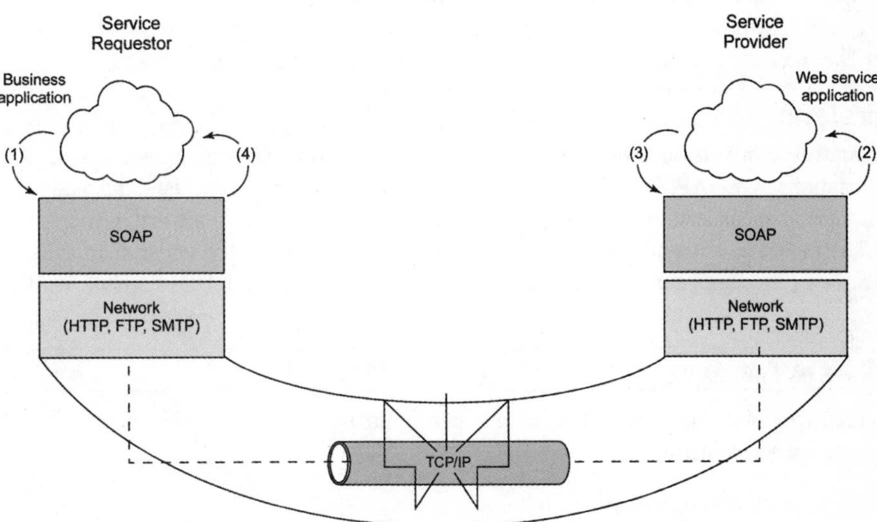

Figure 3-6: The SOAP interaction is very simple. A SOAP message is created and transported over the network and delivered to a SOAP server. The request is processed, packaged in a SOAP message, and returned through the network to the application.

The SOAP architecture follows these steps:

1. A service requestor creates an application that utilizes SOAP messaging. The message contains the information needed to invoke the process described by the service provider. The provider might specify that the invocation is via a SOAP Remote Procedure Call (RPC) request or an XML message format that satisfies the providers requirements to service the request. The message and target address are forwarded to the SOAP transport mechanism. The SOAP message is sent via HTTP to the provider's node.
2. The message is delivered to the provider's SOAP server. The server routes the request over to the Web Service. The SOAP runtime optionally uses the encoding schemes in the message to convert the XML message into a programming language that satisfies the service.
3. The Web Service processes the request and prepares a response. This response must be in the form of a SOAP message. The message is handed over to the SOAP runtime environment with the new destination which points back to the requestor.
4. The response message is received by the requestor via HTTP. The message is routed through SOAP, and the message is potentially converted to the proper target language. The message is then given to the application.

The SOAP interaction is simple. You format the message and forward it to the provider's target address. The provider's SOAP interface extrapolates the message and passes it to the service. The response performs the same steps to return the results to the requestor.

Understanding UDDI

UDDI stands for Universal Description, Discovery, and Integration. Of the three implementations — SOAP, WSDL, and UDDI — UDDI is governed by a standards body. UDDI is a set of specifications produced by the UDDI project, an open-industry initiative that enables businesses to find and transact among themselves quickly, easily, and dynamically with their respective applications. UDDI can also be referred to as the UDDI registry for Web services.

> **NOTE**: See `www.uddi.org` for more details about the UDDI project.

UDDI creates a global, platform-independent, open framework to enable businesses to facilitate the following actions:

- Locate (or discover) each other
- Define how they interact/cooperate over the Web
- Share information in a global registry

Three public UDDI registries, sponsored by IBM, Microsoft, and HP, exist on the Web. You can register for free, and your registration entries are replicated to other nodes. Figure 3-7 shows the UDDI entities and some types of information contained in each.

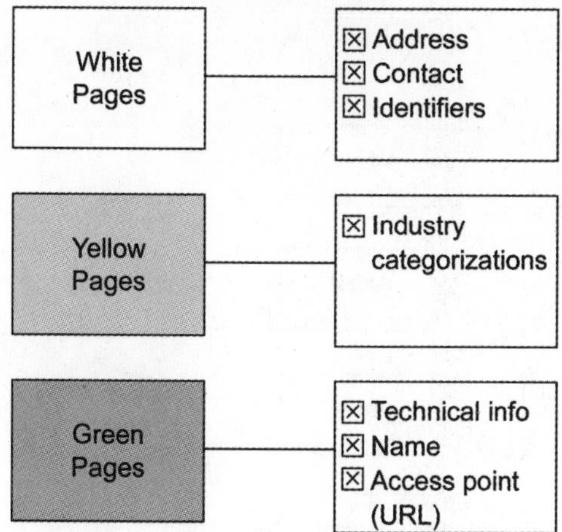

Figure 3-7: UDDI entities are often considered analogous to white pages, yellow pages, and green pages.

The information provided in a UDDI business registration is analogous to the phone book. Within the phone book, there are three components:

- White pages include address, contacts, and known identifiers.
- Yellow pages include industrial categorizations based on standard taxonomies.
- Green pages provide the technical information about services that are exposed by the business.

Web service providers and requestors use a SOAP API to communicate with a UDDI registry.

A UDDI registry contains four data types. They are: *businessEntity*, *businessService*, *bindingTemplate*, and *tModel*. Figure 3-8 shows the relationship between the data types.

A businessEntity contains information about the party who publishes information about a family of services. Information includes contacts, URLs, and addresses. They also contain all services that the business offers, as well as identifiers and categories for the business.

As shown in Figure 3-8, a businessService is contained with a businessEntity. It contains descriptive information about a particular service. It can contain bindingTemplates and CategoryBags. The businessService is exclusive for the businessEntity (meaning it is not shared).

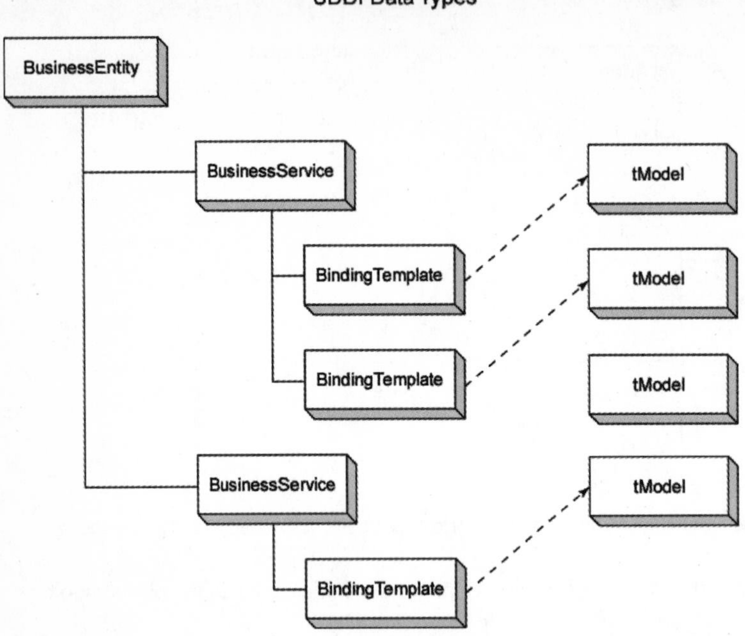

Figure 3-8: In a UDDI data-type hierarchy, a Business entity is demarcated as a business service. The technical details are contained in binding templates that reference technology models (tModel).

A bindingTemplate provides a reference for technical information about a service. You might call it a technical fingerprint. Information, such as the entry point (URL, email, phone number, and so on), and information about the tModel are contained in the bindingTemplate.

TModel stands for Technology Model. It contains the descriptions of specifications for services or taxonomies.

Understanding XML's role in the Web services model

XML is the key enabler to Web services. Although you can develop Web services with minimal experience in XML, you must understand a few important concepts:

- XML basics, such a tags, DTDs, and validation
- XML namespace concept
- XML schema (XSD)

WebSphere Studio Application Developer provides tooling for developing XML documents.

NOTE: For more information on XML visit `http://www.w3c.org/XML` and `http://www.w3c.org/XML/Schema`.

Understanding other Web services initiatives

Web services do not compose a complete architecture. As new requirements are discovered, new initiatives are often started to attempt to address the need. Some of the current initiatives being investigated are Web Services Flow Language (WSFL), Web Services Experience Language (WSXL), and HTTPr.

Understanding WSFL

Built on top of WSDL, WSFL addresses composition of existing Web services. The WSFL specification draft was first proposed by IBM and is shipped with the Web Services Toolkit (WSTK 3.1), a product downloaded from IBM's Alphaworks.

> **NOTE**: You can find specifications at `http://www-4.ibm.com/software/solutions/webservices/pdf/WSFL.pdf`.

Understanding WSXL

WSXL defines an aggregation of existing services through publication using multiple channels. WSXL builds applications based on the MVC (Model View Controller) pattern.

> **NOTE:** Find more at `www.106.ibm.com/developerworks/webservices/library/ws-wsxl`.

Understanding HTTPr

HTTPr is a recently published proposal from IBM for a reliable messaging protocol. HTTPr is built upon HTTP 1.1 so the benefits of HTTP are inherited. HTTPr is an extension to the standard HTTP protocol that adds reliable messaging capabilities.

Supporting Web Services with WebSphere 4.0

The following product versions are installed with WebSphere Application Server 4.0:

- Apache SOAP 2.2
- Apache Xerces 1.2.3
- Apache Xalan 1.1
- IBM UDDI4J 1.0.2

Apache SOAP 2.2 is supported in WebSphere to provide a SOAP server and client application environment. This support gives WebSphere applications the capability to send and receive SOAP messages.

The capability to interface with UDDI registries is provided through integration of UDDI4J. This enables WebSphere applications to communicate with UDDI-compliant registries to publish and locate Web services. Figure 3-9 shows the services supported within WebSphere.

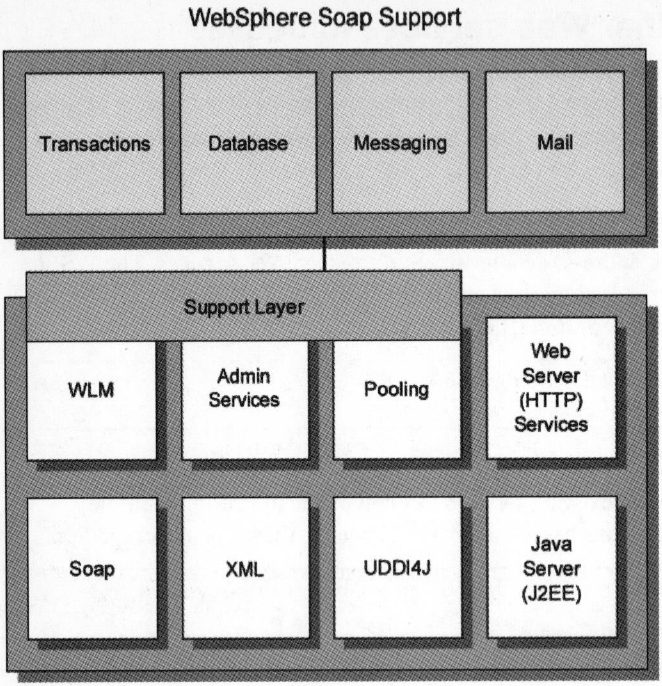

WebSphere Soap Support

Transactions
Database
Messaging
Mail

Support Layer
WLM
Admin Services
Pooling
Web Server (HTTP) Services
Soap
XML
UDDI4J
Java Server (J2EE)

Figure 3-9: Web services on WebSphere (WoW) provide you with all the necessary tooling and functionality to develop Web services.

Using Apache SOAP 2.2 on WebSphere

Support for Apache SOAP 2.2 is implemented in WebSphere Application Server 4.0. The Java-based version of SOAP version 2.2 is based on the specification for SOAP 1.1 with support for SOAP with attachments. This means attachments can be bundled with the SOAP message and passed along. Attachments are binary items.

In addition, WebSphere also enables you to create services from Java classes, EJBs, DB2 stored procedures, and scripts supported by the Bean Scripting Framework (BSF). The XML-SOAP Admin tool, which is covered in Chapter 19, enables you to manage your SOAP-enabled services.

NOTE: WebSphere Application Server supports SOAP over HTTP only.

Figure 3-10 shows how a client/browser accesses a SOAP-enabled application server.

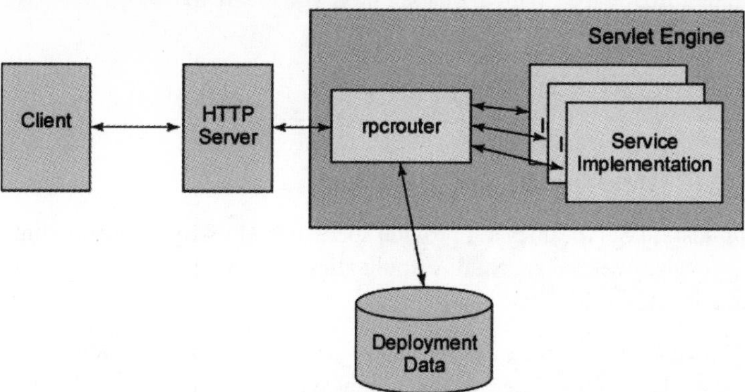

Figure 3-10: WebSphere supports SOAP requests through a mechanism known as the rpcrouter. The rpcrouter manages the basic runtime architecture for SOAP-based messages.

The SOAP servlet handles two types of requests. In Figure 3-10, the rpcrouter handles all requests that are RPC-based. The rpcrouter uses the XML namespace of the first element of the body to identify the service to execute. The deployment data is configured using `dds.xml`. The actual deployed services are stored in the `DeployedService.ds` file. Message-based requests are handled by the message router.

WebSphere also enables you to create services from Java classes, EJBs, DB2 stored procedures and scripts supported by the Bean Scripting Framework (BSF). It supports these different types of services through pluggable providers, which you define using deployment descriptors. Figure 3-11 shows where pluggable providers sit within the architecture.

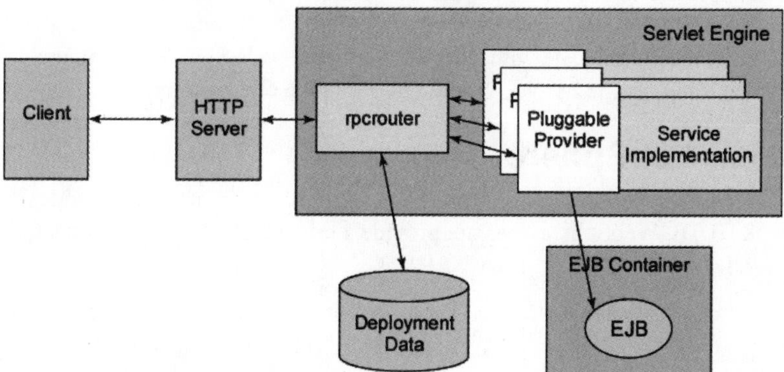

Figure 3-11: Adding pluggable providers extends the SOAP runtime environment to allow for services with different types of implementation.

Pluggable providers are Web services you have created. You describe them with SOAP deployment descriptors and, utilizing the SoapEarEnabler tool, you create a deployable Enterprise archive (EAR) that is installed on WebSphere.

CROSS-REFERENCE: You learn more about creating Web services in Chapter 19.

Generating WSDL files on WebSphere

Actually, WebSphere Application Server does not provide specialized tooling for generating WSDL files. Instead, you can use WebSphere Studio Application Developer or generate the WSDL file manually using `java2wsdl`.

To support a SOAP implementation, you need a SOAP deployment descriptor, the WSDL interface, and implementation definitions. One tool that comes with the WSTK is `java2wsdl`. This utility generates the WSDL documents and SOAP deployment descriptors by using your existing Java objects.

The tool also generates serializers for complex data types. The Apache client and server use serializers to serialize and deserialize complex objects being transported. `java2wsdl.bat` is a tool that performs the following functions:

- Provides a utility that uses existing code and generates WSDL documents
- Supports EJB, Java, and COM objects
- Generates WSDL interface and implementation files
- Generates SOAP deployment descriptors
- Generates SOAP serializers for complex data types
- Lets you select methods to be provided as service

Remember that SOAP needs to send a SOAP request to a server to interpret the result. The client proxy is the mechanism that performs that operation. The WSTK includes a generator for client proxy classes that communicate with a service specified by WSDL. By using the WSDL document as input in to `wsdl2java`, you can generate the client proxy.

Using UDDI on WebSphere

UDDI is supported in WebSphere by UDDI4J. UDDI4J is a Java class library that provides APIs to interface with UDDI. WebSphere does not provide a private UDDI registry. Chapter 19 shows how to install a private UDDI registry.

Introducing Web Services Tooling

This section introduces two Web services enabling tools: the IBM Web Services Toolkit (WSTK) and WebSphere Studio Application Developer (WSAD). The IBM Web Services Toolkit is a preview product that you can download from IBM AlphaWorks. Before WebSphere Studio Application Developer, the WSTK was the only set of tooling available for Web services from IBM.

Understanding IBM Web Services Toolkit

At the core of the Web Services Toolkit are the following tools, which make it easy to create, publish, and invoke Web services:

- A client runtime API that implements both service discovery and service proxy functionality by building on top of IBM's open source UDDI4J (UDDI for Java) and WSDL4J (WSDL for Java) open source projects, as well as Apache's SOAP implementation
- A server-side, runtime environment for deploying and exposing services based on Apache's AXIS SOAP implementation
- A number of samples and code-previews designed to help you get a better understanding of how Web services and Web services technology will evolve in the future

CROSS-REFERENCE: In Chapter 19, you install and try out some of the tools.

Understanding WebSphere Studio Application Developer

Chapter 2 briefly introduces WebSphere Studio Application Developer (WASD). Chapters 5 through 8 cover it in more detail. This chapter introduces you to the Web services supported software and specifications.

The Web service tools, provided with WebSphere Studio Application Developer, enable you to create, deploy, test, and publish Web services. WebSphere Studio Application Developer provides the following:

- Capability to generate a WSDL document from a JavaBean, Document Access Definition Extension (DADX) document, Enterprise JavaBeans (EJB), and URLs
- Capability to generate a Java artifact from a WSDL document
- Capability to create a Web service from a JavaBean, DADX, enterprise bean, or URL
- Capability to discover and publish Web services

WebSphere Studio Application Developer provides the following Web services wizards:

- The Web Services Client Wizard is used to create the Java client access and to test an existing deployed Web service.
- The Web Services DADX Group Configuration Wizard is a DADX Web service that enables you to wrap DB2 extender or regular SQL statements inside a standard Web service.
- The Web Services Wizard is used to create, deploy, test, and publish Web services based on artifacts such as JavaBeans, URLs, EJBs, and DADX files.
- The IBM UDDI Explorer assists you in discovering and publishing your Web service descriptions.

The Web service tools provided in WSAD 4.02 generates code that complies with the following specifications:

- Simple Object Access Protocol (SOAP) version 1.1
- Universal Description, Discovery, and Integration (UDDI) version 2.0
- Web services Definition Language (WSDL) version 1.1

The WebSphere 4.0 release of Web service tools supports the Simple Object Access Protocol (SOAP) version 2.2 runtime environment.

Introducing the Web Services Development Process

This section is designed to give you a general idea about how the Web services development process is conducted and provide you with an introduction to the development process. With this understanding, you should know where to begin and have a mental map to follow. When you actually do some Web services development in Chapter 19, this section will be a good reference.

Understanding the development lifecycle

The Software Development Life Cycle (SDLC) for Web services includes the design, deployment, and runtime requirements for multiple roles: service provider, service requestor, and service registry. Each role has specific requirements to support the operations within the components specified in the Web services architecture.

You can approach development in the following four ways:

- *Fresh:* Many terms are used for starting from scratch, including the green-field scenario, but it basically gets down to the developer starting fresh. That means beginning from scratch, creating not only the Web service but also the application functionality you are exposing as a Web service.

- *Bottom up:* The bottom-up scenario is for enterprise developers who are working to migrate their existing applications to the Web services architecture.
- *Top down:* The top-down scenario starts with an already existing Web services interface description, and the work creates application functionality capable of supporting that interface.
- *Meet in the middle:* The meet-in-the-middle scenario is a combination of the bottom-up and top-down scenarios. In this situation, you have an interface you need to meet and an existing application that you need to set up to comply with the Web Service.

The development lifecycle takes you through one or all of these phases:

- *Discovery*: You need to find a service and support the necessary interface.
- *Creation or transformation*: You either create your own service or transform your application to comply with a discovered interface.
- *Building:* The building phase of the lifecycle includes development and testing of the Web service implementation, the definition of the service interface description, and the definition of the service implementation description. Web service implementations can be provided by creating new Web services, transforming existing applications into Web services, and composing new Web services from other Web services and applications.
- *Deployment:* The deployment phase includes publishing the service interface and service implementation definition to a service requestor or service registry. You also have to deploy the executables for the Web service into WebSphere.
- *Testing:* You need to test your service. You can use a private UDDI registry if you are publishing your service.
- *Development:* In this phase, you create the service and generate the appropriate interfaces and implementations.

Chapter 19 does a thorough job of walking you through the development process. But to get acquainted with the steps involved in the Web services development process, see Figure 3-12.

Figure 3-12 shows the bottom-up lifecycle, which means you have an existing service you want to make available as a Web service. You should take the following steps:

1. Create or modify an existing application server (using SOAP interfaces/implementations).
2. Package the service into a EAR file (use `SOAPEarEnabler.bat`).
3. Deploy the EAR file to WebSphere.
4. Generate the description in the form of a WSDL document (use `wsdlgen or wsad`).
5. Publish the specification to a UDDI registry.

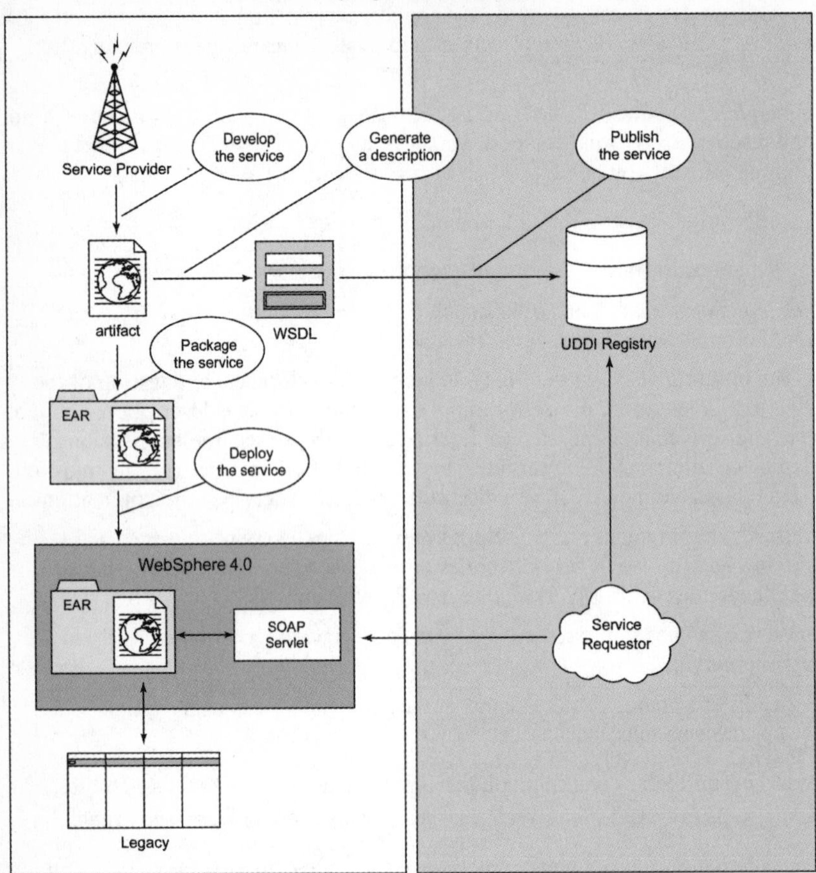

Figure 3-12: Developing a Web service from an existing application requires generating a WSDL description of the application interfaces and publishing them to a UDDI registry. After the description is published, a requestor can utilize the information to access the service.

Introducing the development-process wizards

WebSphere Studio Application Developer comes with a set of wizards to make it easier to develop Web services. Many of the manual tasks that need to be implemented are similar, so the wizards come in handy as ways to reduce the keystrokes and ensure proper adherence to the protocols. Figure 3-13 shows the New Wizard dialog box. In Figure 3-13, you can see three of the wizards that are available under the Web services category.

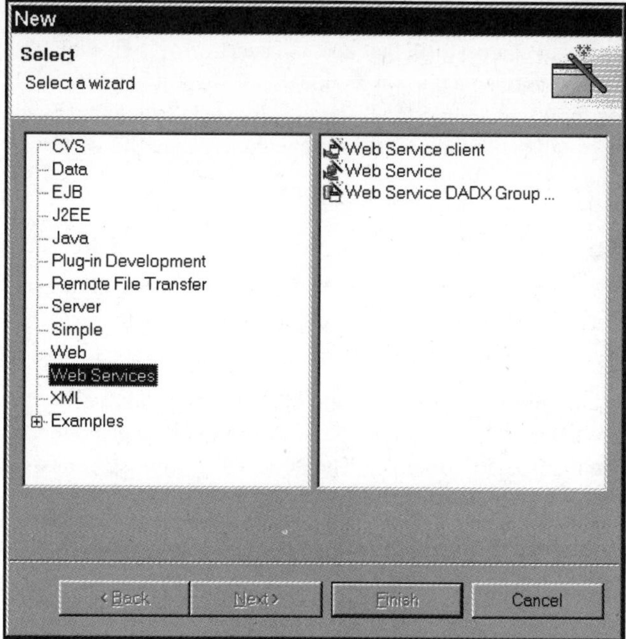

Figure 3-13: You can access the WebSphere Studio Application Developer Web Services wizards by clicking Open the New Wizard⇨Web Services.

The following is a complete list of helpful wizards in WSAD:

- Web Service
- Web Services client
- Java beans for XML Schema
- Web services DADX Group Configuration
- UDDI Browser (which is found using the File⇨Import⇨UDDI)

You utilize some of these wizards in Chapter 19 when you actually do some development with WSAD.

Introducing debugging

Chapter 19 discusses debugging options, but for now this section introduces you to one product (`TcpTunnelGui`) that you should use for your SOAP debugging.

Bugs happen. Because SOAP messages travel between networks, it is often handy to have a tool to review the messages. The tool that can perform that task is `TcpTunnelGui`, which is a Java Swing application that enables you to open a port on the machine where it was started. It tunnels traffic through a remote host/port where the SOAP server is located. The output is your originating message displayed side by side with the returning message from the SOAP server. You see an example of its use in Chapter 19.

Introducing deployment tools

To deploy to WebSphere Application Server, you need an EAR file. With Web services, you need some additional information in the EAR file so it can be deployed properly in WebSphere. WebSphere includes the `SOAPEarEnabler` tool.

Enabling an application EAR file to use the SOAP environment in WebSphere takes an additional step. You need to add a Web module containing the SOAP router servlets to the EAR file. You can add this by using the SOAPEarEnabler. The `SOAPEarEnabler` is passed the EAR file and the SOAP deployment descriptor file.

The SOAP deployment descriptor describes the service provided by the Web services application. The deployment descriptor contains the following:

- The identifier used by the Web service requestors
- The operations available from the service
- The class that implements the Web service

Understanding what occurs at execution time

A final walkthrough of the development process closes out this chapter. Figure 3-14 shows an example of a Web service that provides the temperature of a city.

The process follows these steps:

1. A service requestor creates a weather application that utilizes SOAP messaging. The message contains the necessary information to invoke the `fetchTemperature` process described by the service provider. The provider has specified that the invocation was via a SOAP RPC request. The requestors are presented a page where they select a city for which they will receive current temperature information. On submission, the servlet utilizes the SOAP client to route the message to the target address. The SOAP message is sent via HTTP to the providers node.
2. The message is delivered to the provider's SOAP server. The server routes the request to the Web service.
3. The Web service processes the request and prepares a response, in this case the current temperature. The message is handed over to the SOAP runtime environment with the new destination which points back to the requestor.
4. The requestors receives the response message via HTTP. The message is routed through SOAP, and the message is passed on to a JSP for presentation to the requestor.

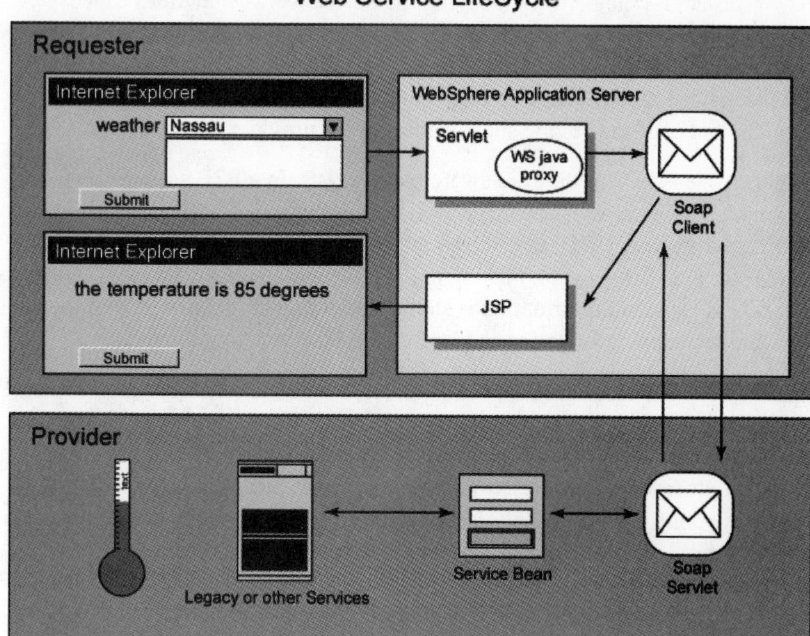

Figure 3-14: To access a Web service for the current temperature, the application server uses a SOAP client to interact with the SOAP servlet. The SOAP servlet is responsible for processing the SOAP request and returning the results to the requestor.

Summary

Web services promise to be the next major leap in application development on the Web. Web services are vehicles for extending existing applications and new standards-based applications to the Web. The key word is *standards-based.* Web services are based on the Simple Object Access Protocol (SOAP), Web Services Description Language (WSDL), and Universal Description, Discovery, and Integration (UDDI) open standards. Together these three enablers provide the capability for businesses to dynamically mix and match Web services to perform complex transactions with minimal programming. Web services allow buyers and sellers all over the world to discover each other, connect dynamically, and execute transactions in real time with minimal human interaction.

The Web services model is comprised of an architecture (or stack) that layers additional services on top of Web infrastructure (the network). SOAP provides the standardized transport protocol to move objects across the network. Moving the objects between entities cannot be done unless the entities have a common interface that describes the features, which is accomplished with WSDL. WSDL provides the description of the services and the means to locate and bind to the service. If a WSDL is presented to a developer, he has the means to develop an application that conforms to the specification of the provider of the service.

Developers can only utilize WSDL if they are aware that it exists. In a B2B scenario, it requires that the provider and requestor exchange WSDL information. To alleviate this need to discover and describe the service, UDDI became an important initiative. UDDI provides a way for businesses to register their information making it available to potential customers. Business entities are described and technical information is stored, providing the requestor with the necessary business and technical information to choose a Web service to implement.

WebSphere 4.0 has built in Web services support. With all these wonderful services, it was only a matter of time before tools entered the market. IBM provides two such toolkits. The first is the IBM Web Services Toolkit and the other is WebSphere Studio Application Developer. WebSphere Studio Application Developer provides wizards that make creating Web services easy. It supports top-down, bottom-up, and meet-in-the-middle development. You learn a lot more about Web services development in Chapter 19.

Chapter 4

Installing WebSphere Application Server

In This Chapter

- Planning the installation
- Handling the preparation tasks
- Determining the steps for migration
- Installing the IBM HTTP Server
- Installing DB2
- Installing WebSphere
- Verifying the installation
- Installing the InfoCenter

Chapters 1 through 3 have provided background on WebSphere Application Server. If you read those chapters, you now have an understanding of the different flavors of WebSphere Application Server. Now, it's time to actually install the product. Because WebSphere Application Server can run on several platforms — Win2000/NT, AIX, HP/UX, Solaris, and Linux — we had to decide which platform to use for the purpose of demonstration. We decided to walk you through the installation process on the Windows platform. Whenever possible, we provide tips along the way to describe the differences you'll find if you're installing on a different platform. But for detailed information, be sure to check the Readme file on the installation CD and the IBM Web site (`www.ibm.com/webservers/appserv`).

One final note before you get started. As you know, WebSphere Application Server comes in three flavors. In this installation chapter, we're focusing exclusively on the installation of WebSphere Application Server Advance Edition (AE).

Preparing for the Installation on Win2000/NT Platforms

As you prepare to install WebSphere Application Server, your primary goal is a successful implementation the very first time. As you learned in Chapter 2, the Web architecture contains a number of key components, carefully woven together to appear as one to the end user. As an administrator, you know each of these components adds complexity. Installing in a methodical, organized manner should provide you solid feedback about problems and failing components. For example, you will be installing a relational database (DB2), a Web server (IBM HTTP Server), and an application server. Each has its own configuration and authorization mechanism. Knowing that each works separately prior to integration should help you determine problem areas.

One area — migration — requires you to do some additional preparation. Migration is discussed in the section "Migrating from an earlier WebSphere version." As you proceed with your installation preparation, keep in mind that they do not take migration into consideration. When you reach the migrating section, we give you specific directions on what you need to do to migrate an existing WebSphere Application Server.

It's always nice to have a checklist to know where you are going and what you are doing. The checklist in Table 4.1 outlines the steps you follow to successfully install WebSphere from scratch. It takes into account that you want to ensure components are working properly before you begin integrating them as one cohesive environment.

Table 4.1: Installation Checklist

Task	*Description*
Hardware prerequisites	Verify that the hardware requirements are met prior to installation.
Software prerequisites	Verify that the hardware requirements are met prior to installation.
Knowing where to look	You will be installing many different application components. You need to know where to install the components. You should become familiar with the shorthand reference as it is used throughout the chapter.
Setup Userids	You need to have proper authorization to utilize administrator functions for WebSphere and DB2
Verify Readme files and FixPaKs	You should refer to the Readme file for further instructions prior to installation. Furthermore, always check for FixPaKs on the IBM Web site.

Task	***Description***
Pre-Install	Do you have all the tasks completed?
Ports	Have you verified that the ports you want to use are available?
Migration	When you begin to install, you need to know what your plan of action will be. The WebSphere install program prompts you for actions.
Choose a Web server	In the installation, you will be asked for the Web server plugin to install. You should know which Web server you will be integrating with. You will be installing the IBM HTTP Server in this chapter.
Web server installation	You install the individual components so you can verify each is working separately. You begin with the Web server.
Install and test DB2	The next component is the database. You install IBM DB2 and test that it was successfully installed.
Switch to JDBC 2.0	WebSphere requires that you utilize the new features of JDBC 2.0 for pooling. You run the batch file that switches from JDBC 1.0 to JDBC 2.0.
Install WebSphere Application Server	You install the application server that collaborates with the other components installed (Web server and database).
Start WebSphere and validate	Finally you start WebSphere and validate that it is operating correctly.

To begin the installation preparation, you need to become familiar with the system requirements.

Evaluating system requirements

WebSphere Application Server is no lightweight when it comes to installation. Given its robust features, it should be no surprise that it comes with beefy hardware and software requirements. With that in mind, you should install it on the biggest, fastest, most awesome machine you have available. After all, it's the gateway to your e-business solution.

The following lists display the minimum hardware and software requirements for the installation components needed by WebSphere Application Server (AE).

Hardware

Here are the minimum hardware requirements for installing AE:

- 500 Mhz pentium
- 200MB disk space (minimum) for WebSphere Application Server
- 350MB disk space (minimum) for IBM DB2 Enterprise Edition
- 50MB disk space (minimum) for IBM HTTP Server
- 135MB disk space (minimum) for TEMP directory
- More than 128MB RAM

Software

Here are the minimum software requirements for installing WebSphere Application Server (AE):

- *Operating system:* Microsoft Windows 2000 Server, Service Pack 1 or Service Pack 2 with128 encryption or Microsoft Windows NT Server with Service Pack 6a
- *Application server:* IBM WebSphere Application Server V4.01, Advanced Edition (AE) or Single Server Edition (ASSE)
- *Database:* IBM DB2 Universal Database V7.2.1, Enterprise Edition for Windows
- *Web server:* IBM HTTP Server 1.3.19
- *IBM GSKit 5.0.3.52.*
- *Java Development Kit:* JDK 1.3 with JDBC 2.0

> **TIP:** Having more than 128MB of RAM does not necessarily mean WebSphere Application Server will meet your needs, but it is enough to install WebSphere. A good rule is an additional 512MB per application server (Win2000/NT) and 768MB (UNIX). Plan accordingly.
>
> In production environments, a single CPU may not satisfy your requirements. Mileage may vary depending upon your applications.

Keep in mind the requirements listed are minimums. You need to consider factors such as the operating system, paging space, a database server, a Web server, and various log files in your total system requirements.

> **CROSS-REFERENCE:** You can find the latest information on software and hardware requirements at the following URL: `www.ibm.com/software/webservers/appserv/doc/latest/prereq.html`.

Now that you know the minimum requirements, it's time to determine where you are going to install the software. Table 4-2 shows the components that you want to install and their default directories. This table also provides an Install Reference column so that you can refer back to product locations because your installation paths may be different based on your hardware configuration.

Table 4-2: Location and References of Installation Components

Component	***Default Install Folder***	***Install Reference***
WebSphere	C:\WebSphere\AppServer	`<was_home>`
WebSphere HTTP plug-in	C:\WebSphere\AppServer	`<plugin_home>`
DB2 client DB2 server	C:\Program Files\SQLLIB	`<db2_home>`
IBM HTTP Server	C:\Program Files\IBM HTTP Server	`<http_home>`

Creating authorized userids

Even though you haven't yet installed any of the components, it is an important security practice to utilize userids with significant authority to prevent unauthorized persons from manipulating your environment and to have enough authorization to administer the environment. You need to create an authorized userid to keep the bad boys out.

Actually, you need to identify three users: one to manage the WebSphere Application Server, one to administer DB2, and another to manage the WebSphere access to databases.

You create the following userids in order:

1. `httpadmin` for the Web server administrator
2. `db2admin` for the DB2 administrator
3. `wasadmin` for WebSphere administrator

NOTE: You could use the same administrative userid for the installation; but in general, this is not a good practice.

Userid creation

Because not everyone is familiar with how to add userids to Windows 2000, a brief walkthrough is in order. To create new users, follow these steps:

In Windows 2000

1. On the Windows desktop choose Start⇨Settings⇨Control Panel.
2. Double-click Administrative Tools and double-click Computer Management.
3. Expand the Local Users and Groups and select Users
4. Then choose Action⇨User.

5. Enter a name, password, and descriptions for the user. Also check that the user never changes the password and the password never expires. Of course, this can be adjusted to meet your security preferences. Click Create.

In Windows NT

1. On the Windows desktop click Start⇨Programs⇨Administrative Tools⇨User Manager
2. Then choose User⇨New User.
3. Enter a name, password, and descriptions for the user. Also check that the user never changes the password and the password never expires. Of course, this can be adjusted to meet your security preferences. Click OK.

> **TIP**: For the sake of consistency with the examples, please make the password for each userid the same as the userid.

Create each of the userids listed first. After completing these, you set specific characteristics to allow them to function differently under security.

> **CROSS-REFERENCE**: Refer to the Windows 2000 user guide for more details on local security and policy rights.

Userid characteristics

Now that you have the userids, you need to apply certain policies to them to ensure that you have enough authorization to perform certain administrative functions. You must set up a considerable number of local policies for the WebSphere administrative user (`wasadmin`) and the DB2 administrative user (`db2admin`) userids. The `wasadmin` and the `db2admin` have the following common characteristics:

- ♦ Are locally defined
- ♦ Are part of the Administrators group
- ♦ Set the policy-level rights to "Act as Part of the Operating System"
- ♦ Can "Log on as an NT service"

Your `db2admin` should add the following characteristics:

- ♦ Increase quotas
- ♦ Create a token object
- ♦ Replace a process-level token

To apply the appropriate policies, you can perform the following steps:

In Windows 2000

1. On the Windows desktop choose Start⇨Settings⇨Control Panels.
2. Double-click Administrative Tools and double-click Local Security Policy.

3. Expand Local Policies; right-click the appropriate policy, and double-click Users Rights Assignment to display a list of policies.
4. Select a policy and double-click.
5. Add the user to the policy by clicking Add and choosing the appropriate userid. After adding, repeat the prior step for as many policies as were listed previously. Don't forget that `db2admin` has some additional policies above and beyond the common policies.

In Windows NT

1. On the Windows desktop click Start⇨Programs⇨Administrative Tools⇨User Manager.
2. Choose the local user and then click Policies⇨User rights.
3. When presented with the next page, check the Show Advanced User Rights check box; then select the policy and add the user by clicking Add and selecting the user.
4. Repeat the prior step for as many policies as you specified earlier.

> **TIP**: The `db2admin` userid is automatically created when WebSphere Application Server is installed and you have chosen to install DB2 as your database repository.
>
> DB2 requires that all userids be eight characters or fewer. This restriction is based on compatibility with existing DB2 systems.

Now that you have set the proper userids, you can continue with the other preparation steps.

Remembering the Readme file

It is amazing how many times the authors have been involved with troubleshooting installation problems that were related to poor preparation. One of the first things any person should do to prepare for an installation of WebSphere Application Server is to read the Readme file.

Two Readme files are located in the root path of the installation CD: One is for WebSphere Application Server (`README.HTML`) and the other for IBM HTTP Server (`IHS_README.HTML`).

Both Readme files contain licensing information referring to terms and conditions, notices, and information. They also provide links to specific Web sites where you can obtain more information about the products.

Within the WebSphere Application Server, Readme is a link to the WebSphere Application Server's InfoCenter:

```
www.ibm.com/software/webservers/appserv/doc/v40/ae/infocenter/
```

The InfoCenter is an excellent WebSphere reference that contains release notes, in-depth documentation, step-by-step installation procedures, and other updates, such as tutorials, code samples, and help file updates. The InfoCenter that ships with WebSphere is a limited subset. Although you can always link to the InfoCenter on the Web, we highly recommend that you download the InfoCenter JAR file and run the procedures to replace the existing InfoCenter with the complete InfoCenter.

The IBM HTTP Server Readme file contains detailed information about required patches and differences among the installation platforms, particularly Solaris. As with the WebSphere Readme file, this Readme file points you to the IBM HTTP Server Web site:

```
www-4.ibm.com/software/webservers/httpservers
```

While you explore the CD prior to installation, open the `license.txt` file to learn some new terminology and buzz words that you can use to impress your friends.

The first things to note are the references to the Apache Foundation. The IBM HTTP Server is actually the Apache Web server with the added functionality of Secured Sockets Layer (SSL) support. The Apache Foundation is an open-source community that provides you with some wonderful tooling such Xalan, Xerces, SOAP, and Jasper. You can find more information about these tools at `www.apache.org`.

Also, notice the other agreements and partnerships. The bottom line is that although WebSphere is an IBM product, it is comprised of many supporting open-source community projects that ensure its openness and robustness.

Keep reading to investigate what else you need to do to install WebSphere.

Introducing FixPak 4.0.3

A FixPak is set of fixes often referred as Program Temporary Fixes (PTF). When a PTF is released, it represents fixes that correct critical problems immediately with a guarantee that it will be included in the next full version of the software. At the present time, the latest version on the IBM support page is FixPak 4.0.3.

> **NOTE:** Unless this is the initial release of the product, it is highly likely that FixPaks are available for download. Fixes come in two flavors: Program Temporary Fixes (PTF) and patches. PTF is an acronym used by IBM to denote temporary fixes. All temporary fixes are eventually incorporated into the next release level. You can find fixes in the support area of `www.ibm.com/webservers/appserv`.

So what is new with FixPak 4.0.3? The best way to find out what is within a FixPak is to look at the release notes. Release notes are generally available on the Web along with the associated FixPak.

Just what do the release notes have to say about version 4.0.3? Here is what you will find:

Version 4.0.3 provides new functions. Included in 4.0.3 is support for the following:

- Concurrency control support for CMP EJBs (4.0.2)
- Support for Oracle 9i (4.0.3)
- Multi-domain work load management support (4.0.3)
- IBM Software Development Kit 1.3.1 on IBM and HP platforms (4.0.3)

- Merant Type-4 JDBC driver for SQL Server (4.0.2)
- SSL with iPlanet Web Server (Solaris) (4.0.2)
- Administrative database failover tolerance for Advanced Edition (4.0.2)
- PTFInstaller usability and reliability improvements (4.0.3)
- J2EE connector architecture v1.0 specification (AE only) (4.0.2)

In addition, version 4.0.3 provides prerequisite upgrades for the following:

- Informix Dynamic Server 7.31, 9.21, 9.3
- the iPlanet Directory Server 5.0, iPlanet Web Server 4.1 with SP8
- Sybase Adaptive Server Enterprise 12.0 (for AEs only)
- IBM DB2 Enterprise Edition 7.2 FP5
- XML4J Parser from 3.1.1 to 3.2.1, includes JAXP1.1, DOM1 and 2, SAX1 and 2
- LotusXSL 2.0 to version 2.2.0 (Xalan2.2.0)
- SuSe 7.2.4
- HP-UX 11i
- JDK 1.3.0_04(Solaris)

The release notes section is a great place to learn everything you need to know about the FixPak. It also contains installation instructions specific to the installation, as well as known problems.

> **TIP:** Reviewing the "Possible Problems and Suggested Fixes" section of the release notes is highly recommended.

FixPak 4.0.3 corrects a number of problems with version 4.01. How do you know whether FixPak 4.0.3 corrects an outstanding problem you have encountered? The best way is to review the defects list. Figure 4-1 shows an HTML page that contains the list of defects corrected in the FixPak.

You can access this page on the download support page for FixPak 4.0.3. Go to `http://www.ibm.com/support/` and follow the links and instructions that position you on the page to download the FixPak. You will find a `List of Defects (HTML)` link. Choose that link to see the list. Another way to quickly access the List of Defects is to enter the following FTP:

```
ftp://ftp.software.ibm.com/software/websphere/appserv/support/
fixpacks/was40/fixpack3/docs/403defectlist.html
```

> **TIP**: Go to `www-4.ibm.com/software/webservers/appserv/support.html` is the URL for WebSphere support.

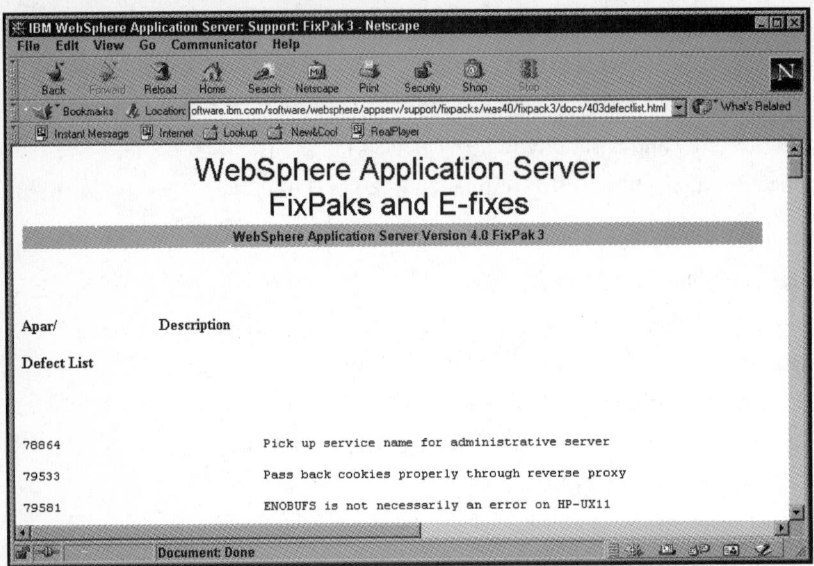

Figure 4-1: The page that tells you about WebSphere FixPak and E-Fixes.

FixPaks are accumulations of previous FixPaks, so upgrading from version 4.0 to version 4.0.3 should contain version 4.01. If you are upgrading from version 4.0 to 4.0.3, we highly recommend that you always make it a habit to read the Readme file. Sometimes a previous FixPak is required before you can apply the newest FixPak. For instance, PTF 4.0.3 requires that version 4.01 is the base. This is found under the prerequisites heading of the Readme. That's why it's always important to read the Readme.

Now that you understand all about FixPaks, you should go ahead and download FixPak 4.0.3 from the IBM support Web site. You install it at the completion of the full installation.

> **NOTE**: If you are upgrading from version 4.01 to FixPak 4.0.3, when prompted you should install the support for the J2EE connector architecture v1.0 specification.

Preinstall checklist

At this point, you have collected and assembled most of the necessary components to perform the install. You should have completed the following:

- Downloaded or purchased the WebSphere Application Server version 4.01 software.
- Verified that you have the appropriate hardware configuration.
- Checked the Web site for FixPaks and downloaded any relevant fixes. Version 4.0.3 was the FixPak that was most current.

- Created three local userids:
  - WebSphere administration (`wasadmin`)
  - Web server administration (`httpadmin`)
  - DB2 administrator ID (`db2admin`)
- Read the Readme file.

> **NOTE**: At this point, it is assumed you are installing from scratch and do not have any migration issues. If you are planning a migration from an existing copy of WebSphere ensure you read the section "Migrating from an earlier WebSphere version" prior to starting the WebSphere installation.

Now that your preparations are complete, you are ready to move to more specific details about the environment you are about to create.

Choosing a supported Web server

Although it is possible to connect directly to the WebSphere Application Server with the use of a Web server, that is not the case in this installation. You need to select which supported Web server you will be installing. After you have a Web server selected, the WebSphere plug-in needs to be installed in the installation directory of the Web server.

> **NOTE:** The terms HTTP server and Web server are used synonymously throughout this book.

WebSphere uses an XML-based Web server plug-in that enables communication between the Web server and the application server. The plug-in refers to an XML file named `plugin-cfg.xml`. The primary services provided by the plug-in are the following:

- Pass requests between the Web server and WebSphere
- Decide which tasks are the Web server's and which are WebSphere's
- Handle errors

> **CROSS-REFERENCE:** You learn more about the plug-in later in section "Plug-in regeneration" and in Chapter 20.

WebSphere supports the following HTTP servers:

- Apache
- Microsoft IIS
- IPlanet
- Lotus Domino
- IBM HTTP Server (that is shipped with WebSphere)

During the WebSphere installation process, two decisions are made about Web servers:

- Do you want to install the IBM HTTP Server as your Web server?
- Which Web server plug-ins need to be generated for the Web servers found on the local machine?

The system is checked for the presence of Web servers. If none are found, you are asked whether you want to install the IBM HTTP Server, which comes with WebSphere.

TIP: If you have already installed one of the supported Web servers, the WebSphere typical installation does not ask if you want to install the IBM HTTP Server. Installing the IBM HTTP Server is optional. The installation program detects the presence of the installed Web servers and is only interested in which plug-in should be generated.

At this point, you are prepared for the decisions that need to be made about Web servers and plug-ins. Because you will be installing the IBM HTTP Server in this chapter, you already know which plug-in you will select.

Your next important step on the checklist is to verify the TCP/IP ports you will be reserving.

Identifying ports to use

A number of default ports are well-known standard ports, and a few ports are IBM product defaults. Table 4-3 shows the list of ports that have been set as defaults.

Table 4-3: Port Addresses Commonly Used with WebSphere

Component	*Address*
HTTP	80
HTTP Administration	8008
Secure Socket Layer (SSL)	443
WebSphere built-in HTTP server	9080
Administration Console (AEs)	9090
Administrative Server Location Service daemon, which is used for persistent object references	9000
Administrative Server Bootstrap Server, which is used for JNDI naming and security	900
DB2 database	50000

TIP: When you are installing on UNIX systems, port addresses below 1024 require root access.

You might consider changing some of the port addresses to add increased security or to resolve conflicts. However, if these addresses are currently available you should take the defaults on your first installation of WebSphere. After you are comfortable with the process and understand the big picture, you should work with your security personnel to develop an overall security plan.

> **TIP:** You can use `netstat -an` to display currently used ports.

You now know which ports you will be utilizing when you install the components. You next need to provide a host name for your new environment.

Updating the host filenames

When you install a Web server, you need to configure a unique host name based on a unique address. Your system administrator usually handles this function for your organization, but if you are installing WebSphere on your personal machine you need to be aware of a few necessary facts.

First, you should verify with the system administrator that TCP/IP networking is correctly configured for your organization and your workstation. You should also reserve the host name you desire (for example, AlmostFreeCruise.com) and request that it is added to the Domain Naming System (DNS) or your local host's file. As a reminder to your system administrator, the IP address of the node should never change, so do not use Dynamic Host Configuration Protocol (DHCP) to dynamically assign an address.

> **TIP:** The local host's file in Win2000/NT is found under `winnt\system32\drivers\etc`.

Second, if you are planning to run WebSphere on a laptop to demonstrate its usefulness to management or impress your friends, you need to configure the MS loopback adapter, which emulates the LAN adapter and enables you to configure a private IP address. After you configure this adapter, add the host name and address to the local host's file.

> **NOTE:** The MS loopback adapter emulates the LAN adapter and enables you to configure a private IP address. This is often confused with the TCP/IP loopback address (127.0.0.1). They are not the same. With the MS loopback adapter you configure an unique address for your machine that makes your system believe that it's functioning within a LAN environment.

You will not be instructed on how to configure the MS loopback adapter. If your situation requires you to run on a single standalone machine and you need the loopback adapter configured, ask your system's support group to show you how to add the MS loopback adapter and configure it with the proper settings. Your next decision is choosing where to create your repository database.

Choosing the location of the WebSphere administration repository

One of the differences between the AE and the AEs/AEd versions is that the AE version requires you to create a repository database to contain all the administration information, which is needed to configure WebSphere domains with information about nodes, applications, servlet engines, security, and other configurable items. With AEs/AEd, there isn't a database requirement. You control your single node with the help of an XML file (`server-cfg.xml`), which is located in `<was_home>\config`.

> **NOTE:** Configuration using AEs is performed by updating `server-cfg.xml` or by using the Administrative Console.

So what is a WebSphere domain? A WebSphere domain is a collection of WebSphere application servers that share a common repository. Through this common repository, you can configure and manage WebSphere application servers remotely. Actions, such as starting and stopping servers, setting up workload management, and updating resources, can all be managed from anywhere provided you have access.

Because this book is focused on WebSphere Application Server Advanced Edition (AE), determining where to locate the repository database is important. The repository database should not reside on the same server as the WebSphere server. Having your administrative database on the same server poses a security risk. If a hacker is somehow able to gain access to your machine, having your repository on the same machine could expose you to unwanted situations. For example, if your Administration Server goes down, your entire domain goes down.

Another important consideration is performance. If you have your database on the same physical device, the application server and the database compete for resources. Database engines often attempt to acquire all available memory to improve performance. A setup in which WebSphere and DB2 fight for resources is not optimal. So given that fact, it's best to place your database repository on another physical machine. With that configuration, you have added protection.

The best practice is to place your administration repository in a safe location behind a firewall and access it using client software such as DB2 client. If your configuration is for a development environment and your budget is limited, you can get away with a single machine performing both operations. Just remember your mileage may vary.

Installing databases other than DB2

Companies are not alike, and the types of databases that organizations use vary. To accommodate this fact, WebSphere supports a number of popular database engines. Following is a list of supported databases:

- IBM DB2
- Informix Dynamic Server
- Oracle 8i
- MS Sql Server
- Sybase Adaptive Server
- Merant Sequelink

In this chapter, you install the IBM DB2 database as the repository database. Any of the databases listed here could be used as the repository and can certainly be used as a business data server. The important fact to remember is that each vendor provides drivers and FixPaks for its respective product. You should ensure that you have the appropriate supported levels downloaded. You should consult the Readme file for more information about specific product installations.

> **NOTE:** In previous editions of WebSphere, you could utilize a database engine called Instant DB. Instant DB is no longer supported. Primarily users, running a single-server implementation, who did not want to exploit the full capabilities of a full-featured database engine, used Instant DB. AEs provides a simpler solution with their XML-based configuration.

Modifying port addresses for security concerns

The "Identifying ports to use" section of this chapter listed the ports associated with WebSphere components. For security reasons, you might want to consider changing some of the ports. For instance, any well-documented port address is an advertisement for mischievous behavior. This includes internal as well as external hackers. For example, the port to access DB2 is port 50000. Any person with this knowledge could gain access to your remote database. Is that something you want? Not likely.

So what should you do? First, before you start changing ports, it is best to implement the base system to ensure that all components are working and that you fully understand where the problems might surface. After you understand the ramifications, you can start making changes for security reasons.

Obviously, there is a lot to take into account when you start considering changing port addresses. Will you be using Secure Socket Layer (SSL)? How many firewalls are implemented? Is Network Address Translation (NAT) utilized? Are proxy servers being utilized? All these questions and more will need to be discussed. This activity is something you should do sitting down with your network administrator, security professional, and system administrator.

There are a lot of books and references on this subject. You may want to check the IBM Redbooks for specific resources on this subject. `www.ibm.com/redbooks`.

Planning for directory services (LDAP)

Although this chapter focuses on installation, it should make mention of directory services. One of the first steps toward enforcing security restrictions is to require users to authenticate before allowing access to applications. For example, you can require users to submit information, such as passwords or certificates, to prove their identities. The security system then checks the information against a database of known users. If the submitted information matches the information in the database, the user successfully authenticates.

Compiling a list of valid users and passwords is a time-consuming task. Putting together an LDAP directory is an equally lengthy process. During the installation phase, it is wise to begin setting aside time to devote to these authentication methods. WebSphere provides three methods of implementing directory services:

- OS (operating system)
- LDAP
- Custom

The WebSphere Administrative Server is responsible for interfacing with these services in a component called the Security Server. This book does not show you how to install any of the LDAP products, although you learn how to integrate them. In Chapter 23, you learn how to integrate a LDAP directory with WebSphere using IBM's Secure Way.

Migrating from an earlier WebSphere version

If you're migrating from a prior version of WebSphere, this section is for you. If you're installing WebSphere on your system for the first time, you can skip to the "Installing IBM HTTP Server 1.3.19" section and continue with the installation preparation.

IBM took a better approach to migration in this version than in previous versions. It provides migration assistance and automates much of the migration. For instance, the install program calls the migration tool, which performs the backup and migration. Figure 4-2 shows the two options for migration: version upgrades and version 4 AEs to AE.

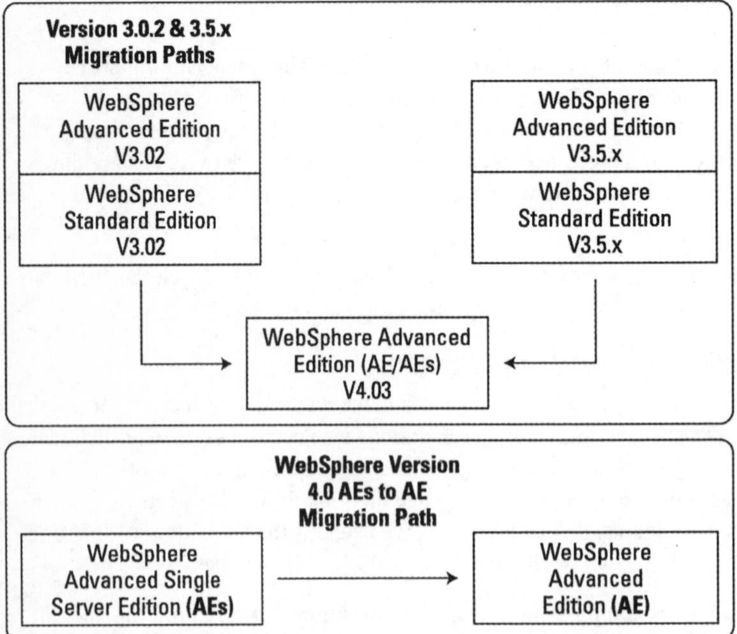

Figure 4-2: The WebSphere migration flavors.

Figure 4-2 depicts how the migration handles version and edition migration that includes migrating Enterprise JavaBeans (EJB) and redeploying and creating Enterprise Application for EJBs and servlets. The first things to consider when migrating are the changes in Java and J2EE API standards. Your application code migration is likely to contain some errors, but that is something that you do not need to address right now.

These are your primary responsibilities as administrator in the migration process:

- Verifying that product prerequisites are supported
- Upgrading to IBM WebSphere Application Server v4.0
- Migrating administrative configurations

> **TIP:** We highly recommend that you visit URL `http://www.ibm.com/webservers/appserv/doc/latest/prereq.html` to review the necessary prerequisites.

The next few sections review the process. At this point, you should have properly downloaded the proper prerequisites for WebSphere version 4.0.

Preparing for a common migration

It is important to know the versions of the components that integrate with WebSphere. If you are new to administration, or are unaware of which levels of software you have installed, this section can help you identify the software release levels.

The following components may need to be upgraded in the migration:

- DB2 7.2
- Java Development Kit (JDK)
- Java Database Connectivity (JDBC) driver.
- IBM HTTP Server

To determine which version of DB2 you have installed, simply type the following in a Windows command window:

```
C:\>db2level
DB21085I  Instance "DB2" uses DB2 code release "SQL07021" with level
identifier "03020105" and informational tokens "DB2 v7.1.0.43",
"n010504" and "WR21254a".
```

Compare the results to the prerequisites for DB2. If you are back level, you have to upgrade DB2 with the appropriate FixPak.

Most likely, you are running at a different level of the JDK than is required for WebSphere 4.0. When you finally run the migration, the JDK is upgraded to version 1.3. The way to check your current version of the JDK is to type:

```
C:\>java -version
java version "1.3.1_01"
Java(TM) 2 Runtime Environment, Standard Edition (build 1
Java HotSpot(TM) Client VM (build 1.3.1_01, mixed mode)
```

This shows you the current runtime environment. As you can see this is at the correct release level for WebSphere 4.0. As mentioned previously, the WebSphere installation ensures that you are upgraded to the proper version of the JDK.

WebSphere 4.0 also requires the use of Java Database Connectivity (JDBC) 2.0. DB2 7.2 supports JDBC 2.0. Assuming you have DB2 installed, you might have already run the batch file (`usejdbc2.bat`) to switch from JDBC 1.x to JDBC 2.0. To see whether DB2 is utilizing JDBC 1.x or 2.0, type the following:

```
C:\>type c:\program files\SQLLIB\java12\inuse file.
```

The response from the window should be JDBC 2.0. Verify that it contains JDBC 2.0. After you determine that you are at the correct level for JDBC, continue checking the version of the Web server.

You will be shown how to determine the IBM HTTP server version. If you are running any of the other supported Web servers, consult their documentation on how to check for version number.

> **NOTE:** UNIX users should browse the WebSphere Application Server `<was_home>/bin/admin.config` file. Check the `adminServerJvmArgs` setting. If it includes the `DB2 java12` directory, it's JDBC 2.0. For JDBC 1.x, it includes the `DB2 java` directory.

To determine the version of IBM HTTP Server, type the following code:

```
X:\IBM HTTP Server>apache -v
Server version: IBM_HTTP_SERVER/1.3.19
Server built:   Jul 11 2001 17:22:19
```

Again, compare the version to the version required for installation. If it is back level, you have to apply the proper FixPak.

Now that you have checked your configurations and acquired and upgraded to the proper releases, you are ready to begin the migrations.

Migrating from version 3.x to 4.0

The migration follows a step-by-step process. Follow these steps exactly, or you might run into problems:

1. Start your current version of the WebSphere Administrative Server.
2. Start the install program. It detects that a prior version exists.

3. When prompted, check the Migration check box that signals the migration process.
4. Use `WASPreUpgrade` to run the migration.
5. After the migration is complete, you must install WAS 3.X.
6. Install Version 4.0, which runs `WASPostUpgrade` and an `XMLConfig` import.

> **TIP:** When using Windows 2000, you can verify that the Administrative Server program is running by checking Start⇨Setting⇨Control Panel⇨Administrative Tools⇨Services.
>
> To verify that the Administrative Server program is running in UNIX, use `ps -ef`.

The XMLConfig command-line tool provides administrators with the capability to back up and restore the WebSphere Administration Server.

> **CROSS-REFERENCE:** You learn more about the XMLConfig tool in Chapter 28. To learn about migrating from version 2 of WebSphere, or to understand more about migration, see section 3, "Migration," in the WebSphere InfoCenter.

Installing IBM HTTP Server 1.3.19

IBM HTTP Server is based on the Apache Web Server (the most popular server on the Web). The IBM HTTP Server can run on the following platforms:

- Windows NT
- Windows 2000
- AIX
- HP-UX
- Linux
- Solaris

IBM has enhanced Apache Server with Secure Socket Layer (SSL), which gives you the capability to secure transactions. In addition to SSL , some other benefits you get with the IBM HTTP Server are its fast-response Cache Accelerator (FRCA), administration capabilities through a browser-based administration server, and its ease of installation. Best of all, it's free with WebSphere.

You are guided through the installation process as you walk through the wizard. After it's installed, you test it to see if it works. To prepare the Web server for the integration with WebSphere, you learn about specific configuration directives for the Web server.

Performing the installation

As mentioned previously, installation is fairly simple. This section outlines installing IBM HTTP Server separately from WebSphere. Although the WebSphere installation program automatically installs the IBM HTTP Server, you install it separately here.

Separate installation provides several benefits. First, you can test the installation and verify that the HTTP Server is functional. This helps you debug installation problems. Another benefit to separate installation is that you probably will be installing the HTTP Server on another workstation anyway. Separating the HTTP Server from WebSphere enables you to implement more security precautions, such as a firewall.

With the WebSphere Application Server (AE) CD in the machine, you can get started with setup, following these steps:

> **NOTE:** On the WebSphere CD in the `NT` folder is another folder named `HTTPD`. This is where the IBM HTTP Server installation programs exist.

1. Start the `setup.exe` program; choose the language, and click Next on the Welcome page. You are presented with the Choose Destination Location panel.
2. Ensure that the Destination Folder points to the location `x:\Program Files\IBM HTTP Server` and click Next.
3. The next page asks you to enter one of the userids that you previously created locally. The information you enter is used to provide authentication for the NT service that starts IBM HTTP Server at bootup. Type **httpadmin** along with the password you assigned.
4. Complete the rest of the wizard when prompted and click Finish to complete the installation.

> **NOTE:** We have deliberately left out some screen shots that we felt were insignificant (Welcome, Type — Typical, Custom, Licensing — and so on) and that we knew you could handle yourself. We continue with that process throughout the installation sections of the book.

Reboot your workstation to finish the installation. Your goal should be to reduce the number of places where errors can occur by verifying that the Web server was installed properly.

Verifying IBM HTTP Server installation

After you reboot your machine and log on, it is time to verify that your Web server is functioning properly. Because the installation set up your Web server as a Windows service, you should check the service to see whether it is actually running. By default, the two services (IBM HTTP Administration and IBM HTTP Server) should be automatically started. Figure 4-3 shows the IBM HTTP Administration and IBM HTTP Server services both started.

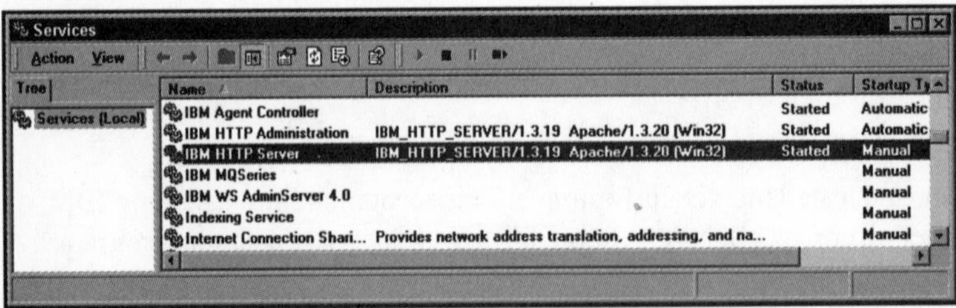

Figure 4-3: The Services screen window in which services are running.

The Services window (Figure 4-3) is a good place to look for potential problems. The status column shows the status of services. The Startup column shows which services are started automatically and those that must be started manually. In the event that you want to change the startup options or perhaps have the IBM HTTP Server started manually, you can right-click the service, select Properties, and change Startup Type from Automatic to Manual.

If you do not see the services running, you probably received a start-up error message. You can attempt to start the service from the Services screen by selecting the service, right-clicking, and selecting Start.

> **TIP:** If you received a cryptic error message while trying to start the HTTP Server, try going to a command prompt and navigating to `<http_home>` and typing in **apache -f <http_home>\conf\httpd.conf** to display startup errors.

If the service starts successfully, as shown in Figure 4-3, you should test to see whether it's working for your node. Try accessing the Web server by using the host name of the machine; for instance, if your machine's name is Foo, you type **http://Foo/index.html**. You can also use the loopback address of `127.0.0.1` to access the Web server. In this case, you type **http://127.0.0.1/index.html**. You can also bring up the same page by typing **http://localhost/index.html**. If everything works properly, you see the Welcome to the IBM HTTP Server page.

You should definitely try accessing the Web server using the appropriate host name to verify that you are properly set up. For instance, if your DNS has not been updated, you cannot access it via the host name. If that is the case, try using the IP address of your Web server to see whether that works. If that doesn't work, it's back to the drawing board.

Preparing to configure the Web server

The configuration of IBM HTTP Server is basic. To configure the server to perform more advanced functions, such as virtual hosting, you need to update the `httpd.conf` file.

The `httpd.conf` file is found within the `<http_home>\conf` folder. You can manually update the file with an editor, or you can use the Administration page to configure the Web server. Most Webmasters update the configuration file with an editor, but a developer configuring the Web server for the first time might appreciate a user interface. The Administration server that comes with the IBM HTTP Server provides such an interface. Before you can utilize the Administration page, you need to have authorization.

> **TIP:** To use the Administration page of IBM HTTP Server, you first need to create a password file to contain valid users.

Setting up a Web server administration account

To do advanced administration work, you must have authorization. Using the IBM Administration Server requires a system administrator to create a HTTP password file. To create the password file, run the program `htpasswd.exe` located in the `<http home>` folder. Each time you call this program, it adds the new userid and prompts you for the user password. Figure 4-4 shows the prompting sequence after the user types:

```
htpasswd -c conf\admin.passwd MyUserid
```

You are prompted for a password twice. You can type in **`mysecret`** as your password.

```
Select C:\WINNT\System32\cmd.exe

D:\Program Files\IBM HTTP Server>htpasswd -c conf\admin.passwd MyUserid
Automatically using MD5 format on Windows.
New password: ********
Re-type new password: ********
Adding password for user MyUserid

D:\Program Files\IBM HTTP Server>
```

Figure 4-4: Adding a userid using htpasswd.

After you create the password file, you should try to access the Administration page for the IBM HTTP Server. You access that page by entering the following in your browser:

```
http://localhost:8008/admin/
```

As an alternative you can type:

```
http://<machine_name>:8008/admin/
```

or

```
http://127.0.0.1:8008/admin/
```

You are challenged by the system to provide a valid userid and password (MyUserid and mysecret).

> **NOTE:** Exposing your administration through the Web is security breach.

The IBM Administration Server is displayed when a user successfully passes the logon challenge. The page that displays provides you with a browser-based method of updating the `httpd.conf` configuration file.

The navigation bar on the left side of the page has the following options:

- Getting Started
- Basic Settings
- Configuration Structure

- Indexing
- Authentication files
- Access Permissions
- Security
- Logs
- Mappings
- Scripts
- Performance
- MIME
- Fast CGI
- File Systems
- Proxy
- View Configuration

You learn how to configure some of these options, but you make those changes using an editor. For more information on how to use the Administration Server, click the question mark symbol located on the Getting Started page in the IBM Administration Server page.

Now that you established authorization and validated that the administration server is accessible, you can learn about some of the HTTP directives set in the `httpd.conf` file that directly impact WebSphere.

Using key directives

The HTTP configuration file can be large because it contains many directives (keywords). You need to change only the following directives initially:

- `Port`: The TCP/IP port that Apache listens to
- `HostnameLookups`: Allows reverse lookup on requesters IP address
- `ServerAdmin`: E-mail address of Web master
- `ServerName`: Host name sent back to HTTP client
- `DocumentRoot`: Base of the Web Server document tree
- `Alias`: Includes documents from other locations in Web server's document tree
- `Directory`: Groups directives to apply to a directory path
- `DirectoryIndex`: Specifies the default filename to serve when a request does not specify a file

Some of these directives are covered in the sections that follow. For more information about configuring IBM HTTP Server, visit the following site:

```
http://www-4.ibm.com/software/webservers/httpservers.
```

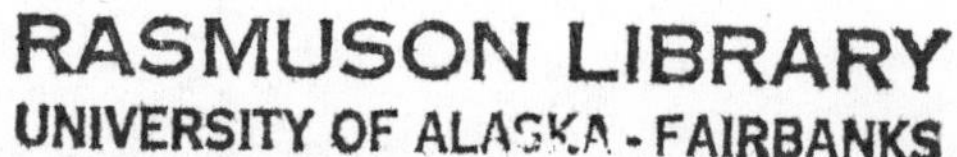

Setting up virtual hosting

You add some virtual host directives to the `httpd.conf` file to customize your configuration for the Web server. Virtual hosts give the Web master the capability to maximize utilization of a server by creating what appears to be many separate hosts. In fact if the server is big enough, the number of hosts seems endless.

In a development environment with multiple hosts, you can subdivide your testing environments on one machine each with separate host names, for example, `development`, `qualityassurance`, and `acceptancetesting`.

If you are running an inexpensive cruise brokerage business on the Web, having the capability to create virtual hosts enables you to create new business entities with different host names so they appear different but actually direct you to the same physical machine. In that scenario, you are maximizing your hardware investment by logically making it seem as though you have many Web sites. Some examples could be `www.reallycruisecheap.com`, `www.stowawaycruise.com`, and `www.almostFreeCruise.com`.

You should now add two additional virtual hosts to `httpd.conf` file. Open the `<http_home>/conf/httpd.conf` file with an editor. WordPad is a sufficient choice of editors. Enter the configuration directives shown in Listing 4-1.

> **NOTE**: When creating multiple virtual hosts for a same IP address, you must use the `NameVirtualHost` directive.

Listing 4-1: Adding Virtualhost to the httpd.conf file

```
NameVirtualHost    131.107.6.1
<VirtualHost www.reallycheapcruise.com>
ServerAdmin webmaster@reallycheapcruise.com
ServerName www.reallycheapcruise.com
DocumentRoot "x:/Program Files/IBM HTTP Server/htdocs/cheapcruise"
ErrorLog logs/cheapHost-error.log
TransferLog logs/cheapHost-access.log
</VirtualHost>

<VirtualHost www.almostFreeCruise.com>
ServerAdmin webmaster@almostFreeCruise.com
ServerName www.almostFreeCruise.com
DocumentRoot "x:/Program Files/IBM HTTP Server/htdocs/almostFreeCruise"
ErrorLog logs/freeHost-error.log
TransferLog logs/freeHost-access.log
</VirtualHost>
```

The process of setting virtual hosts doesn't end with changing the `httpd.conf` configuration. You also have to ensure that you update the x:`\winnt\system32\drivers\etc\hosts` file to contain something similar to the code lines that follow:

```
# Copyright (c) 1993-1995 Microsoft Corp.
#
# This is a sample HOSTS file used by Microsoft TCP/IP for Windows NT.
#
#
# For example:
#
# 102.54.94.97     rhino.acme.com    # source server
# 38.25.63.10      x.acme.com        # x client host
127.0.0.1    localhost
131.107.6.1  kafemocha
131.107.6.1  www.reallycheapcruise.com
131.107.6.1  www.almostfreecruise.com
```

When you finish typing in these directives, you have to stop and attempt to restart the IBM HTTP Server service in order to test your changes. (You were instructed on how to start and stop services in a prior section, "Verifying IBM HTTP Server installation.") You also need to stop the HTTP server and restart it to invoke the changes.

> **TIP:** You can restart gracefully by issuing the <http_home>/`apache -k restart` command.

Setting up the document root

The `DocumentRoot` directive sets the directory from which Apache serves files. The default document root for IBM HTTP Server is the `htdocs` folder.

```
DocumentRoot "x:/Program Files/IBM HTTP Server/htdocs"
```

The document root is where you deploy all your Web resources (HTML, images, and so on). Document roots are just folders in the file system. They form the base or root level where the Web server looks for Web resources. You will most likely set the document root directory to another location to separate your different Web applications. When creating additional `virtualhosts`, you should specify new `DocumentRoots`.

Later in this chapter, in the "Web Containers in WebSphere Application Server" section, you run across another document root. This document root is contained in the internal HTTP server built into the WebSphere Application Server, but more on that later.

Setting up aliases

The `Alias` directive allows documents to be stored somewhere in the file system other than under the `DocumentRoot`. Normally, the default location for Web resources is the document root. The following is an example of the format of this directive:

```
Alias /WSSamples x:/WebSphere/AppServer/WSsamples/
```

If, for example, you go to `www.almostfreecruise.com/WSSamples/`, you see the list of resources occupying that directory. You also see `Parent Directory`. If you select `Parent`

`Directory`, you actually return to the document root of the server and not to `x:/WebSphere/AppServer`. `Parent Directory` really means parent URL.

HTTP error codes

Browsers and Web servers communicate through requests and responses. As actions are performed on the Web server, there needs to be a way to provide the status of the request. The Web server handles that through HTTP error codes. The IBM HTTP Server returns these codes whenever a request is made.

There are numerous error codes. There are codes for successful requests (200), security failures (403), and fatal server errors (500). Following is a short list of the available codes. For a full listing of the codes, consult the IBM HTTP Server help documentation.

- 200 OK
- 302 Found
- 304 Not modified
- 400 Unauthorized
- 403 Forbidden
- 404 Not found
- 500 Server error
- 501 Not implemented
- 502 Bad gateway
- 503 Out of resources

These error codes come in handy as a debugging step. As vendors create Web servers and Web containers, they utilize these error codes as mechanisms to return state. Browsers recognize these codes and can provide useful messages back to the user. Unfortunately, not all conditions are covered, so you may find yourself reviewing these error codes to assist in troubleshooting. For instance, you may receive a 404 Not Found error if a particular Web resource points you to a location that does not exist.

Installing DB2 7.2

In this section, you install DB2 Universal Database 7.2. DB2 UDB version 7 is a powerful relational database-management system that serves not only large corporations, but is flexible enough to serve small- and medium-sized businesses (SMB). Included in UDB version 7 are data warehousing, multimedia, XML extensions, and Web connectivity tools.

If you recall from the checklist at the beginning of the chapter, you will be installing four components (a Web server, a Java Development Kit (JDK), a relational database, and WebSphere). The primary reason for installing a database (DB2 in this case) is so you can use it as the database for the administration repository. You learn about which databases are supported by WebSphere, as well as actually install the database.

Normally you don't install the database on the same physical machine as WebSphere. To access a database that resides on another physical machine, you need some form of client access. In this section, you learn the steps to add the client software to your WebSphere machine. Although you learn these steps, you do not actually implement a remote database.

Understanding databases for the Administration repository

Although only a single server is required to install WebSphere, to build a scalable highly efficient domain, you probably need more that one server. When you build a system that has multiple servers all operating under the administration, it is called a WebSphere domain. To manage a domain requires an Administration repository accessible to all WebSphere application servers. Because of the sheer importance of this information, WebSphere makes use of relational-database technology to manage the persistence of this information.

WebSphere supports the following database types:

- Oracle 8i
- MS SQL Server
- Informix Dynamic Server
- Sybase Adaptive Server
- Merant Sequelink
- DB2 Universal Database (UDB)

Previous versions of WebSphere included the InstantDB database. This database was replaced with the XML file used in AEs. The InstantDB database was allowed in only single-server installations.

NOTE: AEs does not require a database for the WebSphere Administration Repository. It uses, instead, an XML configuration file.

Installing the DB2 Administration database

Installing DB2 for the first time should be rather easy provided you have the necessary space. The minimal requirements stated in the "Evaluating system requirements" section do not account for disk space for your application data. That really isn't a concern as you install DB2 initially. The primary reason you are installing DB2 on your server is to use it as the Administration database. The Administration database doesn't require much disk space.

To start you must load either the WebSphere Application Server CD labeled on this CD - DB2 Universal Database or a DB2 Universal Database Enterprise Edition CD. The following instructions guide you through the installation:

1. Run `setup.exe` on the CD. You are presented with the DB2 Welcome Page.
2. With the mouse, find the Install menu and click Install.
3. When asked to check which products to install, select DB2 Enterprise Edition only and click Next.
4. If by chance you are reinstalling DB2 or had a prior version of DB2 installed, you might be warned about DB2 processes already running on your system. It is highly recommended that you exit the install and manually close each of these services.
5. The next screen is the Installation Type screen. In a normal situation, you could just select Typical, but for this installation, you should select Custom so you can remove features that are unnecessary for WebSphere administration.
6. In the Select Components screen, remove check marks from the DB2 Query Patroller Client, the DB2 Connect Server Support, Data Warehousing Tools, and the OLAP Starter Kit check boxes. These are features that are need for data warehousing. Remember you are trying to install the minimum database with the least amount of system resources. You should also change your destination folder on this page.

> **WARNING**: If you forget to remove the Data Warehousing Tools and OLAP Starter kit, you may see an additional screen asking you to define your local Warehouse Control Database. If this is the case, accept the defaults and use `db2admin` as the userid and password; then click Next.

7. When asked whether you want to create the default DB2 instance, you should answer Yes.
8. When you reach the Enter Username and Password screen enter **`db2admin`** in both the userid and password fields. To make life easier as you continue, check the Use the Same Values for the remaining DB2 Username and Password settings check box.

> **NOTE:** Because you already created the userid, you should not be prompted to create one. If you are prompted, the install creates a userid named `db2admin` with the same policies as discussed in the section "Userid creation."

9. Continue with the installation until you reach the Setup Complete screen. At that point, you need to reboot your system to complete the installation.

> **NOTE:** If you see the Install OLAP Starter kit prompt, you most likely didn't remove it from the Components list. Simply select Do Not Install the OLAP Starter Kit and continue.

10. When your system restarts, you should be presented with the First Steps (Congratulations) window. You can also confirm installation success by verifying in the Window services window that the following DB2 services have started.
    - DB2 – DB2
    - DB2 – DB2CTLSV
    - DB2 – DB2DAS00
    - DB2 Governor (not started)
    - DB2 JDBC Applet Server

- DB2 JDBC Applet Server – Control Center (not started)
- DB2 License Server
- DB2 Security Server

You have completed the DB2 installation. The next section discusses what to do if you do not want to have a local database resident on the same server as WebSphere.

Installing a DB2 remote client

The WebSphere Administration database can be implemented locally on the same physical machine or remotely on another machine. Local implementation is fine for development environments or environments in which memory and security are not major concerns. But in many cases, you need multiple servers in your domain, and the best way to implement the Administration database access is with a remote client.

> **WARNING**: The instructions in this section assume you have not installed DB2 previously. Some of the behavior and prompts change if you attempt to add the remote client to an existing system with DB2 already installed. This additional behavior does not cause problems, but you have to make some additional decisions when you are prompted.

You do not install the DB2 client in your learning environment, but it is important to understand the steps, so you can install the remote client when you are ready to install your "real" system. If you want to, you can skip this section and jump to section "Setting up for JDBC 1.1 or JDBC 2.0."

A DB2 remote client is a client/server implementation of database access. Having client code on the WebSphere Application Server reduces the overhead of maintaining the database engine and provides the flexibility to move the database engine to other servers.

> **NOTE**: Ensure your local userid used for installation has the proper administration rights as discussed in the section called "Key Directives."

You install the Administration client using installation procedures similar to those you use to install the DB2 Enterprise Edition.

1. After starting the installation when you reach the Select Products window, you check only the DB2 application Development Client.
2. On the Select Installation Type page, select the Typical option and then click Next.
3. On the Destination Location page, enter the destination folder. This probably defaulted to the proper folder. Ensure that it points to `<db2_home>` and click Next.
4. Continue with the installation by entering the **db2admin** userid and password and clicking Next. You are presented with the confirmation screen of the files that will be copied. After you click Next, the files are copied and at its completion you answer the final page by clicking Finish. You may be asked to reboot.

5. After rebooting, you should check your Windows services to verify that the DB2 components have started. You should see DB2 JDBC Applet Server and DB2 Security Server started.

Your final steps configure the client to have access to the Administration database. To access the database, you need to update the TCP/IP services file with the port address of the database and then the catalog the database location. You perform these steps as follows:

1. Using the windows explorer or a Windows command window, open `c:\winnt\system32\drivers\etc\services` with WordPad.
2. Add the line **db2cdb2 50000/tcp #Port** of remote instance of db2. This line informs the client program which port to connect to when using a remote client. Save the file.
3. Now, you need to catalog the database. To do this open a DB2 command window by clicking Start⇨Programs⇨IBM DB2⇨Command Window. This opens a command window with the title DB2 CLP.
4. In the DB2 CLP window enter **db2 catalog tcpip node was remote cruisedb server db2cdb2**. Press Enter. This command catalogs a remote node called `was` that points to a remote server named `cruisedb`. These are fictitious names used for the book. You should use the machine name of your database server in place of `cruisedb`.
5. Next you catalog the database (which means inform this machine of the remote database). In the DB2 CLP window, type **db2 catalog db was40 as wasalias at node was.** Press Enter. This line creates an alias named `wasalias` to a database called `WAS40` that is located on the remote node you called `was`.

NOTE: The WAS40 database is the default database name when WebSphere is installed. If you changed the name to something other than WAS40, you should specify that name instead of WAS40.

After you successfully enter these commands, you can connect to the database and run queries. To connect to the database you type **db2 connect to wasalias user db2admin using db2admin**. You get a confirmation display informing you that you connected successfully.

The last thing you need to do before you actually start WebSphere is ensure that you are running JDBC 2.0.

Setting up for JDBC 1.1 or JDBC 2.0

WebSphere Application and J2EE 1.2 require the use of JDBC 2.0. The default implementation of DB2 installs JDBC version 1.1. To successfully install WebSphere, you must update the JDBC level. Luckily, the DB2 folks provided a simple bat file to change from JDBC 1.1 to JDBC 2.0.

The bat file is located in the `<db2_home>\java12` folder. To run the batch file, open a Windows command window and go the `<db2_home>\java12` folder. Run the batch file by typing **usejdbc2** at the command prompt and pressing Enter.

> **NOTE:** If you run only usejdbc2.bat and do not have all the DB2 services shut down, the conversion fails. It is best to first shut down all DB2 services prior to running `usejdbc2.bat`.

Running the `usejdbc2`.bat batch file produces output like that shown in Figure 4-5.

```
C:\WINNT\System32\cmd.exe

D:\Program Files\SQLLIB\java12>usejdbc2
UnZipSFX 5.31 of 31 May 1997, by Info-ZIP (Zip-Bugs@lists.wku.edu).
  inflating: db2java.zip
  inflating: db2jdbc.dll
  inflating: db2ccs.exe
  inflating: db2jd.exe
  inflating: db2jds.exe
        1 file(s) copied.
        1 file(s) copied.
        1 file(s) copied.
        1 file(s) copied.
        1 file(s) copied.
        1 file(s) copied.

D:\Program Files\SQLLIB\java12>_
```

Figure 4-5: Output from usejdbc2.bat.

It is important that you do not receive any errors. If you see any error messages, one of the files being copied is probably in use. You need to correct the error and try again. Most likely, you have DB2 running as a service, and you must not have any DB2 services running. Do not consider installation complete until you get a clean run.

> **TIP:** Check the `inuse` file in the `SQLLIB/java12` folder to determine which version of JDBC you are using.

These are the types of errors that drive first-time installers crazy. Breaking the installation into separate components makes it easier to create a simple path to follow and validate.

Preparing for session persistence

Persisting sessions is an advanced configuration topic. A *user session* is an interaction between the browser and the Web server. A session is an object that contains information about a user session. Therefore, persisting session means keeping relevant information about an ongoing conversation between a browser and the Web server. Persisting sessions is discussed briefly only because it has an impact on the location of the database.

Sessions are a way of maintaining state between HTTP requests. Unlike cookies, in which information is stored on the client, sessions remain in memory on WebSphere. In a situation in which you are load balancing between multiple WebSphere nodes, session persistence must be turned on to ensure the safe return of application-state information to your application.

In a single server environment where you cannot load balance between multiple machines, you probably don't need session persistence. In a multinode environment, you must evaluate your applications and determine whether session persistence is necessary.

> **CROSS-REFERENCE:** Rules governing the use of session persistence are transparent to WebSphere application developers; some basic rules developers need to follow are discussed in Chapter 11.
>
> See Chapter 20, "Configuring WebSphere" and Chapter 11, "Understanding Session Management," to gain a full understanding as to why you use sessions and how to write programs that utilize them. This chapter also discusses the impact of increased reads and writes to the database and the many ways to set up session persistence.

Verifying the DB2 7.1 installation

DB2 is an important component that needs to be running successfully. If it is not working properly, WebSphere fails to install. You install WebSphere Application Server next so it is important to check one more times to ensure DB2 is running properly.

Verify that your installation was successful by opening the Win2000 Services panel:

1. Click Start⇨Settings⇨Control Panel.
2. Double-click Administrative Tools and double-click the Services icon.
3. The following DB2 services should have the status of Started:
   - DB2 – DB2
   - DB2 – DB2CTLSV
   - DB2 – DB2DAS00
   - DB2 JDBC Applet Server
   - DB2 License Server
   - DB2 Security Server

If all these services have a Started status, you can proceed with the WebSphere installation.

> **NOTE**: If you are using the DB2 Client only, you see only the DB2 JDBC Applet Server, DB2 JDBC Applet Server – Control Center, and DB2 Security Server in the Services window.

Installing WebSphere Application Server

Now that you have all the other components installed and verified you are ready to install WebSphere. The assumption being made is that you have not installed the DB2 Client software and will be running with the administrative repository locally. If you did install the DB2 Client, you need to ensure that the database machine is running and that you can connect to it successfully.

Everything should be ready to go, but go over the checklist in Table 4-4 one more time to ensure you have performed all the steps.

Table 4-4: Installation Checklist

Steps	***Description***
Userids	You created userids for `httpadmin`, `wasadmin`, `db2admin`, or userids of your own choice.
IBM HTTP Server	You installed and verified and now *stopped* IBM HTTP Server. You have also noted where you have installed the product — in particular the `httpd.conf` file.
DB2 Local or Remote Database	If you performed a remote installation, you assigned a port number.
JDBC 2.0	You ran and verified `usejdbc2.bat`.

Okay, you're ready to go. IBM HTTP Server has been stopped and JDBC 2.0 has been verified.

This section guides you through a custom installation:

1. Run `setup.exe` on the WebSphere Application Server Advanced Edition (AE) CD and follow the wizard until you reach the Choose Application Server Components page shown in Figure 4-6.

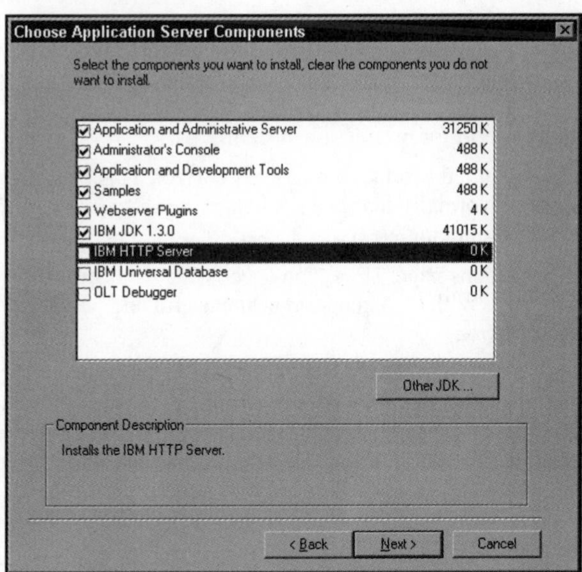

Figure 4-6: Choosing Application Server Components.

2. Because you already installed and verified IBM HTTP Server, you can deselect IBM HTTP Server. You can also uncheck the IBM Universal Database as well as the OLT Debugger. Click Next.
3. Figure 4-7 shows the known Web servers installed on your server. Figure 4-7 shows not only the IBM HTTP Server and Apache, but also Lotus Domino V5.05 and Microsoft IIS. Your particular situation may differ. You should select IBM HTTP server.

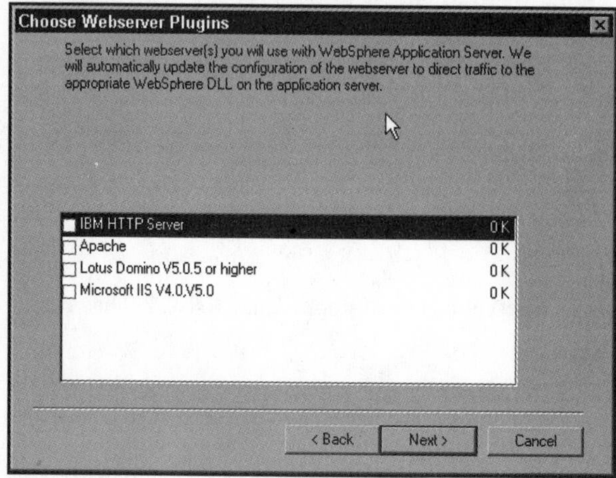

Figure 4-7: Choosing WebSphere plug-ins.

4. Click Next to proceed to the Security Options page. The userid entered is used for starting the WebSphere Application Server. Enter **wasadmin** as the userid for this server. For development environments, this userid is probably fine. Consult your security department to establish a secure userid for production systems.
5. Click Next and ensure that the defaulted Product directory is correct. This path is prefilled with the default location. Normally that is `x:/WebSphere/AppServer`. Accept the default and continue by clicking Next.
6. Figure 4-8 shows the Database Options page. Here, you specify the WebSphere Application Server DB2 repository. With the exception of the userid and password, the information has been defaulted for you.
7. You also specify the userid (`db2admin`) and password (`db2admin`) to start the Administration repository and provide a path to where the product is installed. Even though the URL is empty behind the scenes, it is `jdbc:db2:was40`. If the Remote Database check box is checked, the Server and Port boxes should be filled in.

CAUTION: Because you already installed IBM HTTP Server, you may be asked for the location of the `httpd` configuration file. That file is found in `<http_home>/conf`.

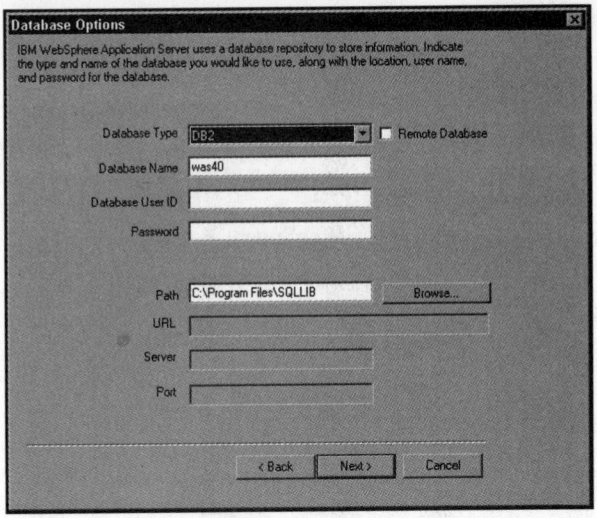

Figure 4-8: Setting the database options.

8. Clicking Next on the Database Option page takes you through the final pages of the wizard. The Select Program Folder and Install Options Selected are self-explanatory. Clicking Next on the Install Options page starts the copying.

> **NOTE:** Did you know that the persistence used for the repository is actually using entity beans and bean-managed persistence?

Voilà! You're done. If you want to look at the Readme file, have a look. Remember you must restart your system.

When your system returns, logon with your `wasadmin` userid. The following services should be started:

- DB2 – DB2
- DB2 – DB2CTLSV
- DB2 – DB2DAS00
- DB2 JDBC Applet Server
- DB2 License Server
- DB2 Security Server
- IBM HTTP Server
- IBM HTTP Administration

The WebSphere Administration Server (shown in the Services window as IBM WS AdminServer) is not started by default. You have to manually start this service.

Before you start the IBM WS AdminServer 4.0 service for the first time, take a moment to learn what happens the first time. When you reboot, the `WAS40` database that was defaulted in the wizard is created. You might see a command prompt temporarily display because the system issued a DB2 command-line processor to create the `WAS40` database and its supporting tables. Right after the bootup, you should also see the WebSphere Application Server — First Steps page. You can close that page for now.

Whew! That was a lot of work. At this point, you have completed the installations of not only the WebSphere Application Server, but also IBM HTTP Server and DB2 Universal Database.

Verifying a Successful Installation

You have installed all the products, and the process you followed provided instant feedback after each component was installed. The following sections take you through some of the common ways to look for errors and ways to validate that your implementation is successful. The following list shows some of the common ways:

- Reviewing installation log files
- Reviewing the admin.config file
- Starting the Administrative Server for the first time
- Seeing whether the Default Server Application operates properly

Checking the installation logs

A few logs are related to installation. You might check these files for error messages if your installation hangs or you have problems starting the servers. Review the following files:

- `<was_home>\logs\wssetup.log (win2000)`
- `<was_home>\logs\wasdb2.log (NT)`

You can use WordPad to open these files.

> **UNIX TIP:** In UNIX, `install.log` is the same as Windows `wssetup.log`.

Figure 4-9 shows a sample of the `wssetup.log` for an Advanced Edition (AE) installation.

The `wssetup.log` lets you know that you installed WebSphere 4.0 Advanced Edition. It shows details about the hardware you installed on and provides other relevant information, such as host name, Web servers present, and available disk space.

> **TIP**: If you are unsure whether errors were encountered during installation, check the end of the `wssetup.log` file for "Total Errors" and "Total Warnings."

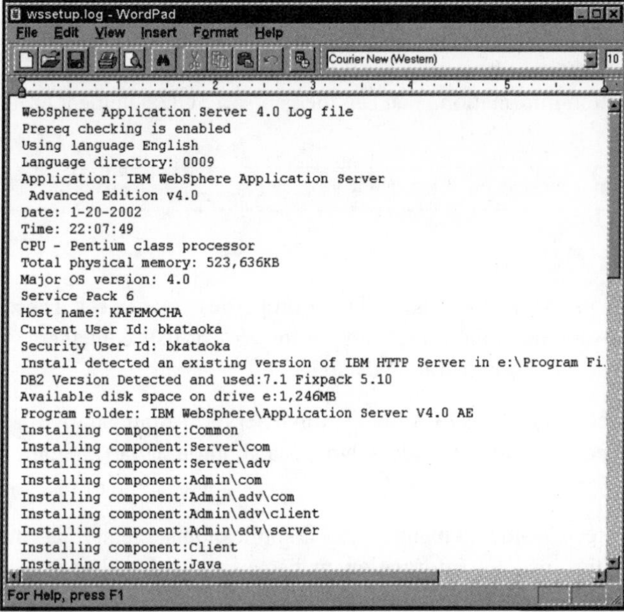

Figure 4-9. The WSSetup.log lets you know which edition of WAS is installed.

The `wasdb2.log` files shows different information. Remember that a DB2 command window is displayed right after you reboot for the first time. When that command runs, it starts DB2 using the `db2start` command and then creates the `WAS40` database using the `DB2 CREATE DATABASE` command. After this file creation, the command file updates the database configuration for the `WAS40` database. The output from these commands is logged into `wasdb2.log`.

Another tool you can use to check out setup and installation problems is the `jdbctest` tool. This Java application tests the connectivity between WebSphere and DB2 or Oracle databases. You can download the code from the following URL into a directory called `x:\javatools`:

```
ftp://ftp.software.ibm.com/software/websphere/info/tools/jdbctest/jdbctest.java
```

You need to compile the Java source code (`jdbctest.java`) so that it can run against the installed database (DB2 or Oracle). To compile the Java code, open a command window, change directories to `x:\javatools`, and type the following:

```
<was_home>\java\bin\javac jdbctest.java -classpath <was_home>\java\lib
```

The code should compile. You can test by executing the following from the command prompt:

```
<was_home>\java\bin\java jdbctest -classpath <was_home>\java\lib
```

When it executes, you are prompted for which database to test. Select 1 for DB2. It then asks for the name of the database. Type **was40** and press Enter. Finally, it asks for a userid and password; use **db2admin** and **db2admin**. After you press Enter, it should show Connection Successful and display the connection information. You can then enter a SQL statement or just type **quit** to end.

> **NOTE**: You must adjust the classpath to include the JDK found in WebSphere.

Reviewing admin.config

The `admin.config` file contains many Administrative Server properties you can set. These properties are specifically for the Administration server and not for Web or EJB containers. That information is stored in the `WAS40` Administration database.

At this point, you have probably seen references to Administrative Server, Administrative Console, HTTP Administration, and DB2 Administrators. Now is a good time to explain the differences.

The *Administrative Server* is the mechanism that manages J2EE application servers. It has the responsibility to start and stop applications, log information, manage workload, and so on. Unfortunately, IBM named the service IBM WS AdminServer. Therefore, you often find references in the documentation to the Admin server. They are one and the same.

The *Administrative Console* (also sometimes referred to as the Administrator's console) is a Java swing application that can be used to control the Administrative Server. Often this application is referred as the Admin console. The Administrative Console writes the configuration information to the repository. The repository is called the Administrative repository. The repository can be updated not only by the Administrative Console but also by tooling, such as XMLConfig and the WebSphere Control Program (WSCP).

With the clarifications complete, look deeper into the `admin.config` file. The `admin.config` file is found within the `<was_home>\bin\  folder.`

> **NOTE:** AEs does not have an `admin.config`. It does provide an XML file that is used to configure the admin server. That file name is `admin-server-cfg.xml`.

Figure 4-10 displays the `admin.config` file. The presentation of the file looks a bit ominous, but some explanation should clear things up. The `admin.config` file is a properties file. Properties files provide information to Java applications — in this particular case, the information that the enterprise server requires to find files, change program behavior, and places to log information.

The first five lines are fairly self-explanatory; they show how the Administrative Server finds or references its needed components (classpath, earfile, path, and JVM parameters).

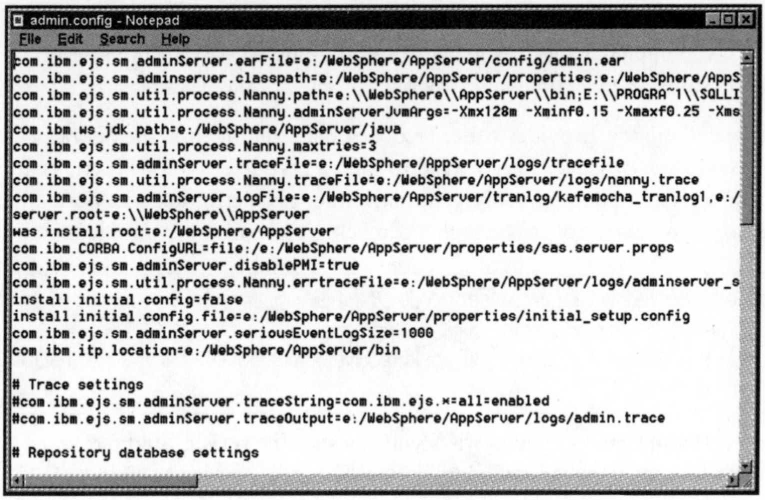

```
admin.config - Notepad
File Edit Search Help
com.ibm.ejs.sm.adminServer.earFile=e:/WebSphere/AppServer/config/admin.ear
com.ibm.ejs.sm.adminserver.classpath=e:/WebSphere/AppServer/properties;e:/WebSphere/AppS
com.ibm.ejs.sm.util.process.Nanny.path=e:\\WebSphere\\AppServer\\bin;E:\\PROGRA~1\\SQLLI
com.ibm.ejs.sm.util.process.Nanny.adminServerJvmArgs=-Xmx128m -Xminf0.15 -Xmaxf0.25 -Xms
com.ibm.ws.jdk.path=e:/WebSphere/AppServer/java
com.ibm.ejs.sm.util.process.Nanny.maxtries=3
com.ibm.ejs.sm.adminServer.traceFile=e:/WebSphere/AppServer/logs/tracefile
com.ibm.ejs.sm.util.process.Nanny.traceFile=e:/WebSphere/AppServer/logs/nanny.trace
com.ibm.ejs.sm.adminServer.logFile=e:/WebSphere/AppServer/tranlog/kafemocha_tranlog1,e:/
server.root=e:\\WebSphere\\AppServer
was.install.root=e:/WebSphere/AppServer
com.ibm.CORBA.ConfigURL=file:/e:/WebSphere/AppServer/properties/sas.server.props
com.ibm.ejs.sm.adminServer.disablePMI=true
com.ibm.ejs.sm.util.process.Nanny.errtraceFile=e:/WebSphere/AppServer/logs/adminserver_s
install.initial.config=false
install.initial.config.file=e:/WebSphere/AppServer/properties/initial_setup.config
com.ibm.ejs.sm.adminServer.seriousEventLogSize=1000
com.ibm.itp.location=e:/WebSphere/AppServer/bin

# Trace settings
#com.ibm.ejs.sm.adminServer.traceString=com.ibm.ejs.*=all=enabled
#com.ibm.ejs.sm.adminServer.traceOutput=e:/WebSphere/AppServer/logs/admin.trace

# Repository database settings
```

Figure 4-10: The admin.config file.

The following line is important:

```
com.ibm.ejs.sm.adminServer.traceFile=x:/WebSphere/AppServer/logs
/tracefile
```

When you turn on tracing, this is the location of the trace's output.

The following lines are also noteworthy:

```
install.initial.config=false
install.initial.config.file=x:/WebSphere/AppServer/properties/
initial_setup.config
```

The first line, when set to `true`, performs the operations to create the `WAS40` database. The second line contains the configuration information for the initial setup. You may remember that when you installed WebSphere and rebooted, a few command files were launched at startup. That was the execution of the initial configuration described here.

CROSS-REFERENCE: There are a lot more lines of `admin.config` to review; but those are covered in Chapter 20.

Starting the Administrative Server

You learned that the Administrative Server is the mechanism that manages J2EE application servers. You have not yet validated that the Administrative Server is working properly. Up to this point, you have just checked some log files (`wssetup.log` and `wasdb2.log`) and verified in the `admin.config` file that the `initial.config` was set to `false` (which means the database was created after bootup).

The installation does not set the Administration server Windows service to automatically install. Although you could open the Services window and start the IBM WS AdminServer from there, it's better to run it from a command window.

Running from a command window provides better feedback than running it in the Services window. The Services window produces only a window with a cryptic error code if errors do occur. In the command window, you minimally get a stack trace if an error occurs. More often than not, you get some reasonable error message that can help you resolve any problems.

> **TIP**: In the Windows Services window, you get an error code 10 if the Administrative Server does not start due to a JDBC 2.0 requirement. If you started the Administrative Server using `<was_home>\bin\adminserver.bat`, you would receive output that informs you that the JDBC level was back level.

It's important to become familiar with the two ways you can start the server. Start the Administrative Server using the command window option. Using a command window, navigate to your `<was_home>\bin` folder. Find the batch file called `adminserver.bat`. You may also see the `adminclient.bat`, which is covered later in this section.

Start the Administrative Server by invoking `adminserver.bat`. A lot of text displays in your window. When you see the message `adminServer open for e-business`, you have successfully started the Administrative Server.

> **NOTE**: After you have started the Administrative Server from a command window, do not close the window. This crashes the Administrative Server.

Next, you need to start the Administrative Console (Admin Console). You could use the `adminclient.bat` file to start the console, but use the Windows desktop menu system instead to learn an alternative.

Click Start⇨Programs⇨IBM WebSphere⇨Application Server 4.0 AE⇨Start Administrator's Console. This may take some time to display. A lot is going on behind the scenes. New Java Virtual Machines (JVM) are being started, the Administrative repository is being accessed, logs are being updated, and transports are being initialized. Finally, you see the Administrative Console.

That completes the installation verification. You have successfully installed WebSphere Application Server, and it is happily connected to most of the other products. You haven't really verified that WebSphere works in conjunction with the IBM HTTP Server. You cannot verify that integration until you start an application server.

You are ready now to look at the default server application server that is installed with WebSphere.

Starting the default server

WebSphere Application Server comes with an application server already configured. That application server is the Default server. The Default server has a Web container and an EJB container. Within the Web container are some servlets that you use to test WebSphere. You need to start the Default server so you can test the integration with the Web server.

1. Expand the Nodes folder and the node for your machine. You should see the Application Servers item.
2. Expand the Application Servers node to view the Default server. You may notice a small icon next to the name. That icon shows whether the server is up. If you see the little green arrow next to Default Server, the server is running. A red X next to Default Server on the left side of the screen means the server is not started. Figure 4-11 shows the Administrative Server expanded to show the Default Server.

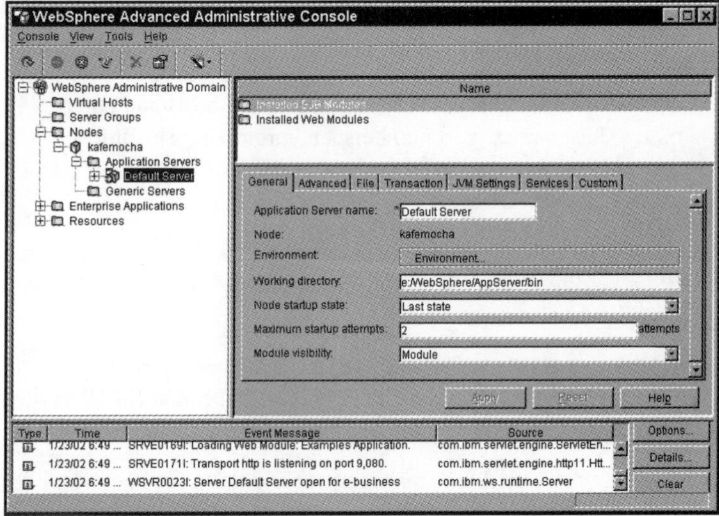

Figure 4-11: Verifying that the default server is running.

3. Right-click the default server and select Start to start the application server. If the Default server shows a red X, it becomes a green arrow after you start the application server.

> **TIP**: Clicking the Refresh icon refreshes the screen. Sometimes the screen does not repaint properly and a refresh can help.

In this case, the server should be running. Another way to test whether the server is running is to ping the server. Pinging is not like your TCP/IP `ping` command. It's just a way to see whether a particular application server is running and can be used by administrators who want to see whether various application servers are actually running. The TCP/IP `ping` command sends a message to an IP address and, in response, a reply is returned informing the user that the address is valid.

Try pinging the Default server. Highlight the default server and select the ping item from the smart icons or right-click.and select Ping. A message displays providing status.

At this point, you have the Default Server started, so there are really very few reasons to believe your WebSphere installation isn't happy. There is one critical task that needs to be discussed if you have separated your Web server from WebSphere. That task is the regeneration and distribution of the WebSphere plug-in.

Regenerating plug-ins

The WebSphere 4.0 plug-in is different from prior versions. This version supports the 1.1 level of the HTTP protocol, which allows for HTTP communication with the application server directly or through Secure Sockets Layer (SSL). In prior versions, the communication was done through the Open Servlet Engine (OSE) protocol.

The plug-in contains information about the configuration of virtual hosts and other configurations that pertain to host names, port numbers, and protocols. This information in version 3.5 used to be stored in vhosts, rules, and queues properties files. Now it is stored in XML format in a file called `plugin-cfg.xml`.

The new plug-in allows direct communication to the application server. The plug-in creators added an internal HTTP Server (port 9080) to the application server Web container, which is how the plug-in supports SSL.

Having this internal HTTP server can come in handy for troubleshooting. If you are having problems accessing your application, you can go directly to the embedded HTTP server to see whether you can access it. If you can, the problem is outside of the application server.

In a multiserver environment, where workload management and fail-over support are required, the Web server needs to know how to route the specific requests to the proper servers. The plug-in configuration must agree with the configuration of the application server — more specifically, with specific transport host, transport port, transport protocol, and SSL. Whenever you change one configuration parameter that affects the way information is routed, you need to update the plug-in and ensure it gets reloaded.

Troubleshooting Installation Problems

The InfoCenter is a handy place to search for specific information that can help you understand and correct problems. Of the chapters in the InfoCenter, Section 8.1 Problem Determination is very informative.

Most of the problems you encounter probably have to do with setup and ensuring that your network is working properly. You learned the proper way to install all the components and verified that your installation was correct along the way. If you are encountering problems, refer to the `wssetup.log` and `wasdb2.log`.

As mentioned previously, the InfoCenter has a whole section (Problem Determination) dedicated to troubleshooting. If looking at the logs doesn't immediately point out the problem, turn to the InfoCenter for assistance.

The InfoCenter that is installed with WebSphere is incomplete. The full InfoCenter documentation is required to see most of the important information. You walk through the implementation of the full InfoCenter in the next section.

Loading the full InfoCenter

The InfoCenter contains release notes, in-depth documentation, step-by-step installation procedures, and other updates, such as tutorials, code samples, and help file updates.

> **NOTE:** `www.ibm.com/software/webservers/appserv/infocenter.html` is the URL where you can view the InfoCenter on the Web.

It can be cumbersome to link to the Web to get information, so we recommend downloading the full InfoCenter JAR file and installing in your environment. This section shows you how to do just that.

> **CAUTION**: Be sure to update your PATH environment variable to point to the JRE in WebSphere by adding `x:\WebSphere\Appserver\java\jre\bin` to the PATH statement.

The full version of the InfoCenter installs in your WebSphere install directory — `<install_drive>\WebSphere\en\InfoCenter`. To actually get it there takes a little work. Follow these steps to begin:

1. First, you must navigate with your browser to `www.ibm.com/software/webservers/appserv/infocenter.html`. From there, you download the applicable InfoCenter for your particular install base. Of course, your options are Advanced Edition (AE), Advanced Edition Single Server Edition (AEs), and Enterprise Edition (EE).
2. For purposes of this example, you use `<download_folder>` as the location in which to save the downloaded file. After you download the file, you might notice that the filename is sort of funny looking. The InfoCenter JAR file is actually a ZIP file. Be aware that the filenames have changed between versions, but it really doesn't matter much. The latest version has a file name of `infocenter_en_wasa.jar.zip`.

> **CAUTION:** Don't use WinZip to unzip the file. The results are incomplete. Instead, you need to rename the ZIP file to a JAR file.

3. Rename the file from `infocenter_en_wasa.jar.zip` to **infocenter_en_wasa.jar**. Rename the ZIP file by entering the following command into a command window:

```
ren infocenter_en_wasa.jar.zip infocenter_en_wasa.jar
```

4. Open a command window and issue the following command:

```
<was_home>\java\bin\java -jar <download_folder>\infocenter_en_wasa.jar
```

5. Type **accept** to accept the licensing. Eventually, you are prompted for the location of the WebSphere Installation. Make sure your installation folder is at the `\WebSphere\AppServer\en\` level, for example `C:\WebSphere\AppServer\en\`.

6. After completion, you can check the `InfoCenterInstall.log` file found in the folder where you ran the command.

> **TIP**: A common error is trying to unjar using a JDK version lower than version 1.2.2. If you have problems, try checking your JDK version. Type **java –fullversion**.

Taking the InfoCenter for a test drive

Now that the InfoCenter has been created on your machine, take it for a test drive.

1. Start Internet Explorer 5.5 (Netscape has problems) and use File⇨Open, and click Browse. Locate the InfoCenter's `index.html` file in the `x:\WebSphere\en folder`.

2. On the left navigation pane, expand the Application Server AE and expand the About This Information to learn how to use the InfoCenter.

3. Undoubtedly you will want to research a subject that you feel the InfoCenter has buried. The InfoCenter has a Java applet that acts as your search engine. Try using the search engine to find some of the new features of Version 4. Click the Search link on the top level navigation bar to start the search.

> **CAUTION:** Sometimes there are problems using search with browsers other than Internet Explorer. If you cannot access search with another browser, try Internet Explorer.

4. When you are presented with the Search page, type **Troubleshooting**; you should see all the sections that discuss troubleshooting.

That completes the introduction of the InfoCenter. You will find that the InfoCenter becomes your friend. You can close your browser now. It's time to run some sample applications using the Default server.

> **NOTE**: At this time, you should install the WebSphere Application Server Fixpak 4.0.3. Refer to the section "Introducing Fixpak 4.0.3."

Running Sample Applications

WebSphere comes with sample applications, so you can see some examples running on your server. Provided you started the Default server, those samples should be available. Begin by ensuring that the Administrative Server is started and that the Administrative Console is running:

1. Check the Windows Services to see if IBM WS AdminServer is started. If it isn't highlight it and right-click and select Start.
2. Start the WebSphere Administration console. Click Start⇨Programs⇨IBM WebSphere⇨Application Server 4.0 AE⇨Start Administrator's Console.
3. When the console is visible, expand the Nodes, your machine name, and then Application Servers.
4. Verify that Default Server has a green arrow beside it. That symbolizes that it is running.
5. Open a browser window and enter the following URL: `http://localhost/WSsamples/index.html` This path is case sensitive.

When the Samples Gallery page opens, you see the Getting Started with IBM WebSphere Application Server Samples, which contains the following samples:

- YourCo
- Bean Scripting
- StockQuote
- HelloEJB
- IncrementEJB

It is up to you to try some of the applications. To run these samples, you must follow the instructions on the first page. The following steps summarize those instructions:

1. Create a new user named **wsdemo** with a password of **wsdemo1**.
2. Create the Sample database by opening a Windows command prompt. Change to `<was_home>\bin`. Type **importsamplesdb2 db2admin db2admin** and press Enter
3. When completed, you need to go to the Administrative Console and select the Default server. Right-click and select Stop. When you get confirmation that it stopped, right-click again and select Start.
4. After it is started, select Enterprise Application in the Administrative Console. Click the Refresh button on the toolbar. You see a new enterprise application called yourMachine/Samples.
5. You can now try some samples. Try the HelloEJB sample. Select HelloEJB and when the screen displays select Run This Sample. You should see Hello EJB Sample in a new browser window.

You should try some of the others examples at your leisure.

The next section exposes you to the one servlet that is not on the sample list but that you should become familiar with: the Snoop servlet.

Running Snoop servlet

Perhaps the tool administrators use most to determine whether WebSphere is running properly is the Snoop servlet. Snoop is part of the default application server. It is useful for examining HTTP request parameters received from a browser and for verifying the operation of the servlet engine. You start the Snoop servlet by entering into a browser the URL `http://localhost/servlet/snoop`. Figure 4-12 shows the results.

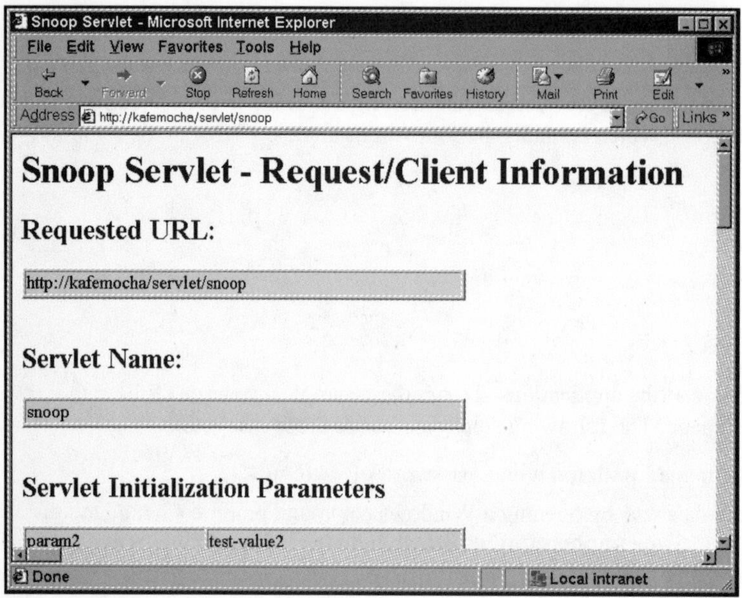

Figure 4-12: The Snoop servlet is a application that interrogates the HttpRequest object to display information about the servlet.

You can find out information about the following:

- Request method
- Request Uniform Resource Identifier (URI)
- Servlet path
- Server name
- Server port
- ServletContext

Snoop contains a lot more useful information that a developer or administrator can use to find out more about the servlet world. This is perhaps one of the most notable tools to validate whether an application server is running. Now that you have Snoop running, it's time to celebrate!

Exploring the Silent Install

You have reached the final segment in the installation chapter. You have learned how to install multiple products (IBM HTTP Server, DB2 and WebSphere Application Server). One feature you can utilize for all three products is the silent install.

You may have heard about the silent install mode. For those of you who believe it is a way of sneaking in code without anyone looking, you're wrong. The silent install is a way of installing WebSphere without having to use the wizard.

Can you imagine having to install (or better yet reinstall) WebSphere on three or four servers? That would take a lot of time. The silent install automates that task by providing a file in which you can enter the answers to all the wizard questions and just submit that file as a parameter to the `setup.exe`.

Using the silent install is easy: The WebSphere CD contains a file within the `<cd_drive>\NT\` folder called `setup.iss`, which is known as the response file. This is where you provide your responses to the wizard questions, as the following steps demonstrate:

1. Copy `setup.iss` to a known directory, and open the file with a file editor (such as WordPad).
2. Next, you have to change the responses in the file to match your answers to the wizard screens. Table 4-5 helps you select the appropriate responses. After you finish entering the parameters, you must make sure you have uninstalled any version of WebSphere Application Server or any back-level versions of IBM HTTP Server on the targeted machine.

Table 4-5: Response File Parameters

Installation Option	*Keyword/Heading*	*Value*

Language	`[ Application]`
	`Name`
	`Application Server`
	`Version`
	`Company`
	Lang
		`[ Application]`
		`Name=WebSphere`
		`Application Server`
		`Version=4.0`
		`Company=IBM`
		Lang=0009

Reboot after installation	`[ RebootDialog-0]` Result	`[ RebootDialog-0]` Result=1 to reboot
WebSphere Application Server Directory	`[SelectTargetDir]`	`[SelectTargetDir]` `szDir = <was_home>`

Table 4-5 *(Continued)*

Installation Option	***Keyword/Heading***	***Value***
Component	[Components] Enter a **1** next to the components you want to install.	[Components] Server=1 Tools=1 Admin=1 Java=1 Samples=1
Security	[Security]	[Security] szUser=userid szPassword=password szHostName=kafemocha
Database	[Database] *Tip:*URL, server, and port are used with Oracle databases.	[Database] szType=DB2 szName=was40 szUser=db2admin szPassword=db2admin szPath=<db2_home>
IBM distributed debugger	[OLT] Result	[OLT] Result=1 installs the debugger
Other JDK	[SelectJdkDir] Specify the home directory of the other JDK in szDir.	[SelectJdkDir] SzDir=<blank>
IBM HTTP Server plug-in	[SelectIBMHttpServer] Result	[SelectIBMHttpServer] Result=1 to install the plug-in. szDir = <http_home>
Apache plug-in	[SelectApache] Result	[SelectApache] Result=1 to install the plug-in. szHttpDir = <http_home> szSrmDir = directory of srm.conf.
IIS plug-in.	[SelectIIS45] Result	[SelectIIS45] Result=1 to install the plug-in. szDir = <http_home>

Installation Option	***Keyword/Heading***	***Value***
Lotus Domino plug-in	`[ SelectDominoDir]` Result	`[ SelectDominoDir]` Result=1 to install the plug-in. `szDir` = <http_home>

IPlanet 4.0 plug-in	`[ SelectiPlanet40_Dir]`
	Result
	Also set `UseSSL` to turn on SSL.
	Warning: Enabling SSL on a non-secure Web server prevents the plug-in from working.
		`[ SelectiPlanet40_Dir]`
		Result=1 to install the plug-in.
		`Result=0`
		`szDir=`
		`UseSSL=0`

Install IBM HTTP Server	`[ HTTPServer]` Result Leave the `szInstallDir` alone.	`[ HTTPServer]` Result=1 to install the plug-in. `szDir` = <http_home>

You are now ready to run setup. This time when you run setup, you have to start it at a command prompt and provide the location of the modified response file:

1. Begin by typing **setup <full path of setup.iss>\setup.iss –s**.
2. At the completion of setup, reboot your system. If you receive errors, check the `wssetup.log` file.

Summary

Wow, this is a big chapter! Installation is the most critical activity an administrator must deal with. Getting off to the right start can save days of effort and heartache. It all begins with the right approach to getting started.

This chapter included the processes to install and test each product. To have the best chance of a successful installation requires that you do your homework. It all begins with understanding the minimal hardware and software configurations necessary to install WebSphere. WebSphere is feature-rich and requires optimal hardware resources.

Planning is important. You learned that planning ahead saves time. Planning ahead means creating proper userids for security and with proper system credentials, preparing for migration, or just preparing by reading all the proper documentation prior to doing an install.

It was suggested that the proper order of installation begins with installing IBM HTTP Server followed by DB2 (Server or Client). Installing the Web server is very easy because few parameters need addressing. After it was installed, you learned about some key directives that help customize the Web server. You learned about the document root, server name, and virtual host directives.

With the DB2 installation, you learned that you must be running the JDBC 2.0 driver before WebSphere can work properly. It was also suggested that the database should reside on a separate machine to be accessed with DB2 client software. You were provided instructions about how to install the client software, although the examples were geared for a single machine containing all three products (Web server, database, and application server). After you verify the proper installation of these products, your confidence that WebSphere will install correctly should be high. Finally, the chapter discussed some other methods of validating your implementation, offered troubleshooting tips, introduced the InfoCenter, and discussed the silent installation feature.

Chapter 5
Preparing a Development Environment

In This Chapter

- ♦ Exploring installation options
- ♦ Planning for version control
- ♦ Defining CVS
- ♦ Installing and configuring a CVS system
- ♦ Installing a new JDK
- ♦ Installing WebSphere Studio Application Developer and/or WebSphere Studio Site Developer
- ♦ Creating the Cruise database and tables
- ♦ Installing Distributed Debugger
- ♦ Verifying the installation
- ♦ Planning for testing

Now that you have created an environment to which you can deploy, you can focus on preparing the environments for development. Because WebSphere AEd and AEs have been targeted for developers, the focus and graphics in this chapter are based on a Win2000/NT deployment. This chapter assumes that you have already installed WebSphere AEd. This chapter introduces and shows you how to install WebSphere Studio Application Developer and WebSphere Studio Site Developer. Topics that are important to development, such as version control and debugging are also discussed. After introducing the development environments, this chapter discusses change-management preparation to complete the development setup. The chapter focuses on why a change system is necessary and provides some typical environments you can establish.

This chapter discusses installing WebSphere Studio Application Developer version 4.0.2 and WebSphere Studio Site Developer version 4.0.2, choosing and installing a Java Development Kit (JDK) and Version Control System (VCS), and creating a test environment. You also load the Cruise database and tables required by many of the exercises found in later chapters. In addition, we discuss using a distributed debugger to debug your server code.

Introducing WebSphere's Development Tools

Although WebSphere Application Server 4.0 provides an abundance of development tools that you can use for developing enterprise applications, only one family of tools shares the same name, the WebSphere Studio family of tools. WebSphere Studio Application Developer and WebSphere Studio Site Developer are the latest tools to fall under the WebSphere Studio brand. Developed by IBM with an entirely new code base and built upon IBM's Eclipse tools platform, WebSphere Studio Application Developer and WebSphere Studio Site Developer were released as replacements for IBM's VisualAge for Java and WebSphere Studio products, respectively. Before WSAD, you used VisualAge for Java to develop the Java for your Web applications such as servlets, applets, and JavaBeans; and you used WebSphere Studio to create dynamic Web pages for your Web application. You could then deploy the resulting Web application to WebSphere Application Server. WebSphere Studio Application Developer incorporates most of the popular functionality in VisualAge, WebSphere Studio (and WebSphere Studio Site Developer, for that matter) into one development environment.

NOTE: Version 4.0 of VisualAge for Java and version 4.0 of WebSphere Studio are the last planned releases of these two development tools.

Eclipse provides an open-platform architecture used in developing integrated development environments that utilize a plug-in tools framework. The Eclipse framework makes it possible for you to acquire plug-in tools that you can then integrate into WebSphere Studio Application Developer. Currently, more than 100 software tools providers are developing tools using Eclipse.

NOTE: This chapter references WebSphere Studio Application Developer using its acronym, WSAD or its short name, Application Developer. Likewise, it refers to WebSphere Studio Site Developer as either WSSD or Site Developer.

Do not get confused if you hear of another development tool called WebSphere Studio Workbench. WebSphere Studio Worbench is actually the development tool used to build WSAD and WSSD. Many of the tools built into WebSphere Studo Workbench are available in WSAD, so if you want, you can use WSAD to create your own plug-in modules.

Understanding Installation Permissions

To install WSAD successfully in a Windows 2000 environment, the logged-in user must have Administrative rights to install software into the `c:\Program Files` directory. By default, users without Administrator rights in a Windows 2000 environment are not permitted to write to the `c:\Program Files` directory or any the files and folders within that folder. The same is true in an NT environment, if the logged-in user does not have the proper permissions. This presents a potential problem when you try to launch WSAD for the first time. WSAD creates the default workspace when you start it for the very first time. Improper file permissions cause the startup to fail.

You can skirt permissions problems in several ways:

- One option is to add write permissions to the `IBM` folder located in `c:\Program Files` for the users who will use WSAD. You may not have this option if you installed WSAD onto a NTFS files system.
- A second option is to bypass the write-permissions issue altogether by defining a separate workspace. To do this, find and modify all the shortcuts that launch WSAD to use the following scheme for their targets:

  ```
  c:\Program Files\IBM\Application Developer\
  wsappdev.exe -data c:\myworkspaces\workspace2
  ```

  where

  ```
  c:\myworkspaces\workspace2
  ```

  is a new workspace location.

Figure 5-1 shows how the shortcut settings should look when you are done modifying the target field. The next time you use the same shortcut to run WSAD, the workspace defined in the target is created and opened.

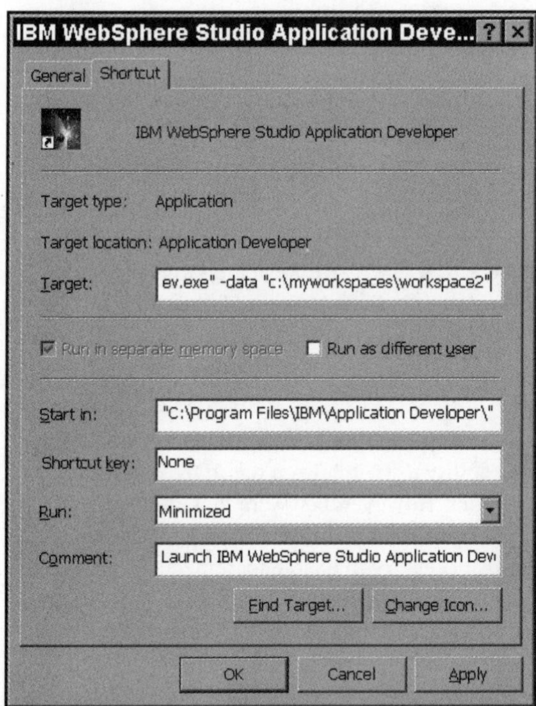

Figure 5-1: This is how the modified shortcut used to invoke the new WSAD workspace should look.

The modified shortcuts call the new workspace every time they are launched. To edit the WebSphere Studio Application Developer shortcut file, do the following.

1. Find the shortcut file that starts WebSphere Studio Application Developer by pointing your file explorer to the Programs folder that holds your Start menu's shortcut files. For example, the shortcut file in my computer is located in `C:\Documents and Settings\All Users\Start Menu\Programs\IBM WebSphere Studio Application Developer`.
2. Right click the shortcut file and choose the Properties option from the pop-up context menu.

CROSS-REFERENCE: By creating multiple shortcuts that point to different workspace locations, you can maintain multiple workspaces. Creating multiple workspaces is a useful function and is discussed in Chapter 7. One advantage of utilizing multiple workspaces is that you can keep your unrelated applications organized and separated into their own workspaces. You can quickly switch from developing one application to the other simply by opening a shortcut to the application's workspace.

Choosing a Version of JDK

Before the discussion of Java Development Kit (JDK) and Java Runtime Environment (JRE) versions, you need to understand the working definitions this chapter uses for both, because there's often some confusion as to what each one is. *JDK* is a set of files necessary to create applications for an associated runtime environment. Files in a JDK include `.class` files and sometimes `.java` source files that you can use to build your applications. A JDK comes with a compiler and other utilities, such as a javadoc generator. *JRE*, on the other hand, can be considered a subset of a JDK. A JRE contains only the necessary files to run and debug Java applications and does not contain a compiler. Even though JREs and JDKs contain common class files, they are not the same. Just because a JDK and a JRE have the same version number, it does not necessarily mean that they share the same number of class files or even the same files.

NOTE: Refer to the documentation that comes with your choice of a JDK for more information.

A key improvement in WSAD in comparison to its predecessors, VisualAge for Java and WebSphere Studio, is that it gives you the capability to switch from one JDK version to another, and thus from one JRE version to another. However, be aware that although you can switch among JDK versions, WSAD always uses its internal compiler to compile your code. This is always the case, because the compiler is necessary to enable incremental compilation of your code. The ability to switch JDK versions means that you could potentially develop applications using one JDK version and test the applications against a different JRE version. This is useful if you want to see how your code works when using another JDK version, provided by multiple vendors. WSAD currently supports JDK versions ranging from 1.1.7 to 1.4.

Preparing to Install WebSphere Studio Application Developer

Before you attempt any of the ways to install WSAD, make sure that you perform the following tasks and ensure that the following requirements are met:

- If you have a beta version of WSAD installed on your machine, uninstall it using the Add/Remove programs function in the Control Panel. Uninstalling WSAD does not remove any working directories, ensuring that the uninstall process does not erase any of your existing work. However, you can remove the working directories at your discretion. Also, some versions of WSAD do not uninstall if you do not first install a FixPak, available at IBM's Web site (`www.ibm.com`).

> **CAUTION:** You should never attempt to uninstall WSAD by simply deleting the WSAD installation directories.

- Make sure that file system of the disk drive where you will be installing WSAD is not the High Performance File System (HPFS) or Novell Netware.
- Make sure that you have either a TEMP or TMP environment variable set to a valid folder. The disk drive containing the folder should have at least 50MB of free disk space.
- If installing to Windows 2000, log on using an Administrator account with permission to install software on your machine. The default installation directory is `c:\program files`, but only users with Administrator rights are allowed to install programs into the directory.
- Make sure that IBM HTTP Server is stopped.
- Make sure that WebSphere Application Server is stopped.
- Make sure that the Services window is closed.
- Although you are not required to implement source control in WSAD, we highly recommended that you choose support for at least one type. Concurrent Versions System (CVS) is a good choice if you are looking for a simple and easy-to-implement solution.

> **NOTE:** WSAD comes installed with a local history to keep track of your changes to code, but is limited in its capabilities and should not be considered as a source control solution.

Review tables 5-1 through 5-3 to determine whether you meet the minimum requirements for installing WebSphere Studio Application Developer version 4.0.2 on your computer.

Table 5-1: Minimum Hardware Requirements for Installing WSAD Version 4.0.2

Harware	*Minimum Reqirements*
TCP/IP	Installed and configured
Processor	Pentium(R) II processor
Display	SVGA (800x600)
RAM	256MB
Hard drive space	Depends on file system. 400MB in NTFS.

Table 5-2: Minimum Software Requirements for Installing WSAD

Software	*Minimum Requirements*
Operating system	Windows 98, ME, XP, NT 4.0 Service Pack 6a, or Windows 2000 Professional, Server, or Advanced Server Service Pack 1, or later
Browser	Internet Explorer 5.5, Service Pack 1, or later

Table 5-3: Software Support in WSAD

Software	*Requirements*
Application servers	WebSphere Application Server 4.0.x, or Apache Tomcat 3.2, 4.0
Source control management	CVS or Rational ClearCase LT, 4.2
Browsers	IE 5.5, or Netscape Navigator 4.7.3
Additonal software support	Merant SequeLink JDBC Driver 5.1

Installing WebSphere Studio Application Developer

After you have determined that you meet all the requirements, you are ready to begin installation. This section includes several ways to install WSAD:

- From the install CD
- From the WebSphere Studio Application Developer file images
- Silent install from CD

> **CAUTION:** A copy of the IBM Agent Controller is automatically installed during the installation of WSAD to support the Performance Analyzer. The Agent Controller may present a security concern because it has no network security. To avoid the possibility of it being used as a Trojan horse, place the Agent Controller behind a firewall. In addition, leaving the Services window open while installing WSAD might prevent the Agent Controller from installing.

If you're migrating from other versions of WSAD, refer to the following subsection, which covers migration issues. When you're ready, choose one of the installation methods previously listed and follow the appropriate instructions located in one of the subsequent subheadings.

> **NOTE:** The instructions for installing WebSphere Studio Application Developer and WebSphere Studio Site Developer are virtually the same.

Installing from the installation CD

Insert the install CD into the CD-ROM drive. The auto-run feature should automatically launch the `setup.exe` program from the CD's root directory. If the auto-run doesn't launch the installer, you can manually start `setup.exe`. After you open `setup.exe`, follow these steps:

1. When prompted select a primary user role that best suits you. The role you choose becomes the default for this WSAD installation and is first perspective to be displayed; however, you can change this at any time after the installation. Figure 5-2 shows the installation screen for choosing the default user role set to WSAD.
2. Click Next to advance the wizard.
3. When prompted to select a source-control management system to install with WSAD, choose the one that fits your needs. Figure 5-3 shows the source-control management support choices available to you during the installation of WSAD.

Again, what you will be installing is support for a source control management system and not the actual source control management software. You will need to install the software separately, before or after installing WSAD:

- Choose CVS to install support for a concurrent versions system.
- Choose Rational ClearCase if you plan to or already are using the LT or Full version of ClearCase.
- If you choose Other, the default behavior of the installer is to install support for CVS. If you have another version control provider, you can install the support for it later. Visit `www-3.ibm.com/software/ad/studioappdev/partners/scm.html` for a list of Source Configuration Management providers.

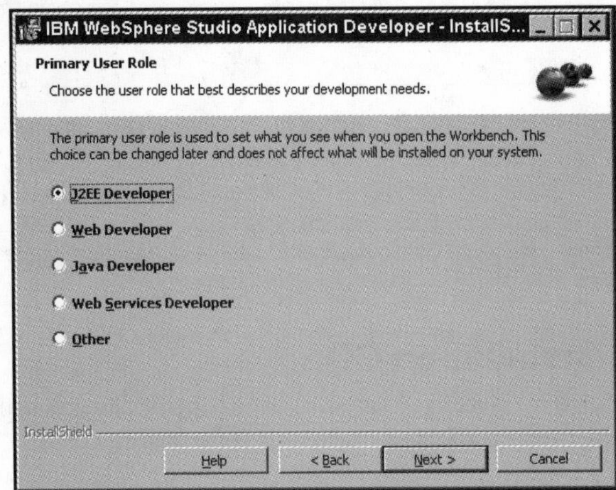

Figure 5-2: Selecting a default primary user role during installation.

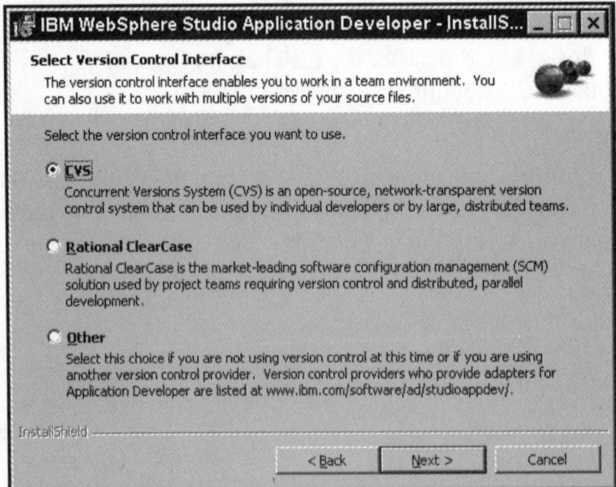

Figure 5-3: Select the version control support for WebSphere Studio Application Developer.

CAUTION: Keep in mind that many of the exercises covered in this book use CVS as the main mechanism for source control; thus this chapter discusses installing a CVS system but does not cover installing ClearCase. Also, be aware that if you change your mind about the type of source-control support you want after installation, you may need to reinstall WSAD altogether to make the switch.

Installing from the installation CD in silent mode

Make sure the installation CD is in your CD-ROM drive and the install program is not already running; then follow these steps:

NOTE: If you install WSAD in silent mode, you do not get any installation prompts. Also, silent installation does not overwrite an existing installation of WSAD. If you want to reinstall WSAD, you cannot use the silent setup option to do so.

1. Bring up a command prompt window. One way to do this in Windows is to choose Run from the Start menu. Enter **CMD** in the dialog box and click OK.
2. Change to the CD-ROM drive and run one of the following commands from the drive root:
    - To install to the default `c:\program files\ibm\application developer` directory, type **setup /s /v/qn**.
    - To install to another directory, where `<TARGET_DIR>` is the target directory, type **setup /s /v"installdir=\"<TARGET_DIR>""/qn**.

NOTE: The silent installation does not work if an existing version of WSAD 4.0.x is already installed. You must run the `setup.exe` from the CD to uninstall it first.

Installing from the WebSphere Studio Application from developer image files

WSAD is also available in five separate self-extracting installation files, which you can download from IBM's Web site, most likely at a hefty price (of course). Only the image files Parts 1 though 4 are required to install WSAD 4.0.x. Part 5 of the set of install files contain the files for installing Rational's ClearCase LT. If you choose to install using the image files, do the following:

1. Optionally create a temporary folder to store the extracted installation files.
2. Double-click each of the image files Parts 1 through 4 (Part 5 is optional) to extract them. When prompted for a folder to extract the files to, enter the path to the temporary folder.
3. Run the `setup.exe` program in the temporary folder.

Migrating from other versions of WebSphere Studio Application Developer

This section covers the following migration scenarios:

- Migration from a beta version of WebSphere Studio Application Developer to WebSphere Studio Application Developer 4.0.x.

> **CAUTION:** WebSphere Studio Application Developer 4.0.x does not officially support migrating from beta versions. You lose any settings that you have in the beta version, such as EJB mappings and associations. System-specific code, such as EJB generated code, is also lost. Your choices when installing the WebSphere Studio Application Developer 4.0.x also affect migration. For example, if you chose to use CVS for source-control management during the beta installation, but choose to use ClearCase when installing WebSphere Studio Application Developer 4.0.x, you might encounter errors during the migration.

- Migration from WebSphere Studio Application Developer 4.0 to WebSphere Studio Application Developer 4.0.x.
- Reinstallation of WebSphere Studio Application Developer 4.0.x.

To migrate from a beta version of WSAD, do the following:

1. Export your projects into a directory or JAR file.
2. Uninstall the beta version of WebSphere Studio Application Developer using the Add/Remove programs function in the Control Panel. After uninstalling, restart your computer.
3. Install the 4.0.x version of WSAD.
4. Create a project to store your resources.
5. Import the contents of the JAR into that project.

You can choose to migrate from WSAD 4.0 to 4.0.x. To do so, you do not have to uninstall 4.0. The installation program automatically uninstalls 4.0 before installing 4.0.x. WSAD 4.0.x also picks up the default workspace from the 4.0 installation. To reinstall WSAD 4.0.x, do the following:

1. Either use the Add/Remove program function in the Control Panel or run the `setup.exe` program to uninstall the existing copy of WSAD.
2. After the uninstall is finished, restart your computer, and then run the `setup.exe` program to start the reinstallation.

> **NOTE:** Uninstalling any version of WSAD does not remove any of your existing workspaces. If you choose to reinstall WSAD 4.0.x into the same location as a previous installation, the previous installation's default workspace is renamed to
>
> `workspace_installdata_installtime`
>
> and a new default workspace is created.

Because the old installation's default workspace is renamed, the new installation of WSAD does not automatically incorporate the old installation's default workspace. That feature is only available when upgrading from 4.0 to 4.0.x. However, you can work around this by doing either of the following:

- Modify any of your shortcuts to WSAD to point to the old installation's default workspace.
- Rename the new default workspace to something else and then rename the old default workspace to take its place. The next time you start WSAD, you open the old default workspace.

Verifying the install

Now that you've successfully installed WSAD onto your computer, review the components included in the installation.

- WebSphere Studio Application Developer development environment
- The integrated local/distributed debugger that enables you to debug your code directly from the workspace or debug code on a remote debug process
- The Agent Controller, which is a daemon process that supports and facilitates key features, such as remote testing, host process launching, and applications profiling
- The support for a source-control management system, if you chose to install one during the installation process
- A local copy of the WebSphere Application Server 4.0 Single Server Edition (for multiplatforms) to facilitate local testing
- Support for using Apache Tomcat Server 3.2 and 4.0 for local testing

NOTE: WSAD does not currently support testing on remote instance of Apache Tomcat. During the installation, if you encounter any errors, you can refer to the installation guide on the CD or unpackaged from the image files for a list of error codes and their possible solutions. The installer might also write an error to the installation directory.

If all went well and you did not get errors during installation, launch WSAD by either using the shortcut in the Start menu (Start⇨Programs⇨IBM WebSphere Studio Application Developer⇨IBM WebSphere Studio Application Developer) or find the executable (`ex: C:\Program Files\IBM\Application Developer\wasappdev.exe`) and run it. You should see a screen similar to the one in Figure 5-4. Figure 5-4 shows the WSAD workspace in the J2EE perspective after being launched for the first time.

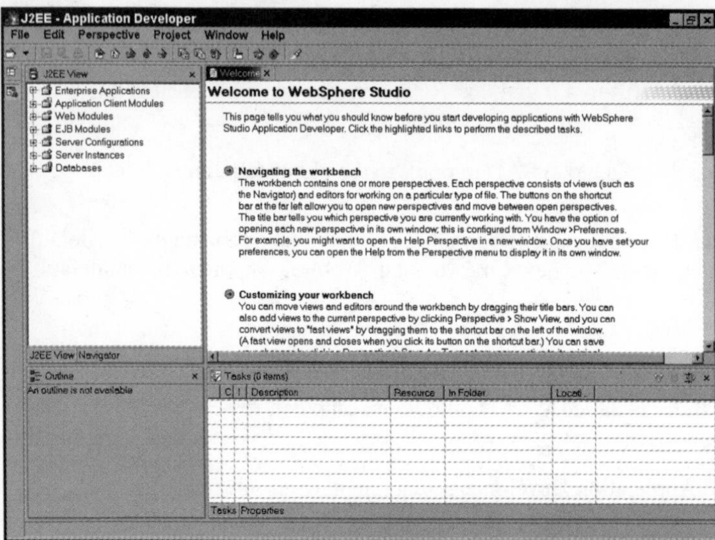

Figure 5-4: The WebSphere Studio Application Developer workspace, when opened for the first time, opens in the perspective you chose during the installation process.

If you encounter errors at this time, an error log is saved to the workspace and an error message displays in the Error Log viewer. The Error Log view does not show automatically. To see the error in the Error Log viewer, do the following.

1. Click Perspectives from the menu bar and select Show Views.
2. Select Other from the list of views to display all the available views.
3. Navigate to and open up the PDE Runtime folder.
4. Select Error Log from the folder and click OK.

In Figure 5-5, the Show View window lists all the available views in categorized folders.

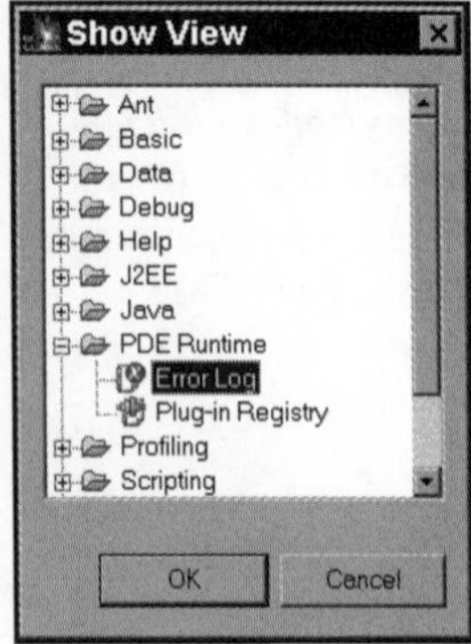

Figure 5-5: A list of all the views to choose from in the Show View window.

The Error Log view should now display in your workspace. If there are any errors, the Error Log view displays the message as well as the plug-in that may be causing the error.

Understanding JDK Java 1.3

Now that you have WSAD installed, take a few moments to look at the JDK that comes along with WSAD. The default JDK installed in WSAD is version 1.3. This JDK is attached to each of the projects that you create when using WSAD. Depending on the type of project that you create, WSAD includes default JAR files and resources appropriate to that type. For example, when you create a Java project, WSAD, by default, includes the `rt.jar` file in the project's build path. The `rt.jar` file contains the base library of classes you need to build a Java application. However, if you chose to create a Web project, the files automatically included in the build path would not only include the file but also the `j2ee.jar`, `webcontainer.jar`, `ivjejb.jar`, and `websphere.jar` files. The additional default JAR files included with the Web project provide additional class libraries to create a Web application. The default JAR files included in each project are specified in the customizable build path. Because the build path is completely in your control, you can also change them to suit your needs.

> **NOTE:** The compiler that comes with WSAD cannot be changed. Although you are allowed to switch JDK versions, the compiler used to compile the code within a project's build path is integrated into WSAD. This is required because the built-in compiler supports the incremental compilation feature in WSAD.

Creating the Cruise database and tables

Now you need to create the database and tables required to do many of the exercises found throughout this book. You need to create the database and table and load test data into the tables. We've created a set of files to help you in creating the database and importing the data. To create the database, follow these steps:

1. Using a command prompt window, navigate to the folder containing the createdb.ddl file. (You can download the file from this book's companion Web site. You'll find the file in the Chapter 14 folder.)
2. Type **db2cmd** and press Enter.
3. Another window opens. In the new window, type **db2 –tvf createdb.ddl** and press Enter.
4. Close both command windows by typing **exit**.

That concludes the setup for the Cruise database. You are now ready to start developing the AlmostFreeCruise applications utilizing the data in the database for the rest of this book.

Understanding the Team Repository

WSAD gives you the choice of installing support for a source-control management (SCM) system, also commonly referred to as a Team Repository. You should consider your long-term needs when choosing a SCM. The CVS system support is a good choice if you are looking to apply version control only to your resources. CVS offers a simple, quick, and easy-to-implement solution for projects, but lacks mechanisms, such as change control. If you expect that you'll need such a mechanism, you should consider installing support for either ClearCase LT 4.2 or the full version of Rational ClearCase. In addition to supporting many of the features found in CVS, ClearCase also adds additional management controls and an optional change-control mechanism.

CVS is by far the easiest to implement and requires the least amount of resources and effort to start; whereas ClearCase is a more complete SCM and includes features you won't find in a CVS. CVS runs as a service on a computer to support source control for both a single user or for a team. To support a team repository using ClearCase, you must be a user on an existing domain. Table 5-4 outlines the various ways to switch SCMs.

Table 5-4: Methods for Switching from One SCM to Another

From	*To*	*Steps*
None	CVS	Surprise, none. Support for CVS is automatically installed if you choose not to add an SCM
None	ClearCase	Uninstall and then reinstall a new copy of WSAD.
CVS	ClearCase	Uninstall and then reinstall WSAD.
ClearCase	CVS	Uninstall and then reinstall WSAD.

Installing CVS

Many different implementation of CVS are out there in the world, but the one this installation session works with is CVSNT 1.11.1.2 (Build 41), which is downloadable from the Web at `www.cvsnt.org`. Although it is called CVSNT, the version 1.11.1.2 of the server application seems to work as well (if not better) in Windows 2000. If you want to install CVSNT 1.11.1.2 on an NT machine, you need to have at least service pack 6 applied. The following list provides a little information about how CVSNT works:

- CVSNT runs as a service on Windows NT or 2000 and listens on port 2401 for client connections.
- CVSNT comes with a command-line client to enable you to make client connections.
- CVSNT supports all CVS functions.
- CVSNT supports NT and Kerberos authentication in both client and server modes.
- CVSNT supports pserver and ntserver protocols for authentication. However, WSAD supports only pserver and extssh protocols.

> **CAUTION:** There are known security holes with using the pserver protocol. Make sure that you and your administrator are aware of them. For example, when using pserver data, packets are not encrypted and thus, your authentication password and source code are at risk of being seen by attackers using packet-sniffing software. You can use a VPN to encrypt the data packets, but packets within the VPN firewall are still susceptible to a packet sniffer.

Installing CVSNT

The following are the basic steps to install the CVSNT server on a computer using the pserver protocol. For more comprehensive installation instructions and explanation of features, refer to the download site for details (`www.cvsnt.org`):

1. Download a copy of the CVSNT install program at `http://www.cvsnt.org`.
2. Run the install program to install CVSNT your computer. If you plan on using CVSNT for team development, install the CVSNT on a server.
3. Follow the installation prompts to install the program.
4. When prompted for a setup type, choose Typical. The other options let you turn off and on such services as Kerberos and included documentation. Figure 5-6 shows the available set-up types for installing CVSNT.

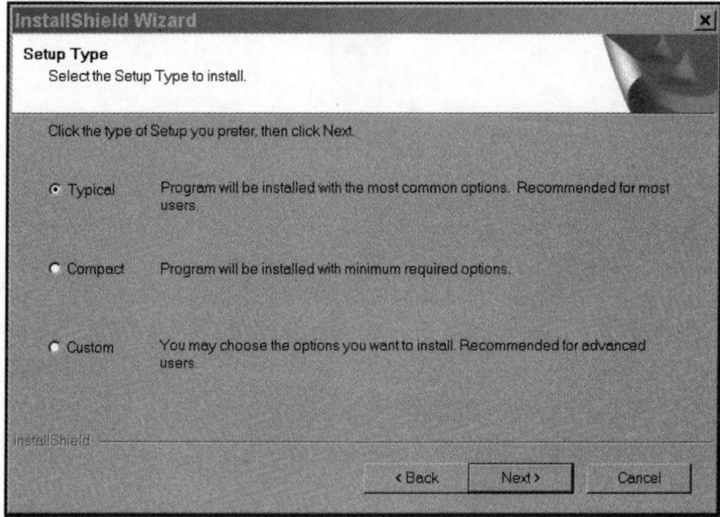

Figure 5-6: Setup type options when installing CVSNT.

5. After installation, run the Configure server application by clicking Start⇨Programs⇨CVS for NT⇨Configure server. (You can also access this from the Control Panel as CVS for NT.)

6. Click the Install button to install CVSNT as an NT Service.
7. If you get the warning, `cvsservice.exe not in path. can't Install`, you need to add the directory in which `cvsservice.exe` exists to the PATH environmental variable. The default directory is `C:\Program Files\CVS for NT`. Figure 5-7 shows the CVSNT Control Panel after installation and prior to being configured for use.

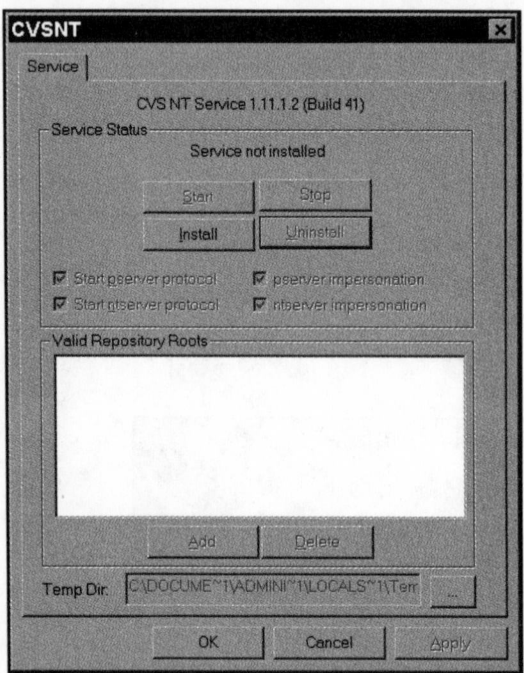

Figure 5-7: The CVSNT Control Panel enables you to install and uninstall the CVS as an NT service, and start and stop the CVS NT Service.

8. Create the directory for your repository. Create a new folder for CVS (`c:\cvs`) to act as the root folder for CVS (see Figure 5-8).

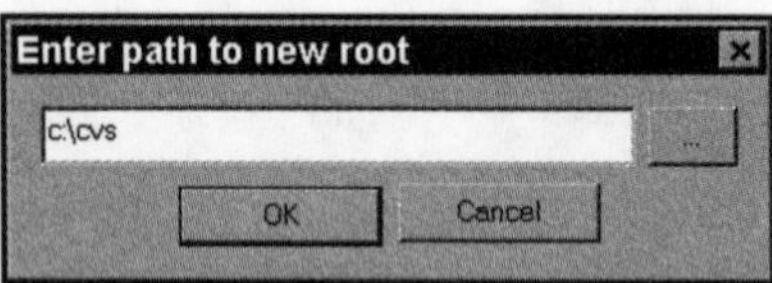

Figure 5-8: Enter the path to the new folder that will be the root of your repository.

9. Initialize your repository.
10. Click the Add button and point it to your new repository root (`c:\cvs`). Click Yes if asked whether to initialize the folder.
11. Set up the environment variables for the system users or the user who will run the CVSNT service:
    - Add a CVSROOT environment variable and set it to **local:c:\cvs.**
    - Add a HOME environment variable and set it to **c:**.
    - Make sure that a TMP or TEMP environment variable is present, and set it to **c:\winnt\temp**.
12. Restart the computer to ensure that all these changes take effect.
13. Open the Configure Service program again by clicking Start⇨CVS for NT⇨Configure server, and click the Start button if the service is not already started.

Pserver can authenticate users against the NT domain or against its own CVS passwords. CVS passwords are recommended because pserver sends passwords in an easily reversible format when authenticating against the domain. You need to decide which one to use. Nothing needs to be done to authenticate against the NT domain when initially installed. To enable CVS password authentication, follow these steps:

1. Stop the CVSNT service if running.
2. Obtain an encrypted password using the Generate Passwords program by clicking Start⇨Programs⇨CVS for NT⇨Generate passwords.
3. Create a passwd file in the CVSROOT directory (c:\cvs\cvsroot) and enter a line for each user where systemusername is the logon name to the system, encryptedpassword is the result of using the Generate passwords program, cvsusername is the CVS alias (can be the same as the systemusername), and domain is the name of the computer or network:
    - `systemusername:encryptedpassword`
    - `systemusername:!domain`
    - `cvsusername:encryptedpassword:systemusername`

NOTE: If pserver doesn't find a user the passwd file, it attempts to fall back on the system for authentication. This is not recommended, because the password is sent in clear text. To disable this fallback option, open the config file located in the `c:\cvs\cvsroot` in a text editor like WordPad, and uncomment the line containing the `SystemAuth` variable and make sure the value is set to No.

Setting up WSAD for use with CVSNT

Now that you have CVSNT installed as a service, you can take advantage of CVS support in WSAD. The following instructions teach you how to setup your CVS source control environment in WSAD:

1. Select Perspective from the WSAD menu bar.Select Open from the menu and choose Team. (If Team is not on the list, select Other to view a list of all the perspectives and then choose Team). Figure 5-9 shows the WebSphere Studio Application Developer workspace in the Team perspective.

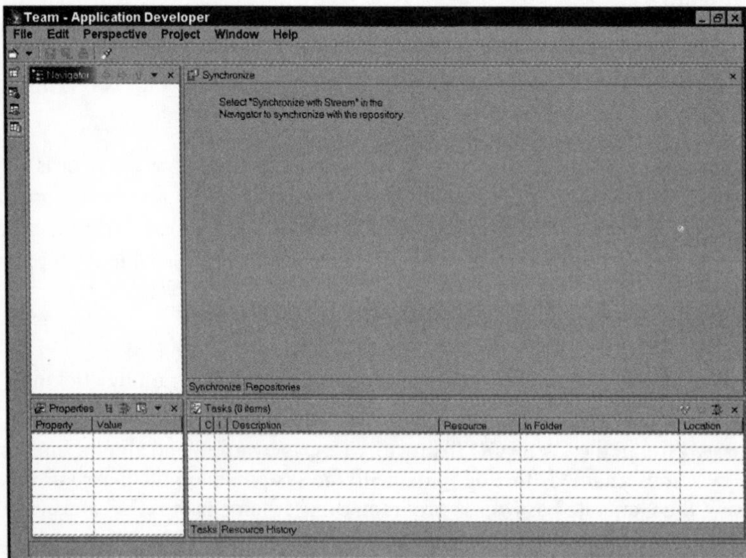

Figure 5-9: WebSphere Studio Application Developer workspace opened to the Team perspective

2. Choose File⇨New⇨Other.
3. Select CVS from the left panel and then Repository Location from the right panel. Figure 5-10 shows the window that displays when you choose the Other option after selecting to create a new object.
4. Click the Next button.
5. Enter the following information to configure the repository location. Table 5-5 shows the new repository location information.

NOTE: CVS support must be installed for you to see CVS in the list in Figure 5-10.

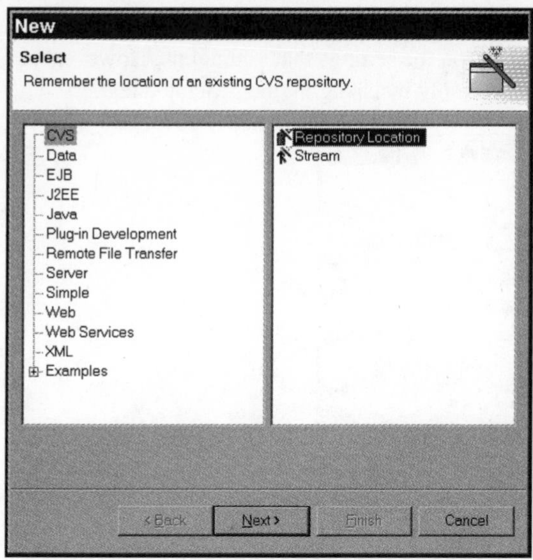

Figure 5-10: The New window with the list of CVS objects to create in focus.

Table 5-5: Settings for a New Repository Location

Field	*Setting*	*Example*
Connection type	pserver	pserver
User name	cvs user name or system user name	brainy_smurf (the user that you setup in the passwd file)
Host name	url of host to connect to	papa_smurf (or 127.0.0.1 if CVS is on the current computer)
Repository path	directory path to repository root	c:/cvs
CVS location	Generated based on the connection type, user name, host name, and repository path settings.	:pserver:brainy_smurf@papa_smurf:c:/cvs
Validate location	Make sure this is checked.	Checked

Figure 5-11 illustrates the sample settings for setting up a new CVS repository location. The CVS location is generated based on the settings that you define. However, you can manually change the CVS location simply by changing the generated text.

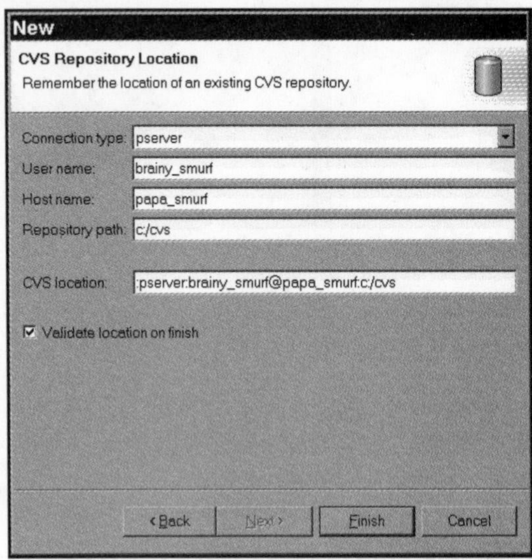

Figure 5-11: Use the New CVS Repository Location window to create a new repository connection.

6. Enter the unencrypted password and username when prompted and click OK.
7. Click Finish to create the repository. Figure 5-12 shows the new repository location added to the Repositories view.

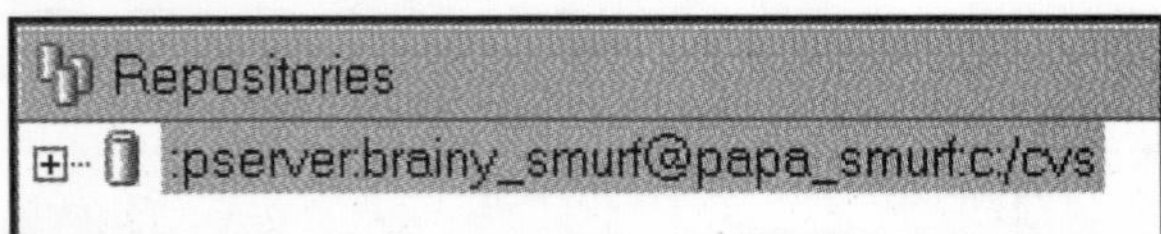

Figure 5-12: The Repositories view with the new repository location added.

Installing a Different Version of the JDK

You might not know it, but you might have a different version of a JDK already installed on your machine. If you're the type who likes to live life in the extreme, you can follow the instructions in this section to install a new JDK on your computer and then make use of it in WSAD. However, keep in mind that the JDK package that you download and install may have special installation instructions. So read the installation instructions for the JDK you choose to install before attempting the following:

1. Download a copy of a JDK package from one of the many JDK vendors (for example, Sun or IBM).
2. If the package comes with an installer, run the installer and follow the prompts. If the package comes in a compressed Zip file, unzip the contents into a temporary folder and run the install program.

CROSS-REFERENCE: Configuring WSAD to use a different JDK for development or a different JRE for runnning and testing an application is discussed in a Chapter 6.

Introducing Distributed Debugger

WebSphere Studio Application Developer's built-in debugger has replaced the IBM distributed debugger for debugging source code on remote applications. Prior to WSAD, the distributed debugger was installed in a separate step and was necessary for WebSphere Studio (not WSAD) because Studio did not have an integrated debugger. WSAD takes care of this by integrating both the local and distributed debugger into one. In later chapters, we discuss the ways you can use the WSAD debugger to debug local as well as remote application code.

Understanding Roles and Responsibilities

WSAD introduces role-based perspectives to help in the division of concerns. Division of concerns simply means that your development environment should only show you a view of an application that applies to your role as a developer. Of course, you can play many roles when developing an application. You might be required to play the role of a Web developer and Java developer when developing an application, but to work effectively, you should play one role at a time and switch between roles. WSAD enables you to do this with the Web and Java perspectives. The Web perspective's default views (as illustrated in Figure 15-13) are those that you, in the role of Web developer, would most commonly use. These include a gallery view of button art, Web animation and pictures, and a style and color view for designing Web pages. The Java perspective offers more tools and views designed for your role as a Java developer for developing of Java code.

Figure 5-13, which shows the Web perspective, is an example an interface a Web developer might be accustomed to using. Notice that all the menus and tools in the perspective are related to Web-development tasks.

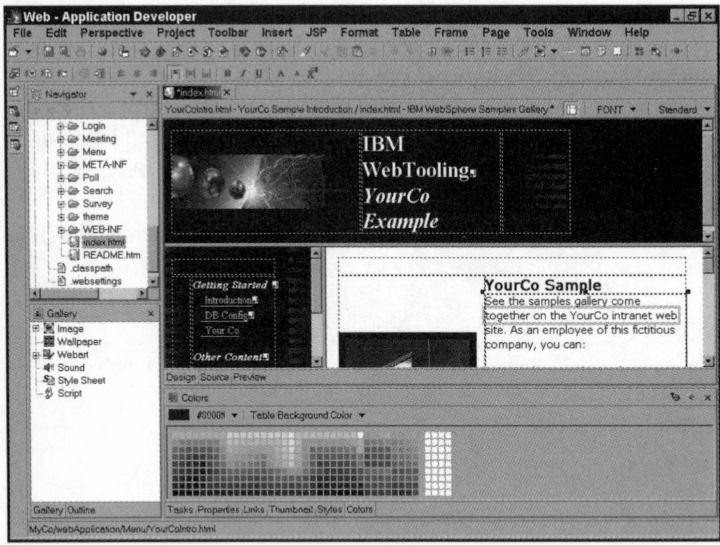

Figure 5-13: WebSphere Studio Application Developer in the Web perspective.

A Java developer probably isn't interested in the default views in the Web perspective because they don't show the Java code in the projects in terms of Java, such as packages, and classes. But a Java developer would be interested in using the Java perspective's default views, such as the package view and class hierarchy view because they do show the Java code in terms of Java packages and classes. These views help you, the Java developer, write Java code more effectively. Figure 5-14 illustrates what is a user sees while in the Java perspective in WSAD. The various options available are all geared towards Java code development.

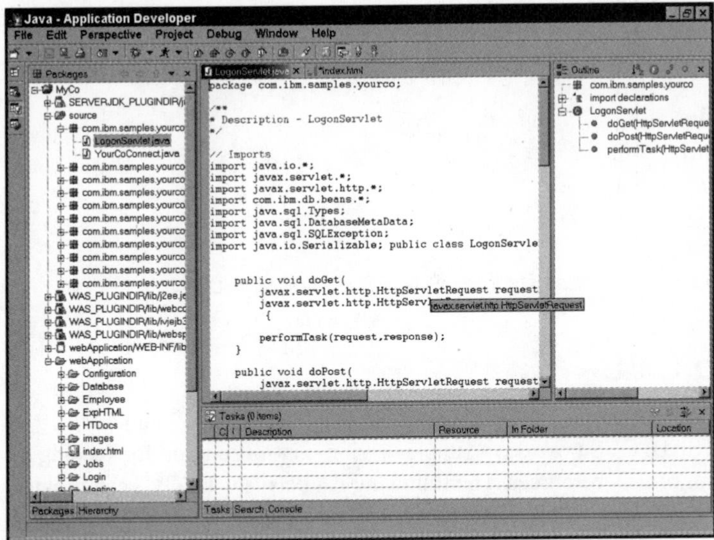

Figure 5-14: This WebSphere Studio Application Developer workbench opened to the Java perspective.

In short, a perspective in WSAD is a combination of views, tools, and workspace settings that are considered relevant and necessary for a certain type of user. Additionally, all of the perspectives are customizable. You could use views and tools interchangeably between perspectives by explicitly invoking the view or tool. The Java perspective in Figure 5.14 enables you not only to view your Java resources, but the Web resources as well. The HTML editor in the Web perspective is also available in the Java perspective.

CROSS-REFERENCE: Refer to Chapter 7 for a more comprehensive coverage of perspectives, views, and the tools available to you in WSAD.

WSAD currently supports the perspectives shown in Figure 5-15. The perspective marked (default) is determined during the installation, but can be changed at any time.

Figure 5-15 lists all the available and customizable perspectives that you can find in WebSphere Studio Application Developer. To view this list and change your default perspective, choose Window⇨Preferences⇨Workbench, and select Perspectives. Highlight one of the views and click the Make Default button.

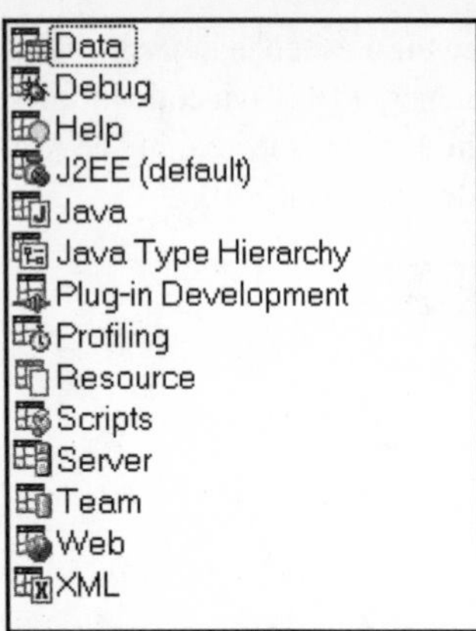

Figure 5-15: A list of the available perspectives found in WebSphere Studio Application Developer.

Understanding CVS

Concurrent Versions System (CVS) is a version-control system and is one of the SCMs systems supported by WSAD. CVS provides a simple version-control solution for keeping a history of changes to your project resources. The following list details what CVS can provide you as an SCM. (If you're looking for more comprehensive coverage of CVS, visit `www.cvshome.org`:)

- CVS provides a shared repository where you and others can share and work concurrently on each other's code. In WSAD, you can retrieve from and release resources into a CVS repository shared with other developers through constructs that you define called streams. CVS always provides a head stream (also called the main trunk) that all developers can use to share changes to resources in the repository with one another.
- In some situations you wouldn't want to share your changes with other developers, but you would still like to be able to keep versions of these changes in the repository. An example of this is if you have a work in progress that you would like to keep in the repository, but you don't want other developers to have access to until you are finished. CVS enables you to create a stream separate from the head stream where you can release and store the work in progress without affecting the contents of the head stream.
- CVS enables multiple developers to work on a common file by providing a local copy to each user. This feature is different from other SCMs that lock out other users from working on a common file. Changes to the local copies can be merged at check-in. At that time, the developer checking in the file is responsible for making sure that the changes he or she made do not overwrite someone else's changes.
- CVS keeps a log of all the changes to a file, so that you can easily roll back to an earlier version of the same file.
- CVS includes compare utilities, so you can see the changes between an original and modified file.

- CVS works by saving only the changes to your code in a separate file. The changes that CVS detects and saves are purely textual and not logical. This means that CVS cannot detect logical relations between one file and another. One file is treated independently of any other.

Following is a list of services that CVS does not provide.

- CVS is not a change-management system. It is does not store reported bugs and their resolution status.
- CVS is not a build system.

Planning Testing Environments

Although the 4.0.x release of WSAD supports using only WebSphere Application Server 4.0 Single Server Edition for local and remote testing, and Apache Tomcat 3.2 and 4.0 for local testing, the plug-in support nature of the Eclipse platform makes it possible to add additional test environments into WSAD. But of course, you can always just export your resources and run the application without involving WSAD.

> **NOTE:** WSAD does not currently support remote testing for Tomcat.

If you plan on testing your applications on either Tomcat 3.2 or 4.0, you need to download and install the server separately, because only the support is installed and not the actual implementation. Installing Tomcat 3.2 is beyond the scope of this book, so refer to the installation documentation that comes with Tomcat for instructions on how to install the server

One thing to keep in mind when planning for testing on a remote version of WebSphere Application Server is that the default test environment is WebSphere Application Server 4.0 Single Edition. It does not automatically register an application with another version of WebSphere Application Server as the Enterprise edition does, mainly because WebSphere Application Server 4.0 Enterprise edition uses a database repository to store its configuration information, whereas, the single server edition uses XML deployment descriptor files. To solve this problem, WSAD can package your enterprise application into an EAR file that you can use to deploy to the Enterprise edition.

Finally, to test your application on a remote instance of the WebSphere Application Server, you must also have the IBM Agent Controller installed on the same computer. The installation files for the IBM Agent Controller are located in the `RAC_Install` folder of the WSAD install CD or from the image files.

> **CROSS-REFERENCE:** Test environments are discussed in more detail in Chapter 8.

Summary

This chapter discussed the issues and concerns involved in setting up a development environment, which included setting up WebSphere Studio Application Developer, WebSphere Studio Site Developer, CVS, ClearCase, JDKs, Distributed Debugger, and WebSphere and Tomcat test environments. The chapter exposed some of the pitfalls, problems, and possible resolutions that can arise before and during installing the development environment. It also introduced you to some of the advantages that WebSphere Studio Application Developer can offer, such as the capability to switch JDK versions and test against multiple test environments.

This chapter also covered the possible version-control systems that are available to you prior to installing, so that you can choose the one that best fits your long-term needs. Follow-up sections illustrated, in detailed steps, how to install and configure CVSNT to work within WSAD.

The chapter also examined the many installation options available to you when installing WSAD and ran though the step-by-step process of implementing the installation. Congratulations, you have a newly created WSAD development environment, ready to rock.

Part II

Application Development

Chapter 6
Web Application Analysis and Design

Chapter 7
Working with WSAD and WSSD

Chapter 8
Testing with WSAD

Chapter 9
Java Servlet Development

Chapter 10
More Servlet APIs

Chapter 11
Understanding Session Management

Chapter 12
Developing JavaServer Pages

(Continues)

Chapter 13
Introducing Enterprise JavaBeans

Chapter 14
Developing Enterprise Java Beans with WSAD

Chapter 15
Additional CMP and Transaction Processing

Chapter 16
Deployment Descriptors and EJB Security Overview

Chapter 17
EJB Best Practices

Chapter 18
Using XML/XSLT in WebSphere

Chapter 19
Developing Web Services

Chapter 6
Web Application Analysis and Design

In This Chapter

- Understanding how the Web development process works
- Understanding how various development models impact the development process
- Understanding how deployment and topology affect an application

The cost of developing a software application is said to account for only 20 percent of the total cost. The other 80 percent of the cost lies with the maintenance and enhancements you need to perform on the application. With this in mind, proper analysis and design can cut costs significantly by creating an application that is flexible enough to update or add to easily, but written in such a way as to be easily understood.

It's like any project you might undertake: The more time you spend analyzing the problem and brainstorming the different options available to you as solutions, the better the end result is. The key is to find the balance between too much analysis and too little. Both can negatively affect your software application process. With the number of solutions available today for software development, it's not as hard as you might think to get caught in the analysis and design infinite loop. At some point, you must draw a line in the sand and begin to implement your solution. This usually is only a problem for large-scale, complex systems. More often, too little forethought is given to the design of an application, and this leads to applications that do not scale well and are hard to change.

Several design approaches and models have been developed that you can leverage to help you design flexible Web-based applications. Each has its advantages and disadvantages. There is no one right answer for all situations. This is why it is imperative that you take the time at the beginning of the development process to research the best solution for your specific need.

Understanding the Web-Development Process

The World Wide Web (WWW) has grown from a small network for sharing documents into a network of networks connecting millions of computers and computer users. Its evolution was not only eruptive in nature, but the time span of the transformation was extremely disproportionate to its bounds.

The World Wide Web, once used merely for exchanging documents, is now used to run business and financial operations. It is both a huge repository of information and a marketplace for commercial and financial transactions. With this shift, the demands of software designers, the tools they use, and the way in which they interact with other team members have been forced to change in order to adapt to the changing times. With the push to a distributed environment, today's Web applications must be designed to interact with external systems seamlessly.

Understanding roles and responsibilities

Today's Web applications have forced the simple data-entry screens, with little or no user interaction, to become much more interactive and visually esthetic to the end user. This shift puts a high demand on servers. The role of the Web server has gone from serving static content, to running Web applications, to serving live (dynamic) content — evolving from a basic static publishing model into an interactive application model.

Having distributed systems that can divide the responsibilities among the different application components is a powerful tool, but this also adds more importance to the interaction among the components. The basic components of an application are the client component used for the user interface, the server component used for the business logic, and the database or backend component used to store the application data. The overall responsibilities of applications have not changed much; however, with this new paradigm, figuring out where the responsibility should lie within the application has become the challenge. Because the number of possible configurations for distributing responsibility is so large, the need for proper analysis and design is imperative.

Introducing the IBM e-business application framework

To help accommodate the complexity of these new requirements, IBM introduced an application framework for e-business. It outlines the different application components and the roles and responsibilities for each. This framework is a comprehensive, scalable platform that supports all the services you need to develop and support an e-business solution. It is a server-centric solution that pushes many of the responsibilities onto the server component. Leveraging this framework during your development process benefits you in the following ways:

- *Leverage and extend existing assets:* A server side-solution enables you to utilize any legacy or core applications that are currently in production.
- *Maximize ease and speed of development and deployment:* By utilizing a Java-based model, your applications can be developed quickly by people, ranging from nontechnical graphic designers to programmers with a wide range of skills.
- *Support any client device*: The server-side solution enables the application to return different data for multiple client devices. This capability is important for coping with the growing popularity of many hand-held devices and cell phones.

- *Ensure portability across server environments:* Using the Java platform, you can deploy your application to systems that best meet your needs.

Web applications are applications that utilize Web clients (such as Web browsers), Web application servers, and standard Internet protocols. They usually access data from non–Web-based legacy systems for some types of service. Figure 6.1 illustrates the major elements of a Web-application topology supported by the IBM application framework for e-business. The Web-application server and external services are logical tiers capable of running on the same physical machine. Functionality of the Web application server can be spread across multiple physical machines. Typically, you split your front-end and business-logic parts between separate server machines.

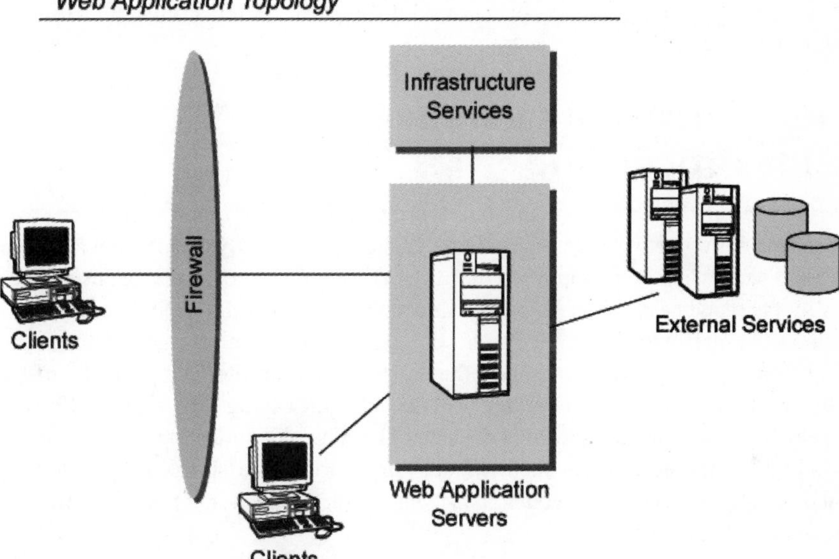

Figure 6-1: The Web application topology supported by IBM's e-business application framework.

The components of this model are as follows:

- *Web application servers*: The Web application server is the brains of the whole operation. Generally, for any sizable application, the Web application server is split (logically and/or physically) into a Web server, which handles the more static content, and the Application server, which handles the business functionality and dynamic content. The Web server is a type of pass-through server, handling the static requests, and passing along all the requests for dynamic content to the Application server for processing. The Application server performs the computations needed to generate a response to the user and sends the response back to the Web server — which, in turn, sends it back to the user.

- *External services*: These services are most often existing applications that handle some of the the core business processing. They can be legacy systems, databases, or other applications.
- *Clients*: Clients can be users connected via the Internet or an intranet, utilizing Internet standards to communicate with the Web application servers. Their basic function is to accept and validate user input and display the results received from the server.
- *Infrastructure Services*: These are services that the Web application server utilizes for functions such as load balancing, caching, security, and so on.

This framework describes the best way to configure your components and helps you determine which component handles which types of services (where the responsibilities lie). One of the key principles of the application framework is that the business logic of a Web application runs on the server and not on the client. This allows for a much more powerful and flexible solution then a client-side solution.

Client-Side Processing versus Server-Side Processing

In the early 1990s, *client/server* was a major buzzword in the software industry. The idea was to distribute responsibility between the server and the client. Many early distribution attempts constructed fat clients, which were supposed to move the solution closer to the end user. The term *fat client* was coined because this approach downloads and runs all the application software on the client machine. These fat clients soon reached their limitations. Writing Java applets to download onto client machines gave the user a quick user interface with a lot of bells and whistles; however, the user interface was the only quick thing Java applets offered. The demands of complex applications drove the size of the download files to increase, forcing long download times. Applets ran into bandwidth or transaction-processing problems. The enhanced GUIs created expectations about enhanced end-user productivity, but fell short of the expected outcomes.

Another challenge of client-side solutions was maintenance. If your application needed to alter the GUI, which was almost inevitable, the applet code had to be recoded by someone with programming skills. With a server-side solution, it's possible to utilize the client for displaying the results of your server processes. With this approach, you can have a nonprogrammer HTML resource change the look and feel of the HTML, and the underlying server process can remain unchanged. The data going to the browser stays the same, it's just rendered with a different HTML look.

A common pitfall that companies encountered was modeling their new client/server system to “front-end” an existing legacy system. This approach allowed for minimal system enhancements. The GUIs could be enhanced; however, the systems were still limited by the constraints of the back-end legacy application. It is kind of like putting earrings on a pig. She may look better, but she's still a pig. A server-centric solution solves many, if not all, of the fat-client problems by providing the following benefits:

- A broader range of client devices can be supported because the dependency on client capabilities is reduced.
- The Web application server integrates access to resources, such as databases; this improves scalability and provides greater security.
- Business logic running on the server is easier to protect, upgrade, and maintain.
- Application environments can be centrally managed.

The advantages of server-side processing over client-side processing give the client very little responsibility. The client can accept user input and display results. The server handles all the processing needed to create the dynamic interaction and updates.

Understanding Remote Presentation

Remote presentation keeps all the application logic on the server and uses the client to display the results (generally HTML) the server returns. The server also contains the view-controller logic (navigation). The client interacts with server applications through a browser that uses HTTP as a communication vehicle.

This approach is often referred to as a *thin client*, as opposed to a fat client that runs everything on the client machine. Following are the primary benefits of implementing a thin-client solution:

- All critical application processing and data remain protected behind a corporate firewall.
- Your code base is in one central location, so updates and maintenance are much easier to manage.
- The server-side controller provides dynamic content to the client.
- The legacy systems are protected behind the firewall and usually require little or no change.
- The client hardware/software investment is minimal, and distribution becomes much simpler.

As with any solution, this one also has some drawbacks. People run a variety of browser versions and configurations, which can cause irregular responses among the different browsers. It is almost impossible to test all browser variations; therefore, many companies limit testing to the more popular browsers and fairly recent versions of them. You can minimize testing if your application is written as an in-house solution because you might be able to control browser variables; but keep in mind that future visions always need to be considered.

Another limitation is that of HTML itself. With the applet solution, the programmer has a variety of tool sets to use to enhance the GUI with lots of bells and whistles, which end users like to see. HTML controls are less interactive and impose a more primitive data-entry screen on users. The gap between HTML screens and applet screens is closing due to newer and better language techniques such as DHTML and JavaScript.

Because the application is running mainly on the server side, it utilizes servlets. A *servlet* is a standard server-side Java program that extends the functionality of a Web server. The server handles requests for servlets from the client browser. The Web server loads the servlet (if it is not already loaded) and sends the request it receives to the servlet for it to process. After the servlet completes its task, it sends any generated output to the browser for display to the client.

One power of servlets is that they are written in a full-fledged programming language (Java), which enables them to interface with existing JavaBeans or Enterprise JavaBeans (EJBs) that can then access a database or any other transaction-based program for any needed services. Servlets are the controllers for Web-based applications. They stand and mediate the interactions between the HTML forms (client) and the application business objects.

Servlets perform better than Common Gateway Interface (CGI) programs do. After a Web server loads a servlet, the servlet stays in memory waiting for more requests. When a new request comes in, a new Java thread starts, and the servlet code runs in that thread. Java threads are lightweight, and their creation has much less overhead than standard CGI, which loads a new operating process for each new request. Servlets also have a `Session` object that can be used to track data across multiple requests for a given user. The `Session` object is also a way to pass data that is used by more than one servlet, which cuts down the overhead of having to recreate that data each time.

Because servlets run within the Web server context, they can use the authentication and authorization features of the Web server. Consequently, servlets give you better ways to implement security in your system than you get with a CGI program.

Understanding Distributed Logic Objects

Distributed logic objects provide a flexible solution for developing systems. They are used to split the application processing across the client and the server. Although this solution is flexible, the development team must develop and maintain code built on two different platforms. This section discusses two types of distributed-logic solutions: remote procedure calls (RPC) and messaging.

Implementing RPCs

RPC communications look like subroutines or function calls to the application's programmer. The call return is usually synchronous, and the calling program is blocked until the procedure returns, hiding communication from the application unless there is some type of network failure. This solution offers a simple programming solution to the programmer, but requires a complex administrative solution supporting the runtime environment. RPCs are implemented in several ways:

- Remote method invocation (RMI)
- Common object request broker architecture (CORBA)
- Enterprise JavaBeans (EJBs)

RMI enables Java objects to send messages over the network to remote objects. RMI includes a naming registry, which tracks instances, associates them to an object name, and enables client objects to locate remote objects. The remote objects use the RMI activation service to activate a server object. RMI also uses a remote reference manager to support the runtime transport of objects. Proxies, or references, are what objects use to communicate with other objects on a remote machine. RMI can communicate over the Internet Inter-ORB Protocol (IIOP), thus enabling RMI clients to work with CORBA objects. These CORBA objects may or may not be written in Java. When programming an RMI application, you include the following steps during your development cycle:

1. Create a type that extends the `java.rmi.Remote` interface. This interface defines the remote methods that can be invoked by the client object.
2. Define a server class that implements the newly defined subtype that extends the `java.rmi.Remote` interface.
3. Run the RMI compiler (rmic) to take the subtype of the remote interface and generate client stub and server skeleton classes and object instances.

The CORBA architecture is a popular solution that uses RPC for communications among the client and server objects. CORBA's core architecture and Java RMI share many of the same features. A descriptor of a remote object is used to generate client stub and server skeleton interfaces. A client object uses the client stub to invoke methods on a remote object. The method request is then transmitted through the underlying CORBA communications infrastructure to the server skeleton. The server skeleton then invokes the method on the remote object. Any method return values or exceptions are transmitted back to the client through the CORBA infrastructure.

CORBA contains general distributed object frameworks. The services available include events, naming, transactions, concurrency, relationships, property, trader, collections, and start-up. CORBA components include the following:

- Common facilities, such as printing, document management, database, and e-mail
- Object services for managing the lifecycle of objects
- Domain interfaces, which are services that support the application domains
- Object request broker (ORB), which accepts requests, coordinates communications, and makes them transparent to the application programmer
- Application objects, which perform specific user-defined tasks
- Interface repository for providing dynamic client access to interface definitions to construct a request, dynamic type checking of request signatures, traversal of inheritance graphs, and ORB-to-ORB interoperability

When you are programming an application using CORBA (the process is similar to RMI process.), you include the following steps during your development cycle:

- Specify the remote object by using an interface definition language (IDL) to specify the remote object name, state, and behavior.
- Compile the remote object description into Java by using an IDL to the Java compiler. The compiler generates a Java interface, a Java client stub, and a Java server skeleton.

Another popular RPC solution is the Enterprise JavaBeans framework. The EJB framework separates high-level business logic from low-level infrastructure services. The EJB model contains an RMI object that runs in the EJB container. The EJB container and server provide services for transaction management, security, name services, distribution services, resource pooling, lifecycle management, and object persistence. EJBs have proven to be such a powerful solution, that they are part of the J2EE API.

Regardless of the implementation of the EJB and its container, any client of that EJB has the same view of it, which allows the client application to be portable across all container implementations. An EJB container is where EJBs live. Multiple EJB classes can be contained within a single EJB container. The developer creates a home interface that enables the client to create, look up, and remove EJB objects. An EJB server can host one or multiple EJB containers. The client need not know which container is being used. There is no client API to manipulate the container, and the client can't tell in which container an EJB is found. A client locates an EJB interface by using the J2EE naming service, Java Naming and Directory Interface (JNDI). To fully describe an EJB object to an EJB container, you must implement three classes:

- Home interface, used to specify how to find or to create an EJB
- Remote interface, used to specify the business logic
- Enterprise Bean implementation, used to implement the home and remote interfaces

There are two types of EJBs:

- Session beans, used to manage a session
- Entity beans, used to persist an object

The EJB architecture offers the best of RMI and CORBA. EJBs have rapidly grown in popularity and will most likely become the standard for distributing objects. Using EJBs offers you several benefits:

- EJBs enable developers either to write to a high-level abstract API or dig deep and write to a set of low-level APIs that deal with state management, multithreading, transaction processing, and resource pooling.
- EJBs are portable and can be developed once and deployed on multiple platforms without source-code modification or recompilation. They are simply rebound to the new target system.

- The EJB architecture is open and interoperable with non-Java applications.
- Because EJBs have become so popular, many vendors have produced a wide range of tools to select from when developing and deploying application components.
- EJBs are CORBA compatible.

CROSS-REFERENCE: EJBs and their implementation are discussed in greater detail in Chapters 13-17.

Implementing messaging

A second type of distributed logic solution is *messaging*. The Java message service (JMS) is a J2EE API for working with networked messaging services, such as IBM MQ Series. You use JMS for writing message-oriented middleware solutions. JMS is like a wrapper for vendor-specific messaging middleware, which provides an abstract interface for messaging. JMS supports two models:

- *Point-to-point, which utilizes message queues:* The client creates a message and addresses it to a recipient. The message is put into a message queue. The recipient then pulls the message out of its queue for processing. The point-to-point model is analogous with e-mail.
- *Publish/subscribe, which uses hierarchical content topic trees*: The client publishes messages to a specific node of the topic tree. Clients can get messages from the specific nodes on the trees to which they subscribe. The publish/subscribe model is analogous to Internet newsgroups.

JMS supports transactions, asynchronous processing, and multithreaded processes. Message-oriented middleware quite often works well with other types of Web-based client/server solutions.

Reviewing Transaction-Processing Models

With the move to more distributed and modularized coding practices, the concept of transactions becomes more important. At a high level, a *transaction* is a sequence of processing steps, called a unit of work, that is treated as a unified whole to satisfy a request. The standard definition of a transaction uses the acronym ACID to characterize a unit of work:

- *Atomic:* If this unit of work encounters any type of failure, all changes that were a part of it get undone. This is known as rolling back a transaction.
- *Consistent:* The effects of a transaction preserve the integrity of modified resources.
- *Isolated:* What goes on within the scope of one transaction should not affect any objects involved in other transactions or even be visible until the transaction completes.
- *Durable:* A completed transaction is permanent, and the changes are never lost.

Each transaction should preserve the ACID properties for the system to reflect the correct state. Unlike a centralized computing environment in which application components and resources are located at a single site and transaction management involves only a local data manager running on a single machine, in a distributed computing environment, all the resources are distributed across multiple systems. In such a case, transaction management needs to be done both at local and global levels. A local transaction is one that involves activities in a single local resource manager. A distributed or a global transaction is executed across multiple systems, and its execution requires coordination between the global transaction management system and all the local data managers of all the involved systems. The resource manager and Transaction Manager (TM), also known as a transaction processing monitor (TP monitor), are the two primary elements of any transactional system. In centralized systems, both the TP monitor and the resource manager are integrated into the DBMS server. Separation of the TP monitor from the resource managers is required to support advanced functionalities required by a distributed, component-based system.

Understanding Remote/Distributed Data-Management Solutions

Remote data-management solutions offer methods for accessing remote databases located on different servers. Java Database Connectivity (JDBC) provides a common API to vendor-specific relational databases. Net JDBC drivers support access databases over the network. The JDBC API provides support for the following actions:

- Obtaining a database connection
- Obtaining metadata about the database and its tables from the database server
- Sending SQL query and update statements to a database server
- Storing Java objects in relational databases
- Retrieving and iterating through query results returned by the server
- Managing database connection pools and obtaining pool information
- Treating database query results as JavaBeans
- Batching updates

Applications can use an intermediate DriverManager to access a JDBC driver or access a JDBC driver directly. Most relational-database systems ship with a DriverManager for accessing relational data. The steps required to access and manipulate data are as follows:

1. Load the database driver.
2. Get a reference to the DriverManager and ask for a database connection.
3. Create, prepare, and process(execute) statements.

Distributed data management is used for a fat-client solution. It provides data management for both the client and the server platforms. The difference between this and the remote data management is that the client is not connected to the network. This solution is made possible with some type of synchronization or replication process to keep the remote database and the server database updated. This solution is one that you can use for a client that needs powerful database access, but may be remote and not have connection to the server-based database. With this solution, the user can run a local copy of the database and then periodically connect to the network to replicate the server database to synchronize with the server database any changes (update, deletes, and so on) that the user has made. Any replication conflicts have to be resolved manually by an administrator of type.

Reviewing Useful Web-Development Approaches

In development, it is important to leverage as many diverse experiences with software development as possible. Find out what others have tried and how successful they were. Many times, other developers have struggled through tough times to figure out best practices for development. You, too, could learn the hard way, but with the amount of documentation about development processes available today, it seems like an unnecessary waste of time (and gray hair). Several approaches to Web development, quite common in today's workplace, are worth mentioning. These include implementing the popular Model View Controller pattern or layering your application code. Some tools and techniques, such as refactoring your code for efficiency or using JUnit to help facilitate proper unit testing, are also available to help you create robust code. Any number of these approaches can help your development process flow and ultimately produce a quality product.

Understanding the Model View Controller (MVC) pattern

One of the most commonly used patterns for Web-application development is the Model View Controller (MVC) design pattern. This pattern provides a clean separation between the business-logic implementation (model) and the presentation (view). The third piece of the pattern, the controller, facilitates the interaction between the models and the views. The specific tasks for each component are as follows:

- *Model:* Encapsulates the application state, responds to state queries, exposes application functionality, and notifies views of changes.
- *View:* Renders the models, requests updates from the models, sends user input to controller, and allows the controller to select the view. It is the view's job to keep consistent with any changes to the model. This is done with a *push* type model where the view registers with the model for any change notifications, or a *pull* type model where the view is responsible for calling the model to get the latest data.
- *Controller:* Defines the application behavior; it defines one behavior for each action, maps user actions to model updates, and selects a view for response.

Typically, you implement the Web-based MVC pattern by using JavaServer Pages (JSPs) for the View layer, JavaBeans or EJBs for the models, and servlets for the Controller layer. This pattern allows for independent development. Each layer performs a specific task and is isolated from the "hows" of the other layers. In theory, the business objects don't have any idea how their data is displayed. They only care about the data itself and the business rules behind it. The View components only care about how the data is displayed to the user. They are unaware of the way the data is created or retrieved. It is the Controller layer that controls the way the models and the views interact. Figuring out which view to show next (navigation) is a common task for a controller. The page (view) knows which data beans (models) it needs to pull data out of, and the data beans know how to populate themselves with the data. This pattern promotes easy maintainability and code reuse. If the display (HTML) needs to be reworked, you can update the JSPs with no change to the business objects. Also, because the business objects are isolated, it is possible for other systems to share objects that perform common routines.

The flow of a MVC application starts with a browser request for a specific servlet. The servlet figures out which resources (JavaBeans, EJBs, or other objects) are needed to perform the requested task, instantiates them (if needed), tells them to run their business logic, and finally selects which view to return to the browser.

Layering applications

Application layering involves breaking up the functionality of an application into separate layers that are stacked vertically. Each layer interacts only with the layer directly underneath it. For example, in a three-tier architecture, layer 1 talks only with layer 2, and layer 2 talks only with layer 3. This type of isolation minimizes any side effects of making changes to a specific layer. If you make a change to layer 1, layer 3 never even knows about it. In fact, you could totally replace layer 1, and as long as the contract or API remains the same with layer 2, layer 3 would never know layer 1 was replaced. This property is known as *strict layering*.

Some feel that strict layering sacrifices performance and sometimes extensibility because it requires more activity to propagate down through the layers. Extensibility could potentially be sacrificed if the contracts between layers are not well thought out with regard to future requirements. As with any design approach, there is give and take. The capabilities to distribute application layers, use the domain layer across applications, and easily configure various data sources and user interfaces seem to outweigh the drawbacks of strict layering.

Nonstrict layering allows a higher-level layer to access any layer defined below it. This fixes some of the strict layering shortcomings; however, it also nullifies many of the benefits.

The traditional two-tier client/server-based applications were partitioned into a Presentation layer, and a Data-Access layer. The client application simply queried a database, performed any necessary computing, and then displayed the results to the user. Today's object technology tries to enforce not only abstracting the Presentation layer, but the business logic and data as well. Today's need for scalability and rapid development and deployment, along with the need to react to business changes, make application layering almost imperative. Most commonly, layers of an application are portioned into Presentation, Domain, and Data-Source sections. It is important that the contracts, or messaging, between each layer be well defined and formalized. Each layer should be designed without regard to the other layers' implementations, thus supporting easy layer substituting. It is quite common for projects to divide their teams into "layer teams," such as the presentation team or the database team, where each team works on a specific function (layer) of the application.

With this separation, you need to define and document, not only the contracts between each layer, but also the *services* that are common to all layers. Examples of these services are exceptions handling, logging, and startup/shutdown operations. Merely defining the application layers is not enough. The interaction of these layers must be well defined and applied consistently.

The decoupling of presentation, domain, and data source logic is accomplished with three layers; but by adding two more layers, you can help facilitate a higher enterprise reusability. To help remove all the domain-specific logic from the Presentation layer, a Controller/Mediator layer should be added between the Presentation layer and the Domain layer, which encapsulates more of the GUI interactions. Also, adding a Data Mapping layer (also referred to as a Broker layer) between the Domain layer and the Data-Source layer further hides the implementations of the data source from the domain objects.

Defining and standardizing services

To facilitate reuse and minimize side effects when requirements change, it is important to define and standardize the implementation of application *services* that are common among multiple applications. Some of these application services include error handling, status tracking, application startup and shutdown, access to externalized properties, and application of interface preferences. Because these services are used across applications, a robust design is critical. The design needs to be flexible enough to allow for multiple implementations of the different services. Error handling might utilize log files in one system, whereas another system might want to log the errors and/or also show them to the user at the screen level.

The long and short of services is that they need to be well thought out and flexibly designed. Many projects don't pay enough attention to these common services and then slam in something that "works for now." We all know where those come back to bite you. You must put in place a design that enables developers to consistently apply error handling across all applications but supports the ability to install and change these behaviors on an application basis.

Facilitating communication with design patterns

The goal of patterns within the software community is to create a body of literature to help software developers resolve recurring problems encountered throughout the software-development process. Patterns help create a shared language for communicating insight and experience about these problems and their solutions. Formally codifying these solutions and their relationships lets you successfully capture the body of knowledge that defines your understanding of good architectures that meet the needs of your users. Forming a common pattern language for conveying the structures and mechanisms of your architectures enables you to reason intelligently about them. The primary focus is not so much on technology as it is on creating a culture to document and support sound engineering architecture and design.

The following list summarizes the nature of software design patterns:

- A literary form for documenting best practices
- Recurring solutions to common design problems
- An effective means of (re)using, sharing, and building on existing wisdom/experience/expertise
- Practical/concrete solutions to real-world problems
- Context-specific solutions
- Best-fits for the given set of concerns/trade-offs
- Old hat to seasoned professionals and domain experts
- A shared vocabulary for problem-solving discussions

Some of the more popular design patterns are the Factory, the Façade, the Mediator, and the Singleton. Many publications go into great detail about these and other design patterns. *Design Patterns* by Gamma, Helm, Johnson, and Vlissides (published by Addison-Wesley) is an essential book for every developer's library.

Refactoring

Many software programs begin in a well-designed state; then as new bits of functionality are tacked on, usually right before deployment, they gradually lose that well-designed structure, eventually deforming into a mass spider web. Part of this is scale: You write a small program that does a specific job well; then when you are asked to enhance the program, the program becomes more complex.

One of the reasons for this increasing complexity is that when you add a new feature to a program, you are building on top of the existing program — often in a way that the existing program was not intended to accommodate. In such a situation, you can either redesign the existing program to better support your changes, or you can work around the changes in your additions. Although, in theory, it is better to redesign your program, this usually results in extra work because any rewriting of your existing program introduces new bugs and problems. Remember the old engineering adage: If it ain't broke, don't fix it. However, if you don't redesign your program, the additions will be more complex than they should be. Gradually, this extra complexity exacts a stiff penalty. Thus, you have a trade-off: Redesigning causes short-term pain for longer-term gain. Adding newly defined requirements on top of your existing application provides the short-term gain of meeting deadlines; however this choice suffers the long-term pain of a complex system that is costly to maintain. Schedule pressure being what it is (and managers being who they are), most people prefer to put their pain off until the future.

Refactoring is a term used to describe techniques that reduce the short-term pain of redesigning. When you are refactoring, you are not changing the functionality of your program. You are changing its internal structure to make it easier to work with and understand. Refactoring changes are usually small steps: renaming a method, moving a field from one class to another, or consolidating two similar methods into a super class. Each step is tiny; yet a couple of hours of implementing these small steps can do a lot of good to a program. Refactoring can be made easier by following some basic principles:

- *Do not refactor and add functionality at the same time.* Put a clear separation between the two when you are working.
- *Make sure that you have good tests before you begin refactoring.* Run the tests as often as possible to see whether your changes have broken anything.
- *Take short deliberate steps.* Refactoring often involves making many localized changes that result in a larger scale change. If you keep your steps small and test after each step, you avoid prolonged debugging.
- *Run a regression test.* This can verify that the refactoring didn't break anything.

Unit testing with JUnit

To reduce the time needed to turn around code from user acceptance testing back to the developers unit tests, it is important to make sure you perform a sufficient amount of unit testing before turning your code over for integration.

JUnit is a regression-testing framework written by Erich Gamma and Kent Beck. It's used by developers who implement unit tests in Java. JUnit is open-source software, released under the IBM public license.

Compared to the conventional unit testing that developers perform, JUnit actually helps you write code faster while increasing code quality. When you start using JUnit, you'll begin to notice a powerful relationship between coding and testing, ultimately leading to a development style that involves writing new code only when a test fails.

Here are just a few reasons to use JUnit:

- *JUnit tests enables you to write code faster while increasing quality:* When you write tests using JUnit, you spend less time debugging and have confidence that changes to your code actually work. This confidence enables you to be more aggressive about refactoring code and adding new features. With a comprehensive test suite, you can quickly run the tests after changing the code, confident that your changes didn't break anything. If you detect a bug while running tests, the source code is fresh in your mind, so you can find the bug easily. Tests written in JUnit help you write code at an extreme pace and spot defects quickly.

- *JUnit is elegantly simple:* Writing tests should be simple — that's the point. With JUnit, you can quickly write tests that exercise your code and incrementally add tests as the software grows. After you write some tests, you want to run them quickly and frequently without disrupting the creative design-and-development process. With JUnit, running tests is as easy and fast as running a compiler on your code. In fact, you should run your tests every time you run the compiler. The compiler tests the syntax of the code, and the tests validate the integrity of the code.
- *JUnit tests check their own results and provide immediate feedback:* Testing is no fun if you have to compare the expected and actual result of tests manually, which slows you down. JUnit tests can be run automatically, and they check their own results. When you run tests, you get simple and immediate visual feedback about whether the tests were passed or failed. You do not need to comb manually through a test-results report.
- *JUnit tests can be composed into a hierarchy of test suites:* JUnit tests can be organized into test suites containing test cases and even other test suites. The composite behavior of JUnit tests enables you to assemble collections of tests and automatically regression test the entire test suite in one fell swoop. You can also run the tests for any layer within the test-suite hierarchy.
- *Writing JUnit tests is inexpensive*: Using the JUnit testing framework, you can write tests cheaply and enjoy the convenience offered by the testing framework. Writing a test is as simple as writing a method that exercises the code to be tested and defining the expected result. The framework provides the context for running the test automatically and as part of a collection of other tests. This small investment in testing will continue to pay you back in time and quality.
- *JUnit tests increase the stability of software*: Tests validate the stability of the software and instill confidence that changes haven't caused a ripple-effect through the software. The tests form the glue of the structural integrity of the software.
- *JUnit tests are developer tests*: JUnit tests are highly localized tests that you write to improve your productivity and code quality. Unlike functional tests, which treat the system as a black box and ensure that the software works as a whole, unit tests are written to test the fundamental building blocks of your system from the inside out. You, the developer, write and own the JUnit tests. When a development iteration is complete, the tests are promoted as part and parcel of the delivered product as a way of communicating, "Here's my deliverable and the tests that validate it."
- *JUnit tests are written in Java:*Testing Java software using Java tests forms a seamless bond between the test and the code under test. Your tests become an extension of the overall software, and your code can be refactored from the tests into the software under test. The Java compiler helps the testing process by performing static syntax checking of the unit tests and ensuring that the software interface contracts are being obeyed.
- **JUnit is free.*

> **ON THE WEB:** For more information about the JUnit framework, view the Web site at `www.junit.org`.

Understanding Web Application Programming Models

To make a decision about what type of application architecture you want to implement, you should have an understanding of the different models available. By knowing the pros and cons of each, you are able to make a better decision about which one would best fit your application. After you have your architecture direction defined, you can then begin to develop the subsystem component underneath. No one solution works for all applications. You must ultimately decide which type of system you want to develop.

Implementing client/server versus n-tier development

Today's Web-based applications are best designed with multitiers in mind. You must take many variables into consideration, but for scalable applications that have good performance, we recommend multitier designs.

In some situations, however, pure client/server solutions are appropriate. Signs that a client/server solution may be appropriate are as follows:

- A strong user interface is required. For example your users require data-entry widgets with some complex functionality behind them.
- The application has a small footprint. (Make sure that you scope this with the future in mind.)
- The user doesn't mind the initial download time for the application to run.

Keep in mind, however, that a multitier architecture allows for a more modular, flexible, and scalable application.

Implementing single servlet versus multiple servlets

After the decision is made to use servlets for a large-scale application, the next thing to do is come up with a more detailed design. Do you create a servlet for every function in the program? Keep in mind that your design decisions should not only enhance the reliability and scalability of the application, but also make it easy to understand and maintain. Sometimes developers forget about the wonderful world of maintenance.

As discussed in the "Layering applications" section of this chapter, the servlets act as the controllers of the application and sit in the Controller/Mediator layer. A simple and often effective approach is to use one servlet per action in your application. An *action* can be thought of as an HTML submit button (for example, Continue, Calculate), or an HREF tag. Each unique action performs a unique function. It makes sense that each action should have its own servlet that knows what to do specific to that action.

This single-servlet solution is straightforward and simple — two things that help with training, turnover, and maintenance. However, as simple and effective as this approach is, it's not always the most appropriate choice. Because the role of the servlet is clearly defined as an application-control mechanism, you should be able to identify an abstract role that it fills. In fact, all servlets seem to follow the same design or pattern. Their role is to take a request made over HTTP, extract any arguments passed in, instantiate a process specific to the request made, and provide dynamic results based on the processing performed. The servlet produces basically three results: return HTML directly back to the browser, forward the request onto a JSP for display, or redirect the request to a new page.

Because all the servlets seem to share much of their controlling functionality, another design approach is to have only one servlet that handles all requests and uses helper classes to perform the more action-specific logic. This approach yields several advantages over the multiple-servlet solution. One obvious benefit is that this approach reduces the amount of duplicate code. The multiservlet solution has a fair amount of code duplicated in each servlet. If a change is needed in the controlling logic, every servlet must be updated with the new code. With the single-servlet approach, you handle changes through simple abstractions and change the code in only one place. Another benefit to the single-servlet approach is the capability to add new actions (functions) to your application without reconfiguring the Application server; this is possible because new actions are not defined in individual servlets, but by implementing a simple interface or extending an abstract controller class.

CROSS-REFERENCE: Servlets are discussed in greater detail in chapters 9 and 10, so coding details are deferred until then.

Planning your Web-application topology

Before you can begin to define your Web-application topology, you need to identify your target system requirements. After you identify these, you can design your WAS topology. The components that make up a topology are as follows:

- *Node*: A node represents a physical machine. After the installation of WAS, you have a node representing the machine on which it is installed. You can have more than one node, each of which represents different machines to which various resources can be distributed.
- *Application server*: Application servers are used to extend the capabilities of Web servers to handle requests for servlets, EBJs, and Web applications. There are two main components to an application server in WAS: a Java virtual machine configuration and support for a servlet engine to handle servlet requests.
- *Servlet engine*: A servlet engine is a program that runs within the Application server and handles the requests for servlets, JSPs, and other types of server-side include coding. The servlet engine is responsible for creating instances of servlets, initializing them, acting as a request dispatcher, and maintaining servlet contexts for use by your Web applications. WAS supports only one servlet engine per Application server.

- *Web application*: A Web application represents a grouping of servlets, JSPs, and their related resources. Managing these elements as a unit enables you to stop and start servlets all at once. You can also define a separate document root and class path at the Web-application level, thus enabling you to keep different Web applications separate in the file system. All servlets that run within a Web application share the same servlet context, which enables them to communicate with each other. The notion of a Web application is a J2EE definition. Installing WAS creates three Web applications under the default servlet engine, and each has a number of default servlets: the `default_app`, the `admin`, and the `examples` Web application. The `default_app` Web application can be used to deploy simple servlets for testing. You can also use this as a template for your own Web application. WAS uses the `admin` Web application to install the AdminServer GUI, and you do not normally have to change it. The `examples` Web application contains a few sample servlets that you can run to test your environment and give you an idea of some basic designs.
- *Virtual host*: A virtual host is a mechanism that allows a single physical machine to resemble multiple host machines. Different resources, including servlets, JSPs, and Web applications, are associated with a single virtual host and are not shared with other virtual hosts, even if they are on the same physical machine. You can also specify MIME-type support at a virtual-host level. Each virtual host has a logical name and a list of DNS aliases by which it is known. WAS comes configured with a default virtual host, `default_host`, with some common aliases, such as the machine's IP address, short host name, and a fully qualified host name. All default Web applications and their resources are set up to use this virtual host.

With knowledge of all the components, you should think about several things up front when you begin to define your own topology.

Determining the target JVM

Will you be utilizing Java 1.1, Java 1.2, Java 1.3, or maybe even Java 1.4? Plan to use 1.3 or higher because WAS 4 requires it.

Naming your Application server

What will the `default_app` be? Generally you use the `default_app` that installs with WebSphere Application Server as a model for creating your application-specific `default_app`. You should try not to change the existing `default_app` in order to keep it available to help debug any environment-type problems.

What will the `default_host` be? You should create your default host as an application or departmental default host. As with any naming convention, the name you give to your default host should have some relevancy and be easy to understand. These are organizational-type tasks that help you keep your project well organized and running smoothly.

Selecting a virtual host

How many host machines (virtual) will you want to divide your server into? What will each alias be named, and which users will access which alias? Depending on your hardware constraints, you may have a Unit test alias and an Integration test alias. These issues seem somewhat unimportant as you begin your development efforts, but performing some of these tasks midstream can cause unnecessary lag time. Granted, adding a virtual host doesn't take all that much effort, but defining your structure up front helps your development process flow better.

Determining the number of nodes to use

You must also give thought to the number of nodes or physical machines you will be running. If at all possible, your development environment should mirror production as closely as possible to avoid any unforeseen issues after deployment. What is your target user base and how many machines will you need to support it? Will you be load balancing? Will you use cloning? If so, will you use vertical or horizontal cloning?

Vertical cloning involves creating additional application-server processes on a single physical machine. Horizontal cloning involves creating additional application-server processes across multiple physical machines. Vertical cloning provides for process isolation and application software failover. However, it does not provide any type of hardware failover, because everything resides on one machine. The main advantage to vertical cloning is that the executables for an application have to be distributed to only one machine. With horizontal cloning, you are required to distribute your application executables across multiple machines.

Determining your servlet engine parameters

What will your directory structure be? (What will the root be?) You must define these, because programmers have to account for them. It is best to externalize much of this coding into some type of properties file; however, the structure needs to be defined and communicated from the very start.

Where will your system files go (for example: logs, errors, and so on)? WebSphere Application Server enables you to change where standard out and standard error files are written to. You can even rename them if that helps you better organize your file system.

Determining the type of EJB container to use

Some up-front questions about EJBs are things such as whether you will use CMP or BMP for persisting your data. What type of security levels do you want to impose? If you will have a somewhat complex structure for the machines that need to communicate with your EJBs, make sure that all the access and configuration avenues are well thought through.

The answers to all these questions influence the design of your topology. It is extremely important to put in the time up front for topology analysis. Changes you make midstream can have rippling effects through your whole system and cause unwanted downtime. Your topology is the *foundation* for your application. Make sure it is sturdy enough to hold up your house (application), and flexible enough to add more rooms to, if and when you need them.

Introducing AlmostFreeCruise

The rest of this book uses Almost Free Cruise as its sample application. The sample enables you to actually see coding practices in use. You build upon this application, until, at the end, you have a working online reservation system that utilizes some of the more popular patterns for Web development.

You start with the main page (shown in Figure 6-2) and add functionality as you cover the different technical aspects of the different chapters. This application utilizes the Model View Controller architecture. It uses JavaServer Pages (JSPs) as the View component and a single-servlet solution for the controller mechanism.

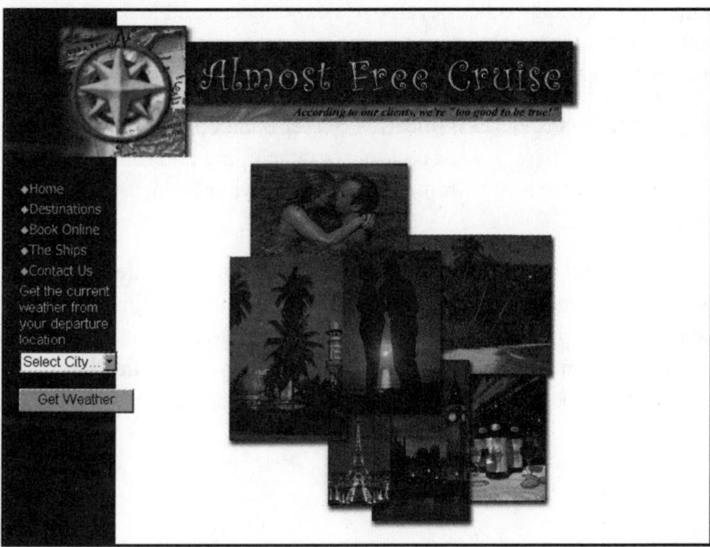

Figure 6-2: The Almost Free Cruise sample application.

As you build on this application, you see how the different technologies relate to a real-world application and the possible tradeoffs. Seeing models and coding techniques in a real-world application can help you learn much more than simple textbook examples. Although these textbook examples illustrate the fundamental points, they don't get into much detail.

Summary

This chapter discussed how the creation of the World Wide Web has opened many opportunities for creative and powerful applications, but has forced us to rethink the process in which we develop these systems. We discussed the different roles and responsibilities that have been formed by this new paradigm and offered some road maps to help you design robust and scalable Web-based applications. The IBM e-business application framework is a solid foundation on which you can build.

Although sharing many similarities, all Web-based applications have different requirements and different constraints that need to be evaluated before coming up with a target architecture. Knowing the different styles and approaches for remote systems arms you with the necessary ammunition to make an educated decision about the architecture that best fits your application. This chapter discussed distributed logic objects, transaction-processing models, and remote data management to help you understand more about distributed systems.

This chapter also discussed techniques that you, as a developer, can utilize to help you write better code. Utilizing popular design patterns, such as the Model View Controller pattern and application layering, can help you leverage other developer's experiences and kick-start your development process. It also discussed the importance of proper unit testing and offered details about the powerful JUint tool to help facilitate this.

The chapter discussed how to take WebSphere Application Server components into account before you begin development. WebSphere is a strong tool for developing and running Web-based applications that can scale and perform extremely well to give your business users an advantage.

Performing the necessary analysis and design at the front end of the application-development process is essential for creating applications that will scale and grow to the changing needs of your users. With 80 percent of development costs attributed to the maintenance and updates of the system, the time you spend up front will pay for itself quickly after your application goes live. Preparation and planning are the key ingredients in software development.

Chapter 7
Working with WSAD and WSSD

In This Chapter

- Introducing WSSD and WSAD
- Comparing WSSD and WSAD
- Overview of functions, features, and wizards
- Introducing Web development with WSAD
- Introducing EJB development features and wizards
- Introducing Java development features

WSAD is the new development tool from IBM. This chapter takes you through an overview of the product and its features and briefly discusses how to use the tools. The remaining chapters in Part II delve into more details and examples as you actually do some development.

In Chapter 5, you learned how to install the WSSD and WSAD development environment. You also got a nickel tour of WSSD and WSAD so that you would know what you were about to install on your computer. However, please don't skip this chapter believing that it is nothing more than a rehash of Chapter 5. It contains a good deal of useful material about WSSD and WSAD that wasn't covered previously.

So far, you know that WSAD and WSSD are built using a tool-building platform called Eclipse; thus, they inherit the flexibility of the plug-in architecture. But what functions, features, and advantages do WSAD and WSSD provide you over other development environments? This chapter discusses how to use the tools in WSAD and/or WSSD to create your Web, EJB, and Java applications. It walks you through the necessary steps to create an application, beginning with creating the project to publishing the project to the WAS test environment for unit testing.

Introducing WSSD and WSAD

WebSphere Studio Site Developer (WSSD) and WebSphere Studio Application Developer (WSAD) offer some powerful tools and features for developing enterprise applications using Java, JSPs, HTML, servlets, XML, and more. The features and tools that you find in both of these development environments are robust, comprehensive, and fairly complete. To help you decide which of the two development environments is best for you, the following section compares the two.

Comparing WSSD and WSAD

Up to this point, you've heard that WSSD and WSAD are interrelated because WSAD supports all of WSSD's functionality. Although you work exclusively with WSAD in this book, you should know what you're getting with WSAD over WSSD. This section discusses the similarities and differences between the two development tools, and, at the same time, gives you an overview of the functions and tools that are included in each tool.

Because WSAD is essentially WSSD plus additional development tools, the section starts by introducing to you the features you find in WSSD and talks about the additional features found in WSAD.

WSSD is specifically created for Web developers. The tools and features that you find in WSSD include the following:

- *Web services*: Support building and publishing Web services for the Web utilizing the SOAP, UDDI, WSDL technologies and protocols
- *XML:* Enables you to build XML, XML Schemas, DTDs, XSLT, and XSL files, often through a WYSIWYG editor; the XML tooling also enables you to validate your XML documents using its XML validator and to create XML mappings between XML files and against relational database stores and queries
- *Support for JavaServer Pages 1.1 and Servlet 2.2 specifications*
- *Support for file-based storage of all your resources*
- *Customizable, role-based perspectives of your projects*
- *Page Designer*: Enables you to author Web documents (such as HTML, and JSP) using a WYSIWYG editor or from the source
- *CSS Designer*: Enables you to author cascading style sheets for your Web documents
- *Image Creator/Editor:* Enables you to create or edit your Web images
- *Design Gallery*: Provides a set of image, sound, style sheet, and JavaScript files that you can use in conjunction with Page Designer to enhance your Web pages
- *JavaBean and servlet wizards*: Provide a form-based editor for creating JavaBeans and servlets quickly and easily
- *Java Integrated Development Environment:* Provides tools for building and editing Java source files, with such features as code assist, syntax highlighting, and code refactoring
- *JDK switching:* Enables you to switch compilation of your Java code against multiple Java Development Kit versions

- *JRE switching:* Enables you to run your Java code against a different Java runtime environment, which might be from a different Java Development Kit version
- *Database:* Enables you to connect to and view existing databases, as well as create and edit your own databases for deployment; this feature also includes an SQL statement editor that enables you to build and execute SQL statements against relational databases
- *Integrated Web browser*: Enables you to preview your Web documents
- *Team support:* Provides plug-in support for source control (for example, CVS and ClearCase LT)
- *Link Manager:* Enables you to view and edit the link relationships between the Web documents in your projects
- *Text and Java search*: Enables you to search the files in your project for matching text or in the context of the Java language
- *Server configuration*: Enables you to create and edit the server configurations of the servers you want to use to deploy your Web applications
- *Unit test environments*: Provide a full version of the WebSphere Application Server 4.0 Single Server Edition (for multiple platforms) as a unit test environment; also provided is support for Apache Tomcat for local unit testing, and testing on remote instances of WebSphere Application Server 4.0 Single Server or Advanced Edition
- *Web application archive packaging*: Enables you to package your Web applications as archive files for easy deployment to WAS 4.0
- *HTTP/FTP import and FTP export*: Enable you to import Web resources either using the HTTP or FTP protocol straight into your workspace and to transfer your resources to a remote location using the FTP protocol

In addition to the tools and features available in WSSD, WSAD also adds the support for working with EJB and enterprise applications. Some of the additional features and tools are described in the following list:

- A complete set of tools for creating and testing Enterprise JavaBeans according to the EJB 1.1 specification, which includes mapping your entity beans against a database and providing an EJB test client for testing your EJBs straight from the workspace
- Packaging according to J2EE specification, which enables you to package your Web, EJB, and enterprise applications according to J2EE specifications for easy deployment to a J2EE-compliant server environment
- Profiling, which enables you to do performance analysis and tracing of your Web applications

Although WSSD and WSAD share a common set of tools and features, they were created to satisfy two different markets, so you might see some minor differences in some of those features and tools.

Overview of Functions, Features, Wizards and Tools

Now that you know what is available to you in WSAD, this section gives you an overview of the functions, features, tools, and wizards. It also explains what the concepts of a workspace and a workbench. You explore the views and perspectives that help you work with your application resources.

Understanding the workspace

WSSD and WSAD provide a workspace for storing all your projects and resources. Not to be confused with the WSAD *workbench*, which is the main development window you use in WSAD, the *workspace* is actually a folder located in the file system. A default workspace aptly named `workspace` is created the first time you start WSAD. You can find the default workspace in the installation folder of WSAD (`c:\program files\ibm\application developer`). However, WSAD also enables you to define other workspaces as well. This is a nice feature to have if you want to keep two different development tracks for one application, or you want to maintain unrelated applications separate from one another. The first example is useful because most applications go through release cycles, and keeping these releases separate from one another enables you keep one release in maintenance mode while you work on the next release. The latter example is useful because keeping applications separate keeps the workspace size small and helps minimize the time it takes to start WSAD.

To create and use multiple workspaces in WSAD, execute the following command in the Run window, which you access by selecting Start⇨ Run:

```
"<installation path>wsappdev.exe" -data "<base path to workspace><name
of workspace here>"
```

In this command, `<installation path>` is the path to your installation of WSAD, and `<name of workspace here>` is the name of the workspace to create, for example, `"c:\program files\ibm\application developer\wsappdev.exe" -data "c:\myworkspaces\newworkspace"`

The double quotes (") are necessary, because the Run command window might not recognize the spaces in paths like `program files` and `application developer`.

However, for convenience, we recommend that you create shortcuts to each of your workspaces. Simply make copies of the original shortcut to WSAD and modify each target to use the command line shown previously. Your shortcuts should look like the example in Figure 7-1.

The shortcuts that you create open the specified workspace in WSAD. If the target workspace doesn't exist, WSAD creates a new one. If you want to branch off one workspace into two separate development tracks, take the following steps:

1. Locate and make a copy of the workspace you want to make into two separate workspaces.
2. Rename the copy of the workspace.
3. Make a copy of the shortcut that opens the old workspace. You can optionally rename the shortcut to better represent the new workspace that it opens.
4. Modify the properties of the new shortcut to point to the new copy of the workspace.

Each shortcut opens to an independent but identical copy of the same workspace. With WSAD, you can run multiple workspaces at the same time. In fact, you can even have multiple copies of the same workspace opened simultaneously. However, having the same workspace opened at the same time means that anything you modify in one workspace gets out of sync with the other. In this case, you need to refresh the other workspace to pick up the changes.

NOTE: Although you can have multiple workspaces open simultaneously with WSAD, doing so is resource intensive.

To show the properties for a shortcut, right-click the shortcut to modify it and choose Properties from the drop-down list.

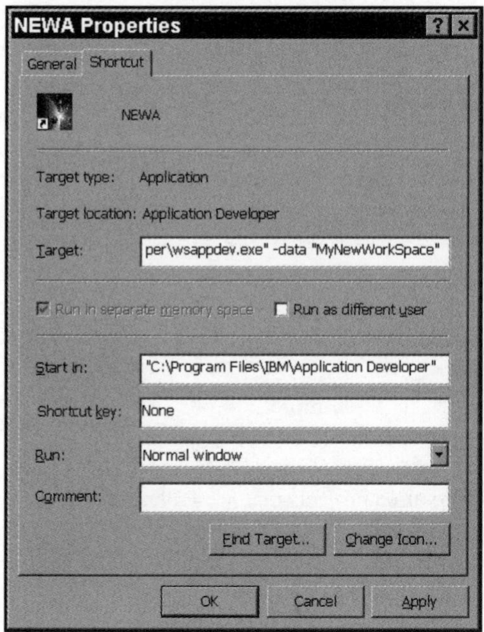

Figure 7-1: This shortcut creates or opens a workspace called MyNewWorkSpace in the directory where you installed WSAD.

The workspace folders that you create using WSAD are used by WSAD and are not defined by the J2EE specification; however, they are specific to the Eclipse framework. Along with all your projects and resources, the root of the workspace folder also contains a `.metadata` folder where WSAD stores all your preferences and settings for that workspace. The settings and preferences can be changed easily because most of them are stored in XML text files. However, we highly recommend that you do not change the files in the `.metadata` folder because it might corrupt the workspace, make it unusable, or at the very least cause some unexpected behavior.

NOTE: If you cannot find the default workspace in the installation directory, either you have not started WSAD for the first time, you deleted the workspace folder, or you had to change the shortcuts to WSAD (as instructed in Chapter 5) to bypass some permissions issues with your WSAD installation. To create the default workspace for the first time or to create a new default workspace (in case you deleted the original one), run the WSAD application. If you changed the targets of your shortcuts for running WSAD and you already ran WSAD once, you will find the workspace in the location defined by the shortcut target.

Understanding projects

Projects, like workspaces, are not part of the J2EE specification but are used for organizational purposes. However, the types of projects that you create affect how WSAD represents and provides resources. For example, the default classes and deployment descriptors provided for a Web project differ from those provided for an EJB project. The menu choices that WSAD presents to you also depend on the type of project that you create. After you create a project in WSAD, you cannot change its type. You might be able to change the resources that the project references to mimic another project type, but WSAD continues to treat the project differently. You can create the following types of projects with WSAD:

- Web
- EJB
- Enterprise application
- Application client
- Java
- Plug-in
- Plug-in fragment
- Plug-in component
- Server
- Simple

To illustrate how WSAD treats projects differently according to their types, see Figure 7-2 to see how WSAD organizes your projects. Notice the three projects that are organized under an Enterprise Application Project.

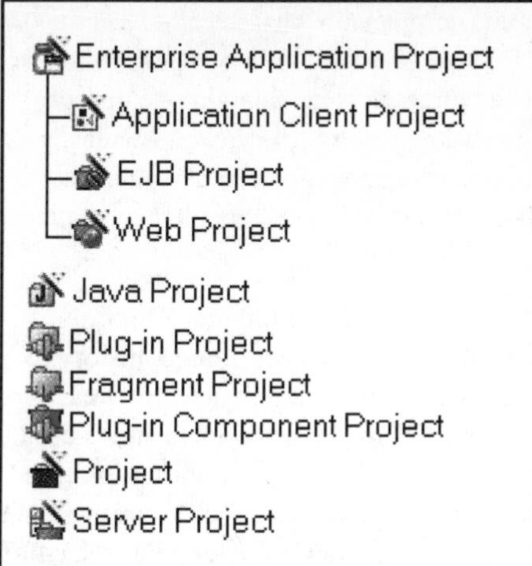

Figure 7-2: This figure illustrates how projects are organized in WSAD. Web, EJB, and Application Client projects are stored in Enterprise Application Project.

The Application client, EJB, and Web project types are always added to an enterprise application project. If an enterprise application project is not present in the workspace, you can choose to create one along with your new project. Although the projects are added to an enterprise application project, the physical project folders can be placed anywhere. By creating one of the three projects in an enterprise application, you associate the project with the enterprise application. Specifying the association modifies the enterprise application's deployment descriptors to include the projects when you choose to export to an .EAR file.

Understanding the workbench

The word *workbench* is used to describe two different environments in the context of WebSphere Studio. One environment is the WebSphere Studio workbench, which is the tooling development application that tool builders can use to build new plug-in tools for WSAD and WSSD. The workbench in WSSD and WSAD is the main window in which you do all your development work. Throughout this chapter and book, unless otherwise stated, you can assume that when we refer the workbench we're using the latter of the two definitions.

> **NOTE**: Adding to the confusion over the definition of the *workbench* is that fact that the WebSphere Studio workbench tooling development environment is also included in WSAD. WSAD provides the same plug-in development environment that you can find in WebSphere Studio workbench.

The main function of the workbench is to show you your projects in what is called a perspective. You learn about perspectives later, but for now just think of a perspective as a set of viewing windows that make up the workbench. The workbench can contain one or more perspectives. If you're starting WSAD for the first time, the primary role you chose during installation determines the first perspective to open. As you change between perspectives, so does the workbench. However, the pattern by which the workbench presents the perspectives windows and editors remains relatively constant.

The workbench is divided into different regions. A small region on the left side of the workbench window is reserved for the Perspectives toolbar, which shows a quick history of the perspectives that you have already opened and also makes switching perspectives easy. The status bar located at the bottom of the window is also part of the workbench and is used to display information about the items that you select. The center and biggest region is reserved for the editors and views, toolbars, and menu bars that make up a perspective. You use them to edit and view your files. Depending on the perspective that you work with, and thus the editors and views, the workbench adapts by changing the menu bar, toolbar, and options available to you. You can change the behavior of the workbench by changing the workspace preferences. The following are the to steps change preferences:

1. Open the workbench preferences by choosing Window from the menu bar and then Preferences from the drop-down menu.
2. If it's not already selected, click Workbench in the left panel to show the workbench options, as shown in Figure 7-3.

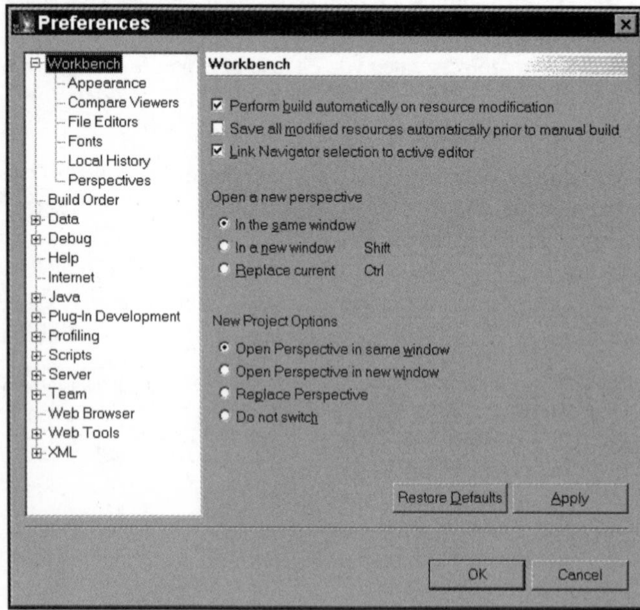

Figure 7-3: Use the Preferences window of the WSAD workbench to set your preference settings.

Here is a list of some of the available options:

- Workbench
  - *Perform build automatically on resource modification*: Check this box to perform a build every time you save your changes.

> **NOTE:** To perform a build in WSAD is to request that WSAD validate the selected resources according to constraints and to create or modify files necessary for testing and running applications. For example, performing a build on a Java project executes the Java builder to validate the Java source code and to generate the class files that result from compiling the source code.

  - *Save all modified resources automatically prior to manual build:* Check this box if you want the workbench to save any modifications to files when you choose the Rebuild All Functions from the Project menu.
  - *Link Navigator selection to active editor:* Check this box if you want the editors and the navigator views to interact. For example, if you choose a file in the navigator view that already has an editor open, the editor comes into focus. The reverse is also true; selecting an editor brings the associated file into focus.
  - *Open a new perspective in the same window:* Select this option to open new perspectives in the same workbench window. Your new perspectives is added to the toolbar of perspectives.
  - *Open a new perspective in the a new window:* Select this option to open new perspectives in their own workbench windows.
  - *Open a new perspective to replace the current window:* Select this option if you want the workbench to close the active perspective and open a the new perspective in its place.

> **NOTE:** You can use the Shift and Ctrl keys to control how new perspectives open in the workbench. Hold down either key to quickly change this behavior.

  - *New project options: Open in the same window*: The default perspective for the project type opens in the same workbench window.
  - *New project options: Open in a new window:* The default perspective for the project type opens in a new workbench window.
  - *New project options: Replace the current window*: The default perspective for the project type opens in the current window. If the perspective is not listed in the Perspectives toolbar, the perspective opens and is added to the toolbar.
  - *New project options: Do not switch:* Creating a new project does not switch to the default perspective.

Click the (+) sign next to the Workbench option to reveal a list of other options:

- Appearance
  - *Tab position: Editor:* Select whether to show the tabs used to access your editors at the top or bottom of the editor views.

- *Tab position: Vie* : Select whether to show the tabs used to access your views at the top or bottom of the view windows.

◆ Compare Viewers

- *Synchronize scrolling between panes in compare/merge viewers:* Select this if you want the compare or merge windows to scroll together, keeping the corresponding lines of code in focus.
- *Show Psuedo conflicts:* Select this to show conflicts that occur when two developers make the same changes in the compare viewer.
- *Show Ancestor Pane initially:* Check this option to always show the original parent resource when comparing two child resources.
- *Text font:* You can change the default text font for the compare viewers.

◆ File Editors

- *File types: Add*: Adds a new file type to the list of file types that the workbench is aware of. If you choose to add, you are asked for the file extension for the type.
- *File types: Remove:* Removes a select file type from the list.
- *Associated editors: Add:* This enables you to add an editor that you can use to edit a file of a selected type. First select a file type from the file types panel and then choose Add. You can choose from a list of built-in editors by selecting Internal or External from a list of supported editors. If you choose an external editor, you need to provide the location of the editor.
- *Associated editors: Remove:* Removes the selected editor for a selected file type.
- *Associated editors: Default*: Makes a selected editor the default editor for a selected type. Double-clicking the selected file type invokes the default editor.
- *Fonts:* Enables you to change the fonts for text in the workbench.

◆ Local history

- *Days to keep file:* Enter the number of days that you want the workbench to keep a history of the changes to your resources.
- *Entries per file*: Specify the number of change entries the workbench stores in its history for a file.
- *Maximum file size (MB):* Specify how big the history file can become before forgetting old changes.
- *Perspectives:* Shows you a list of all the default perspectives available to you through the workbench, including the any custom perspectives that you create. You can change the default perspective here by choosing a perspective and clicking Default. Also, you can delete any perspectives you may not want to keep.You can only delete perspectives that you create, not the default perspectives. Deleting perspectives that you create is permanent.

Figure 7-4 shows the workbench in WSAD, the main window used for all your development.

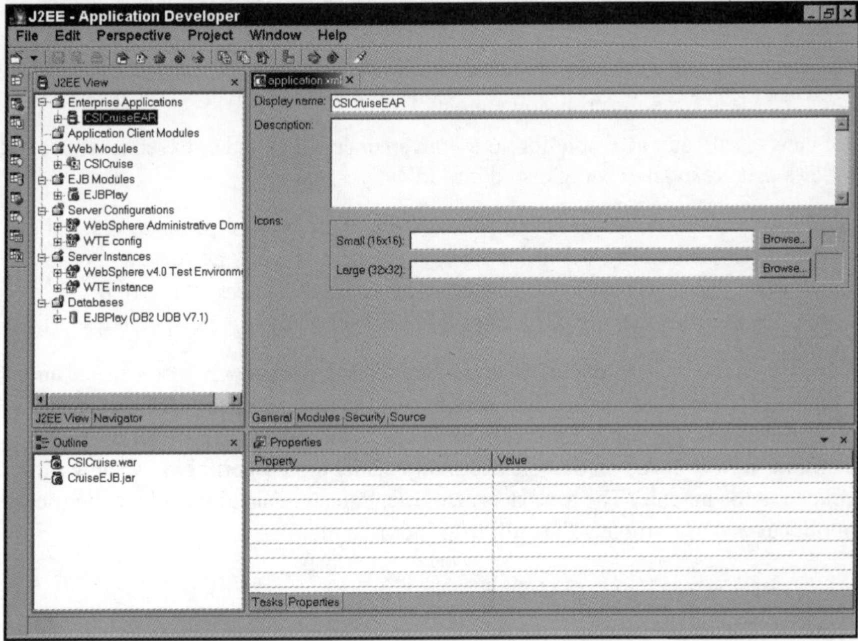

Figure 7-4: This is the workbench window in WSAD and WSSD. It is currently opened to the J2EE perspective, with the application.xml editor for the CSICruiseEAR project in focus.

Understanding views

Before you start exploring the many perspectives that WSAD has to offer, take a brief look at the views in WSAD. A view in WSAD, like the Servers view shown in Figure 7-5, is a window pane that can show you your WSAD resources in a useful way. A perspective is often comprised of several view windows put together, all aimed at supporting the editors that you use in WSAD. In fact, all the default and customer perspectives that you design get their view windows from a common set of views.

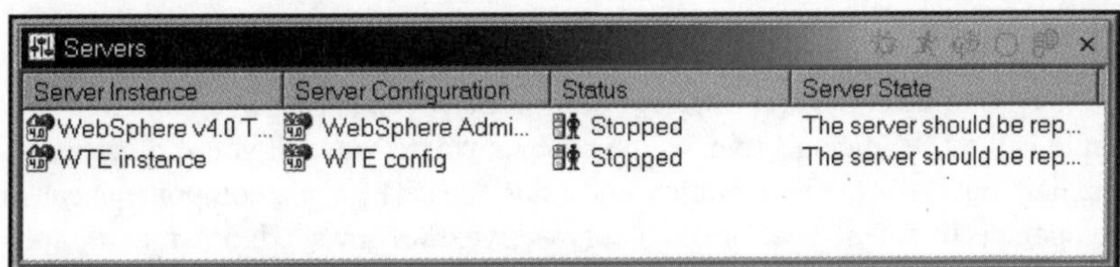

Figure 7-5: The Servers view window showing two server instances listed as Stopped. The Server State for each indicates that the servers are not current and their associated projects should be republished.

To see a list of the views available in WSAD, perform the following steps:

1. Choose Perspective from the menu bar.
2. Choose Show View from the drop-down menu.
3. A list of views is already available for your convenience. Click Other to see an entire list of the views that are available, organized into folders.

There are more than forty views that you can choose from to use in your perspectives. All of them serve a specific function. Try to familiarize yourself with as many as you can, because you never know when you might need one of them. The views that make up a certain perspective are often the ones that are most helpful to the user whom the perspective services.

The views can also interact with other views and editors in the workbench. You can see an example of this interaction while in the J2EE perspective. When you open a J2EE module through the J2EE window, the editor for that module opens into focus. The selection also triggers the outline view to focus on the selected module, and the Properties view shows any properties related to the module. The reverse is also true. Selecting an editor brings the file in the editor into focus and also triggers the outline to focus on the file.

Understanding perspectives

One of the key features in WSAD is the way it presents resources to you. Development tools are often designed with a specific type of user in mind. WebSphere Studio is an example of a development tool designed with Web developers in mind, and VisualAge for Java is an example of a development tool designed with Java developers in mind. The tools, features, and settings in each development environment were created to aid the developer in doing highly specialized tasks. Because WSAD combines all these tools and features into one, the challenge is to continue to provide the division of concerns that separate development environments, such as Studio and VisualAge for Java.

WSAD helps in the serration of concerns by implementing role-based views of your project resources. These role-based views are called perspectives. This section introduces you to three of the perspectives — the J2EE, Web, and Java perspectives — to give you a better understanding of what perspectives are meant to do.

A perspective in WSAD is nothing more than a combination of view windows, editors, and settings targeted to a type of user. Several different built-in perspectives are available in WSAD. An example is the J2EE perspective, which enables you to view all you projects as J2EE components, like WAR files, EJB modules, and EAR files. The same components can be viewed in the Web perspective. However, in Web perspective, the views, editors, menus, and tools showing, by default, are all related to Web development. Figure 7-6 shows all the available perspectives.

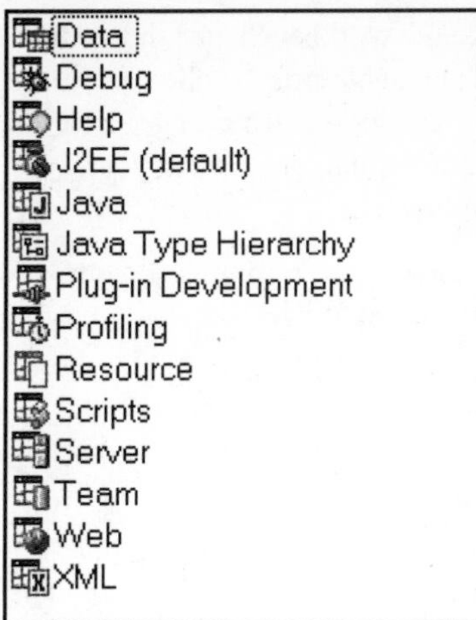

Figure 7-6: In this list of the default perspectives, J2EE is marked as the current default perspective.

To open the workbench to a different perspective, do the following:

1. Choose Perspectives from the menu bar.
2. Choose Open from the drop-down list.
3. Select the perspective to open from the quick list of perspectives. If the one you want to open is not in the quick list, choose Other to open a list of all the available perspectives.
4. You can also swap bidirectionally through the Perspectives toolbar by holding the ALT key and pressing the Up or Down arrows (depending on which direction you want to scroll).

CAUTION: Having more than one perspective open at the same time can cause your files to be out of sync if you have the same file opened in separate perspectives. This problem is compounded if you have more than one version of the same perspective open at the same time. Although it defeats the purpose of being able to have multiple perspectives open at the same time, try to keep the number open to a minimum, or you can choose to have only one perspective open at a time by changing the workbench preferences.

Now that you have a pretty good idea about what a perspective is and how to open to a perspective, take a look at some of the more common perspectives and make a few comparisons.

Using the J2EE perspective

The J2EE perspective is customized for the role of an application assembler. An application assembler is normally the user in charge of setting up an application for deployment by making the necessary modifications to deployment descriptors and gathering the resources to be deployed. The default tools, editors, and options available while in this perspective are specific to building and packaging J2EE applications.

When you switch to this perspective, you immediately notice the workbench adapting to the change. For example, the toolbar contains buttons for creating an enterprise application, an application client project, an EJB project, an EJB, and so on. The views also change. You should see the J2EE view, which shows you all the J2EE modules that you have in your workspace. The J2EE perspective, by default, includes the following.

- *J2EE view:* This view window (shown in Figure 7-7) shows your resources in your workspace as J2EE modules, such as EAR files, WAR files, and EJB jars.

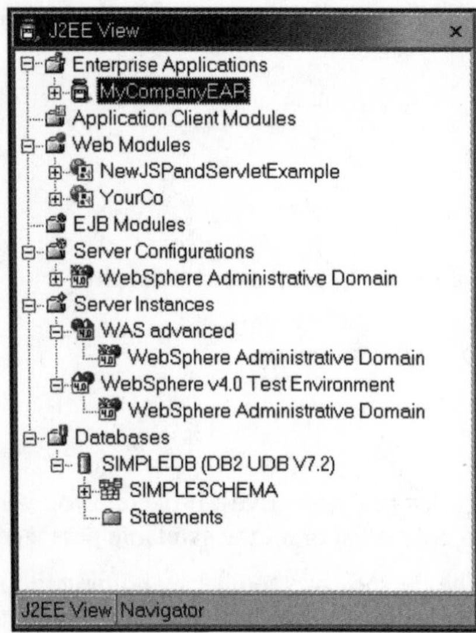

Figure 7-7: Use the J2EE view to quickly navigate and edit your J2EE applications.

- *Navigator view:* This view window is stacked together along with the J2EE view and shows your projects as folders and files.
- *Outline view:* This view window, depending on the editor that is opened and in focus, by default shows the currently selected resource in an outline form. For example, by opening a Web module into the Web.xml editor, you set the outline to focus on the Web module. You can see the Web module and the servlets contained within in an outline form.
- *Tasks view:* This view window is common among almost all the perspectives that you will work with. This view window's main purpose is to display all the errors and warnings in your files as tasks. You can even create your own tasks.
- *Properties view:* This view window is also common among perspectives and shows you the properties of some known file types, such as HTML and XML files. It enables you to not only see the properties for a selected file but also to change its properties.

Using the Web perspective

The role of the Web developer often spans the boundaries of being a GUI designer and a Java developer. The Web perspective in WSAD is a perspective that you can use to work with both your Web and Java resources. The default views in this perspective include the Navigator view, Outline view, Properties view, and Task view found in the J2EE perspective. However, the Web perspective also provides the following additional views.

- *Gallery view:* The Gallery view shows a gallery of sample images, wallpaper, Web art, sounds, style sheets, and JavaScript files that you can choose from when designing HTML and JSP Web pages.
- *Links view:* The Link view, when the Page Designer editor is in focus, maps out the links in an HTML or JSP document relative to itself. Through this view, you can see graphically where you have broken links and how documents are linked.
- *Thumbnail view:* The Thumbnail view is used to support the Gallery view. When you select a gallery from the Gallery view, the contents of the gallery show automatically as thumbnail items in this view. The Thumbnail view also includes a File Filter drop-down box that you can use to show only the file types that you want.

Using the Java perspective

The Java perspective is designed for the role of the programmer. The main purpose of this perspective is to show you your Java files as Java artifacts, such as classes, interfaces, packages, and so on. The default view windows for the Java perspective are Packages, Hierarchy, Outline, Tasks, Search, and Console. These views are explained in the following list:

- *Packages view:* The purpose of this view is to display your Java resources as they appear in their own package hierarchies. This view looks similar to the Navigator view; however, unlike the Navigator view, the Packages view not only shows your source files but also the Java libraries found in the build path set to each project. You can choose to hide these reference libraries by clicking the solid down arrow on the top-right corner of the view and deselecting the Show Reference Libraries option.
- *Hierarchy view:* The purpose of this view is to show the hierarchy of a selected Java type when you choose the Open to Type Hierarchy option. The Hierarchy view can show you a Java type in a type, supertype, or subtype hierarchy. A lower section of the Hierarchy view is reserved for the members of the type, including variables and methods.
- *Outline view:* The Outline view in the Java perspective serves to show the currently selected type in an outline form. The outline shows the code for the Java artifact graphically.
- *Tasks view:* This view shows all the errors and warnings related to all the resources in your workspace as tasks that you can prioritize. You can also add your own tasks through this view.

- *Search view:* This view lists the results of a Java or text search against your resources in the workspace. Double-clicking a result in this view takes you to the location where the match was found.
- *Console view:* This view is where a Java application's `system.out` statements display.

Introducting infopop

A useful feature of WSAD is infopop, a help feature that provides help on any item in focus. Infopop can be useful when working with settings in wizards and other WSAD interfaces. You can use infopop by setting focus on the item you want help with and pressing F1. Infopop displays the information about the item as well as provides links to the Help perspective for additional assistance.

Understanding editors

WSAD comes installed along with an extensive collection of editing tools that you can use to edit your resources. There are essentially two types of editors in WSAD: internal editors and external editors. *Internal editors* are editing tools integrated into WSAD that appear as editor windows within the WSAD workbench; *external editors* are editors are not installed with WSAD and run outside of the WSAD workbench. Page Designer is an example of an internal WSAD editor; whereas, the WordPad editor that comes installed with most Microsoft operating systems is an example of an external editor.

> **NOTE:** WSAD also supports Active X controls in Microsoft Windows by enabling you to open documents as an OLE (Object Linking and Embedding) document. For example, Microsoft Word supports opening Word documents as an embedded OLE document in WSAD. Be careful; some versions of Word might not function properly with WSAD, including the XP version of Word. If you choose to edit a Word document in one of your projects through WSAD, WSAD opens the Word document as an internal editor but with Word's own toolbars showing within the editor.

Internal editors in WSAD open in the area reserved for editors at the top-right region of the workbench. If there is more than one editor opened at the same time, the editors are stacked on top of one another. The toolbars and menu options available in the workbench depend upon the internal editor that is currently in focus and dynamically change as you switch from one editor to another. Some editors, such as the Page Designer editor (shown in Figure 7-8) for editing HTML and JSP files, provide additional tabs layered within the editor to offer additional functions, such as a Preview tab for previewing an HTML page.

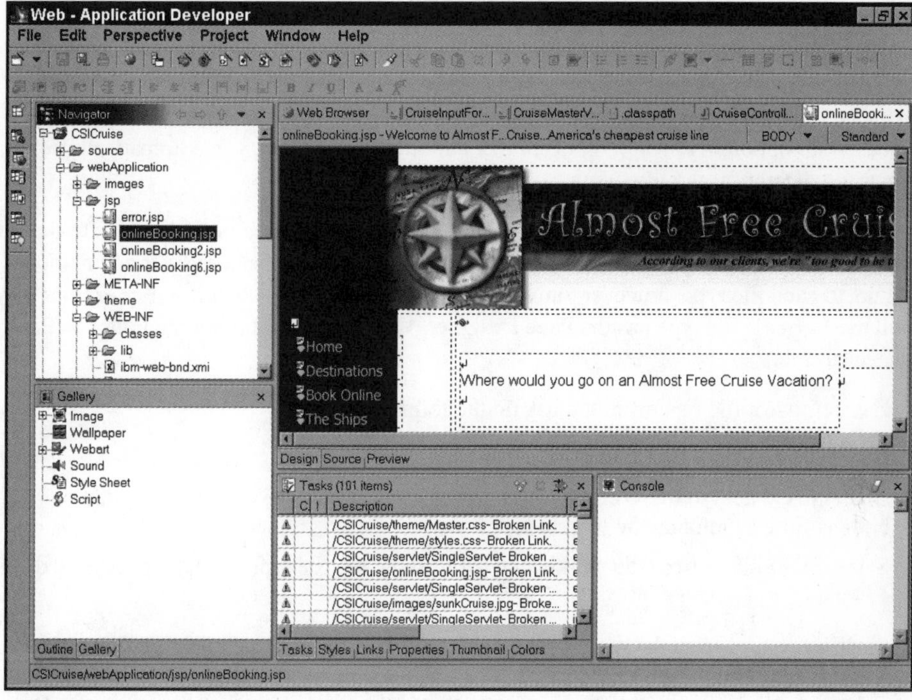

Figure 7-8: This is a Web perspective in WSAD with the Page Designer editor opened and with the Design tab in focus.

When you make changes to a document in an editor, the tab of the editor indicates that the document has changed by placing an asterisk (*) before the name of the file. The asterisk remains until you save changes by choosing Save from the File menu.

WSAD enables you to associate multiple editors for each file type in the workbench. Each file type is assigned a default editor for editing files of that type. Double-clicking a file automatically opens the file in the default editor. If the file type is not registered in the workbench or does not have an associated editor assigned, WSAD searches for a system default editor for that type and opens the file in that editor. Also, WSAD lets you quickly switch from one associated editor to another when you right-click a selected file and choose the Open With option. By switching to another editor in this manner, you automatically set the editor as the default for the file type.

WSAD enables you to add and remove file types and also to associate internal and external editors to each file type by editing the Workbench preferences. You can register any number of editors to each file type; however, only one editor can be the default editor. For example, by default the `*.html` file type has the Page Designer, Web browser, and Source Editor as the available editors.

To add or remove a file type from the list, do the following:

1. Choose Preferences from the Window menu.
2. Click the (+) next to the Workbench option on the left panel to access the additional options for customizing the workbench.
3. Select File Editors from the workbench list to show the file types and their associated editors.

To remove a file type from the list, select the file type from the list and click the Remove button to the right of the list. To add a new file type, click the Add button and enter either the filename or the file extension in the pop-up window. Click OK to accept the change. To add an editor to a file type and select a default editor, do the following.

1. Choose Preferences from the Window menu.
2. Click the (+) next to the Workbench option on the left panel to access the additional options for customizing the workbench.
3. Select File Editors from the workbench list to show the file types and their associated editors (as shown in Figure 7-9).
4. From the file types list, select the file type to add, remove, or set a default editor for. The associated editors display for the selected file type.

To remove an associated editor for the selected file type, select the editor from the Associated Editors list and click the Remove button. To add an associated editor for the selected file type, click the Add button. To add an internal editor, make sure the Internal Editors radio button is selected; select the editor from the list as shown in Figure 7-10, and click OK to associate the editor with the selected file type.

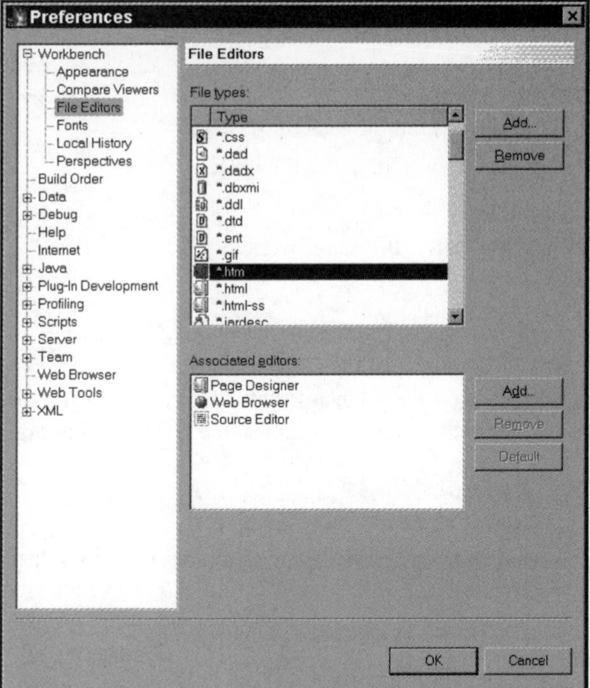

Figure 7-9: Web perspective in WSAD with the Page Designer editor opened and the Design tab in focus.

Figure 7-10: In the Editor Selection window, choose either an internal or external program for editing an associated file type.

To add an external editor program for the selected file type, make sure the External Programs radio button is selected.

1. Select the program to use for editing the file type from the list and then click the Browse button to located the executable (`*.exe`) program in your file system.
2. Click OK to associate the selected program for editing the file type.
3. The editor you select should display as an associated editor.
4. To make the new editor the default editor, select the editor from the list of associated editors and then click the Default button.
5. Finally, click the OK button to accept all the changes.

Now that you've associated an editor for the file type and made the editor the default, every time you double-click a file of that type, the file opens in the associated editor. The editor also appears in the pop-up menu list when you right-click a file and choose the Open With option.

Customizing the workbench perspectives

You can customize the default perspectives provided by WSAD or create new ones. You can create new perspectives by taking a starting perspective, modifying it, and saving it as a new perspective.

The following steps show how you can create a new perspective called NewWeb:

1. Open your workbench to the Web perspective.
2. To illustrate the difference between the old Web and the new perspective, add the Server view to the new perspective by doing the following:
   - Choose Perspective from the menu bar.
   - Choose Show View from the drop-down list.
   - Select Servers from the quick list of available viewing windows.

3. A Server view window like the one shown in Figure 7-11 appears in the workbench.

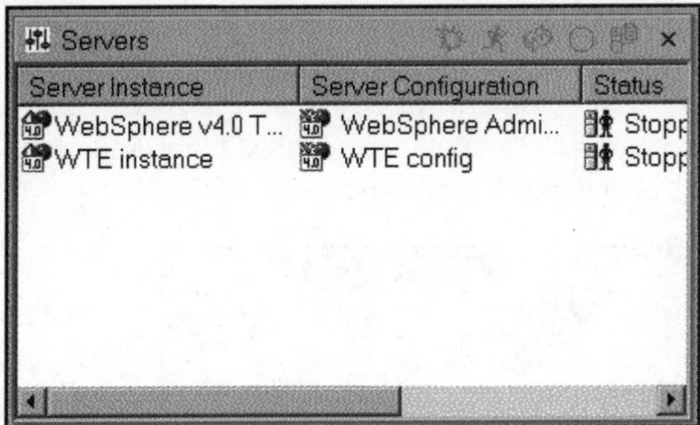

Figure 7-11: The Servers view window displaying two WebSphere Application Server 4.0 server instances.

Next, you save the new perspective by doing the following:

1. Choose Perspective ⇨Save As.
2. Enter **NewWeb** as the name of the new perspective in the prompt window and click OK to save it.
3. The title bar of the workbench should now read NewWeb.

The NewWeb is added and is available in the list of perspectives. To see the difference between the Web and the NewWeb perspectives, open the Web perspective and then the NewWeb perspective. Notice that the Server view is available in the NewWeb perspective. To delete a perspective that you created, do the following.

1. Choose Window⇨Preferences.
2. Click the (+) sign next to the workbench.
3. Select Perspectives from the list of options for customizing the workbench.
4. Select the perspective to remove and click the Delete button.

NOTE: Deleting a perspective affects only the list of perspectives that you can choose to open. Any perspective that you already have open or that is listed in the Perspectives toolbar is still accessible.

Using fast view

WSAD supports creating shortcuts to view windows called fast views. Fast view shortcuts appear as buttons on the perspective toolbar. You can quickly open a view window by clicking the button that represents the fast view. A view window, when accessed as a fast view, appears glued to the side of the Perspectives toolbar and cannot be repositioned for as long as it remains a fast view. Figure 7-12 shows how the fast view looks.

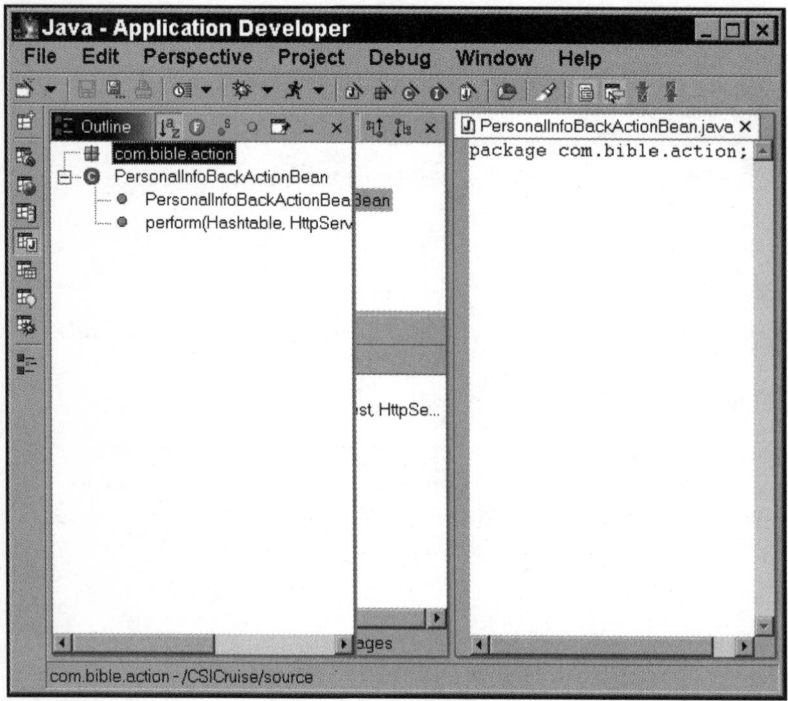

Figure 7-12: The Outline view is stored as a fast view in the perspectives toolbar. Notice the icon listed lowest on the Perspectives toolbar. By clicking the Outline fast view icon, you can hide and show the Outline view window.

To make a view window into a fast view, right-click the title bar of a view and choose the Fast View option from the pop-up menu. You can also make a view window into a fast view by dragging the window by its title bar into the Perspective toolbar.

To turn off fast view for a view window, bring the view window into focus by clicking its Fast View button. Then either click the Restore button that appears in the view windows title bar or right-click the title bar and select Restore.

Introducing Web Development with WSAD

To help you develop your Web applications, WSAD provides the Web perspective for developing all your Web application resources. The Web perspective is ideal for viewing and editing your resources. The wizards for creating your resources include an HTML Wizard, Servlet Wizard, JSP Wizard, and a Style Sheet Wizard. In this section, you walk through some examples to learn about some of these wizards and how you can use them to create a Web project.

Creating and working with Web projects and perspectives

There are several ways to create a project in WSAD. The following example takes you through creating a Web project called `CSICruise`.

1. Choose File⇨New.
2. From the quick list of project types, select Create a New Web Project.
3. If the project you want to create is not listed, choose Project to see a window of all the projects that you can create, as shown in Figure 7-13.

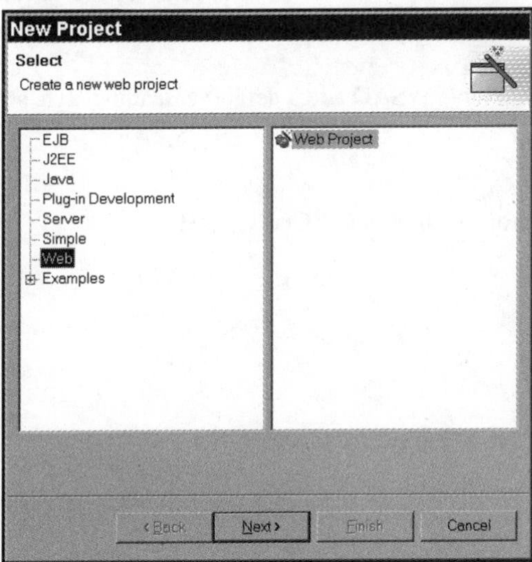

Figure 7-13: The New Projects window lists all the types of project wizards that you can use to create projects in WSAD.

4. The Web Project Wizard walks you through creating the project. You will, at the minimum, need to specify a name for the project and the location in which to create the project. Other options and settings are required depending on the type of project to be created. Notice that you are required to add a Web project to an enterprise application project. Many of the default settings are sufficient to create a project, but for this example, enter the information as shown in Figure 7-14.
   - *Project name:* Enter the project name here to identify the Web project in the workspace.
   - *Use default location:* Check this box to create the Web project under the WSAD installation directory (`c:\program files\ibm\application developer\<WEB PROJECT FOLDER>`).
   - *Location:* This option enables you to override the default location. Uncheck the Use Default Location check box, and enter the location in which to create the project.
   - *Enterprise Application project name:* Either choose an existing enterprise application project from the drop-down list to add the Web project to or enter a new name to create a new associated enterprise application project.
   - *Context root:* Enter the Web application root here. The Web application root is the top-level folder name of your application when it is deployed to your Web server. The context root is used by Link Manager to ensure that the links in your Web documents are consistent. You can always change the context root for a Web project by changing the properties of the project.
   - *Create CSS file:* Check this box to have WSAD add a default cascading style sheet to the Web project.
5. Enter **CSICruise** as the Project name.
6. Change the enterprise application project name to **CSICruiseEAR**.
7. Click Next to accept the changes.

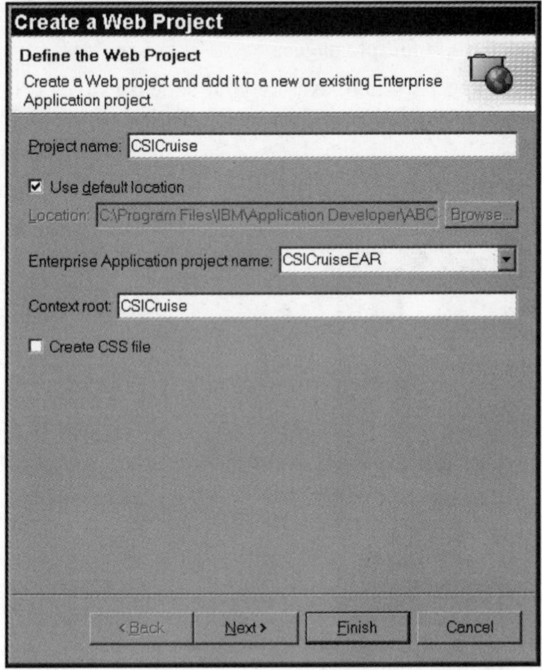

Figure 7-14: This is the first page of the wizard for creating Web projects in WSAD.

8. The next screen in the wizard enables you to select any existing modules that you want to include when building this project. If the enterprise application defined in the previous screen contained any modules (EJB JARs), you see a list of them here. For now, click Next to skip this screen.

9. The next screen you encounter enables you to define the Java build settings. The screen, as shown in Figure 7-15, is divided into multiple pages.
   - The Source page enables you to specify where to store your code packages. You have the option of storing your code into the Project folder or of creating new folders for organizing your code packages.
   - The Build Output folder also enables you to specify where to store the compiled versions of your source code when you do a build.

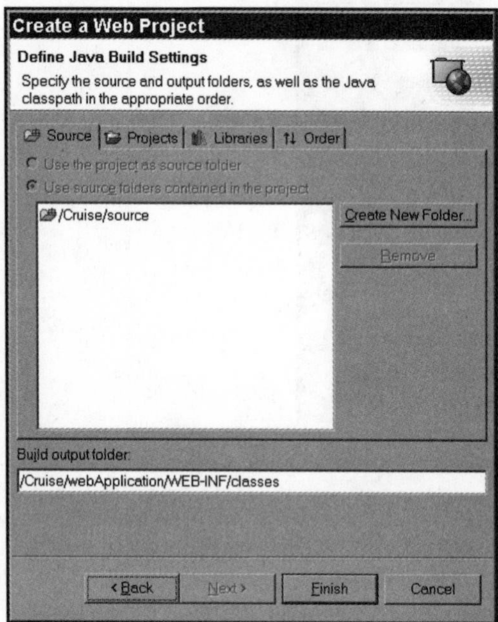

Figure 7-15: This page of the wizard enables you to create additional folders for storing your Java source code. The source folders that you create participate in the build path for the new project.

   - The Projects page enables you to choose any projects in the workspace that your new Web project may require to do a build.
   - The Libraries page shows you all JAR files and folders that your project may need to do a build.
   - The Order page enables you to shift the build order of your project's resources. WSAD builds your resources sequentially, so it is important that you keep dependent resources closer to the bottom of the list. Otherwise, you may encounter problems when you build. To shift a resource up or down in the list, select the resource and click the Up or Down button.

10. Click Finish, and WSAD creates a new project of the selected type in your workspace and automatically switches to the appropriate perspective with the new project in focus.

Congratulations, you just created the CSICruise Web project.

Using proof-of-concept wizards

Before venturing into a project, often a proof of concept is done to test and demonstrate the viability of the ideas in the project. A proof of concept is a scaled-down version of the project with the main goals in mind at the end of development. The WSAD wizards can help you to create a fast and simple proof of concept. The following section shows you the database and JavaBean wizards for creating Web pages from existing JavaBean classes and Web pages for accessing databases. The wizards generate all necessary components, such as Java classes, HTML pages, and JSPs.

Using Web application wizards that create Web resources from database queries and JavaBeans

You begin by using the Database Web Page wizard for creating a Web page that accesses a database and displays the results. To continue the cruise theme, this exercise steps you through creating a Web page that displays the results of a database search against the Cruise database. You use the CSICruise Web project you created previously. Before you begin this exercise, you should make sure that you have the Cruise database already loaded into your DB2 database and that DB2 is currently running.

> **CROSS-REFERENCE:** Refer to Chapter 5 for instructions on loading the Cruise database and tables.

There are actually two models of database Web pages that you can generate with the wizard. One model utilizes Java view bean classes generated by the wizard to connect, retrieve, and display data from the database. The other type utilizes a tag library to connect, retrieve, and display data from the database. In this exercise, you learn to create database Web pages that utilize the Java classes.

If you choose to create database Web pages using the view bean model, the wizard can automatically generate the following resources for you:

- *Input HTML page:* This page is the starting page for submitting requests to the cruise database for information.
- *Master View JSP page:* This page displays the results of the database request.
- *Details View JSP page:* This page displays details about one of the items in the master view page.
- *MasterViewBean class:* This class is used to access the database for the information in the master view JSP.
- *DetailViewBean:* This class is used to access the database for the detail view JSP.
- *Controller servlet class:* This is the servlet class that handles your requests for action.

This exercise uses the Database Web Page Wizard to display all the cruises and the ships that will sail for each cruise in the cruise database:

1. Begin by selecting Open The New Wizard. Select File⇨New. Select Other from the drop-down list. Select Web from the left panel list of resource types. Then select Database Web Pages from the right panel.
2. Click the Next button to start the wizard
3. From the first page of the wizard, click the Browse button next to the Definition Folder dialog box.
4. Open the CSICruise project. Select the `WebApplication` folder, and click OK to close the window. The first page should look like Figure 7-16.

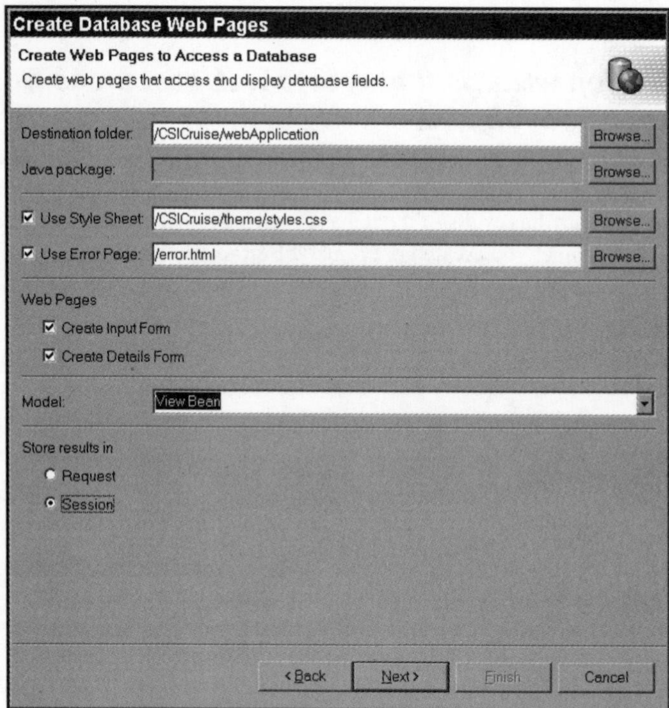

Figure 7-16: This page of the wizard lets you define the style sheet and error page that the generated Web pages use and to determine whether to create an input form and/or a details form for displaying results.

The Java Package dialog box enables you to specify the Java package in which you would like to store the Java classes that the wizard generates. On that page, you set the following options:

- The Use Style Sheet check box indicates whether to use a style sheet for the pages that the wizard generates. If you check the box, you can either enter or browse for the style sheet to use.
- The Use Error Page check box indicates whether to use a Web page to display errors. If you check the box, you can either enter or browse for the Web page to use.
- Check the Create Input Form to indicate whether the wizard should generate an input HTML page.
- Check the Create Details Form to indicate whether the wizard should generate a detail HTML page that can display information for an individual record.
- The Model drop-down list enables you to select the model that you want the wizard to use when generating the classes and JSPs. You have two model options:
  - *View Bean:* This model creates Java classes for connecting and displaying information from the database.
  - *Tag Lib:* This model utilizes a set of custom JSP tags for connecting to and displaying database information.
- The Store Results In option specifies to the wizard whether to store your results in the session or request.

5. Click Next to advance the wizard.
6. The Choose an Existing Select Statement Page of the wizard enables you to select an existing SQL statement in your Web project to use for creating your Web pages. You can skip this page because you will be specifying your own SQL statement. Click Next to advance the wizard.
7. On this page you specify how to create your SQL statement. Selecting the Be Guided through Creating an SQL Statement option enables you to create the statement with the wizard. The Manually Type an SQL Statement option enables you to type the SQL statement. If you have a database model in your project, you can use it to construct the SQL; otherwise, you can connect to the database to create the statement. For this exercise, choose to Be Guided through Creating the SQL Statement and Connect to a Database, and then select Next.
8. The Database Connection wizard page, as shown in Figure 7-17, enables you to enter the connection information for making a connection to the cruise database. Change the connection name to **CruiseCon.**
9. Enter **Cruise** in the Database field. This is the name of the database you want to connect to.
10. If you're not currently logged on as a valid database user, you can enter the user ID and password for connecting to the database.

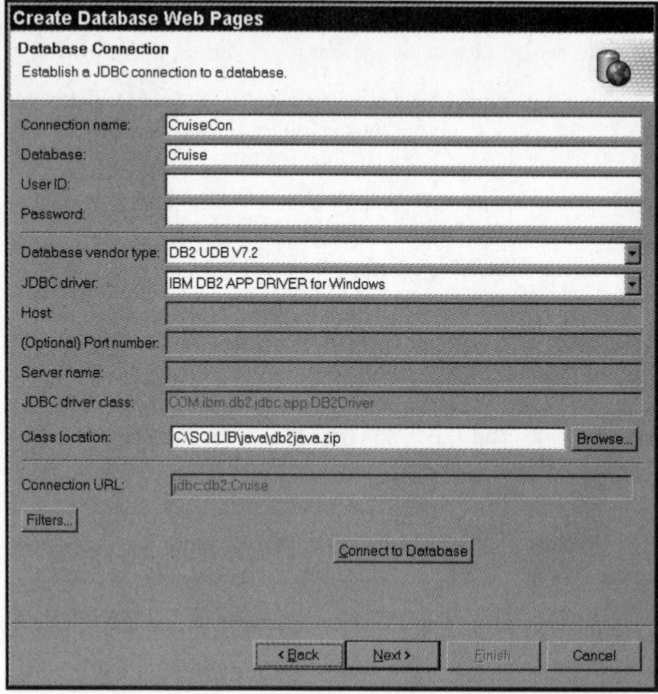

Figure 7-17: This page of the wizard lets you enter the information to connect to the Cruise database.

11. Click the Connect to Database button to connect to the Cruise database; after the database has successfully connnected, click Next.
12. The Construct an SQL Statement page helps you create the SQL statement visually. This page is divided into multiple tabs. Start at the Tables tabs. From the Available Tables panel on the left, click the (+) next to the schema, in this case Administrator. Then click the (+) sign next to the Tables folder to show all the tables in the database.

13. Select the Cruise table from the list of tables and click the > button to add the table to the Selected Tables list.

14. Select the Ship table from the list of tables and click the > button to add the table to the Selected Tables list, as shown in Figure 7-18.

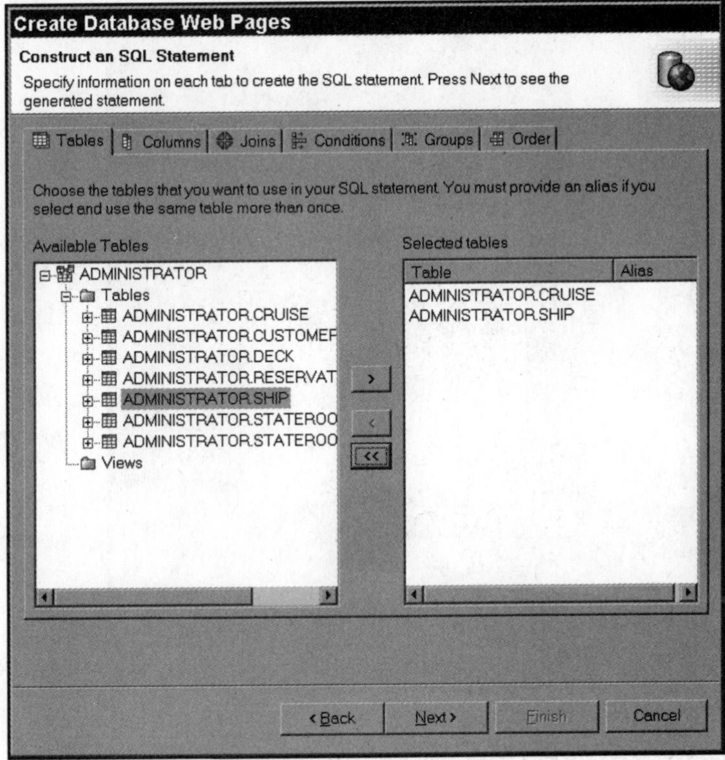

Figure 7-18: This page of the wizard lets you add the tables containing the data you want to query for information.

15. Now click the Columns tab to show the columns panel as shown in Figure 7-19.

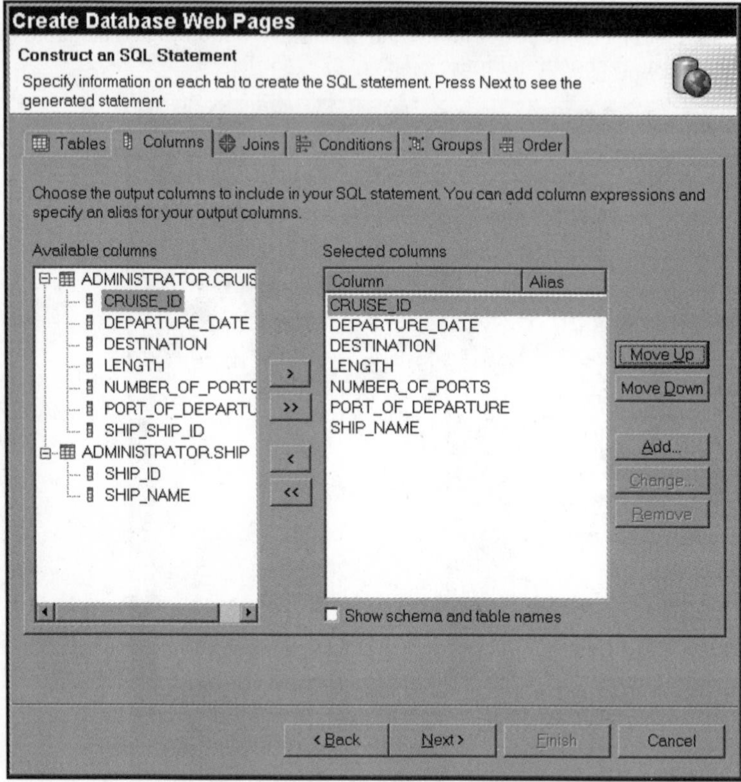

Figure 7-19: This page of the wizard lets you choose the columns from the selected tables that you want to show when displaying the results.

16. From the Available Columns panel on the left, click the (+) signs to open the Cruise and Ship tables to show their columns. By highlighting and clicking the > button, add the following fields from each table to the Selected Columns panel.
    - *Cruise table:* **CRUISE_ID, DEPARTURE_DATE, DESTINATION, LENGTH, NUMBER_OF_PORTS, PORT_OF_DEPARTURE**.
    - Ship table: **SHIP_NAME**
17. Click the Joins tab to display the Joins panel (see Figure 7-20). You use this panel to define how the tables should be joined. Both tables should display in the wizard. Right-click the title bar of the Cruise table and choose Create Join from the drop-down list.

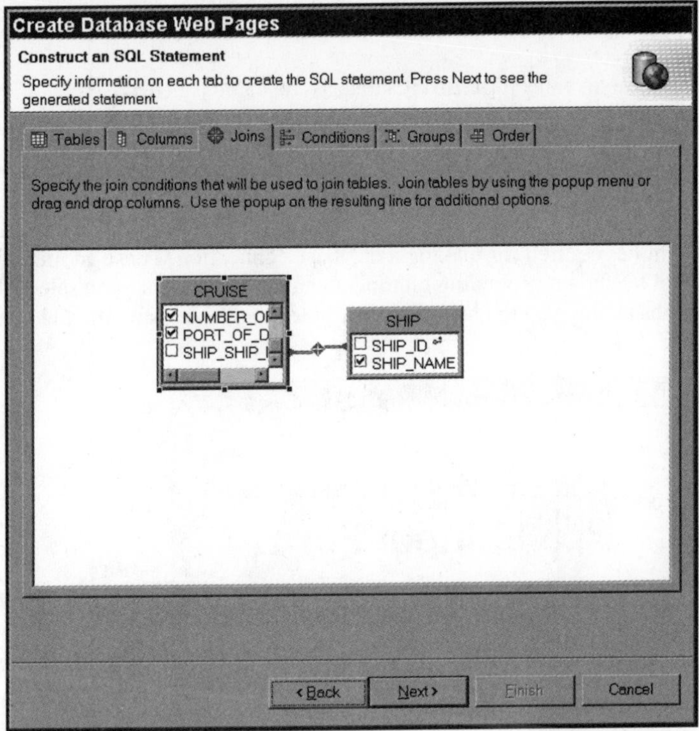

Figure 7-20: This page of the wizard shows you the tables in the database that contains the data to be retrieved. The tables in the example are joined via the SHIP_ID field in each table.

18. From the Source and Target window, select SHIP_SHIP_ID from the Source column drop-down list, and select SHIP as the target table and SHIP_ID as the target column. The join is represented by a line linking the two tables. It should look like the one shown in Figure 7-20. If the line joining the two tables appears different, right-click over the line that joins the two tables and choose Specify Join Type. Choose Inner Join from the list of joins and click OK to modify the join.
19. Click OK to close the window.
20. Click Next to advance to the next page of the wizard.
21. From the Specify Runtime Database Connection Information page, you can specify how the generated classes open a connection the database. Click the Use Driver Manager Connection radio button to choose to use a driver manager for making a database connection.

22. If it is not already present, enter **COM.ibm.db2.jdbc.app.DB2Driver** as the driver name.
23. If it is not already present, enter **jdbc:db2:Cruise** as the database URL.
24. Click Next to advance the wizard.
25. The Design an Input Form page, as shown in Figure 7-21, enables you to customize the input form that you use to submit a request for data from the database. The Host Variables panel enables you to check the host variables, such as database name and other variables that might be required for making a database connection. These additional variables might not be shown depending on model and the options that you select. The Page and Fields tabs enable you to change the attributes of the page and the fields in the input page.

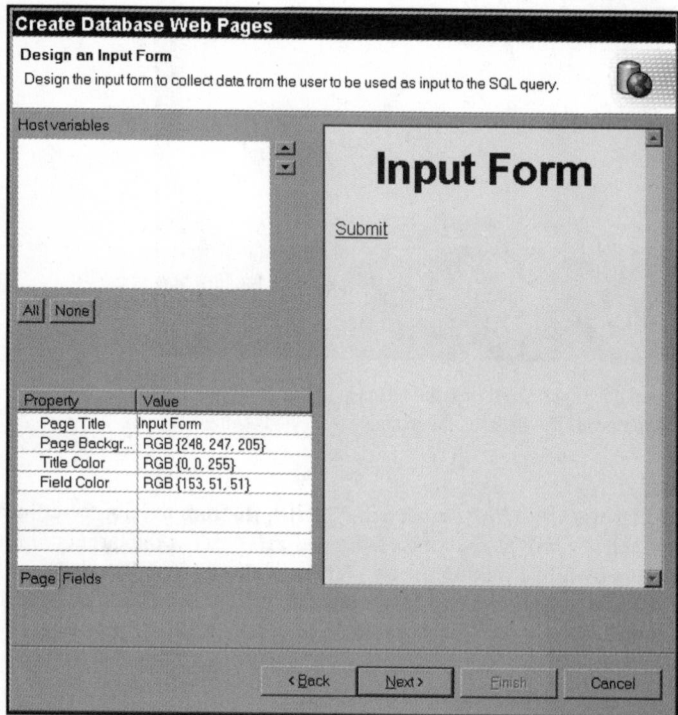

Figure 7-21: Use this window to design the input form that gets generated by the database Webpage Wizard.

26. Click Next to see the Result Table page like the one shown in Figure 7-22. This page of the wizard enables you to change the attributes of the Results Web page that displays the results of your request. The Result Set Columns panel enables you to select the database columns from the results set that you want to see on the Web page. The Page and Fields tabs enable you to change the page and field attributes in the Web page.

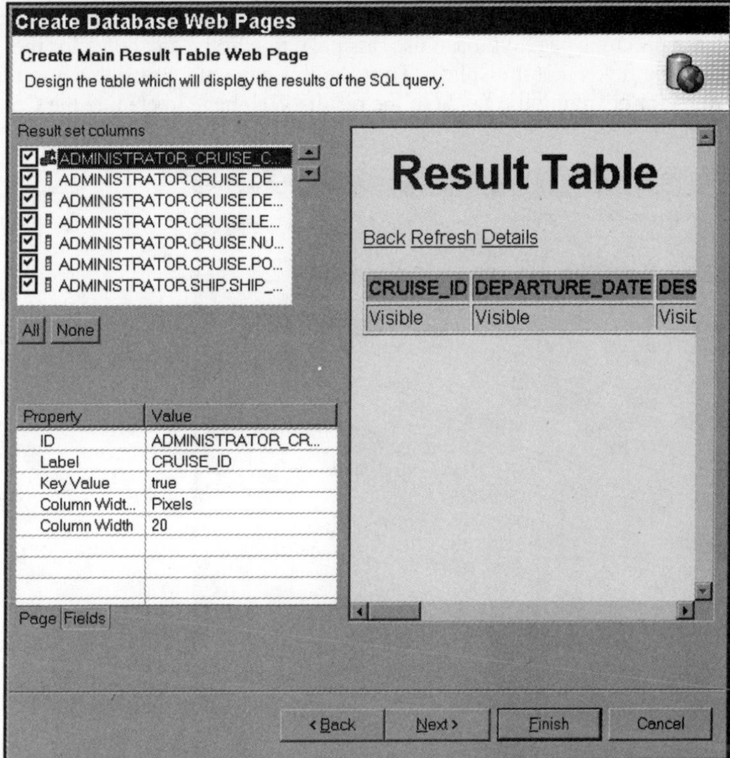

Figure 7-22: This page of the wizard enables you to modify the way the generated result pages appears.

27. Click the Fields tab, if it is not already in focus, and click the first column from the Result Set Columns to display the field's properties.
28. Depending on the way the database was created, the schema name might be included with the column name. This can make it hard to see the results, so customize the Web page to make it more readable. From the Field tab, click the Value field of the Column's Label property and remove the Schema and table name from the value. After you press Enter to accept the change, the preview pane on the right updates automatically.
29. Repeat the previous step for the rest of the columns of the Results set.

NOTE: You can use the All or None buttons under the Result Set Columns panel to include or exclude all of the columns from the list. Also, you can use the Up and Down buttons to the right of the same panel to shift the order in which each columns appears in the Web page.

30. Click Next to advance to the Record Detail design page of the wizard as shown in Figure 7-23. As with the previous page, you can use this page to edit the attributes for the Details page and the fields that it displays. To make this page more readable, use the same instructions for changing the fields of the results Web page to change the Column Labels for this page.

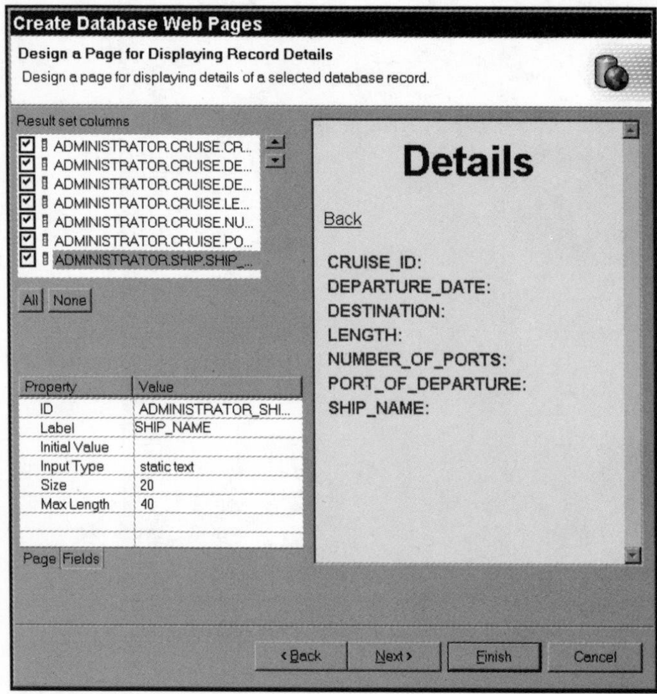

Figure 7-23: This page of the Database Web Page Wizard enables you to modify how the Details Web page displays the data that comes back from a search.

31. Click Next to advance to the Front Controller and View Bean page. This page enables you to choose the methods that you want to use to interact with the database and with the Web pages that get generated.

32. Make sure that the Create a New Front Controller radio button is selected. The Front Controller is a special Java class called a servlet. The servlet is the class that processes your requests via the HTML Forms and Results pages. You can use a pre-existing controller to handle your actions, or you can choose not to create one at all. However, from a design standpoint, it is recommended that you create a controller to handle your actions.

CROSS-REFERENCE: Servlets, also often referred to as Controllers, are discussed in length in Chapter 9.

33. Make sure that the Create View Bean(s) to Wrapper Your Data Object(s) check box is checked. Checking the box tells the wizard to create a set of Java classes that follow a standard pattern for displaying the data from the database. Using View beans for displaying data makes for a more manageable system beacuse it tends to hide the Java code from the Web pages.
34. Click Next to advance to the Specify Prefix page of the wizard and change the value in the Prefix Input box to Cruise. The prefix that you enter is the prefix used for each of the files that the wizard generates.
35. Click the Finish button to generate the files. From the Navigator view window, you see the generated files, as shown in Figure 7-24.

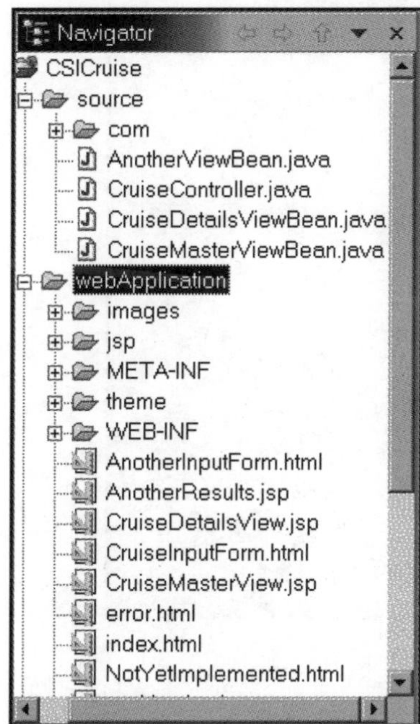

Figure 7-24: This is the Navigator window showing you the newly generated .Java, .html, .jsp files generated by the wizard.

Congratulations, you've just created a set of Web pages and Java classes to interact with the Cruise database to return Cruise data. Now you need to test the new Web pages. But before you can do that, you should perform a build on the Cruise project to make sure that your resources are built properly. The concept of a build is discussed in the next section, "Building projects in WSAD." For now, simply choose Rebuild All from the Project menu.

1. From the Web perspective, open the CSICruise project folder in the Navigator view.
2. Locate and select the `CruiseInputForm.html` file in the WebApplication folder.
3. Either click the Run On Server button from the tool bar, or right-click the file and choose Run On Server from the pop-up menu. WSAD automatically publishes the page and launches it in its internal browser.
4. Click the Submit link to execute the database search and see the results as shown in Figure 7-25.

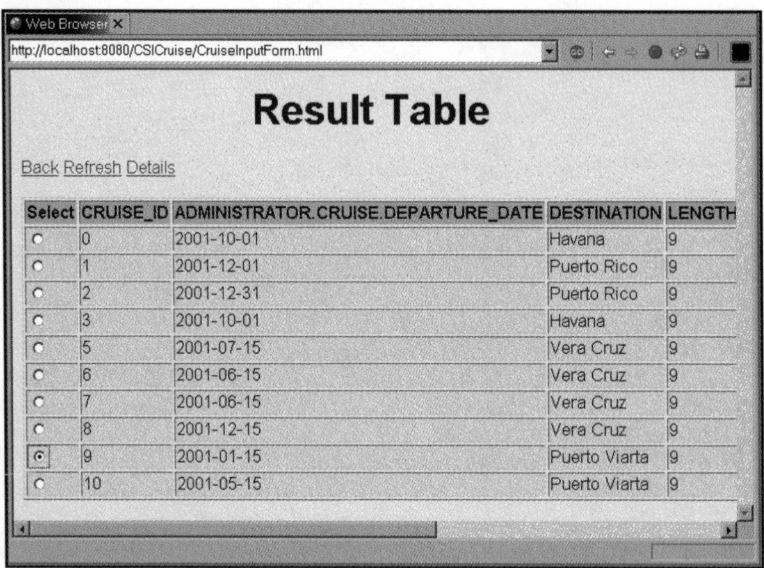

Select	CRUISE_ID	ADMINISTRATOR.CRUISE.DEPARTURE_DATE	DESTINATION	LENGTH
○	0	2001-10-01	Havana	9
○	1	2001-12-01	Puerto Rico	9
○	2	2001-12-31	Puerto Rico	9
○	3	2001-10-01	Havana	9
○	5	2001-07-15	Vera Cruz	9
○	6	2001-06-15	Vera Cruz	9
○	7	2001-06-15	Vera Cruz	9
○	8	2001-12-15	Vera Cruz	9
◉	9	2001-01-15	Puerto Viarta	9
○	10	2001-05-15	Puerto Viarta	9

Figure 7-25: This is the Results Web page that displays the results of executing the SQL statement against the Cruise database.

5. Select one of the cruises by clicking the radio button next to the corresponding cruise record; then click the Details link to display detailed information regarding the selected cruise. You should see a Web page much like the one shown in Figure 7-26.

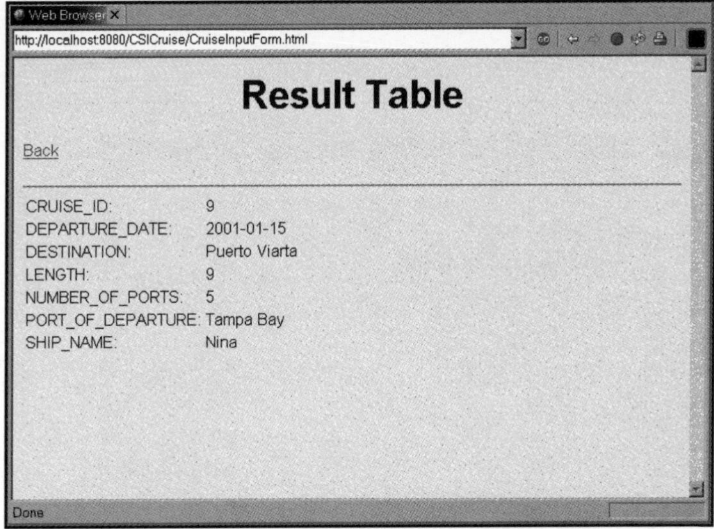

Figure 7-26: The Details page generated by the Database Web Pages Wizard shows you more information for an individual item listed in the Results page.

Building projects in WSAD

A build in WSAD is nothing more than a request for WSAD to validate your resources against a set of rules and to modify or create files based on other resources in your workspace. There are several types of builders in WSAD, including a Java and a Web link builder. The Java builder in WSAD is used to convert your Java source files into Java executable class files. The Web link builder validates and modifies your links as file locations changes. Depending on how you customize your workspace, you can change the way the builders behave.

Building in WSAD is dependent on the Java build path defined for your projects. Not all projects require you to define a build path, such as an enterprise application project. However, any Web or Java project contained in the enterprise application project requires you to define a build path for each project. Build paths are similar to classpaths in Java. Build paths, like classpaths, define the location of required resources. Unlike classpaths, build paths require that you define the order in which the resources should be accessed.

The build path's order is important in WSAD. The builders in WSAD check for resources sequentially. The resources that order lower in the build path depend on the resources defined higher in the classpath. Thus, if you have a class that depends on another class in your project, you should place the dependent class higher in the order of the build path.

To modify the build path for a project, do the following:

1. Select and right-click the project to modify its build path for, and choose Properties from the pop-up menu. A Properties window like the one shown in Figure 7-27 appears.

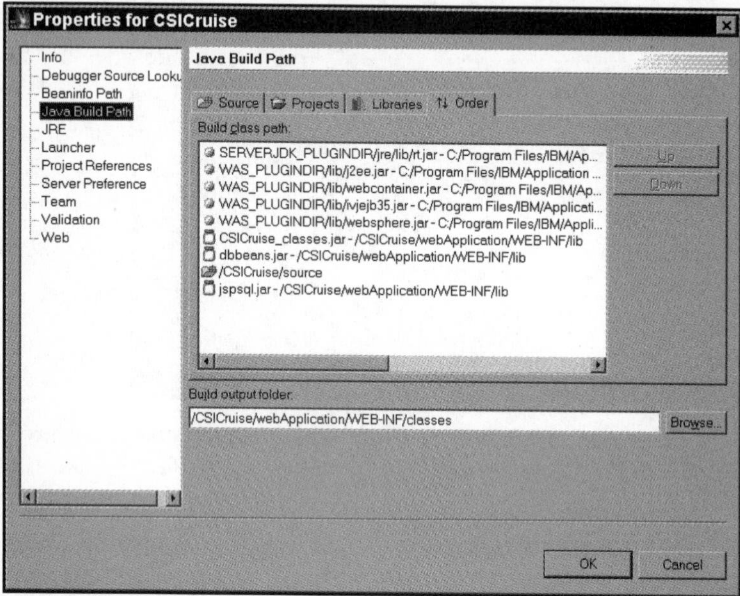

Figure 7-27: This is the Properties page of the CSICruise Web project with the Java Build Path property in focus. The Order tab is opened showing you the order in which the resources are built.

2. In the Properties window, select Java Build Path from the left panel to display the build path for the project.

CROSS-REFERENCE: For a more detailed explanation of each panel for defining the Java Build Path, refer to the earlier section that covers creating and working with projects.

3. Click the Order tab to view how the build path is currently ordered. To manipulate the order of the build path, select the resource to shift and then click the buttons marked Up and Down to reorder their sequence when doing a build.
4. Click OK to apply the change.

Now that you know what a build is and how to prioritize the resources involved in a build, it is time to learn about the different kinds of builds that you can execute in WSAD. There are essentially two ways to perform a build in WSAD: manually and automatically. There are also two types of builds in WSAD: incremental and full builds.

An automatic build is a build that occurs every time a resource is saved and a change is recognized in a resource. A manual build is a build that occurs when the user chooses to execute a build command. There are advantages to using each build type. The automatic build makes it convenient because your build files are kept current and ready for testing. However, a manual build lets you determine when to do a build. You might want to do this if you do not want to incur the extra overhead of building every time you change a resource, especially if the automatic builds present no value.

An incremental build is a build that affects only the resources that are changed and saved in the workspace. WSAD modifies the previous state of the resource to reflect the changes in the build. A full build disregards the previous state of a build and simply builds all the resources from the beginning. Performing incremental builds help to minimize the time it takes to do a build. However, at times, a full build is necessary, especially if your resources were updated externally and you want to refresh your build files.

To use automatic builds, make sure that the Perform Build Automatically on Resource Modification option is checked in the Workbench Preferences window. Every time you modify and save a resource, WSAD builds the resource that changed.

NOTE: To access the Preferences window, choose File⇨Preferences.

To perform a manual build on an individual or group of projects, select the project or projects in the workspace that you want to build and right-click them. From the pop-up menu, choose the Rebuild Project option to perform a build on the selected projects.

Many of the builds that WSAD performs are incremental builds. A manual build and automatic build are by default incremental builds. To perform a full build on a project or a set of projects, highlight all the projects on which you want to perform a full build, and select the Rebuild All option from the Project menu. To perform a full build on the entire workspace, do not select any project and select the Rebuild All option from the Project menu. When installed, WSAD uses automatic builds by default to build your resources.

NOTE: The automatic build performs an incremental build every time you modify and save a resource.

Performing an HTTP/FTP import

WSAD provides a set of wizards that enable you to import your files using the HTTP or FTP protocol. All the import functionality in WSAD can be found by choosing Import from the File menu. You need to have an existing folder to hold the files that you want to import.

To import using HTTP do the following:

1. Choose the Import option from the File menu. Select HTTP from the list of import options and click Next.

2. Enter the URL of the target files or Web site to import in the HTTP URL dialog box. If you need a proxy for making connections, you can click the Advanced button to define the proxy settings:
   - The Host and Default page enables you to enter any host names that you want the Import Wizard to import if it encounters references to them in the target site's Web pages.
   - Depth Limit enables you to specify the number of layers of links the import wizard follows when importing files.
3. Enter the folder to hold the imported files by entering the folder name or browsing to the folder. Click Next to advance to the next page.
4. On the Import Options page, you can specify whether the wizard should convert the links between files to file paths relative to the files themselves. You can also specify whether the wizard should overwrite existing resources without warning or follow the links in the parent folder of the starting URL. Lastly, you can change the timeout (in milliseconds) that the wizard waits for a connection to the target URL.
5. Click the Finish button to begin the file import.

To import using FTP do the following.

1. Choose the Import option from the File menu. Select FTP from the list of import types and click Next.
2. Enter the URL of the FTP site in the FTP URL input box.
3. If the FTP site requires you to authenticate, enter the login and password. Some other options include the following:
   - Check the Use PASV mode to go through the firewall if your network enables you to make only outgoing network connections. The PASV mode specifies that WSAD initiates file transfer activities.
   - Check the Use Firewall check box to specify that you want to use a Socks host server or an FTP proxy server for making connections. If you want to use a Socks server, you must enter the hostname and port number for the server. If you select to use an FTP proxy, you need to specify the firewall type, hostname, port number, and authentication credentials.
   - The List of folders to be excluded from the import input box and Add button enable you to add any folders at the target site that you want WSAD to ignore during the import.
   - The Depth Limit radio buttons and input box enable you to specify the number of layers of folders you want WSAD to dig into before stopping. For example, if you choose No Limit, WSAD explores every folder and subfolder of the target site. However, if you choose the Limit to option and enter a limit of 1, WSAD imports the contents of the root folder of the target site, and if the root folder contains any subfolders, WSAD imports only the subfolders and the files in the folders.

4. In the Folder input box, you can enter the folder name or browse to find the folder from which you want to add the imported files and folders. Click Next to advance the wizard.
5. The Identity Import Options page of the wizard is similar to the one used by the HTTP Import Wizard. The Convert Links to Document Relative specifies that WSAD should automatically convert the links that it finds in the imported files into links relative to other files in the workspace. Otherwise, WSAD leaves the links alone. The Overwrite Existing Resources with Warning check box specifies whether WSAD should ask you if it is okay to overwrite a files that already exist in the folder that you want to import into. The Connection Timeout input box enables you to enter the time (in milliseconds) that you allot to WSAD for making a connection with the FTP site.
6. Click the Finish Button to commence importing.

You've now imported a Web site into your workspace using the FTP protocol.

Importing ZIP/JAR/WAR/EAR files into WSAD

You might know what a ZIP file and JAR file is, but you might not know what WAR or EAR files are. WSAD supports all these files types. This section discusses EAR and Jar files briefly before continuing to talk about importing them in WSAD.

A *JAR file* is the acronym for a Java Archive file and is similar to a ZIP file. As with a ZIP file, you can create and store an entire set of files into one single compressed file. However, JAR files are not ZIP files. JAR files do more than serve as a storage device. JAR files are used mainly for packaging the resources that a Java application needs to run (including the application itself) into a single file or multiple files. You can point to a JAR file in a class or build path to make its contents available to the runtime environment.

> **NOTE:** Unlike a ZIP file, a JAR file can also contain a MANIFEST.INF files which are text files that contain additional information about the contents of the JAR. One important piece of information found in the MANIFEST.INF file is the Main-Class entry. The Main-Class entry specifies the name of the file in the JAR that contains the necessary code to launch the application. With this entry, you can use the `java -jar <jar file name>` to run an application contained within a JAR, without having to know the name of the application to launch.

A *WAR file* is the acronym for a Web Application Archive file and is similar to a JAR file. Both file types are used for packaging application resources and applications. However, unlike a JAR file, a WAR file must conform to an additional set of rules for packaging its applications. The WAR file type is defined in the J2EE specification to help speed up the configuration, packaging, and deployment of Web applications. WAR files not only contain the HTML, JSP, JAR, image, and other resource files for an entire application, they also contain special deployment descriptor files that tell the server where they will be deployed and how to configure itself to receive the application. This feature makes it possible for you to configure an application and see these changes implemented after you deploy a WAR file to the target server environment. It also makes your development environment similar to the actual target environment.

An *EAR file* is the acronym for an Enterprise Application Archive. An EAR file is similar to a WAR file because an EAR file is also used to package applications. However, an EAR file can contain one or more WAR files. An EAR file can also contain JAR files. EAR files are a part of the J2EE specification and, like a WAR file, they must adhere to a set of rules for packaging its content. EAR files are used to make configuring, packaging, and deploying enterprise applications easier. You can package multiple applications into an EAR file and deploy them all to an application server, such as WebSphere Application Server 4.0.

In short, EAR files are used to package WAR files, JAR files, EJB JAR files, and other resources that are needed to deploy your applications successfully. A WAR file is used for deploying only Web applications. JAR files are mainly used for packaging Java applications and resources.

To import a JAR or ZIP file, do the following:

1. Select the Import option from the File menu. Select the ZIP file option from the list of import types and click Next to advance to the ZIP file import window as shown in Figure 7-28.

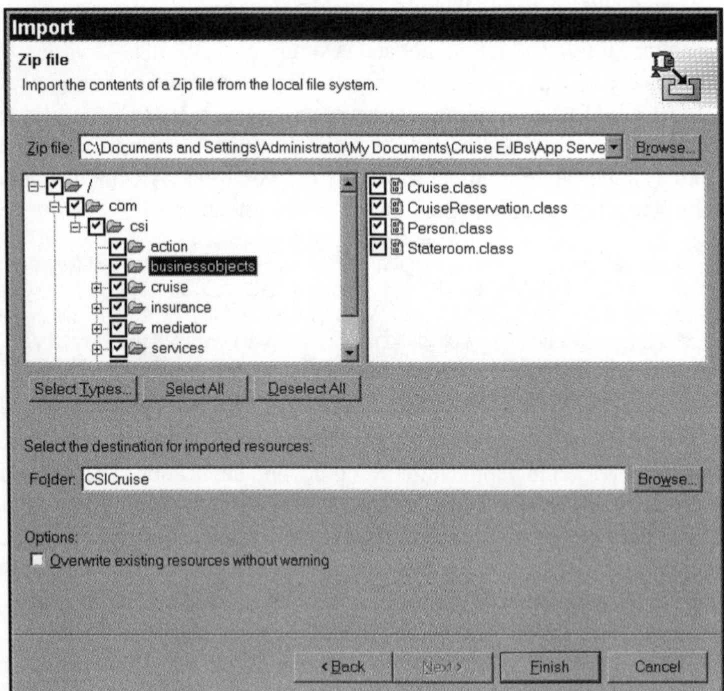

Figure 7-28: This is the page of the ZIP File Import Wizard where you can browse for the ZIP or JAR file to import into your projects.

2. Either enter or browse the path to the ZIP or JAR file.
3. From the left panel, you can check the folders and subfolders that you want to include in and exclude from the import. You can also use the shortcut buttons to select or deselect the folders to import.
4. The right panel shows the contents of a folder or subfolder that you can choose to include in and uncheck to exclude from the import.
5. In the Folder input box, you need to enter the folder in your workspace to which you want to import the selected files.
6. Check the Overwrite Existing Resources without Warning option if you want WSAD to overwrite any resources without ask you.
7. Click the Finish button to begin importing the contents of the files.

> **NOTE:** When importing JAR files into the same folder, you might be asked whether you want to overwrite the `MANIFEST.INF` files that were imported in previous import sessions. If you want to keep separate `MAINFEST.INF` files, you should consider importing JAR files into separate folders.

To import a WAR file, do the following:

1. Select the Import option from the File menu.
2. Select the WAR file option from the list of import types and click Next to launch the WAR File Import Wizard as shown in Figure 7-29.
3. Enter the path to the WAR file or browse the file system for the file.
4. Enter the name of the Web project that you want to use for the application that you're going to import.
5. Enter the context root name for the application. The context root is usually the name of the top-level directory for your application after it is deployed to the server. By default, the context root is the same as the Web project name.
6. Enter the name of the enterprise application project that will contain the imported Web application.
7. Again, you can select the option to have WSAD overwrite any existing resources without notification.
8. Click the Next button to advance to the next page.
9. If there are any available JAR files that the application depends upon, you can select them using the Module Dependencies page.

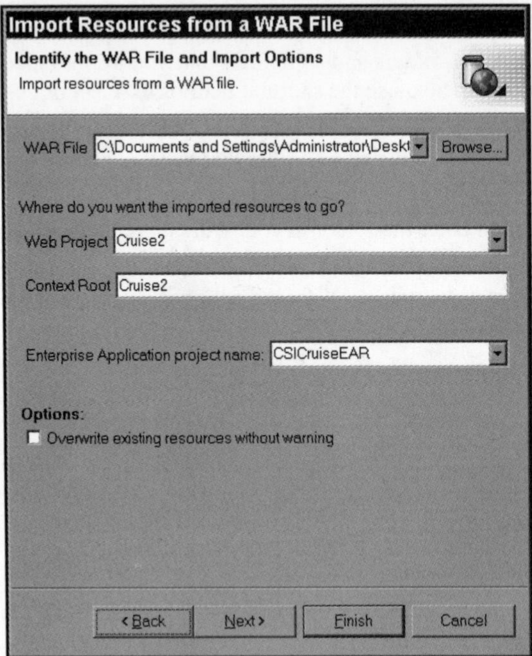

Figure 7-29: This page of the WAR File Import Wizard lets you define the name of the Web project and the context root name used to access the Web application.

10. Click the Next button to advance to the Define Java Build Settings page.
11. This page and the layered tabs within it enable you to define the resources that are available to the application when doing a build of its resources. The Source tab enables you to create additional source folders. The Projects tab enables you to select any projects in the workspace that you want to include in the build path. The Libraries tab enables you to add additional resources in the form of folders and JARs to the build path. Finally, the Order tab enables you to define the order in which the resources are accessed and compiled in the build.
12. Click the Finish button to begin importing the WAR files into your workspace.

To import an EAR file, do the following:

1. Select the Import option from the File menu.
2. Select the EAR file option from the list of import types and click Next to launch the EAR File Import Wizard as shown in Figure 7-30.

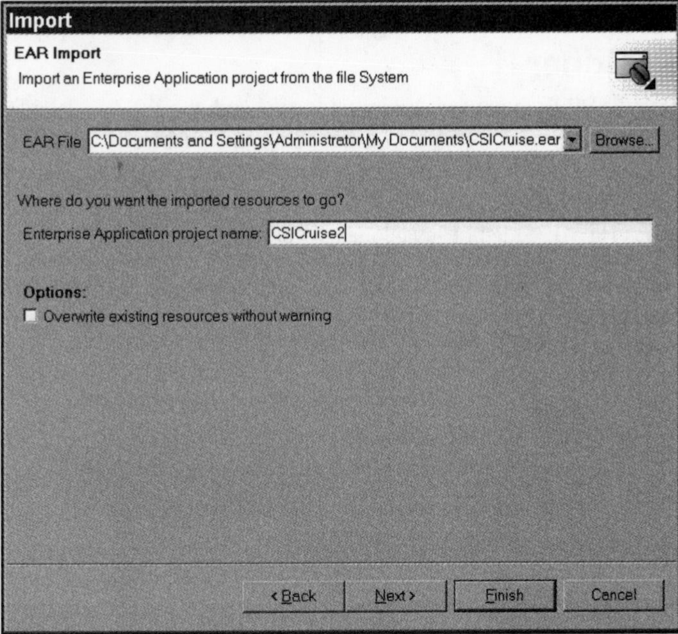

Figure 7-30: This page of the EAR File Import Wizard lets you browse for the EAR files to import.

3. Enter the path to the EAR file in the EAR File input box or browse the file system for the file.
4. Enter the name of the EAR project that you want to create or use for the enterprise application in the Enterprise Application project name input box.
5. Click Next to advance to the next page of the wizard.
6. The Manifest Class-Path page enables you to select the available dependent JAR files for each module file found in the EAR file, thus making the JAR files available in the build path for the module. You can always do this after importing the EAR file by modifying the build path for each imported module. To add an available dependent JAR for a module file, simply select the module from the left panel and then select the JAR files that the module depends upon. By setting the dependent JAR files for each module, you are also modifying the classpath in the module's `MANIFEST.INF` file.
7. Click Next to advance to the last page of the wizard.
8. The EAR Modules page enables you to rename the project names for each module that you are importing. To rename a project, click the default name under the New Project Name column, and type the new project name.
9. Click Finish to begin importing the EAR file.

Now that you are more familiar with JAR, WAR, and EAR files, you should be able to follow the instructions to import the all the sample files for this book.

Developing JSP and HTML pages in WebSphere Studio Page Designer

Development of HTML and JSP Web pages is mainly done through the WSAD Page Designer editor. Page Designer is a what-you-see-is-what-you-get editor that enables you to see the resulting Web page as you are designing it. In combination with the views in the Web perspective and the editor's toolbars and menu options, you can quickly put together a Web page that not only includes HTML code but Java code as well.

To demonstrate how you can develop your own HTML and JSP Web pages in WSAD, this section shows you how to use WSAD to create a simple HTML page and then modify the same page into a JSP page:

1. First, make sure that you are currently in the Web perspective. Then choose File⇨New⇨Other.
2. From the New window, as shown in Figure 7-31, select Web from the left panel and HTML page from the right panel.

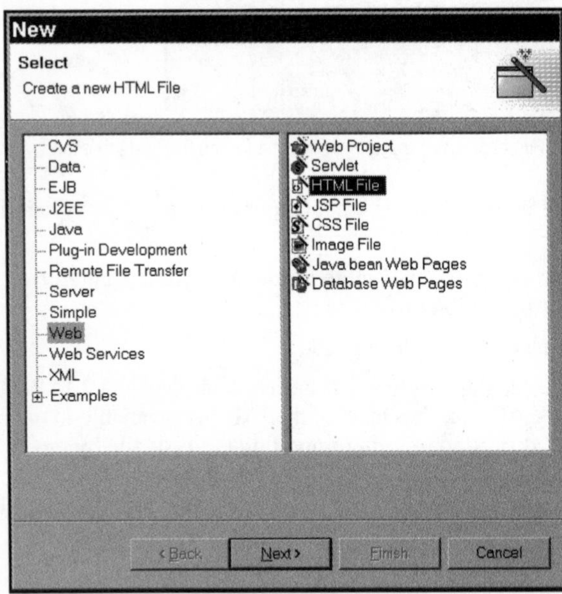

Figure 7-31: This window shows you a list of all the wizards that you can use in WSAD.

3. Click the Next button to advance the wizard to the Create an HTML File window as shown in Figure 7-32.

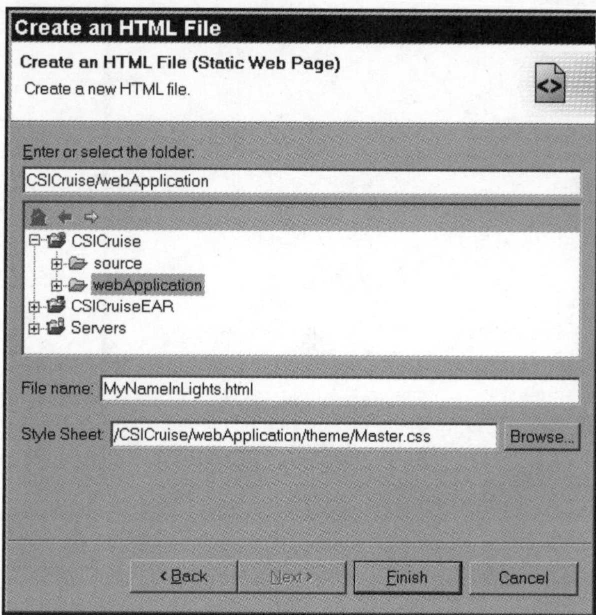

Figure 7-32: This page of the HTML Wizard enables you to name the new HTML file and also to define where you would like to store the generated file.

4. Enter or select the folder in which you want to put the new HTML file.
5. In the File Name box, type the filename for the new HTML file.
6. Click Finish to add the file to your project. The new HTML file should open automatically in the Page Designer editor as shown in Figure 7-33.
7. If Page Designer is not already opened with the new file displaying in the Design tab, locate the file via the Navigator view and double-click the file to open the file in a new Page Designer editor. Make sure the editor is currently opened in the Design tab.

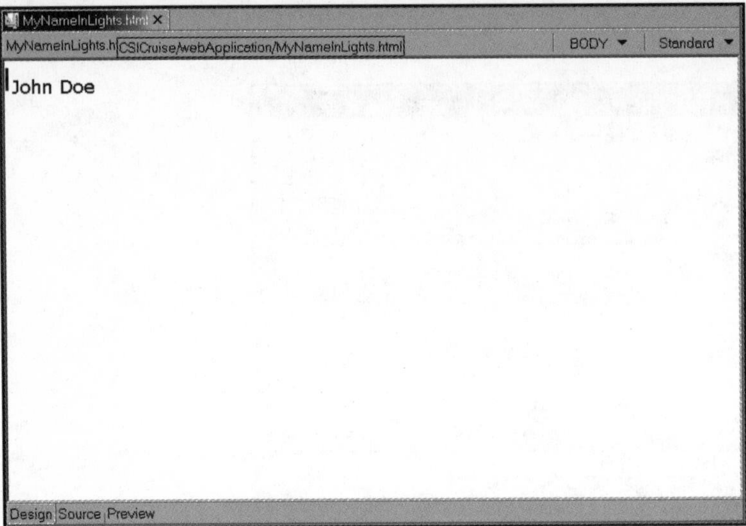

Figure 7-33: Use the Page Designer editor to edit your HTML page. The Design tab is currently in focus.

8. Replace the default text in the body of the Web page to include your full name.
9. Save the Web page by choosing Save from the File menu.

Now that you have created the HTML page, you can test it by right-clicking the file from the Navigator view and choosing the Run on Server option from the pop-up menu. WSAD publishes your page to the test environment and opens the page in the internal Web browser, as shown in Figure 7-34.

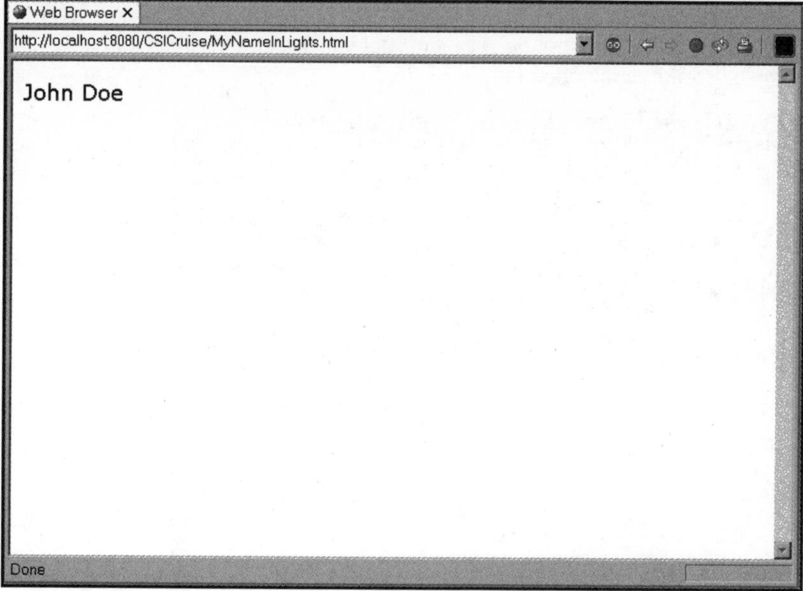

Figure 7-34: This is how your new HTML page looks in the WSAD Web browser when you choose the Run on Server option.

Now turn your HTML page into a JSP by generating your full name through Java scriplet code:

1. Switch back to the Web perspective by choosing Open⇨Web from the Perspectives menu.
2. Switch to the Page Designer editor that has the new HTML file already opened.
3. Remove all the text from the body of the HTML page. With the cursor in the body of the HTML page, select the Insert Scriptlet option from the JSP menu.

4. From the Script window, locate the library panel at the lower-left side, and double-click the Display a String on the Page option. The scriptlet panel on the right should now contain a sample script like the one in Figure 7-35.

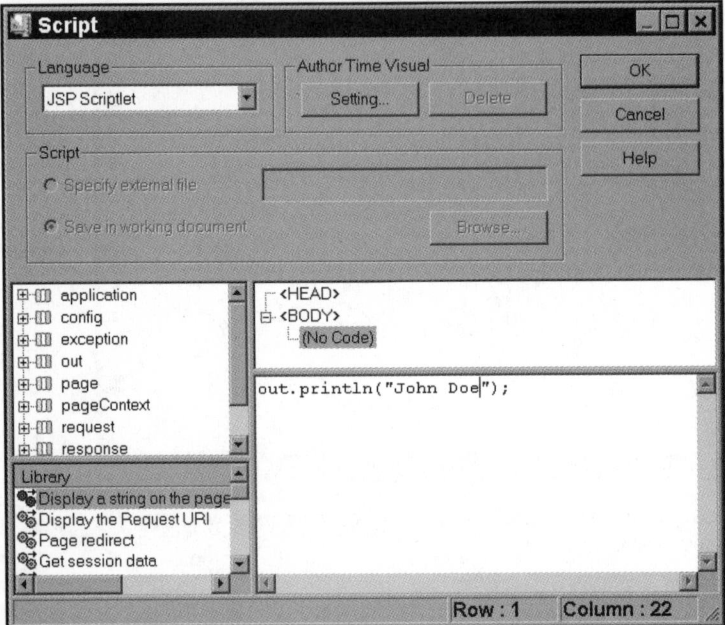

5. **Figure 7-35:** This window helps you add your scriptlets to your JSPs.

6. Replace the words within the parentheses with your full name surrounded by double-quotes:

```
out.println(“Type your string here”);
```

The scriptlet should now looks something like this:

```
out.println(“John Doe”);
```

7. Click the OK button to insert the scriptlet into the body of the HMTL page. The scriptlet shows up as an icon in the body of the page. Choose File⇨Save to save the changes.

8. For the server to treat your new page as a JSP, you need to rename the file with a `.jsp` extension. Locate the HTML file from the Navigator view and right-click the file to open the pop-up menu.

9. Choose Rename from the pop-up menu, replace the `.html` extension with the `.jsp` extension, and press Enter to accept the change.

You just turned your HTML page into a JSP page. Retest your changes by repeating the steps you used to test the original HTML page. You should notice a delay while the server compiles the JSP file into a servlet class and runs the new code scriptlet you inserted. However, the output in the browser should look the same as before.

Editing support for cascading style sheets (CSS)

WSAD's internal CSS editor enables you to design your cascading style sheets in many different ways and with the help of many different views. The CSS editor, in conjunction with the Outline and the Styles views, lets you see, create, and edit your style rules. When you open a `.css` file in WSAD, the CSS editor opens in the Source view, showing you the actual code that defines the style rules. You can edit the source of the style sheet directly; however, you can have the tool do the work for you. For example, invoking the CSS editor also changes the outline editor to display your style rules as a tree of rules and their properties. You can quickly navigate to a style rule or the rule's property from the Navigator view, and the editor automatically highlights the correct line of code. The Style view also lists the names and descriptions of each style rule in the document. Double-clicking a style name in the Style view invokes a Style Rule editor window for that rule and lets you change its properties. This makes it much easier to edit style sheets because it can be a challenge to remember all the properties that you assign to a rule. The Style view also contains a lot of shortcut buttons that you can use to edit, open, and create style rules for the opened style sheet.

Creating servlets

WSAD makes creating servlets almost painless. A servlet is an application that runs on an application server and waits for requests from client programs. In fact, you already created a servlet in the previous exercise. The JSP that you created in the previous exercise, when accessed, is automatically converted into a servlet by the test environment server. WSAD provides a Servlet Wizard that walks you through creating a servlet for a Web project in your workspace. WSAD does most of the work of creating the `Servlet` class and registering the servlet to the Web application. For fun, try creating a servlet that mimics the JSP you created in the prior exercise.

Follow these steps to create the servlet:

1. Choose File⇨New ⇨Servlet to launch the Servlet Wizard shown in Figure 7-36.

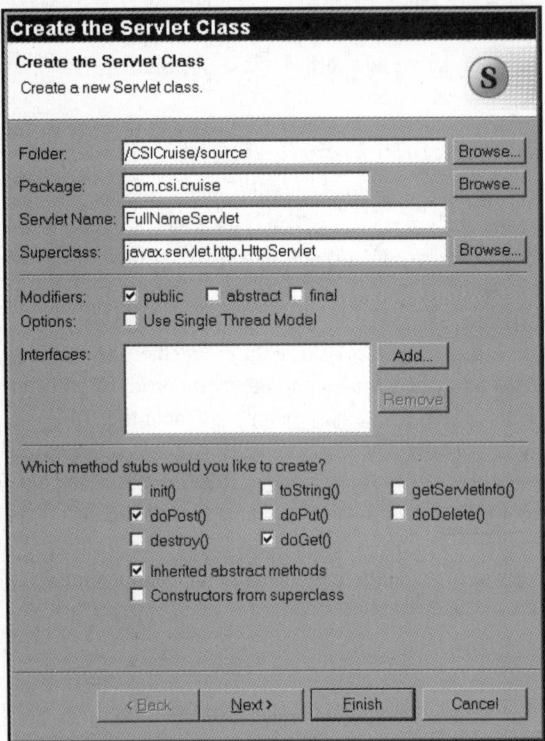

Figure 7-36: This page of the Servlet Wizard enables you to define the servlet that you want to create.

2. Enter or browse the source folder for the project to which you want to add the servlet code.
3. Enter the package name for the servlet to create and enter a name for the servlet to create.
4. Click the Next button to accept all other default options.
5. The Define the Servlet in the Deployment Descriptor menu is where you can change the way you want the servlet to be deployed to the test server.
   - Check the Add to Web.xml check box if you want WSAD to add the servlet to the Web application's deployment descriptor. This automatically makes the servlet available to your Web application.
   - Enter the display name in the Display Name dialog box to identify the servlet.
   - The Mappings table enables you to map different URLs for the same servlet.
   - The Init Parameters table enables you to set any initialization parameters to the servlet that gets generated.

6. Finally, click Finish to add the servlet to the Web application.

The new Servlet file should automatically open in a Java editor. To have the servlet return your full name, you need to add scriptlet of code into the servlet just as you did when you worked with the JSP:

1. Modify the `doGet()` method body of the servlet to include the following line of code.

```
public void doGet(javax.servlet.http.HttpServletRequest request,
javax.servlet.http.HttpServletResponse response ) throws
javax.servlet.ServletException, java.io.IOException {

    response.getWriter().println("John Doe");

}
```

2. Save the servlet by choosing Save from the File menu.
3. Now test your new servlet as before. Only this time, you need to locate the new servlet, right-click the servlet class, and choose the Run on Server option. The servlet is published to the server, and the browser responds with the same page that was generated by the HTML and JSP pages, as shown in Figure 7-37.

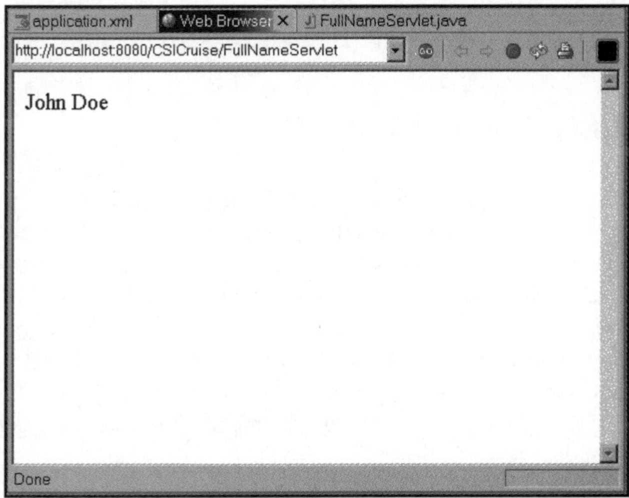

Figure 7-37: The output that your new servlet should generate when you point your browser to the servlet's URL in the WSAD Web browser.

Deploying with WebSphere Studio Application Developer

Before deploying your applications to WAS 4.0, you need to make sure that the deployment descriptors for your application are configured correctly. Deployment descriptors are XML files that store configuration information for the modules in your application. The perspective most suited for editing these descriptors is the J2EE perspective because the perspective is geared for the role of an application assembler.

You should be concerned with two deployment descriptors when deploying your applications: the `web.xml` and `application.xml` descriptors. The `web.xml` stores the configuration information for a Web application, whereas the `application.xml` deployment descriptor stores configuration information for an enterprise application. The descriptors are actual files located in the `WEB-INF` folder of each project. To edit the `web.xml` or `application.xml` descriptor while in the J2EE perspective, choose to open the module from the J2EE view and the default editor for each descriptor opens automatically. You can also open the descriptors from other perspectives by opening the file straight from the Navigator view. The `web.xml` and `application.xml` editors enable you to edit the deployment descriptor graphically. However, you can also choose to edit the file manually by changing to the Source tab while in each editor.

Deployment of your applications with WSAD is accomplished through exporting WAR, and EAR files. The WAR and EAR files that WSAD generates meet the J2EE specification and require little configuration after the files are created. The target server need only import the WAR or EAR file. However, if your intention is to test your application on a remote test server, such as WebSphere Application Server Advanced Single Server Edition 4.0, you can deploy to the server by transferring the files over an FTP session or export and then import WAR and EAR files.

Using FTP to transfer files to a server

WSAD provides two mechanisms for transferring your files to a remote instance of WAS 4.0 Advanced Single Server Edition: copying the files directly or using FTP. Each mechanism is supported through remote transfer instances. A remote transfer instance is nothing more than an XML configuration file that stores information, such as the target directory, password information, and the host address. The remote transfer instances are then assigned to remote server instances. Any time you create a remote server instance, you are prompted to create a remote transfer instance or to choose an existing one to use for publishing to the target server. After your server instance is set up with a remote transfer instance, you can begin testing your applications on the remote server. WSAD handles the transferring of your files every time you start your remote test server.

CROSS-REFERENCE: Refer to Chapter 8 for instructions on creating server instances and configurations.

Introducing Java Development Features

Java development in WSAD can be done in many perspectives in WSAD. Although you can open a `.java` file into a Java editor from any perspective, the perspective of choice for developing Java classes is the Java perspective. The views that comprise the Java perspective are the most suited for developing Java code. In addition to views and editors, WSAD provides wizards for creating projects, packages, classes, and interfaces. The wizards walk you through a series of windows prompting you for such information as method modifiers and return types.

By default the Java perspective comprises the Packages, Hierarchy, Outline, Tasks, Search, and Console views. The Enterprise Bean Java editor is the default editor for all your `.java` files. The views in the perspective are used to support the Java editor. For example, selecting an item in the Outline view automatically highlights the section of the source code that the item occupies.

Another feature that you might find useful for Java code in WSAD is Content Assist. Content Assist shows you all the methods and variables available to you at the time you requested assistance. To access Content Assist while working with JSP code or Java source code, press and hold the Ctrl button and then press the spacebar.

WSAD also offers some tools for refactoring your Java code, such as changing package names and method names. *Refactoring* is the term used to describe the process of transforming your Java code so that it adheres better to object-oriented best practices while preserving the original behavior of the code.

Using the Java editor

The default editor for your Java source code is the Enterprise Bean Java editor. The editor is much like an ordinary text editor, but it offers some powerful features and tools for viewing and editing your Java code. One such feature of the editor is its capability to highlight your Java code based on syntax. Each piece of code is highlighted based on whether it is a Java keyword, method name, comment, and so on.

The default behavior of the Java text editor is to show you the entire content of your source code file. This may be undesirable if you are used to working with a Java development tool, such as VisualAge for Java, which shows you only the section of source code that you selected in an outline similar to the Outline view. WSAD enables you to mimic this behavior when you select Show Source of Selected Element Only. When the Show Source of Selected Element Only feature is turned on, and you select an element from the Outline view to show in the Java editor, the editor displays only the selected element.

NOTE: The Show Source of Selected Element Only button is available only when the Java editor is in focus.

Understanding Java elements

A Java element is a unit of code that represents something. For example, an import statement in your Java source is considered a Java element. A series of import statements is also considered a Java element. A method is considered a Java element. The Outline view shown in Figure 7-38 lets you work with the Java elements in your Java code by displaying them as an outline. You can quickly navigate from element to element as you edit them.

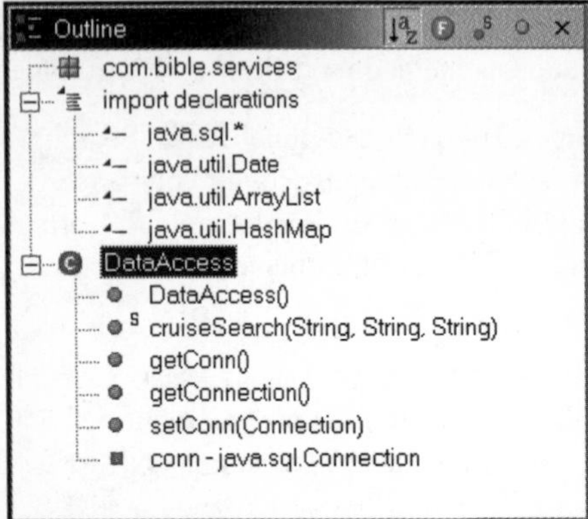

Figure 7-38: The Outline view window shows you all the elements in the Java editor in an outline form. You can easily navigate to an element by selecting it.

Java elements are displayed in the Outline view by special symbols in an outline form that shows how each element is related to the others. For example, a green solid circle next to an element indicates that the element has a public modifier. A green solid circle with an *s* superscript indicates that the element has a public static modifier. Outline view also enables you to filter some of these elements by their modifiers. You can hide or show fields in a class, static members of a class, or nonpublic members of a class by selecting one of the three filter options located on the Outline view's title bar. You will become familiar with each modifier as you begin to create Java classes in the Java perspective.

Specifying alternative JREs

WSAD supports the testing of Java code on different versions of the Java runtime environment. When installed, WSAD provides a default JRE for building and running all your Java programs within your workspace. You can override the default JRE by installing another JRE and making it the new default. This means that you can install other versions of Java on your computer and develop and test your Java code against each version.

NOTE: Refer to Chapter 5 on a refresher on JREs and JDKs.

To do this, you need to have each version of the Java runtime environment that you would like to test installed first. You then need to perform the following steps to set up WSAD for testing using the new JREs. First you need to add the JREs to WSAD by doing the following:

1. Choose Preferences from the Window menu. From the list of preferences on the left panel, expand the Java preferences by clicking the adjacent (+) sign.
2. Select Installed JREs from the list of Java preferences to show a list of installed Java Runtime Environments like the one in Figure 7-39.

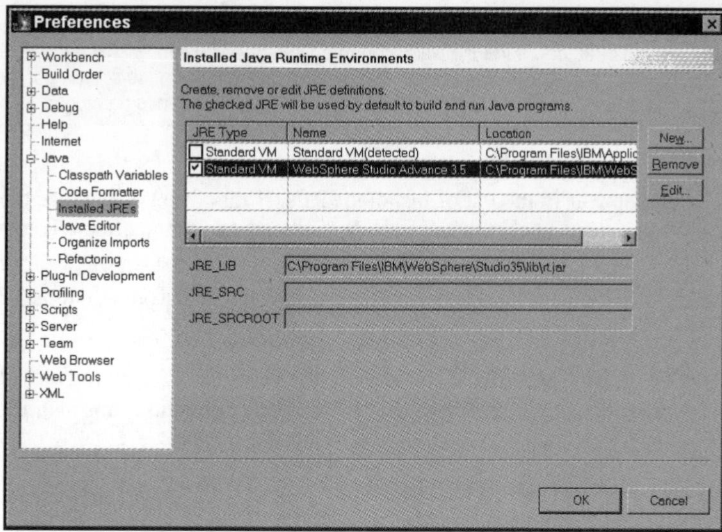

Figure 7-39: The Preferences page for the WSAD workbench, shown here with the installed JRE's Preference page currently in focus. Use it to define any new JREs that you want to add to the current WSAD workbench.

3. Click the New button to define a newly installed JRE. The Add JRE window, as shown in Figure 7-40, enables you to define the JRE.

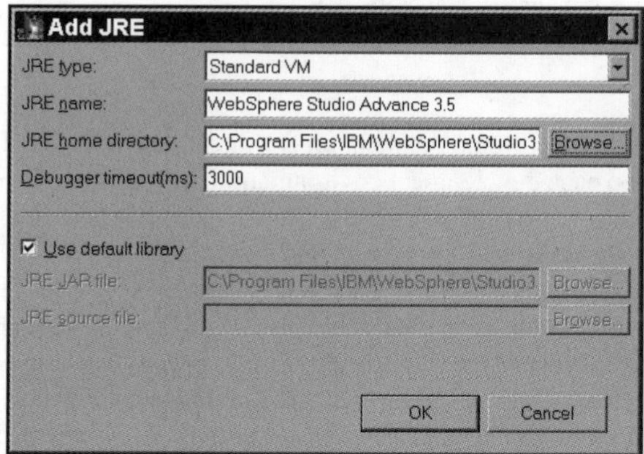

Figure 7-40: To add an installed JRE to the WSAD workbench, you need to define the type of JRE that you want to add, including the name of the JRE and the location of the files for the JRE.

4. Select Standard VM from the JRE type drop-down list. Enter the name that you want to use to display for this JRE.
5. Enter the installation path where you installed the JRE into the JRE Home directory input box or click the Browse button to locate the folder.

TIP: If the Use Default Library check box is checked, WSAD attempts to locate the `rt.jar` file in the path entered as the JRE Home directory. If the file is located in a directory, you can uncheck the box and define your own path to the `rt.jar` file. Also, you can optionally define a path to the source code of the JRE. This can be useful if you need to see the source code of the `rt.jar` file while debugging.

6. Click OK to add the JRE to WSAD.
7. The new JRE should appear in the list of installed JREs. But before you can use the new JRE as the default, you need to check the check box adjacent to it and click OK to accept the changes.
8. You can repeat these same steps to add any number of other JREs from versions 1.1.7 to 1.4.

Your workspace is set up to use a new JRE. You can use the new JRE for running any of your Java applications in your workspace. To change the JRE that an application runs against, do the following:

1. While in the Java perspective, select the project that holds the Java application that you want to run from the Packages view.
2. Right-click the project and choose Properties from the pop-up menu.
3. From the list of properties on the left panel, choose JRE. Click the radio button adjacent to the Use Custom JRE for Launching option.
4. From the list of JREs, select the JRE that you want to use to run your application against and click OK to accept the changes.

Your application is set up to test and run against a custom JRE.

Summary

This chapter introduced you to WebSphere Studio Application Developer and WebSphere Studio Site Developer and compared each development environment. It also discussed the concepts of and differences between a workspace and the workbench in WebSphere Studio Application Developer. One of the significant concepts in WSAD is the notion of a perspective, which is the attempt to show you, the developer, a view of your resources in term of your role. This concept is supposed to help keep your concerns isolated to your particular role. To introduce you to perspectives, this chapter discussed the many pieces that come together to form a perspective: its views, editors, and menus. After getting acquainted with some of the concepts, features, and tools, you began using WSAD to build new projects and explore some of the wizards that WSAD has to offer. You used the same wizards to create Java applications using HTML, JSPs, and servlets to pull data from the Cruise database. You were then introduced to the Java development tools and features that WSAD has to offer.

Chapter 8
Testing with WSAD

In This Chapter

- Understanding the WebSphere test environment
- Using the default server instance
- Adding a server instance
- Adding a server configuration
- Adding a project to a server configuration
- Adding a data source to a server configuration
- Publishing and testing a project
- Introducing the debugging tool

As a developer you probably spend as much time, if not more, testing and debugging than you do actually writing code. Most of this testing and debugging happens as you're coding. To facilitate this testing, a local full version of the WebSphere Application Server Single Server Edition comes pre-installed with WebSphere Studio Application Developer (WSAD) 4.0.

With the WebSphere test environment, you can test and debug your live server code, JavaServer Pages (JSPs), servlets, Enterprise JavaBeans (EJBs), and JavaBeans as though you were on an actual implementation of the full WAS 4.0 (Advanced Edition) version.

The main focus of this book is WebSphere, so this chapter deals exclusively with the WebSphere test environment. In this chapter, you set up the WebSphere test environment to test your Almost Free Cruise Web Application straight from your workbench. You create a new server project, server instance, and server configuration. You add your Cruise Enterprise Application (EAR) project to your new server instance, publish the project to the server, and then launch the application.

> **NOTE:** The exercises used in this chapter require that you already have all the Almost Free Cruise projects imported into your WebSphere Studio Application Developer workspace. Refer to Chapter 7 for instructions on importing the Almost Free Cruise enterprise application EAR file.

Setting Up the Test Environment

You have the options of testing your code either straight from the workbench, on a local server installation, or on a remote server installation. When testing your code from the workbench, you're actually testing your code straight from the file system, which enables you to add, remove, or change those resources without having to restart the test server. WSAD has the potential to support many other test environments via its plug-in capabilities. However, currently the only application server environments supported by WSAD are WebSphere Application Server and Apache Tomcat. Apache is available for download on the Web for free, and its server code is open source. Before deciding on which of the two environments you would like to use, you should be aware of the types of projects and server instances that the runtime can support, as illustrated in Tables 8-1 and 8-2.

NOTE: WSAD's server tool feature currently supports only Tomcat versions 3.2 and 4.0. However, some beta versions of WSAD support only the beta 5 version of Tomcat 4.0.Features such as SSL and HTTPS are fully supported by WebSphere Application Server, but are not enabled in the WebSphere test environment.

The WebSphere test environment does not function if the WSAD workbench is installed in a directory with a $ in its name.

Table 8-1: Types of Server Instances Supported by the WAS and Tomcat Runtime Environments

Server Instance Type	*WebSphere Application Server*	*Tomcat*
Test environment	Yes	Yes
Local server	Yes	Yes
Remote server	Yes	No

WebSphere Studio Application Developer enables you to test your applications in different ways depending on the type of server instance that you use. The following list shows how WebSphere Studio Application Developer publishes and runs your applications.

- Test environment runs your project within the workbench.
- Local server publishes and runs your project on a server installed on the same machine that has your workbench.
- Remote server publishes and runs your project on a server installed either on the same or another machine.

> **NOTE:** WSAD currently supports testing locally and/or remotely on WebSphere Application Server Single Server Edition for multiplatforms only. To test on a local or remote installation of WebSphere Application Server, you must have IBM Agent Controller installed on the server machine first. Agent Controller is automatically installed with each copy of WSAD; however, you can install the application by itself. There are many reasons why WSAD supports testing only on WebSphere Application Server Single Server Edition, but a simple reason is that WSAD uses XML files (for example, `server-cfg.xml`) to store all its configuration information; whereas, the Advanced Edition of WebSphere stores its configuration information in a DB2 7.2 database. However, if you want to, you could always export your projects as EAR files and then import them into another version of WebSphere Application Server, such as the 4.0 advanced. You just won't be able to start and stop the server through WSAD.

Table 8-2: Project Types and RunTime Environments

Project Type	*WebSphere Application Server*	*Tomcat*
Enterprise Application projects	Yes	No
EJB projects	Yes	No
Web projects	Yes	Yes

Managing your server objects with the Server perspective

WSAD provides a Server perspective to aid in managing server files. The Server perspective presents these files as objects in the workbench that you can easily manipulate with the help of editors and menu options. The Server perspective lets you easily configure, start, and stop your test environments. To open the workbench to the Server perspective, do the following:

1. Choose Perspective⇨Open.
2. From the drop-down menu, choose the server if it is present.
3. If you do not see server in the list, choose Other; then choose Server from the Select Perspective window. Figure 8-1 shows the Server perspective in WSAD.

The two main concerns when working in the Server perspective are the server instance and server configuration. A server instance represents the target server environment you want to use, such as WebSphere Application Server or Tomcat. Actually, a server instance in WSAD is nothing more than an XML file stored in your server projects. The server environment that the instance represents doesn't even need to reside on the same computer. When you modify a server instance in WSAD, you're actually modifying the server instance file. The settings that you make against the server instance are applied to the actual server environment at the time you choose to publish and test your applications. A server configuration contains the information required to set up and publish to a server. However, as a server instance, a server configuration in WSAD is also a file stored in your server projects. Server configurations are designed to make configuring your test environments more flexible by implementing a plug-in type relationship between server instances and server configurations.

Server instances and server configurations are intimately related. You can think of a server configuration as a group of settings that you want to apply to a server instance. By making different versions of server configurations, you can easily reconfigure a server instance by simply applying the server configuration that you want to use. You can even apply the same server configuration to more than one server instance at the same time. This feature is invaluable feature, because reconfiguring server instance settings can be a pain in the neck. While in the Server perspective, you can see all your server instances and server configurations. You can easily add or delete a server instances or configurations while in the Server perspective.

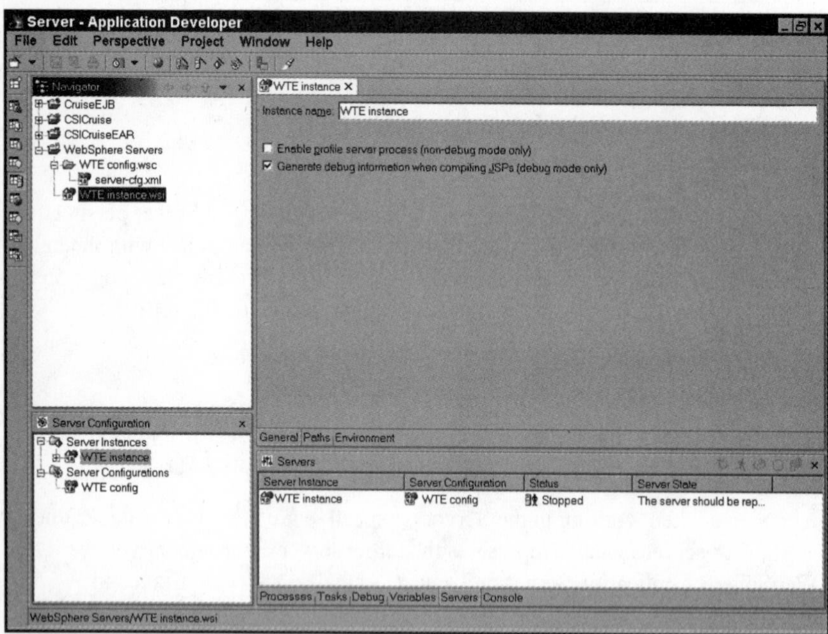

Figure 8-1: The Server perspective is designed to make configuring your test environment faster and easier. The view windows specific to this perspective are Server Configuration and Servers.

Preparing the WebSphere test environment requires the following steps:

1. Create a server project.
2. Create the server instance.

3. Create the server configuration.
4. Configure the server instance.
5. Modify the server configuration.
6. Set the server configuration to a specific instance when necessary.
7. Assign projects to a configuration.

This chapter discusses these steps in detail. Most of these steps should be done while in the Server perspective, because the view windows and toolbars are conveniently laid out for you already. However, WSAD is flexible enough to let you perform any of these steps from any perspective. For example, you can easily create a server project from the Java perspective, but doing so also automatically places you in the Server perspective.

> **TIP:** If you're looking for a quick and easy way to set up a test environment, you can simply right-click the Web or Enterprise application project you want to test and choose Run on Server from the pop-up menu.

Creating a server project

Before you can create a server instance or server configuration, you need to create a server project. Create a new server project and call it WebSphere Servers by performing the following steps:

1. From the Server perspective, choose File⇨New.
2. From the drop-down list, select Server Project to start the Project Wizard for creating a server project.
3. Type **WebSphere Servers** in the Project Name text box.
4. Click Finish to create the new server project.

Any new server instances and configurations and other server configuration files that you create should be placed in server projects. WSAD treats server projects and their contents as resources; therefore, you can apply version control to them later.

As the many other types of projects in WSAD, server projects come with a validator to validate their resources. The WebSphere Server Configuration Validator checks the syntax of the server project's configuration files and the consistency of its resources. However, unlike the validators for most projects, the WebSphere Server Configuration Validator does not support automatic validation. To manually validate a server project, make sure you're in the Server or Web perspective and locate the server project to validate in the Navigator view. Right-click the server project to validate and choose to Run Validation.

You can now create the server instances and server configurations to set up your test environments and store them in the WebSphere Servers server project.

Creating server instances and configurations

To test your Web applications in WSAD, you first need to create the server instance that represents the server that you want to use when you publish the Web application. So if your target deployment platform is WebSphere Application Server 4.0, you should choose to create a WebSphere Application Server 4.0 server instance. Creating a server instance is not enough to begin testing. You also need to create a server configuration to use with the server instance. The server configuration contains more application-specific settings to use on a server instance.

WSAD offers several ways to create server instances and configurations. The easiest way is to let WSAD create a default server instance and configuration automatically. To have WSAD create these, right-click a project or a file in the project, and select Run on Server. WSAD checks for an existing default server. If the default server already exists, the project is published to it and the server is automatically started for you.

NOTE: Run on Server is available if you're using testing for the first time and haven't created any instances and configurations, or if a project does not have a server instance assigned. This feature is equally convenient for testing EJBs. The EJBs are automatically deployed to the server. After deploying, the server starts up automatically, and depending on your server configuration settings, the EJB client used to test the EJBs launches automatically.

Using the Run on Server feature on a project that does not have a valid Welcome page set in its deployment descriptor (`web.xml`) causes a 404 File Not Found error.

If WSAD finds an existing default server instance and/or configuration, WSAD does the following:

- Launches the Server perspective
- Creates a server project if it finds no server project in the workspace
- Creates the default server instance and configuration and adds them to the server project
- Adds the configuration to the instance
- Publishes the selected project to the default server
- Starts the default server instance
- Opens the Debug and Source views if there are breakpoints set to the file

NOTE: The default server instance and configuration are always created in pairs. For example, if a default instance is deleted from the server project leaving default configuration behind, the "orphaned" configuration is not automatically used the next time you choose Run on Server. Instead, when you choose Run on Server again, a new default server instance and default server configuration (2) are created.

Another method for creating a server instance and server configuration is to create them at the same time. Creating both objects simultaneously gives the instance and the configuration the same name. Also, WSAD automatically sets the new server configuration to the new server instance.

Another alternative is to create a server instance and server configuration in separate steps. Using this technique requires you to set configurations manually to each instance. However, as Figure 8-2 illustrates, you are not tied down to any one technique. Whether you create the instances and configurations together or separately, you have the opportunity to change their associations at any time. To see how these server objects relate to one another in WSAD, this chapter example shows you how to create the server instance and server configuration in separate steps.

> **TIP:** Creating the server instances and configurations in separate steps and using a naming scheme (for example, `WTEinstance` and `WTEconfig`) to differentiate instances and configurations can help you understand the separation between the two.

The diagram in Figure 8-2 shows how server configurations can be reused on multiple server instances and vice versa.

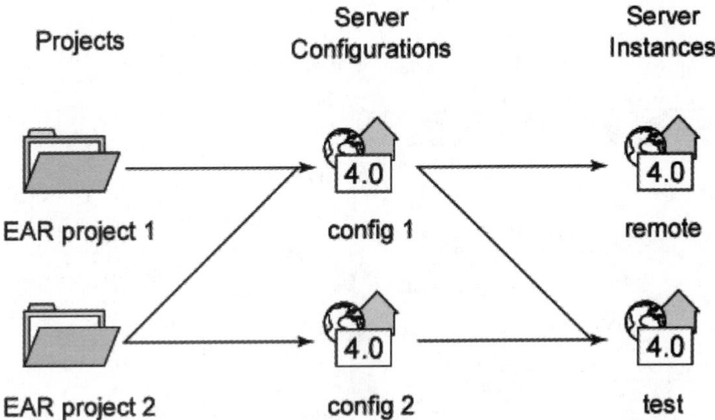

Figure 8-2: The relationship between server instances and server configurations and your projects. You can add EAR project 2 to both server configurations 1 and 2. Server configuration 1 is also set to both the remote and test instances.

Creating the server instance

After you create the server project, select to add a new server to the project by doing the following:

1. Select the server project in the Navigator view.
2. Choose New from the File menu.
3. Select Other from the drop-down menu.
4. Select Server from the list of wizard types in the left panel.
5. Select Server Instance from the list of wizards for creating server objects in the right panel.
6. Click Next to start the wizard.
7. Enter the **WTE instance** as the name of the server instance you want to create.

8. Make sure that the server project, WebSphere Servers, is selected in the Folder drop-down box.
9. From the panel marked Instance Type, expand the list of WebSphere Server instance types that you can create by clicking on the (+) sign.
10. Select WebSphere v4.0 Test Environment from the list of instance types.
11. Optionally, you can choose a server instance template to use for creating your server instance from the Template drop-down list. A template contains base settings that you can use to create and configure a server instance at the same time.
12. Click the Finish button to create the server instance.

You now have a server instance that you can configure and use to test your enterprise and Web applications.

Figure 8-3 shows the setting for the new WebSphere test environment instance.

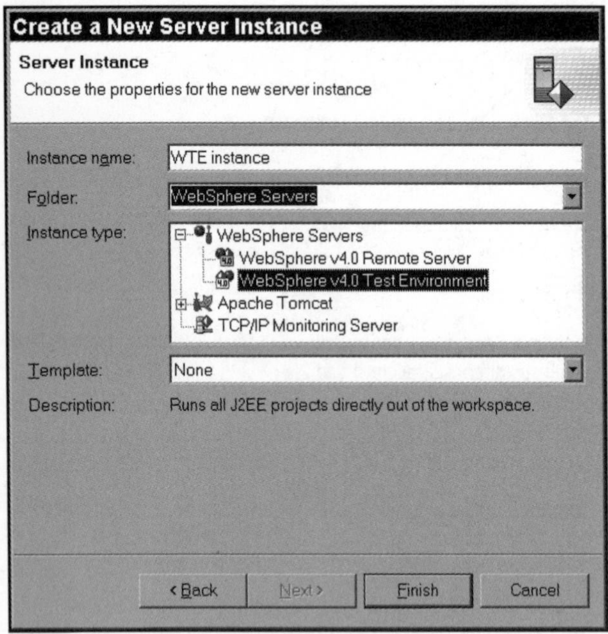

Figure 8-3: Use the settings in the New Server Instance Wizard to create a WTE instance server instance.

Creating the server configuration

Now that you have created your server instance, you need to give it a server configuration. You can create a new server configuration by doing the following:

1. Select the server project in the Navigator view.
2. Choose File⇨New⇨Other.
3. Select Server from the list of wizard types in the left panel.
4. Select Server Configuration from the list of wizards for creating server objects in the right panel.
5. Click Next to start the wizard.
6. Type **WTE config** as the name of the server instance you want to create.
7. Make sure that the server project WebSphere Servers is selected in the Folder drop-down list.
8. In the Configuration type panel, expand the list of WebSphere Server configuration types that you can create by clicking on the (+) sign.
9. Select WebSphere v4.0 Configuration from the list of configuration types.
10. Optionally, you can choose a server configuration template to use for creating your server configuration from the Template drop-down list. A template contains base settings that you can use to quickly create and configure a server configuration at the same time.
11. Click the Finish button to create the server configuration. If you need to change the HTTP port settings for this configuration, click the Next button to see the next page.

Figures 8-4 shows the settings for the new server configuration.

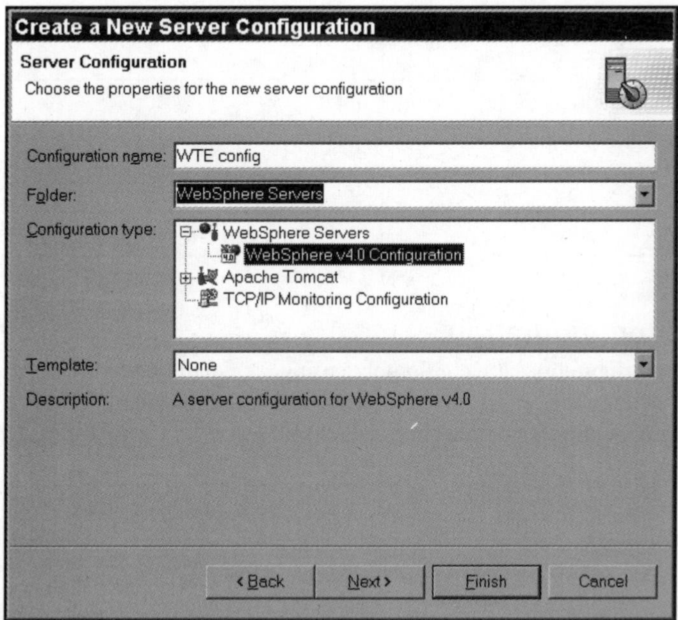

Figure 8-4: This is the first page of the Server Configuration Wizard. Here, you define a new server configuration.

Now that you've created your instance and configuration, take a moment to examine the files that were generated, which depend on the type of instance and configuration you chose to create:

- The WTE instance is defined by the `WTE instance.wsi file` located in the `WebSphere Servers project` folder. The file contains the settings for the WTE instance server instance in XML and can be edited using the default WebSphere Instance Editor, XML editor or even a text editor.
- The WTE configuration is defined by the `server-cfg.xml` file in the `WTE config.wsc` folder of the `WebSphere Servers project` folder. The `server-cfg.xml` file contains the settings information for the server configuration in XML. You can easily edit this file, and thus the server configuration, using the default WebSphere Configuration Editor, XML editor, or text editor.

Table 8-3 shows the different types of files that are generated for instances and configurations.

Table 8-3: Server File Extensions

File	*Extension*
WebSphere server configuration	.wsc
WebSphere server instance	.wsi
WebSphere remote instance	.wrsi
Remote file transfer	.rft
TCP/IP Monitor server configuration	.msc
TCP/IP Monitor server instance	.msi
Tomcat server configuration	.tsc
Tomcat server instance	.tsi

Modifying the server configuration

Like server instances, server configurations are configurable using the default editor or a text editor. To modify a server configuration, either open the server configuration listed in the Server Configuration view or open the `.wsc` file in the server project.

The view in Figure 8-5 shows the default editor for a WebSphere Application Server configuration.

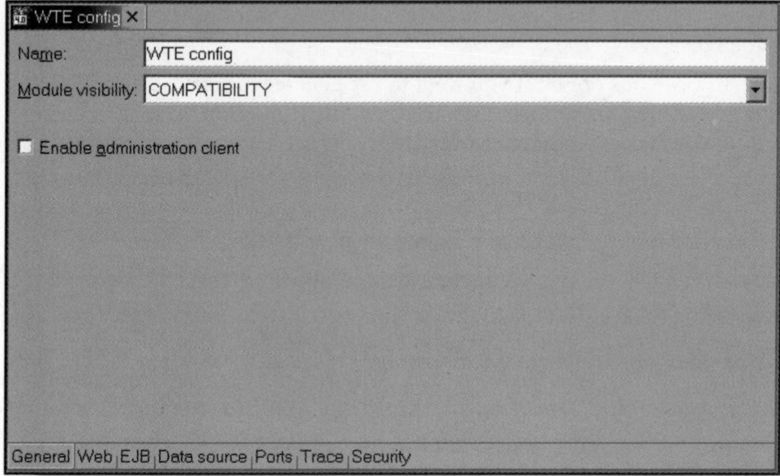

Figure 8-5: The default editor for a WebSphere Application Server configuration enables you to make modifications to the server configuration through a graphical user interface.

The General tab enables you to change the following:

- *Name:* This is the name that identifies this server configuration in the Server Configuration view. Changing this name changes only what appears in the Server Configuration view and does not affect any filenames and vice versa.
- *Module visibility:* This setting enables you to specify the classloader isolation mode to use for the server that implements this configuration.
  - *COMPATABILITY:* Choose this option if you want compatibility for applications from WebSphere Application Server 3.5.x and 3.0.2.x, and for situations in which code running in one application needs to see code running in others, such as when you want to exchange application logic at development time from one EAR file and another.
  - *APPLICATION:* Choose this option if you want to use one classloader for each EAR file.
  - *SERVER:* Choose this option if you want to use one classloader for the entire server.
  - *MODULE:* Choose this option if you want to use one classloader per module.
- *Enable administration client:* Check this option box to use the Web-based administration client to change settings in a configuration that is defined to use WebSphere Application Server.

The Web tab enables you to change the following:

- *Mime types:* Add or edit mime-types and their extensions for a server configuration.
- *Enable session manager:* Choose this option to use Session Manger in WAS to store and manage your session.

- *Enable URL rewrite:* Choose this option to have Session Manager use rewritten URLs to carry the session ID.
- *Enable cookies:* Choose this option if you want to use cookies to carry session IDs. If this option is disabled, Session Manger uses URL rewrite if the URL rewrite option is enabled. Using cookies takes precedence over URL rewrite.

The EJB tab enables you to change the following:

- *Default data source:* Select a defined data source for your EJBs.
- *Enable EJB test client:* Choose this option to use the Web-based Test Client provided by the server tools to test the interfaces for your EJBs.

The Data Source tab enables you to change the following:

- *JDBC driver list:* Add, remove, and delete the drivers available for creating data sources.
- *Data sources defined in the JDBC driver:* This list shows the data sources defined for a specific driver. To add a data source, you must select a driver from the JDBC driver list first.
- *Resource properties defined for a data source:* This option enables you to define the properties for a selected data source, such as port number and connection URL, in the case of a data source for a remote database.

The Ports tab enables you to change the various port settings for your server, including host aliases, HTTP ports, OLT ports, a location service daemon port, a trace service port, a naming service port, an ORB bootstrap port, and an optional administrative host port.

> **TIP:** The Ports tab is important when you're looking to run multiple test environments simultaneously, because all the new server configurations created in WSAD share the same default port settings. Servers running on the same computer cannot share the same port settings. For each test environment to function properly, you need to make each port setting in the server configurations unique.

The Trace tab enables you to do the following

- *Enable checkbox:* Enable or disable tracing in the workbench.
- *Trace string*: Enable and disable various monitors by entering the detail string into the dialog box. For example, to enable monitoring of EJB lifecycle events, change the string to `com.ibm.ejs.container*=all=enable`.

The Security tab enables you to do the following

- *Enable security:* Enable the WebSphere Application Server Security feature.
- *Local OS Authentication:* Enter the authentication information to use to log into the local OS for the server.

Configuring the server instance

You can configure your server instances in several ways. The easiest method is to use the default WebSphere Instance editor for each type of server instance. Some alternatives to using the default editor are to edit the XML in the `.wsi` file with a text editor or with the built-in XML editor. The code in Listing 8-1 shows the `WTE instance.wsi` file in a text editor. Needless to say, the preferred way of editing your server instances is to use the default instance editor associated with each type of server instance.

Listing 8-1: WTE instance.wsi File in Default Text Editor

```
<?xml version="1.0" encoding="UTF-8"?>
<webSphere-instance
   INSTANCE_CONFIG_REF="/WebSphere Servers/WTE config.wsc"
   INSTANCE_DEBUG_PORT_NUM_ID="-1"
   INSTANCE_EXTRA_WS_EXT_DIRS_APPEND_FLAG_ID="0"
   INSTANCE_EXTRA_WS_EXT_DIRS_ID=""
   INSTANCE_FILE_KEY="WebSphere v4.0 Test Environment Server Instance"
   INSTANCE_JSP_SRC_DEBUG_ID="true" INSTANCE_PROFILE_PROCESS="false" "
   name="WTE instance">
   <configuration-ref ref="/WebSphere Servers/WTE config.wsc"/>
   <classpath/>
   <system-properties/>
   <vm-arguments/>
</webSphere-instance>
```

NOTE: For simplicity's sake, this chapter uses the default editor to configure servers.

To configure your new WTE instance server, switch to the Server perspective and double-click the WTE instance server instance in the Server Configuration view. The view in Figure 8-6 shows the default editor for a WebSphere Application Server instance.

The General tab of the instance editor enables you to change the following:

- *Instance name:* This is the name that identifies this server instance in the Server Configuration view of the Server perspective. Changing this name changes only what appears in the Server Configuration view and does not affect any filenames and vice versa.
- *Enable profile server process* Select this option to indicate whether the server instance allows the WSAD profiling tool to analyze its performance. This feature is not available and disabled if the server is explicitly started in debug mode.
- *Generate debug information when compiling JSPs:* Select this option if you want to see the JSP source for your compiled JSPs when in debug mode.

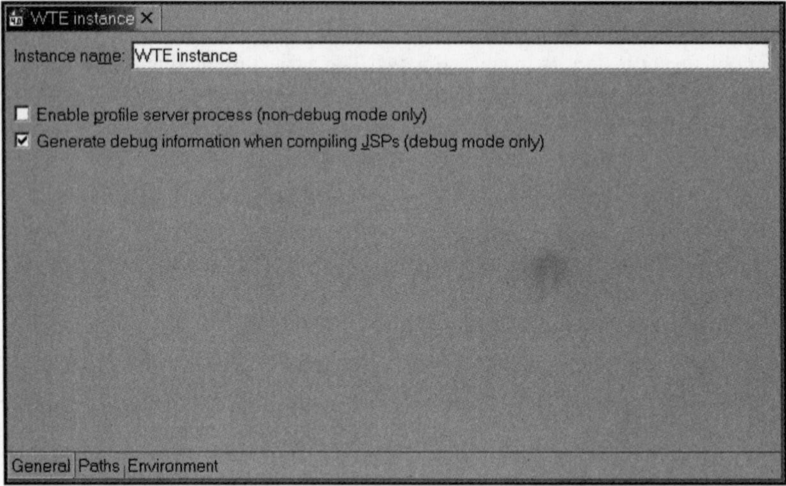

Figure 8-6: The default editor provides three tabs for adding and changing configuration settings.

The Paths tab enables you to point to the resources that the runtime may need to provide to its published applications. The Environment tab enables you to add the following:

- Arguments to the command line used to launch the Java VM.
- System properties you want to pass to the runtime.

Remember to save any changes to the server instance configuration.

Setting a server configuration to an instance

Before a server instance can be used for testing, you must set a server configuration to the instance. By setting a configuration, you're basically applying the settings stored in the configuration to the instance. Follow these steps for setting a server configuration to an instance while in the Server perspective.

1. To set a configuration to the WTE instance, right-click the instance in the Server Configuration view and choose Set Configuration.
2. From the list of available configurations, choose the WTE config. In the future, to unset a server configuration from an instance, simply choose Set Configuration and select No Configuration from the list.

The WTE instance is now available for testing your projects.

Adding a project to a server configuration for testing

In WSAD, you add projects to server configurations. The types of projects you can add to a server configuration depend on the type of server configuration. Because server configurations are set to server instances, by adding a project to a server configuration, you're specifying that the server instances (that the server configuration is set to) are also the locations to which the project publishes. For example, if you add a project to a server configuration and then set the configuration to two separate server instances, the project publishes to both server instances.

1. To add the AlmostFreeCruiseEAR project to a server configuration, right-click the WTE config server configuration and click Add a Project.

> **NOTE:** The list of projects that you can add to a server configuration depends on the type of server it is. Because Tomcat server configurations support only Web projects, only Web projects show in the list of projects to add. Because applications are deployed to WAS 4.0 as EAR files, projects are added as EAR files to WebSphere server configurations.

2. Next, select the AlmostFreeCruiseEAR project to add it to the configuration from the list of applicable projects.

> **NOTE:** As illustrated in Figure 8-2, it is possible to have a project belong to more than one server configuration. When a project is added to a server configuration for the first time, that server becomes the default server used for a Run on Server command. You can change the default server setting by opening the project's Properties window and selecting the desired default server from the server preferences panel.

3. The project is now set to the server configuration. The project publishes to the server instance to which you set the server configuration.

Adding a data source to a server configuration

In WSAD, a data source is defined in a server configuration, which is assigned to a server instance. To add a data source to a server configuration do the following.

1. Open the server configuration in the default editor.
2. Change to the Data Source tab.
3. Select the type of driver to use for the data source from the JDBC driver list. In this example, be sure to select the Db2JdbcDriver.
4. Choose Add to define a data source.

> **CROSS-REFERENCE:** Refer to Chapter 4 for instructions on how to install the cruise database. You can install the database after creating the data source described in the following instructions.

5. Click in the Name text box and enter **CruiseDB**. This is the name used to display the datasource.
6. In the JNDI name text box, enter **jdbc/cruise** as the JNDI name that you want to use when using a naming server to locate this data source.
7. In the Database name text box, enter **cruise** as the name of the database to connect to.
8. If your database requires a user ID for connections, enter the user ID in the Default user ID field.
9. If you entered a user ID, enter the accompanying user password.
10. Leave all the default values for pool size and timeout information as they are.
11. Click the OK button to create the new data source. Figure 8-7 shows the entry form for creating or editing a data source.

12. Save your changes to the server configuration by pressing Ctrl+S.

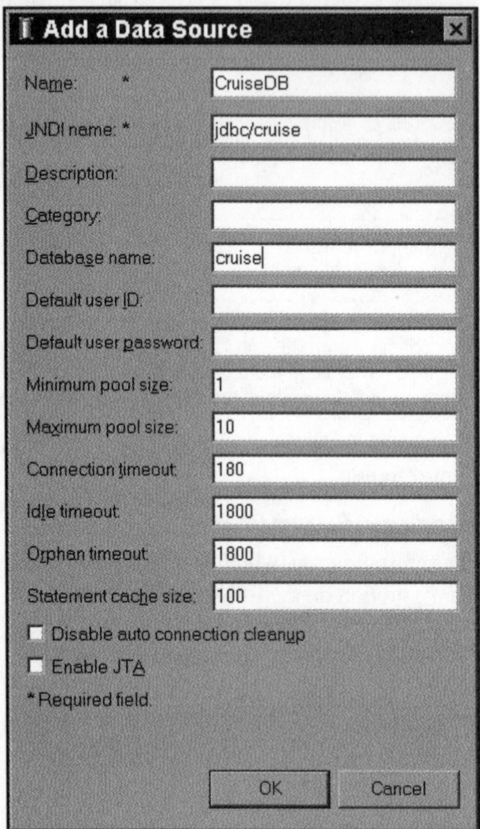

Figure 8-7: Data source settings should look like this.

Here is a list of all the settings and their descriptions for defining a data source.

- *Name:* Enter the display name for the data source.
- *JNDI name:* Enter the JNDI name including any naming context that you would like to use to retrieve the datasource from the JNDI naming server.
- *Description:* Enter an optional description.
- *Category:* Enter an optional category used to group the resource.
- *Database name:* Enter the name of the database that the data source connects to. For example, **cruise** where cruise is the name of the db2 database you would like to connect to in this datasource.

- *Default user ID:* Enter the user ID for the database to connect to. If you enter a user ID, you must enter a user password. The user ID and password you enter will be used if no user ID and password is specified by the application using the data source.
- *Default user password:* Enter the password to use for the user ID specified in the Default user ID field. Entering a password requires you to enter a user ID.
- *Minimum pool size:* Enter the minimum number of database connections that this data source must provide in the connection pool.
- *Maximum pool size:* Enter the maximum number of connections that can be in the connection pool. If the limit is reached and all connections are being used, all other requests need to wait until a connection is freed and returned to the pool.
- *Connection timeout:* Enter the number of seconds that a request for a connection from the pool of connections has to wait if the maximum pool size limit is reached and all available connections are in use.
- *Idle timout:* Enter the maximum number of seconds that a connection can be in the connection pool without being allocated. If the connection is idle for the specified number of seconds, the connection is removed to free up resources.
- *Orphan timeout:* Enter the maximum number of seconds that a connection is allowed to be unused by the application that has it opened. If the application does not use the connection for the maximum amount of seconds specified, the connection is terminated and placed back into the connection pool.
- *Statement cache size:* Enter the maximum number of prepared statements that the datasource can retain for connections within the connection pool. This limit is shared among all connections.
- *Disable auto connection cleanup:* To keep connection pooling from closing connections from a data source after each transaction, select the Disable Auto Connection Cleanup check box. This setting is useful if you want to keep the connection open over multiple transactions. However, if you enable this feature, you must make sure to close the connection programmatically when you're through using it.
- *Enable JTA:* The Enable JTA check box enables you to use the Java Transaction API to connect to the database.

Applications defined in the project that are set to this server configuration can now use this data source to make a connection to the Cruise database.

Testing the application on the test environment

In this section, you test the HTML pages, JSPs, and servlet that comprise the Almost Free Cruise application. But, before you can begin to test using your new test environment, you need to add the `SingleServlet` object to the application's deployment descriptor:

1. To do this, open the CSICruise Web project and then the `WebApplication` folder.
2. Open the `web.xml` file in the `WEB-INF` folder. The `web.xml` editor opens on the General tab.

3. Switch to the Servlets tab.
4. If the SingleServlet is already listed in the Servlet list, you can remove it by selecting it from the list and clicking the Remove button.
5. Click the Add button below the Servlets list box to add a new servlet.
6. From the list of available servlets to add, double-click SingleServlet.
7. Click the Add button to the right of the URL mappings list box and enter **/CSICruise/SingleServlet** as the URL.
8. Save the `web.xml file` by pressing Ctrl+S. The application is now ready for testing.

To get your testing started, right-click the CSICruise Web or EAR project and choose Run on Server. The server tool publishes the project to the server and starts it.

NOTE: At times, your test environment's resources might not have all the latest changes. Any server instance that is out of sync will indicate in the server state column of the Server view that its associated contents should be republished. To resolve this problem, you can right-click the server instance and choose to publish.

The view in Figure 8-8 shows a server instance with an out-of-sync server state.

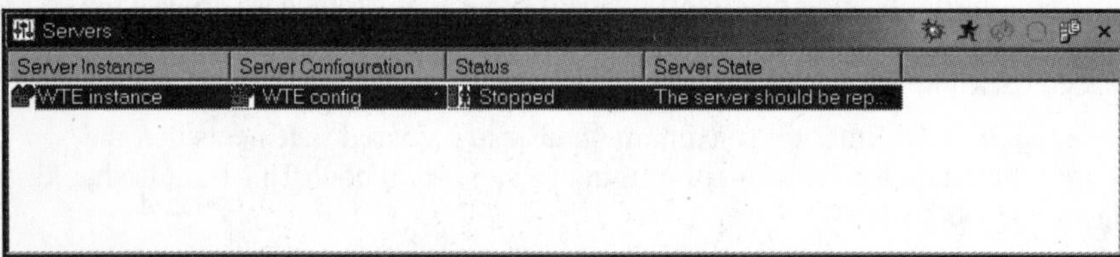

Figure 8-8: The contents of the WTE instance here is out of sync. The server state indicates that the server should be republished to update its content.

The perspective automatically switches to the Server perspective and a browser launches to the project URL. A second way to do this is to start the testing environment manually:

1. First, right-click the WTE instance from the list of server instances and choose Publish to the Server.
2. Right-click the WTE instance and choose Start to start the server, or Debug to start the server in Debug mode.
3. Next, start a Web browser, and point the browser to `http://localhost:8080/CSICruise/index.html`. The `index.html` file that you point to can be found in the `webApplication` folder of the CSICruise Web project.
4. Select Book Online and start testing the application. If you do discover a problem, skip to the following section, "Debugging the application," to learn how to debug it.

The browser in Figure 8-9 shows the Welcome page of the Almost Free Cruise Web application.

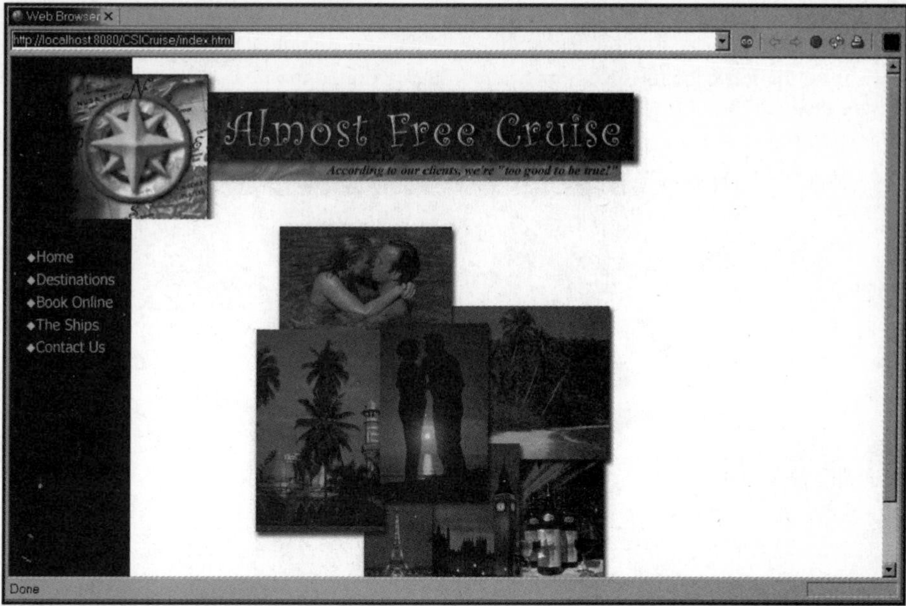

Figure 8-9: After you install your application, you should see this Almost Free Cruise Welcome page.

> **CAUTION:** Your Web project must have a Welcome file defined when running a Web project at the project level, otherwise you encounter 404 errors.

Debugging the application

Before attempting to debug your application, make sure you've checked the Generate debug information when compiling JSP's check box for the server instance that will run the application:

1. Begin by opening the `onlineBooking2.jsp` file in the CSICruise Web project into an editor.
2. Place a breakpoint on the first scriplet in the file by right-clicking the line number and choosing Add Breakpoint.
3. Now open the `SingleServlet.java` file located in the `CSICruise  source` folder into an editor.

Place a breakpoint onto the first line in the `doPost()` method of the servlet, by doing the following:

1. Position your mouse pointer over the left edge of the Java Source Editor window next to the first line of the `doPost()` method.

2. Right-click the left edge of the editor and select Add Breakpoint. You can also add the breakpoint by double-clicking the left edge of the editor window. A blue dot should appear on the left edge of the editor where you positioned the mouse pointer, indicating where the breakpoint is assigned. The screen in Figure 8-10 shows how to add a breakpoint in an editor.

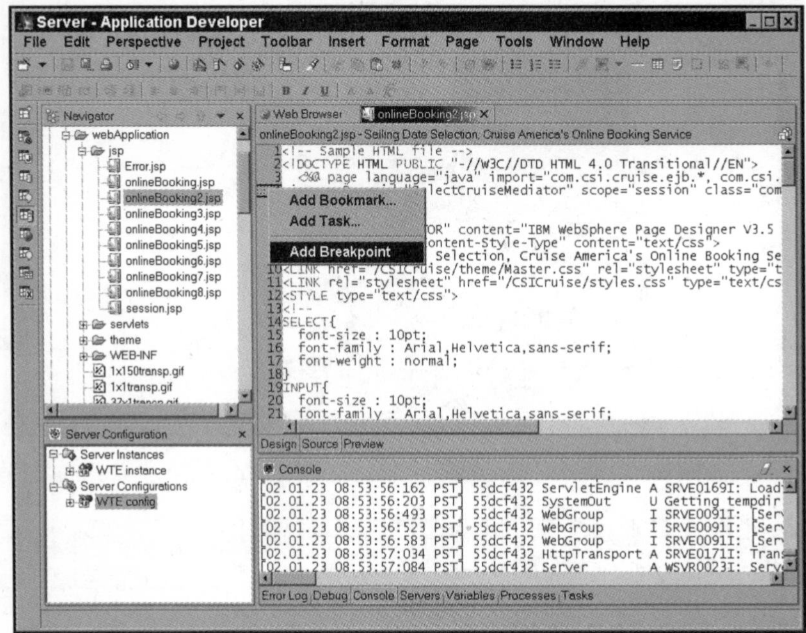

Figure 8-10: Adding a breakpoint in the Java Source Editor window to debug jsp and Java source code.

3. If the server has not already started in Debug mode, launch the application in Debug mode by choosing Run on Server for the CSICruise project. The server tool automatically publishes to the server and turns on Debug mode. If the server is already started, you need to stop it first by selecting the server in the Servers view. Right-click the server and choose Stop.
4. The main page of the Almost Free Cruise Web application, showing in Figure 8-9, automatically opens in a Web browser.
5. Choose the Book Online option from the main pages menu on the left of the Web page to begin booking a cruise.
6. From the Web application's Cruise Search page, make a search by filling out the search form and clicking the Forward button
7. The debugger tool automatically opens the `SingleServlet.java` file to the breakpoint for debugging and sets focus to the Debug view with the current thread in focus.

8. You can now debug the servlet by using the various controls on the upper-right corner of the Debug view. The window in Figure 8-11 shows the debugger at a breakpoint.

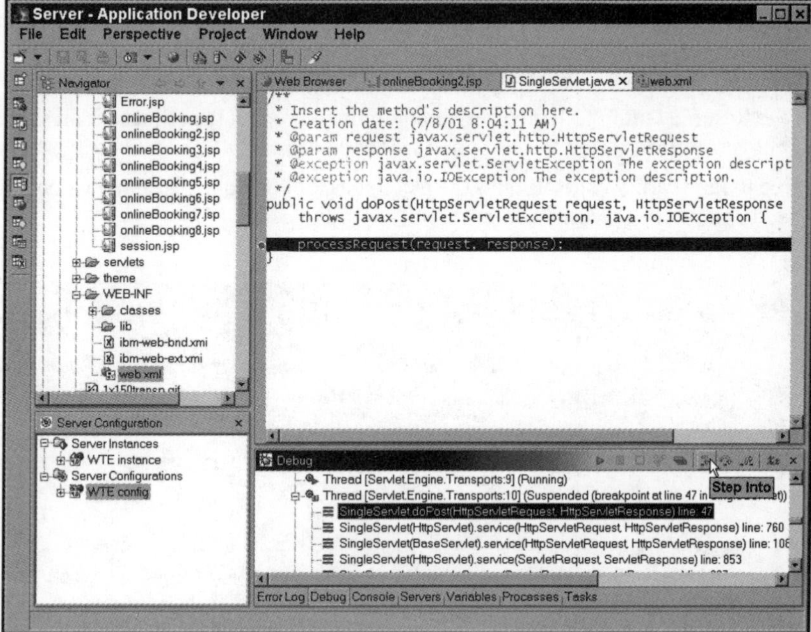

Figure 8-11: Debugging a servlet is made simple with WSAD's integrated debugger. This figure shows how the debugger is integrated with other views to make debugging more convenient.

9. Click the Step Into button in the upper-right corner of the Debug view window to drill into the `processRequest()` method.

   Now you can examine the contents of the `processRequest()` method. This method does the following.

   - It instantiates a `CruiseController` object to perform the search.
   - It executes the process method of the CruiseController object to perform the search.
   - Finally, it calls the CruiseController object's `sendNext()` method to send the user to the next Web page of the Web application.

10. Click the Step Over button to step over to the line of code that reads `controller.process();`.

11. Change from the Debug view to the Variables view by selecting the Variables tab. Click the (+) sign next to each variable to see its contents; examine the variables that have been declared thus far by opening each one.

12. Switch back to the Debug view and click the Step Into button located at the upper-right corner of the Debug view window to examine the code in the `controller.process()` line. You should be in the `process()` method of the controller instance. This method may seem complex, but it does some very basic things. Based on some hidden fields in the page, the method instantiates an object called the Mediator, which is used to process the form information checks for errors.
13. Click the Resume button to let the server continue to process the request. You should see the debugger stopped inside the compiled JSP code of `onlineBooking2.jsp`.
14. Feel free to familiarize yourself with the Debugger tool and click Resume when you're satisfied to allow the server to continue.

Running Multiple Test Environments Simultaneously

The Server tool in WSAD enables you to run more than one test environment at the same time. For this feature to work, you need to do the following. For each server instance that you want to run simultaneously, you must modify the server configurations of each to have unique port numbers for the ports listed below. You can find the port settings for each server configuration in the Ports tab of the Server Configuration editor.

The draw back of running multiple server instances is that you cannot set the same server configuration to more than one server instance that you want to run simultaneously. You have to create one server configuration for each server instance that you want to run simultaneously, and modify their port numbers as specified. You may experience other port conflicts depending on certain features that you enable. Be careful not to use ports already used by your system. Try incrementing the HTTP port, the Trace service port, and the ORB bootstrap port numbers by 1 or 2.

Summary

This chapter covered the basics of setting up a WebSphere test environment for testing and debugging your future applications. The topics included how to work with the server tooling to create a server project, server instance, server configuration, and ultimately to tie them together to build your test environment. A server project is used to store the files for your test environments. A server instance represents a server that you would like to test your application with. A server configuration is a group of settings that you want to apply to a server instance. Server configurations make it quicker and easier to change how a server instance is configured.

After setting up your test environment, you walked you through a basic test of the Almost Free Cruise application and an overview of what the debugger can offer to you. As you can tell, there are many different approaches to and different levels on which you can set up your test environments. WebSphere gives you the flexibility of being able to work at own skill level in forming your test environment.

Chapter 9
Java Servlet Development

In This Chapter

- Servlets flow and lifecycle
- The Servlet API
- Servlet coding examples
- Comparison to CGI
- The HttpServletRequest
- The HttpServletResponse

To best explain servlets, this chapter starts with a little history about Web development. Early in the World Wide Web's history, the Common Gateway Interface (CGI) was defined to allow Web servers to process user input and serve dynamic content. CGI programs can be developed in any script or programming language, but Perl is by far the most commonly used language. Virtually all Web servers support CGI, and many Perl modules are available as freeware or shareware to handle most tasks.

But CGI is not without drawbacks. Performance and scalability are big problems because a new process is created for each request, which quickly drains a server's resources. Sharing resources, such as database connections, between scripts or multiple calls to the same script is far from trivial, leading to repeated execution of expensive operations.

The Web server vendors defined Application Program Interfaces (APIs) to solve some of these problems. But an application written to these proprietary APIs is tied to one particular server vendor. If you need to move the application to a server from another vendor, you have to start from scratch. Another problem with this approach is reliability. The APIs typically support C/C++ code executing in the Web server process. If the application crashes, for example, due to a bad pointer or division by zero, it brings the Web server down with it.

The Servlet API was developed to leverage the advantages of the Java platform to solve the issues of CGI and proprietary APIs. It's a simple API that is supported by virtually all Web servers by allowing extensions to load-balancing, fault-tolerant application servers to handle the servlet request for them. It solves the performance problem by executing all requests as threads in one process, or in a load-balanced system, in one process per server in the cluster.

The `javax.servlet` and `javax.servlet.http` packages provide developers with the power to write robust server-side applications that utilize the request-response paradigm. Because most servlets are written for servers that use the HTTP protocol, the `HttpServletRequest` and the `HttpServletResponse` objects provide the basic foundation for communication between clients and servers.

This chapter provides you with the information necessary for deciding whether to use servlets in your development. In addition to explaining the reasons why you might want to use servlets, utilizing some basic coding examples, it also provides you information about how to create servlets.

Comparing Servlets with CGI Programs

Everything you can do with servlets, you can also accomplish by implementing CGI programs. CGI programs can be written in any language, but are most commonly written in Perl or C/C++. The major difference between servlets and CGI programs is that CGI programs create a new server process for each client request. Figure 9-1 illustrates three requests for the same CGI process. Each request spawns its own new child process. Having each request create a new process puts a heavy load on server resources, and this can affect the number of requests a server can handle concurrently.

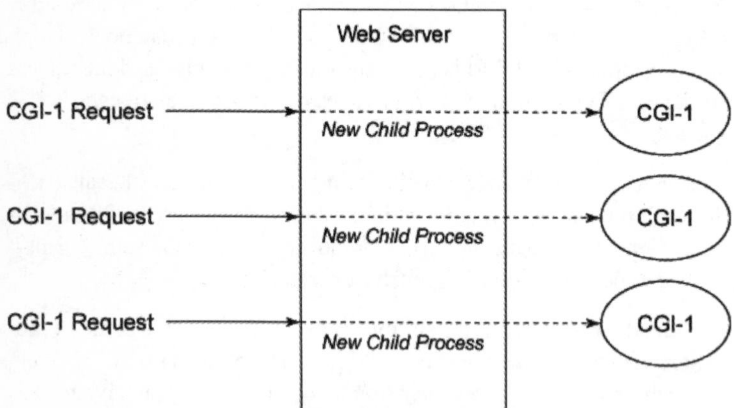

Figure 9-1: How a server handles CGI processing.

Because servlets stay loaded in memory, one servlet can handle multiple requests. Servlets use threads, which are much lighter and have lower overhead than individual server processes. Figure 9-2 illustrates three requests for the same servlet process. Each request is run through the single instance of the servlet in its own thread.

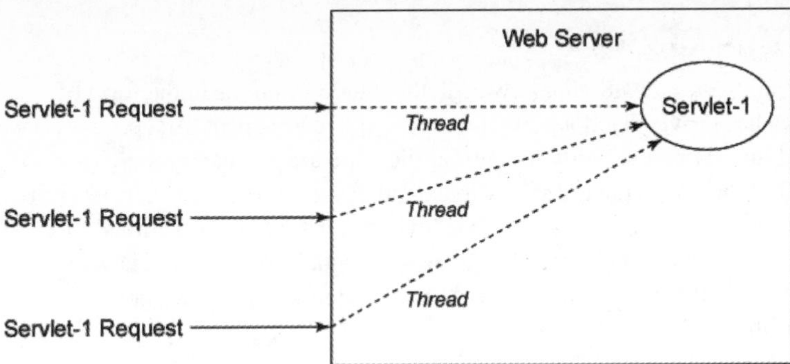

Figure 9-2: How a server handles servlet processing.

Another problem with CGI programs is that they cannot interact with the Web server or take advantage of the server's capabilities after they begin execution because they are running in a separate process. CGI programs cannot, for example, write to the server log files. Because servlets run within the Web server, they have access to its services and can build on top of them.

There are many reasons why you would use servlets instead of CGI programs. The following list summarizes the major advantages to servlet implementations:

- *Portability*: Servlets are inherently portable because they are written in a platform-neutral language, Java.
- *Power*: Servlets have access to the full Java API with RMI, CORBA, JNDI, and so on.
- *Efficiency*: After a servlet is loaded into memory, there is no reload overhead because it stays running in memory waiting for multiple requests. Servlets use threads, which are lightweight, to handle requests.
- *Safety*: Servlets are inherently secure because they are written in Java. They get strong typing because Java allows for extensive compile-time checking for potential type-mismatch problems, garbage collection, and critical error handling. Servlets can also utilize the Java Security Manager.
- *Elegance*: The code is clean and object oriented. The Servlet API has methods and objects available for development, such as session handling.
- *Integration*: Servlets integrate with Web servers and provide logging and tracking, and they work with the Web server to check request path and handle types.
- *Extensibility/flexibility*: Because servlets are Java based, they are easily extensible. Servlets are flexible, so they can be used to generate purely dynamic content or invoke other servlets to generate partial dynamic content.

Although the same functionality can be built with CGI programs, it is easy to see why servlets have gained so much popularity and seem to be the predominant choice among server-side developers.

Understanding Servlets

Java was originally intended for developing powerful client-side solutions in the form of applets. However, Java has proven itself a powerful server-side component. A *servlet* is a Java class written to add additional functionality to a server. Servlets are most commonly used to extend a Web server, but they have the capability to extend any kind of server. Servlets run inside a servlet engine within a Web server and allow dynamic content to be returned to a client via the request-response paradigm. Servlets have been widely adopted and have been used as a replacement for CGI scripts. The Servlet API is a required API of the Java 2 Platform Enterprise Edition (J2EE).

Understanding the servlet process flow

At a basic level, servlets are to a server what applets are to a client. They run on the server and perform specific tasks needed to process applications. Examples of servlet processes are to compute the totals for a given set of numbers or figure out what the next page in your application should be, based on the user request. Servlets can be designed to perform any number of processes for your application, but they should be limited to performing one specific process that they specialize in. Applets are designed to enhance client-side processing, whereas servlets are designed to enhance (and extend) server-side processing. Generally, a server has multiple servlets associated with a Web application and uses each of their services for specific tasks.

From a high-level perspective, the servlet process flow follows these steps (see Figure 9-3):

1. The client sends a request to the server for some type of service.
2. The server passes the request information it received from the client to the servlet.
3. Using data from the request, the servlet performs its task and dynamically builds a response for the client.
4. The server sends the response to the client.

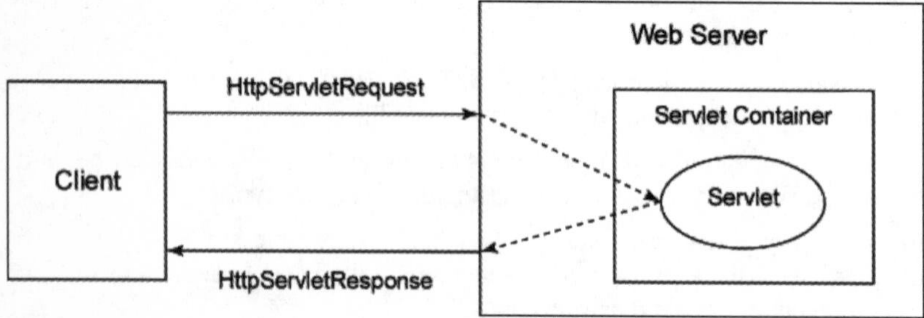

Figure 9-3: The Servlet process flow for handling user requests.

Introducing the Java Servlet API

The Servlet API is defined as an extension to the standard JDK and contains the following packages:

- `javax.servlet`
- `javax.servlet.http`

The `javax.servlet` package contains classes to support generic servlets. These classes are extended by the classes in the `javax.servlet.http` package to add functionality specific to the HTTP protocol. The servlet interface provides methods that manage the servlet and its communication with clients. When a servlet gets a call from a client, it receives two objects: One is a `ServletRequest` and the other is a `ServletResponse`. The `ServletRequest` object encapsulates the communication from the client to the server, and the `ServletResponse` object encapsulates the communication from the server back to the client. If you are using the `javax.servlet.http` package, the servlet receives an `HTTPServletRequest` and returns an `HTTPServletResponse`.

For your class to be recognized and treated as a servlet by the servlet engine, you must implement the `javax.servlet.Servlet` interface. Most accomplish this by extending either `javax.servlet.GenericServlet` or `javax.servlet.http.HttpServlet`. If your servlet needs to be protocol-independent, you extend `GenericServlet`. If, however, you are writing an HTTP servlet, you extend the `HTTPServlet`, which itself is a subclass of the `GenericServlet`.

A servlet does not have a `main()` method as regular Java programs have. Instead, servlets have methods that are invoked by the server when processing requests from a client. When a server invokes a servlet, it calls the `service()` method. This method accepts, as its two parameters, the `request` object and the `response` object. The `service()` method is generally overridden by servlets that extend `GenericServlet`. Although the `service()` method can also be overridden for servlets that extend `HTTPServlet`, it is not recommended. Servlets that override `HTTPServlet` should override its `doGet()` and or `doPost()` methods depending on what type of action is required. These methods are covered in more detail in the `HttpServlet` interface section later in the chapter. The `service()` method is the method that gets the original request. In turn, it calls the specific `doXXX()` method. HTTP servlets can also override the `doPut()` and `doDelete()` methods to handle `put` and `delete` requests. In addition, the `doHead()`, `doTrace()`, and `doOptions()` methods can be overridden; however, for HTTP servlets, the default implementations are usually sufficient.

Two other useful servlet methods that can be overridden are `init()` and `destroy()`. The `init()` method runs when the servlet is first loaded, just before the `service()` method. Because this method is called at the beginning of the servlet lifecycle, it is generally used to load data dynamically that the servlet uses at a global level during its processing. A good example would be for the `init()` method to read an external file for environmental information. The `init()` method is called only once, when the servlet first gets loaded. If you want to change the data in the file and have the servlet code pick it up, the servlet must be unloaded and then reloaded to pick up the new values.

The `destroy()` method is the cleanup method. The server calls a servlet's `destroy()` method when the servlets is about to be unloaded. The `destroy()` method frees up any resources that the servlet has acquired that the garbage collector won't free up. This method is also a good place to persist any unsaved data that has been cached that will be used for later `init()` method calls.

Understanding the servlet lifecycle

Each servlet has the same lifecycle:

- A server loads and initializes the servlet.
- The servlet handles zero to many client requests.
- The server removes (unloads) the servlet.

When a server loads a servlet, it runs the servlets `init()` method. Even though most servlets run in multithreaded servers, there are no concurrency issues during servlet initialization, because the server calls this method only once when it is loaded and does not call it again unless it reloads the servlet. The server cannot reload the servlet until after the `destroy()` method runs. Initialization is allowed to complete before client requests are handled or the servlet is destroyed.

After the server loads and initializes the servlet, the servlet is able to handle client requests. It processes them with its `service()` method. Each client request runs in its own thread. Servlets can run multiple `service()` methods at a time. It is important, therefore, that the `service()` method is written in a thread-safe manner. A good rule of thumb is never to use class variables unless they are for constant values. Method variables are thread safe because each thread gets its own copy of them as they run, but class-level variables are shared by all the servlet threads. Sharing can be a good thing, but inevitably, data is overwritten and mixed between threads. If it turns out that a server should not run multiple `service()` methods concurrently, the servlet should implement the `SingleThreadModel` interface. This interface guarantees that no two threads execute the servlet's `service()` method concurrently. This cures your threading problems; however, you lose many of the servlet's performance benefits.

Servlets run until they are removed from the service — for example, at the request of a system administrator. Because servlets stay running in memory, they can quickly respond to client requests and return their response without having to load every time. When the servlet is unloaded, the server runs the `destroy()` method of the servlet. Figure 9-4 illustrates a servlet lifecycle.

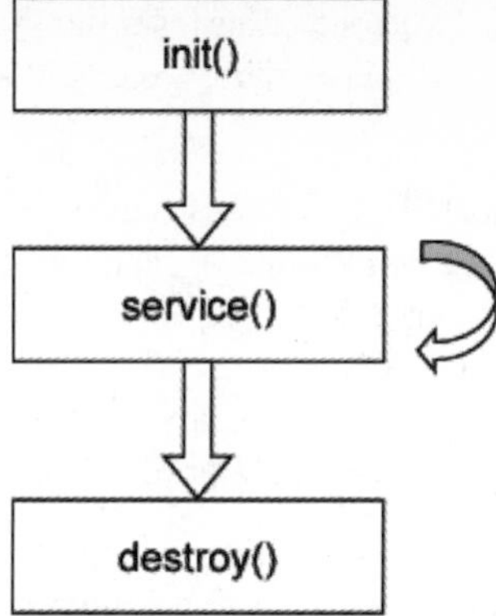

Figure 9.4: The lifecycle of a servlet.

Examining basic servlet examples

So you can better understand some of the points talked about thus far, this section includes some basic servlet coding examples. Those of you who are more experienced with servlets might want to skip this section; however, these few simple examples illustrate some of the fundamental concepts of servlets.

Looking at the obligatory Hello World

This wouldn't be a technical book without our good friend Hello World. Although it is very basic, it illustrates some of the most common features of servlets. The most basic servlet returns a HTML page as its response. Listing 9-1 illustrates a servlet that returns a simple HTML page that says, "Hello World!"

Listing 9-1: The Hello World Servlet

```
import java.io.*;
import javax.servlet.*;
import javax.servlet.http.*;
public class HelloWorldServlet extends HttpServlet {
 public void doGet(HttpServletRequest req, HttpServletResponse res)
    throws ServletException, IOException {
   res.setContentType("text/html");
   PrintWriter out = res.getWriter();
   out.println("<HTML>");
   out.println("<HEAD><TITLE>Hello World</TITLE></HEAD>");
   out.println("<BODY>");
   out.println("<BIG>Hello World!</BIG>");
   out.println("</BODY></HTML>");
}
}
```

This servlet extends the `HTTPServlet` and overrides its `doGet()` method. Whenever the Web server receives a `Get` request for this servlet, the server invokes this method, passing in a `HttpServletRequest` object and a `HttpServletResponse` object.

The `HttpServletRequest` represents the request from the client. The servlet uses this to get information about the client, the parameters for this request, header information, and other items that help it know what to do. Later on in this chapter, the "Using the HttpServletServletRequest and HttpServletResponse protocols" section covers `HttpServletRequest` in greater detail. For this basic example, it is not necessary to interrogate the request because the servlet always returns the same data: Hello World!

The `HttpServletResponse` represents the reply from the servlet. The servlet uses this object to send back the information that was requested from it. It can return any content type, but the type needs to be specified as part of the response. The servlet also has the capability to update attributes of the response headers. We cover responses in more detail in the "Using the HttpServletServletRequest and HttpServletResponse protocols" section of this chapter. The Hello World example has no need to update any response header information because it is a basic example and always returns a simple HTML page.

The first line of code in the `doGet()` method sets the content type of its response to `text/html` by calling the `setContentType()` method of the response object. The `text/html` type is the standard MIME content type for HTML pages. Next the servlet uses the `getWriter()` method to obtain a `PrintWriter` from the response object. The `PrintWriter` converts Java's Unicode characters to a locale-specific encoding. The servlet then uses the `PrintWriter` to return a Hello World HTML page to the client. The browser receives the response and renders the HTML to the user. That's it. Using the request-response paradigm, the client requested an HTML page, and the servlet responded with the HTML page. The result is shown in Figure 9-5.

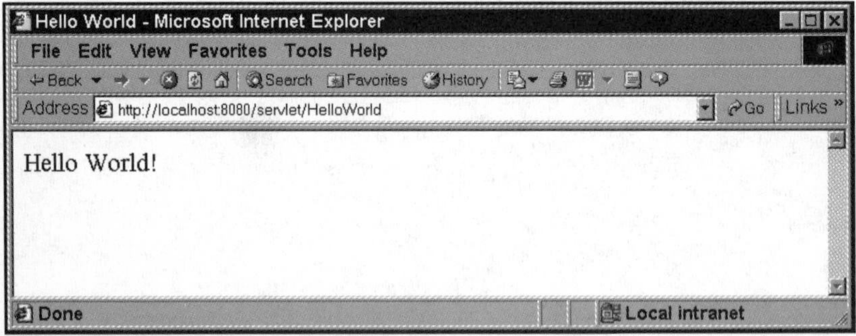

Figure 9-5: The code in Listing 9-1 produces the Hello World output.

Looking at a simple counter servlet

This next example takes you through another basic servlet that displays the number of times it has been called since the server was last booted (or loaded the servlet). It uses a class variable to hold the count and displays the count to the user as HTML. Remember class variables generally should be constants (variables that are used for reference and are never changed), but sometimes threading issues aren't a concern. This is a basic example not intended for high-volume processing. Listing 9-2 shows you the source for this servlet.

Listing 9-2: Simple Counter Servlet

```
import java.io.*;
import javax.servlet.*;
import javax.servlet.http.*;
public class SimpleCounterServlet extends HttpServlet {
  int count = 0;
public void doGet(HttpServletRequest req, HttpServletResponse res)
    throws ServletException, IOException {
    res.setContentType("text/html");
    PrintWriter out = res.getWriter();
    count++;
    out.println("Since loading, this servlet has been called " +
count + " times.");
}
```

As in the Hello World servlet, this servlet first sets the content type of its response, obtains a `PrintWriter`, and then uses the `PrintWriter` to write the data to the client. This servlet includes a class variable (`count`), which it increments each time the `doGet()` method is called. Remember, servlets stay loaded in memory after they are loaded, so the count variable won't be reinitialized to zero each time it processes a request. Each thread that runs through this servlet accesses the same variable. Figure 9-6 shows the output that results from a call to this servlet. If you try this servlet, keep clicking the Refresh button on your browser and notice the count incrementing each time. The refresh action causes the browser to submit another request to the servlet. Figure 9-7 shows the output from this servlet after clicking the Refresh button two times.

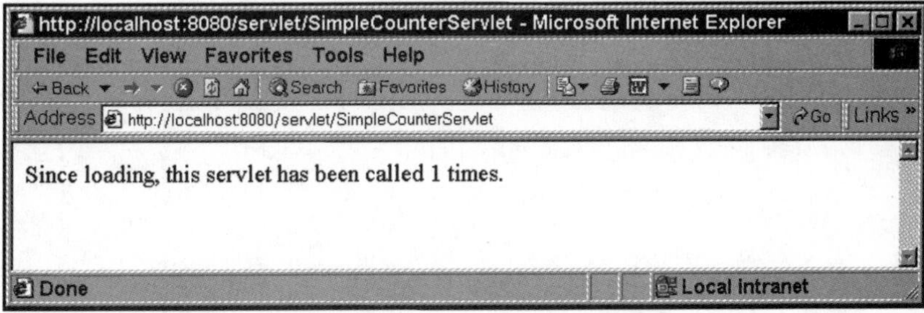

Figure 9-6: SimpleCounterServlet output.

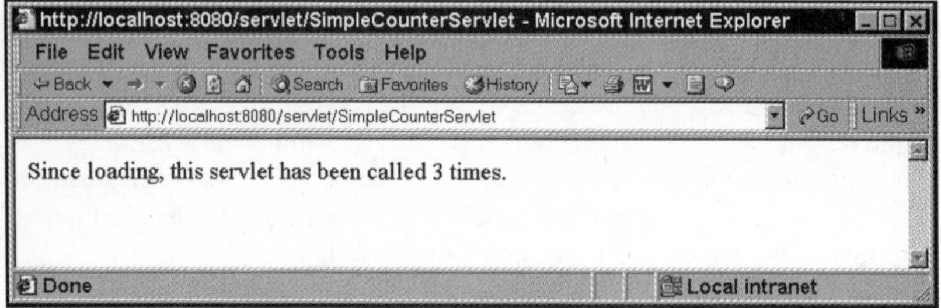

Figure 9-7: More output from the SimpleCounterServlet.

Looking at a simple HTTP servlet

Still keeping it simple, this next example adds a little bit more interaction with the user. This servlet imitates a search facility by accepting a name to search for and returns results based on what it finds. To keep things simple, this example stubs out the results and returns a hard-coded list. First, you need to present the user with an HTML entry form to capture the search criteria. Use the HTML code in Listing 9-3 to gather user information. Figure 9-8 shows how form looks.

Listing 9-3: Coding the HTML Entry Form

```
<HTML>
<HEAD>
<TITLE>Search Screen</TITLE>
</HEAD>
<BODY>
<FORM METHOD=GET ACTION="/servlet/SimpleHTTPServlet">
Please enter the first name of the person you wish to search for:
<INPUT TYPE=TEXT NAME="name"><P>
<INPUT TYPE=SUBMIT VALUE="Search">
</FORM>
</BODY>
</HTML>
```

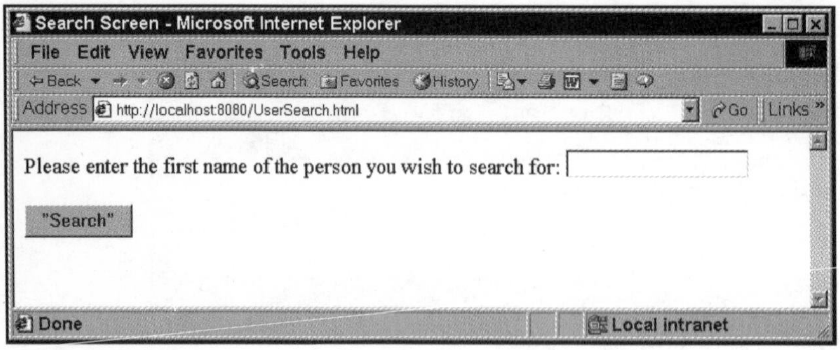

Figure 9-8: The code in Listing 9-3 produces this search criteria form.

When the user submits this form, the name is sent to the SimpleHTTPServlet servlet because the form's `ACTION` attribute tells it to do so. The code also tells it to use the `GET` method. In the `doGet()` method, you can get the form parameter(s) from the `HttpServletRequest` object. This example gets the `name` parameter from the request so you can use it in your mock query. The source code for the SimpleHTTPServlet is shown in Listing 9-4.

Listing 9-4: Source Code for SimpleHTTPServlet

```
import java.io.*;
import javax.servlet.*;
import javax.servlet.http.*;
public class SimpleHTTPServlet extends HttpServlet {
public void doGet(HttpServletRequest req, HttpServletResponse res)
     throws ServletException, IOException {
 res.setContentType("text/html");
 PrintWriter out = res.getWriter();
 String userName = res.getParameter("name");
 //Here you could query a database with the username and return
 //the result set back to the user.
 //Instead we will just stub out the results for our example.
 out.println("<HTML>");
 out.println("<HEAD><TITLE>Search Results</TITLE></HEAD>");
 out.println("<BODY>");
 out.println("<TABLE>");
 //assure userName not null before trimming
 if( userName != null && userName.trim().length() > 0)
 {
   out.println("<TR><TD><BIG>");
   out.println("The following people were found that fit your criteria:");
  out.println("</BIG></TD></TR><TR><TD>");
  out.println( userName + " Jones");
  out.println("</TD></TR><TR><TD>");
  out.println( userName + " Smith");
  out.println("</TD></TR><TR><TD>");
  out.println( userName + " Warner");
  out.println("</TD></TR>");
  }
  else
  {
 out.println("<TR><TD>");
 out.println(" You did not enter a name to search for. Please try again.");
 out.println("</TD></TR>");
  }

  out.println("</TABLE></BODY></HTML>");
} //end of doGet()
}
```

This servlet looks a bit more complex than the previous examples, but the only major difference is the call to `req.getParameter("name")` to find out what the user entered on the form. The `getParameter()` method of the request allows the servlet access to the query string that was passed. It returns the parameter's value for the parameter that you ask for, or it returns null if the parameter is not on the query string. If the parameter was sent but without a value (for example an empty entry field), the `getParameter()` returns an empty string. You check for both a null value and an empty string to determine whether anything is entered.

Because this simple form only has one entry field, you only have to check for the presence of one field, and you can dynamically generate an error message if nothing was entered. Figure 9-9 displays the resulting HTML page if `John` is entered in the form.

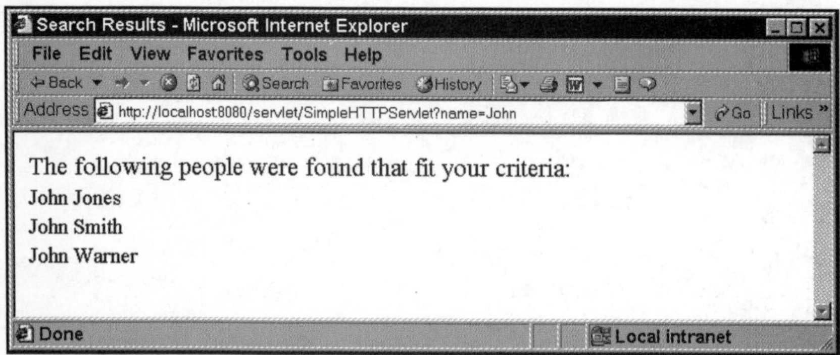

Figure 9-9: SimpleHTTPServlet output if John is entered in the form.

This example shows a stubbed result set. It takes the name that is entered, appends last names to it, and writes them to the buffer. In a real-world example, you would most likely run some type of JDBC call to a database to query on the name entered or use some type of EJB to perform the search. You can then display the result set that is returned, or if the result set is empty, you can return a message to the user stating that no results were found.

Understanding the GenericServlet interface

The `GenericServlet` class implements the `Servlet` interface and, for convenience, the `ServletConfig` interface. Servlet developers typically subclass `GenericServlet`, or its descendent `HttpServlet`, unless the servlet needs another class as a parent. If a servlet needs to subclass another class, the servlet must implement the `Servlet` interface directly because of the Java-wide restriction that Java is unable to support multiple inheritances. This would be necessary when, for example, RMI or CORBA objects act as servlets.

The `GenericServlet` class was created to make writing servlets easier. It provides simple versions of the lifecycle methods `init()` and `destroy()` and of the methods in the `ServletConfig` interface. It also provides a `log()` method, from the `ServletContext` interface. The servlet programmer must override only the `service()` method, which is abstract. Although not required to do so, the servlet programmer should also override the `getServletInfo()` method, and he will also want to specialize the `init()` and `destroy()` methods if expensive servlet-wide resources need to be managed.

Understanding the HttpServlet interface

Because most servlets extend the capabilities of Web servers that use HTTP to interact with clients, the most common way to develop servlets is by specializing the `java.servlet.http.HttpServlet`. This class implements the `Servlet` interface by extending the `GenericServlet` base class.

`HttpServlet` is an abstract class that simplifies writing HTTP servlets. An abstract class cannot be instantiated. Abstract classes are used to provide the foundation for the declarations of any subclasses. Because HttpServlet is an abstract class, servlet programmers must subclass it and override at least one of its methods. The following methods are generally overridden:

- The `service()` method is called each time the servlet is requested. Typically, most developers do not use the `service()` method, but instead use the `doGet()` and `doPost()` methods supplied by the `HttpServlet` class.
  - The `doGet()` method is invoked in response to a request from the server through the `GET`, the `conditional GET` and `HEAD` methods, typically from a URL request or an HTML form. `GET` methods should be used whenever the request will not modify any information on the server. Because `doGet()` calls pass parameters on the URL, the amount of data passed to the `doGet()` method is limited to the number of characters allowed in a URL. Because the information is passed on the URL, the end user can see the values being passed in the browser. If you are passing sensitive data, you should either encode it before it is passed or consider using the `doPost()` method.
  - The `doPost()` method is invoked in response to a request from the server through the `POST` method, typically from an HTML form. `POST` methods should be used whenever the request will modify some information on the server. In contrast to implementing the `doGet()` method which limits the amount of data you can send to the servlet, `POST` requests can pass an unlimited amount of data directly over the socket connection as part of its HTTP request body.
- The `init()` method executes only once when the Web server loads the servlet. Even though most servlets are run in multithreaded servers, there are no concurrency issues during servlet initialization because the server calls the `init()` method once, when it loads the servlet, and it does not call it again unless it is reloading the servlet. A servlet continues to run until it is removed from the server.

- The `destroy()` method is called when the servlet is removed from the Web server. This method allows you to clean up or free the resources that you obtained in the `init()` method, and also perform any type of proper shutdown of services.
- The `getServletInfo()` method should be implemented by developers to return imformation about the author, version, and copyright of the servlet. This method is basically an information method that returns a string populated with organizational type data.
- The `doPut()` and `doDelete()` methods enable servlet developers to support HTTP/1.1 clients, which support these features. In containers that support only HTTP/1.0, only the `doGet()`, `doHead()`, and `doPost()` methods are used because HTTP/1.0 does not define the `PUT` or `DELETE` methods.

Using the HttpServletRequest and HttpServletResponse protocols

The `HttpServletRequest` and `HttpServletResponse` are the mechanisms that servlets use to implement the request-response paradigm. Each time a client requests an action of a servlet, it passes its request in the form of an `HttpServletRequest(`*`subclass of ServletRequest`*`)`, along with a `HttpServletResponse(`*`subclass of ServletResponse`*`)` object for the servlet to populate and return. Each have methods and attributes to which the servlet developer has access.

Using HttpServletRequest

The `HTTPServletRequest` object transmits the data from the client to the server by the HTTP headers and the message body of the request. The servlet engine stores the information submitted, either via the URL or form fields, as a set of name-value pairs. Multiple parameter values can exist for any given parameter name. The following methods are supplied by the interface for accessing parameters:

- `getParameter()`
- `getParameterValues()`
- `getParameterNames()`

The `getParameter()` method returns a string object representing the value of the parameter, or null if no parameter with that name was sent. The simple HTTP servlet example uses an HTML form with a `Name` input field. When the user submits this form, the servlet inspects the request object for the value of `req.getParameter("name")`. The result of this call is whatever the user entered in the input field. If the user doesn't enter anything into the field and then submits the form, the `getParameter("name")` call returns an empty string, not a null string. The form submits whatever is in the text box.

Because it is possible to have multiple values for each parameter name, a developer can use the `getParameterValues()` method, which returns an array of string objects that represent the values for the given key. If the `getParameter()` method is used for a parameter that has multiple values, it returns the first element in the array of values.

These two methods give you the capability to selectively ask for parameters by name or get all the values submitted on the form. Another useful method enables you to get all the names of the parameters submitted. The `getParameterNames()` method returns an enumeration of string objects containing the names of the parameters contained in the request. Listing 9-5 shows how a program can cycle through the parameters that were submitted on the request and print them to standard out.

Listing 9-5: Using getParameterNames()

```
Enumeration myParameters = req.getParameterNames();
while(myParameters.hasMoreElements())
{
 String paramName = (String)myParameters.nextElement();
 System.out.println("Parameter name =  " + paramName);
 System.out.println("Parameter value =  " +
req.getParameter(paramName));
}
```

The request object can also have attributes associated with it. Attributes can be set by the engine to express information that otherwise couldn't be expressed via the API, but, most commonly, attributes are used when one servlet wants to communicate information to another servlet (via RequestDispatcher). You must use the RequestDispatcher to forward the request to the next servlet to preserve the data; otherwise, a new request gets generated, and the attributes of the original request are lost. An example of passing an attribute on the request to another servlet might include passing a name entered on one screen that you want to default on another screen, or your second servlet may just want access to it. Attributes can be any type of Java objects, such as a string for use in the previous example. Attributes are accessed by the following methods:

- `getAttribute()`
- `getAttributeNames()`
- `setAttribute()`

Unlike the `getParameter()` and `getParameterValues()` methods that return `String` objects, the `getAttribute()` methods return values of type `Object`, so you must cast them to the appropriate type when you want to use them. Listing 9-6 illustrates this:

Listing 9-6: Getting and Setting Request Attributes

```
Servlet A {
HashMap myDrivers = new HashMap();
myDrivers.put(…)
req.setAttribute("Drivers", myDrivers);
}
Servlet B {
(HashMap) myHashReceived = (HashMap) req.getAttribute("Drivers");
}
```

The receiving servlet that pulls out an attribute must know what type the initiator put it in as. In Listing 9-6, the initiator built a HashMap loaded with drivers and set it on the request. The next servlet pulls the HashMap off the request and casts it so that the servlet can then use the HashMap for whatever it may want to do with it. You can associate only one value with each attribute name (unlike parameters).

The `HttpServletRequest` object also has methods that a servlet developer can use to access header information. A servlet can access the header information of an HTTP request with the following methods:

- `getHeader()`
- `getHeaders()`
- `getHeaderNames()`

The `getHeader()` method returns the value of a header of the supplied name. Multiple headers can be present in an HTTP request. If there are multiple headers with the same name, the `getHeader()` method returns the first header contained in the request. The `getHeader()` methods are analogous to headers as the `getParameter()` methods are to parameters. The `getHeaders()` method allows access to all the header values associated with a particular header name returning an enumeration of string objects. Using the `getHeaderNames()` method, you can obtain an enumeration of all the header names the request contains. From this list, you can loop through the header names and obtain each header value.

If headers contain data that can best be expressed as an `int` or a `Date` object, the following methods simplify access to these values:

- `getIntHeader()`
- `getDateHeader()`

If the `getIntHeader()` method cannot translate the header value to an integer, a `NumberFormatException` occurs. If the `getDateHeader()` method cannot translate the header into a `Date` object, an `IllegalArgumentException` occurs.

Path elements are another part of the request. You can obtain the following URI (Uniform Resource Identifier) elements from the request object:

- *Context path:* This is the path prefix associated with the `ServletContext` that the servlet is a part of. If the servlet is running in the default context, this path is an empty string because the default context is rooted at the base of the Web server's URL namespace. If the servlet is running in any other context, this path starts with a forward slash (`/`) character but does not end with a / character.
- *Servlet path:* This is the path section that directly corresponds to the mapping that activated this request. This path starts with a / character.
- *Path info:* This is the part of the request path that is not part of the context path or the servlet path.

The following methods exist in the `HttpServletRequest` interface to access this path information:

- `getContextPath()`
- `getServletPath()`
- `getPathInfo()`

These methods can be useful tools to your servlets for reconstructing URLs or passing along values, via the URL, via the path info other than parameter values. Figure 9-10 illustrates a few examples that should help clarify some of these points.

Context Path = /csi

Servlet1 Mapping	Servlet2 Mapping	Servlet3 Mapping
Pattern: /employees	Pattern: /clients	Pattern: *.jsp

Request 1: * /csi/employees/index.html*
ContextPath = /csi
ServletPath = /employees
PathInfo = /index.html

Request 2: */csi/clients/bio/*
ContextPath = /csi
ServletPath = /clients
PathInfo = /bio

Request 3: */csi/home/intro.jsp*
\ContextPath = /csi
ServletPath = /home/intro.jsp
PathInfo = null

Figure 9-10: Examples of accessing Pathing elements from the request object.

HttpServletResponse

The response object encapsulates all information to be returned from the server to the client. In the HTTP protocol, this information is transmitted from the server to the client either by HTTP headers or the message body of the request.

To improve efficiency, a servlet engine is allowed to buffer output going to the client. The following methods are provided in the `ServletResponse` interface to allow a servlet access and to set the buffering information:

- `getBufferSize()`
- `setBufferSize()`
- `isCommitted()`
- `flushBuffer()`
- `reset()`

These methods are provided on the `ServletResponse` interface to allow buffering operations to be performed whether the servlet is using a `ServletOutputStream` or a writer.

The `getBufferSize()` method returns the size of the underlying buffer being used. If no buffering is being used for this response, this method returns the `int` value of `0` (zero).

The servlet can request a preferred buffer size for the response by using the `setBufferSize()` method. The actual buffer assigned to this request is not required to be the same size as requested by the servlet, but must be at least as large as the buffer size requested. This method must be called before any content is written using a `ServletOutputStream` or a writer. If any content has been written, this method throws an `IllegalStateException`.

The `isCommitted()` method returns a Boolean value indicating whether any bytes from the response have yet been returned to the client.

The `flushBuffer()` method forces any content in the buffer to be written to the client.

The `reset()` method clears any data that exists in the buffer as long as the response is not considered to be committed. All headers and the status code set by the servlet prior to the reset being called must be cleared as well. If the response is committed and the `reset()` method is called, an `IllegalStateException` is thrown. In this case, the response and its associated buffer remain unchanged. A response is considered committed after it has already had its status code and headers written and is no longer available to be updated.

After the buffer in use is filled, the engine must immediately flush the contents of the buffer to the client. If this is the first time that data is sent to the client in response to this request, the response is considered to be committed at this point.

A servlet can set headers of an HTTP response with the following methods of the `HttpServletResponse` interface:

- `The setHeader()` method sets a header with a given name and value. If a header already exists with this name, it is replaced by the new header. In the case in which a set of header values exist for the given name, all values are cleared and replaced with the new value.
- `The addHeader()` method adds a header value to the set of headers with a given name. If no headers are already associated with the given name, this method creates a new set.

To be successfully transmitted back to the client, headers must be set before the response is committed. The servlet engine ignores any headers set after the response is committed.

The following convenient methods exist in the `HttpServletResponse` interface:

- `sendRedirect()`
- `sendError()`

The `sendRedirect()` method sets the appropriate headers and content body to redirect the client to a different URL. It is legal to call this method with a relative URL path; however, the underlying engine must translate the relative path to a fully qualified URL for transmission back to the client. If a partial URL is given and, for whatever reason, cannot be converted into a valid URL, this method throws an `IllegalArgumentException`.

> **NOTE**: Using `sendRedirect` creates a brand new request object for the target URL. Any attributes on the old request are lost.

The `sendError()` method sets the appropriate headers and content body to return to the client. An optional string argument can be provided to the `sendError()` method, which can be used in the content body of the error.

Calling these methods commits the response, if it has not already been committed, and terminates it. No further output to the client should be made by the servlet after these methods are called. The data is ignored if it is written to the response after these methods are called.

If data has been written to the response buffer, but not returned to the client (for example, the response is not committed), the data in the response buffer must be cleared and replaced with the data set by these methods. If the response is committed, these methods throw `IllegalStateException` errors.

It is also possible for a servlet to set the language attributes of a response back to a client. This information is communicated with the `Content-Language` header along with other mechanisms described in the HTTP/1.1 specification. You use the `setLocale()` method of the `ServletResponse` interface to set the language of the response. Examples of different possible languages are `en` (English), `fr` (French), or `ja` (Japanese) This method correctly sets the appropriate HTTP headers to communicate the locale to the client accurately.

For maximum benefit, the `setLocale()` method should be called by the developer before the `getWriter()` method of the `ServletResponse` interface is called. This ensures that the returned `PrintWriter` is configured appropriately for the target locale.

If the `setContentType()` method is called after the `setLocale()` method and there is a charset component to the given content type, the charset specified in the content type overrides the value set with the call to `setLocale()`.

The following events can indicate that the servlet has provided all the content to satisfy the request (`HttpServletRequest`) and that the response object (`HttpServletResponse`) can be considered closed:

- The termination of the `service()` method of the servlet
- The amount of content specified in the `setContentLength()` method of the response has been written to the response
- The `sendError()` method is called
- The `sendRedirect()` method is called

When a response is closed, all content in the response buffer, if any remains, is immediately flushed to the client.

Summary

You should now understand why servlets have gained such widespread popularity with server-side developers. This chapter covered the servlet flow and lifecycle events, talked about which objects are generally utilized from the Servlet API, and illustrated some basic techniques with code examples.

This chapter introduced you to the `javax.servlet` and `javax.servlet.http` packages, which are defined as extensions to the standard JDK. Because most servlets extend Web servers that use HTTP to interact with clients, the chapter concentrated on the `javax.servlet.http` package. It explained the `HttpServlet` Interface and the abstract methods it contains. And because the fundamental design of servlets uses the request-response paradigm, this chapter provided details about the `HttpServletRequest` and the `HttpServletResponse` objects.

Each servlet receives a `HttpServletRequest` and `HttpServletResponse` object when it gets a call from a client. It is through these two objects that the server (servlet) and the client interact. These objects have many useful helper methods that allow you to manipulate and transform data to offer a dynamic environment for server-side processing.

> **ON THE WEB:** To see some of these techniques applied to a real-world application, the Chapter 9 folder on this book's companion Web site (`www.wiley.com/extras`) contains the entire source code file (`CSICruiseFinal.ear`) for the Almost Free Cruise application.

Chapter 10
More Servlet APIs

In This Chapter

- Using the `ServletContext`
- Using the `RequestDispatcher`
- Understanding servlet interaction techniques
- Using cookies

In many situations multiple servlets are running as part of a Web application. An important part of servlet programming is knowing how these servlets interact. Some servlets depend on other servlets to help them with their specific task; some servlets share common data among themselves, and some servlets may not care about any other servlets.

The Servlet API includes tools that enable you to control the manner in which servlets interact and share data. These methods are important for consistency and performance. If each servlet needs to access the same piece of data stored in a database, you wouldn't want each one to have to run the expensive I/O to do a database query for the same data. Instead, the first servlet that needs the data could perform the query and then share this information with the rest of the servlets in the application.

Servlets are generally used to control application flow. The Servlet API has methods that allow the servlets to pass control around to the different components of the application. Because developers want their applications to behave in many different ways, the API provides multiple methods that enable you to tailor the way your servlets navigate.

Using the tools of the Servlet API, such as the `ServletContext` and the `RequestDispatcher`, enables you to effectively build and manage the interaction and behavior of your application servlets. It is vital that you know how your servlets relate to each other and the interaction that must take place in order for them to run as efficiently and accurately as possible. This chapter explains some of the more popular approaches to enabling servlet interactions and gives you an understanding of the costs and benefits of each.

Reviewing Controller Issues

When servlets are used to handle the application control, you need to consider some issues before you design your navigation infrastructure. Some design approaches use a servlet for each page of the application, allowing each servlet to perform a distinct service related to a specific page. The knowledge of how the page should interact is isolated to each individual servlet. Another popular design is to have one application servlet handle the navigation and have specialized classes handle the specific business logic for each page. This design decreases the number of class files your application requires and centralizes the navigation logic to one place.

Security is an issue that needs to be well thought out. Because application servers enable you to define security down to the servlet level, you need to determine whether the single-servlet approach is going to give you the flexibility you need to keep your application secure. You may want to implement the multiple servlet design creating a servlet for each page, splitting your controller logic, so that each can have its own security level defined. This design would best fit an application that has multiple security roles defined within each page. If your security level is at the overall page level, the single servlet approach offers a streamlined solution.

Another issue that could be a factor in your decision-making is the way your development team is organized. This team structure might dictate the best type of controller design for you. If your application uses a servlet controller for each page in the application, it is easier to divide tasks among team members. You can define a unit of work to be at a screen level. Each developer can have one or more screens assigned to him or her. In a Model View Controller (MVC) architecture, each developer can be responsible for all three modules for the screens assigned. If multiple developers need to work on the controller piece of an application at the same time, the single servlet design poses a potential bottleneck in development.

Each development project is unique and can utilize the controller design that best fits its application and environment. There is no single way to code your application controller layer.

Using the ServletContext

The `ServletContext` interface provides a common area for multiple servlets in a Web application to share information. Using the `ServletContext` object, a servlet can log events, obtain URL references to resources, and set and store information for the other servlets in the context to access.

Each Web application deployed into a container has only one instance object of the `ServletContext`. If an application is distributed among multiple virtual machines, there is one instance object of a `ServletContext` per virtual machine. If a servlet is not deployed as part of a Web application, it is implicitly part of a default Web application and has a default `ServletContext`. A default `ServletContext` is nondistributable and must exist in only one virtual machine.

Just like servlets, the `ServletContext` can have initialization parameters defined to be loaded at start up. The following two `ServletContext` methods give you access to these parameters:

- *getInitParameter(String name):* This method returns a string object of the value of the named initialization parameter, or `null` if the parameter does not exist.
- *getInitParameterNames():* This method returns an enumeration of `string` objects with the names of the context's initialization parameters, or an empty enumeration if the context didn't have any initialization parameters defined.

Typically developers use initialization parameters to load setup information for things that will be accessed by multiple servlets. A servlet can add an object attribute into the context by name. A servlet can get and set variables (attributes) out of and into the `ServletContext`. The following methods are available for manipulating the values:

- *setAttribute(String name, Object object):* This method binds an attribute to the context with the given name. If an attribute is already bound with that name, it replaces the old value with the newly supplied value.
- *getAttribute(String name):* This method returns the attribute value that corresponds with the given name, or null if no attribute with that name exists.
- *getAttributeNames():* This method returns an enumeration of string objects that represent the names of all the bound attributes.
- *removeAttribute(String name):* This method removes (unbinds) the attribute from the context for the given name.

Context attributes are local to the virtual machine in which they are created. If your application is running in a distributed environment, you shouldn't use the `ServletContext` to share data. Instead, the information should be put into a session object (discussed in Chapter 11), stored in a database, or set in an Enterprise JavaBean component.

The `ServletContext` interface provides direct access to the hierarchy of static content documents that are part of the Web application, including HTML, GIF, and JPEG files, via the following methods of the `ServletContext` interface:

- *getResource(String path):* This method returns a URL to the resource that is mapped to a specific path. The path must be a relative path (beginning with a /).
- *getResourceAsStream(String path):* This method returns the resource located at the given path as an `InputStream` object.

The `getResource()` and `getResourceAsStream()` methods take a string with a leading forward slash (/) as an argument, which gives the path of the resource relative to the root of the context. This hierarchy of documents can exist in the server's file system, in a Web application archive file, on a remote server, or at some other location.

These methods are not used to obtain dynamic content. For example, in a container that supports JSPs, a method call of the form `getResource("/login.jsp")` returns the JSP source code, not the generated output.

Using the RequestDispatcher

Typically when developing Web applications, you need to perform forward processing of a request to another servlet or include the output of another servlet in the response. These actions are made possible by the `RequestDispatcher` interface. Use the following two methods to obtain a `RequestDispatcher`:

- *ServletContext.getRequestDispatcher(String path):* This method returns a `RequestDispatcher` object for the resource located at the given path.
- *ServletContext.getNamedDispatcher(String servletName):* This method returns a `RequestDispatcher` object that acts as a wrapper for the given servlet.

The `getRequestDispatcher()` method accepts a string argument describing a path within the scope of a `ServletContext`. The path must be relative to the root of the `ServletContext` and begin with a forward slash (/). The method looks for the servlet in the path supplied, wraps it in a `RequestDispatcher` object, and returns it to the caller. If no servlet can be resolved based on the given path, a `null` is returned.

If you need a `RequestDispatcher` object that can be obtained using a path that is relative to the path of the current request, instead of the root of the `ServletContext`, the following method is provided in the `ServletRequest`:

```
ServletRequest.getRequestDispatcher()
```

This method is similar to the method of the same name in the `ServletContext`. The servlet container uses the information from the request object to translate the given path into a complete path. For example, if a context is rooted at / and a request is rooted to `/images/list.html`, a request dispatcher returned from `ServletRequest.getRequestDispatcher("total.html")` behaves exactly like a call to `ServletContext.getRequestDispatcher("/images/total.html")`.

The `getNamedDispatcher()` method takes a string argument indicating the name of a servlet known to the `ServletContext`. If a servlet is found, it is wrapped with a `RequestDispatcher` object, and the object is returned to the caller. If there is no servlet with the given name, the method returns a null.

The `RequestDispatcher` has two methods that you can utilize:

- *forward(ServletRequest req, ServletResponse res):* This method forwards a request from one servlet to another servlet (or JSP or HTML file).
- *include(ServletRequest req, ServletResponse res):* This method includes the content of a resource (servlet, JSP, HTML file) in the response.

The parameters to these methods can either be the request and response arguments passed into the service method of the `Servlet` interface, or instances of subclasses of the request and response wrapper classes (new with the 2.3 specification). The container must ensure that the dispatch of the request to a target servlet occurs in the same thread of the same virtual machine as the original request.

The `include()` method can be called at any time. When you include the output of another servlet, that servlet has access to all the aspects of the request object as the original servlet, but its access to the response object is limited. It can write information only to the `ServletOutputStream` or writer of the response object and commit a response by writing content past the end of the response buffer, or by explicitly calling the `flushBuffer()` method of the `ServletResponse` interface. It cannot set headers or call any methods that affect the headers of the response.

Except for servlets (wrapped in a `RequestDispatcher` object) obtained by using the `getNamedDispatcher()` method, a servlet being used as a result of calling the `include()` method on that servlet has access to the path by which it was invoked. The following request attributes are set:

- *javax.servlet.include.request_uri:* This returns the URI of the included file.
- *javax.servlet.include.context_path:* This returns the servlet context path used by the included file.
- *javax.servlet.include.servlet_path:* This returns the servlet path of the included file.

- *javax.servlet.include.path_info:* This returns a string object with the value of the path information of the included file.
- *javax.servlet.include.query_string:* This returns a string object with the value of the query string that was sent to the included file.

These attributes are accessible from the included servlet by using the `getAttribute()` method of the request object. The following list illustrates the results of these calls:

- *Context Path:* `/csi`
- *Servlet Mapping:* `*.jsp`
- *Request URL:* `http://WASBible/servlet/MyServlet?a=1&b=2`
- *MyServlet Include Call:*

```
getServletContext().getRequestDispatcher("/jsp/error.jsp")
.include(req,res);
```

Given the this example, the return values for `req.getAttribute("<key>")` returns the following:

```
javax.servlet.include.request_uri =     "/jsp/error.jsp"
javax.servlet.include.context_path =     "/csi"
javax.servlet.include.servlet_path =     "/jsp/error.jsp"
javax.servlet.include.path_info =    null
javax.servlet.include.query_string =     "a=1&b=2"
```

If the `RequestDispatcher` was obtained with the `getNamedDispatcher()` method, these attributes are not set.

The `forward()` method of the `RequestDispatcher` interface can be called by the calling servlet only when no output has been committed to the client. If output data exists in the response buffer that has been committed, the content must be cleared before the target servlet's `service()` method is called. If the response has been committed, an `IllegalStateException` is thrown. The only exception to this is if the `RequestDispatcher` is obtained with the `getNamedDispatcher()` method. In this case, the path elements of the request object must reflect those of the original request.

Before the `forward()` method of the `RequestDispatcher` interface returns, the servlet container must send, commit, and close the response content.

Forwarding versus Response Redirection

After a servlet is done processing its logic, it generally sends the user to another page in the application. You accomplish this in two ways: One is to use the `forward()` method of the `RequestDispatcher`, as discussed in the previous section, and the other is to use the `sendRedirect()` method of the `Response` object, which is covered in Chapter 9.

Using the `forward()` method of the `RequestDispatcher` interface is a good way to pass data to another resource because the request and response are kept alive and passed on. It is possible to set attributes on these objects, and they can be utilized by the target page. Remember that the `forward()` method should be used to give another resource the responsibility of replying to the user. An example of this would be if a servlet is responsible for validating data input by a user and finds an error (such as relational field edits). The servlet can set an error message as an attribute in the request and forward the request to a JSP view, which could then display the error message while still retaining the data submitted in the original request.

The `forward()` method never leaves the server machine. You are forwarding from one server resource to another. In contrast, the `sendRedirect()` method returns to the client and tells the browser to go to another URL before displaying to the client. This creates a brand new `request` object, so any attributes of the old request are lost. You can, however, pass parameters in the URL string to which you redirect. Figure 10-1 illustrates the flow of the `forward()` method, and Figure 10-2 illustrates the `sendRedirect()` flow.

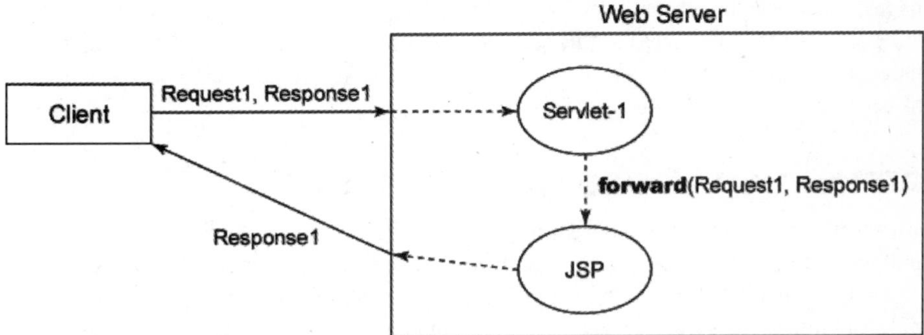

Figure 10-1: The RequestDispatcher forward() method.

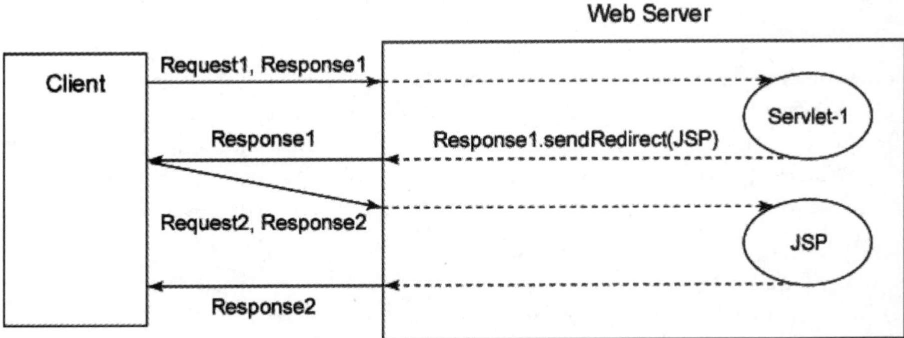

Figure 10-2: The flow of a client request using the Response sendRedirect() method to ultimately send back a client response.

Servlet programmers heavily utilize these methods. Deciding which to method to use depends on the requirements of the transaction. Following are bits of code that show you the correct syntax for these methods:

`//forward` example:

```
RequestDispatcher dispatcher =
getServletContext().getRequestDispatcher("/csi/employees.jsp");
  request.setAttribute("EmpName", "John");
  dispatcher.forward(request, response);
```

`//redirect` example:

```
request.setAttribute("EmpName", "John");
response.sendRedirect("/csi/employees.jsp");
```

As mentioned previously, using the `sendRedirect()` method ends up creating a new request object that gets sent to the `employees.jsp`. Any attributes that are set on the original request are lost. In this case, a call in the `employees.jsp` to get the `EmpName` attribute returns `null` because the attribute was set on the first request. If you would like for the `employees.jsp` to have access to this attribute, use the `forward()` method so that the original request is preserved and a call in the `employees.jsp` to get the `EmpName` attribute returns `John`.

Understanding Cache Complications

Because most servlets are ultimately returning data to be rendered in a browser, you must be aware of the different browsers and the way they behave. Browsers have their own Back and Forward buttons to aid the user with navigation. As you develop applications, browser navigational buttons can cause problems if your application screens are not fully decoupled from each other. The browser's caching function poses another potential problem. Because your servlet application is dynamic in nature and most likely uses some type of dynamic front end (JavaServer Page), caching is not always preferred. Sometimes the caching mechanism hides the updated results.

Most of the time, you want your browser to reload the page every time it displays the page to the user to verify it has all the latest updates. It is possible for you to set header information into the `HttpServletResponse` object to notify the browser to do just that. You need to set the appropriate HTTP header attributes to prevent the browser from caching the dynamic content output by the JSP. The following code displays the proper attributes to set:

```
response.setHeader("Cache-Control","no-cache"); //HTTP 1.1
response.setHeader("Pragma","no-cache"); //HTTP 1.0
response.setDateHeader ("Expires", 0); //prevents caching at the proxy server
```

You should you use both `setHeader` statements to allow for older browser versions. If setting the Cache-Control to `"no-cache"` does not work, try setting the Cache-Control to `"no-store"`. To enable your client to run in a browser, you must not only be aware of your software design but also of the browser's design.

Using Precondition Processing

With the rise in popularity of remote devices, such as PDAs, handhelds, and cell phones, the Web-based developer needs to allow for a flexible presentation layer. You should abstract your presentation from the actual business logic as much as possible. One way to accomplish this is to implement precondition processing. Here are some common examples of precondition processing:

- *Decrypting an input stream:* The incoming data is encrypted for security purposes.
- *Decompressing a stream:* The incoming is compressed for more efficient transfer over the network.
- *Translating various encoding schemes to a common format:* Multiple encoding schemes require different handling.

If each encoding is translated to a common format, the core request-handling mechanism can treat every request in the same manner. You can think of it as putting a filter in front of all your requests so the core logic only has to deal with one type. You could even put user authentication or authorization in precondition processing; however, it is usually handled as a part of the controller.

A common implementation of preconditioning processing is to have the `doPost()` method of your servlet handle any of the filtering needed to create a common request format and then call a method such as `processPost()`, which handles the core logic. Even if you don't plan to use any type of filter when you first design your servlet, it is a good habit not to put your core logic into your `doPost()` method. By having `doPost()` call `processPost()`, you are adding a layer in between the entry point of your servlet and the core logic layer. After your core logic is coded, if you ever need to allow for multiple client requests, you can use the `doPost()` method to filter or decode each request type into a common format to be processed by the core logic.

Using Post-Condition Processing

Just as you can put filters on requests, the same holds true for putting filters on the replies. Common examples of this are as follows:

- *Encrypting an output stream:* Encrypting the outgoing data for security purposes
- *Compressing a stream:* Compressing the outgoing stream for efficient transfer over the network
- *Transformation of data for different clients:* Transforming into HTML, XML, or WML

Post-condition processing is a powerful pattern when you have multiple possible clients for whom you need to adapt your presentation. If your servlet runs all its output through a post-conditioning method, such as `processResponse()`, you can isolate the filtering of output to this method. Again your core logic only needs to understand how to process data in a generic manner, and then the specific display results can be transformed by the post-processing.

Like precondition processing, post-condition processing simply adds a layer between your core logic and the client response. Using this type of abstraction keeps the clutter of any filter-type code out of your core logic processing. This technique helps keep your code clean and more easily understood (not to mention flexible).

Understanding Servlet Interaction Techniques

An individual servlet can create content by generating a full page for returning to the client, but it can also cooperate with other servlets in the application to create content. You can use several different techniques to facilitate servlet interactions.

Enabling servlet collaboration

Servlets can share information with other servlets (collaborate) by saving strings to the system Properties list, using a shared object, such as a singleton found in the server's classpath, or by using inheritance.

A basic way for servlets to share information is by using Java's system wide Properties list in the `java.lang.System` class. This list holds standard system properties, such as `java.version` and `path.separator`, but can also hold values for applications. Servlets can use this list to share data among themselves. One servlet can put a value in the list using the name-value paradigm, and another servlet, running in the same Java Virtual Machine (JVM), can get the property that the preceding servlet set. You use the following methods to manipulate values in the Properties list:

- `System.getProperties().put("key","value");`: This method sets a system property into the Properties list with the given name to the value specified.
- `System.getProperty("key");`: This method returns the system property value from the Properties list associated with the given key name.
- `System.getProperties().remove("key");`: This method removes the given property value from the system Properties list.

It is good practice to name the key for a property value with a prefix that contains the name of the servlet's package and the name of the collaboration group, for example, "`com.csi.servlet.ShoppingCart`". The Properties list intends that the key and value of a property should be objects, such as strings.

Using the Properties list for collaboration has some drawbacks. The data isn't persisted between server restarts, so you can potentially lose data; other classes in the servlets' JVM have access to this information and can modify or delete it, and some servlet security managers may not even grant servlets access to the system Properties list.

Another form of servlet collaboration is for the servlets to use a shared object. The Properties list is, in a sense, a shared object; however, if you create your own shared objects, you can specify them to your exact needs. You can write to a shared object, and the other servlets in your JVM can access it as long as it is kept in the classpath. Generally, this would be a singleton object, so that every servlet would get the same instance. The challenge to this approach is to keep the shared object from being garbage collected. The Garbage Collector can reclaim the shared object if, at any time, the object isn't referred to by a loaded servlet. With this in mind, it is a good idea to have each servlet save a reference to the shared object.

Probably the cleanest and easiest way for servlets to collaborate is to use the object-oriented technique of inheritance. All the servlets that want to share information can subclass off the same parent class, which can hold a reference to the information. All the servlets would inherit this reference. This method simplifies the code for collaborating servlets and limits access to the shared information to the proper subclasses.

In addition to holding shared references, the parent class can hold data and business logic that is common to the collaborating servlets. Each child class can access this information through the parent class's access methods.

Using servlet chaining and filtering

Another servlet interaction technique is to use servlet chaining. This process allows a request object to be handled by a sequence of servlets. The request and response that come into the first servlet are passed down the list of servlets. Each servlet has the capability to update the response object, but ultimately the last servlet in the chain has control over what is returned to the client via the response object.

There are two common ways to implement servlet chaining. One is to tell the server that certain URLs should be handled by a predefined list of servlets. The other way is to tell the server to send all output of a particular content type through a certain servlet before it is returned to the client. When a servlet converts one content type into another, it is called *filtering*. You may choose to use filtering if one servlet can handle the conversion needed; however, sometimes the updates that need to occur are somewhat involved and need multiple servlets to help with the process. In this case, simply defining a filter would be insufficient. Also with filtering, you must be able to identify all the content type(s) that could possibly require the filter to be applied to them.

With servlet chaining, the header information gets passed to the servlets in the chain, other than the first servlet, if the header information is from the preceding servlet, not the client. The first servlet in the chain gets the request and response from the client, with the original header information. It then does its thing and sends the request and response onto the next servlet in the list. The header information is not preserved from the client. The first servlet has the opportunity to add response headers and update, or even remove, existing values. Unless a chained servlet specifically reads the previous servlet's response headers and sends them as part of its own response, the headers are not passed and the client does not see them. A good design for chained servlets is always to pass the previous servlet's headers on to the next servlet, unless you have a specific reason not to do so. If, for example, you know that the last servlet in the chain updates the language type based on some logic, there is no need for you to preserve the value between the intermediary servlets in the chain.

Understanding Cookies

Cookies are small bits of textual information that a Web server sends to a browser and that the browser returns unchanged when visiting the same Web site or domain later. Cookies are used to save small bits of data for future use. Cookies are a good way to save small bits of data that need to be shared among different components of your application. Using cookies is a way to persist data for later use. The major drawback of relying on cookie data as your sole persistent mechanism for the data is that browsers allow the user to disable cookies. This can make your application unable to save any data to that machine. Because many of today's Web sites use cookies, many users have enabled their browsers to accept them, so they can be helpful as a source for persisting data. You should, however, always have an alternative way to save this data so your application can still function on browsers that do, in fact, disable cookies.

Using the Servlet Cookie API

To send cookies to the client, a servlet creates one or more cookies with the appropriate names and values via `new Cookie(name, value)`, sets any desired optional attributes via `cookie.setXxx`, and adds the cookies to the response headers via `response.addCookie(cookie)`. To read incoming cookies, call `request.getCookies()`, which returns an array of cookie objects. In most cases, you loop down this array until you find the one whose name (`getName`) matches the name you have in mind, and then call `getValue` on that cookie to see the value associated with that name.

Creating cookies

You create a cookie by calling the `Cookie` constructor, which takes two strings: the cookie name and the cookie value. Neither the name nor the value should contain whitespace or any of the following characters:

- Square brackets []
- Prentheses ()
- Equal sign (=)
- Quotation marks (")
- Forward slash (/)
- Question mark (?)
- Ampersand (@)
- Colon (:)
- Semicolon (;)

After you create the cookie, you are unable to change the cookie name. You can overwrite the value in the cookie by calling the `setValue()` method, but you must create a new cookie in order to change the name. The syntax for creating a new Cookie is as follows:

```
Cookie userCookie = new Cookie("user", "uid1234");
```

Reading and specifying cookie attributes

Before adding the cookie to the outgoing headers, you can look up or set attributes of the cookie. Here's a summary:

- *getComment()/setComment():* Gets or sets a comment associated with this cookie.
- *getDomain()/setDomain():* Gets or sets the domain to which cookie applies. Normally, cookies are returned only to the exact host name that sent them. You can use this method to instruct the browser to return them to other hosts within the same domain.
- *getMaxAge()/setMaxAge():* Gets or sets the amount of time (in seconds) that should elapse before the cookie expires. If you don't set this, the cookie lasts for only the current session (for example, until the user quits the browser), and is not stored on disk.
- *getName():* Gets the name of the cookie. The name and the value are the two pieces you virtually always care about. Because the `getCookies()` method of `HttpServletRequest` returns an array of cookie objects, it is common to loop down this array until you find a particular name, and then check that cookie's value with `getValue()`.

- *getPath()/setPath():* Gets or sets the path to which this cookie applies. If you don't specify a path, the cookie is returned for all URLs in the same directory as the current page as well as all subdirectories. This method can be used to specify something more general. For example, `someCookie.setPath("/")` specifies that all pages on the server should receive the cookie. Note that the path specified must include the current directory.
- *getSecure()/setSecure():* Gets or sets the Boolean value indicating whether the cookie should only be sent over encrypted (SSL) connections.
- *getValue()/setValue():* Gets or sets the value associated with the cookie. Again, the name and the value are the two parts of a cookie that you almost always care about, although in a few cases a name is used as a Boolean flag, and its value is ignored (meaning, the existence of the name means `true`).
- *getVersion()/setVersion():* Gets or sets the cookie protocol version with which this cookie complies.

Placing cookies in the response headers

You add a cookie to the `Set-Cookie` response header by means of the `addCookie()` method of `HttpServletResponse`, as shown in the following example:

```
Cookie userCookie = new Cookie("user", "uid1234");
response.addCookie(userCookie);
```

Reading cookies from the client

To send cookies to the client, you create a cookie and use `addCookie()` to send a `Set-Cookie HTTP` response header. To read the cookies that come back from the client, you call `getCookies()` on the `HttpServletRequest`. This call returns an array of cookie objects corresponding to the values that came in on the `Cookie HTTP` request header. After you have this array, you typically loop down it, calling `getName()` on each cookie until you find one matching the name you have in mind. You then call `getValue()` on the matching cookie, doing some processing specific to the resultant value.

Using CookieCounterServlet

Listing 10-1 is a basic counter servlet that implements the Cookie API. This code calls `request.getCookies` to obtain the array of cookies on your computer. It then calls `extractCookie`, which loops through the array looking for a match on the name of the cookie (`cookiecounter`). If the method successfully finds the cookie, you set the count variable to the value in the cookie, otherwise you initialize it to zero.

Next the code creates a new cookie with the new count, and sets it on the response. After it is created, the `setMaxAge()` method is called with 86400 seconds (24 hours) as an expiration date. This expiration date enables you to close your browser completely, and if you come back within 24 hours to the same URL, the count is still preserved. The code then generates some HTML to display results to return to the client.

Listing 10-1: Using CookieCounterServlet to Implement the Cookie API

```
package com.bible.servlet;
import java.io.*;
import javax.servlet.*;
import javax.servlet.http.*;
public class CookieCounterServlet extends HttpServlet {
public void doGet(HttpServletRequest request, HttpServletResponse response)
throws ServletException, IOException
 {
  int counter;
  Cookie cookies[] = request.getCookies();
  if(cookies == null)
  {
   counter = 0;
  }
  else
  {
   Cookie cookie = extractCookie(cookies, "cookiecounter");
   if(cookie == null)
   {
    counter = 0;
   }
   else
   {
    counter = Integer.parseInt(cookie.getValue());
   }
  }

  Cookie newCookie = new Cookie("cookiecounter",
       String.valueOf(counter+1));
  newCookie.setMaxAge(86400); //24 hours
  response.addCookie(newCookie);

  response.setContentType("text/html");

  ServletOutputStream out = response.getOutputStream();

  out.println("<html>");
  out.println("<head><title>Cookie Counter Servlet</title></head>");
  out.println("<body>");

  if(counter == 0)
  {
   out.println("The cookie counter cookie did not exist");
  }
  else
  {
   out.println("The cookie counter is now " + counter);
```

Listing 10-1: ***(Continued)***

```
  }

  out.println("</body>");
  out.println("</html>");
  out.close();
} //end of doGet method
public Cookie extractCookie(Cookie[] cookies, String name) {
 Cookie returnCookie = null;
 for(int i=0; i<cookies.length; i++) {
      Cookie myCookie = cookies[i];
      if (name.equals(myCookie.getName()))
        returnCookie = myCookie;
    }

  return returnCookie;
 } //end of extractCookie method
} //end of CookieCounterServlet Class
```

The first time this servlet is called from your browser, you see the output in Figure 10-3.

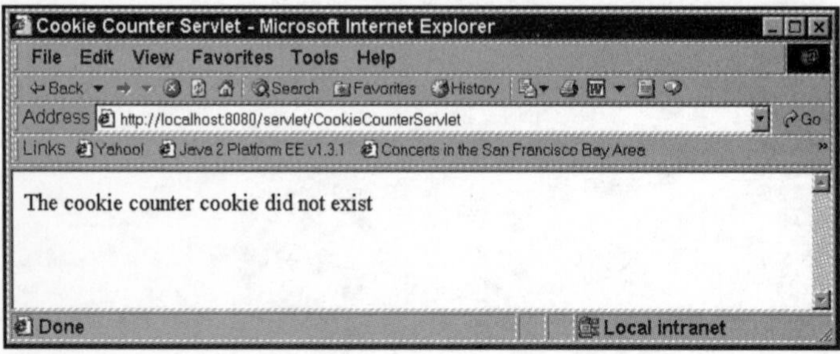

Figure 10-3: The output from the CookieCounterServlet after the first time a browser calls the servlet.

The cookie didn't exist on your computer, so the servlet created one and stored it there. If you click Refresh on your browser one time, you should see the output shown in Figure 10-4.

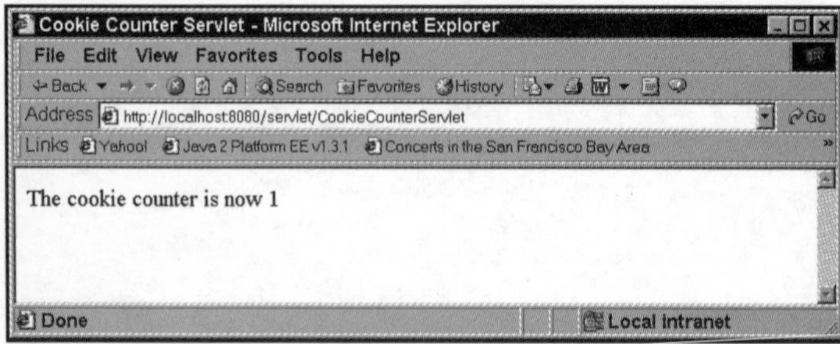

Figure 10-4: The output from the CookieCounterServlet after the the cookie has been set and the user returns.

Every time you access this servlet the number increments by one. If you click the Refresh button, you can watch it increment. Remember this cookie lives on your computer, so you can surf to other sites, or even turn off your computer; as long as you come back to this servlet within 24 hours (before the cookie expires), your count is preserved.

Summary

The Servlet API enables you to implement multiple techniques that allow your servlets to work together. Servlets can share information by saving it in an area of memory to which the servlets involved have access. Servlets can share information with other servlets (collaborate) by saving strings to the system properties list, using a shared object (such as a singleton found in the server's classpath), or by using inheritance. The implementation of cookies is yet another API tool that allows servlets to store data that other servlets can access.

Servlets also have the capability to pass data between themselves as method parameters. One way is for the servlet to utilize the `RequestDispatcher`'s `forward()` method and pass along the request and response objects. Another way is to use the servlet's `sendRedirect()` method of the `HttpServletResponse` and append values to the query string. Again, each application can choose which technique to implement and generally uses a combination of techniques.

To allow your servlets to handle requests in a generic sense, pre- and post-condition processing is a valuable pattern to implement. With the gain in popularity of multiple client-type devices, you need to allow your application the flexibility to keep up with these changes.

Because servlets are generally used to control application flow, the Servlet API provides methods that allow servlets to pass control around to the different modules of the application. Because application servlets behave in multiple ways, the API provides multiple methods that enable you to tailor the way your servlets interact together.

> **ON THE WEB:** To see many of these techniques applied to a real-world application, you can download the entire source code file (`CSICruiseFinal.ear`) from the Chapter 10 folder on the companion Web site at `www.wiley.com/extras`.

Chapter 11

Understanding Session Management

In This Chapter

- Understanding session management
- Using the HttpSession object
- Using the IBMSession object
- Implementing large-scale session management
- Using the WebSphere Application Server Session Manager

Internet communication protocols fall into two categories: stateful and stateless. The server associates a state with a connection to a session. A *session* is a series of requests to a servlet originating from the same browser. Stateful protocols can process multiple operations before closing a connection. An example of a stateful protocol is File Transfer Protocol (FTP). The server knows that all requests came from a single user. Stateless protocols have no way to decipher one connection from the next. HTTP is a stateless protocol. Each time a request is made for a Web page, the protocol opens a separate connection to the server, and the server doesn't know the context from one connection to the next.

Because Web-based applications utilize HTTP, you as the developer must be able to track which request came from which user. Can you imagine having to write an application without knowing who is requesting each command? If, for some reason, you have an application that has only one long data entry form, and the only function your program needs to perform is accept the data a user enters on the form and store it in a database somewhere; you don't have to worry about session tracking. However, in reality, the need for this kind of system is slim to none. Most applications require several pages of user interface with some complex logic happening on the server in between requests. Imagine writing a simple Web-based bank account application. When a user submits a request to debit his account, you don't know which account to debit. At the same time, another user may want to credit his account. You may end up debiting the account that should be credited and crediting the account that needs to be debited. This is kind of a raw example, but you begin to see the problem.

This chapter explains to you the ways in which WebSphere Application server enables you to gracefully handle session management. It explains the different Java APIs that are used for session management, such as the `HttpSession` object, and shows you how to use the WebSphere Application Server Administrative Console to configure your server to handle these objects. By configuring your server to handle session management, your application can not only track user requests but also enable you to add a certain level of fall tolerance to your application. By turning on things, such as session persistence, you can persist any data that is saved in the `HttpSession` object. Then, if your application crashes, you can recover the session data and not lose any valuable application information.

Introducing Session Management

To implement systems via HTTP, some type of session management is needed. You must design your application in such a way that you can identify individual users and know what application state they are in. To handle session management well, you must design it into your system from the beginning. To scale well, your application must be able to track many users through multiple application states. For session management, the first thing you must be able to do is link each user request with the user that sent it. It's up to you to determine how you want to generate a unique ID for the user and, ultimately, how the ID is submitted with each request. One alternative for generating unique session IDs is to use the Remote Method Invocation (RMI) class UID, which is designed for just that. It guarantees a unique number. The following example shows what your code would look like:

```
Sting myId = new java.rmi.server.UID().toString();
```

After you obtain the unique ID (`myId`), you can send it with each request a specific user makes, so your servlet knows who sent the request.

Sounds easy enough. The tricky part is figuring out how to submit the user ID with each request. Web developers can use several techniques to implement ID submission. Techniques for tracking sessions and associating data with them over multiple connections include using cookies or hidden fields, implementing URL rewriting, or utilizing the `HttpSession` object. With each solution, you as a developer can choose to create a unique session ID (user ID) and pass it back and forth to your servlet, or you can choose to create actual data objects to be passed between each request.

Using the Cookie API to handle session tracking

Utilizing the Cookie API is a common technique Web developers use to handle session tracking. Cookies can store the unique ID on the client machine on the first request; then with each subsequent request, your servlet can access the cookie to uniquely identify the user. This technique can get a little complicated if your application uses multiple cookies. You then have to keep track of which cookies to use and which to expire and when. Because a cookie cannot grow to be more than 4K in size, and you can only have a maximum of 20 cookies per domain on a user's machine, the amount of information you can store about each user is limited. By using cookies to store only the unique session ID for the user, your servlet can derive the rest of the user information from some type of data store and still keep the size of your cookies to a minimum.

Some users view cookies as an invasion of privacy. They don't like the idea of someone writing data (any data) to their personal machines. Because of this fear, your application should not depend on cookies as its sole mechanism for session tracking.

CROSS-REFERENCE: More details about the Cookie API can be found in Chapter 10.

Using hidden fields to handle session tracking

Another way to handle session tracking is to use hidden fields that store user-specific data. You can add hidden fields to a HTML form, but the client's browser doesn't display them. When the form is submitted to a servlet, these fields are submitted to the server the same way the visible fields are submitted. You can then retrieve the hidden field by using the servlet's `HTTPServletRequest` object. The following form uses an HTML hidden field:

```
<FORM ACTION="/servlet/MyServlet" METHOD="post">
<INPUT SIZE="20" TYPE="text" NAME="classes">
<INPUT TYPE ="submit" NAME ="action" VALUE="Continue">
<INPUT TYPE ="hidden" NAME ="userId" VALUE ="228">
</FORM>
```

When the user submits this, the three input fields become available to `MyServlet`. Although only the first two fields are displayed in the user's browser, the hidden field, named `UserId`, is also submitted with the `HTTPServletRequest` and is accessible to the servlet via the `getParameter()` method. You can put as many hidden fields on a form as needed. However, using hidden fields for session tracking does have some drawbacks. To make them unique to a user session, they must be generated dynamically; thus, you are limited to putting them on dynamically generated pages. If your application uses static HTML pages, the session ID is lost after these static pages are displayed. Because they are not dynamic, they cannot add the dynamic session ID. Another drawback is security. Although they are not displayed in the user's browser, hidden fields do show up if the user decides to view the HTML source. Any data stored in hidden fields cannot be protected from being viewed.

Using URL rewriting to handle session tracking

URL rewriting is yet another way to implement session tracking. With URL rewriting, every application-specific URL must be dynamically generated to include the unique identifier for tracking. The data is appended to the end of the URL string. Because of the limitation of URL lengths, usually only a unique user ID (session ID) is passed. The extra information is commonly passed in one of two ways: extra path information or added parameters.

You can pass extra path information by extending the URL with the unique data. An example of this is if the original URL were `http://server:port/servlet/MyServlet` and the session data that you want to pass is a unique ID of `XJ6`, the rewritten URL would be http://server:port/servlet/MyServlet/XJ6. Using extra path information works on all servers, and it works as a target for forms that use both the get() and post() methods. However, it doesn't work well if your servlet has to use the extra path information as true path information.

You can pass added parameters by appending the URL with your unique data preceded by a question mark and separated by ampersands. For example, if you have the original URL http://server:port/servlet/MyServlet, and the session data that you want to pass is a unique ID of XJ6 and a limit of 5, the new URL after rewriting would be http://server:port/servlet/MyServlet?uniqueID=XJ6&limit=5. Using added parameters works on all servers as extra path information does, but it only works with servlets that don't implement the post() method. Also, depending on the number of parameters you want to pass, the URL string can very quickly become really long. A security issue (from having data passed on the URL for all to see) is another consideration.

URL rewriting also has the same drawback as hidden fields. It must be part of dynamically constructed pages. With URL rewriting, every application-specific URL in the program must be rewritten each time the page displays.

Using the HttpSession object for session management

Because of the integral part that sessions play in Web applications, the Java Servlet API has classes and methods that are specifically designed to help your servlets handle session tracking. Every user of a site gets associated with a javax.servlet.http.HttpSession object that a servlet can use to identify each user request uniquely and store or retrieve pertinent information from. Because each session object automatically generates a unique session ID, you, as a developer, don't need to generate one programmatically. You can store any Java object in a session object. However, the objects that you store in the session need to implement the java.io.Serializable interface so they can be persisted. A servlet obtains the user's HttpSession from the request object via the getSession() method. This method returns the current session associated with the user making the request. The getSession() method with no parameters looks for an existing user session and, if one is not found, creates a new one and returns it. The getSession(boolean) method call allows you to tell the Session Manager whether to create a new session if one is not found or to return a null. The following examples illustrate what gets returned from the different getSession() method calls:

- HttpServletRequest.getSession() always returns an HttpSession.
- HttpServletRequest.getSession(true) always returns an HttpSession.
- HttpServletRequest.getSession(false) returns an HttpSession if one already exists, or null if one does not already exist.

Accessing sessions and state data

The `HttpSession` object has methods to enable you to access state data. The following methods are used to deal with the details of the connection of the user to the Web server:

- *isNew():* This method enables you to determine whether the session is new. A session is considered new if the server uses only cookie-based sessions, and the client disables the use of cookies. Otherwise, a session is considered not new when the client joins the session.
- *getId():* Every `HttpSession` is assigned a unique identifier by the servlet engine. This method returns a string object, representing the unique session ID that has been assigned to the session object.
- *setMaxInactiveInterval(int interval):* This method enables you to set the maximum number of seconds that a session can remain inactive before it is discarded. This is an improvement over the JSDK 2.0 where you managed this yourself. Now the servlet engine takes care of this for you. If the time expires, the session itself expires.
- *getMaxInactiveInterval():* This method returns an integer representing the maximum number of seconds that the session can remain inactive without being disposed of.
- *getCreationTime():* This method enables you to get the time that the session was created. The oddity of this method is that it returns the time in milliseconds since midnight January 1, 1970 GMT. To make use of this data you, have to do some fancy math calculations.
- *getLastAccessedTime():* This method enables you to find out the last time the session was accessed. This, too, has the oddity of returning time based on January 1, 1970 GMT.
- *invalidate():* This method can be called to invalidate the `HttpSession` object. All objects that are set as attributes are unbound when this method is called.

It is good practice to invalidate and release your `HttpSession` objects when you are finished with them. WebSphere enables you to configure a finite number of `HttpSession` objects. WebSphere can reuse an `HttpSession` when the application invalidates it or when WebSphere reclaims it after a configured idle timeout period. The default configuration is to keep sessions alive for 30 minutes before reclaiming them. Quite often, an application performs session invalidation as part of a log-off routine.

Running Snoop servlet

To illustrate some of the common methods of the `HttpSession` object, you create a Snoop servlet that will snoop into the session object and display some of the values that are contained in it. It is a basic example that returns HTML to display the values. This simple example illustrates how a servlet can access the *state* data of the `HttpSession` object.

Listing 11-1 implements the `doGet()` method and uses the `PrintWriter` to return HTML to the browser to display the various values that are accessed from the session object.

Listing 11-1: Implementing doGet() and PrintWriter to Display Session Object Values

```
package com.bible.servlet;

import java.io.*;
import java.util.*;
import javax.servlet.*;
import javax.servlet.http.*;
public class SnoopServlet extends HttpServlet {
    public void doGet (HttpServletRequest req, HttpServletResponse res)
    throws ServletException, IOException
    {
 HttpSession aSession = req.getSession();
 PrintWriter        out;
 res.setContentType("text/html");
 out = res.getWriter ();

 out.println("<html>");
 out.println("<head><title>Session Snoop Servlet</title></head>");
 out.println("<body>");
 out.println("<h3>Request information:</h3>");
 out.println("<pre>");

 out.println( "Request method = " + req.getMethod());
 out.println( "Request URI = " + req.getRequestURI());
 out.println( "Request protocol = " + req.getProtocol());
 out.println( "Servlet path = " + req.getServletPath());
 out.println( "Path info = " + req.getPathInfo());
 out.println( "Query string = " + req.getQueryString());
 out.println( "Content length = " + req.getContentLength());
 out.println( "Server name = " + req.getServerName());
 out.println( "Server port = " + req.getServerPort());
 out.println( "Remote host = " + req.getRemoteHost());

 out.println("<h3>Session State information:</h3>");
 out.println("<pre>");

 out.println( "Is new? = " + aSession.isNew());
 out.println( "Session ID = " + aSession.getId());
 out.println( "getMaxinactiveInterval() = " + aSession.getMaxInactiveInterval());
 out.println( "getCreationTime() = " + aSession.getCreationTime());
 out.println( "getLastAccessedTime() = " + aSession.getLastAccessedTime());

 out.println("<h3>Session Data information:</h3>");
 out.println("<pre>");

 Enumeration e = aSession.getAttributeNames();

 int dataCount = 0;
```

```
while (e.hasMoreElements())
{
 String name = (String)e.nextElement();
 out.println(" " + name + ": " + (String)aSession.getAttribute(name) );
 dataCount++;
}
if( dataCount == 0 )
{
 out.println("There is currently no data attributes on the session.");
}

out.println("</body></html>");
   }
}
```

Figure 11-1 shows the output that the servlet displays when a user accesses it for the first time. Notice the `isNew()` method returns `true` because this is the first time the user has accessed the server, creating a new session. The `getLastAccessedTime()` method returns a `-1` because it has only been accessed once and there is no previous access.

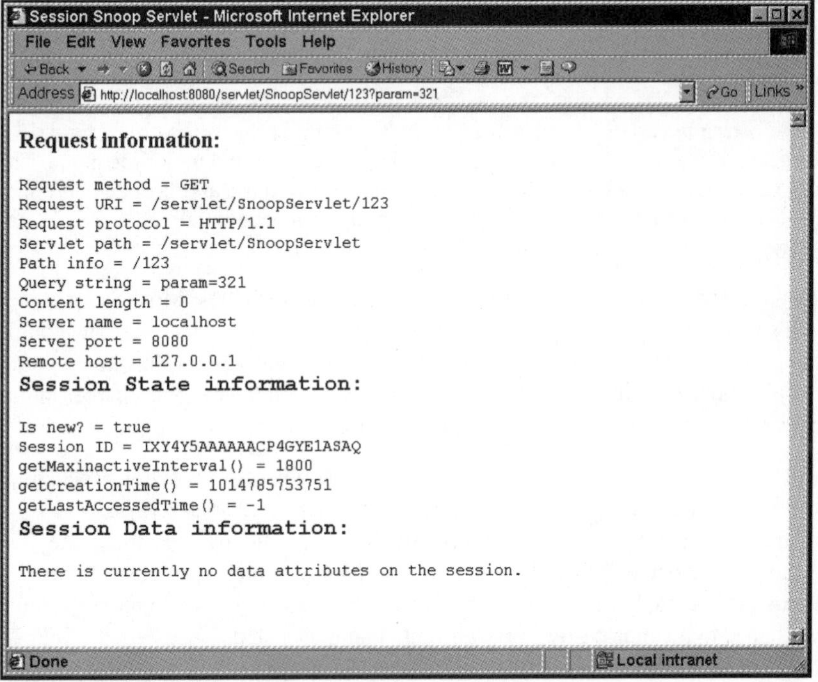

Figure 11-1: The snoop servlet finds no data.

Notice the bottom portion of the snoop servlet cycled through all the attributes of the session. Figure 11-1 shows that nothing is found because this is the first servlet to use the session, and `setAttribute()` of any data values was not performed. The example in the next section illustrates application session data. The example in this section was presented to show you the different state attributes that are a part of the `HttpSession` object. You did not add any data attributes that pass data objects to be utilized by your application. State attributes are methods, such as `isNew()` or `getCreationTime()`, that can also be utilized by your application but refer to the *state* that the session is in, not the data that it contains.

Accessing sessions and using application data

After you obtain the user session object, your servlet has the capability to get or set values or *application data* in it. Application data is available to all servlets that are part of the same Web application (`ServletContext`) and is not visible to components in another context. The values that you set or get from the `HttpSession` object are stored as attributes of the object. The accessor methods for session values are as follows:

- *setAttribute(String name, Object value):* The `setAttribute()` method binds an object to the session using the name specified. Remember, you can put any Java object into the session, but it needs to implement `Serializable` in order to be persisted. If an object of the same name is already bound to the session, the object is replaced. If this method is called on a session that has been invalidated, a `java.lang.IllegalStateException` is thrown.
- *getAttribute(String name):* The `getAttribute()` method returns the object bound with the specified name in the session, or null if no object is bound under the name. This call returns an instance of object, and the caller must cast it to the appropriate class in order to use it. If this method is called on a session that has been invalidated, a `java.lang.IllegalStateException` is thrown.

Passing data between servlets is easily accomplished via session attributes. Most string objects and objects with small object graphs are stored into the session for future access. You should try to keep your session object as small as possible. The size plays a bigger role when it comes to large-scale applications that utilize persistent sessions (discussed later in this chapter in the "Understanding Large-Scale Session Management" section).

You can also retrieve a `java.util.Enumeration` of string objects representing the names of all the objects that are bound to the session by calling the `getAttributeNames()` method. You can use this enumeration to loop through all the attribute names and get the corresponding values associated with them. Generally, you know which attributes you are expecting to be in the session, but this method gives you the flexibility to write more dynamic code that doesn't need to be updated for every attribute that gets added.

One of the main challenges of working with `HttpSessions` is keeping the correct data with the correct user. If you ignore the multithreading capability of servlets, your data can quickly become out of sync between users. Because servlets are multithreaded, the `get()` and `set()` methods to the session object should be synchronized to force the servlet to perform these methods using the single-thread model and, thereby, prevent the mixing of user data. The following shows an example of synchronizing a `get()` method:

```
HttpSession aSession = req.getSession(true);
String userId = "";
synchronized (aSession) {
userdId = (String)aSession.getAttribute("uID");
}
```

Because using the synchronized block forces the servlet into the single-thread mode, make sure you limit the amount of code implemented inside the block and the number of synchronized blocks you use in your code.

Running the Hit Count servlet

Chapter 9 shows a servlet example that displays the number of times that a particular servlet had been called. It uses a class variable for keeping track of the total count and displays it to the user when it is called. Because there is only one instance of a servlet running for multiple requests, this count is a total count of the number of times that a servlet was called by *all* users. To keep track of the number of times a particular user has accessed the servlet, the class-level variable does not suffice. In this next example, you add functionality to your Snoop servlet to keep track of the number of times a specific user calls the servlet and then set the count variable into the session as an attribute.

By using an `HttpSession` object, you can increment a counter that gets carried around with each user. Because the session is unique to a specific browser, users can hit this servlet, leave your page, surf the Internet for a while, and return later to your servlet, and you get an accurate count of the number of times they specifically visited your page. The count stays in the user session until the browser is closed (or the session expires/invalidates, whichever happens first).

Listing 11-2 is the source code for a servlet that implements a hit count utilizing an `HttpSession`.

Listing 11-2: Using the HttpSession Object to Keep Track of User Visits

```
package com.bible.servlet;

import java.io.*;
import java.util.*;
import javax.servlet.*;
import javax.servlet.http.*;

/**
 * Hit Count servlet. This servlet uses the session to keep a counter of
 * how many times it has been accessed by the same user.
 *
 * @author   CSI
 */
```

Listing 11-2: *(Continued)*

```
public class HitCountServlet extends HttpServlet {
    public void doGet (HttpServletRequest req, HttpServletResponse res)
    throws ServletException, IOException
    {
  //Get the current session object for the user or create a new one
  HttpSession aSession = req.getSession(true);
  PrintWriter        out;

  res.setContentType("text/html");
  out = res.getWriter ();

  out.println("<html>");
  out.println("<head><title>Hit Count Servlet</title></head>");
  out.println("<body>");
  out.println("<h3>Request information:</h3>");
  out.println("<pre>");

  out.println( "Request method = " + req.getMethod());
  out.println( "Request URI = " + req.getRequestURI());
  out.println( "Request protocol = " + req.getProtocol());
  out.println( "Servlet path = " + req.getServletPath());
  out.println( "Path info = " + req.getPathInfo());
  out.println( "Query string = " + req.getQueryString());
  out.println( "Content length = " + req.getContentLength());
  out.println( "Server name = " + req.getServerName());
  out.println( "Server port = " + req.getServerPort());
  out.println( "Remote host = " + req.getRemoteHost());

  out.println("<h3>Session State information:</h3>");
  out.println("<pre>");

  out.println( "Is new? = " + aSession.isNew());
  out.println( "Session ID = " + aSession.getId());
  out.println( "getMaxinactiveInterval() = " + aSession.getMaxInactiveInterval());
  out.println( "getCreationTime() = " + aSession.getCreationTime());
  out.println( "getLastAccessedTime() = " + aSession.getLastAccessedTime());

  out.println("<h3>Session Data information:</h3>");
  out.println("<pre>");

  int count;
  synchronized (aSession) {
   if( aSession.getAttribute("COUNT") != null )
   {
    count = ((Integer)aSession.getAttribute("COUNT")).intValue();
   }
   else
```

```
 {
   count = 0;
 }
 count = count + 1;
 //Put the counter into the session so it is available later on
 aSession.setAttribute("COUNT", new Integer(count) );
   }
 out.println("You have visited our site " + count + " times.");
 out.println("</body></html>");
   }
}
```

When a distinct user hits this servlet for the first time, the output is that shown in Figure 11-2.

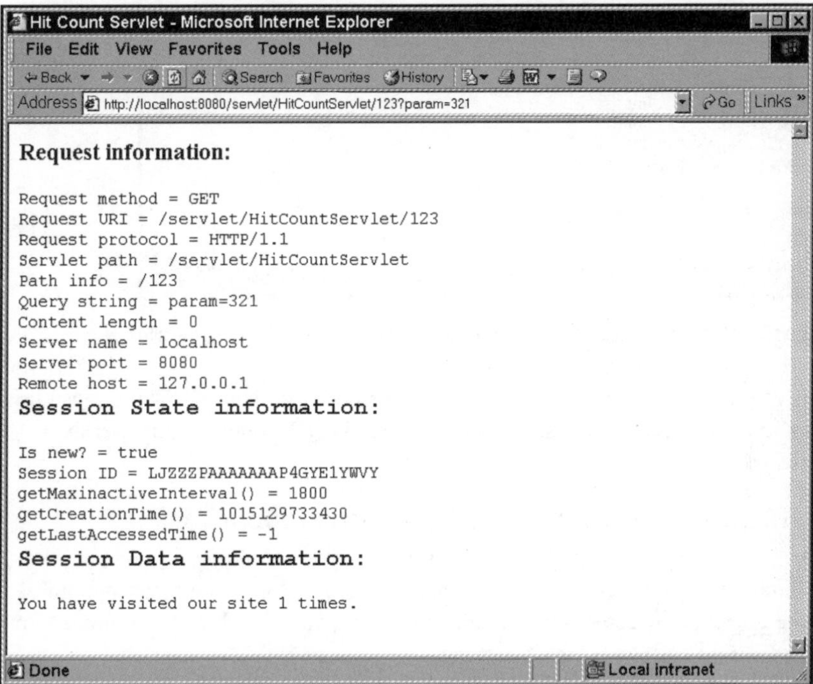

Figure 11-2: The Hit Count servlet displays counter information.

After the user hits the servlet, the `count` variable is stuck in that user's session and remains with that browser even when visiting other sites. When the user comes back to your page, the servlet pulls the variable out of the session and increments it by one for display and then puts it back into the session. This process can continue until the session is terminated or invalidated. Figure 11-3 shows the count after the user has returned to your site two more times (for a total of three).

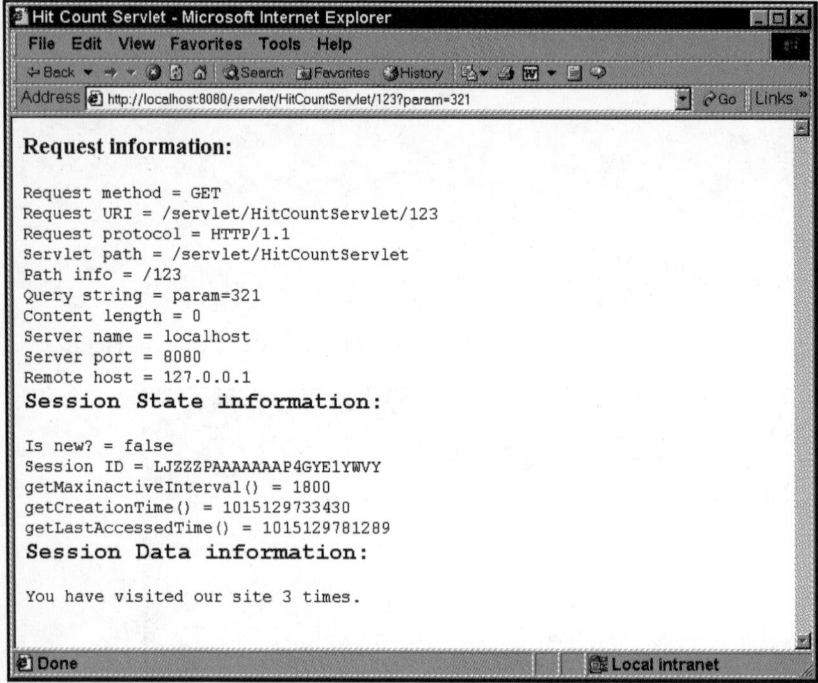

Figure 11-3: The Hit Count servlet tracks the number of times this user has returned to the site.

Remember, this count lists only the number of times a specific user comes to your page during one browser session. You need to persist this count data to keep a count for this user over multiple browser sessions.

Using the HttpSessionBindingListener interface

When using the `HttpSession` object for session tracking, you should perform clean-up routines. You should invalidate session objects when they are no longer being used and free up any resources the object might reference. To handle cleanup, you use objects that implement the `HttpSessionBindingListener` interface.

When an HttpSession contains an object that implements the `HttpSessionBindingListener`, the listener notifies the object when the object is being bound and unbound from a session. Use `HttpSession.setAttribute()` to bind an object to a session and `HttpSession.removeAttribute()` to unbind it from a session. Session invalidation also implies that any objects currently bound to a session are unbound.

Because the `HttpSession` object itself is passed as part of the `HttpSessionBindingEvent`, the `HttpSessionBindingListener` interface lets you save any part of the session before the session is removed. It does not matter whether the session ends automatically or by a specific request. The interface contains two abstract methods, which you can override with your own processing:

- `valueBound()` is called when the object is being bound to a session.
- `valueUnbound()` is called when the value is being unbound from a session.

By overriding either of these methods, you can programmatically react to objects being put into or removed from a session object. So as you can see, the `HttpSession` object of the Servlet API is a strong tool for implementing proper session tracking.

Using com.ibm.WebSphere.servlet.session.IBMSession

The `IBMSession` interface extends the `HttpSession` interface of the Servlet API to enable you to maintain sessions in a clustered environment, via object serialization, and to provide a measure of security when a servlet attempts to access a session.

WebSphere Application Server includes the notion of an authenticated or unauthenticated owner of a session. If a session is marked as being owned by an authenticated user with the username provided by the WebSphere Security APIs and management, a servlet must be operating under the credentials of the same user in order for WebSphere to return the requested session to the servlet. WebSphere Application Server includes the `com.ibm.websphere.servlet.session.`

`UnauthorizedSessionRequestException` interface, which is used when a session is requested without the necessary credentials. Session Manager uses the WebSphere security infrastructure to determine the authenticated identity associated with a client HTTP request that either retrieves or creates a session.

A session gets denoted one time with the first authenticated username the Application server sees while processing the session. This can occur if the user has already been authenticated on the `HttpRequest`, which leads to the creation of the session, or it can happen on the first authenticated username seen after an anonymous session is created. In a database environment, the WebSphere runtime defaults to updating any changes to a given `HttpSession` and unlocking the session after the completion of the service method. Through the configuration options in the WebSphere runtime, you can turn this off. By turning off this option, you can control when servlet updates to a session are sent to the database and when the session is unlocked. To allow the database to be written to, you must explicitly call the `sync()` method. To turn off the association of user identity with a session, set the `HttpSessionSecurity=false` system property.

You can manually control when modified session data can be persisted to the data store by using the `sync()` method in the interface `com.ibm.websphere.servlet.session.IBMSession`. By calling `sync()` from the `service()` method of a servlet, you send any changes in the session to the database. If neither the manual update nor the time-based write option is enabled, the `sync()` method call performs no updates. It merely returns.

Ideally, you should call `sync()` after all updates have been made to the session so that the session will not be accessed any more. In other words, wait until the end of the servlet `service()` method to call `sync()`.

Understanding Large-Scale Session Management

Although using `HttpSessions` is a powerful way to develop Web-based applications, if you are developing a large-scale application, you need to follow some best practices to get the performance you need. You should know how WebSphere Application Server handles `HttpSessions` and the different settings you can apply to tailor your server. To get the desired performance from your application, you must determine whether to turn on session persistence, which is usually turned on for applications of substantial size. If your application needs to store large amounts of data in the session object, you might want to utilize WebSphere's multirow access feature. Also, depending on the design of your application, you might choose to limit the number of session objects held in memory by the server, or you may choose to allow session overflows. The following sections discuss these issues in more detail in the sections, so you can evaluate the best settings for your application. After explaining why you might use one option over another, this section shows you how to set these options in WebSphere using the WAS Session Manager.

Using persistent sessions

When developing Web-based applications, keep in mind what your target environment will be. Many times for large-scale applications, the servers are cloned and multiple machines are used to handle the workload. Your application should be load balanced between several machines. Load balancing affects the way you need to look at configuring your servers and your session handling. With session persistence enabled, the data that you store in your user sessions is persisted to a designated datastore, so your application can access the information at any time, from any machine.

It is not recommended that you put large data objects into your `HttpSession`. Doing so severely affects the performance of your application. Most large applications need to turn on persistent `HttpSessions`. However, doing this costs you in performance. An `HttpSession` must be read by the servlet whenever it is used, and then rewritten whenever it is updated. WebSphere serializes when writing it back to a database, which is why to use session persistence successfully, objects stored in the session must implement `java.io.Serializable`. In most cases, your servlet needs only part of the data that is stored in the session, but by storing large object graphs in the session, WebSphere Application Server is forced to process the entire object each time.

When using persistent sessions in the WebSphere Application Server, use a dedicated data source for the session data. To avoid contention for Java Database Connectivity (JDBC) connections, don't reuse an application data source or the WebSphere Application Server repository for persistent session data.

Using multirow access

The default setting for WebSphere Application Server session management is single row access. A single session maps to a single row in the database table used to hold sessions. This setup limits your sessions to the amount of application data that can be stored within them. The maximum size for session data in a single row setting is 2 megabytes. WebSphere Application Server supports the use of a multirow schema option, in which each piece of application-specific data is stored in a separate row of the database. This option enables you to store as much data as your database can handle.

Using the multirow schema potentially has performance benefits if your application is storing large amounts of data in sessions. With this schema, if a servlet needs only a subset of the large amount of data stored in the session, only the small amount needed by the servlet has to be fetched from the database. The entire session object does not need to be read from the database, and this cuts down on the amount of Java serialization that occurs.

The decision to use single-row session persistence or multirow session persistence is mainly dependant upon how much data you want to store for each session. The following list contains some high-level guidelines you should use to help you determine when to use single versus multirow access:

Reasons to use single row:

- You can read or write all values with just one record read/write.
- This option takes up less space in a database because you are guaranteed that each session is only one record long.

Reasons to use multirow:

- The application can store an unlimited amount of data (limited only by size of database and 2 MB per record limit).
- The application can read in individual fields instead of the whole record. When larger amounts of data are stored in the session, but only small amounts are specifically accessed during a given servlet's processing of an HTTP request, multirow sessions can improve performance by avoiding unneeded Java object serialization.

It is generally advised that you not store mass amounts of data in a session object, but if this is the design you feel best fits your needs, multirow access is a good way to define your data into more logical pieces and give you performance benefits. If you leave the default (single row) setting, but store large objects into your sessions, performance may be compromised. A well-defined session architecture provides performance benefits.

Understanding overflows

When using session persistence in WebSphere Application Server, you can set the number of session objects that the server keeps in memory by setting the `Max In Memory Session Count`. An overflow occurs if the maximum number of sessions has already been allocated and another request for a new session comes in. If the overflow option is activated, the server allows the number of allocated session to exceed the maximum session count. If this option is not selected, your server is limited to the user-specified number in the `Max In Memory Session Count`.

The decision whether to allow overflow is dependent on the administrator and the resources of the WebSphere server. You want to allow overflow if you do not want to be limited by the amount of memory specified in the base memory field (`Max In Memory Session Count`). One reason for turning off overflow is to protect your server from malicious users. With overflow turned on, a hacker who turns off cookies and uses a script to make multiple new session requests can cause the server to use all its resources to fill those requests and bring your server to a crawl. You might want to turn off overflow so you can limit the amount of physical memory used as a cache.

Using WAS Session Manager

In WebSphere Application Server's (WAS) Administrative Console, you use Session Manager to configure the way your Web container handles session objects. You access the Session Manager by selecting the Services tab in the Server view and clicking the Edit Properties button. Figure 11-4 shows the Administrative Console with the Session Manager selected.

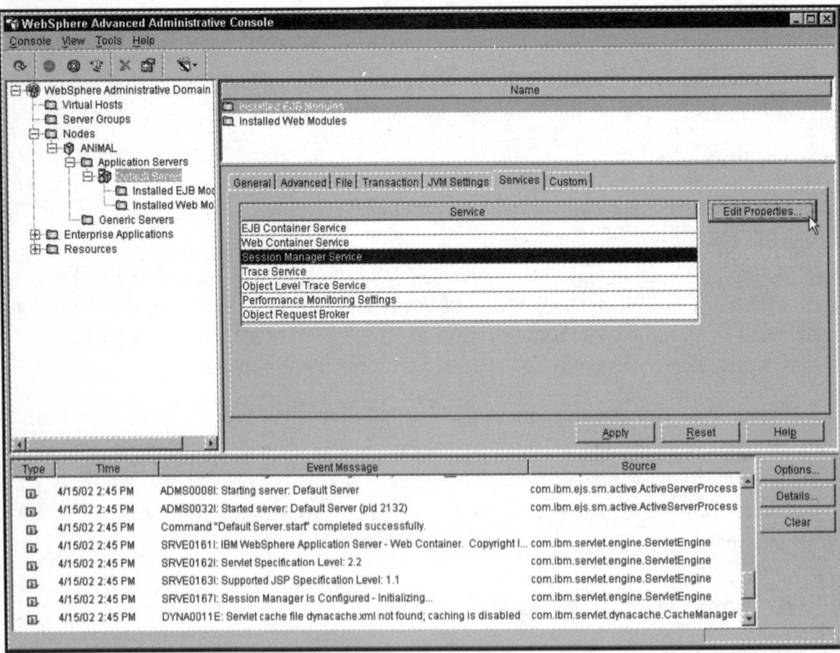

Figure 11-4: Selecting the Session Manager service with the WebSphere Administrative Console.

The Session Manager has a notebook interface with five tabs: General, Advanced, Cookies, Persistence, and Database.

From the General tab, you configure the settings to define the session tracking mechanism you would like the server to use for your application. The possible mechanisms are SSL ID tracking, Cookies, or URL rewriting. Figure 11-5 displays the different options for this page.

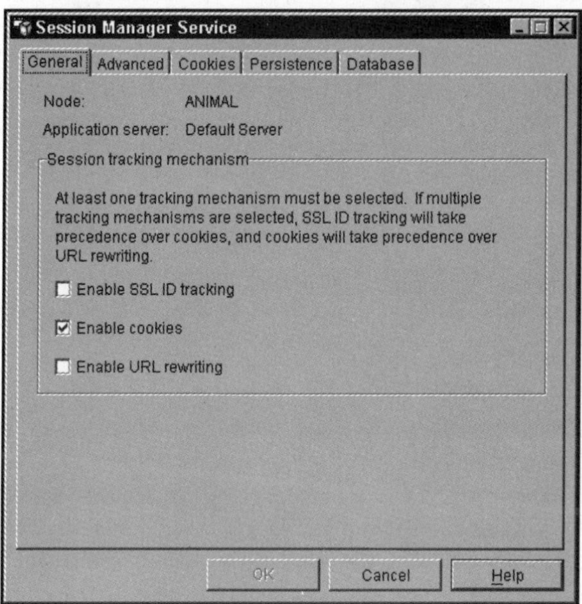

Figure 11-5: Session Manager General tab.

From the Advanced tab, you select the maximum number of session objects that the server keeps in memory. If you want this limit to be exceeded if more sessions are requested after the max is reached, you can select the session overflow option here. From this page you also set whether to integrate with WebSphere security, enable protocol switch rewriting, and set the session timeout interval. Protocol switch rewriting is used to add session IDs to URLs in transition from HTTP to HTTPS and back. It is the equivalent to URL rewriting, except it is used between two different types of protocols. An `HttpSession` object can either be programmatically invalidated, or it can be invalidated by the server after it times out. You can set the timeout to a certain amount of time, or you can select the No Timeout option, which allows your session to stay in memory and never timeout. Generally, this is not a good practice because you want to keep your server's memory as fresh as possible. Figure 11-6 shows the Advanced tab and all its options.

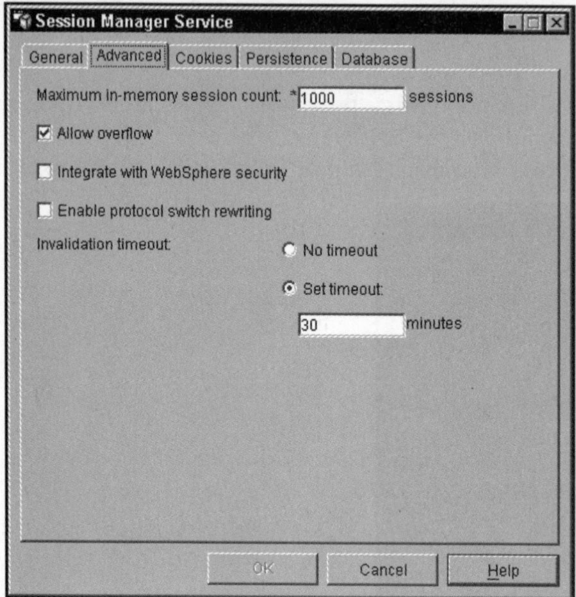

Figure 11-6: Advanced Session settings in the WAS Session Manager.

Cookies are one of the most common ways to implement session tracking. Within the Session Manager, you have the ability to set the various cookie settings that will be used by the server, the cookie domain, and the cookie path. You also determine whether you want to exchange cookies to secure session and set the lifetime of each cookie. The cookie name is already determined for you, but you can change the domain and path. You can set the default age of a cookie by entering a max number of seconds that this cookie will live on the client machine. By default, the cookie only lives as long as the browser session is alive. After the user exits the browser session, the cookie expires. Figure 11.7 shows the Cookie tab and all its options.

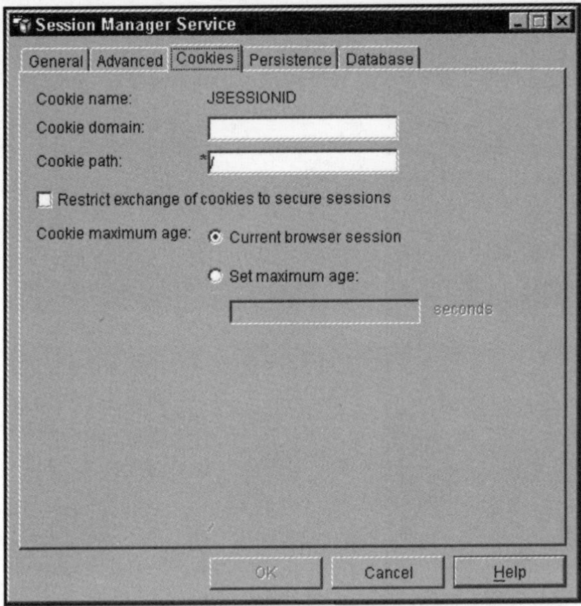

Figure 11-7: Setting the default behavior of session cookies.

Because most large-scale applications need to turn on session persistence, the Persistence tab of the WAS Administrative Console enables you to turn on this feature and configure the parameters for writing to the database. After you enable persistent sessions, you can then select at what point the persist occurs. You have the ability to persist the entire session data or only the data that has changed. You can also configure whether you want the session to be persisted every time the service method has completed, or you might want it to persist automatically after a set amount of time. Figure 11-8 shows the Persistence tab with the available settings.

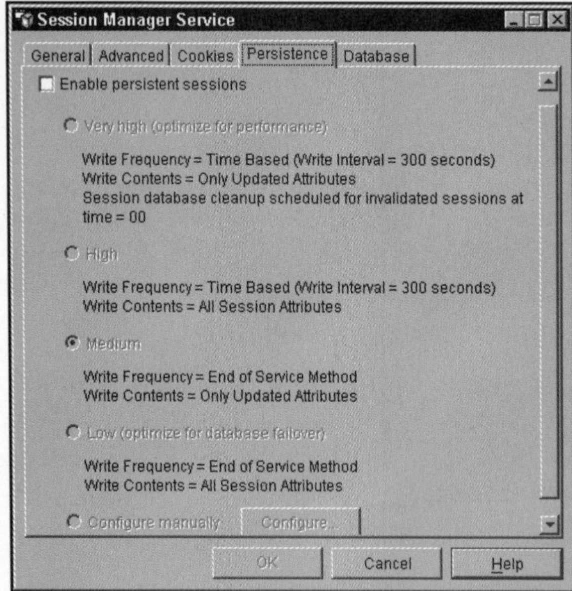

Figure 11-8: Configurations for session persistence.

If you don't feel these available options for session persistence are good enough for your application, WebSphere enables you to configure the settings manually by selecting the Configure manually radio button and clicking the Configure button. Figure 11-9 displays the Manual Configuration tab.

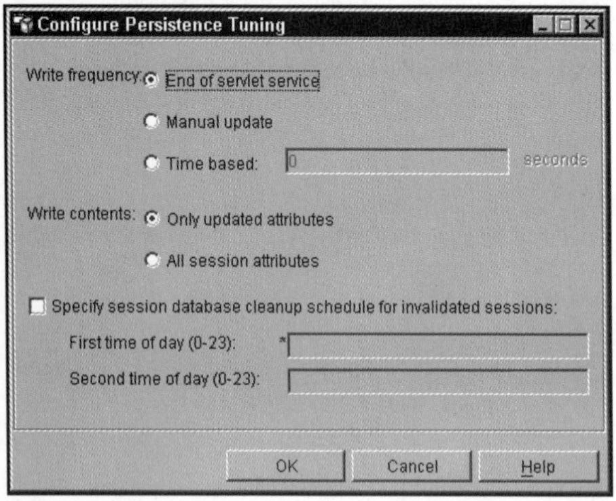

Figure 11-9: Configurations for manually setting session persistence.

Manual settings enable you to have the same control as the provided options but also enable you to provide a cleanup schedule for cleaning up any invalidated session objects.

After you have chosen to enable session persistence, you can select the Database tab of the Session Manager and define the database to be used to store the persisted data. This tab is also where you would override the default single-row session to use multirow sessions. Figure 11-10 shows the Database tab and its options.

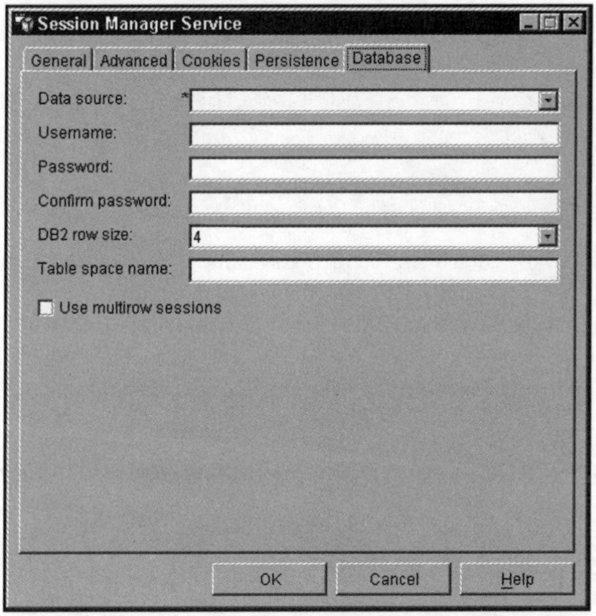

Figure 11-10: Setting up your session persistence database options.

The WAS Session Manager gives you a user-friendly interface for controlling how the server deals with session objects for your application. It is important to understand what the server is doing under the hood with its own session management so you can configure it to handle the application session management effectively. Each setting can affect the performance of your application in a negative manner if not given enough attention.

Setting Session Support in the Sample Application

The sample Almost Free Cruise application uses the `HttpSession` object to pass data objects to the requested JavaServer Page (JSP). Each JSP has a related mediator class that is used as the View/Data bean. It is responsible for controlling the data manipulation for its specific page. These objects hold most of the business logic that determines how the screens should interact with the data.

Because this sample implements the single-servlet design, each submitted request has two hidden fields that the servlet uses to instantiate the specific controller and ultimately the specific mediator. The servlet first uses the `action` hidden field to determine which type of controller bean to instantiate. After the correct action controller is instantiated, the servlet passes the request and response to it and tells it to process the request.

The controller uses the hidden field `PageDesc` that was submitted from the form to determine which type of mediator to pull from the `HttpSession` object, using the following code:

```
//ForwardController builds a mediator object from Hidden field:
 String pageDesc = getRequest().getParameter("PageDesc");
 String myMediator =  MEDIATOR_PATH + pageDesc + "Mediator";

 // get the Mediator from the session
 Mediator aMediator =
    getMediator(getSession(), myMediator);
```

Within the `getMediator()` method of the controller, the mediator name is derived and then used to get an attribute off the session with that name. If an attribute is present, this method returns it so the controller can use it in its present state; if one is not present in the session object, the `registerMediator()` method is called to create a new mediator of the required type, and then sets it as an attribute on the session with that name before returning it to the controller, as shown in Listing 11-3.

Listing 11-3: Checking the Session for a Data Object or Creating a New Object to Return

```
private static Mediator registerMediator(HttpSession aSession, String mediatorName) {
 String name, prefix = null;
 Mediator aMediator = null;
 try {
  aMediator = (Mediator) Class.forName(mediatorName).newInstance();
  int index = mediatorName.lastIndexOf(".");
  if (index == -1)
   name = mediatorName;
  else {
   name = mediatorName.substring(index + 1);
   prefix = mediatorName.substring(0, index);
  }
  aSession.setAttribute(name, aMediator);
 } catch (ClassNotFoundException e) {
  AppService.handle(e);
 } catch (InstantiationException e) {
  AppService.handle(e);
 } catch (IllegalAccessException e) {
  AppService.handle(e);
 }
 return aMediator;
}
```

Because these objects are placed in the `HttpSession` object, the JSP can grab them using the `jsp:useBean` tag (discussed in Chapter 12). Basically, you use the session object to pass the databean between the JSPs and the servlets. The databean (mediator) can hold a superset of all the data required for running business logic for the page, and the JSP can capture a smaller subset that the servlet can put together with the mediator and then use to perform necessary processing. If the larger set of data isn't passed in the session object, the JSP has to perform I/O procedures to gather the data needed to display itself to the user; then on submission of the form, the servlet has to again perform I/O to gather the same data to perform its business logic.

Using the `HttpSession` object enables you to pass data objects easily between the Model (servlet) and the Views (JSP).

Summary

This chapter covered the problems with using a stateless protocol (HTTP) and some solutions that you can use to overcome these problems. You must be able to link each request with a unique user. After you have a unique ID for each user, there are several ways in which you can pass this information along with each request: cookies, hidden fields, URL rewriting, or by using the unique session ID from the `HttpSession` object.

The `HttpSession` object has many built-in functions that enable you to work with WebSphere Applications and track session activities. WAS supplies built-in session *state* attributes, and you can store *application* data for access by other servlets. Don't forget to keep your session objects as simple as possible to avoid having large object graphs that slow down your application.

IBM has extended the `HttpSession` object to enable you to maintain sessions in a clustered environment and to provide a layer of security for accessing sessions.

Your design for large-scale applications needs to account for session handling in a distributed environment. Sessions need to be able to be persisted without heavy I/O costs. Each object that you choose to store into a user session needs to implement the `java.io.Serializable` interface for the session to be persisted.

WebSphere Application Server provides configuration for handling sessions, which enables you to tailor your session needs. Using the WebSphere Application Server's Session Manager, you can set the different session techniques and parameters that best fit your application needs.

Chapter 12
Developing JavaServer Pages

In This Chapter

- ♦ Understanding the benefits of using JavaServer Pages
- ♦ Using Web application models with JavaServer Pages
- ♦ Using WSAD for JavaServer Pages development
- ♦ Understanding JavaServer Pages syntax
- ♦ Understanding JavaServer Pages interactions
- ♦ Understanding tags
- ♦ Creating JavaServer Pages custom actions

Today's end users like dynamically generated screens that can give them a personalized Web-based application. Web browsers were designed to render static HTML pages that allow for little to no personalization. JavaServer Pages (JSPs) provide you a way to generate dynamic views programmatically and create a more interactive end-user experience. JSPs enable rapid development of Web pages that can interface with existing systems. This technology allows the view to be separated from the business logic that generates the data for the screens, enabling Web designers to change the look and feel of a page without having to change the underlying logic for generating the content.

This chapter discusses how JSPs can enable you to easily code an interactive Web-based application and how JSPs play an integral part in many of today's popular Web-application models. Using the WebSphere Application Developer (WSAD) tool, we walk you through creating your own JSPs and explain the syntax along the way. In addition to detailing the syntax, this chapter also discusses the use of JSP tags and how you can create your own tag libraries to help you create reusable components for all your JSP pages. This chapter also covers how to get your JSPs to interact with each other and other components of the application.

JSPs are extensions to the Java servlet technology Sun Microsystems developed as an alternative to Microsoft's Active Server Pages (ASPs). JSPs have a dynamic scripting capability that works in tandem with HTML code, separating the page logic (dynamic) from the actual design and display (static) of the page. Embedded in the HTML page, the Java source code and its extensions help make the HTML more functional. JSPs are not restricted to any specific platform or server because they are written in the Java programming language.

JSPs enable you to separate the model from the view. Thus, your Web designers can write the HTML look and feel for the application, while your systems programmers can concentrate on the complex business logic. With JSPs, Web designers can change the look and feel of the application as much as they want and the underlying business logic remains untouched. This is a very strong feature because, in reality, user interfaces change quite frequently. JSPs don't sever the ties between Web designers and system programmers entirely, but they make the interaction between the two much less complicated. Ideally your Web designers will have some basic knowledge of how JSPs work so they can minimize the interaction even more. It is always important for the system developers to interact with the Web designers, but having your developers waste a lot of time redoing look-and-feel–type logic takes away from their work with the core business logic.

Today's users like to feel that the application has been tailored to their specific needs. Personalization is a trend that is gaining a lot of momentum in Web-based applications. Utilizing the power of JSPs, you can show individual users only the data that is relevant to them. An example might be an online magazine or newspaper. Most people concentrate on only one or two sections. If a user is interested in the only business section (to check stocks) and the sports section, he or she doesn't want to have to navigate through the application to find each section separately. With dynamically generated pages (JSPs), users can register the sections they are most interested in; those pages would then be displayed on the front page when readers access the site, giving them a personalized view. They would not need to navigate unless they wished to read other sections.

Because JSPs are written in Java, you have access to the powerful Java API, such as JavaBeans. JSPs have the capability to load JavaBeans to help them with heavy business processing. You can leverage the server capabilities and interact with external services to handle the business logic; then the bean can represent the results of all your processing. The JSP can then display the data from the bean using the surrounding HTML tags. The content generated by the JSP can be dynamic in nature, and this provides maximum flexibility for your pages.

With the use of JSPs, you can rapidly develop Web pages for your application. After the HTML pages are created, you can add the specific JSP tags and create an interactive page quite quickly. JSPs increase the speed of development and also, by separating of the model from the view, allow for easy maintenance.

JSP technology speeds the development of dynamic Web pages in several ways:

- *Separates content generation from presentation:* Utilizing JSPs, Web page developers use HTML or XML tags to design and format the results page. They use JSP tags or scriptlets written by Java developers to generate the dynamic content. The business logic that generates the content is encapsulated in the beans and tags, which are executed on the server side. With this logic encapsulated into the beans and tags, you can have a Web-page designer change the overall look of the screen, and the business logic can remain the same. The Web designers can update the JSPs with the new HTML and use the existing bean calls and special JSP tags for the content generation.
- *Emphasizes reusable components:* Most JSP pages rely on reusable components (JavaBeans or Enterprise JavaBeans components) to perform the more complex processing required for the application. These components can be shared among developers utilizing the common operations. A component-based approach enables you to speed up overall development and leverage existing expertise and development efforts.
- *Simplifies page development with tags:* Because the more complex logic is hidden from the page designer, people who may not be familiar with scripting languages can design your Web pages. JSP tags can access and instantiate JavaBean components, set or retrieve bean attributes, and perform other functions that a page designer would otherwise have to be able to code.

Led by Sun Microsystems, the JSP specification was designed with the collaboration of industry leaders in the enterprise software and tools markets. Sun makes the JSP specification available at no cost to the development community with the goal that every Web server and application server support the JSP interface. JSP pages share the "Write Once, Run Anywhere" characteristics of Java technology. JSP technology is a key component in the Java 2 Platform, Enterprise Edition.

Understanding Web Application Models

When a JSP is called for the first time, it is compiled into a Java servlet. The servlet stays loaded in memory to handle multiple client requests. If the timestamp of the JSP changes, the server recompiles the JSP and runs the `init()` method to instantiate the new servlet file. Because JSPs are compiled into servlets, they run on the server and have full access to all Java runtime environment benefits.

You can choose from several main application models when developing JSP-based applications. The first model is the basic model, allowing the JSPs to accept the request from the user and generating the return content itself. The JSP can access a data store via Java Database Connectivity (JDBC) to gather any necessary data needed to generate the dynamic content, but the JSP itself is responsible for generating all the return content. Figure 12-1 illustrates this basic model. This model works fine for smaller applications that don't have a lot of components. This model does not scale well and gets somewhat confusing after your JSPs fill with business logic coding.

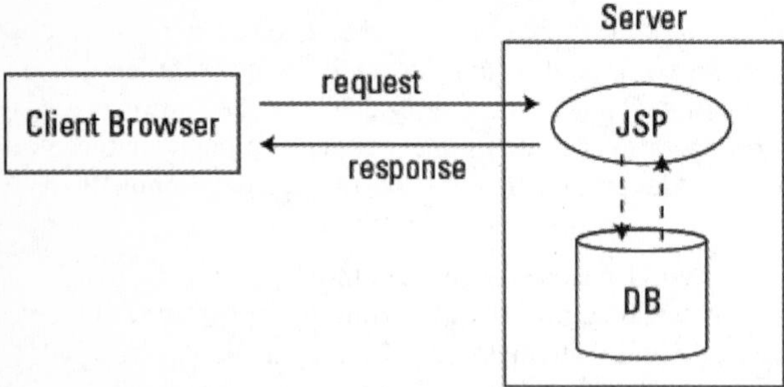

Figure 12-1: The very basic application model using a JSP to dynamically generate return content for a browser-based client.

Another model, the scalable application model, uses a servlet to accept the users requests. The servlet can then process any business logic that is needed by utilizing multiple external services. It then generates a databean with its results and passes it to a JSP to display the data to the user. Figure 12-2 illustrates this application model. This approach scales well and allows the JSPs to be simpler and easier to maintain.

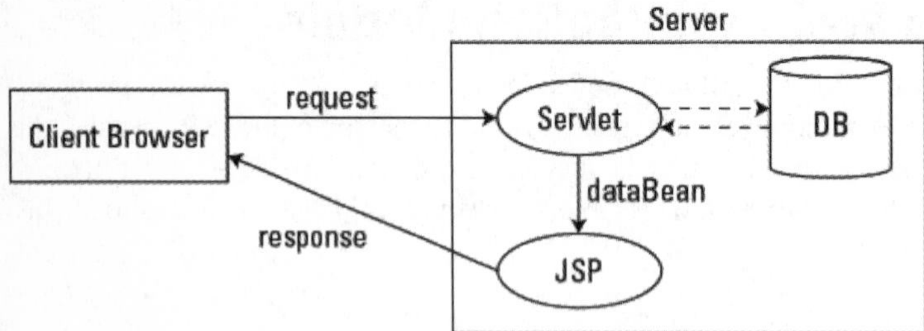

Figure 12-2: A scalable application model using a JSP, servlet, and JavaBean to generate dynamic content for a browser-based client.

A third popular model, the EJB model, uses JSP as the proxy between the client and an Enterprise JavaBeans (EJB) architecture. The EJBs handle all the business logic and security, and the JSPs utilize them for any needed services. Figure 12-3 illustrates this EJB style model. This model is supported by the Java 2 Enterprise Edition (J2EE) platform.

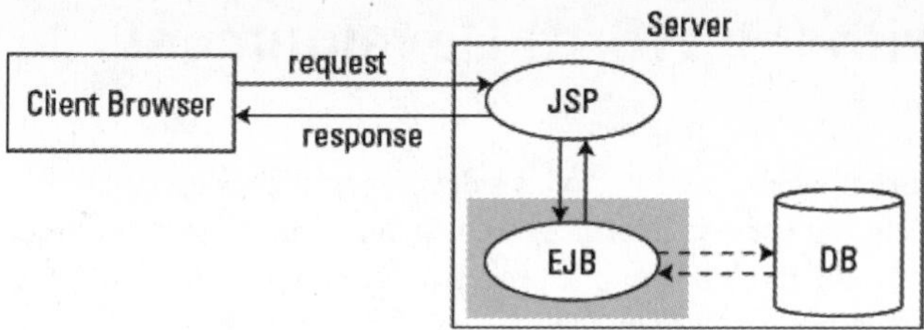

Figure 12-3: An EJB application model using a JSP interacting with an EJB to generate dynamic content for a browser-based client.

After you have determined the requirements for your application, you can begin to evaluate which of these models best fits your needs.

Java2 Enterprise Edition (J2EE) is a set of related specifications that provide a single standard for implementing and deploying enterprise applications. The current J2EE specification level that WebSphere Application Server fully supports is 1.2. The J2EE platform is designed to provide server- and client-side support for developing enterprise, multitier applications. A typical J2EE environment configures a client-side tier to provide the user interface, one or more middle-tier modules for handling the business logic and services, and a back-end tier to provide the data-management layer. The client tier supports a variety of client types. The middle tier supports the business logic and services through Web containers (HTML, Servlets, JSPs, and XML) and Enterprise JavaBeans (EJBs) containers. The back-end tier or enterprise-information tier supports the access to existing systems.

The notion of containers is a key element in the J2EE development model. *Containers* are standardized runtime environments that provide specific component services. Every J2EE server provides runtime support for a standard set of container services. Each server supports the request/response paradigm for handling processing between each container, automated support for transaction and lifecycle management for EJB components, and provides access to enterprise information systems (for example, JDBC access to a database).

The J2EE standard is defined through a set of related specifications. Three of the many key elements of the J2EE architecture are the EJB specification, the servlet specification, and the JSP specification.

NOTE: Chapter 6 discusses the Model View Controller (MVC) architecture, a popular and powerful design approach. JSPs are extremely popular with this approach because they can represent the view component well. With a JSP application model, the JSPs act as the views; the data beans or EJBs act as the models; and the servlets act as the controller mechanisms. Each component can perform the application function that it does best without regard to the manner in which the rest of the application is implemented. This method provides an object-oriented approach for software development. By creating individual reusable components in this manner, your application will gain scalability, power, and ease of maintenance.

Developing JSPs with the WSAD Development Environment

Chapter 7 mentions that WSAD is a powerful tool for today's developer. It enables you to organize your development projects and use one interface to update all your project resources. You can code your servlets, JSPs, and EJBs all from one program. By simply switching your perspective, you can view each container of your application.

The Web perspective is a powerful tool that JSP editors can use. With WSAD, you can develop your JSPs in a snap. Context-sensitive help enables you to view the API as you type; it also has a built-in browser so you can view your changes immediately as you incrementally develop. This section walks you through the coding of two basic JSP files using the WSAD developing environment. Although they are simple JSPs, they illustrate how to create new JSP files, enter your code, and test your changes.

Coding the obligatory Hello World

The first of the two JSPs is, of course, our good friend Hello World. After you have started your WSAD environment, select the Web perspective view. From within this perspective, select File⇨New ⇨JSP File (see Figure 12-4).

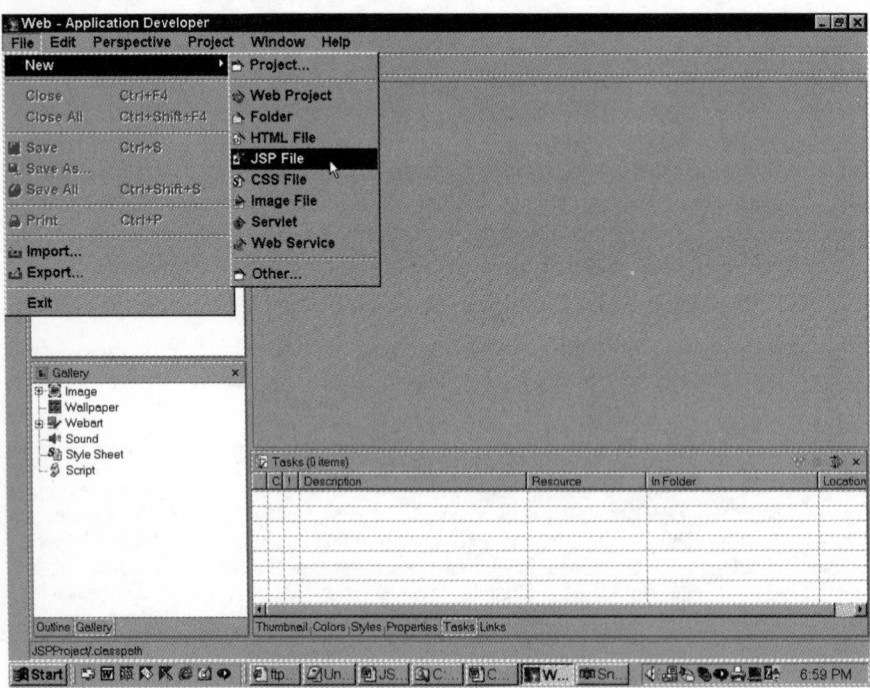

Figure 12-4: Creating a new JSP in WSAD.

This opens the Create a JSP File Wizard to guide you through defining your new JSP. Select your Web Application directory and enter **HelloWorld** as the name of your JSP file in the File Name entry field (see Figure 12-5).

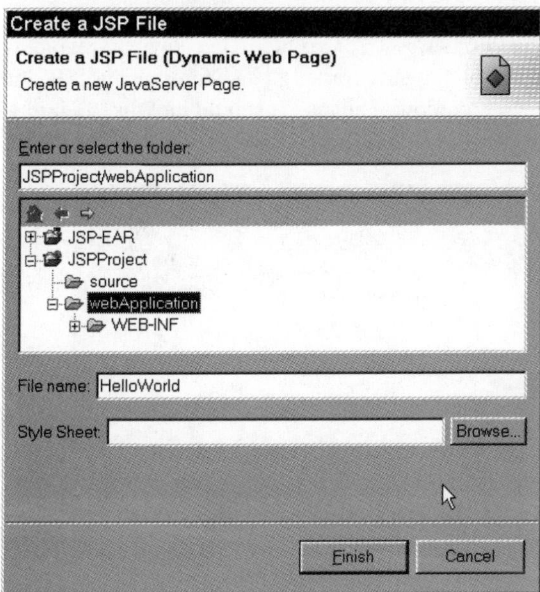

Figure 12-5: Naming the HelloWorld JSP.

After you click the Finish button, your JSP file is created and loaded into your main WSAD window. The default tab shown is the Design tab. Select the Source tab at the bottom of the window so you can update the code WSAD generated.

You are going to add a JSP scriptlet and a JSP expression (discussed later in this chapter) to your JSP to provide output for the page. Insert the lines from Listing 12-1 into your JSP.

Listing 12-1: Adding a JSP Scriptlet and JSP Expressions to the Hello World JSP

```
<!DOCTYPE HTML PUBLIC "-//W3C//DTD HTML 4.01 Transitional//EN">
<HTML>
<HEAD>
<%String title = "Hello World JSP!"; %>
<META name="GENERATOR" content="IBM WebSphere Studio">
<TITLE><%= title %></TITLE>
</HEAD>
<BODY>
<%= title %>
</BODY>
</HTML>
```

As you type the string in your scriptlet (`<% String title = "Hello World JSP!"; %>`), the context-sensitive help window pops up and shows you the possible API calls you can make. After you enter this scriptlet, the variable *title* is accessible to the other JSP expressions (`<%= title %>`). You use it to update the HTML title and body text at runtime.

To test your changes, simply right-click the `HelloWorld.jsp` file in the Navigator window, select Run on Server to start the server (if it is not already started), parse through the JSP, and return the resulting HTML in its own Browser window. The results should look like Figure 12-6.

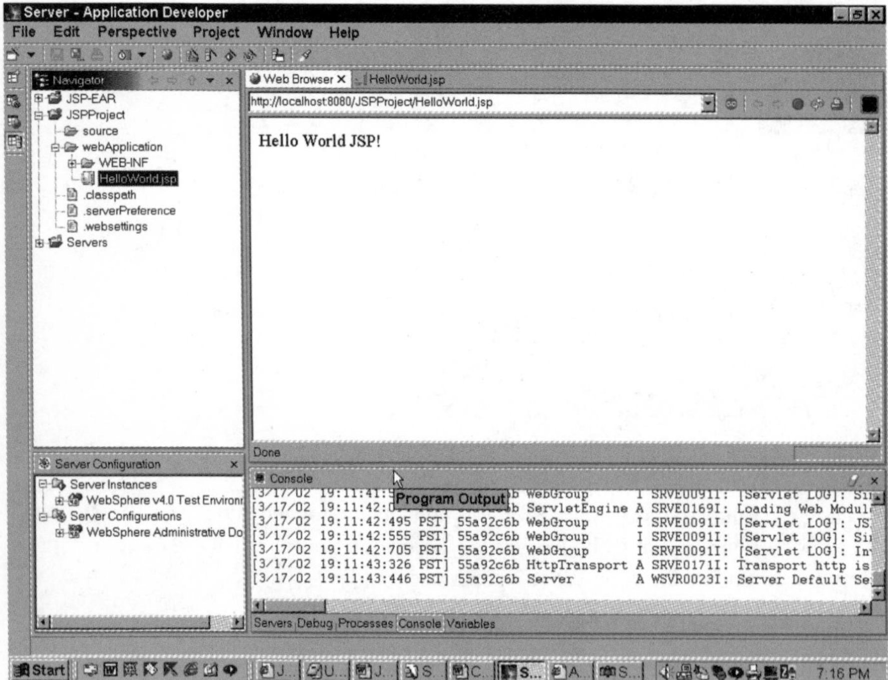

Figure 12-6: Output from HelloWorld.jsp.

If everything is coded correctly, you should see `Hello World JSP!` in the window. Congratulations. That's all there is to writing your first JSP. You are now ready to join the wonderful world of JSPs.

Running the simple JSP

Next, you build another JSP with more dynamic content. For this example you use an HTML form to accept user input. In your JSP, you inspect the data that gets passed into the JSP via the `HttpServletRequest` object and display it to the screen.

Select your Web Application folder, create a new JSP, and name it **SimpleJsp**. In the source window, update the code to look like Listing 12-2.

Listing 12-2: Creating a More Interactive and Dynamic JSP

```
<!DOCTYPE HTML PUBLIC "-//W3C//DTD HTML 4.01 Transitional//EN">
<HTML>
<HEAD>
<META name="GENERATOR" content="IBM WebSphere Studio">
<TITLE>SimpleJsp.jsp</TITLE>
</HEAD>
<BODY>
<FORM action="/JSPProject/SimpleJsp.jsp">
<TABLE>
<TR>
  <TD>What is your Name?</TD>
  <TD><INPUT size="40" type="text" name="tf_name"></TD>
</TR>
<TR>
  <TD>What is your favorite JSP?</TD>
  <TD><INPUT size="20" type="text" name="tf_jsp"></TD>
</TR>


<%
String name = request.getParameter("tf_name");
if(name != null && name.trim().length() > 0 )
{
%>
  <TR><TD colspan="2">Hello <%= name %></TD></TR>
<%
}
String favJsp = request.getParameter("tf_jsp");
if(favJsp != null && favJsp.trim().equalsIgnoreCase("SimpleJSP"))
{
%>
  <TR><TD colspan="2">You have very good taste in JSPs!</TD></TR>
<%
}
%>
<TR>
<TD colspan="2"><BR><INPUT type="submit" value="Continue"></TD>
</TR>
</TABLE>
</FORM>
</BODY>
</HTML>
```

Run this new JSP in the WSAD test environment. The resulting HTML file that displays is illustrated in Figure 12-7.

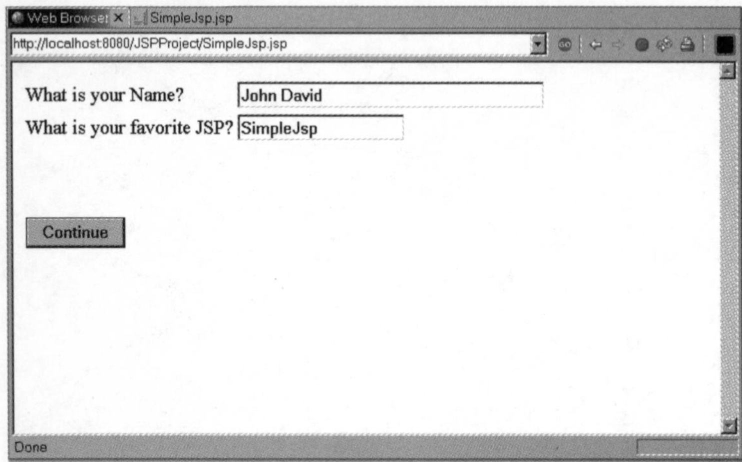

Figure 12-7: SimpleJsp.

When the user clicks the Continue button, the JSP calls itself and displays the results shown in Figure 12-8.

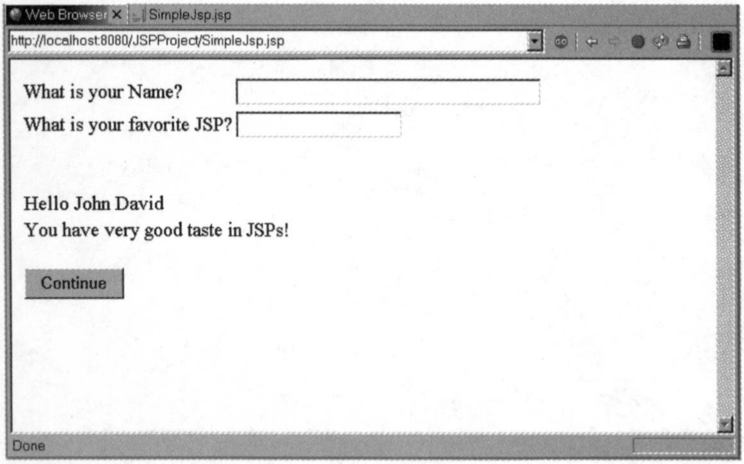

Figure 12-8: Results of SimpleJsp.

This example uses scriptlets to set variables with the data that the user entered (name and favorite JSP). You use the implicit request object of the JSP to check for the data. You then do a check to see whether parameters were sent. If so, you display the name that the user entered. You always show the name of the person if it is present; however, because you are a little biased, you only tell users they have good taste in JSPs if they chose the SimpleJSP as their favorite. This simple example illustrates how to dynamically generate HTML content depending on user requests.

Creating Dynamic Content in JSPs

JavaServer Pages have their contents (HTML tags, JSP tags, and scripts) translated into a servlet by the Application server. This process translates both the dynamic and static elements declared within the JSP file into Java servlet code that delivers the translated contents to the browser. Because JSPs are server-side technology, the processing of both the static and dynamic elements of the page occurs on the server. The JSP/servlet architecture is often referred to as thin-client because most of the business logic is executed on the server. The following list outlines the tasks performed on a JSP file on the first invocation of the file or when the underlying JSP file is changed by the developer:

- The Web browser makes a request to the JSP page.
- The JSP engine parses the contents of the JSP file.
- The JSP engine creates temporary servlet source code based on the contents of the JSP. The generated servlet is then used for rendering the static elements of the JSP specified at design time in addition to creating the dynamic elements of the page.
- The servlet source code is compiled by the Java compiler into a servlet class file.
- The servlet is instantiated. The `init()` and `service()` methods of the servlet are called, and the servlet logic executes.
- The combination of static HTML and graphics combined with the dynamic elements specified in the original JSP page definition are sent to the Web browser through the output stream of the servlet's response object.

Any subsequent calls for the JSP file simply invoke the `service()` method of the servlet created by the process to serve the content to the browser. As a result, the servlet produces the remains in service (memory) until the Application server is stopped, the servlet is manually unloaded, or a change is made to the underlying file causing recompilation.

Understanding JSP syntax

JavaServer Pages are composed of standard HTML tags and JSP tags. The available JSP tags are categorized as follows:

- Directives enable you to define global definitions.
- Declarations enable you to declare classes or methods for use by the JSP code.

- Scriptlets enable you to embed Java code directly into your HTML.
- Comments give you a mechanism to comment your JSP code.
- Expressions allow your JSP to render a value directly into your HTML.

Using directives

JSP *directives* are global definitions sent to the JSP engine that remain valid regardless of any specific requests made to the JSP page. Because of the way the JSP parsing engine produces servlet code from the JSP file, directives always appear at the top of the JSP file before any other JSP tags.

The syntax of a directive is as follows:

```
<%@directive directive_attr_name =value %>
```

Directives fall into three groupings: `page`, `include`, or `taglib`.

The page directive defines page-dependent attributes to the JSP engine.

```
<%@page ... %>
```

The following are attributes of the page directive:

- *language* : Identifies the scripting language used in scriptlets in the JSP file or any of its included files. JSP supports only the value of `java`.
- *extends*: The fully qualified name of the superclass for which this JSP page is derived. Using this attribute can affect the JSP engine's capability to select specialized superclasses based on the JSP file content. The `extends` attribute should be used with care.
- *import*: When the `language` attribute of `java` is defined, the `import` attribute specifies the additional files containing the types used within the scripting environment.
- *session "true" | "false"*: If the value of this attribute is `true`, it specifies that the page will participate in an HTTP session and enables the JSP file access to the implicit session object. The default value is `true`.
- *buffer "none" | "sizekb* : This attribute dictates the buffer size for the JspWriter. If `none`, the output from the JSP is written directly to the `ServletResponse PrintWriter` object. Any other value results in the JspWriter buffering the output up to the specified size. The buffer is flushed in accordance with the value of the `autoFlush` attribute. The default buffer size is no less than 8kb.
- *autoFlush "true" | "false"*: If the value of this attribute `true`, the buffer is flushed automatically. If `false`, an exception is raised when the buffer becomes full. The default value is `true`.
- *isThreadSafe "true" | "false"*: If the value of this attribute is `true`, the JSP processor can send multiple outstanding client requests to the page concurrently. If `false`, the JSP processor sends outstanding client requests to the page consecutively, in the same order in which they were received. The default is `true`.

- *info*: The attribute allows the definition of a string value that can be retrieved using `Servlet.getServletInfo()`.
- *errorPage* : This attribute specifies the URL to be directed to for error handling if an exception is thrown and not caught within the page. In the JSP 1.0 specification, this URL must point to a JSP page.
- *isErrorPage "true" | "false* : This attribute identifies that the JSP page refers to a URL identified in another JSP's `errorPage` attribute. When this value is `true`, the implicit variable exception is defined, and its value is set to reference the throwable object of the JSP source file that causes the error.
- *contentTyp*: This attribute specifies the character encoding and MIME type of the JSP response. Default value for `contentType` is `text/html`. Default value for `charSet` is `ISO-8859-1`.

The `include` directive allows substitution of text or code to occur at translation time. You can use the `include` directive to provide a standard header on each JSP page, as follows:

```
<%@include file="header.html"%>
```

The `include` directive has `file` attribute, which tells the JSP engine which content will be substituted into the JSP. This include file could be another JSP file.

The `taglib` directive allows custom extensions to be made to the tags known to the JSP engine. This tag is an advanced feature and is covered in more detail later in this chapter in the "Understanding JSP Tags and Tag Libraries" section.

Using declarations

`Declarations` are fragments of code that are called from an expression block written directly within the JSP file. Code within a declaration block is usually written in Java; however, WebSphere Application Server supports declaration blocks containing other script syntax. Code within a declaration block is often used to perform additional processing on the dynamic data generated by a `JavaBean` property. The syntax of a declaration is as follows:

```
<%!declaration(s)%>
```

The following is a more complete example:

```
<%!
private int hitCount =0;
private String generateRandomNumber(request)
{...method body here...}
%>
```

Be aware that when using declarations, you are creating processing or variables that are treated at a global level for all requests being processed by the JSP. Using declarations is equivalent to using class variables when coding a Java servlet.

Using scriptlets

JSPs also support embedding Java code fragments within the JSP by using a scriptlet block. Scriptlets are used to embed small code blocks within the JSP, rather than to declare entire methods as performed in a declarations block. The syntax for a scriptlet is as follows:

```
<%scriptlet %>
```

Listing 12-3 shows the logic used in the `SimpleJSP`, which uses a scriptlet to output an HTML message based on which JSP the user entered as the favorite. You can see that the HTML elements appear outside the script declarations.

Listing 12-3: Adding a Scriptlet to a JSP to Create Dynamic HTML Content

```
<%
 String name = request.getParameter("tf_name");
 if(name != null && name.trim().length() > 0 )
 {
%>
  <TR>
   <TD colspan="2">Hello <%= name %></TD>
 </TR>
<%
 }

 String favJsp = request.getParameter("tf_jsp");
 if(favJsp != null && favJsp.trim().equalsIgnoreCase("SimpleJSP"))
 {
%>
 <TR>
   <TD colspan="2">You have very good taste in JSPs!</TD>
 </TR>
<%
 }
%>
```

Many times, developers clutter their JSPs with lines and lines of scriptlet code, which overrides many of the benefits of separating the business logic from the view. The idea is to encapsulate most of the business logic into beans or custom tags, so the JSP is mostly HTML. Cluttering up your JSPs with a lot of code makes it more difficult for a Web designer to make HTML changes because the HTML is so spread out among all your scriptlets.

Using comments

You can use two types of comments within a JSP. The first comment style is known as an *output comment*, which enables the comment to appear in the output stream on the browser. If users select the View Source option in their browsers, these comments are visible. This comment is an HTML formatted comment with the following syntax:

```
<!--comments ...-->
```

The second comment style is used to fully exclude the commented block from the output and is commonly used when uncommenting a block of code so that the commented block is never delivered to the browser. This style is known as a *no-output comment*. The syntax is as follows:

```
<%--comment text --%>
```

You can also create comments containing dynamic content by embedding a `scriptlet` tag inside a `comment` tag, as follows:

```
<!--comment text <%=expression %>more comment text ->
```

Using expressions

Expressions are pieces of scriptlet code whose results can be converted to string objects and sent to the output stream for display in a browser.

The syntax for an expression is as follows:

```
<%=expression %>
```

Typically, expressions are used to execute and display the string representation of variables and methods declared within the declarations section of the JSP or from JavaBeans that are accessed by the JSP. If the conversion of the expression result is unsuccessful, a `ClassCastException` is thrown at the time of the request. All primitive types, such as `short`, `int`, and `long` can be automatically converted to strings. Your own classes must provide a `toString()` method for string conversion.

Using JSP scripting

WebSphere Application Server offers a number of enhancements over the JSP 1.0 specification and includes the capability to use non-Java scripting languages within JSP pages or use multiple scripting languages within the same JSP file.

You can use any of the Bean Scripting Framework (BSF) 1.0-compliant languages, such as JavaScript, JPython, or Perl, in your JSP by specifying it within the `language_name` attribute of the page directive.

Accessing implicit objects

When you are writing scriptlets or expressions in your JSPs, there are a number of objects that you automatically have access to in your code as part of the JSP standard without having to fully declare them or import them. The following is a list of the implicit objects that are available to you in your JSP. You can use these implicit objects directly in your code:

- *request:* This is the `javax.servlet.HttpServletRequest` that triggered the service invocation.
- *response:* This is the `javax.servlet.HttpServletResponse` to the request.

- *pageContext:* This is the `javax.servlet.jsp.PageContext` of the JSP. By accessing this object, you have access to a number of convenience objects and methods, such as `getException()`, `getPage()`, and `getSession()`, providing an explicit method of accessing JSP implementation specific objects.
- *session:* This is the `javax.servlet.http.HttpSession` object created for the requesting client.
- *application:* This is the `javax.servlet.ServletContext` as obtained from the servlet configuration object.
- *out:* This is the `javax.servlet.jsp.JspWriter` output stream writer.
- *config:* This is the `javax.servlet.ServletConfig` for the JSP.
- *page:* This is the `java.lang.Object` instance of this 'page's implementation class processing the current request.

Understanding JSP Interactions

JSPs, like other components of a Web application, need the capability to interact with each other. A JSP can use a number of methods to accomplish this. JSPs usually use a JavaBean object to present dynamic content. However, a JSP can also invoke another JSP page by URL, by including another JSP or HTML page in the include directive or by calling a servlet.

Invoking a JSP by URL

A JSP can be invoked via a URL from within the `<FORM>` tag of a JSP or HTML page, or from another JSP. To invoke a JSP by URL, use the syntax `http://servername/path/filename.jsp`. An example of invoking a JSP via a URL is as follows:

```
http://localhost/csicruise/ShowDates.jsp
```

Calling a servlet from a JSP

You can invoke a servlet from a JSP either as an action on a form, or directly through the `jsp:include` or `jsp:forward` tags.

It is quite common to call a servlet from a `HTML<FORM>` tag to process the data that was entered by the user. In the `<FORM>` tag, you set the *action* to the URL of the servlet and set the `method` attribute according to whether you want the `doPost()` or the `doGet()` method of the servlet to be called. The syntax for calling a servlet from a JSP is as follows:

```
<FORM METHOD="POST|GET"ACTION="applicationURI /servletURL ">
...
</FORM>
```

Listing 12-4 is an example using this syntax.

Listing 12-4: Writing Your HTML to Send Its Content to a Servlet for Processing

```
<HTML>
...
<FORM action="/CSICruise/servlet/SingleServlet" method="post">
  <TR>
    <TD>First Name:</TD>
    <TD><INPUT size="20" type="text" name="tf_first_name"></TD>
  </TR>
  <TR>
    <TD>Last Name:</TD>
    <TD><INPUT size="20" type="text" name="tf_last_name"></TD>
  </TR>
  <INPUT type="submit" name="action" value="Forward">
</FORM>
...
</HTML>
```

This code calls the `SingleServlet` servlet's `doPost()` method passing it an `HttpServletRequest` with the data that was entered in the form fields `tf_first_name` and `tf_last_name`.

You can also include the output of a servlet in a JSP using the `jsp.include` tag. The syntax for this is as follows:

```
<jsp:include page="applicationURI /servletURL"/>
```

Listing 12-5 is a coding example of the include tag being used:

Listing 12-5: Embedding the jsp:include Tag into Your JSP to Include the Results from a Servlet

```
<HTML>
...
<TR>
  <TD>Your Results are:</TD>
  <TD>  <jsp:include page="/CSICruise/servlet/DisplayResultsServlet"/>
</TD>
</TR>
...
</HTML>
```

When you run this JSP, the output from the `DisplayResultsServlet` servlet is imbedded in the JSP output, enabling you to perform the heavy logic in the servlet and use the JSP only to display the results.

JSPs also gives you the ability to forward process from a JSP to a servlet using the `jsp.forward` tag. The syntax is as follows:

```
<jsp:forward page=" applicationURI /servletURL "/>
```

Listing 12-6 is a coding example of the forward tag being used:

Listing 12-6: Embedding the jsp:forward Tag into Your JSP to Include the Output of the Processing Servlet

```
<HTML>
...
<jsp:forward page="/CSICruise/servlet/SHTMLServlet"/>
...
</HTML>
```

When this JSP runs, the output of the processing servlet (`SHTMLServlet`) replaces the output of the JSP. All output of the JSP is lost.

Calling a JSP from a servlet

Most often a JSP is called from a servlet to display the results of the servlet's processing. There are two methods you can use to call a JSP from a servlet. One way is to call the `sendRedirect()` method of the `HttpServletResponse` object, directing the response to the desired JSP. This method sends a message back to the browser to send a redirect to the JSP before returning the output to the user. It creates a brand new request object to send to the JSP.

However, sometimes you may want to preserve some of the data in the existing request object. For cases like this, you call a JSP from your servlet using the `RequestDispatcher` object and forward the `HttpServletRequest` and `HttpServletResponse` objects onto the JSP.

The syntaxes for both of these actions are as follows:

```
response.sendRedirect ("http://servername/path/filename.jsp "); //
creates a new request
getRequestDispatcher("/path/filename.jsp ").forward(request,response);
// preserves request data
```

The decision of whether to use `Forward()` or `Redirect()` is based on whether you need to preserve any of the `HttpServletRequest` attributes. If your resulting JSP needs data from the originating request, you need to use the `Forward()` method. If your JSP is designed in such a way as to stand alone, using the `sendRedirect()` is preferred.

Invoking a JSP from a JSP

Calling a JSP from another JSP is similar to calling a servlet from a JSP. You can call a JSP from another JSP in four ways:

- You can specify the target action of your HTML `<FORM>` tag to go to the second JSP:

```
<FORM action="/CSICruise/jsp/MyNextJSP.jsp">
```

- You can specify the URL of the second JSP in an anchor tag HREF attribute:

```
<a href="MyNextJSP URL"> Click here to go to my second JSP </a>
```

- You can use the `javax.servlet.http.RequestDispatcher.forward` method to invoke the second JSP file. This is the same as using the `jsp:forward` tag.
- You can use the implicit request object within your JSP and use the `request.sendRedirect()` method to invoke the second JSP file.

Generally, you use a servlet to handle the processing for the JSP data, but there are times when you will want to go from one JSP to another without using any type of pass-through servlet. More times than not, the URL style for linking JSPs is implemented.

Understanding JSP Tags and Tag Libraries

When people first begin to work with JSPs, they end up using mostly JSP scriptlets and embedding a lot of Java code within the JSP. Remember part of the power behind JSPs is the power to remove the business logic from the view and make it easy for page designers to change the look and feel of a page with ease. Cluttering your JSPs with scriptlets makes it harder for the page designer to move things around in the JSP file. Because there are a lot of common tasks that JSP developers share, JSPs use tags, which enable developers to remove scriptlet code from the actual JSP file into a tag; then the only piece that gets added to the JSP is the actual tag that represents the logic that it performs. The JSP specification has a set of common tags that are built in, and there are a wide variety of tag libraries available to use. Following is a list of useful JSP development tags that are part of the JSP specification:

- *jsp:useBean*: This tag declares the usage of an instance of a JavaBeans component. If it does not already exist, the instance is created and registered in the servlet environment.
- *jsp:setProperty*: This tag can be used to set all the properties of a bean from the request parameter stream with parameters of the same name, or it can be used to set individual properties.
- *jsp:getProperty*: This tag gets the property of the bean, converts it to a String, and puts it into the implicit "out" object.
- *jsp:forward*: This tag forwards the request to another JSP or servlet.
- *jsp:include*: This tag includes another JSP.
- *jsp:plugin*: This tag loads into the specified plug-in of the browser.

The advantage of tags is that they are easy to use and share between applications. The real power of a tag-based syntax comes with the development of custom tag libraries, in which tool vendors or others can create and distribute tags for specific purposes.

WebSphere Application Server provides the following custom tags that you can use in conjunction with the standard JSP specification:

- *tsx:getProperty*: The IBM extension implements all the `<jsp:getProperty>` function and adds the capability to introspect a database bean that was created using the IBM extension `<tsx:dbquery>` or `<tsx:dbmodify>`.
- *tsx:repeat*: Use the `<tsx:repeat>` syntax to iterate over a database query results set or a repeating property in a JavaBean.
- *tsx:dbconnect*: Use the `<tsx:dbconnect>` syntax to specify information needed to make a connection to a JDBC or an ODBC database. The `<tsx:dbconnect>` syntax does not establish the connection. Instead, `the <tsx:dbquery> and <tsx:dbmodify>` syntax are used to reference a `<tsx:dbconnect>` in the same JSP file and establish the connection.
- *tsx:userid and tsx:passwd*: Instead of hardcoding the user ID and password in the `<tsx:dbconnect>`, you can use `<tsx:userid>` and `<tsx:passwd>` to accept user input for the values and then add that data to the request object where it can be accessed by a JSP that requests the database connection.
- *tsx:dbquery*: Use the `<tsx:dbquery>` syntax to establish a connection to a database, submit database queries, and return the results set.
- *tsx:dbmodify*: Use the `<tsx:dbmodify>` syntax to establish a connection to a database and then add records to a database table.

WebSphere Application Server also adds three language tags that enable you to specify different language types for different JSP elements:

- `<jsp:scriptlet language="language_name">`
- `<jsp:expr language="language_name">`
- `<jsp:declaration language="language_name">`

In addition to the tags within the JSP specification and the custom tags defined by WebSphere, multiple tag libraries are available from vendors for you, as a JSP developer, to use. In fact, a wealth of available custom tag libraries is available today. The Apache Jakarta project has many of the more popular libraries used today. They have application taglibs, which contain tags that can be used to access information contained in the `ServletContext` for a Web application. They have the Jakarta BSF Taglib, which integrates scripting languages, such as JavaScript, VBScript, Perl, and Rexx. They also have the Jakarta Input Taglib, which generates HTML form elements that preset their values from the `ServletRequest`. Yet another is the Jakarta JDBC Taglib, which has tags that can be used to read from and write to an SQL database. The list goes on. You begin to see that even Apache has an abundance of taglibs available to you. Chances are that someone else has experienced some of the same problems as you have with your application and has written custom tags to help facilitate the separation of coding logic from the JSP.

Developing JSP Custom Actions

The JSP 1.1 specification supports the development of reusable modules called custom actions. A custom action is invoked by using a custom tag in a JSP page. A tag library is a collection of custom tags.

To use a custom tag in your JSP, you must use the `taglib` directive to tell the JSP which taglib you are referencing. The directive must be placed in the page before any of the custom tags defined in it can be used. The syntax for the `taglib` directive is as follows:

```
<@ taglib uri="/taglibURI" prefix="tlb" %>
```

The `uri` attribute refers to a Uniform Resource Identifier (URI) that uniquely identifies the taglib you want to use. You can declare a relative URI or an absolute URI. If you use a relative URI, it must be mapped to an absolute location in the taglib element of a Web application deployment descriptor.

The `prefix` attribute defines the prefix that is associated with the tags for the given tag library. This attribute notifies the JSP that any tag that uses the specified prefix is contained in the specified tag library and helps it to distinguish those tags from those provided by other tag libraries.

Custom actions use the XML syntax, having a `start` tag and `end` tag, and possibly a body. It is possible for the `start` tag of a custom action to contain attributes. You can use the attributes to customize the behavior of the tag. Attributes are set in custom JSP tags much like HTML tags: `attr="value"`. You can simply set an attribute to a string constant or, to build a more dynamic action, you can use parameters from the request object being passed in. Attributes can be set with values of the following types:

- *String:* As indicated in *`java.lang.String`*
- *Boolean:* As indicated in `java.lang.Boolean.valueOf(String)`
- *byte or Byte:* As indicated in `java.lang.Byte.valueOf(String)`
- *char or Character:* As indicated in `java.lang.Character.valueOf(String)`
- *double or Double:* As indicated in `java.lang.Double.valueOf(String)`
- *int or Integer:* As indicated `in java.lang.Integer.valueOf(String)`
- *float or Float:* As indicated in java`.lang.Float.valueOf(String)`
- *long or Long:* As indicated in `java.lang.Long.valueOf(String)`

Tag attribute values can also be set by using a `<%= scriptlet_expression %>` that is computed at request time. Using request time expressions, you can assign attributes of any type. No automatic conversion is preformed as with the types shown in the preceding list.

In lieu of using attributes for customizing your tags behavior, you might want to use a tag that has a body. The body of the tag is the logic that is contained between the start tag and the end tag:

```
<tlb:tag>
   body
</tlb:tag>
```

You can put scriptlet code in your tag's body the same way you would use a scriptlet to set your tag's attribute. Using scriptlet code to set tag attributes and using scriptlet code in the tag body give you the power to pass the dynamic content to your tag logic to be used at generation time. Generally, any data that is a simple string or that can be generated by evaluating a simple expression is best passed as an attribute. The use of a tag body is generally used for more complex data structures or logic.

Tags can also work together. Tags cooperate with each other via shared objects. In the following example, the first tag creates an object called `myObject` and sets the value of its attribute with `myValue`. The second tag can then use the object that was created by the first tag by calling it by name. The JSP specification encourages you to create a tag with an `id` attribute that creates and names an object that is then referenced by other tags using a `name` attribute that corresponds with the ID of the object that was created.

```
<tlb:tag1 id="myObject" attr="myValue" />
...
<tlb:tag2 name="myObject" />
```

It is also possible to nest tags together to allow all inner tags access to the value of the outer tag. In this case, you do not need to name the object, which can reduce the opportunity for naming conflicts.

To write a custom action, there are two things that you must implement. The first thing you need to do is define a tag handler and any needed helper classes. The second thing that must be done is to define a tag library descriptor.

Defining tag handlers

A tag handler is a class that gets called by the JSP container to handle the actions for the custom tag during runtime. When the JSP container encounters a `start` tag for a custom tag, it calls the methods of the handler to handle initialization and then the `doStartTag()` method. When the JSP container reaches the custom end tag, the handler's `doEndTag()` method is invoked. To implement a tag handler, you must implement the methods that the JSP container invokes to handle different stages of the tag lifecycle. Tag handlers must implement either the `Tag` or `BodyTag` interfaces defined in the JSP specification. You can utilize Interfaces to make tag handlers out of pre-existing Java objects. For newly created tag handlers, you can use the `TagSupport` and `BodyTagSupport` classes as base classes.

If you want to write a basic tag that has no attributes and does not implement a body, you need to implement the following methods:

- `doStartTag()`
- `doEndTag()`
- `release()`

To write a tag handler for a tag that still does not have a body but does use attributes, you need to implement the following methods:

- `doStartTag()`
- `doEndTag()`
- `setAttribute()` / `getAttribute()` (for each attribute)

For tags that implement a body, but do not require the JSP container to interact with the body, you need to implement the following methods:

- `doStartTag()`
- `doEndTag()`
- `release()`

Finally, if you want to write a tag handler for a tag that uses a body that has interaction with the JSP container, you must implement the following methods:

- `doStartTag()`
- `doEndTag()`
- `release()`
- `doInitBody()`
- `doAfterBody()`

A tag handler should reset its state and release any private resources in the `release()` method.

Tag handlers communicate with the JSP page via the page-context object, which allows the tag handler access to all other implicit objects that are accessible from the JSP (request object, session object).

Using tag library descriptors

A tag library descriptor (TLD) is an XML document that describes a tag library. If you are familiar with XML, it is analogous to a document type definition (DTD). TLDs describe information specific to the tag library and to each of the tags contained in it. The JSP container uses the TLDs to validate the tags.

The elements that make up a tag library are as follows:

- *<tlibversion>:* The version of the tag library
- *<jspversion>:* The JSP specification version the tag library implements
- *<shortname>:* A simple default name that could be used by a JSP page authoring tool to create names with a mnemonic value
- *<uri>:* The URI that uniquely identifies the tag library
- *<info>:* Any descriptive information about the tag library
- *<tag> ... </tag>:* Definition for each tag in the library

The TLD element used to specify a tag handler's class is required for each tag. You must fully qualify the classname attribute:

```
<tag>
   <tagclass>classname</tagclass>
   ...
</tag>
```

For each tag attribute, you must specify whether the attribute is required and whether the value can be determined by an expression. If the tag attribute is not required, you should provide a default value, as follows:

```
<tag>
   ...
   <attribute>
      <name>attr1</name>
      <required>true|false|yes|no</required>
      <rtexprvalue>true|false|yes|no</rtexprvalue>
   </attribute>
</tag>
```

If your tag does not use a body, you must declare that its body content is empty:

```
<tag>
   ...
   <bodycontent>empty</bodycontent>
</tag>
```

If your tag does have a body, you must specify the type of the body content:

```
<tag>
   ...
   <bodycontent>JSP|tagdependent</bodycontent>
</tag>
```

Custom actions can be very powerful for a JSP-based application. To use custom actions, you must be running the JSP 1.1 specification. It is important to keep up with the latest releases of the specification so that you can leverage the latest capabilities and add benefit to your development process. The JSP specification has evolved over the years and is becoming more and more powerful as part of a Web developer's tool set.

Understanding Differences between JSP Specification .92, 1.0, and 1.1

The change between the JSP 9.2 specification and the JSP 1.0 specification was the first major jump for the specification. JSP 1.0 built upon the 9.x specification and added some very useful tools.

Understanding changes between JSP V.92 and JSP V1.0

Following is a summary of the changes that were made from the JSP 9.2 specification and the JSP 1.0 specification:

- The `jsp:request` action element was added to provide runtime forward and include capabilities of active resources (based on the `RequestDispatcher`).
- The `jsp:include` action element was added to provide runtime inclusion of static resources.
- Buffering was added.
- The page directive now collects several attributes.
- `jsp:plugin` was defined.
- An equivalent XML document for a JSP page was provided.
- The `jsp:include` action was merged with the `jsp:request` include action. The `jsp:request` forward action was been renamed to `jsp:forward`.
- SSIs were replaced with a `<%@ include` directive.
- Tags became case sensitive, as in XML and XHTML.
- Standard tags now follow the mixed-case convention from the Java Platform.
- `jsp:setProperty`, and `jsp:getProperty` were defined.
- `<SCRIPT> </SCRIPT>` were replaced by `<%! ... %>`.

Understanding changes between 1.0 and 1.1

The JSP 1.1 specification was built upon the JSP 1.0 specification. A summary of the major changes that were made are listed here:

- Use of Servlet 2.2 instead of Servlet 2.1.
- `jsp:plugin` can no longer be implemented by just sending the contents of `jsp:fallback` to the client.

- The `flush="false"` option was removed in `jsp:include` because it cannot be implemented with Servlet 2.2.
- A Tag Library Descriptor (TLD) file was added.
- Parameters to `jsp:include` and `jsp:forward` were added.
- The `JspException` and `JspError` classes were added.
- A parent field to the `Tag` class to provide a runtime stack was added.
- `pushBody()` and `popBody()` were added to the `PageContext` class.
- The `Tag abstract` class was split into two interfaces and two support classes.
- Tag handlers are now JavaBean components in which attributes are properties that have been explicitly marked as attributes in the TLD.

Each revision allows the JSP specification to integrate with the latest Servlet API specification and keep it heading towards the J2EE platform. There was a big push to get the JSP syntax to become more like XML tags. Again trying to bring together some of the latest technology trends and align developers towards a common J2EE "philosophy" around software development. As with all software, the JSP specification has gone through trial and tribulation, and the developers at Sun have constantly been improving their code and adding new functionality to create a robust and very useful tool for software developers.

Adding JSPs to the Almost Free Cruise Application

The architecture of the Almost Free Cruise application utilizes servlets and JSPs. You now build upon the application to add a new page. The ease with which you can add a new page to your application illustrates some of the benefits of using the JSP and servlet design approach.

One way to distribute work among a development team is to assign each developer a screen, or set of screens, for which he or she is accountable. Developers have the most intimate knowledge of their individual application components and, because of the object-oriented approach, can interface with the other components of the application without needing to understand which functions they may or may not perform. In the case of the Almost Free Cruise application, you are assigned the task of implementing the Personal Information page that accepts personal data about your potential cruise mate. You need to create the following files:

- *onlineBooking6.jsp:* A new JSP for data entry
- *PersonalInfoMediator:* A new mediator object to handle the storage and manipulation of the page data
- *PersonalInfoForwardActionBean:* A forward action bean used to handle the forward navigation for the page
- *PersonalInfoBackActionBean:* A back action bean used to handle the back navigation for the page

> **ON THE WEB:** To obtain the base code for the following example, go to this book's companion Web site at `www.wiley.com/extras` and download the `CSICruiseStart.ear` file from the Chapter 12 folder.

In the following example, assume that the Web designer has developed the HTML file for you to demonstrate the way he wants the page to look (see Figure 12-9). Follow these steps to add your new page to the application:

1. *Rename file:* Your first step is to rename it to a .JSP instead of an .HTML file.

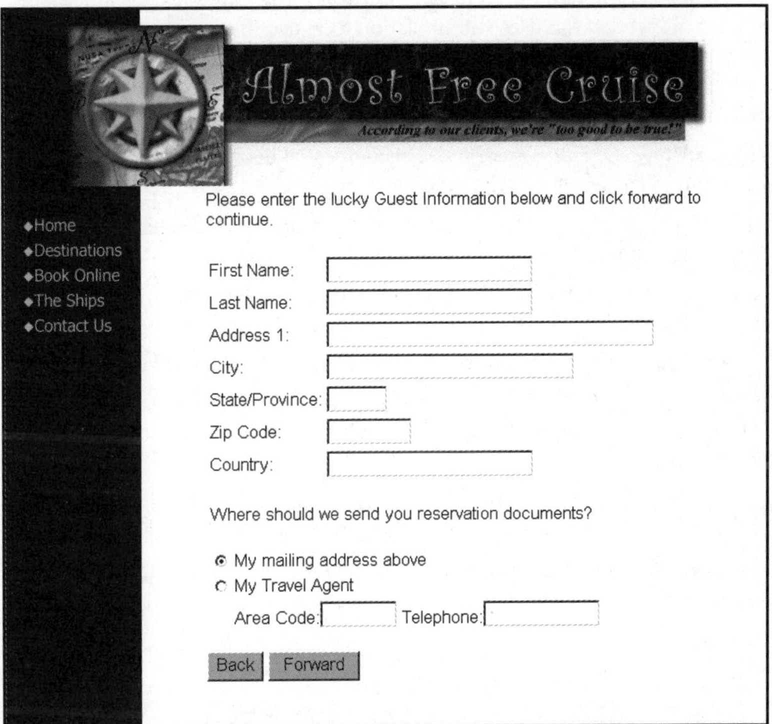

Figure 12-9: The Personal Information HTML page.

2. *Create bean:* Next you write your mediator class, which represents the data that needs to be captured from this page. You create a subclass of the base `Mediator` class and name it **PersonalInfoMediator**. You need to add getters and setters for each of the data entry fields:
   - First Name
   - Last Name
   - Address
   - City

- State/Province
- Zip Code
- Country
- Where to send documents
- Area Code
- Telephone Number

3. *Call setter methods:* You call the setter methods for these variables passing them the data off the request object that the user submits. You then use these variables to run page edits, to make sure you have clean data before updating the mediator's copy of its business object. Implement bean methods: Because you subclassed the `Mediator` class, you have to implement the following abstract methods:
   - *copyFromBusinessObject(Object businessObject):* This is used to copy the data out of the actual business object into the mediator variables.
   - *copyToBusinessObject():* This method is used to copy the validated data into the actual business object.
   - *getBusinessObject():* This method is used to obtain the business object that this page updates.
   - *setBusinessObject(Object businessObject):* This method is used to set the business object that this page updates.
   - *hasErrors(HttpServletRequest req):* This method is where you code any page edits that need to be run.
   - *processArguments(Hashtable aHashtable):* This method is used to copy the data from the *HttpServletRequest* into the mediator's variables.
   - *processLogic(HttpServletRequest req):* This method is called by the single servlet for every mediator.
4. *Add static fields to the bean:* You also want to add static variables for each of the fields used to add the HTML `name` attributes for each.

```
public final static java.lang.String FIRST_NAME = "tf_firstname";
```

5. *Embed JSP expressions in HTML:* You use JSP expressions to populate the values of the HTML field attributes dynamically. The following is a code snippet that generates the HTML for the First Name text field:

```
<TR>
  <TD>First Name:</TD>
  <TD><INPUT size="20" type="text"
name="<%= PersonalInfoMediator.FIRST_NAME%>"
value="<%= PersonalInfoMediator.getFirstName()%>">
  </TD>
</TR>
```

At runtime, the HTML *name* resolves to `tf_firstname`, and the *value* is set to the bean's value. The first time through the user will not have entered anything, so the bean fields are blank. You need to add an expression for the name and value fields for each data entry field.

6. *Update the form action:* The next piece you add is the action attribute of the HTML `<FORM>` tag. Because you are using the single-servlet design approach, all JSPs submit to it via the `post()` method.

```
<FORM action="/CSICruise/servlet/SingleServlet" method="post">
...
<INPUT type="submit" name="action" value="Back">
<INPUT type="submit" name="action" value="Forward">
```

7. *Add an HTML Submit button:* You also need to create your Submit buttons for back and forward actions. These values are used to dynamically generate the required objects at runtime.

8. *Add a hidden field:* The last JSP change that you need to make is to add the HTML hidden field that the JSP needs to identify itself to the application. The application also uses this value to dynamically generate the correct Mediator object and corresponding Back and Forward beans.

```
<INPUT type="hidden" name="PageDesc" value="PersonalInfo" >
```

9. *Create Forward and Back action classes:* Now that you have your page mediator and your JSP (model and view), you need to subclass the `CruiseActionBean` to implement your specific back and forward navigation. In each class, you create an `ActionNavigator` object that has attributes defining where the application needs to navigate to. The `PersonalInfoForwardActionBean.perform()` code is simple(and it's the most complex of the two). It creates a new `ActionNavigator` class to return, and then depending on whether there are page errors (for example, `mediator.isValid() returns false`), sets the appropriate values for navigation.

10. After you have developed all your pieces, all you need to do is notify the developer of the screen that precedes yours, so he can update `ForwardActionBean` (SelectForwardActionBean) to include your page as the next page and to remove the stubbed out page. That's it. The next time the user clicks the Forward button on the Cruise Select screen, the single servlet automatically generates the correct mediator needed for your page and navigates to it with any needed data.

If all the developers follow the same construct, adding new pages and even changing navigation should be at minimal cost to the overall deadline. JSPs are powerful for rapidly developing Web-based applications.

ON THE WEB: To obtain the complete code base for the preceding example, go to the companion Web site at `www.wiley.com/extras` and download the `CSICruiseFinal.ear` file from the Chapter 12 folder.

Summary

The power of JSPs lies in their capability to separate the view logic from the complex business logic. This allows the look and feel of the application (HTML) to change as often as necessary without touching the underlying business logic that generates the page content. The JSP specification promotes the concept of reusable parts, which greatly enhances a project's capability to deliver in a timely manner.

Several types of application models work well with JSPs. The most basic model simply uses the JSP for both generating the required data and for displaying the data back to the user. The more scalable models use the JSP as a mechanism for implementing the view component of a Model View Controller (MVC) architecture, utilizing servlets or EJBs to perform the heavy business-logic processing.

The JSP technology enables developers to develop dynamically generated pages for their Web applications rapidly. By using XML-like tags defined in the JSP specification, developers can utilize existing logic that has been created for common tasks. JSPs have different types of syntaxes to perform their services. You can simply use scriptlets to embed Java code directly into your JSPs, or you can choose to encapsulate some of your JSP logic into custom tags. In addition to creating your own custom tags, numerous tag libraries, which can further increase the speed of development, are available from outside vendors.

With today's sophisticated users, a developer must be able to quickly respond to user needs and code dynamic interactive Web applications. The JSP technology provides a means for Web developers to work with Web designers and keep up with the rapidly changing Web application requirements.

Chapter 13
Introducing Enterprise JavaBeans

In This Chapter

- Introducing Enterprise JavaBeans
- Understanding Enterprise JavaBean characteristics
- Understanding Enterprise JavaBean architecture
- Understanding object persistence
- Using entity beans
- Understanding session beans

This chapter introduces you to Enterprise JavaBeans (EJBs). The material covered in this chapter touches only the surface of EJB, but it should be sufficient for you to understand the Enterprise JavaBean-related subjects in the following chapters. Also, note that the version of the EJB specification covered in this chapter is Enterprise JavaBean 1.1 because it is the only version supported by WebSphere Application Server 4.0.

> **NOTE:** Before you continue, we must establish some naming conventions. EJB can have more than one meaning. For example, EJB can refer to the architecture or to more than one instance of an EJB. This chapter uses the abbreviations EJB or EJBs to describe an instance of an Enterprise JavaBean. However, when referring to an Enterprise JavaBean container and server, it uses EJB container or EJB server, respectively. Always be aware of the context of the term *Enterprise JavaBeans* or its abbreviation in a sentence because it can be used ambiguously.

Understanding Enterprise JavaBeans

Enterprise JavaBeans (EJBs) are a specification and an architecture created by Sun Microsystems for developing and deploying component-based, object-oriented, distributed systems in Java. A distributed system enables applications located remotely from each other to work together. The Enterprise JavaBeans architecture, like other distributed architectures such as CORBA, the Common Object Request Broker Architecture, offers enterprise services, such as distribution, security, transaction management, persistence, lifecycle, and many other services for an enterprise application. Enterprise JavaBeans offer a standard solution that enables developers to build on these service layers.

Enterprise JavaBeans support many of the services found in enterprise solutions. Enterprise JavaBeans offer a standard server-side component model that vendors of component transaction monitors can use to build their products. A component transaction monitor is a powerful application server that can offer automatic management of your server resources, security, data persistence, transactions, distributed objects, and concurrency.

Before Enterprise JavaBeans, about the only component transaction monitors around were developed by Microsoft, including Microsoft's Transaction Server (MTS), which didn't offer all the features that business systems needed. Other vendors tried offering alternatives, such as CORBA, to Microsoft's Transaction Server but struggled because each vendor designed its component transaction monitors based on different server-side component models. Sun Microsystems eventually drafted the Enterprise JavaBeans specification to solve this problem. By designing your components according to the Enterprise JavaBeans specification, you can be assured that they will work on any component transaction monitor that complies with the full Enterprise JavaBeans specification.

NOTE: Enterprise JavaBeans are not JavaBeans. Although the two technologies share the same name and are both specifications for differing component models, they are very different. Unlike JavaBeans, Enterprise JavaBeans are distributed objects by specification. JavaBeans are a component model for developing reusable components for building graphic user interfaces and for representing business logic; whereas Enterprise JavaBeans are mainly used to represent the business objects and business logic in a distributed system.

Understanding the Reasons for Using Enterprise JavaBeans

Prior to EJB, existing technologies, such as CORBA, MTS, and DCOM, satisfied most of the complex service requirements of enterprise applications. However, they required extensive time and resources (translating to money) to build and maintain. EJB is a solution that fulfills enterprise application requirements and, at the same time, minimizes time and resource expenditures. Using Enterprise JavaBeans is a robust and scalable, object-oriented, enterprise application solution. It offers many of the services that enterprise applications require — such as distribution, transaction management, security, persistence, concurrency, resources management, and more — while taking the complexity out of designing, building, and maintaining those services. Enterprise JavaBeans, like most distributed solutions, are interoperable, reusable, portable, and location transparent.

One of the many examples of why you would use Enterprise JavaBeans is to make the cruise application from the previous chapters available to other departments in the company. The billing department might want to have access to the reservation information to bill the customer. You could share the business objects in the cruise Web application among all departments and let each department build its own applications. However, this approach would make it difficult to keep each department's code up to date. A better solution is to build the cruise application as a set of Enterprise JavaBeans and let each department connect to them.

All you need to do is distribute a set of well-defined interfaces that each department can use to access the Enterprise JavaBeans.

Besides being reusable, Enterprise JavaBeans also offer interoperability by adopting CORBA, another standard distributed technology, into their lower architectural layers. It is a widely supported, standardized, object-oriented framework for building distributed systems. Actually, Enterprise JavaBeans use subsets of different distributed frameworks in their architecture. Enterprise JavaBeans, prior to version 1.1, used Java Remote Method Invocation (RMI) as the main distributed framework. Although powerful, Java RMI, a purely Java solution, isn't compatible with other distributed systems. CORBA, on the other hand, is language neutral, which makes it a perfect solution for offering interoperability. This is one of the reasons why CORBA was incorporated into the Enterprise JavaBeans specification and why it is an example of how Enterprise JavaBeans take advantage of existing and proven technologies.

Location transparency is a feature found in all distributed systems. Enterprise JavaBeans have this feature. An EJB server, so long as it is on a network, is available to any client with the necessary interfaces to communicate with it. The interfaces not only hide the possibility that an Enterprise JavaBean is located on a remote server but also hide the underlying implementation involved in communicating with the remote server and its Enterprise JavaBeans. This makes Enterprise JavaBeans powerful. You can make an Enterprise JavaBean available to all who wish to use it, so long as they have the interfaces for locating the Enterprise JavaBean over the network.

Enterprise JavaBeans is a Java technology, making its EJB servers and containers portable to multiple environments with heterogeneous operating platforms. Because EJBs are pure Java, they are maintainable in a development environment that is familiar to a Java developer.

CAUTION: Although the Enterprise JavaBean classes that you develop are portable, meaning you can deploy them to any compliant EJB container, the support code generated by deployment tools (such as WAS 4 Application Assembley Tool) is not portable. The code generated by each deployment tool is specific to a targeted vendor's (WAS 4) EJB container.

Another advantage of using Enterprise JavaBeans is that they make the job of managing remote objects a less formidable task. Enterprise JavaBeans are deployed to EJB containers. The containers do most of the work of managing their own Enterprise JavaBeans. The container is responsible for managing the lifecycle of its beans, storing their state, and making available the services of the surrounding EJB server. A deployment tool generates the RMI, CORBA, and other code necessary to support the remote interactions. This makes the job of programming Enterprise JavaBeans almost elementary because much of the plumbing is already generated for you. You need only create the business object and make its methods available in the Enterprise JavaBean interfaces.

Introducing EJB Architecture

Now that you have an idea of what Enterprise JavaBeans can offer as a distributed object solution, this section discusses what makes up the Enterprise JavaBean architecture and includes discussions of CORBA, RMI, and the characteristics of Enterprise JavaBeans.

Enterprise JavaBeans, like all other distributed solutions, adopt proxy patterns to describe how a client communicates with a distributed object. A proxy is a stand-in for something. In this case, the proxy is a stand-in for the remote object or subject that a client wants to use. The proxy pattern commonly consists of a client, an interface, a subject, and a proxy (a stand-in for the subject). The client is the client application that wants to use a subject. The interface in Enterprise JavaBeans is a Java interface that contains a view of the services or methods that the client wants to use against an instance of the subject. The proxy is located on the client side, and the subject is located on the server side. Both the proxy and subject implement the Java interface. The interface is basically a contract between the proxy and subject to provide a symmetric connection point, although allowing each side to provide its own implementation. The proxy is thus in charge of creating the implementation called the stub; whereas the subject provides the implementation called the skeleton. The stub is in charge of marshaling requests from the client to the skeleton, and the skeleton, in turn, unmarshals the request and makes the appropriate call to the server-side object.

Enterprise JavaBeans incorporate a combination of proven distributed technologies in their architecture to fulfill the proxy pattern. Enterprise JavaBeans build upon the Java version of RMI and OMG's CORBA. RMI and CORBA are both widely used distributed object systems, each with their strengths and weaknesses. For example, CORBA is a language-neutral solution, whereas Java RMI or Java Remote Method Invocation is strictly Java. To take advantage of CORBA's language neutrality, the EJB architecture incorporates CORBA at its lower layers to facilitate communication with systems written in languages other than Java. On the other hand, Java RMI is a Java standard, making it much easier to use for programming your Enterprise JavaBeans than CORBA's interface definition language (IDL). With Java RMI, you develop in a language that you're already familiar with.

NOTE: There are drawbacks to incorporating both Java RMI and CORBA in the Enterprise JavaBeans architecture. For example, distributed garbage collection, which is a feature of Java RMI, is not supported by CORBA and is not available.

The combination of Java RMI and CORBA in the EJB architecture is known as RMI over Internet Intra-ORB Protocol (IIOP) and is the framework that Enterprise JavaBeans use to communicate with other distributed systems (including other Enterprise JavaBeans) over a network. IIOP is defined and used by CORBA as the primary method for marshaling server invocation requests over a network.

Figure 13-1 illustrates how the Enterprise JavaBean architecture incorporates other technologies, such as Java RMI and CORBA, into its many layers. Data flows bi-directionally up and down the layers from the client program down to the TCP/IP layer and vice versa.

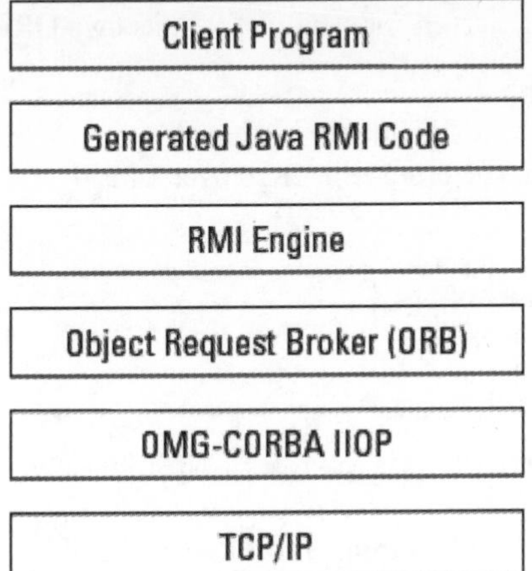

Figure 13-1: RMI over IIOP is the framework for communication for Enterprise JavaBeans.

The CORBA and Java RMI code is generated at deployment time. A deployment tool, such as WebSphere Application Server's Application Assembly tool, is used to deploy and thus generate the Java RMI and CORBA code that supports intercommunication between client and server code.

Introducing CORBA

CORBA is an important piece of the EJB architecture. It helps to make up the underlying communications framework for Enterprise JavaBeans. Because Enterprise JavaBeans are written strictly in Java, they are not compatible with other systems not written in Java. However, CORBA is a standard architecture for distributed object systems defined by the Object Management Group (OMG). The OMG is a collaborative of over 700 companies helping to provide standards for a wide range of industries. By building your distributed systems according to the CORBA specification, you can be assured that your distributed objects can interoperate with other distributed objects of other CORBA-distributed systems.

CORBA works by defining interfaces to the services of distributed objects. Some of the goals of CORBA are interoperability, and portability. CORBA defines the interfaces that compliant platforms can use to communicate over a network. This means that two disparate distributed systems can use a common interface to facilitate communication. CORBA is portable because the language used to define the interfaces is not bound to any programming languages, such as Java, C++, or Ada. This means you should be able to define a CORBA interface and use it to generate code in any of the seven currently supported programming languages. This also extends CORBA's interoperability because CORBA standardizes how ORBs communicate, whether that communication occurs between a system written in C++ or in Java.

CORBA uses a structure called an ORB as the mechanism for communication over a network. CORBA enables vendors to provide their own ORBs, but the ORBs must adhere to the interfaces defined by CORBA. WebSphere Application Server, for example, uses its own ORB for communicating with other ORBs on foreign systems.

Figure 13-2 shows where each piece of the CORBA puzzle fits into the picture. A stub communicates with a skeleton through CORBA ORBs. The protocol is IIOP over TCP/IP.

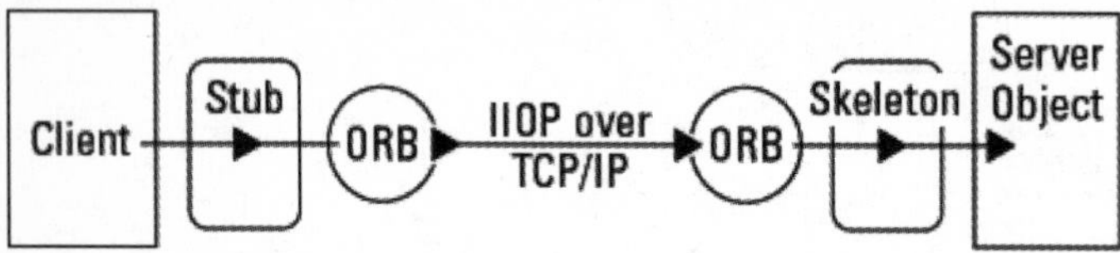

Figure 13-2: This diagram illustrates how communication flows from client to a remote object using CORBA IIOP.

In respect to Enterprise JavaBeans, CORBA is what makes Enterprise JavaBeans so flexible. Enterprise JavaBeans uses strictly Java RMI, which is Java specific. By interfacing the Java RMI with CORBA at its lower communication layers, Enterprise JavaBeans can take advantage of CORBA's language neutrality and wide support.

CORBA specifies an interface definition language (IDL) that you can use to define the interfaces that a CORBA client and the target CORBA object (server) use to communicate with each other. The IDL is not language specific. However, the syntax of the language is similar to that of C++ and Java. The language consists of keywords, modifiers that can map to any one of the seven supported languages' keywords and modifiers.

When you develop an Enterprise JavaBean, you are required to create a remote interface for the Enterprise JavaBean instance that you want to use. The remote interface contains all or a subset of the Enterprise JavaBean instance's methods. When you create an Enterprise JavaBean, a CORBA IDL is also generated. The IDL is compiled using an IDL compiler specific to the programming language (Java). The result of the compilation is the implementation for the stubs and skeletons. The generation and compilation of the IDL file(s) is often done with a deployment tool when the Enterprise JavaBean is deployed to an Enterprise JavaBean container.

Understanding RMI

By now you should know that Enterprise JavaBeans communicate over a network using a few well-known protocols, namely Java RMI, CORBA, and TCP/IP. You've also heard mention of an RMI or Java-specific version of it called Java RMI. Remote Method Invocation, or RMI for short, is a protocol used by distributed objects to invoke the methods of other distributed objects over a network and possibly return a result. You can write RMI applications in many languages, including C++ and Java. RMI is the basis for building distributed objects and for making them location-transparent. The following is a simple explanation of RMI.

The interaction between a client application and server application over the RMI protocol is accomplished by objects called the stub and skeleton. The stub and skeleton contain the implementation required to communicate with one another using RMI over a network. The client uses the stub to communicate the server's method and any parameters to the skeleton. The instruction to invoke the server's method is sent over the network according to the RMI protocol. Upon receiving the instructions, the skeleton invokes the request method against the server application that it is associated with. If the method invoked returns a value, the skeleton returns the value to the stub and thus to the client.

Enterprise JavaBeans developed following the Enterprise JavaBean 1.1 specification use the IIOP protocol defined by CORBA to communicate RMIs over a network. This is an important concept because CORBA and RMI are related but separate technologies. Each technology can stand by itself, but both are utilized by Enterprise JavaBeans to take advantage of each technology's strengths. Java RMI and CORBA IIOP occupy different layers in the Enterprise JavaBeans framework. Java RMI is still the main method of remote communication for Enterprise JavaBeans. The code generated for invoking a remote method when an Enterprise JavaBean is deployed is still Java RMI code, but the code generated for communicating the RMI call is CORBA.

Understanding the Object-Persistence Dilemma

One of the primary uses of Enterprise JavaBeans is to manipulate data stored in a database in terms of remote objects called Entity JavaBeans. Entity JavaBeans compared to session JavaBeans, which you learn more about in the "Understanding Session Beans" section of this chapter, represent real-life objects, such as the ships in the cruise examples, and contain information about those objects. The information in these objects is most commonly stored in a database. This presents some challenges. One challenge is to decide how the information should be stored. This section discusses this and some other challenges when using Enterprise JavaBeans to represent data in a database.

For the information in an object to be retrieved and saved so that it is readily available, it needs to be saved to a database. You can accomplish this in several ways, but the two most common mechanisms involve mapping the entity bean's fields to a database or persisting the entire entity bean to a database. Persisting the entire entity bean is considered the more sophisticated of the two options because you are relieved of the complexities of mapping the entity bean's fields to a database. However, although object databases have been around for a while, they are not as widely supported and standardized as relational databases.

To save the state of entity JavaBeans to a relational database, the JavaBean developer is required to map the fields of the JavaBean to the columns in a table on the database. There are several challenges to mapping the entity beans. One such challenge is that the fields in an Enterprise JavaBean might not map nicely to a database either because of differences between an Enterprise JavaBean field's type and the type designated by a database column. WebSphere Studio Application Developer offers some solutions to some of these problems. One such solution is a list of persistence converters to help you convert your Java types to database types and vice versa. Another solution, discussed in the "Understanding object-to-relational mapping," section, enables you to develop your Enterprise JavaBeans with different approaches depending on your situation.

Understanding the Bean Container Contract

Enterprise JavaBeans "live in" and communicate with the EJB server through an intermediary environment called an EJB container. An EJB container is not a physical object but a concept. An EJB container's job is to make services, such as lifecycle, security, and transaction management, available to the Enterprise JavaBeans in its care. An EJB server can hold many containers and is the door to the outside for the containers and their Enterprise JavaBeans.

The contract between the Enterprise JavaBeans and their containers is defined by the Enterprise JavaBean specification. For example, the specification requires that the container implement the `javax.ejb.EJBContext` interface and that entity beans and session beans implement subclasses of the same interface, `javax.ejb.EntityContext` and `javax.ejb.SessionContext`, respectively. This element of the contract ensures that the Enterprise JavaBeans created by the container has access to information about the beans themselves, the container that houses them, and the clients that use the beans.

An EJB container is also responsible for managing its Enterprise JavaBeans. The container, depending on the type of Enterprise JavaBean, creates and removes instances when necessary. You learn more about how the container does this for each type of Enterprise JavaBean in more detail in the sections, "Understanding the lifecycle of an entity bean," "Understanding the lifecycle of a stateless session bean," and "Understanding the lifecycle of a stateful session bean." Besides helping to manage the Enterprise JavaBeans that it stores, the container also makes callbacks on the bean instance, giving the developer the opportunity to use the callbacks to set up the Enterprise JavaBean before it is made available to the client.

Understanding the Characteristics of Enterprise JavaBeans

Now would be a good time to review some of the characteristics of Enterprise JavaBeans:

- Enterprise JavaBeans are distributed objects that are deployed to an EJB container, and their lifecycles are managed by an EJB container(s).
- Enterprise JavaBeans utilize RMI over IIOP for remote communication.
- EJB containers are intermediaries for Enterprise JavaBeans in their care.
- EJB containers provide services to Enterprise JavaBeans.
- An Enterprise JavaBean's bean class and remote interfaces are defined by the bean developer.

Another characteristic of Enterprise JavaBeans is that they can be customized during deployment by modifying a deployment descriptor file packaged in each Enterprise JavaBean JAR file. For example, Listing 13-1 shows the `ejb-jar.xml` deployment descriptor for the cruise EJB JAR. Imagine that after you jarred up all your Enterprise JavaBeans, a change was made to the cruise database: The departure date field in the database was renamed to `depart_date`. Do you have to go back, modify the Cruise entity bean, and rejar? No, that's what the deployment descriptor is for. Simply open the `ejb-jar.xml` file in a text editor; find the field name tag for `departure_date`, and change it to `depart_date`.

Listing 13-1: Altering the ejb-jar.xml Deployment Descriptor

```
<cmp-field id="CMPAttribute_2">
  <field-name>departure_date</field-name>
</cmp-field>
```

Introducing Enterprise JavaBeans

You should now have a good understanding of the Enterprise JavaBean architecture and how various technologies, such as CORBA and Java RMI, are used to offer a fairly complete distributed object solution. This section now introduces you to the different types of Enterprise JavaBeans, the EJB container, and the many services that the container provides.

There are two types of Enterprise JavaBeans that you can create: session beans and entity beans (see Figure 13-3). Additionally, you can also create two flavors of each type of Enterprise JavaBean: stateless and stateful session beans, and container-managed persistence (CMP) and bean-managed persistence (BMP) entity beans. You learn more about each type later on, in the sections, "Understanding Entity Beans" and "Understanding Session Beans."

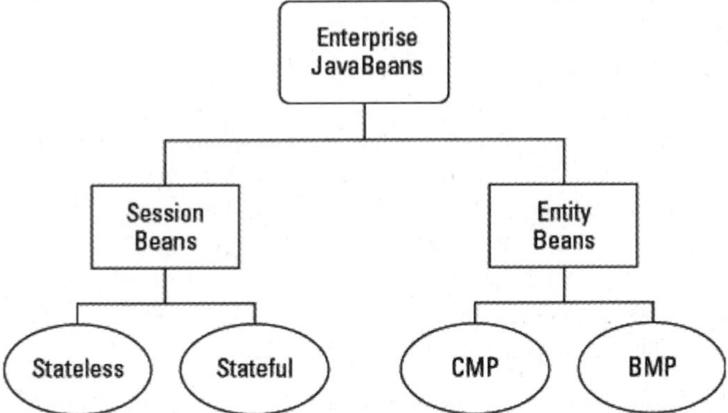

Figure 13-3: The various types of Enterprise JavaBeans and their relationships.

Each Enterprise JavaBean that you create with WebSphere Application Developer generates the following:

- *A remote interface:* A Java interface that exposes the business methods of an Enterprise JavaBean's bean class to the client.
- *A home interface:* A Java interface associated with an Enterprise JavaBean that the client can use to find a specific instance of an entity bean or stateful session bean and to create an instance of an entity bean or stateless and stateful session bean
- *A bean class:* The actual Java class that implements the logic that the client would like to use.
- *A primary key class (only for entity beans):* A Java class used to uniquely identify an entity bean to the client and in the database.

The bean class is the object located on the EJB server that actually contains the business model or logic that a client wants to use, and depending on the type of Enterprise JavaBean you want to create, it implements either the `SessionBean` or `EntityBean` interface.

Entity beans and session beans share a common bond. Both types of Enterprise JavaBeans indirectly implement the `EnterpriseBean` interface, as shown in Figure 13-4. However, only session beans implement the `SessionBean` interface, and only entity beans implement the `EntityBean` interface.

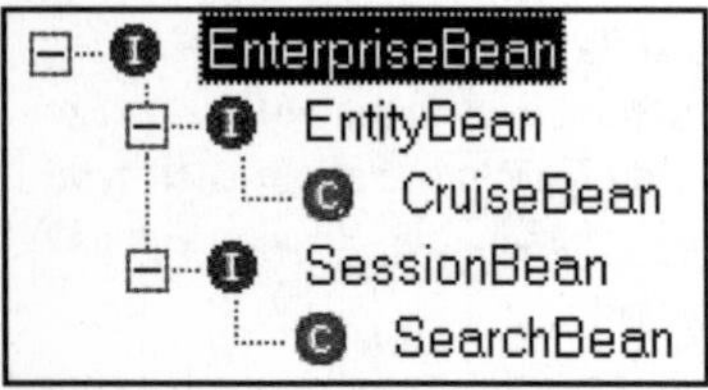

Figure 13-4: This diagram shows how entity beans and session beans fit in the class hierarchy.

The remote interface is what the client uses to interact with the bean class. In fact, the remote interface often, but not always, contains the same method signatures as those found in the bean class, because the interface is supposed to represent the bean class itself. For example, the `getDepartureDate()` method found in the cruise bean class of the cruise application is also in the cruise remote interface. In fact, each Enterprise JavaBean that you create generates, at minimum, two interfaces: the generated home interface implements the `EJBHome` interface, and the generated remote interface implements the `EJBObject` interface.

As you can see from Figure 13-5, all remote interfaces indirectly extend the `Remote` interface. However, only home interfaces extend the `EJBHome` interface and only remote interfaces extend the `EJBObject` interface.

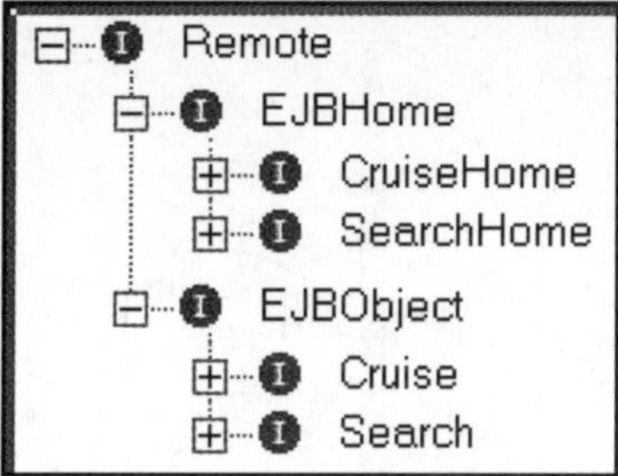

Figure 13-5: This diagram illustrates how the remote interfaces for an Enterprise JavaBean fit in the class hierarchy.

For each interface that you create, several other objects that you probably will not ever see are also created. For example, the `home` interface is associated with an EJB home stub on the client side and an EJB home object on the server side. The `remote` interface is also associated with an EJB object stub on the client side and an EJB object on the server side. The stubs contain the code to send data across the network from the client to the server.

Before an Enterprise JavaBean can be used, you must first find its `EJBHome` object and return a remote reference to it. The `home` interface can, as the name indicates, be considered the home for an Enterprise JavaBean, because the client must first look up the home interface for an Enterprise JavaBean. In a method similar to looking up a phone number in the phone book, the client uses a directory to look up the home, in this case a JNDI service. After the client has a remote reference to the `EJBHome` object, the client can use it to create new instances of the Enterprise JavaBean or, in the case of entity beans, to find them.

Figure 13-6 shows how a client locates and creates an entity bean. The client application begins by locating a home interface to the `EJBHome` object on the server. The client then invokes the `create()` method of the home interface, triggering the container to instantiate an instance of the entity bean object. The container proceeds to add the entity bean to the database and then returns a remote reference to the entity bean. The client application has successfully created an entity bean and can continue to use it to make modifications to its state.

Also, every entity bean must have a primary key class that is used to uniquely identify the entity bean in the database. The primary key is a serializable class that stores a public ID attribute. Similar to a primary key in the database used to return a database record, the primary key of the entity bean is used to locate and retrieve an entity bean. For example, in the cruise example, the client can retrieve a specific entity bean by calling the `findByPrimaryKey()` method of its `home` interface. The `findByPrimaryKey()` method takes an instance of the primary key class that the client needs to instantiate and set with the `cruise_id` value.

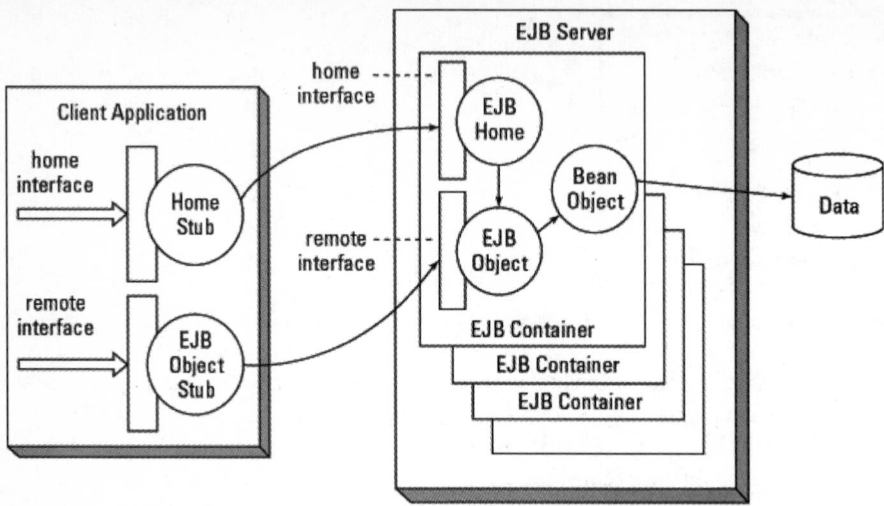

Figure 13-6: Enterprise JavaBeans communicate with clients through interfaces and stubs. This simplifies the client's interaction with the remote object by completely shielding the client from any of the implementation.

You now know a little more about what Enterprise JavaBeans can do, how they work, and what makes them useful as distributed objects; but Enterprise JavaBeans alone cannot provide the most important services of a distributed object system. These services include persistence, security, transactions, and others. All these services are provided by the EJB container, which you learn more about in the rest of this section. You also learn how to use the container's services when developing a client to Enterprise JavaBeans in the section, "Developing Enterprise JavaBean clients."

Understanding containers

A *container* is the environment that houses Enterprise JavaBeans on an EJB server. An EJB server contains one or more containers. Each container can contain one or more Enterprise JavaBeans. Each container is also in charge of managing the lifecycle, persistence, security, and other services for the Enterprise JavaBeans that it maintains. The container, in turn, interacts with the EJB server to answer requests for services from Enterprise JavaBean clients.

Relationships between the container and the EJB server are implementation specific. In other words, unlike the contract between an Enterprise JavaBean and its container, the contract between an EJB container and an EJB server hasn't yet been defined. When the contract is defined, a container vendor can then follow the details of the contract to create a container that works on any compliant EJB server.

Understanding services

An EJB container provides a variety of services necessary to make a distributed system work, as well as a robust environment in which to operate. These services include persistence, transactions, security, and naming.

Persistence

For container-managed persistence (CMP) Entity Beans, the container provides automatic persistence of their state. The container does this by automatically generating most of the persistence logic used to save and retrieve an entity bean's state from the database. For example, when you call the `create()` method of a CMP entity bean's home interface, the container automatically executes a `select` statement against the database to check to see whether the entity bean already exists. If the `select` statement is successful, the container instantiates a new instance of an entity bean and loads it with the results. If the container cannot find the entity bean, it then executes an `insert` statement to create the entity bean. This all happens without your having to code any of the logic.

Transactions

To provide a robust and scalable distributed enterprise solution, Enterprise JavaBeans provides services for transaction management. A transaction is a unit of work that must be wholly successful. If a transaction fails, all changes within the scope of the transaction are backed out. You normally would provide the logic for doing all this. An EJB container frees you from having to provide transaction logic by automatically managing it for you. All you have to do is modify the deployment descriptors for your Enterprise JavaBeans, specifying how the container should enforce transactions. For example, you can modify the deployment descriptor for the search session bean's `searchCruise()` method to require that each invocation of the method requires a new transaction. As a result of this action, the container always executes the `searchCruise()` method within a new transaction.

Security

Enterprise JavaBean security enables you to define who can access the methods of an Enterprise JavaBean. For example, you might not want just anybody to be able to book a reservation, but you want everybody to be able to search for a cruise. In this scenario, you have two roles: the role of a booking agent and the role of a general user. EJB security enables you to define this set of roles and assign each role to the methods that each one can execute. First you define the booking agent role and then the general user. You then assign each role to the methods of an Enterprise JavaBean. In the cruise example, you assign the general user role to the method that searches for a cruise. The booking agent role is assigned to both the method that creates a reservation and the method that searches for a cruise because a booking agent should also be able to search for cruises.the Enterprise JavaBeans are deployed to a container, the container takes control of monitoring security. The container ensures that a client trying to execute a method has the proper role. If it doesn't, the code throws an exception.

Naming

The EJB container is also responsible for providing a JNDI naming service for registering an Enterprise JavaBean remote object to a name. Similar to a telephone book, the JNDI naming service binds the name of an Enterprise JavaBean to the actual remote object. An example is the JNDI name for the cruise home remote object, which is `CruiseHome`. Using JNDI, a client application can look up and retrieve a reference to the `CruiseHome` object. The client can then use the `CruiseHome` object to create or find cruise objects.

Developing Enterprise JavaBean clients

The client to an Enterprise JavaBean can be an application, such as an HTTP servlet, an applet, or even another Enterprise JavaBean. Whatever the form the client application takes, however, the classes that you must use to develop the client must include a `home` interface and its generated stub classes, or a `remote` interface, its generated stub classes, and a primary key class if the Enterprise JavaBeans is an entity bean. The bean class is not visible to the client.

When developing Enterprise JavaBeans, you must keep in mind that you're dealing with distributed objects. So even though the Enterprise JavaBean architecture shields you from most of the implementation involved in working with the objects, you still need to treat them as distributed objects. One clear example of this is that you cannot simply instantiate an instance of an Enterprise JavaBean. By specification, Enterprise JavaBeans do not expose their default or any other lifecycle constructor to the client. Forcing the client to use an Enterprise JavaBean's `home` interface to create bean instances allows the container to properly manage its Enterprise JavaBeans.

To locate the `home` interface to an Enterprise JavaBean, you must use a JNDI service to locate it first. Locating the `home` interface to an Enterprise JavaBean is resource intensive and can take time. To save yourself some time and resources, you should cache the `home` interface after you've located it. Caching the `home` interface enables you to reuse the interface to create more Enterprise JavaBean instances without paying the heavy price of a JNDI lookup. Additionally, after using the `home` interface to get a remote reference to a bean instance, CORBA requires that you explicitly cast the remote reference to the correct type. Enterprise JavaBeans also require that all return types and method parameters be either primitive types or objects that implement the `Serializable` interface because, for an object reference to stream, it must first be serialized. Another issue of note, when developing an Enterprise JavaBean client is that objects returned and passed as parameters of methods are passed by value. Objects returned by and parameters passed to methods, unless they are remote references to an Enterprise JavaBean, are not distributed objects. Any changes that you make to these objects are not reflected on the remote server. So you cannot treat any of those objects as you would other Java objects.

Locating an Enterprise JavaBean and data sources with JNDI is fairly simple. Only an Enterprise JavaBean's home interface is registered with the JNDI service because the container and the home interface are responsible for initiating the lifecycle of an Enterprise JavaBean. If you bypass using the `home` interface, you also bypass the lifecycle requirement, which should never happen.

To locate the `home` interface to an Enterprise JavaBean, you must first create a `Context` object from the `javax.naming` package, as illustrated in Listing 13-2. To create the context object you need to follow these steps:

1. Load a properties or hashtable object with a list of settings required by the context, such as the host name of the server providing naming services, the port number for the service, and the fully qualified class name of the context factory class that will generate the `Context` object.

> **NOTE:** The properties that you add to the properties object are vendor specific. Please check the documentation for the deployment environment that you want to deploy to so you can to load the appropriate settings.

2. After creating the context, you then call the `lookup()` method of the `Context` object, passing in the JNDI name of the `home` interface you want to find. If a match is found, the `Context` object returns a reference to the home object.
3. You need to explicitly narrow the object reference to the correct type using the `PortableRemoteObject'` s static `narrow()` method. This action is required as CORBA IIOP doesn't support casting because not all languages supported by CORBA support the concept of casting.
4. Now that you have the `home` interface, you use its `create()` methods and, for entity beans, `find()` methods as well to retrieve a remote reference to an Enterprise JavaBean. Notice that this time you don't have to do any narrowing because each `home` interface (and stub) is associated with an Enterprise JavaBean and knows exactly the type that it should return.
5. With the `remote` interface at your disposal, you can now make calls to the Enterprise JavaBean's business methods.

Listing 13-2 :Implementing a Lookup Function to Locate and Create a Remote Reference to an Enterprise JavaBean

```
try {
 // load the JNDI properties
 java.util.Properties props = new java.util.Properties();
 props.put ( java.naming.Context.PROVIDER_URL, "iiop://localhost:900");
 props.put ( Context.INITIAL_CONTEXT_FACTORY,
com.ibm.websphere.naming.WsnInitialContextFactory);

 // instantiate an initial context
 javax.naming.Context ctx = new java.naming.InitialContext(props);
```

Listing 13-2 *(Continued)*

```
 // lookup and get a handle to the Cruise EJBHome object
 Object objRef = ctx.lookup("CruiseHome");

 // explicitly narrow the handle to the correct type, CruiseHome.
 CruiseHome cruiseHome = (CruiseHome)javax.rmi.PortableRemoteObject.
narrow(objRef, CruiseHome.class);

 // use the CruiseHome interface to find and get a handle to
 // a cruise object by its primary key
 CruiseKey cKey = new CruiseKey( new Integer(1) );
 Cruise cruise = cruiseHome.findByPrimaryKey( cKey );

 // use the remote interface to the Entity Bean instance to get the
 // destination of the Cruise
 String destination = cruise.getDestination();
 System.out.println( "Destined for: " + destination );

} catch ( Exception e ) {
 // Not the best way to handle an exception
 // but should suffice for this example.
 e.printStackTrace();
}
```

Understanding Entity Beans

Entity beans are used to represent real-world (business) objects that require their internal state to be saved for retrieval at any time. The ship bean in the cruise example application is an entity bean. The ship bean contains the `ship_id`, which uniquely identifies the ship that it represents, and the `ship_name` field. The `ship_id` and `ship_name` are columns in the ship table of the cruise database.

There are two kinds of entity beans: bean-managed persistence (BMP) and container-managed persistence (CMP). BMP and CMP entity beans are discussed in the following sections. BMP entity beans enable the bean developer to provide the code to persist the state of their instances, whereas CMP entity beans delegate the responsibility of persisting the state of their instances to the EJB container.

Whether it's a CMP or BMP entity bean, each bean class is accompanied by a primary key class that serves as a wrapper for the primary key field that uniquely identifies an Enterprise JavaBean in a database. The primary key class is what you use.

An entity bean does not usually contain any business logic; that job is left to session beans. An entity bean is used to represent a business object that a client might want to retrieve from a database. The client application can operate on the entity bean to ask for its internal state.

Understanding the lifecycle of the entity bean

Entity beans are managed in an EJB container as a pool of bean instances. Each bean instance goes through a series of states during its life. An entity bean's lifecycle begins as a set of files and deployment descriptors deployed to an EJB server. At this stage, the entity bean doesn't exist yet. However, after the EJB server is started, the EJB container creates several instances of each entity bean and places them into an instance pool. At this stage, the entity beans are in a pooled state; however, each bean instance does not yet have any state. The entity beans wait in the pool until the EJB container needs to use them. When a client calls a `create()` or `find()` method of an entity bean's home interface, the EJB container places the entity bean in a ready state by loading the bean instance with state information from the database. The container then instantiates an EJB remote object and assigns it to the bean instance. At this point, the bean instance is ready to service the client.

An entity bean continues to be available to the client until either the container determines that the entity bean can be reclaimed and returned to the pooled state or the client calls the `remove()` method of the entity bean's `home` interface. An entity bean is eligible to be reclaimed any time that it is not invoking a method. When an entity bean is reclaimed or removed, the container disassociates the bean instance from the EJB object. After an entity bean is returned to the pooled state, it is immediately available as a candidate for another or the same client. All the while, the container monitors its pool of entity bean instances to determine whether it needs to add to or remove from the pool.

Describing container-managed persistence

An entity bean that uses container-managed persistence relies on its EJB container to do almost all of the work of servicing an Enterprise JavaBean's needs. The container not only automatically handles the persistence of the entity bean's state to a database but also activation and passivation of the entity bean. The container accomplishes this by performing persistence functions that match a client's actions. For example, when a client calls the `create()` method of an entity bean's `home` interface, the container automatically executes an `insert` statement that creates the database record for the new entity bean. Likewise, for an entity bean, the container executes a `select` statement for any `find()` method, a `delete` statement for any `remove()` method, and an `update` statement for any `set()` method called against the bean's `remote` interface.

Describing bean-managed persistence

Bean-managed persistence leaves it up to you to handle the work of providing the implementation to persist the state of an entity bean. To do this, you must add the persistence code to all the BMP entity bean's EJB methods, which include `ejbLoad()`, `ejbStore()`, `ejbRemove()`, all `ejbCreate()` methods, and all `finder` methods. The container is guaranteed to call these methods as it does for CMP beans. The basic difference in the use of these methods between BMP and CMP entity beans is that in CMP beans, these methods are overridden but not often implemented because the container is responsible for handling the persistence.

Understanding object-to-relational mapping

The data in entity beans is stored in relational database tables. To indicate where the data in the entity beans will be stored, each field in the bean needs to be mapped to a corresponding column in the database. WSAD offers three approaches for doing the mapping of your Enterprise JavaBeans: top down, meet in the middle, and bottom up. WSAD does much of the work of mapping your entity beans for you depending on the type of approach you choose. The following sections discuss each approach briefly.

Starting from top down

You normally use the top-down approach to mapping Enterprise JavaBeans when you do not yet have a relational database created to store the data for your entity beans. In the top-down approach, you first create the entity beans you want to use and then use the new entity beans to generate the database tables that represent each entity bean. The top-down approach is a good way to start an Enterprise JavaBean solution because WSAD does a lot of the work for you. However, this may not always be a viable approach because most enterprise applications already have a relational database that dictates how you need to map your Enterprise JavaBeans.

Meeting in the middle

You can use the meet-in-the-middle approach for mapping your entity bean if you already have a set of beans to map and a relational database to which to map them. As the name of the approach indicates, your goal is to map the existing database to your entity beans and vice versa. Although WSAD can assist in the mapping, much of the work is up to you. This approach can be complicated because your entity beans might not map exactly to a table in the database. For example, your entity bean might contain fields that are stored in separate tables in the database, or the database might not support the type of field defined in the bean.

Starting from bottom up

Your can probably guess what the bottom-up approach to mapping entity beans might be by now. The bottom-up approach is used to generate your entity beans from a relational database. WSAD creates an entity bean for each table in the database. The bottom-up approach is an attractive method for starting an EJB solution because most enterprise applications are data driven. However, you lose control, if not flexibility, in the structure of your entity beans because you're allowing the database to dictate the entity beans you will have.

Understanding Session Beans

Session beans are used to represent the business functions in an enterprise application. An example of a business function in the cruise application is the act of saving a cruise reservation. In the cruise example, the save action is implemented as a save session bean. The session bean's main task is to take the reservation data and create the necessary entity beans to save the data. The save session bean is an example of a stateless session bean.

A session bean is initially created as either a stateless or stateful session bean. However, you can always change the flavor of a session bean by changing the session bean's deployment descriptor.

The following sections introduce you to stateful and stateless session beans. You learn the differences between the two types of session beans, the different uses for each type of session bean, and their unique lifecycles.

Using the stateless session bean

A stateless session bean does not store keep any information (state) about a client's interaction with the session bean. Thus when a stateless session bean falls out of the scope of a method where it is used or the connection to the session bean is lost, there is no risk of losing any information.

A stateless session bean is meant for client interactions where the client does not need to maintain a session with a certain instance of the session bean. The interaction between a client and stateless session bean is normally, but not necessarily, short and compact.

Understanding the lifecycle of a stateless session bean

Session beans, like all other Enterprise JavaBeans, are stored in and managed by an EJB container. Unlike other Enterprise JavaBeans, stateless session beans, as their name indicates, do not save their state (information) to a database. This means that if the session bean falls out of the scope of the method in which it was created or the client connection is lost, the client cannot determine which instance of the session bean it was interacting with even if it wants to.

Initially, when the EJB server is started, its EJB container(s) automatically generates a number of instances of each stateless session bean and places them into a pool. This is similar to the way entity beans are managed. However, unlike entity beans, stateless session beans only have two states: a nonexistent state and a method-ready state. The method-ready state is where stateless session beans are pooled. Unlike entity beans where an instance can serve the client for more than one method invocation, stateless session beans are only used for one method invocation.

A stateless session bean transitions from the nonexistent state to the method-ready state when the container determines that more instances of the session bean are necessary to handle the current workload. In the method-ready state, a stateless session bean waits until a client asks for a reference to an instance of the session bean by calling the its home interface's `create()` method. The container then assigns an EJB object to the stateless session bean, making it accessible to the client.

The EJB container reclaims a stateless session bean after every method invocation. Finally, a stateless session bean transitions from the method-ready state to the nonexistent state when the container deems that it can reduce the number of stateless session beans. The container calls the `ejbRemove()` method of the stateless session bean instance and reclaims the memory.

Understanding the stateful session bean

A stateful session bean, as opposed to a stateless session bean, maintains its state over multiple method invocations and services the same client for the life of the bean instance. A stateful session bean is often considered an extension of the client. A common example and use of a stateful session bean is a shopping cart. A shopping cart is associated with a shopper. The shopper places items into the shopping cart and requires that the items be there for as long as the shopper wants. The items in the shopping cart are sometimes stored on the client or on a database on the server. Storing the data ensures that the items in the shopping cart are available to the shopper across any number of shopping sessions. The behavior of the shopping cart describes how stateful session beans behave. Like the shopping cart, once created, a stateful session bean is associated with a client. A stateful session bean, like a stateless session bean, also provides business methods for the client; but unlike a stateless session bean, a stateful session bean can store information that the client might need in a later session.

Understanding the lifecycle of a stateful session bean

The core difference between the lifecycle of a stateful session bean and a stateless session bean is that stateful session beans are not pooled and are not swapped between different clients. As previously stated, a stateful session bean is associated with a client for the life of the stateful session bean. Also a stateful session bean's EJB object remains connected to the client even if the bean instance associated with it is no longer in memory because the EJB container is responsible for passivating and activating the stateful session bean on the demand of the client. Passivating a stateful session bean is the process of saving the bean's state to a secondary database. Activating is the process of setting the stored state back to the stateful session bean. All this requires that the fields of the stateful session bean be serializable.

Stateful session beans have three states: a nonexistent state, a method-ready state, and a passive state. The stateful session bean starts its life like all other Enterprise JavaBeans in the nonexistent state. After a client invokes the `create()` method on the stateful session bean's home interface, a new instance of the stateful session bean is created and a remote interface to the session bean's `EJBObject` is returned to the client. The stateful session bean is now in the method-ready state and is ready for use by the client. The client has a continuous connection to the client. However, the container may passivate a stateful session bean to conserve resources or when a stateful session bean is inactive for a period of time defined in its deployment descriptor. During passivation, the container saves the state of the session bean to a database and removes the stateless session bean instance from memory. After the client attempts to interact with the stateful session bean, the container automatically retrieves the state from the database and refills the stateful session bean.

Summary

This chapter introduced you to Enterprise JavaBeans. It discussed what Enterprise JavaBeans are and why they might be useful to you. It gave you a little background on Enterprise JavaBeans and where they evolved from and the technologies that are behind them, including a brief explanation of RMI and CORBA.

As a distributed object system, Enterprise JavaBeans offer the flexibility of CORBA and the power of Java RMI. Enterprise JavaBeans can free you from having to worry about all the complexities that are inherent in a distributed-object system. Obstacles, such as persistence, location transparency, and lifecycle, are either removed or simplified — making Enterprise JavaBeans an easy choice for implementing distributed objects.

To explain how Enterprise JavaBeans can do all these things, this chapter also provided an overview of the architecture behind Enterprise JavaBeans and how all the pieces fit together to create a distributed application. It included an explanation of home interfaces, remote interfaces, and stubs, which are the underlying components that Enterprise JavaBeans use to communicate with other distributed objects. Enterprise JavaBeans cannot do all that they can do without the help of an EJB container. This chapter introduced you to the concept of an EJB container and its role in the Enterprise JavaBean architecture. You learned about some of the services that an EJB container provides for your Enterprise JavaBeans, including its capability to help persist the data for your CMP entity beans and to enforce security for the Enterprise JavaBeans in its care. This chapter then discussed some of the issues worth considering when developing an Enterprise JavaBean client and continued by showing how a client would use the JNDI naming service to locate a remote reference to an Enterprise JavaBean. It also pointed out the importance of caching your `home` interfaces to avoid having to do a JNDI lookup for the same `home` interface for an Enterprise JavaBean. It then discussed, in brief, the differences between CMP and BMP entity beans and explained the lifecycle of an entity bean. You also learned about the differences between a stateful session bean and a stateless session bean and how the container treats each type differently. It concluded by explaining the lifecycle of both types of session beans.

Chapter 14

Developing Enterprise JavaBeans with WSAD

In This Chapter

- Tutorial using WebSphere Studio Application Developer
- Using EJB-RDB mapping
- Creating a CMP entity bean
- Using the EJB Test Client
- Creating a session bean
- Using access beans

In Chapter 13, you learned that an enterprise bean is a Java component that can be combined with other resources to create distributed client/server applications.

There are two types of enterprise beans:

- Entity beans store data in a database or by other means depending on which type you choose. There are two types of entity beans: container-managed persistent beans and bean-managed persistent beans. Entity beans with container-managed persistence (CMP) require database connections. Entity beans with bean-managed persistence (BMP) manage permanent data in whichever manner is defined in the bean code. This can include writing to databases or XML files, for example.
- Session beans do not require database access, although they can obtain it indirectly (as needed) by accessing entity beans. You might think of session beans as business logic. Session beans can also obtain direct access to databases (and other resources) through the use of resource references.

All beans requiring data access use the JDBC 2.0 data sources that provide resource pools of database connections. All beans reside in enterprise bean containers, which provide an interface between the beans and the application server on which they reside.

In this chapter, you take the existing AlmostFreeCruise servlet application and enhance it to utilize Enterprise JavaBeans (EJBs). The process you follow is tutorial based. You are guided through all the steps necessary to create an EJB project in WebSphere Studio Application Developer all the way through creating and deploying EJBs for testing.

Preparing for the Tutorial

You need to do some housecleaning prior to coding the application. If you haven't downloaded the code from the Web site, you should download the code segments at this time. Place all the downloaded code into a folder called `x:/Bible/chapter14/code`. Then create a WebSphere Studio Application Developer project located in `x:\code\ejb` where `x` is the drive where you want to place your code. You should create this folder on your hard drive before starting the next section.

> **NOTE**: In most cases, we refer to Enterprise JavaBeans as EJBs. In WebSphere Studio Application Developer, they are referenced as enterprise beans. You can consider both to be referring to an Enterprise JavaBean.

Creating a WebSphere Studio Application Developer workspace

You should have already created a folder called `x:\code\ejb`. What you should do next is to create a shortcut on your desktop that launches WebSphere Studio Application Developer and points to the location of the workspace (`x:\code\ejb`). Follow these steps to create the shortcut:

1. Create a shortcut on your Windows desktop by right-clicking the desktop and selecting New⇨Shortcut.
2. Enter with quotes **"x:\Program Files\IBM\Application Developer\wsappdev.exe" -data "x:\code\ejb"**, and click Next.

> **NOTE**: Use the drive letter and folder in which you installed WebSphere Studio Application Developer.

3. Name the shortcut **Chapter 14 EJB** and click Finish.

You now have a shortcut ready to start WebSphere Studio Application Developer. You need to start WebSphere Studio Application Developer and import the Enterprise Archive file (EAR) from the downloaded code folder.

1. Double-click your Chapter 14 EJB shortcut.
2. When WSAD starts, select File⇨Import and select EAR File as the type of file to import.
3. Using the file browser, navigate to the `x:\Bible\Chapter14\code` and select CSICruiseStart.ear. Call the project **AlmostFreeCruiseEAR**. Click Finish to import the EAR file.

You have imported the Web module for this tutorial. Figure 14-1 shows the outcome of your import.

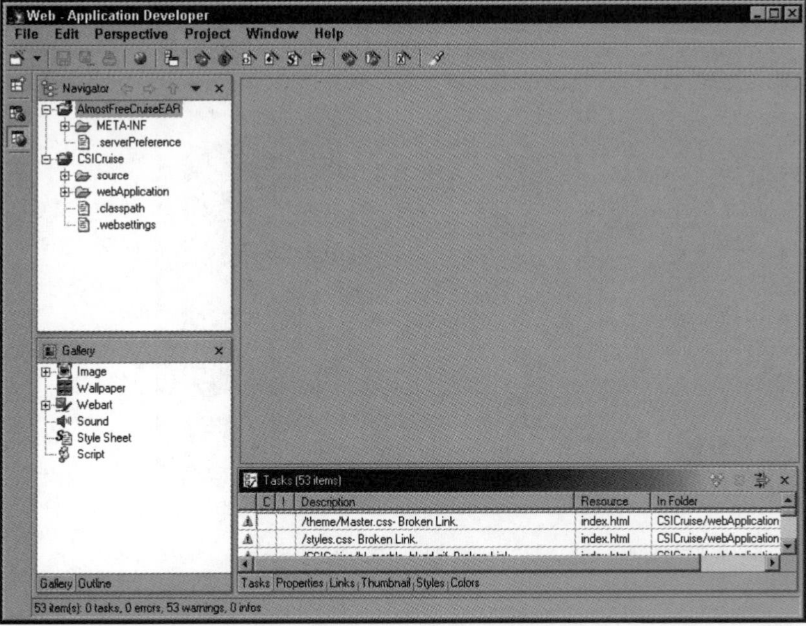

Figure 14-1: After you import your file, the AlmostFreeCruiseEAR project appears in the Navigator pane.

Included in the EAR file is the CSICruise Web Project. This is the application that contains the AlmostFreeCruise Web application.

> **NOTE**: You could have used the workspace from the previous chapters, but for those who choose to hop among various chapters, we decided to have separate projects for each chapter to maintain continuity.

Creating the necessary database and tables

You will be creating entity bean in this chapter by using a bottom-up development process. Bottom-up development is where you begin with an existing database and table structure and create entity beans from the table definitions.

You need to create the database and table and load test data into the tables. A set of files has been created to aid in creating the database and importing the data. To create the database, follow these steps:

1. Navigate to the `x:\Bible\chapter14\code` folder by using a command window.
2. Type **db2cmd** and press Enter.
3. Another window opens. In the new window, type **db2 –tvf createdb.ddl** and press Enter.
4. Output similar to Figure 14-2 is displayed.
5. Close both command windows by typing **exit**.

```
DB2 CLP
DB20000I  The DROP DATABASE command completed successfully.

create database CRUISE
DB20000I  The CREATE DATABASE command completed successfully.

connect to CRUISE

   Database Connection Information

 Database server        = DB2/NT 7.2.1
 SQL authorization ID   = WASADMIN
 Local database alias   = CRUISE


create schema DB2ADMIN
DB20000I  The SQL command completed successfully.

import from ./cruise.ixf of ixf messages ./msg.txt create into DB2ADMIN.CRUISE

Number of rows read         = 10
Number of rows skipped      = 0
Number of rows inserted     = 10
Number of rows updated      = 0
Number of rows rejected     = 0
Number of rows committed    = 10


import from ./customer.ixf of ixf messages ./msg.txt create into DB2ADMIN.CUSTO
ER

Number of rows read         = 3
Number of rows skipped      = 0
Number of rows inserted     = 3
```

Figure 14-2: Output from running a DB2 script to create the CRUISE database.

That concludes your setup. You are now ready to start creating entity beans for the AlmostFreeCruise applications.

Creating an EJB

You change hats quite a few times in this tutorial. In some cases, you will be a Java developer looking at the Java perspective; and at other times, you will be in the J2EE perspective. Near the end of the tutorial, you use the Web perspective to modify some of the JavaServer Pages (JSP) and servlet code.

You need to create an EJB project. Switch to the J2EE perspective (on the left toolbar) and perform the following:

1. Click Open The New Wizard in the upper toolbar, and select Project. In the dialog box, select EJB ⇨ EJB project.
2. Use the name **AlmostFreeCruiseEJB** and click Finish.

Under the EJB Modules item within the tree view, you should have the new EJB project called AlmostFreeCruiseEJB.

An EJB module is the smallest deployable and usable unit of an enterprise bean. An EJB module is packaged and deployed as an EJB JAR file. It contains the following:

- *Java class files for the enterprise beans and their remote and home interfaces:* If the bean is an entity bean, its primary key class must also be present in the EJB module.

- *Any non-J2EE Java classes and interfaces that the enterprise bean code depends upon:* This includes super-classes and the classes and interfaces used as method parameters, results, and exceptions.
- *A EJB deployment descriptor:* This descriptor provides both the structural and application-assembly information for the enterprise beans in the EJB module.

An EJB JAR file differs from a standard JAR file by the addition of a meta-file that is the deployment descriptor. The deployment descriptor in WebSphere 4.0 is different from previous versions in that, in previous versions, there was a deployment descriptor for each EJB.

Now that you have the project to hold your components, review the steps you will be following:

1. You learn about mapping database tables to container-managed persistence (CMP) entity beans, and you create an CMP entity bean.
2. Using the IBM Extension editor, you update the deployment descriptors with JNDI bindings.
3. You learn you how to prepare to test your entity bean. This entails setting up a server instance using WebSphere Studio Application Developer, establishing a datasource, and finally, testing your EJB with the EJB Test Client.

Mapping EJB-RDB

EJB relational database (EJB-RDB) mapping provides the components necessary for editing the mapping between EJBs and relational database tables. The EJB-RDB tools support the following:

- Inheritance
- Associations between enterprise beans mapped as foreign-key relationships
- Conversion from database columns to attributes within a bean
- Complex bean mapping to multiple columns within the database

The mappers provide the capability to map in one of three ways:

- *Top-down:* Generates a database schema after defining an entity bean. The bean is created first, and the table is mapped on a one-to-one basis. `META_INF/Schema/Schema.dbxmi` contains one table for each CMP EJB. Any association is mapped as a foreign-key relationship. EJB inheritance is mapped to a single table. When you map in this fashion, you are required to implement the schema on the database.
- *Bottom-up:* Assumes the database exists. You import the database schema and generate the entity EJBs with the mapping between the entity EJB and the database schema.
- *Meet in the Middle:* In this case, you not only create the schema but also create the entity beans. You import the table structure from the database and map each field of the

enterprise bean to a corresponding column in a table within the selected schema. You do this until all fields are mapped.

Creating your first CMP entity bean

As mentioned previously, you will be creating an entity bean using the bottom-up approach. To start the bottom-up process, follow these steps:

1. Select the EJB project AlmostFreeCruiseEJB and right-click.
2. Select Generate⇨EJB to RDB Mapping. You are presented with the screen that enables you to select the type of mapping you want to establish. In this case, you should select Bottom Up to generate an enterprise bean and map to an existing database schema. Click Next.
3. On the Database connection page, enter **CRUISE** as the database name and **db2admin** for both the userid and password. Leave the defaults for the vendor type and JDBC driver as DB2 UDB and IBM DB2 APP DRIVER. Click Next.
4. When you get to the Selective Database Import page, for this example check all of the the tables. Click Next.
5. On the Create new EJB/RDB Mapping page, change the Java package name from cruise to **com.bible.cruise.ejb**. Leave the prefix for generated EJB classes blank. Click Finish.

Using the EJB Extension editor

Extensions are additions to the standard J2EE deployment descriptors. They enable the use of enterprise extensions, older systems, or behavior not defined by the specification. This editor is used to modify IBM-specific extensions to the EJB 1.1 specification. These extensions are only used when deployed to WebSphere Application Server. The EJB Extension Editor is divided into six pages

- The Methods page defines access intent, isolation level, and security identity settings for methods.
- The Inheritance page is where you change the enterprise bean's inheritance structure.
- The Relationships page is used to add, modify, and remove relationships.
- The Finders page is used to define Home methods. You define the metadata for container-managed entity finders for find methods that are already defined on the Home interface.
- The Container page is used to define bean cache, locale location, and local transaction settings. You can choose from the following bean cache settings:
  - Activate at
  - Load at
  - Pinned for

  For local transaction settings, you can apply the following settings:

- Boundary
- Resolver
- Unresolver action

♦ The Bindings page is used to set JNDI name and data source access permissions.

> **TIP**: Do not edit the XML documents by hand. Instead use WebSphere Studio Application Developer's built-in editors to modify deployment descriptors. That way, all references are updated. Otherwise, you need to update all references by hand.

When you set the bindings the output for the JNDI binding is written to `ibm-ejb-bnd.xmi`.

You use the EJB Extension editor to set the Java Naming and Directory Interface (JNDI) name and details about the data source. Figure 14-3 shows how to invoke the EJB Extension editor by highlighting the EJB project (AlmostFreeCruiseEJB), right-clicking, and selecting Open With⇨EJB Extension Editor.

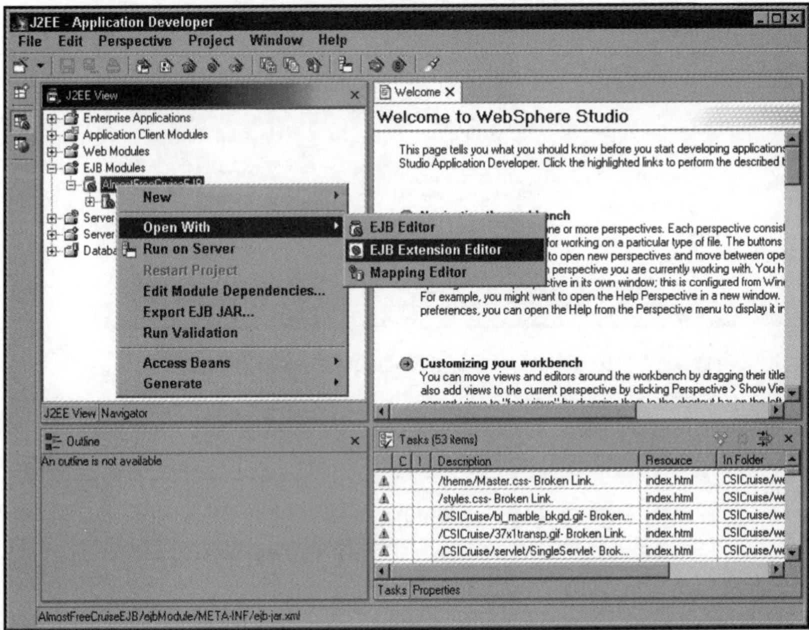

Figure 14-3: To open the EJB Extension editor, select the EJB project, AlmostFreeCruiseEJB; right-click and select Open With, EJB Extension Editor.

To begin working with the EJB Extension editor, follow these steps:

1. Click the Bindings tab to expose the JNDI properties. Highlight the AlmostFreeCruiseEJB project to see the properties set for that project. In the Datasource grouping, enter the following information:

- *JNDI name:* **jdbc/cruise**
- *Default user id:* **db2admin**
- *Default password:* **db2admin**

2. You might see the asterisk next to the EJB Extension Editor tab. That is the reminder that you need to save your work. Do either a File⇨Save or a Ctrl+S to save the EJB Extensions. Figure 14-4 shows the EJB Extension editor with your information entered.

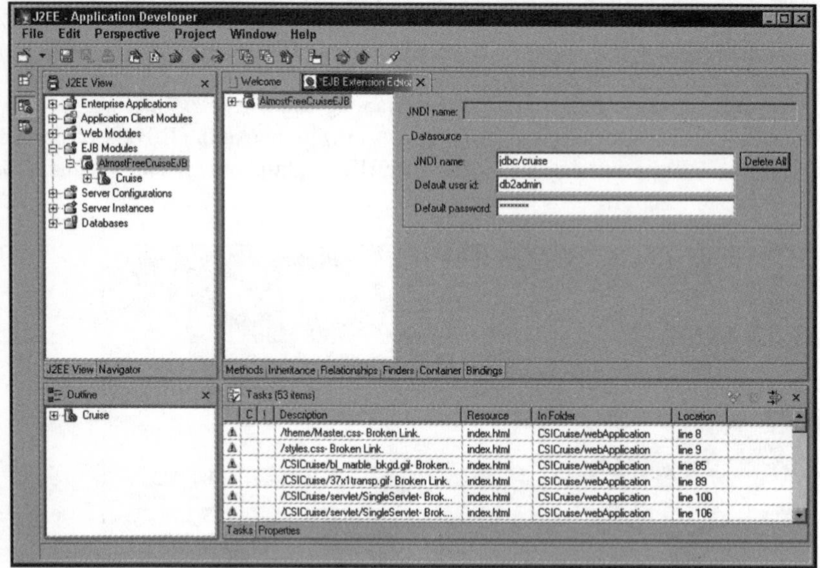

Figure 14-4: The Extension editor should look like this after you enter your information.

> **NOTE:** As an exercise, you might want to click through the other tabs at the bottom of the properties panel.

The XML generated for the IBM extensions found in `x:\code\ejb\AlmostFreeCruiseEJB\ejbModule\META_INF` is shown in Listing 14-1.

Listing 14-1: Generated ibm-ejb-jar-bnd.xmi

```
<?xml version="1.0" encoding="UTF-8"?>
<ejbbnd:EJBJarBinding xmi:version="2.0"
  xmlns:xmi="http://www.omg.org/XMI" xmlns:ejbbnd="ejbbnd.xmi"
  xmlns:commonbnd="commonbnd.xmi" xmlns:ejb="ejb.xmi" xmi:id=
     "ejb-jar_ID_Bnd">
<defaultDatasource xmi:id="ResourceRefBinding_1" jndiName="jdbc/cruise">
```

```
<defaultAuth xmi:type="commonbnd:BasicAuthData" xmi:id="BasicAuthData_1"
   userId="db2admin" password="{xor}OzltPjsyNjE="/>
</defaultDatasource>
<ejbJar href="META-INF/ejb-jar.xml#ejb-jar_ID"/>
<ejbBindings xmi:id="Search_Bnd" jndiName=
   "ejb/com/bible/cruise/ejb/SearchHome">
<enterpriseBean xmi:type="ejb:Session" href="META-INF/
   ejb-jar.xml#Search"/>
</ejbBindings>
</ejbbnd:EJBJarBinding>
```

It is always good practice to verify that your object behaves properly. The way you can test your newly created entity bean is to generate the deployment code and create the remote code to test your bean. You test your bean with the EJB Test Client. Figure 14-5 shows how to invoke the Deploy and RMIC code generator by highlighting the EJB project, right-clicking, and selecting Generate⇨Deploy and RMIC Code.

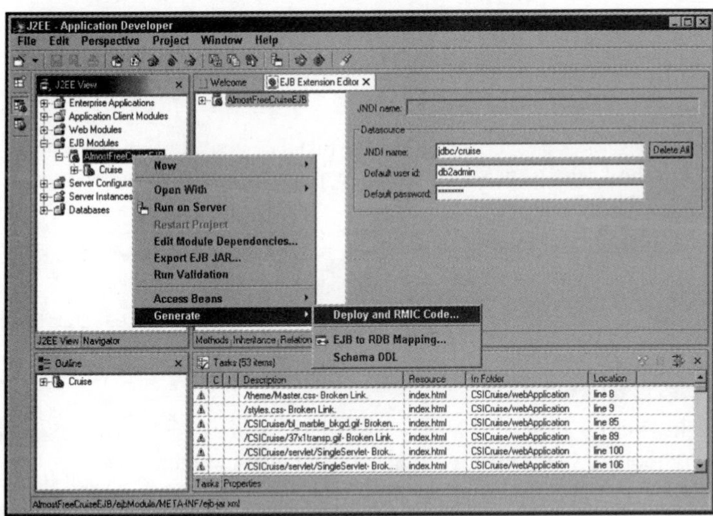

Figure 14-5: To generate the deployment code and RMI stubs, select the EJB project, AlmostFreeCruiseEJB; right-click and select Generate, Deploy and RMIC Code.

To generate your code perform the following:

1. Select the EJB project AlmostFreeCruiseEJB and right-click.
2. Select Generate⇨Deploy and RMIC Code.
3. When the Generate Deploy and RMIC Code window opens, check CRUISE and click Finish. You see an additional window appear as the RMIC compiler runs.

> **NOTE**: RMIC stands for Remote Method Invocation Compiler.

You are almost ready to test. First you need to set up your application server instance and configure it appropriately.

Setting up the server instance

WebSphere Studio Application Developer provides server tooling that provides test environments where you can test JSP files, servlets, HTML files, and EJB beans. The server tool uses server instances and server configurations to test your projects. Server instances identify servers where you can test your projects. Server configurations contain setup information. You need to create a server instance to run your application.

After you set up your server instance, you can associate it with you EJB project. You will be running the AEd version of WebSphere to test your application. To set up your server instance perform the following steps:

1. Switch to the J2EE perspective and select Server Configurations within the J2EE View.
2. Right-click in the J2EE view and select New⇨Other.
3. When the dialog box opens, click Server; select Server Instance and Configuration and click Next. Figure 14-6 shows the New Server Instance and Configuration dialog box. You have some additional instance types from which to choose.

> **NOTE**: WebSphere Studio Application Developer supports the use of WebSphere servers and Apache Tomcat as Server instance types. With WebSphere, you have the capability of using the debugger in WebSphere Studio Application Developer to track down errors.

4. Enter **WAS4Server** as the server name.
5. Type the word **Servers** in the Folder field.
6. Because you are testing locally and using WebSphere, you should expand the WebSphere Servers and select WebSphere v4.0 Test Environment, as shown in Figure 14-6.
7. Click Finish and, when asked to confirm the creation of a new folder, click Yes.

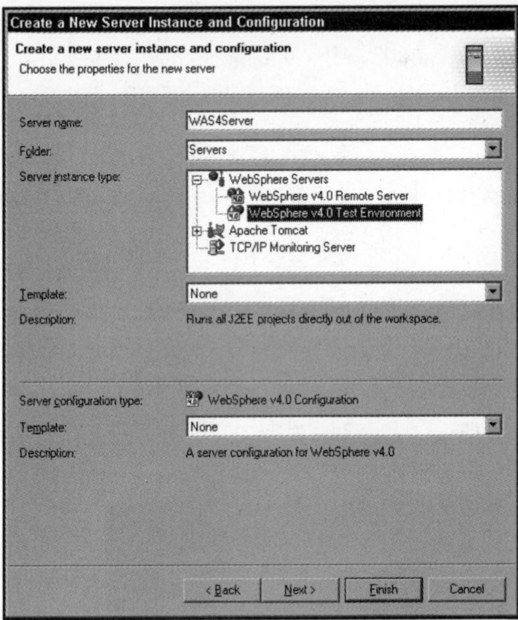

Figure 14-6: Within WSAD, you can choose WebSphere v4.0 Remote or Test environments or Apache Tomcat as your test server.

Setting up the data sources

This is the next step in the process of configuring the WebSphere server to prepare to test your application. You have described the JNDI name you are looking up in the EJB Extension editor. Now, you need to ensure the WebSphere Application Server has a data source that matches your alias. To add the data source to WebSphere, perform these steps:

1. Open a Server perspective by clicking Perspective⇨Open⇨Server.
2. The Server perspective opens to reveal the Navigator, Server Configuration, and Servers panes.
3. Double-click WAS4Server under Server Configurations node. The WAS4Server property sheet opens.

4. Click the Data source tab on the bottom of the WAS4Server pane.
5. You want to add the data source. In the middle of the pane is the `Data source defined in JDBC driver selected above` list. Click the Add button for this list.
6. When the Add a Data Source window opens, enter **CRUISE** for the name.
7. Enter **jdbc/cruise** for the JNDI name. This matches the name you specified in the EJB Extensions editor.
8. Enter **CRUISE** for the database name.
9. You should also enter **db2admin** for the default userid and password.
10. Check Enable JTA and click OK because you want to use the Java Transaction API (JTA) to connect to the database.

Figure 14-7 shows the results of your efforts. You now have a matching data source name defined in WebSphere.

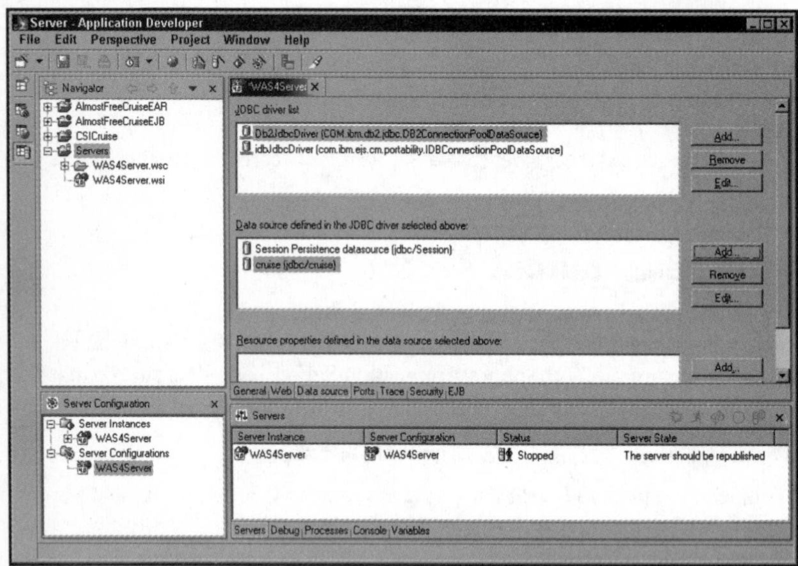

Figure 14-7: The data source you defined appears in the WAS4Server window.

Because this is a property sheet, you need to save you changes. Press Ctrl+S to save WAS4Server and then close the WAS4Server window. You must now associate a project for this customized server:

1. Click WAS4Server under Server Configurations in the Server Configuration view. Right-click and select Add Project⇨AlmostFreeCruiseEAR.
2. If you expand WAS4Server, you can see the association to AlmostFreeCruiseEAR.

You are now ready to test your EJB.

Running the Test Client

Up to this point you have completed the following tasks:

- Created an CMP entity bean using the EJB-RDB mapping tool
- Generated the deploy code and RMI stubs
- Specified the bindings and updated the IBM extensions
- Created a customized server just to test your EJB application
- Configured the server with the appropriate data source

You have done a lot without doing much typing. Now, follow these steps to test:

1. Switch to the J2EE perspective.
2. Expand the EJB Modules and AlmostFreeCruiseEJB project.
3. Right-click the Cruise entity bean and select Run on Server. Two messages appear as your application is published. Your perspective automatically changes to the Server perspective as the server console messages are output. Depending upon the configuration of your workstation, this might take some time. Figure 14-8 shows the EJB Test Client view.

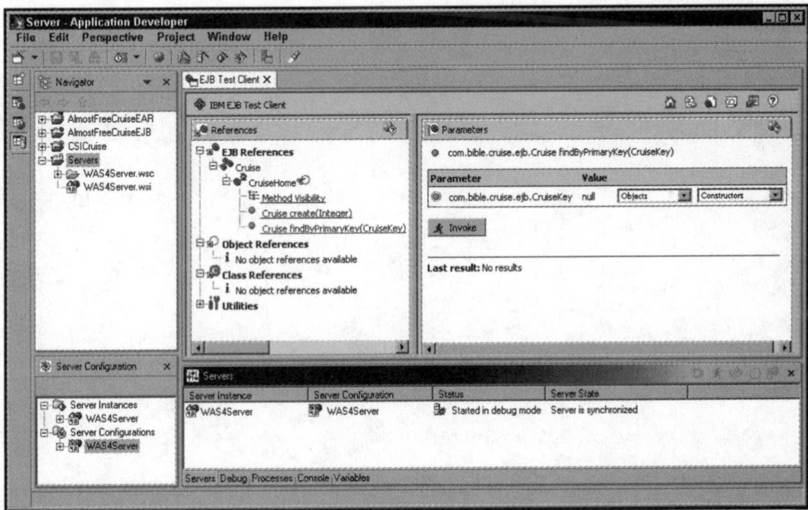

Figure 14-8: From the EJB Test Client, you can find an EJB bean with or without a JDNI name.

The EJB Test Client is a browser-based test client that can be configured to the browser of your choice. It includes the following features:

- JNDI browser for searching namespaces
- Object Clipboard for reusing returned objects
- Dynamic method invocation, including the creation and passing of complex objects

Figure 14-8 shows that the Test Client window is partitioned into two panes: the Reference pane and the Parameters pane. You should expand the Cruise and CruiseHome references to expose the public methods available for your use.

Pausing for a Review

One thing that often confuses people about tools such as WebSphere Studio Application Developer is the number of clicks that produce the results you want but leave you wondering what they did. How often have you followed a tutorial like the one you just did and asked yourself, "I know it works, but what did I do?"

Take a minute to review what you have done so that you can put it within the context of the EJB lifecycle. So far, you have done the following:

- Used a tool to generate the necessary interfaces for a CMP entity bean:
  - Home interface
  - `Create()` method
  - `Finder()` method (`findbyPrimaryKey`)
- Used JNDI to look up a EJB container

To complete the process to access the CMP entity bean, you need to do the following:

1. Perform a JNDI lookup.
2. Perform a "narrow" (in some cases) to get the reference to the EJB Home Interface. Narrowing is performed to accommodate other programming languages that support CORBA such as C++ and COBOL.

   NOTE: Narrowing is used because casting is not native to CORBA. You must, therefore, narrow to get a remote object of CruiseHome.
3. Invoke a `Create()` method on the Home Interface to have the EJB server create an instance of the EJB and return a remote interface.
4. Invoke a `finder()` method to work with existing persisted EJBs.
5. Invoke business methods on the remote interface either passing values to methods or viewing results from method calls.

As you continue with the EJB Test Client, try to keep these steps in mind to help you understand what is being conducted behind the scenes.

> **TIP**: Did you know that you can run the IBM Test Client in debug mode? You can toggle the EJB client to run in debug mode and then invoke it using HTTP://<hostname>:8080/UTC/debug

Referring back to Figure 14-8, the Cruise EJB reference and the CruiseHome interface reference are displayed in the References pane. You have already performed a JNDI lookup and narrow on Cruise, and that is how you obtained the CruiseHome. You have exposed the `create(Integer)` methods and the `findByPrimaryKey(CruiseKey)` method.

Next, you look up a specific primary key in the Cruise EJB. To find by primary key, perform the following steps:

1. Click Cruise findByPrimaryKey(CruiseKey).
2. In the Parameters pane. click the drop-down list that has constructors displayed and select CruiseKey(Integer). This action forces a redisplay of the screen. This new screen is shown in Figure 14-9.

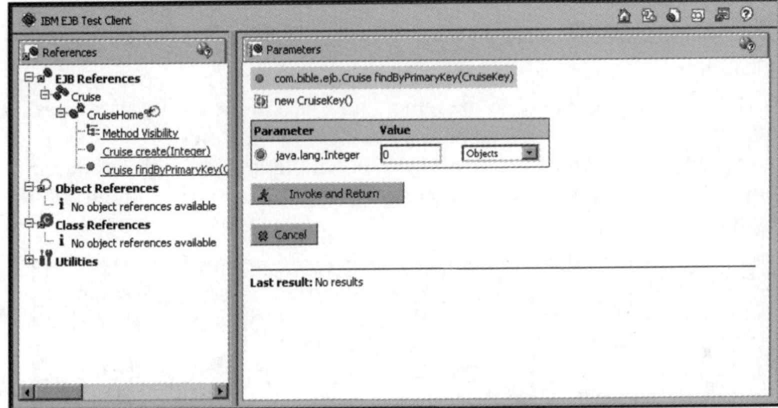

Figure 14-9: By setting a constructor parameter, you are passing in to the constructor the value you wish the object to reference.

3. Enter the value **1** into the Value field. This step sets the key value and requests that the container return a reference to the CruiseKey object.
4. Click Invoke and Return to have the container return the reference. Figure 14-10 shows the CruiseKey reference returned, and now the `findByPrimaryKey(CruiseKey)` can be invoked.

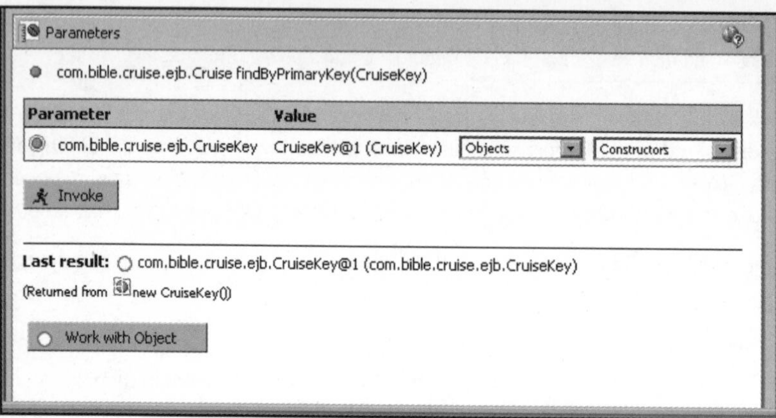

Figure 14-10: After you instantiate the object, a reference is returned of type CruiseKey.

5. Click the Invoke button to execute the `findByPrimaryKey()` method. Your screen refreshes.
6. You now should have a reference to the remote interface of the Cruise entity bean. Click Work with Object to show the Cruise object returned. In the References pane, a new Cruise (com.bible.cruise.ejb.CruiseKey@1) is shown. Figure 14-11 shows the new remote object in the Reference pane. This remote object should have all the public methods exposed.

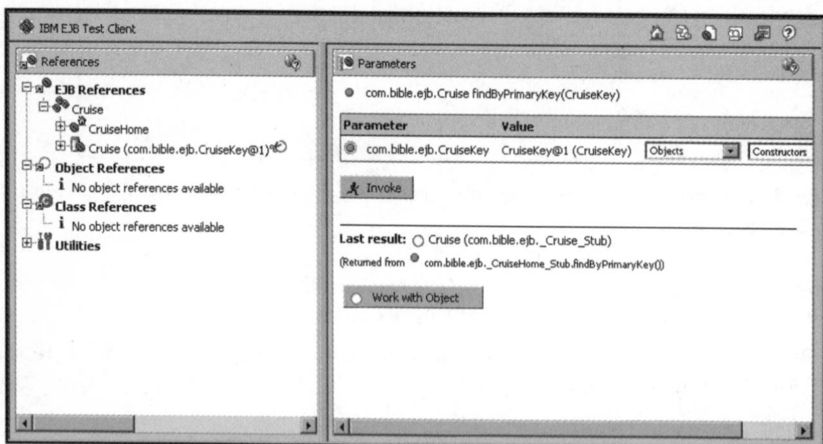

Figure 14-11: After you click Work with Object, a new Object reference of a Cruise object is displayed.

7. You used JNDI to look up and find the EJB and narrowed to get the reference to an EJB Home (in this case the CruiseHome). You retrieved a reference to the `primaryKey` object and used it to pass as a parameter in the `findByPrimaryKey()` method. In turn, the remote interface for Cruise was returned by the `findByPrimaryKey`, so now you can invoke methods on the object. Expand the new Cruise remote object to see the methods. Figure 14-12 shows the methods exposed on the EJB.

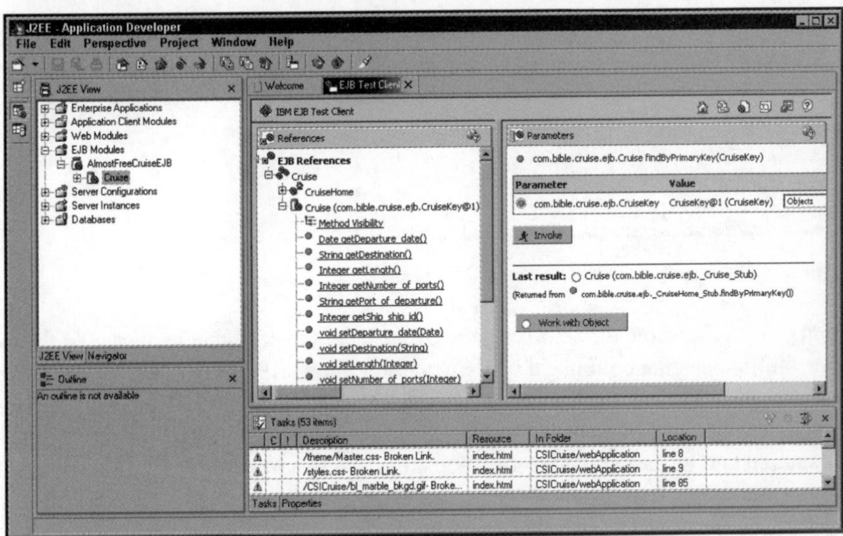

Figure 14-12: By expanding the Cruise object in the references pane, you expose the methods from the Cruise EJB.

8. The last thing you should do is select one of the getter methods and check the results of the fetch. Click the `getDestination()` method, and click Invoke in the Parameters pane. You should see the results of the remote method call displayed in the Parameters pane. Figure 14-13 shows that your results should be `Puerto Rico (java.lang.String)`.

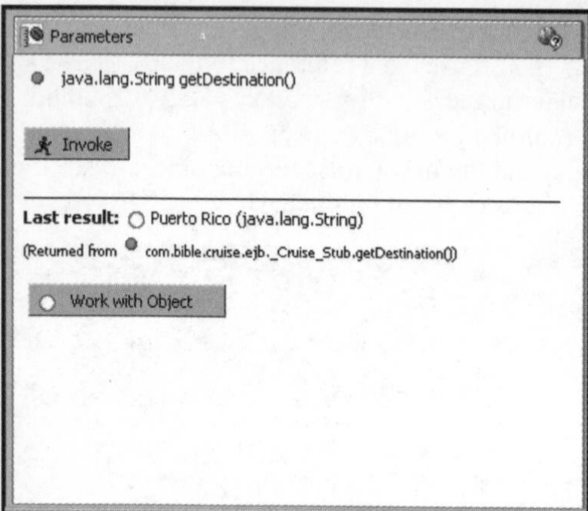

Figure 14-13: Results of the remote call getDestination().

You can try to invoke some of the other getters and setters to see what happens. At this point, you successfully created a bottom-up implementation of a CMP entity bean. You didn't have to code much, in fact not at all. What you learned was how EJBs work. You also learned about how WebSphere Studio Application Developer can speed development. Of course, this is a simple example and you are not done yet. You still need to add your own business logic to your application.

Creating an EJB Session Bean

You now have a CMP entity bean that has information about Cruises. To create an Enterprise Bean that is a session bean, follow these steps:

1. Select the EJB Project AlmostFreeCruiseEJB, and right-click.
2. Select New⇨Enterprise Bean. Figure 14-14 shows an example of the screen. In this screen, you can select whether the new bean is a session bean, an entity bean with bean-managed persistence, or an entity bean with container-managed persistence.
3. Ensure the Session bean radio button is selected and enter **Search** as the bean name. The rest of the fields should be left with their default selections. Click Next.

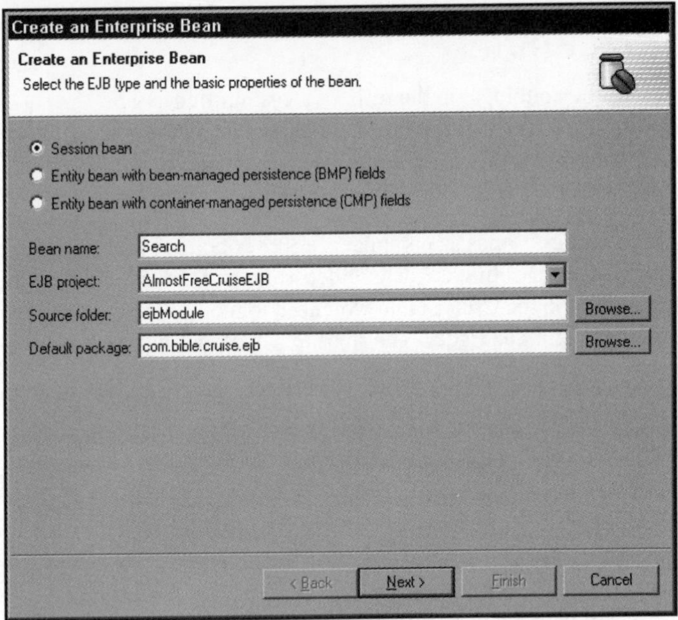

Figure 14-14: Creating an Enterprise Bean is easy with the wizard approach. To select the different types of EJBs, you simply select the type you want.

4. To accept the defaults on the Enterprise Bean Details screen and the EJB Java Class Details screen, click the Next button and finally Finish.

The new bean should display in the J2EE view. The session bean Search is found under the AlmostFreeCruiseEJB project.

You have generated a session bean. To edit the SearchBean, you find the standard interface methods implemented:

- public void ejbActivate()
- public void ejbCreate()
- public void ejbPassivate()
- public void ejbRemove()

You leave the SearchBean for a short period as you continue to enhance and prepare your Cruise entity bean to search for more than one cruise at a time.

Adding a Custom Finder

In this section, you add some custom logic in the form of a custom finder. The AlmostFreeCruise application requires that it return the cruises that leave on a particular date to a particular destination. To provide this feature, you need to update the CruiseHome interface with a new method called `findAllForSearch()`.

The method `findAllForSearch()` has as parameters a `String` value representing the destination and a `Date` object representing the date of departure and the length of the trip. Because this information is kept in the Cruise table, you need to modify the CruiseHome interface before you can implement this finder. The steps to begin your quest are as follows:

1. In the J2EE view, expand Cruise and open the CruiseHome class to add the new finder.
2. You can add the following line of code to CruiseHome or cut and paste the code from the downloaded code found in `x:\bible\chapter14\code\cruisehome.jv`.

```
public java.util.Enumeration findAllForSearch(String destination,
java.sql.Date departdate, String length) throws
javax.ejb.FinderException, java.rmi.RemoteException;
```

3. Save your work. You get error messages, but ignore them for now. The entire CruiseHome interface should look like Listing 14-2.

Listing 14-2: CruiseHome Interface Class

```
package com.bible.cruise.ejb;
/**
 * Home interface for Enterprise Bean: Cruise
 */
public interface CruiseHome extends javax.ejb.EJBHome {
/**
 * Creates an instance from a key for Entity Bean: Cruise
 */
public com.bible.cruise.ejb.Cruise create(java.lang.Integer cruise_id)
throws javax.ejb.CreateException, java.rmi.RemoteException;
/**
 * Finds an instance using a key for Entity Bean: Cruise
*/
public com.bible.cruise.ejb.Cruise
findByPrimaryKey(com.bible.cruise.ejb.CruiseKey primaryKey) throws
javax.ejb.FinderException, java.rmi.RemoteException;

public java.util.Enumeration findAllForSearch(String destination,
java.sql.Date departdate, String length) throws
javax.ejb.FinderException, java.rmi.RemoteException;
}
```

4. The next step is to once again update the IBM extensions. Select AlmostFreeCruiseEJB and right-click.

5. Select Open With⇨EJB Extension Editor.
6. Click the Finders tab located on the bottom of the Extension Editor pane.
7. In the Extension Editor pane, expand the EJB project AlmostFreeCruiseEJB, and Cruise. Next, select the method `findAllForSearch()` as shown in Figure 14-15.

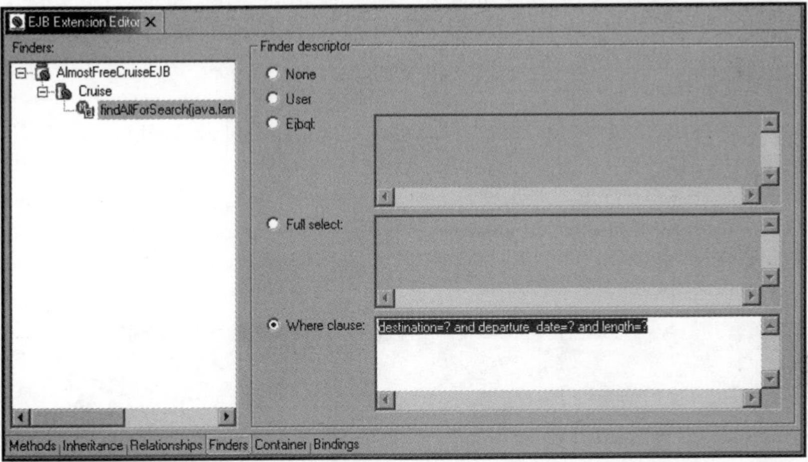

Figure 14-15: When you create a custom finder, you provide the Where Clause selection criteria.

8. Click the Where Clause radio button.
9. Enter **destination=? and departure_date=? and length=?** In the Where Clause text box. Close the window and save when prompted. You updated the IBM extension and also updated the Home Interface. You need to redeploy the code and run the RMIC compiler again.
10. In the J2EE view, expand the EJB Modules and AlmostFreeCruiseEJB project. Right-click Cruise and select Generate Deploy Code.
11. If the WAS4Server is still running. stop the server and restart it by opening the Servers perspective (if not already open), right-clicking WAS4Server, and selecting Restart.

Now that you have created you new finder, you should continue with the good practice of testing. The code that you wrote returns an enumeration of objects from the Cruise table, so you should anticipate some additional references being returned. To test, perform the following steps:

1. Switch to the J2EE perspective and expand the AlmostFreeCruiseEJB project to select the Cruise bean. Right-click and select Run on Server.
2. After a few moments, the EJB Test Client opens. Expand the Cruise and CruiseHome references.
3. Click your new method `findAllForSearch`. As you might recall, your new finder requires you to provide a date to travel. The date field is of type `java.sql.Date`;

therefore, you need to choose a constructor in the Parameters pane that enables you to pass in a valid date.

4. Click the java.sql.Date drop-down list and change from Constructors to Date (int, int, int). The panel changes immediately.
5. In the panel that displays, you see three int fields. Starting from the top, enter the values **101, 5, 15**, and click Invoke and Return. Again the panel refreshes.

NOTE: The interesting date values are based on a starting date of 1-1-1900.

6. The date 2001-06-15 displays. Enter **Vera Cruz** into the first String field to pass the destination to the constructor. Also enter in the value of **9** in the last String field to represent the length of trip. Click Invoke.
7. This should run the constructor. Now click Work with All Contained Objects. The Reference panel updates, showing you two Cruise EJB references. Figure 14-16 shows how the panel should look.

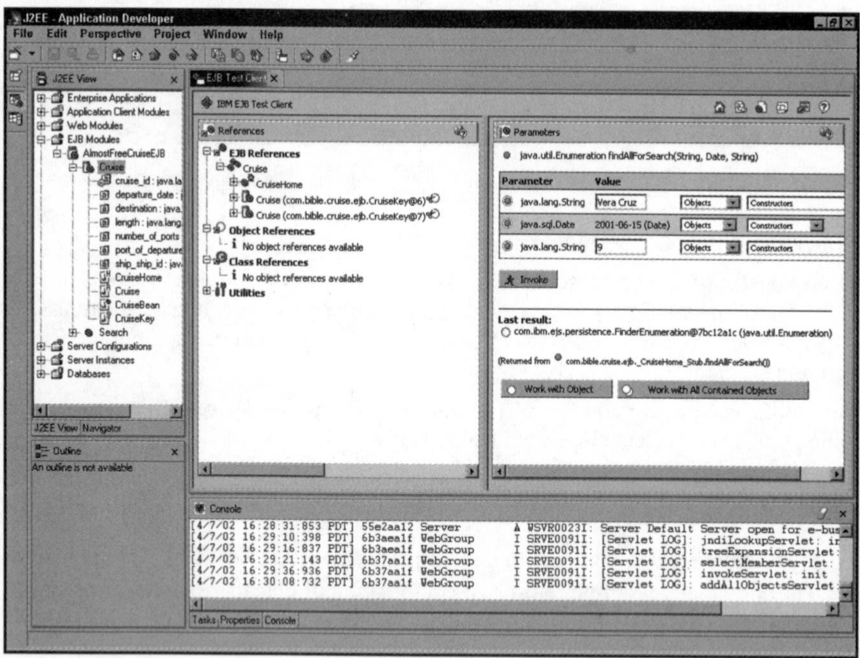

Figure 14-16: When you run a customer finder ,you are able to review the results of your custom finder and evaluate the values returned. You can see how powerful it is to have the Test Client.

8. Try expanding the Cruise objects and clicking getShip_ship_id( ). Click Invoke to see the values returned. For the two Cruise objects, find ship ID 1 and 2.

You now have experience with custom finders and are ready to work on some helper classes to begin the process of hooking in your EJBs to the AlmostFreeCruise Web application.

Creating Access Beans

What do you think happens when an enterprise bean having a large number of attributes gets called across the network? Each remote call for an attribute is called using a getter method in the remote interface. If you have a large number of attributes, you have a large number of network calls. Obviously this eventually builds up to something less than satisfying.

Access beans can greatly simplify client access to enterprise beans and alleviate performance problems associated with remote calls for multiple enterprise bean attributes. Access beans are JavaBean representations of enterprise beans. Access beans solve the performance problem by simply caching server-side data, such as entity data, on the client side. A local cache of enterprise bean attributes significantly improves access speed to an enterprise bean. You use access beans in your AlmostFreeCruise servlets and JavaServer Pages (JSP) to access your enterprise beans.

One of the nice things about access beans is that they shield you from the complexities of managing enterprise bean lifecycles. Again you use the WebSphere Studio Application Developer tooling to create access beans. The following is a review the steps in the EJB process:

1. Obtain a context to the name server using JNDI.
2. Look up the home of the enterprise bean using the name service context.
3. Create an enterprise bean instance from the enterprise bean home, which returns an enterprise bean proxy object.
4. Access the remote methods of the enterprise bean instance through an enterprise bean proxy object using a remote call.

When you have completed this exercise, you will be able to verify that all these steps were addressed in the proper order.

Because the AlmostFreeCruise is accessing the Cruise bean, you need to create a copy helper access bean. A copy helper adds a single copy helper object in the access bean that contains a local copy of attributes from a remote entity bean. To create the access bean, perform the following steps:

1. In the J2EE perspective, expand the EJB Modules and AlmostFreeCruiseEJB project to select the Cruise bean. Right-click and select New⇨Access bean.
2. The Create an Access Bean dialog box opens (see Figure 14-17). Select Copy Helper and click Next.

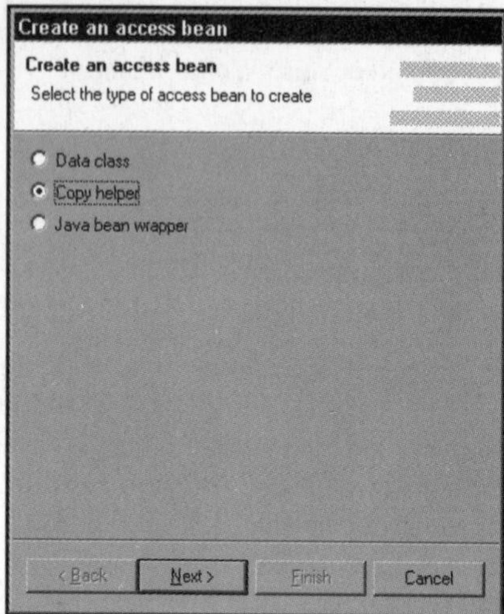

Figure 14-17: WSAD lets you create access beans that improve the design of your EJB interactions.

Before continuing, you should be aware of the other three types of access beans available for your selection:

- *Data classes:* A data class is an access bean that is similar to a copy helper access bean, but it employs a different technology. A data class provides the data storage and access methods for cacheable enterprise bean properties. You can define multiple data classes for an enterprise bean, each with a different set of cached properties.
- *Java bean wrappers:* JavaBean wrapper access beans allow either a session or entity bean to be used like a standard JavaBean. Through lazy initialization, a process that identifies objects but doesn't initially instantiate them, the Java bean wrappers keep the access beans light until the proper moment.
- *Copy helper:* A copy helper access bean has the same basic characteristics as a JavaBean wrapper, with some differences. For example, the copy helper is optimized for use with a single entity EJB instance. Unlike a Java bean wrapper, a copy helper incorporates a single copy helper object that contains a local copy of attributes from a remote entity bean.

3. Next, select the EJB project AlmostFreeCruiseEJB and click Next.
4. You then select the bean you want wrappered. In this case, it's the Cruise bean. Select the Cruise bean and click Next.
5. You can choose between the `create()` method or the `findByPrimaryKey()` method to utilize in the zero-argument constructor. You should select the `create(java.Integer)` method. Click Next to continue.
6. When all properties from the bean are shown, take the default, which is all, and click Finish.

7. You have generated the copy helper, but you must switch to a Java perspective to see the copy helper. Remember the copy helper is a JavaBean. Find a Java class called CruiseAccessBean, which is your helper bean.

> **TIP**: You can see the results of the access-bean generation by switching to the Java perspective, expanding the AlmostFreeCruiseEJB project, and expanding ejbModule. You should find the `CruiseAccessBean.java` class in the `com.bible.cruise.ejb` package.

8. There are some errors in the code because you need to regenerate the code. Switch to the J2EE perspective and select the Cruise bean again. Right-click and select Generate Deploy code.

Updating the Session Bean

With your newly created access bean, you need to update the session bean you created earlier to utilize the access bean to mediate between the entity beans:

1. Expand the SearchBean from the J2EE perspective and edit the SearchBean. You need to add `searchCruise( String destination, String date, String length)` to the class. You can add the following lines of code, shown in Listing 14-3, to SearchBean or cut and paste the code from the downloaded code found in `x:\bible\chapter14\code\searchbean.jv`. You should ensure you also copy in the `convertToDate()` method.

Listing 14-3: Adding SearchBean Methods

```
// Add these methods to the SearchBean
public java.util.Enumeration searchCruise( String destination, String
       destination_date, String length) {

        CruiseAccessBean cab = new CruiseAccessBean();
        java.util.Enumeration enum = null;
        try {
            enum = cab.findAllForSearch(destination,
          convertToDate(destination_date), length);
        } catch (javax.ejb.FinderException fe) {}
          catch (java.rmi.RemoteException re) {}
          catch (javax.naming.NamingException ne) {}
        return enum;
    }

private java.sql.Date convertToDate(String aDate) {
    java.sql.Date date = new java.sql.Date( java.util.Date.parse(aDate) );
    return date;
}
```

2. Save your changes by pressing Ctrl+S.
3. You need to promote the `searchCruise()` method to the remote interface. Right-click the `searchCruise()` method in outline view. Select Enterprise bean⇨Promote to Remote Interface (see Figure 14-18).

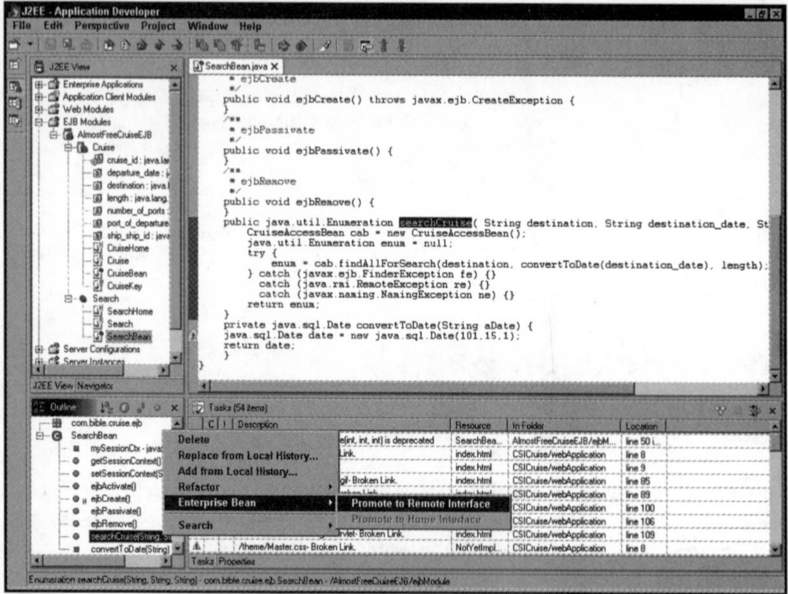

Figure 14-18: Exposing a method to the remote interface.

4. Select the Search Session bean; right-click, and select Generate Deploy code. So far, you have created a new method (`searchCruise`) that utilizes the CruiseAccessBean you created earlier. Now you need to wrap the session bean so you can add it to the servlet. This wrapper relieves you of the tediousness of creating all the proper calls (lookup and so on) to acquire the session bean.
5. Right-click the Search Session bean and select New⇨Access bean.
6. Choose Java bean wrapper and click Next.
7. Accept AlmostFreeCruiseEJB and click Next.
8. Select Search as your enterprise bean and click Next
9. Accept the default constructor, `create()` and click Finish
10. Right-click the Search Session bean and select Generate Deploy Code.

If you feel bold enough, try using the EJB Test Client to test your bean. Otherwise, it's time to start integrating your code into the AlmostFreeCruise application.

Integrating the Beans: The Home Stretch

In this section, you integrate the entity beans, session beans, and supporting access beans into the AlmostFreeCruise Web application. Prior to making the coding changes, you need to add the existing project to the build path. You begin by performing the following actions:

1. Open the Web perspective. Select Perspective⇨Open⇨Web.
2. In the Navigator, select the CSICruise; right-click, and select properties.
3. You want to add the AlmostFreeCruiseEJB project to the build path for your Web application. Figure 14-19 shows the Java Build Path.

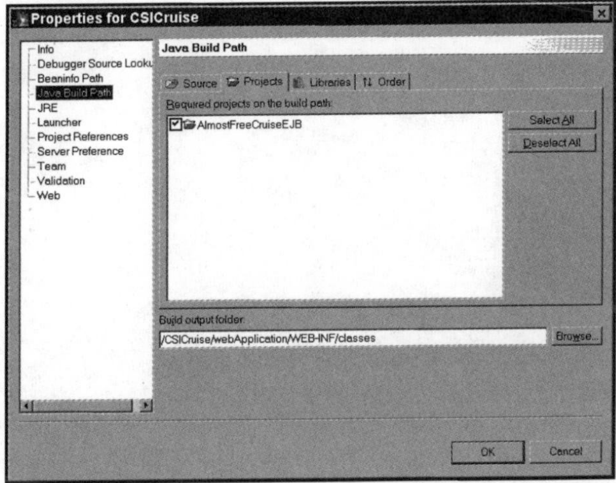

Figure 14-19: Setting up the proper build class path is important; without the correct build path, your code won't compile.

4. Select the Java Build Path, and click the Projects tab. By updating the build path you are setting the classpath for this application. Check the AlmostFreeCruiseEJB project and click OK to accept the changes.
5. Now you are ready to update the code necessary to hook in your enterprise beans. You should switch to the Java perspective to locate the code.
6. Expand the CSICruise project, then the source folder, and then the `com.bible.mediator` package.
7. Edit the `SearchMediator.java` class by double-clicking it.

8. Locate and replace the `copyToBusinessObject()` method with the code provided in Listing 14-4. The code basically uses an access bean to use the search session bean and returns an enumeration of the Cruise access beans. Each enumerated access bean is then used to return the actual results. You can add the code in Listing 14-4 to SearchMediator or cut and paste the code from the downloaded code found in `x:\bible\chapter14\code\searchmediator.jv`. Save the file when you finish.

Listing 14-4: Replacing copyToBusinessObject

```
/**
 * Once the data in the mediator variables has been validated,
 * this method is called to update the business object(s) with
 * the new values.
 * Creation date: (7/10/01 8:42:08 PM)
 */
public void copyToBusinessObject() {
com.bible.cruise.ejb.SearchAccessBean sab = new
com.bible.cruise.ejb.SearchAccessBean();
    Enumeration enum = null;
    try {
     enum = sab.searchCruise( getDestination(), "06/15/2001", "9" );
    } catch (javax.naming.NamingException ne){}
    catch ( javax.ejb.CreateException ce){}
    catch ( java.rmi.RemoteException re){}

    ArrayList results = new ArrayList();
    while ( enum.hasMoreElements() ) {
    try {
     com.bible.cruise.ejb.CruiseAccessBean cab =
(com.bible.cruise.ejb.CruiseAccessBean)enum.nextElement();
    HashMap row = new HashMap();
    GregorianCalendar gc = new GregorianCalendar();
    java.util.Date d = new
     java.util.Date(cab.getDeparture_date().getTime());
    row.put("Departure", d.toString() );
    row.put("Ship", "To be determined");
    row.put("Itinerary", cab.getLength() + " days");
    row.put("EmDisBark", cab.getDestination());
    row.put("Destination", cab.getDestination());

    results.add(row);
    } catch (javax.naming.NamingException ne){}
      catch ( javax.ejb.CreateException ce){}
      catch ( java.rmi.RemoteException re){}
      catch ( javax.ejb.FinderException fe){}
    }

    setBusinessObject( results );

}
```

9. Now you are ready to update the Web pages. Switch to the Web perspective.
10. Locate and select the `index.html` file located in the `webApplication` folder of the CSICruise Web project. You may have to expand the `WEB-INF` folder to find it.
11. Right-click `index.html` and select Run on Server. The output from `index.html` is shown in Figure 14-20.

Figure 14-20 WebSphere Studio Application Developer provides an internal Web browser to help your development. Shown here is the AlmostFreeCruise index.html page.

12. Now test your enterprise beans. On the browser, select the Book Online link to kick off the enterprise bean accesses. After a few seconds as the JSP compiles, you should be presented with a page similar to Figure 14-21.
13. Choose Vera Cruz for the destination and click Forward.

    Forward posts the request to the servlet, and a call to the mediator services the request by looking up the EJB and using your custom finder to locate the cruise ships destined for Vera Cruz. Figure 14-22 shows the final results of your query.

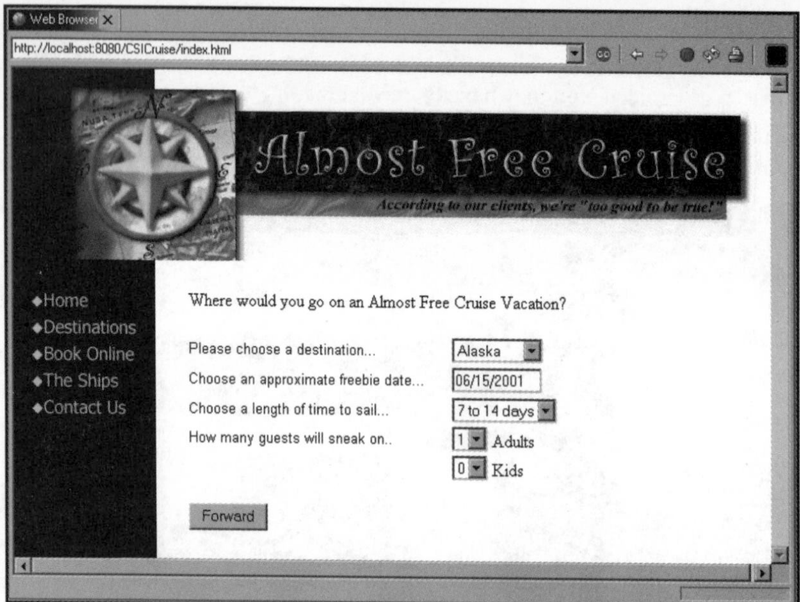

Figure 14-21: When testing the Book Online search Java Server Page (JSP), you need to choose Vera Cruz.

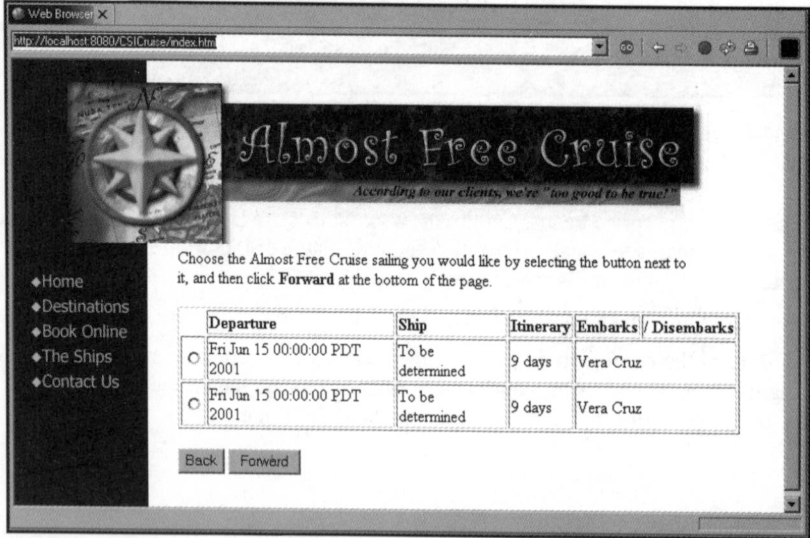

Figure 14-22: The results of your test are successful, and you have successfully developed CMP entity beans and have accessed them using a combination of servlets and Java Server Pages (JSP).

So there you have it. You have completed the exercise from start to finish. Although you did a lot of switching between perspectives and ran a few wizards, you were productive and that's what it's all about. The following list recaps your accomplishments:

- You created a container-managed persistence entity bean.
- You ran the EJB Test Client to verify the contents of your entity bean.
- You created a custom finder where you specified a unique where clause.
- You created a session bean.
- You discovered access beans and learned how they help wrapper EJBs.
- You implemented you EJBs and wrapper classes into the Web application.
- You tested your application.

Not bad!

Summary

Creating Enterprise JavaBeans (EJB) is one of the strengths of WebSphere Studio Application Developer. Enterprise JavaBeans is a component-based technology for writing server-side applications. Enterprise JavaBeans are managed by containers, which provide services for transactions and persistence.

Prior to learning about EJBs and WebSphere Studio Application Developer, a developer needs to understand how to approach EJBs. EJBs can be developed in one of three ways:

- Top down
- Meet in the middle
- Bottom up

This chapter guided through an EJB tutorial that utilized the bottom-up model. You prepared the database by creating the Cruise database. The database was populated with a DB2 script.

After you created the database, you prepared the development workspace to begin development in WebSphere Studio Application Developer. Taking a bottom-up approach, you utilized the EJB-RDB Mapping tool to create a container-managed persistent (CMP) entity bean. You are not responsible for doing any of the JDBC setup or transactions. The container handles it all.

As you create entity beans, there is a requirement to bind the JDBC data source to the particular EJB. This is all done through the EJB Extension editor. Information provided in this editor is persisted to XML files for use by the application server.

After setting up the bindings, all that was left to do was create the data source in the local server. With WebSphere Studio Application Developer, you can create server instances that are customized by EJB project. After the data source was matched to the bindings, you were able to utilize another tool provided by WebSphere Studio Application Developer: the EJB Test Client.

The EJB Test Client enables you to test your EJB. With the EJB Test Client, you can utilize the getter and setter in the remote object to update or query attributes within the bean.

With testing complete, you learned how to begin compiling the components necessary to link into the Web application. You created a session bean to perform a specialized search that returned multiple instances of cruises.

Through the use of access beans, you were able to wrap the EJBs to provide better performance. Access beans come in multiple flavors. You can utilize JavaBean wrappers, copy helpers, and data classes. The capability to cache objects, thereby reducing round trips, is the primary benefit of these objects. Finally the application is updated with the newly generated entity beans, session beans, and access beans.

WebSphere Studio Application Developer is a powerful enabler to the enterprise developer. After you are familiar with the tool, you should find it most valuable.

Chapter 15

Additional CMP and Transaction Processing

In This Chapter

- ♦ Understanding EJB-RDB mapping
- ♦ Understanding EJB relationships
- ♦ Understanding transaction basics

The previous two chapters discuss EJBs and show a simple example of a container-managed persistence (CMP) bean. You created the bean by using the bottom-up approach. The bottom-up approach utilizes existing table structures to create the beans. There are actually three approaches to take. You have already seen the bottom-up approach. In this chapter, you become familiar with the other two approaches (meet in the middle and top down). There is another point to consider. Objects have relationships with other objects. The same holds true for Enterprise JavaBeans (EJB). Establishing these relationships is simplified with WebSphere Studio Application Developer, and you also learn how to use them.

The final part of the chapter discusses the concept of transactions. Transactions are your guarantee that information is persisted in a manner so that it's Atomic (committed or uncommitted); Consistent (where integrity is ensured); Isolated (where changes are not interfered with); and Durable (written to the database). These four qualities are referred to as the ACID qualities of transactions. Transactions are often best described as units of work. As you traverse the method calls, you must maintain the transaction's ACID qualities.

You can initiate transactions in a couple of fashions, but the best way is to use declarative management. Using declarative management improves the flexibility and portability of the transaction. The benefit of using Enterprise JavaBeans is that it allows for declarative transaction management.

You learn how to establish a transaction scope by setting the transaction attributes to one of the following:

- Supported
- Not supported
- Required
- Requires New
- Mandatory

You also learn how to use WebSphere Studio Application Developer to specify declarative management of transactions. First, pick up from where you left off in Chapter 14, where you created a container-managed persistence (CMP) bean by using the bottom-up approach. The next section discusses the approaches you can use to create Enterprise JavaBeans (EJB).

Using the EJB-RDB Mapping Tool

The EJB-RDB mapping tool provides support for associations between EJBs mapped to foreign-key relationships. It also provides for inheritance of EJBs. Whenever you are mapping from an EJB to a relational database, you must have a way to map data types from Java to the data types supported by the database column. The EJB-RDB tool provides some built-in converters for translating single database columns to and from a bean class. Even though there are already prebuilt converters, you have the ability to create your own converters.

WebSphere Studio Application Developer also provides Composers and Converters for mapping individual complex CMP fields with multiple columns in the database. A converter is used to translate a single database column to and from the bean class field, for instance, converting a database data type of Date to a Java String. A composer is used to map a single complex bean field to multiple database columns. You won't be creating your own converters or composers in this chapter. To learn more about converters and composers, refer to the WebSphere Studio Application Developer Help.

Understanding types of mapping

You can use the EJB to RDB Mapping Wizard to develop the following approaches for mapping EJB-to-database tables:

- Top-down mapping
- Bottom-up mapping
- Meet-in-the-middle mapping

Bottom-up mapping

You experienced the bottom-up approach in Chapter 14. The bottom-up approach utilizes existing database tables. These tables are imported into WebSphere Studio Application Developer and mapped automatically. Any foreign keys are created as associations.

Top-down mapping

This chapter demonstrates the top-down approach. This approach assumes that you are creating EJBs first and then creating matching tables from the bean. When you finish defining the beans, you can generate a database schema based on the enterprise bean design.

Tables are generated to support the CMP entities inside the EJB project. Each table has corresponding columns that map to CMP fields in the enterprise bean. Also generated are the mappings that map fields to columns. Any relationship associations are mapped to foreign-key relationships.

In terms of inheritance, EJB inheritance hierarchies are mapped to a single table. This means that the base and all derived EJBs are mapped to the same database table.

Meet-in-the-middle mapping

The third and most common approach comes from a single starting point and works its way back. In the meet-in-the-middle approach, you begin with both ends defined and meet in the middle by matching by name, by type, or not at all.

When you meet in the middle, you have to map a field from the enterprise bean to a corresponding column in the table. By default, when mapping a role (an association between two tables) to a foreign-key, the tool automatically maps the other end to the same foreign key. The mapping document contains metadata that can be re-executed to keep up with changes to the database or class files.

Implementing top-down mapping

You use the completed workspace from Chapter 14. If you completed Chapter 14, double-click the Chapter 14 shortcut and start the tutorial at Creating a Top-Down Bean. Otherwise begin by performing the following steps:

1. Create a shortcut on your windows desktop by right-clicking the desktop and selecting New⇨Shortcut.
2. Enter **"x:\Program Files\IBM\Application Developer\wsappdev.exe" -data "x:\code\ejb"** and click Next. In this case, you must enter the quotation marks.
3. Name the shortcut **Chapter 14 EJB** and click Finish.

4. You need to start WebSphere Studio Application Developer and import the Enterprise Archive file (EAR) from the downloaded code folder. Double-click your Chapter 14 EJB shortcut.
5. Select File⇨Import and select EAR File as the type of file to import.
6. Using the file browser, navigate to `\x:\Bible\Chapter14\code`, and select `CSICruiseStart.ear`. Call the project **AlmostFreeCruiseEAR**. Click Finish to import the EAR file.

Creating a top-down bean

When you use the top-down approach to developing EJBs, you must first have an enterprise bean created. You create a new EJB project to hold your new EJB in WebSphere Studio Application Developer. After creating your EJB, you create some attributes in your EJB and then create the schema and mapping for these attributes.

You use the AlmostFreeCruiseEAR project to create your top-down bean. To generate a schema and map from an existing EJB, follow these steps:

1. Switch to the J2EE view in the AlmostFreeCruiseEAR project and select the EJB Modules element.
2. Click Open a New Wizard in the upper toolbar and select EJB project.
3. Use the name of **AlmostFreeTicketEJBModule** and click Finish. Under the EJB Modules item within the tree view, you should have the new EJB project called AlmostFreeTicketEJBModule.
4. Select AlmostFreeTicketEJBModule from EJB modules folder, and right-click.
5. Select New⇨Enterprise Bean.
6. When the Create an Enterprise Bean panel appears, click the entity bean with container-managed persistence (CMP) fields. Enter **Ticket** as the bean name and enter **com.bible.cruise.ejb** as default package. Accept all other defaults. Click Next.
7. On the Details screen accept the Home Interface and Remote Interface class values. Click the Add button to add CMP attributes.
8. On the Create CMP Attribute panel, type **ticketNumber** for the name and select `int` for the type, and check Key field. Click Apply.
9. Add another field named **cruiseLine** with the type of `java.lang.String`. Ensure that all but the Key field is checked, and click Apply.
10. Add one more attribute named `amount` with a type of `float`. Accept the rest of the defaults, click Apply, and then click Cancel. Your attributes should appear as shown in Figure 15-1.

11. Click Finish.
12. Expand the AlmostFreeTicketEJBModule. Right-click and select Generate⇨EJB to RDB Mapping from the pop-up menu.
13. In the Create new EJB/RDB Mapping dialog box, select Top Down and then click Next.
14. Select the Cruise Database. Type the database name (**CRUISE**) and schema name (**db2admin**) and click Next, as shown in Figure 15-2.
15. Click Generate DDL to generate a Data Definition Language script.
16. Click Finish to create the top-down mapping.

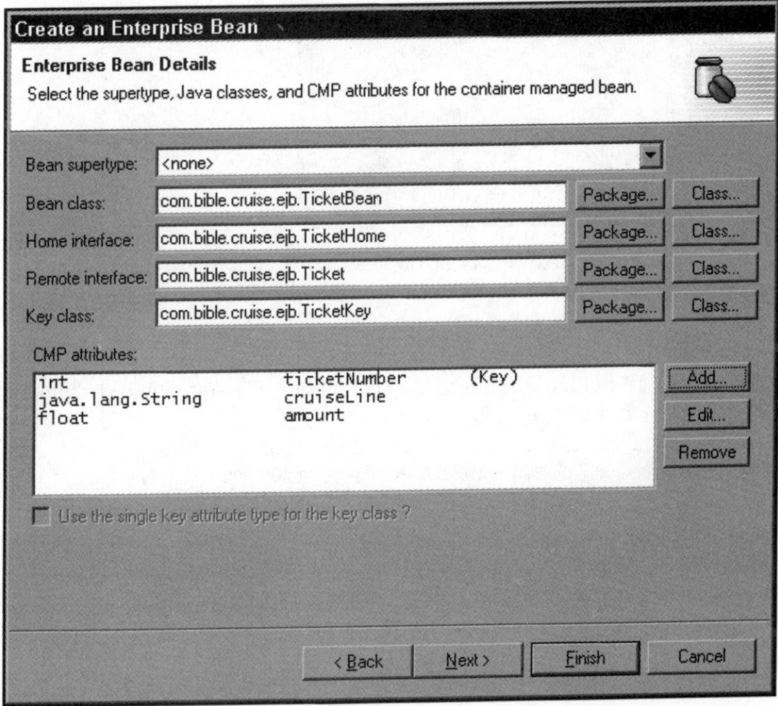

Figure 15-1: When you create CMP entity beans, you must specify the attributes of the bean.

> **NOTE**: Check WebSphere 3.x Compatible only if you are migrating from WebSphere Application Server 3.x deployments.

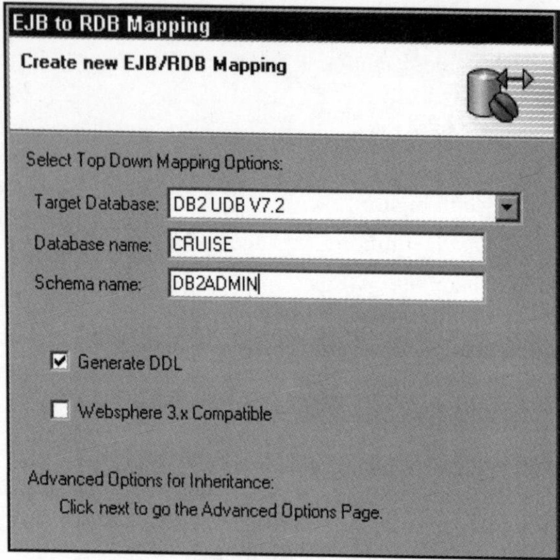

Figure 15-2: When you use the top-down approach to creating CMP entity beans, specify a database and schema to map to the EJB; this generates a DDL script so that you can create your database table.

The EJB tool creates tables, columns, and constraints relating to a CMP bean and its fields, as well as a map of each CMP field to a column. You can then make any required changes to these maps using the EJB-RDB Mapping editor.

> **NOTE**: You can use the relational database tools to modify the tables and columns.

You generated an EJB by using a top-down approach. One way to verify that it has completed successfully is to switch to the Navigator view of the J2EE perspective. Look at the EJB module you just created (AlmostFreeTicketEJBModule) under `META-INF`, and you should see the following panels:

- Schema/Schema.dbxmi
- Map.mapxmi

If you open the Map.mapxmi panel, you see how WebSphere Studio Application Developer mapped the attributes to the database. You can also look at the `Table.ddl` file, which shows the script that can be used to build the database table. Listing 15-1 shows the information from `Table.ddl`.

Listing 15-1: Table.ddl Showing Mapping Attributes

```
-- Generated by Relational Schema Center on Tue Apr 16 21:51:06 PDT 2002
CREATE SCHEMA DB2ADMIN;
CREATE TABLE DB2ADMIN.TICKET
  (TICKETNUMBER INTEGER NOT NULL,
   CRUISELINE VARCHAR(250),
   AMOUNT REAL);
ALTER TABLE DB2ADMIN.TICKET
  ADD CONSTRAINT TICKETPK PRIMARY KEY (TICKETNUMBER);
```

You do not have to test the TicketBean, but if you want to, ensure that you created the database table, defined a data source, set the bindings, and created a test server. All these steps were presented in Chapter 14.

Understanding the meet-in-the-middle process

You won't be running an exercise for meet-in-the-middle process, but you should be familiar with the steps. They are similar to those in the top-down approach, but the approach assumes that you have database tables and schemas already. It also assumes you have existing EJBs that are business objects that need to be mapped to normalized relational databases. To start the process, use the EJB to RDB Mapping Wizard and step through generating a meet-in-the-middle mapping:

1. In the J2EE perspective, select the EJB project.
2. Right-click and select Generate⇨ EJB to RDB Mapping.
3. Select Meet in the Middle and then click Next.
4. If you have not already imported the database tables into the EJB project, the Database Connections page appears. Fill in the connection information or select one from the drop-down list if you already created a connection previously.
5. Select additional mapping options as necessary, and click Finish.

You can do a meet-in-the-middle mapping by matching by name, by type, or no matching. Map each field of the enterprise bean to the corresponding column of a table within the selected schema. You also map each association role to a foreign-key relationship. Continue with the steps until all fields are mapped.

CROSS-REFERENCE: Converters are not covered in this book. A converter is used to translate a single database column to and from the bean class field. Some databases have their own unique data types that do not map exactly to Java primitives. You need to define converters to handle the mapping. Refer to the WebSphere Studio Application Developer Help to learn more about converters.

Defining EJB relationships

You can use the EJB Extension editor to define a relationship among different EJBs. There are three main types of relationships:

- In a one-to-one (1…1) relationship, a CMP entity bean is associated with a single instance of another CMP entity bean. For example, a Ship bean could be associated with only a single instance of an ShipID bean, because a ship can have only one ship identifier on file.
- In a one-to-many (1…n) relationship, a CMP entity bean is associated with multiple instances of another CMP entity bean. For example, a Ship bean could be associated with multiple instances of a Deck bean, because most ships are made up of multiple decks.
- In a many-to-many (n…n) relationship, multiple instances of a CMP entity bean are associated with multiple instances of another CMP entity bean. A many-to-many relationship is created by joining two (1…n) relationships. For example, multiple instances of a Customer bean could be associated with multiple instances of a Cruise bean, because cruises serve many customers, and customers go on many different cruises.

As part of defining a relationship, you assign a *role* to each bean relative to the other bean, and you give that role a name. For example, there is a relationship between a particular cruise and the ship that it will use. The role of shipID within the Cruise bean could be referred as assignedShipID. The role of Cruise within the Ship bean could be cruise or tour. These names are used to derive names in the generated code and become a part of the remote interface.

When CMP fields and relationships are eventually mapped to database tables, foreign keys are used to represent these relationships in the database tables. You can then add relationship roles to the key of an enterprise bean, which makes the foreign key represented in the relationship part of the Key class.

To add a role to the key of a bean, it must be single multiplicity (1 to 1), and it must be required (for example, 1...1). Also, the bean with an established role must have the Foreign Key check box selected.

In the preceding example, the assignedShip role can be made part of the Cruise key if the multiplicity is (1...1) and Cruise has the Foreign Key check box selected. Listing 15-2 shows the generated code.

Listing 15-2: ejbCreate with assignedShip

```
/**
 * ejbCreate method for a CMP entity bean.
 */
public com.bible.cruise.ejb.CruiseKey ejbCreate(java.lang.Integer
cruise_id, com.bible.cruise.ejb.Ship argAssignedShip) throws
javax.ejb.CreateException {
 _initLinks();
 this.cruise_id = cruise_id;
 try {
  setAssignedShip(argAssignedShip);
 } catch (java.rmi.RemoteException remoteEx) {
  throw new javax.ejb.CreateException(remoteEx.getMessage());
 }
 return null;
}
```

> **NOTE**: Marking a role as required (1...x), adds the role's type as a parameter to the Home interface's `create()` method.

You learn how to use the Relationships tab of the IBM Extension editor in the next section.

Creating relationships

You need another EJB to establish a relationship. You should create another CMP EJB in the AlmostFreeCruiseEJB project. To create the CMP, follow these steps:

1. Select AlmostFreeCruiseEJB project and right-click. Select New⇨New Enterprise Bean.
2. Enter **Ship** as the name of the bean and accept all other defaults.
3. Click Finish.
4. Select Ship and right-click. Select the IBM Extension editor.

Use the EJB Extension editor to specify the relationship between two EJBs in your EJB project. The EJB Extension editor generates the appropriate finder methods to support any relationships that you create.

When you define a relationship from one CMP to another, extra CMP fields, based on the key fields from the referencing CMP bean, are added to the owning CMP bean of the forward referencing role. Remember that the Foreign Key check box was selected as the CMP bean owner.

Let's review a scenario. The Ships bean has a 1...n relationship to Decks with the roles ship and deck, respectively. The Ship CMP bean has key fields: `ship_ID` and `ship_Name`. When you create the relationship, the CMP fields that are automatically added to the Deck bean are `ship_ship_ID` and `ship_ship_Name`. These fields are not seen in the EJB editor because they are fields that were added to support the deck relationship role.

WARNING: Problems arise if these CMP fields are removed from the `ejb-jar.xml` file while the relationship still exists. They show up as runtime errors and may be difficult to troubleshoot.

When a relationship is created, additional classes are created to support the runtime in maintaining the links between these two beans. If you look at the `Home`, `Remote`, and `Bean` classes of both EJB, you see the additional methods that were generated.

NOTE: You see compile errors in the EJB Extension editor when a relationship is first created because the generated Link classes need to be compiled.

Expect to see compile errors after you save the EJB editor or EJB Extension editor. This is normal when you are creating relationships. After you compile, the errors disappear.

Establishing the relationship

To create an association between EJB, perform the following steps:

1. Open the AlmostFreeCruiseEJB in the EJB Extension editor (if it's not already showing).
2. Click the Relationships page and then click Add.
3. In the Relationship Name field, type **cruise-ship** as the relationship name.
4. In the left Enterprise bean drop-down list, select Cruise.
5. In the right Enterprise bean drop-down list, select Ship.
6. By default, role names are automatically generated. Just to be different change ship to **assignedShip**.
7. Set parameters for each role, as follows:
   - Navigable means that instances of the other bean in the association can be retrieved using this role. Check both boxes so the beans can access each other.
   - Multiplicity means that the role potentially represents many instances of the other bean. Using 1…x makes the role required, but in this case, make both 1…1.
   - Foreign Key means that the specified enterprise bean of the relationship holds a foreign key for the other relationship role. Check Foreign Key for Cruise.
8. Click Apply. Figure 15-3 shows the results of your efforts.

In Figure 15-3, you see a new cruise-ship relationship. You can also look at the cruiseBean and shipBean to see what was generated. As mentioned previously, you see errors until the beans are compiled. You will not be modifying the AlmostFreeCruise application to implement this relationship. It's time to move on to some other important features.

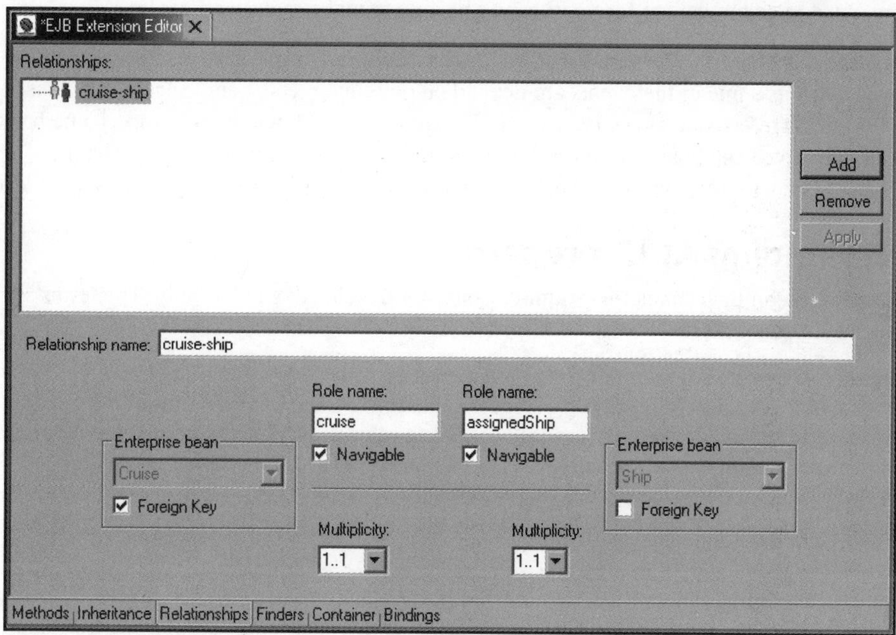

Figure 15-3: With the EJB Extension editor, you can establish relationships between two EJBs. In this figure, a relationship is being established between the Cruise bean and the Ship bean.

Understanding Transaction-Management Basics

Most people with strong backgrounds in database-management systems or transaction processors, such CICS or IMS, have a good understanding about the system interactions with transactions. Unfortunately, not everyone has had this experience, so it is important to provide some business scenarios to set the stage. In this scenario, you are moonlighting as a travel agent in your spare time. You have devised a simple system with which you do business. The scenario goes like this:

1. Stressed out people contact you and want you to book them on a cheap cruise to anywhere but where they are at that moment.

2. You find a cruise that has one room available. You are in competition with other travel agents to reserve that last room so you want to hold it for your customer.
3. When the customer pays money, the room is his and the room is removed from the list of available rooms. If his credit card is no good, the room is made available again.
4. You need to document the reservation and be able to make modifications later.

Each of these listed items represents some basic transactions. Transactions are business events, and as you can see, some of the events are dependent on other events being successful. This chain of events is referred to as a *unit of work*. To participate within a unit of work, some basic properties need to be established to ensure that the transaction is done properly, without compromise. The way you ensure that these properties are met is by adhering to the ACID test.

Understanding ACID properties

ACID is an acronym that stands for: Atomic, Consistent, Isolated, and Durable. The terms' descriptions are as follows:

- *Atomic:* When a transaction must complete successfully or not complete at all, the transaction is said to be atomic. This means that in the business transaction in the unit-of-work scenario, all the events within the scenario must work or be completely undone. When they complete successfully, the transaction is considered committed. When you undo the transactions, the events are rolled back.
- *Consistent:* Consistency is important because you want all the cross-referenced items in sync with each other. You want the room reserved to the right person at the price you quoted. The room should be removed from the available rooms and the proper accounting of the transaction set so that you can earn your commission. From a database perspective, you want to ensure data integrity by enforcing constraints.
- *Isolated:* Wouldn't it be wonderful if you were the only travel agent and everyone came to you? That is not a likely scenario; it's a dog-eat-dog world. When you are ready to book that client, you do not want anyone else stealing the stateroom before you reserve it for your client. When transactions are isolated, you are guaranteed that no one else will affect your transaction.
- *Durable:* Finally, you want your transaction duly noted and placed in a safe place. The safe place is usually some data-storage mechanism. If your transaction is stored only in memory and you have some sort of catastrophic error, you lose your information as well as your commission.

The next section explains how ACID properties impact EJBs.

Understanding transactions

Now that you have an idea about the ACID properties, the next important thing is to understand is how transactions work. Some definition work is in order:

- *Transactional objects:* These are objects whose behavior is affected by being invoked within the scope of a transaction. Transactional objects can be associated with only a single transaction at a time. EJBs can be transactional objects.
- *Transaction context:* The context represents the transaction shared by participating transactional objects. It is automatically passed on to other transactional objects when they are utilized. The context identifies the community of transactional objects that is affected by a commit or rollback.
- *Transactional client*: A transaction client is a program that can invoke operations on many transactional objects using a single transaction. An example would be a stateless session bean operation.
- *Transaction manager:* A transaction manager has the responsibility of managing transactions. The EJS container is an example of a transaction manager.
- *Resource manager:* Resource managers manage the transactions for a single data source. Any database manager, such as DB2, would fit this description.

Understanding the two-phase commit

When people speak of two-phase commit they are not taking about "I love you" and "Will you marry me." Although those are two forms of commitment, two-phase has to do with the capability to allow multiple databases to be updated in a single commit process.

Using some of the definitions in the previous section, this section discusses how their interaction supports a two-phase commit. EJBs are transactional objects. WebSphere supports EJBs as well as an infrastructure that includes database-management systems, such as DB2. The drivers that are supplied with DB2 can act as resource managers. WebSphere implements containers that support the transactional manager requirements.

When you tie all three of these objects together, you have the necessary infrastructure to support two-phase commit. A two-phase commit requires two sets of messages from the transaction manager (containers) to the resource managers (database drivers). Each resource manager temporarily persists the database changes. Then the transaction manager precommits. You might relate this to our marriage analogy as an "I think I'm ready, are you?" When each resource manager responds saying it's ready to commit, the transaction manager sends the final commit. And the transactions live happily ever after.

In WebSphere 4.0, the two-phase commit is even easier to use with the addition of the Merant SequeLink Server and Driver. The Merant SequeLink Server and Driver enhances JDBC Java Transaction API (JTA) functionality. It supports JTA transaction data sources and makes transaction chaining easier by integrating with a variety of data access interfaces across multiple database.

Understanding transaction architecture

With the mention of JTA in the previous section, it might be a good time to introduce some of the groundwork that supports the two-phase commit. That groundwork was set in the form of the X/Open XA specifications, which define a model for distributed transactions. They provide a way to describe the distributed participants and are the foundation for EJB models.

The specifications also outline the interfaces for managing transactions. Vendors, such as Merant, are writing XA-aware JDBC 2.0 drivers, but not all vendors are there yet.

Java Application Programming Interfaces (APIs) participate in the transaction architecture, specifically, Java Transaction Service (JTS) and Java Transaction API (JTA).

Understanding JTS

The Object Management Group (OMG) put out a specification, named Object Transaction Server (OTS), which is based on the XA specification. Many EJB designs are based on the OTS specification. JTS implements the Java mapping of OTS. JTS is considered low level and specifies the implementation of a transaction manger that supports the JTA specification.

Understanding JTA

The Java Transaction API (JTA) specifies local Java interfaces between a transaction manager and interaction involving an application, resource managers, and application server. JTA sits on top of JTS and provides the `UserTransaction` class.

Using Transactions

This section describes how to get the benefits of transactions in your EJB and/or for other vendor applications that utilize EJB. You can choose from the following ways to implement transaction services:

- *Declarative transaction management:* In this case, everything for transactions is done in the deployment descriptors. This is perhaps the simplest way to implement transactions.
- *Explicit Transaction management:* This is where you use JTA/JTS to manage the transaction. This requires significant knowledge as it is more complex to code.

A good rule of thumb when you first get started is to let the EJS container handle transactions and adjust your design to fully utilize it. From this point on, the focus is on utilizing declarative transaction management.

Introducing EJB transaction services

The scope of the transaction is important. When you think of scope of the transaction, it may help to think of it as the unit of work. A unit of work is a thread of a transaction. Furthermore, each transaction, to be a successfully defined transaction, must adhere to the ACID properties. Therefore, transactions must be atomic and thus any failed efforts results in a rollback.

The scope of a transaction includes every bean that participates in the thread (or unit of work). Transactions begin with a starting method. As that method calls other methods in other beans, those beans become part of the thread or transactional context. When the originating method ends, so does the transaction. Transactions can also end with an exception. Would the exception cause a rollback? In some cases that might be correct. The transaction thread is not the only thing that matters when determining whether a bean is part of the scope; some transactional attributes affect transactional control.

Understanding transactional attributes

Luckily, as developers, having declarative transaction management has removed the need to control transactions. With the use of the deployment descriptors, you can set the transaction attributes at deployment. You can set the attributes for a method or for the entire bean.

CROSS-REFERENCE: Chapter 16 provides more details about deployment descriptors.

Within the EJB deployment descriptors is an element named `<container-transaction>`, which contains the methods and transaction attributes that are set. The attributes you can set within the deployment descriptor are shown in Table 15-1

Table 15-1: Transaction Attributes

Transaction Attribute	***EJB 1.1 Value***
Mandatory	Mandatory
Never	Never
Not Supported	NotSupported
Required	Required
Requires New	RequiresNew
Supports	Supports

The EJB 1.1 transaction attributes are described in the following list:

- *Mandatory:* A mandatory bean requires that this method always be within a transaction. If it is called from a nontransactional scope an TransactionRequiredException is thrown.
- *Never:* This is a no-no-no attribute. A bean with this attribute can never be invoked within a transaction. Calling from a nontransaction scope is acceptable.
- *Not Supported:* When a method with this attribute is invoked, the transaction suspends until the method is completed. Any methods that this method calls do not participate in the transaction either. After completion, the original thread continues.
- *Required:* With Required, there must be a transaction in progress. If there is not, a transaction starts and terminates at the end of the executing method.
- *Requires New:* This attribute means a new transaction is always started. The buck starts here. If a transaction is already in scope and a method with `Requires New` is initiated, the prior scope is suspended and a new scope begins. At termination of the executing method, the suspended scope resumes.
- *Supports:* When a method uses this attribute, it is included in the transaction scope if and only if it was invoked within an existing transaction. Any beans the additional beans invoke participate in the transaction. It is okay if a bean that invokes a method with the `Supports` attribute is not part of a transaction.

Understanding isolation and locking

Whenever you hear about isolation levels and locking you should immediately think of databases. Database-management systems have been addressing the effects on transactional processing for some time now. Isolation of data is the process of ensuring that two or more transactions do not operate on the same data. The isolation levels and their descriptions are as follows:

- *Read Uncommitted:* This is also referred to as a dirty read. This happens when a second transaction (T2) reads data that has been uncommitted by another transaction (T1). When the other transaction (T1) issues a rollback, the data is invalid, but the other transaction (T2) thinks its data is fine. Dirty reads and phantom reads (see Read Committed) can occur.
- *Read Committed:* In this case, a transaction is not able to read uncommitted data from other transactions. Phantom reads can occur in this isolation level. A phantom read is one where you read data, and then on subsequent reads within the transaction, the data is no longer there. In this case, dirty reads are prevented, but phantom reads can occur.
- *Repeatable Read*: Using this isolation level guarantees that the data that you read is still the same data if you read it again during the same transaction thread. In this case, dirty reads are prevented, but phantom reads can occur.
- *Serializable:* In this case, all transactions are serialized. No other transaction can read or write to the serialized data.

Normally, you cannot control isolations through declarative attributes, but using WebSphere Extension editor, you can set the isolation levels in the Methods tab, shown in Figure 15-4.

> **NOTE:** You can probably guess that isolations can impact performance. Be particularly careful with Serializable.

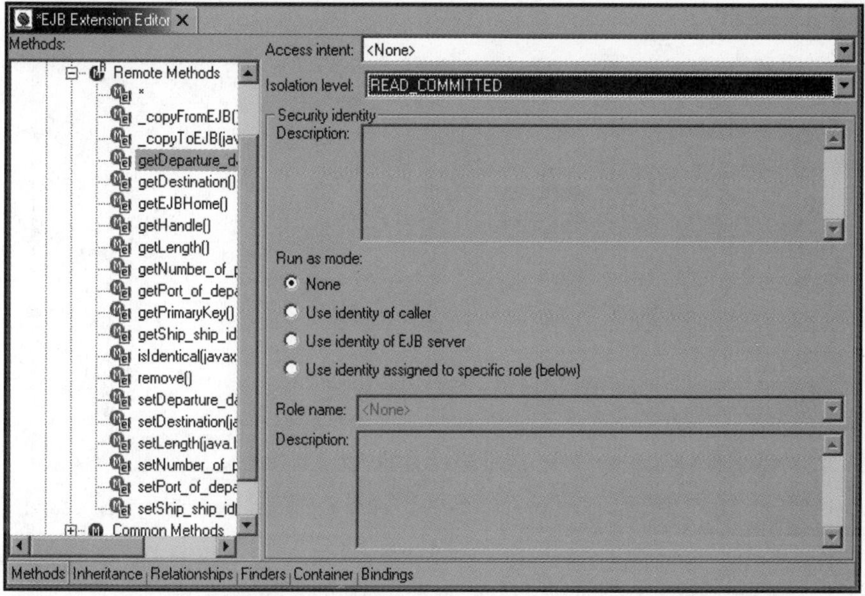

Figure 15-4: The EJB Extension editor makes setting isolation levels easy. This removes the manual updating of XML files, and thereby reduces errors.

Setting Transactions in AlmostFreeCruise

Chapter 16 covers deployment descriptors in some detail. The one element that is not presented is the process for implementing declarative transaction management. You learn how you can set up a transaction using WebSphere Studio Application Developer. Follow these steps:

1. Start your WebSphere Studio Application Developer environment.
2. Switch to the J2EE perspective.
3. Expand the EJB module.
4. Select the AlmostFreeCruiseEJB project.
5. Right-click and select Open With⇨EJB Editor.
6. Select the Transaction tab and highlight Cruise.

7. Click the Add button. You should see the Add Method Transaction dialog box, as shown in Figure 15-5.

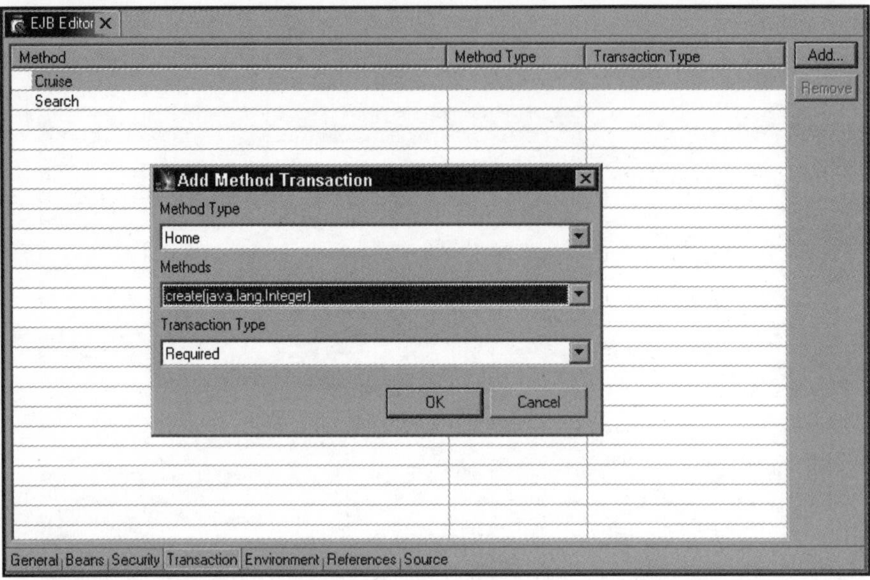

Figure 15-5: To add method transactions, you click the Add button and choose the Method Type, Method, and Transaction Type.

8. Use the Methods drop-down list, and select create(java.lang.Integer).
9. By selecting Required in the Transaction Type field, you are ensuring that this method is running in a transaction scope. In the Transaction Type drop-down list, select `Required`. Click OK.
10. You see that Cruise under the Method column now has an expand icon. If you expand it, you see your method.
11. Save the EJB editor and close the editor.
12. Switch your view to the Navigator view.
13. Expand AlmostFreeCruiseEJB, ejbModule, and schema.
14. Double-click `ejb-jar.xml`.

Scan down the deployment descriptor and you should find the `<container-transaction>` element that matches what you just did. Listing 15-3 shows the output you should find.

Listing 15-3: The <container-transaction> Tag Specifying the Transaction Attribute

```
<container-transaction>
 <method>
  <ejb-name>Cruise</ejb-name>
  <method-intf>Home</method-intf>
  <method-name>create</method-name>
  <method-params>
   <method-param>java.lang.Integer</method-param></method-params>
 </method>
 <trans-attribute>Required</trans-attribute>
</container-transaction>
```

That brings you to an end of the chapter. You now know the steps to prepare for deployment. You will not immediately be deploying this application to WebSphere, as you have a bit more to learn in the next chapter.

Summary

There is a lot to learning how to develop EJBs with WebSphere Studio Application Developer. One of the tools that makes life easier is the EJB-RDB Mapping tool. With the EJB-RDB Mapping tool, you can generate code using one of the three approaches to building EJB:

- Bottom up
- Top down
- Meet in the middle

With bottom up, you work with existing database tables and generate a single enterprise bean for each table. Fields are mapped to corresponding columns within the database table. The tool is database-aware, so it knows how to convert column types to Java types.

When you use the top-down approach, you create an EJB first and then create database tables by running the database script that is generated by WebSphere Studio Application Developer. In the chapter, you ran a small example that utilized top-down development.

Meet in the middle is a hybrid approach. In this case, you have both existing database tables and you have created your own objects. You need to meet in the middle and map attributes between the objects and the tables. This option is a little more work than the other two.

Relationships are needed between objects or databases to establish a link between two objects. WebSphere Studio Application Developer provides the capability to establish these relationships with a simple wizard. When you establish the relationship, WebSphere Studio Application Developer creates the necessary code that includes the role each association has and the capability to reference each other.

After you learned how to create EJB, you were introduced to transactions. Transactions are a series of events that occur to process a business transaction. A transaction must conform to the ACID properties. The acronym stands for Atomic, Consistent, Isolated, and Durable.

When a transaction must complete successfully or not complete at all, the transaction is said to be atomic. Consistency is important because you want all the cross-referenced items in sync with each other. When transactions are isolated, you are guaranteed that no one else can affect your transaction. Finally, you want your transaction duly noted and stored in a safe place. The safe place is usually some data storage mechanism. When your business events meet these requirements, you can safely say you have a good transaction.

Within EJB, transactions are managed at the method level. They are started with a method, and through a facility called the transaction context, they are propagated to other beans making up a unit of work. As transactions are run, some EJBs can be called and either included in the transaction or not included. You can govern the way transactions are scoped by declaring the transaction properties in the deployment descriptors.

Isolation levels have an impact on the integrity side of the ACID properties. Isolation levels govern the way the transactions interact with data freshness. You can configure the isolation levels through the WebSphere extensions.

Finally, you get to work with WebSphere Studio Application Developer to create the deployment descriptors for transaction processing. You are now ready to learn more about deployment descriptors and how they help keep EJB portable and flexible.

Chapter 16

Deployment Descriptors and EJB Security Overview

In This Chapter

- Understanding the application-assembly process
- Understanding deployment descriptors
- Introducing EJB security

The previous three chapters taught you all about J2EE and Enterprise JavaBeans. You learned quite a bit about how to use, create, and test them. To test them, you need to create deployment descriptors. Now that they are all XML-based, deployment descriptors are handled differently than in previous releases of WebSphere. Luckily, WebSphere Studio Application Developer takes on that responsibility and generates all the deployment descriptors for you. But, at times, you might need to update the deployment descriptors without the assistance of WebSphere Studio Application Developer. In this chapter, you learn more about deployment descriptors and some of the details of the specialized extensions of the deployment descriptors needed by WebSphere Application Server that were generated by WebSphere Studio Application Developer.

Also this chapter touches upon how security impacts the deployment descriptors. Chapter 23 is devoted to security, but EJB security affects deployment descriptors so, in this chapter as well, you have an opportunity to learn a little about how security and deployment descriptors function.

Understanding Application Assembly

The J2EE platform enables developers to create different parts of their applications as reusable components. Assembling components into modules is called *packaging*. In WebSphere terminology, this is also known as *application assembly*. Whenever you assemble an application for a specific environment, the process is known as *deployment*. With WebSphere, you are able to assemble and customize your application for deployments that are J2EE compliant.

Understanding J2EE compliance

For WebSphere to become J2EE compliant, it needs to comply with the specifications for deployment of the three types of modules (EJB, Web, and Client).

For EJBs, WebSphere has to perform the following tasks:

- Generate and compile the stubs and skeletons for the enterprise bean
- Set up the security environment to host the enterprise bean according to its deployment descriptor, so that the access to the methods of the enterprise bean can be regulated according to the security policy of the application
- Set up the transaction environment for the enterprise bean according to its deployment descriptor, so that the calls to the methods of the enterprise bean happen in the correct transaction context
- Register the enterprise bean, its environment properties, and its resource references in the JNDI namespace
- Create database tables for enterprise beans that use container-managed persistence (CMP)

Figure 16-1 shows the J2EE deployment architecture. A J2EE application is packaged as an Enterprise Archive (EAR) file. You used EAR files in Chapter 14.

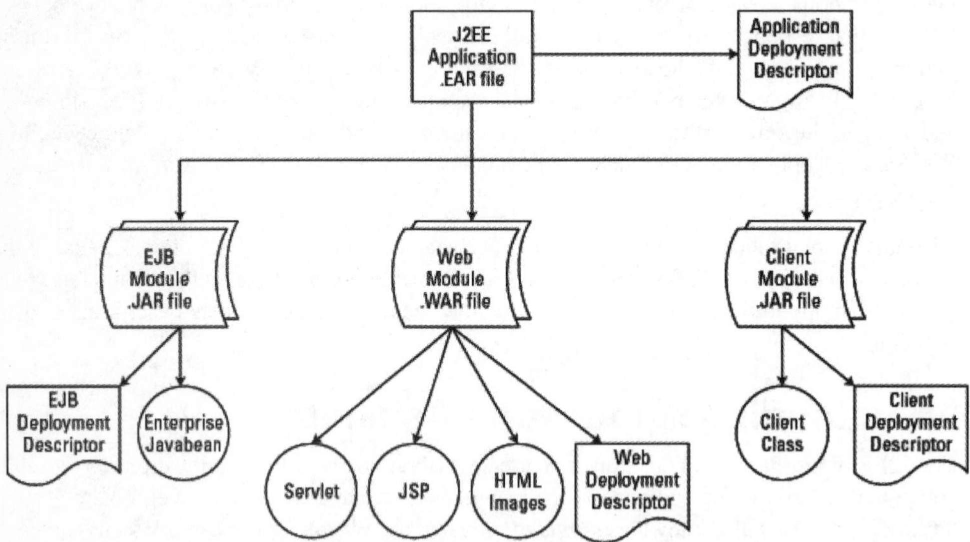

Figure 16-1: In the J2EE deployment architecture an Enterprise Archive file contains JAR files and WAR files that contain the EJB, Web, and Client resources necessary to run an application.

An EAR file is a Java Archive (JAR) file that includes a deployment descriptor. A J2EE application EAR contains one or more J2EE modules and a deployment descriptor. A deployment descriptor is an XML-based text file with elements that describe how to assemble and deploy the application unit into a specific environment, such as WebSphere Application Server. The modules are divided into three types:

- Enterprise JavaBean (EJB) modules
- Web modules
- Client modules

You focus only on the EJB deployment descriptors in this chapter.

Introducing the Anatomy of an EJB Deployment Descriptor

How should you think of deployment descriptors? You might think of deployment descriptors as providing the same functionality as a property file. You can retrieve property information and alter the behavior of your application. The biggest difference between a property file and deployment descriptors is the use of XML. In J2EE 1.2, deployment descriptors must be implemented using XML.

> **CROSS-REFERENCE:** You learn much more about XML in Chapter 18.

XML is similar to HTML. It has tags and attributes, but they are unique to HTML. Instead of seeing `<HEAD>` tags, you might see `<ejb-jar>`, or `<enterprise-beans>`. These tags are defined in a definition document called a Document Type Definition (DTD). For each XML descriptor, there is a DTD that describes its tags and attributes.

You may already know that XML has restrictions. You must conform to the restrictions set forth in their corresponding XML Schema or DTD. In addition, XML documents must be well-formed. For example, each tag must have a closing tag. XML is also case sensitive. HTML could care less if its tags are in uppercase, lower-case, or a combination. When you look at deployment descriptors, you will see that all tags are lowercase. Keep that in mind if you are manually updating a deployment descriptor.

Listing 16-1 shows the `ejb-jar.xml` file, which is the deployment descriptor for the AlmostFreeCruiseEJB project that you developed in Chapter 14. The `<assembly-descriptor>` is an additional set of tags added to illustrate the declaration of security roles.

Listing 16-1: ejb-jar.xml Contains the Deployment Descriptors for AlmostFreeCruiseEJB

```
<?xml version="1.0" encoding="UTF-8"?>
<!DOCTYPE ejb-jar PUBLIC "-//Sun Microsystems, Inc.//DTD Enterprise
JavaBeans 1.1//EN" "http://java.sun.com/j2ee/dtds/ejb-jar_1_1.dtd">
<ejb-jar id="ejb-jar_ID">
  <display-name>AlmostFreeCruiseEJB</display-name>
  <enterprise-beans>
   <entity id="ContainerManagedEntity_1">
    <ejb-name>Cruise</ejb-name>
    <home>com.bible.cruise.ejb.CruiseHome</home>
    <remote>com.bible.cruise.ejb.Cruise</remote>
    <ejb-class>com.bible.cruise.ejb.CruiseBean</ejb-class>
      <persistence-type>Container</persistence-type>
      <prim-key-class>com.bible.cruise.ejb.CruiseKey
      </prim-key-class>
      <reentrant>False</reentrant>
      <cmp-field id="CMPAttribute_1">
        <field-name>cruise_id</field-name>
      </cmp-field>
      <cmp-field id="CMPAttribute_2">
        <field-name>departure_date</field-name>
      </cmp-field>
      <cmp-field id="CMPAttribute_3">
        <field-name>destination</field-name>
      </cmp-field>
        <cmp-field id="CMPAttribute_4">
        <field-name>length</field-name>
      </cmp-field>
      <cmp-field id="CMPAttribute_5">
        <field-name>number_of_ports</field-name>
      </cmp-field>
      <cmp-field id="CMPAttribute_6">
        <field-name>port_of_departure</field-name>
      </cmp-field>
      <cmp-field id="CMPAttribute_7">
        <field-name>ship_ship_id</field-name>
      </cmp-field>
      <env-entry>
        <env-entry-name>MaxVacationDays</env-entry-name>
        <env-entry-type>java.lang.String</env-entry-type>
        <env-entry-value>21</env-entry-value>
      </env-entry>
    </entity>
```

```
  <session id="Search">
  <ejb-name>Search</ejb-name>
    <home>com.bible.cruise.ejb.SearchHome</home>
    <remote>com.bible.cruise.ejb.Search</remote>
    <ejb-class>com.bible.cruise.ejb.SearchBean</ejb-class>
    <session-type>Stateless</session-type>
      <transaction-type>Container</transaction-type>
    </session>
    </enterprise-beans>
    <assembly-descriptor>
     <security-role>
      <description>Any Potential Customer</description>
        <role-name>Customer</role-name>
     </security-role>
     <security-role>
      <description>Our trusted agents</description>
        <role-name>Travel Agent</role-name>
     </security-role>
    </assembly-descriptor>
</ejb-jar>
```

If you peruse the XML, you might decipher some of the attributes, but other attributes may seem strange to you. The following sections break down the file into understandable segments.

Understanding the document header

All XML documents start with a few tags, just as HTML documents do. In Listing 16-2, the first two tags are extrapolated from the full listing.

Listing 16-2: Document Header

```
<?xml version="1.0" encoding="UTF-8"?>
<!DOCTYPE ejb-jar PUBLIC "-//Sun Microsystems, Inc.//DTD Enterprise
JavaBeans 1.1//EN" "http://java.sun.com/j2ee/dtds/ejb-jar_1_1.dtd">
```

The first line is the version tag. This line states that the file adheres to version 1.0 of the XML specification.

The second tag, `DOCTYPE`, contains the URL where you can validate the document. Will you be validating XML documents of this type? The answer is probably not, unless you are a tool vendor. But you can find this DTD in `<was_home>/deploytool/itp/plugins/com.ibm.etools.j2ee/dtds`.

Another important line is the `<ejb-jar>` element. This line identifies the *root element*, which is the beginning of the document. In this case, it's `ejb-jar`. You should find that as the first element after `DOCTYPE`.

Understanding the body

As you learned previously, the root element is the first element. The `<ejb-jar>` tag is the root element, and because XML requires an ending tag for each tag, you find a `</ejb-jar>` tag at the end of the document. Between these tags is the body of the document. The following list contains some of the elements found in the example in Listing 16-1:

- `<display-name>` is optional, but WebSphere Studio Application Developer generated a description for it and that description is the EJB project.
- `<enterprise-beans>` describes the enterprise beans in your application deployment. One and only one enterprise-beans element must be contained within the EJB descriptor.

The following list contains some optional tags you might see and certainly will see when you utilize the Application Assembly Tool (AAT):

- `<description>` is used to provide a description of the deployment descriptor. Putting in a description is not a bad idea for maintaining documentation of your application components.
- `<small-icon>` and `<large-icon>` are tags that identify 16 X 16 and 32 X 32 images that your deployment tool can utilize to display your unique image. Again, if you are a tool vendor you might use this feature, but in general application developers can ignore this tag.
- `<assembly-descriptor>` is an element that contains information about security roles, method permissions, and transaction attributes.

The two elements that you spend the most time with are `<enterprise-beans>` and `<assembly-descriptor>`. Take a closer look at the `<enterprise-beans>` element first.

Understanding enterprise-beans

Listing 16-3 shows the `<enterprise-beans>` element. In the example you created in Chapter 14, you only had one container-managed persistent (CMP) bean. Just because this deployment descriptor has only one bean defined, it doesn't mean you can't have more than one. In fact, defining multiple beans in one deployment descriptor is a good thing. For instance, if you are setting security roles, having the beans that apply to the specified role in the same descriptor makes it easier to maintain. Can you imagine having to search for all the beans that apply to a particular role if they are spread out in multiple files?

Listing 16-3: Using the <enterprise-beans> Element

```
<enterprise-beans>
 <entity id="ContainerManagedEntity_1">
  <ejb-name>Cruise</ejb-name>
   <home>com.bible.cruise.ejb.CruiseHome</home>
   <remote>com.bible.cruise.ejb.Cruise</remote>
   <ejb-class>com.bible.cruise.ejb.CruiseBean</ejb-class>
     <persistence-type>Container</persistence-type>
```

```
      <prim-key-class>com.bible.cruise.ejb.CruiseKey</prim-key-class>
      <reentrant>False</reentrant>
      <cmp-field id="CMPAttribute_1">
        <field-name>cruise_id</field-name>
      </cmp-field>
      <cmp-field id="CMPAttribute_2">
        <field-name>departure_date</field-name>
      </cmp-field>
      <cmp-field id="CMPAttribute_3">
        <field-name>destination</field-name>
      </cmp-field>
      <cmp-field id="CMPAttribute_4">
        <field-name>length</field-name>
      </cmp-field>
      <cmp-field id="CMPAttribute_5">
        <field-name>number_of_ports</field-name>
      </cmp-field>
      <cmp-field id="CMPAttribute_6">
        <field-name>port_of_departure</field-name>
      </cmp-field>
      <cmp-field id="CMPAttribute_7">
        <field-name>ship_ship_id</field-name>
      </cmp-field>
      <env-entry>
       <env-entry-name>MaxVacationDays</env-entry-name>
       <env-entry-type>java.lang.String</env-entry-type>
       <env-entry-value>21</env-entry-value>
      </env-entry>
    </entity>
    <session id="Search">
    <ejb-name>Search</ejb-name>
    <home>com.bible.cruise.ejb.SearchHome</home>
    <remote>com.bible.cruise.ejb.Search</remote>
    <ejb-class>com.bible.cruise.ejb.SearchBean</ejb-class>
    <session-type>Stateless</session-type>
     <transaction-type>Container</transaction-type>
 </session>
</enterprise-beans>
```

Enterprise beans come in two flavors (entity and session). For the sake of saving space, the descriptions of the elements are combined and noted when one applies only to a particular flavor; otherwise, they are valid for both.

`enterprise-beans` provide optional elements just as `ejb-jar` does. You are already aware of description, `display-name`, `small-icon`, and `large-icon`. You can ensure that these elements are specified as needed. Some of the more interesting elements in Listing 16-3 are as follows:

- *<ejb-name>:* This required element is the name of the bean. Whenever the name of an EJB is presented, this is the name that is being discussed.
- *<home>:* This required element specifies the fully qualified class name for the bean's home interface.
- *<remote>:* This required element specifies the fully qualified class name for the bean's remote interface.
- *<ejb-class>:* This required element specifies the fully qualified class name.
- *<persistence-type>:* This is for entity beans only and specifies whether the bean is a container-managed persistence (CMP) or bean-managed persistence (BMP) bean. The value are `Container` or `Bean`.
- *<prim-key-class>:* This required field is for entity beans only. It specifies the fully qualified class name of the primary key class. You can defer the definition to the person deploying by specifying the class as `java.lang.Object`, which is helpful if you are using automatic database primary key generation columns.

> **NOTE**: The `<primkey-field>` is an optional field for entity beans and is used to define which field to use as the primary key. It's never used if you have a customized primary key or if the entity bean manages its own persistence.

- `<reentrant>`: For entity beans this element is required. The re-entrant element is a Boolean (True or False) that specifies whether the bean allows loopbacks.
- *<cmp-field>:* Elements may or may not be present for this bean. They apply only to entity beans. For each container-managed field in a bean class, there must be a `cmp-field` declared.
- *<field-name>:* This is a required field if you have a `<cmp-field>` declared. It declares the name of the field that the container manages.
- *<session-type>:* There must be at least one provided, and it is used for session beans only. The `<session-type>` element declares a session bean to be either stateful or stateless. The valid values are `Stateful` or `Stateless`.
- *<env-entry>:* This field contains zero or more entries. This element declares an environment entry that is available through JNDI. It's similar to properties files that can be accessed during runtime.
- *<env-entry-name>:* This is a required field if you have a `<env-field>` declared. It declares the name of the field that the container manages.
- *<env-entry-type>:* This is a required field if you have a `<env-field>` declared. It declares the Java type of the field.

- *<env-entry-value>:* This is an optional field if you have a `<env-field>` declared. It declares the value of the field.
- *<transaction-type>:* There must be at least one provided, and it is used for session beans only. This element declares that the session bean manages its transaction or allows the container to manage it. The valid values are `Bean` or `Container`.

Referencing other beans

In the simple sample in Chapter 14, you didn't reference any other enterprise beans at all. In an enterprise environment, additional departments might very well be creating reusable components that are shared throughout the organization. Normally, you would interact with other department's enterprise beans by issuing a JNDI lookup on their names and making the remote calls. This hard-coded method works, but isn't the most flexible. What if another department decides to update the name of its enterprise bean? You would be forced to make a coding change.

A better way to approach it would be to use the `<ejb-ref>` element to provide an externalized way of getting the reference. Then you can have the deployment person provide the proper naming and/or renaming to match the target bean. This makes your application more portable and easier to maintain. The following code demonstrates how a typical `<ejb-ref>` declaration might look:

```
<ejb-ref>
  <ejb-ref-name>/Ships</ejb-ref-name>
  <ejb-ref-type>Entity</ejbj-ref-type>
  <home>com.bible.cruise.ejb.ShipHome</home>
  <remote>com.bible.cruise.ejb.Ship</remote>
</ejb-ref>
```

Making environmental entries

Environmental entries are similar to referenced beans. The obvious goal of environmental entries is to decouple the application from hard-coded values and provide a more flexible way to maintain the system. Listing 16-4 shows a sample environmental entry.

Listing 16-4: The <env-entry> Element with Valid Entries

```
<env-entry>
 <env-entry-name>MaxVacationDays</env-entry-name>
 <env-entry-type>java.lang.String</env-entry-type>
 <env-entry-value>21</env-entry-value>
</env-entry>
```

In Listing 16-4, `MaxVacationDays` is externalized outside of the program, so it is easily changed without recoding. The process of externalizing variables is similar to using a properties file in Java. The type is of type `String`. You are limited to certain Java types with `<env-entry-types>`. Those types are `String`, `Integer`, `Long`, `Double`, `Float`, `Byte`, `Boolean`, and `Short`.

Making your programs flexible takes some thought. By using environmental entries, you make your program easy to change. The trick is being proactive and looking for instances where you can take advantage of environmental entries.

Resourcing references

Similar to the environmental entries and referencing to external beans, resource references operate in the same fashion. What types of other resources might you access? You could be accessing Java Message (JMS) connections or JavaMail for instance. If you wanted to implement resource references, environment references, and other EJB references, the JNDI lookup would follow these steps:

1. Get an `initialContext`:

   ```
   InitialContext context = new InitialContext();
   ```

2. Use the lookup method to get your data:

   ```
   // for environmental

   String maximumVacationDays = (String)
        context.lookup("java:comp/env/MaxVacationDays");

   // for references to other beans

   Object ref = context.lookup("java:comp/env/ejb/ShipHome");
   ShipHome home = (ShipHome) PortableRemoteObject.narrow(ref,
        ShipHome.class);

   // for resources

   DataSource ds = (DataSource)
   context.lookup("java:comp/env/jdbc/cruiseDB");
   ```

The preceding Java code snippets show examples of looking up environmental references (`MaxVacationDays`), references to other beans (`ShipHome`), and resource references (`cruiseDB`).

All that effort just covered the `<enterprise-beans>` element. The other important element is the `<assembly-descriptor>`. The assembly descriptor defines the security roles for the EJB.

Using assembly-descriptor

As you might recall, the `assembly-descriptor` element contains information about security roles, method permissions, and transaction attributes. If you do not have any of these requirements, you do not need to a have an `assembly-descriptor`. Listing 16-5 shows the entries in the `ejb-jar` for the `assembly-descriptor`.

Listing 16-5: The Entries in ejb-jar for<assembly-descriptor>

```
<assembly-descriptor>
  <security-role>
    <description>Any Potential Customer</description>
    <role-name>Customer</role-name>
  </security-role>
  <security-role>
    <description>Our trusted agents</description>
    <role-name>Travel Agent</role-name>
  </security-role>
</assembly-descriptor>
```

You use WebSphere Studio Application Developer to create these entries later in this chapter, but first some information about the elements you see in Listing 16-5.

Is the developer the person responsible for assembling applications in your organization? Probably not. You most likely have someone whose responsibility is to understand the ramifications of data integrity. Without data integrity, your information might be incomplete or invalid. Proper transaction processing results in reliable, consistent, and safe processing.

But what if your transactions are unsecured? Would you provide your ATM card to any unknown stranger? The answer is no. So, when you assemble your application, you need to consider not only the transactions, but also the security of those transactions.

This is where the `assembly-descriptor` plays a role. The basic purpose of the `assembly-descriptor` elements is to provide a means of describing the transactional attributes of the beans and the roles and permissions allowed with your beans. The capability to control the transaction management with deployment descriptors is called *declarative transaction management*.

The following elements are contained within the `assembly-descriptor`:

- *<container-transaction>:* This element specifies certain transactional attributes that apply to certain business methods. You can have zero or more container-transactions. For entity beans, you must have `container-transaction` declarations for all the remote and home interface methods. You must have one and only one `<trans-attribute>`. The following `<trans-attribute>` values are allowed:
    - `NotSupported`
    - `Supports`
    - `Required`
    - `RequiresNew`
    - `Mandatory`
    - `Never`
- *<security-role>:* You can define zero or more `<security-role>` elements. Each `security-role` defines the security role that is used to access the bean. A `<security-role>` has only one `role-name`.
- *<method-permission>:* The roles defined in the `<security-role>` are utilized in the `<method-permission>` elements to specify which role(s) are allowed to call the bean's methods.

CROSS-REFERENCE: Transactions are discussed in detail in Chapter 15. That chapter showed examples of the `container-transaction`.

It's time to move on to describing how deployment descriptors participate in security.

Overviewing Security

Security is a big subject, and Chapter 23 is primarily dedicated to security within the WebSphere environment. In this section, you learn about how security relates to deployment descriptors.

There are two principal ways to achieve security within J2EE and WebSphere Application Server as per the J2EE specification.

- The first is to use role-based security defined in XML-based deployment descriptors that get deployed with an EAR file. This conforms to the J2EE specification; whereas in previous versions of WebSphere Application Server this was a serialized file. The deployment descriptors define how a user belongs to a group that is assigned one or many roles. However, you can assign a user to a role directly if you want. In the case of EJBs, methods can be assigned to roles as well.

- The second method to achieve security is programmatically within an API. The primary functionality you can achieve through this is attaining a principal (an authenticated user) and determining whether a principal is within a given role.

You focus on role-based security in this section, and you have an opportunity to use WebSphere Studio Application Developer and let its tooling do the deployment descriptor work for you.

Understanding EJB security

EJB security is role based. Each role is established with the use of the `java.security.Principal` object. The principal represents various logical persons or roles. By using deployment descriptors, you can set these roles at deployment time. So in one case, you can establish student and teacher roles and in another it might be employee and manager roles. Having the capability to change at deployment time makes your application more portable and flexible.

Declaring security-role

The two elements used in declaring `security-role` are as follows:

- *<description>:* You should provide a good description of the role you are creating. This is extemely helpful to the application deployer as she/he tries to map the security role type to the existing operationally defined roles.
- *<role-name>:* This is the logical role name. It has no relationship to any specific security realm.

You can provide as many `<security-role>` elements as you need. Listing 16-6 shows a snippet from the `<assembly-descriptor>` within the `ejb-jar` deployment descriptor.

Listing 16-6: <security-role> in ejb-jar

```
<security-role>
   <description>Any Potential Customer</description>
   <role-name>Customer</role-name>
</security-role>
```

Listing 16-6 describes a role of `Customer` with a description of `Any potential Customer`. In the operational environment, the deployer might assign everyone to this particular role because anyone could be considered a customer.

Describing method-permissions

Establishing a role is not enough to activate role-based security. You also need to describe the methods that are allowed or forbidden for that role. You accomplish this with the `<method-permission>` tag. The format of the deployment descriptor is shown in listing 16-7.

Listing 16-7: Defining <method-permissions>

```
<method-permission>
    <role-name>Customer</role-name>
    <method>
         <ejb-name>Cruise</ejb-name>
          <method-name>getDepartureDate</method-name>
    </method>
</method-permission>
```

This element and information is pretty self-explanatory. When a user with the role of `Customer` accesses the Cruise EJB, the only method that can to be executed is the `getDepartureDate()` method. Any other method calls result in an exception. If you were to put an asterisk (*) in the `<method-name>` element, all methods within the class would be accessible for that role.

> **NOTE**: You cannot use the asterisk in combination with other text, such as `<method-name)get*</method-name>`.

When the application is assembled and ready for deployment, the deployer examines the `<security-role>` tags and maps the roles to corresponding user group(s) in the operational environment. So in a case of an environment of buyers and sellers, you might map buyers to customer and travel agent to sellers.

You have already learned that a single asterisk (*) is a wildcard that allows all methods to be accessible. You can combine the method permissions to form a more complex permission structure. For instance, if you want all travel agents to have access to all methods in the Cruise EJB, but you want limit the access on the same EJB to only `getDepartureDate()` for customers, you can do so. Listing 16-8 shows an example of this scenario.

Listing 16-8: Setting Combined Permissions

```
<method-permission>
    <role-name>Travel Agent</role-name>
    <method>
         <ejb-name>Cruise</ejb-name>
          <method-name>*</method-name>
    </method>
</method-permission>
<method-permission>
    <role-name>Customer</role-name>
    <method>
         <ejb-name>Cruise</ejb-name>
          <method-name>getDepartureDate</method-name>
    </method>
</method-permission>
```

Handling overloaded methods

Perhaps you have noticed that the method names have no signatures. So what happens to methods that are overloaded? The way it works is that any named method automatically applies the method permissions. This can work in a number of cases. You may, however, have overloaded a method and want to apply a role to that specific method. The way you can get the granularity that you seek is to use specific method declarations.

A new element is added that enables you to specify the signature of the method and, thereby, achieve the granularity you desire. Using the `<method-params>` tag in conjunction with the `<method-param>` enables you to add the signature to the method. Listing 16-9 shows an example.

Listing 16-9: Using <method-params> and<method-param> to Increase Method Granularity

```
<method>
    <description>create() method</description>
    <ejb-name>Cruise</ejb-name>
    <method-name>create</method-name>
       <method-params></method-params>
</method>
<method>
    <description>create(int) method</description>
    <ejb-name>Cruise</ejb-name>
    <method-name>create</method-name>
      <method-params>
         <method-param>int</method-param>
      </method-params>
</method>
```

The last `<method-name>` issue has to do with the remote and home interfaces. In both cases, they have the same signature. You need to add a special tag to point to the proper interface. The `<method-intf>` tag specifies whether the method belongs to the `Remote`, `Local`, `LocalHome`, or `Home` interface.

You have been shown how security is prepared within the deployment descriptors. You could add these tags to the descriptors manually, but why do that when WebSphere Studio Application Developer provides a simple way to perform the task? The next section takes you through quick tutorial about how to add the security descriptors.

Adding EJB Security Descriptors

In this section, you use WebSphere Studio Application Developer to add the security roles to your deployment descriptors. At this point, you have two choices about how to prepare for the tutorial.

- You can download the code for the chapter, load the EAR file, and perform the exercises.
- You can utilize the same project that you created in Chapter 14 and make the updates in that project.

If you have forgotten how to create a new workspace and load an EAR file, refer to Chapter 14 for instructions. You should use `CSICruiseStart.ear` as the imported EAR file.

This quick tutorial shouldn't take you long to complete. You create the security roles first and then assign those roles to a particular method:

3. Prepare or start your WebSphere Studio Application Developer environment as stated previously.
4. Switch to the J2EE perspective.
5. Expand the EJB module.
6. Select the AlmostFreeCruiseEJB project.
7. Right-click and select Open With⇨EJB Editor.
8. Click on the Security tab to bring up the Security roles.
9. Click Add and enter **Customer** as the name and **Any Potential Customer** as the description.
10. Click OK and perform the same steps using **Travel Agent** and **Our trusted agents**.
11. Click OK again. Save your work using Ctrl+S. Figure 16-2 shows the results of your work.

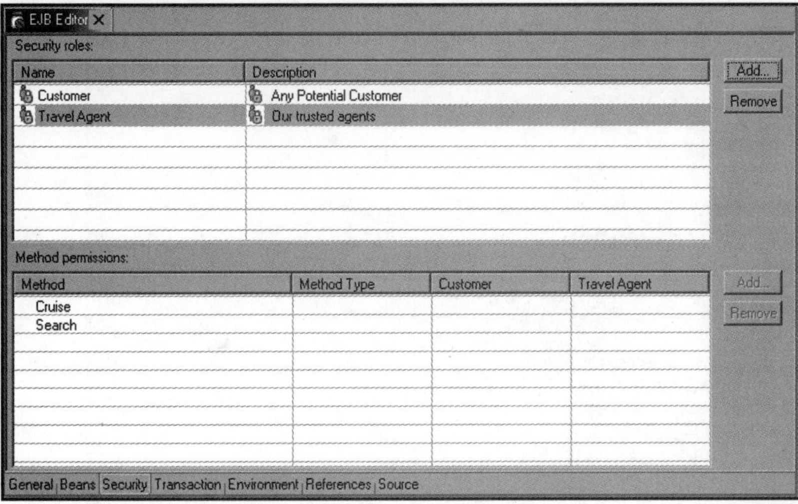

Figure 16-2: With EJB editor in WebSphere Studio Application Developer, it is easy to create security roles.

Now you assign those roles to a specific method:

1. On the navigator, right-click AlmostFreeCruiseEJB, and select Open With⇨EJB Extension Editor.
2. You should be on the Methods tab. Expand the Cruise EJB; expand Remote Methods, and select getDeparture_date().
3. Set the Access intent to READ and Isolation level to REPEATABLE_READ.
4. Under `Run as mode`, select `Use Identity assigned to specific role`, as shown in Figure 16-3.
5. Click on the dropdown menu for Role name and select the Customer role. Enter an appropriate description in the Description field.
6. Figure 16-3 shows an example of your work. Save your work with Ctrl+S.

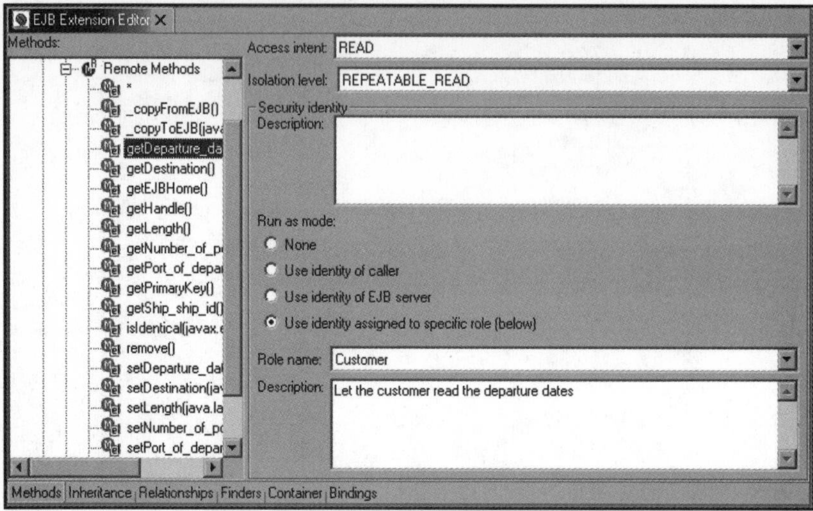

Figure 16-3: The EJB Extension editor is where you reference a role and set Access intent and Isolation levels.

You have successfully assigned a security role to a method. So where are the deployment descriptors? Depending on where you created your WebSphere Studio Application Developer workspace, they are found under the `x:\code\ejb\AlmostFreeCruiseEJB\ejbModule\META-INF`. Figure 16-4 shows the folder structure and files.

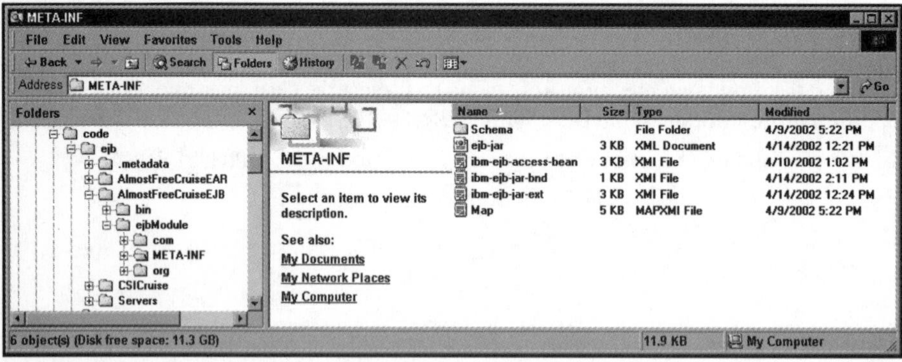

Figure 16-4: You find your deployment descriptors for WebSphere Studio Application Developer in the Project directories under META-INF.

You should review the following files:

- ejb-jar.xml
- ibm-ejb-jar.bnd.xmi
- ibm-ejb-jar-ext.xmi

Examples of all the elements are discussed in this chapter.

Using the Application Assembly Tool (AAT)

In Chapter 22, you learn about the IBM Application Assembly Tool (AAT). The Application Assembly Tool is a utility to assist the J2EE Provider or J2EE Deployer with the generation of J2EE-compliant deployment descriptors and binding attributes.

You could have used AAT to perform some of steps you took in the preceding tutorial, but the focus was on WebSphere Studio Application Developer rather than WebSphere deployment. Following are some of the tasks you use AAT to perform:

- Create an application
- Create an EJB module
- Create a Web module
- Create an application client

You can also run create wizards that walk you through the process.

CROSS-REFERENCE: Chapter 22 shows you how to use the Application Assembly Tool (AAT).

With AAT you can take existing J2EE JAR files and/or WAR files and create the appropriate deployment descriptors and EAR files. With your knowledge of deployment descriptors and some of the tedious entries that you have to perform, using AAT to generate the descriptors is a time saver.

Summary

The J2EE platform enables developers to create different parts of their applications as reusable components. Packaging is the process of assembling components into modules ready for deployment. In WebSphere terminology, this is also known as application assembly. Whenever you assemble an application for a specific environment, the process is known as deployment. With WebSphere, you are able to assemble and customize your application for deployment in a manner that is J2EE compliant.

Implementing J2EE 1.2 deployment descriptors requires using XML. XML is similar to HTML. It has tags and attributes, but they are unique to XML. The benefits of using XML instead the old way of creating deployment descriptors is that it's easy to read and it simplifies building tools to create deployment descriptors. WebSphere Studio Application Developer and the Application Assembly Tool are two tools that can read and write deployment descriptors for you.

Supported by a Data Tag Definition (DTD), deployment descriptors follow a precise pattern of elements that describe data. To make EJB portable, it is necessary to place information that can change into deployment descriptors. The deployment descriptors contain information about external references, environmental references, security, and data mapping.

The EJB deployment descriptors are found in a file named `ejb-jar.xml`. Within the deployment descriptors, the two most important elements are the `<enterprise-beans>` and `<assembly-descriptor>`. These two tags describe the enterprise beans and the beans assembly. You learned how to read and modify the tags.

The `<assembly-descriptor>` and `<enterprise-beans>` tags work in tandem to specify the security roles declared for the beans. You learned that security in EJB is role based. That means you can establish various roles and provide a granular security model to prevent access to classes and methods of classes.

To enhance your knowledge further, a short tutorial was conducted on how to use WebSphere Studio Application Developer to update the deployment descriptors for security.

Chapter 17
EJB Best Practices

In This Chapter

- Examining your design approach and strategies
- Improving Java performance
- Enhancing EJB development
- Optimizing your Web modules

Understanding EJB best practices is about more than enterprise beans. It's about learning from the experience of others. It's always nice to learn from others and not have to reinvent the wheel, especially if you are new to enterprise beans. The goal of this chapter is to present some of the best practices that the authors have utilized over the years. It's not limited to enterprise beans. It covers design approaches, Java performance, EJB best practices, and Web best practices. The chapter is organized in four sections:

- Design approaches and strategies
- Improving Java performance
- EJB module development and implementation
- Web module development and implementation

Each section is divided into three subsections:

- *Proactive practices:* These are topics and practices that proactively guide you to a better solution. You should consider implementing each item.
- *Problem avoidance:* These are known practices that you can use to prevent problems before they occur. Most likely, you have run across these problems before and would like to avoid them when you can.
- *Things to consider:* The items in these sections are meant to make you think and trigger your curiousity. Depending upon your situation, you might want to implement some of these practices.

You do not learn how to implement these best practices in this chapter, but some are scattered throughout the book. Many other books on the market provide detailed examples of the best practices. You are left to explore those on your own. Without further ado, we begin with design strategies.

Introducing Design Approaches/Strategies

This section introduces you to a number of practices that should be thoughtfully considered as you begin a project. There are so many things to think about when you initiate a project; getting off to right start improves your chances of being successful.

Proactive design practices

A lot of factors go into a design. It's very similar to planning a trip. Traveling is like any adventure. Some things you have control over, and some you do not. You need to have some flexibility. So traveling down a road is fine as long as you can reach your destination. Hurrying to reach the destination might mean better spots to vacation or shorter lines. Planning ahead is important, but if your map is old, you might miss a newly created road, or if your nose is always inside a map, you might miss the turn (or hit a Mack truck). If you choose a road that is unsurfaced, you could find yourself going over some bumpy roads. Find the freeway and it's smooth sailing. But watch out! Going too fast can lead to unanticipated delays (for example: a speeding ticket, a missed exit, or an accident).

Today's market is not much different from your summer vacation. You need to be nimble enough to get the job done but aware enough to utilize the best habits possible. Those habits have one thing in common: You need to be able to make modifications that do not hamper the overall design.

Some of the good habits are often taken to extremes where a good habit becomes a burdensome marathon. This section discusses some of the good habits to consider as you try to organize the design iteration. By incorporating these practices into your design, you can be reasonably confidant that you have done a good job of starting your journey.

- *Layers:* Layering provides a separation between vertically stacked services.Your layers could be demarcated by presentation, control, business logic, and supporting services.
- *MVC:* Model View Controller provides a clean separation between the business logic implemented by a model and the view or presentation. In a J2EE implementation, the controller layer is often made up of servlets.
- *Patterns:* Design patterns are proven designs that elegantly implement common programming challenges. Using patterns not only improves your designs but provides a common vocabulary that communicates design decision and implementations. The Gang of Four (GoF) have popularized patterns by identifying and describing the use of various types of design patterns. You will definitely see some of these and other patterns show up in the EJB and Web development sections. The Model View Controller, Façade, and Mediator patterns are three that you see in Chapter 10.

- *UML:* Unified Modeling Language provides a means of documenting behavioral requirements. It's a wonderful way to identify and document requirements, but it's no panacea. Someone must be responsible for ensuring that the documentation is properly archived and updated.

Avoiding design problems

Planning your vacation requires some decision-making. Choosing where to go, how many places to visit along the way, budgeting yourself so you won't be penniless when you return, and getting the kids to buy into the trip are some of the problems you might face. When it comes to design decisions, you need to apply the same thoughtful process. The following list details some thought-providing practices:

- *Identify requirements:* You cannot successfully build a system if you cannot describe what it should do. One of the very first steps is to ensure that your team understands the requirements for your system and that the requirements are properly documented.
- *Prioritize your requirements:* The following steps are included in this part of the process:
  - Determine whether there is value to the business.
  - Always consider the cost to deliver.
  - If time to market is critical, factor in the time to deliver.
  - Evaluate how complex a system you need to develop. You may have many heterogeneous systems to integrate. Try not to underestimate the complexity to deliver.
- *Define your project's scope:* Scope creep is usually a byproduct of the failure to define your project's scope accurately. Strive to document your decisions and get sign-off.
- *Follow a software process:* You need to follow some sort of software practice. Pick one. You have choices, such as the Rational Unified Process (RUP) and extreme programming. Software procesess give you the best chance to ensure that you are able to communicate with your team and the organization. Consider the interaction of a support organization. If supporting organizations don't know your processes, how can they possibly support you?
- *Split large projects into several smaller ones:* There is nothing more frustrating than having your project fail. Projects fail for many reasons, but one of the big reasons is trying to build too much at one time. Avoid that problem by delivering in smaller subprojects or iterations. Your software process should address this problem.
- *Vertical slice:* This is another way to split large projects into smaller ones. Taking a vertical slice is often a good way to to deliver in an incremental way. If your vertical slice satisfies an immediate business need, you achieve two benefits immediately: the satisfaction of delivering and credibility in the eyes of your sponsor.

- *Management buyoff:* Never ever build solutions looking for a problem. So often projects are started based on technology and not on business need. Ensure that your management sanctions the project. With management blessings you get management support and attention. After all, they sponsored it.
- *Test with JUnit:* It is becoming a common practice to develop unit test cases early in the development cycle. JUnit is a testing framework that empowers the developer to create test cases to validate his objects. A common tool for extreme programmers, it's a wonderful way to avoid problems before they happen and it's free! Can't say that happens very often on a vacation.

TIP: You can find information about JUnit by visiting `www.junit.org`.

Things to consider in the design process

You would think when you take a vacation that you would never forget to take the sunscreen. However, it's likely that once or twice you forgot the basic necessities. When starting a new project, it is so easy to get caught up in designing and coding that you dismiss the simple things, such as your work environment. When the project is going hot and heavy is when you'll wish you had spent a little more time to prepare. Don't let that happen. Consider the following:

- *Development environments:* It seems like a no-brainer, but getting a development environment that supports the developer is important. When starting projects that include sophisticated Interactive Development Environment (IDE), you need to have hardware that supports the software and enough memory to ensure that the developer is productive. You should always consider the tooling requirements and procure appropriately.
- *Testing environments:* Do you need more than one testing environment? Surely you need more than a unit test environment. With today's myriad of configurations, you might want to consider creating a testing environment that fairly simulates your production environment. Don't wait until it gets into production to validate your system.
- *Extreme programming:* Many of the items already discussed are common practices of extreme programming. If you have been experiencing some of the problems described, you might want to read up on extreme programming and consider it as your next software process.

Improving Java Performance

Because WebSphere is based upon the Java platform, it is good to discuss some of the good practices that impact Java. First, there is the understanding of how the Java Virtual Machine (JVM) works. Knowing some of the key design points can help you optimize your system operation and code. Also, some known coding efficiencies can help the JVM run your code faster. This section looks at some of them.

Java proactive practices

Proactive practices are really just implementations of good habits. Learned through references or experiences, practicing good habits with Java is your ticket to a better professional life. Nothing is more comforting than knowing that what you are creating is efficient and performs well. (Of course, having a real social life is actually more comforting.) This section points out some of the basics that you should know and practice to instill great habits:

- *Understanding the Java Virtual Machine (JVM).* This area involves the following:
  - *Heap:* The heap is the memory pool where all objects (class instances and arrays) are maintained. You create objects in the heap, but unlike in C/C++, you cannot explicitly remove them. That is left up to the garbage collector. Increasing the size of the Java heap improves throughput until the heap no longer resides in physical memory. After the heap begins swapping to disk, Java performance drastically suffers. Therefore, the maximum heap size needs to be low enough to contain the heap within physical memory.
  - *Initial heap size:* If you know you will be creating large numbers of objects, consider raising the initial heap size in the JVM command-line arguments to a larger number to reduce the times garbage collection attempts to clean up. A side effect is that when the heap is larger, the garbage collector takes longer to run.
  - *Maximum heap size:* In the JVM command-line arguments, you can specify a maximium heap size to limit the amount of physical memory allocated. If the heap size is too large, it gets swapped to disk, which slows the system.
  - *Thread Stacks :*Thread stacks are associated with each Java thread that executes within the JVM. Executing a method within a thread pushes a new method frame on the thread stack. The frame consists of method parameters, local variables defined in the method, and return values. When the method completes, the method is popped off the stack.
- *Understanding coding practices.* These techniques include the following:
  - *Inlining:* Inlining is a performance enhancement technique (often done in C/C++ compilers) where the body of the method is contained within the invoking method (a method in a method). You can help encourage the JVM to take advantage of inlining by keeping your methods small and defining them as private, static, or final. You might consider creating nonbase classes as final, which makes all methods contained as final, too.
  - *Loop termination:* Try not to code methods within a loop condition. A bad example would be `for (int x=0; myObject.size( ); x++);  //.` Use a local variable instead.
  - *Exceptions:* The cost of throwing an exception is relatively high. Throw exceptions on error conditions only and not for normal flow navigation. Proactively try to place multiple catches that support a single `try` statement.

Avoiding Java problems

All along the mantra has been to avoid problems. There are so many other books that discuss Java performance that it won't be covered here. This section presents a few coding practices that are fairly well known but often overlooked. Perhaps Java makes it easy to become complacent. The best way to avoid Java problems is to understand what causes them. The following four coding practices come to mind:

- *String processing:* String concatenation is the textbook bad practice that illustrates the adverse performance impact of creating large numbers of temporary Java objects. Because strings are immutable objects, string concatenation results in temporary object creation that increases Java garbage collection and, consequently, CPU utilization as well. The solution is to use `java.lang.StringBuffer` instead of string concatenation.
- *Efficient file handling:* Buffering data on read and write streams greatly enhances the efficiency of the device.
- *Serialization:* By implementing the serializable interface, you can serialize your object. Keep in mind that if your object is an aggregate object, when the object is serialized, all objects are serialized, and your small object could turn out rather large.
- *RMI:* This remote procedure call is integral to enterprise beans. As objects are sent across the wire they are "flattened" or serialized; therefore, network traffic can be impacted if large objects are sent across the wire. In addition, the objects are deserialized on the other end, so that could take some time. When you are designing enterprise beans, this is the one thing you should aways consider.

Things to consider in Java

Now that you have been introduced to ways of improving your coding, consider another alternative. With tighter budgets, it's easy for your manager to say "No." Undoubtedly you are one of those system professionals who has encountered the manager who is tighter than an airplane bathroom. Always be prepared to present the facts.

Always consider your hardware. When putting up a mission-critical application, always first consider the physical memory, CPU, and I/O. Hardware is cheap and coding improvements rarely exceed the performance you get by increasing memory. Don't spend $10,000 worth of effort for something you can solve for $100.

Enhancing EJB Development

So far the practices have been in areas related to, but not about, enterprise beans. In this section, you learn about some practices that can you utilize as a designer and developer of enterprise applications.

Proactive EJB development practices

As the J2EE specification moves towards 2.0, a lot has changed to improve not only the performance, but also the design practices that improve performance. Performance (or lack thereof) over the network has always been one of the key factors in degradation. This section provides you some design tips to consider before you start coding:

- *Cache initial context:* Getting the initial context is expensive because it is done across the network. If you multiply that by a large number of users, you can guess that performance would be impacted. You might consider using a singleton helper to reduce the impact.
- *Cache EJB homes:* You might consider caching the EJB homes in a helper class that contains a hash table of EJB homes. If the home exists, it is returned; if not, it is created. This practice requires some thoughtful coding as you still need to invalidate the EJB homes and remove the EJB homes from the hash table.
- *Mark EJB methods as read-only:* In cases where you need to read the information, you can cut down on the number of database calls by marking the EJB method as read-only.
- *Rationalize use of transactions:* A good practice is to use session beans as your means of managing transactions and have the session beans access entity beans. If you utilize this practice, you can set all entity bean methods to *<trans-attribute>Mandatory</trans-attribute>*, thereby ensuring that a transaction exists before the invocation.
- *Use a stateless session bean to access entity beans:* You use this practice in Chapter 14 when you let a session bean access the EJB. The benefit is reduced calls across the network.
- *Configure no local copies:* The EJB 1.1 specification states that method calls are to be pass-by-value. *Pass-by-value* means that for every remote method call, the parameters are copied onto the stack before the call is made. This can be expensive. It is possible to specify *pass-by-reference*, which passes the original object reference without making a copy of the object. If the EJB client and EJB server are installed in the same WebSphere Application Server instance, specifying pass-by-reference can improve performance up to 50 percent. See Chapter 24 for more information.

- *Generate access bean design:* Access beans are JavaBean representations of enterprise beans. EJB access beans can greatly simplify client access to enterprise beans and alleviate the performance problems associated with remote calls for multiple enterprise bean attributes. Access beans shield you from the complexities of managing enterprise bean lifecycles. This means that you can program to enterprise beans as easily as you can program to JavaBeans, which greatly simplifies your enterprise bean client programs and helps reduce your overall development time. WebSphere Studio Application Developer provides a wizard to generate access beans.
- *Use object-to-relational mapping with WebSphere Studio Application Developer:* Using tooling that makes developers more productive is a good thing as long as you understand that these tools tend to be propiertary. Proprietary tools have their drawbacks. One is the code generated might be relatively inefficient or inflexible. There are often problems where generated code becomes a black box where errors can occur. As when buying a car, choose wisely based on speed, comfort level, and price.

Avoiding problems in EJB development

The previous section provided you with some predevelopment tips. In this section, you switch from design practices to development best practices. Enterprise beans used unwisely can create serious performance issues. Using these tips as reminders should improve your chances of creating a robust, performance-friendly enterprise application:

- *Avoid tutorial-itus:* Don't assume that a tutorial is necessarily the proper way to implement all enterprise beans. Many tutorials are there to give you a basis for fundamentals and are not necessarily a best practice.
- *Avoid multiple remote calls*: Calling an entity bean from a EJB client causes multiple calls across the network. Network latency then becomes an issue. You can avoid this situation by utilizing session beans (and a single method call) to access your entity beans information.
- *Avoid stateful session EJBs:* Stateful session beans cannot be cached as they are for one user and one user only. Activating or making a stateful session bean passive also takes longer than useing stateless session beans. Stateful session beans also cannot be workload managed.
- *Avoid finders that return large results:* Obviously gathering too much in a results set sends a lot of information across the wire. Depending on how you have implemented your finder, you could be doing multiple queries to obtain a single result. Consider using a session bean or access bean instead.
- *Use entity beans wisely:* Entity beans incur large amounts of overhead. Developing an entity bean with very few attributes just doesn't justify the amount of overhead incurred.

- *Consider JDBC over Entity bean persistence only:* If an entity bean is used as a mechanism to retrieve and store information, consider using JDBC. Entity beans should provide some business logic.
- *Discard stateful session beans when no longer needed:* The EJB container passivates session beans when it reaches the allocated memory. Stateful beans that are no longer used congest the container over time. Write the code to remove stateful session beans when they are no longer needed.
- *Test your enterprise beans*: Enough said.

Things to consider during EJB development

It's decision-making time! During some point within the development of enterprise beans you will be confronted with some key decision you must consider. This section introduces some practices to consider while in the heat of battle:

- *Consider WebSphere EJB caching:* WebSphere supports three levels of caching (levels A-C). Caching level A has exclusive access to data and is therefore faster. Option C enables multiple users to access but is slower. So depending upon your circumstance, you might be able to utilize option A.
- *Consider helper beans:* Often referred as bulk accessors, helper beans create and return value objects to represent the data in the entity bean. These help solve the significant runtime performance penalty that can occur when crossing the network on an RMI-IIOP call.
- *Use two CMPs to one BMP:* If you have multiple container-managed beans calling each other, you might find some performance improvements by moving to a bean-managed persistence bean and eliminating one bean. In this case, you might remove one bean and replace it with a direct call to JDBC.
- *Write JDBC within a session bean:* You don't have to use container-managed persistence or bean-managed persistence. You can write straight JDBC from a session bean to the the job being done.
- *Don't use complex data types:* Complex data types must be serialized if they cross the wire. If there is information that you do not need, you can make use of the transient `keyword`.
- *Utilize profiling tools*: Tools, such as Wily Introscope, Sitraka JProbe, and AltaWorks Panorama, can open up a new window of knowledge. Notice that they don't open Pandora's box. With profiling tools, you are able to see how the Java Virtural Machine (JVM) is reacting to your code. Some of the tools, such as Panorama, do even more than that and reach horizontally across environments showing performance bottlenecks in Web servers and databases. Although some of these tools should not be run in production environments, some of them can run with little degradation.

Optimizing the Web Module

The Web container is where you run servlets and JavaServer Pages (JSPs). The Servlet API provides various methods and models that can impact performance. Consider the best practices described in this section seriously. Because your user interface is what the user sees, his or her perception of performance can mean the difference between a sold customer and a disgruntled user.

Proactive Web-module practices

- *Do not use SingleThreadModel:* SingleThreadModel is a tag interface that a servlet can implement to transfer its re-entry problem to the servlet engine. As such, `javax.servlet.SingleThreadModel` is part of the J2EE specification. The WebSphere servlet engine handles the servlet's re-entry problem by creating separate servlet instances for each user. This slows down processing so SingleThreadModel should be avoided.
- *Use JDBC connection pooling:* Connection pooling can improve the response time of any application that requires connections, especially Web-based applications. When a user makes a request over the Web to a resource, the resource accesses a datasource. Most user requests do not incur the overhead of creating a new connection because the datasource might locate and use an existing connection from the pool of connections.
- *Use* `HttpServlet.init()` *to perform expensive operations that are only done once:* Because the servlet `init()` method is invoked when servlet instance is loaded, it is the perfect location to carry out expensive operations that need only be performed during initialization. By definition, the `init()` method is thread-safe. The results of operations in the `HttpServlet.init()` method can be cached safely in servlet instance variables, which become read-only in the servlet service method.
- *Minimize use of* `system.out.println`*:* Although developers use `println` as a form of debugging, you should not use this in production applications. Because `system.out.println` statements and similar constructs synchronize processing for the duration of disk I/O, they can significantly slow throughput. They also clutter the WebSphere logs.
- *Minimize synchronization in servlets:* Servlets are multithreaded. Servlet-based applications have to recognize and handle this. (See Chapter 9 for more information.) However, if large sections of code are synchronized, an application effectively becomes single threaded, and throughput decreases.

Avoiding problems in Web modules

This section moves on from best practices for enterprise beans over to best practices for Web modules. A majority of your J2EE applications most likely involve Web modules. Chapters 9 through 12 discuss servlets and JavaServer Pages (JSP).

This section provides some best practices that prevent performance problems:

- *Do not store large objects in HttpSessions:* Large applications require using persistent `HttpSessions`. However, there is a cost. An `HttpSession` must be read by the servlet whenever it is used and rewritten whenever it is updated. This involves serializing the data and reading it from and writing it to a database. In most applications, each servlet requires only a fraction of the total session data. However, by storing the data in the `HttpSession` as one large object, an application forces WebSphere Application Server to process the entire `HttpSession` object each time. WebSphere Application Server has `HttpSession` configuration options that can optimize the performance impact of using persistent `HttpSessions`.

CROSS-REFERENCE: The `HttpSession` configuration options are discussed in detail in the WebSphere InfoCenter documentation and in Chapters 11 and Chapter 21.

- *Do not create HttpSession in JSP by default:* By default, JSP files create `HttpSessions`. This is in compliance with J2EE to facilitate the use of JSP implicit objects, which can be referenced in JSP source and tags without explicit declaration. `HttpSession` is one of those objects. If you do not use `HttpSession` in your JSP files, you can save some performance overhead with the following JSP page directive: `<%@ page session="false"%>`.
- *Release HttpSessions when finished:* The application explicitly and programmatically releases `HttpSession` using the API, `javax.servlet.http.HttpSession.invalidate ();` quite often, programmatic invalidation is part of an application log-out function. WebSphere Application Server destroys the allocated `HttpSession` when it expires. WebSphere Application Server can maintain only a certain number of `HttpSessions` in memory. When this limit is reached, WebSphere Application Server serializes and swaps the allocated `HttpSession` to disk. In a high volume system, the cost of serializing many abandoned `HttpSessions` can be quite high.
- *Don't use* `Beans.instantiate()` *to create new beans:* The method, `java.beans.Beans.instantiate()` creates a new bean instance either by retrieving a serialized version of the bean from disk or creating a new bean if the serialized form does not exist. The performance problem is that each time `java.beans.Beans.instantiate` is called, the file system is checked for a serialized version of the bean. As usual, such disk activity in the critical path of your Web request can be costly. To avoid this overhead, simply use `new` to create the instance.

Things to consider with Web modules

Consider adding Web servers and additional application servers. In general, providing the capability to manage workloads helps distribute the workload among multiple machines. Adding additional Web servers and implementing an IP sprayer can improve performance and reduce failover.

CROSS-REFERENCE: Chapter 24 covers adding Web and application servers in depth.

Summary

Best practices fall into many categories. There are best practices for all facets of application development, starting with project initiation through deployment. This chapter presented best practices for design, Java utilization, EJB development, and Web development.

Each best practice was partitioned into one of three categories. *Proactive practices* presents best practices that you can implement to avoid problems. *Problem avoidance* covers known issues that take advantage of the best practice to prevent problems before it's too late. Finally, *Things to consider* sections give you the opportunity to evaluate and plan to implement practices that could improve performance, reduce maintenance, and provide planning and structure to your environment.

Chapter 18
Using XML/XSLT in WebSphere

In This Chapter

- Understanding XML basics
- Getting to know the XML Schema and DTD
- Benefiting from XSLT
- Performing an XSLT transformation using XPath
- Developing an XML application using WSAD
- Building an application using stylesheets

In this chapter, you learn the basics of the Extensible Markup Language (XML) and the Extensible Stylesheet Language Transformation (XSLT) mechanism. XML has quickly become the standard used to structure and describe data, as well as to pass information to and from Web applications. You learn a little of the history that explains why XML is so popular. You also learn about the XML Schema and DTD, which are used to validate XML documents. XSLT transformations are covered, and the basics of XPath are discussed. Finally, you become familiar with the tools that WebSphere provides to help you create applications that use XML and XSLT, and you are guided through building an XML-based application using WSAD.

Introducing XML

XML is a powerful technology concerned with structuring and describing data. Like HTML, it is a markup language. But unlike HTML, it isn't limited to a finite tag set. XML gives you the ability to define tags and the relationships between them.

Before delving into the details of XML, look at an example of a simple XML document in Listing 18-1. XML looks similar to HTML. Although XML is related to HTML, XML is much more powerful and flexible.

Listing 18-1: A Simple XML Document

```
<?xml version="1.0"?>
<city>
 <subdivision>
  <name>Highland</name>
  <block number="1">
   <lot number="20">1474 Cumberland Avenue</lot>
   <lot number="4">1479 Cumberland Avenue</lot>
  </block>
  <block number="9">
   <lot number="3">339 15th Street</lot>
   <lot number="2">411 15th Street</lot>
  </block>
 </subdivision>
 <subdivision>
  <name>Awbrey</name>
  <block number="6">
   <lot number="2">566 Greyhawk Drive</lot>
   <lot number="3">548 Greyhawk Drive</lot>
   <lot number="4">552 Greyhawk Drive</lot>
  </block>
  <block number="4">
   <lot number="9">635 Sonora Avenue</lot>
  </block>
  </subdivision>
</city>
```

Notice that the components of Listing 18-1 have an organized, hierarchal, and descriptive structure. The city element contains multiple `subdivision` elements; each `subdivision` element contains a `name` and one or more `block` elements. Each `block` element includes one or more `lot` elements. Each `lot` element contains a text entry, which is the address of that lot.

Figure 18-1 shows part of the tree structure of the hierarchy from Listing 18-1. Block number 9 of the Highland subdivision element is fully expanded and shows the lots and addresses it contains.

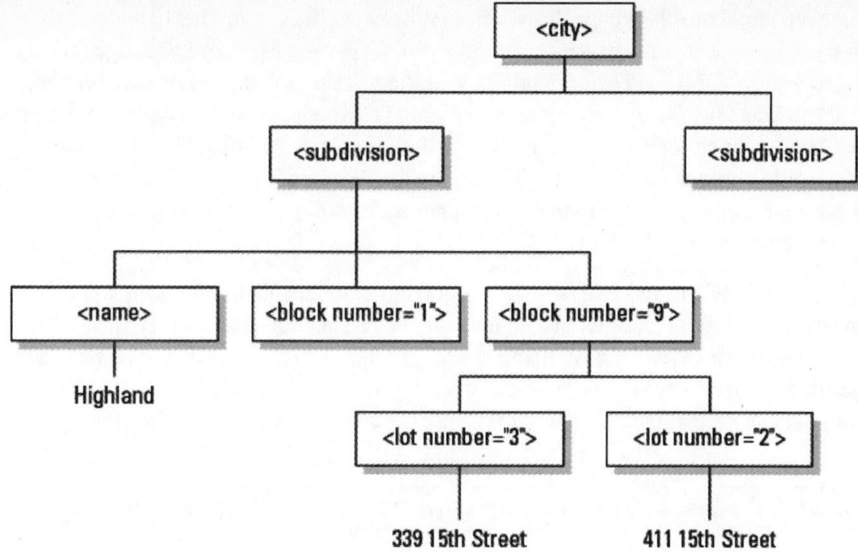

Figure 18-1: This is the data from Listing 18-1 shown in a logical tree structure.

Understanding the need for XML

In a perfect world, any computer program would be able to exchange data with any other computer program on any platform. The data would be understood universally and would have the capability to combine the interchangeability of text files with the efficiency and descriptive advantages of binary format.

For years dating back to the dawn of computers, engineers have sought a common data format. In the 1980s, Standard Generalized Markup Language (SGML) emerged. SGML is a powerful and extensible tool used to mark up data, or in other words, add descriptive metadata. Just like XML, SGML can be used to create infinite numbers of markup languages. SGML took hold because it was useful for cataloging and indexing, particularly in large document-management systems.

SGML is such a complicated language, however, that its capabilities were never added to mainstream word processors or browsers. Around 1990, Hypertext Markup Language (HTML) evolved as a subset of SGML. HTML contains a specific vocabulary and was created as the universal markup language for displaying information. HTML was simple enough that it could be written with any text editor and presented with a Web browser. Although HTML is simpler than SGML, it still is limited to displaying documents in a Web browser. For example, an application cannot extract all the lot numbers for a particular subdivision in a city from an HTML document. But it can with XML.

XML is also subset of SGML but with a different objective: to be able to represent any data using a standard format. For example, in Listing 18-1, there's no question that `Highland` is the name of a subdivision. What's special about XML syntax is that virtually any text can be used to describe the data. For example, you can use `foo` instead of `subdivision`, although most programmers agree that the best choice is to use descriptive and meaningful element names.

NOTE: XML is not considered a programming language. Rather, it describes a particular syntax.

Understanding the advantages of using XML

If the advantages of XML aren't immediately obvious, consider the following example. A programmer needs to read data about a city grid into an application. Initially it might seem easiest to format the data in rows and create some rules that dictate the placement of the data. Each row can represent an address, so part of the data might look like the following:

```
Awbrey 6 2 566 Greyhawk Drive
Awbrey 6 3 548 Greyhawk Drive
Awbrey 6 4 552 Greyhawk Drive
```

At this point, the decision seems reasonable. The program that reads the data knows that the name of the subdivision starts at the beginning of the line. After the first space, a digit represents the block number. Following the second space, a digit represents the block number. Continuing along, after the third space, several digits that make up the address are followed by another space and the street name, which might contains spaces.

The logic works as long as the same program doesn't also have to try to read the addresses in the following data:

```
Northwest Crossings 18 1 4000 Yellowtail Hawk Avenue Apartment 114
Northwest Crossings 18 2 548 1/2 NW Mt. Washington Drive Suite B
Foxborough 50 5 1616 NE Aspen View Court
```

This data causes problems. Some addresses have apartment numbers; others include fractions and subdivisions, and streets have spaces in their names; some lot numbers have two digits, and so on. You need to make a choice: Either complicate the reading program to account for additional address types, or limit the types of addresses that can be handled. Neither is a good choice. The first takes time and will still be unable to handle every address variation and additional changes in the future, and the second fails because complexities in data aren't handled at all.

If the previous addresses were represented in an XML document, part of it would look like Listing 18-2. Although this example is more complex than that in Listing 18-1, it is more flexible because it keeps different parts of the address separate. You will intuitively recognize the reason for this when you read the sections on XSLT and XPath.

Listing 18-2: XML Describes Its Data

```
<city>
. . .
 <subdivision>
  <name>Northwest Crossings</name>
  <block number="18">
   <lot number="1">
     <address>
      <number>4000</number>
      <fraction></fraction>
      <direction></direction>
      <street>Yellowtail Hawk Avenue</street>
       <apartment-suite>Apt 114</apartment-suite>
     </address>
   </lot>
   <lot number="2">
    <address>
      <number>548</number>
      <fraction>1/2</fraction>
      <direction>NW</direction>
      <street>Mt. Washington Drive</street>
      <apartment-suite>Suite B</apartment-suite>
    </address>
   </lot>
  </block>
 </subdivision>
 . . .
</city>
```

Listing 18-2 shows a more flexible description of the city grid data. In XML, elements can be added, removed, or changed without requiring the parsing program to change as well. Better yet, parsers are already available to deal with getting information from XML files. They still work when the XML changes as long as you follow XML syntax.

Aside from the flexibility of its content, XML has other advantages:

- XML content can be delivered in multiple output formats, such as Portable Document Format (PDF), HTML, or PostScript.
- Content is maintained separately from presentation (structure and style). Content and presentation are intermingled in HTML, limiting the capability to extract only the information from the HTML pages and present it in other ways.
- Advanced searching is supported. The hierarchal structure of XML makes XML documents easy to parse and manipulate. And because content is separate from presentation, displaying data based on individual parameters is possible. For example, a county records search might be based on street name or subdivision, or both. Search results can be displayed in groups by subdivision, street name, or city.

Introducing the family of XML technologies

The XML family of technologies includes multiple specifications, each of which covers different aspects of its capabilities. Here is a partial list of some of the specifications you should be aware of:

- XML 1.0 describes syntax that XML documents should follow. It covers most everything you want to know about writing, parsing, and manipulating XML documents. WSAD provides an XML editor.
- Document Type Definitions (DTDs) provide a means for validating XML documents. An XML document is valid when it adheres to the rules defined in its DTD. These are also important when other developers need to produce documents that are compatible with other XML documents. DTDs describe and dictate what an XML document should look like. DTDs are not required; however it is a good idea to use one if your data needs to follow certain rules. This is especially important when XML is displayed or exchanged in wide environments, such as in e-commerce or business-to-business applications. WSAD includes a DTD editor.
- A Schema is similar to a DTD except that Schemas are XML documents themselves. Schemas have several other advantages over DTDs: You can display and manipulate them with the Document Object Model (DOM). They are modifiable at runtime, and because they are XML documents, their syntax is familiar to those who know XML. Schemas also have more advanced features than DTDs. WSAD provides an XML Schema Editor and can even create an XML Schema based on an existing XML document. An example of a Schema is shown in Listing 18-3.

- XPath describes a language that enables different parts of an XML document to be referenced. XPath lets you pick and choose which elements will be processed or displayed. XPath is discussed further in the sections on performing an XSLT transformation.
- Extensible Stylesheet Language for Transformations (XSLT) is used to transform a document from one type to another. WSAD provides an XSL trace editor, which lets you view a transformation in real time.

> **NOTE**: These specifications can be found on the W3C (World Wide Web Consortium) Web site at `www.w3.org`.

The details of each of these technologies are beyond the scope of this book. It is important to understand, however, that XML documents must meet the following criteria:

- They must be valid, meaning that they must conform to the restrictions set forth in their corresponding XML Schema or DTD.
- They must be well-formed, meaning that they must follow the syntax defined in the XML 1.0 specification.

Listing 18-3 shows an example of an XML Schema that can be used to validate the XML shown in Listing 18-1.

Listing 18-3: Schema Document That Can Be Used to Validate XML

```
<xsd:schema xmlns:xsd="http://www.w3.org/2001/XMLSchema">
 <xsd:annotation>
  <xsd:documentation xml:lang="en">
   City Grid Schema for WebSphere Application Server Bible
  </xsd:documentation>
 </xsd:annotation>
 <xsd:element name="city" type="CityType"/>
 <xsd:complexType name="CityType">
  <xsd:sequence>
   <xsd:element name="subdivision" type="SubdivisionType"
minOccurs="1" maxOccurs="unbounded"/>
  <xsd:sequence>
 </xsd:complexType>
 <xsd:complexType name="SubdivisionType">
  <xsd:sequence>
   <xsd:element name="name" minOccurs="1" maxOccurs="1">
    <xsd:simpleType>
     <xsd:restriction base="xsd:string">
     <xsd:enumeration value="Awbrey"/>
     <xsd:enumeration value="Highland"/>
     <xsd:enumeration value="Overturf"/>
     <xsd:enumeration value="Skyliner"/>
     </xsd:restriction>
   </xsd:simpleType>
```

Listing 18-3 *(Continued)*

```
  </xsd:element>
  <xsd:element name="block" type="BlockType" minOccurs="1"
maxOccurs="unbounded"/>
   </xsd:sequence>
 </xsd:complexType>
 <xsd:complexType name="BlockType">
  <xsd:sequence>
   <xsd:element name="lot" type="LotType" minOccurs="1"
maxOccurs="10"/>
  </xsd:sequence>
  <xsd:attribute name="number"
type="xsd:positiveInteger"/>
 </xsd:complexType>
 <xsd:complexType name="LotType">
  <xsd:attribute name="number" type="xsd:positiveInteger"
use="required"/>
 </xsd:complexType>
</xsd:schema>
```

Listing 18-3 shows a particular XML Schema, which is one of many possible variations, depending on the restrictions required for the data. This particular Schema requires that the `<city>` element contain at least one `<subdivision>` element, and that the `<subdivision>` element adhere to the requirements in the `complexType`, and `SubdivisionType`.

Look at the `complexType` for `SubdivisionType`. The `<xsd:sequence>` expression requires the `<name>` element to appear before any of the `<block>` elements. The `<name>` element is further restricted by the `<xsd:restriction>` and `<xsd:enumeration>` expressions to have one of four possible values: `Awbrey`, `Highland`, `Overturf`, or `Skyliner`. Further along in the XML Schema, see that the `SubdivisionType` requires a `<block>` element, which can occur an unlimited number of times and is of type `BlockType`. The `BlockType` type has a `number` attribute, which must be a positive integer.

There are numerous other ways to constrain the format and kinds of data that are allowed in an XML document. For the complete specification, see `www.w3c.org/XML/Schema`.

> **NOTE**: To create an XML Schema, select the Web application; right-click, and choose New, Other, XML, and then XML Schema.

Introducing XSLT

XSLT is used to transform XML documents to other text-based documents. Probably the most common application of XSLT is transforming XML documents to HTML documents.

Here are the two most common uses of XSLT:

- *Turn one XML document into another by changing how data is ordered or adding special formatting:* This feature comes in handy for business-to-business applications, because each company might have its own way of storing information; but when two companies share this information, they can do so using a common format.
- *Display content of an XML file in a Web browser by transforming it to HTML:* You can extract all or only some of the information from an XML document and display it alongside static information. For example, the `address` label might precede the actual value of the address, which is extracted from the XML. Or, an image map can be used to link to a dynamic URL, provided from the XML.

Understanding the benefits of using XSLT

XSLT has numerous benefits over other dynamic Web page technologies. The following list offers some of the most talked about:

- Unlike HTML and JSP, which intermingle content with presentation, XSLT cleanly separates the two. Data can change freely without a Web developer ever having to modify its presentation.
- Unlike JavaServer Pages (JSPs), XSLT is free of side effects. JSP side effects can occur when global variables are accessed by multiple classes in an API, which might cause unexpected results. This leaves a programmer worrying about the order in which functions are called. XSLT and JSPs can be compared in this context, because JSPs have direct access to the Java API.
- Imperative programming languages, such as JavaScript, C++ or Java, need to know exactly *how* to perform some operation. XSLT just needs to know *what* you want done. That is why it's referred to as a declarative language. This frees you from having to worry about whether your code is running optimally. XSLT does all the work.
- Like HTML, XML is simple enough that nontechnical writers can provide its content. But unlike HTML, which mingles content and presentation, formatting and navigation through the written content can be left to programmers (using XSLT).

NOTE: XSL is short for Extensible Stylesheet Language. The 'T' in XSLT refers to the transformation from one XML document to another.

Performing an XSLT transformation using XPath

Three things are necessary to perform an XSLT transformation:

- An XML document that provides the content.
- An XSLT engine that does the actual transformation. This engine includes an XSLT processor and an XML parser. Usually, these resources are accessed by a Java servlet.
- An XSLT style sheet, which contains the instructions about what you want to transform and what the resulting format should be.

Within an XSLT stylesheet, you'll see XSL, which is the language used within the stylesheet and XPath, a language used to reference specific sections of an XML document. XSL and XPath go hand-in-hand, as shown in Listing 18-4.

Listing 18-4: University Course Information Represented in XML

```
<?xml version="1.0"?>
<university>
  <course>
    <subject>Biology</subject>
    <instructor id="649">
      <first-name>Robert</first-name>
      <last-name>Inman<last-name>
    </instructor>
    <classroom>1001</classroom>
  </course>
  <course>
    <subject>Statistics</subject>
    <instructor id="442">
      <first-name>Reva</first-name>
      <last-name>Smith</last-name>
    </instructor>
    <classroom>1002</classroom>
  </course>
</university>
```

Listing 18-4 shows a simple XML document containing information for two courses at a university. You want to use XSLT to display some of this information in a Web browser. You want to display the first and last name of each instructor in one column, and the subject of the course that she/he teaches in the next column. Listing 18-5 shows the stylesheet to do this.

Listing 18-5: The Style Sheet Used to Display Some Course Information

```
<?xml version="1.0"?>
<xsl:stylesheet version="1.0"
                xmlns:xsl="http://www.w3.org/1999/XSL/Transform">
<xsl:output method="html"/>

<xsl:template match="/">
 <HTML>
  <HEAD>
   <TITLE>Instructor and Course List</TITLE>
  </HEAD>
  <BODY>
   <xsl:apply-templates select="university"/>
  </BODY>
 </HTML>
</xsl:template>

<xsl:template-match="university">
 <TABLE>
 <xsl:for-each select="course">
  <TR>
   <TD>
    <xsl:value-of select="instructor/first-name"/> 
    <xsl:value-of select="instructor/last-name"/>
   </TD>
   <TD>
    <xsl:value-of select="subject"/>
   </TD>
  </TR>
 </xsl:for-each>
 </TABLE>
</xsl:template>

</xsl:stylesheet>
```

Listing 18-5 includes some XSL, some HTML, and some XPath. The XSLT engine processes the stylesheet depending on what it finds in its templates. This example shows two templates. The first starts as follows:

```
<xsl:template match="/">
```

This line denotes the document root. The document root is not the same thing as the root element of a tree structure. You can think of the document root as the root of a directory structure. It doesn't specify a single document or directory, but rather a starting point. What this means is that any references to other locations (using XPath) should start from the root of the document. This is demonstrated with the reference to the other template:

```
<xsl:apply-templates select="university"/>
```

This line means that the processor should traverse the tree structure from before the outermost element until it encounters the `university` element. From the current location, or context node, every course element that is encountered undergoes the same processing. This is denoted as follows:

```
<xsl:for-each select="course">
```

A row is created with the `HTML` <TR> element, a column `<TD>`, and then the following lines:

```
<xsl:value-of select="instructor/first-name"/> 
<xsl:value-of select="instructor/last-name"/>
```

This code directs the processor to put the text value of the `first-name` and the `last-name` of the `instructor` element. The `first-name` and `last-name` elements are considered "children" of the `instructor` element. A space is explicitly placed in between them because HTML ignores white space.

Next, you close the column with `</TD>` and a new one starts. The next column extracts the subject of the course (that is, the course in the "context node"):

```
<xsl:value-of select="subject"/>
```

It then closes the column and row. The `for-each` directive closes, and then the table and template close.

The following is output from this transformation:

```
Robert Inman        Biology
Reva Smith          Statistics
```

Although this example shows XPath at work in an XSL stylesheet, it barely scratches the surface of XPath's capabilities. If you are going to be using XSLT, it is important to understand and get to know XPath.

XPath has the following capabilities:

- XPath can extract the attributes from an element by using the `@` operator, such as with `@id`.
- XPath can specify certain elements using a filter. For example, `instructor[ @id=' 442' ]` matches any `instructor` element that is a child of the context node whose `id` attribute is equal to `442`.
- XPath has a number of useful functions, such as `text()` and `comment()`, which select the text of the context node and any comments, respectively. Boolean and positional functions are part of the XPath specification as well.
- XPath can use logical operators. For example, `first-name | last-name` specifies either the `first-name` or the `last-name` element within the context node. Wildcards can also be used. You can use `university/*/*/last-name` to specify the `last-name` element from any course and any instructor in the university.

- XPath can use Boolean functions, which convert the results to a Boolean in the case of `boolean()` and `not()`, or to the number `0` in the case of `false()` or to `1` for `true()`. For example, `not(false())` returns `true`, `boolean(5)` returns `true`, and `boolean(0)` returns `false`.

> **NOTE**: The XPath specification can be found at: at `www.w3.org/TR/xpath`.

Putting the pieces together

So far you have learned the basics of XML and XSLT and some of the advantages of using XML in your applications, and you know where to find details on each of the specifications of XML technologies.

Unfortunately, using XSLT isn't as simple as browsing to a file and seeing the transformed results. That is why the XSLT engine is necessary. You also need to be able to validate XML documents, view and edit XSL documents, and possibly manipulate and compile Java source files to create XML-based applications. Fortunately, WSAD includes tools for performing each of these functions. The next section discusses some of these tools and puts them to work building a sample application.

Developing an XML Application Using WSAD

Applications that use XML and XSLT include a number of necessary components in order to run properly. Fortunately, WSAD comes with a rich set of visual XML development tools. It provides components for creating and editing XML files, building DTDs and XML Schemas, using XSLT, and defining mappings between XML and different data sets. This section describes the XML development tools and puts several of them to work in an XML-based application.

Introducing XML development tools

The following list is a summary of the XML tools that are available with WSAD:

- The *XML editor* is used to create and view XML files. You can create brand-new XML files or use existing XML Schemas or DTDs to build them. The XML editor also lets you validate your XML against a DTD or XML Schema.
- The *XML Schema Editor* is used to create, validate, and manipulate XML Schemas. You can also use it to generate JavaBeans for creating XML instances of an XML Schema.
- The *DTD editor* is a tool used to view and create DTDs or generate XML Schema files from an existing DTD. It also lets you generate a default HTML based on a DTD.
- The *XSL Trace editor* lets you see what happens during a transformation. You can visually step through an XSL transformation script and see each rule execute. You can also use it to view the resulting XML or HTML as it is created.

- The *XML to XML mapping editor* is used to map multiple XML source files to one target XML file, adding XPath expressions, Java methods, conversion functions, or groupings to the mapping. It also lets you delete, add, or edit mappings. XSLT script can be generated from defined mappings, and the generated script can be used to transform XML files.
- The *RDB to XML mapping editor* is used to define a mapping between an XML file and tables in a relational database (RDB). After a mapping is defined, you can generate a document access definition (DAD) script that can be run by the DB2 XML extender, which can either compose XML files from DB2 data, or vice versa.
- The *XML and SQL query wizards* are used to create XML file(s) from results of a SQL query. They can also do the reverse: generate a SQL query based on the resulting XML file. Optionally, you can create a DTD or XML Schema based on the data.

Perhaps the most straightforward way to illustrate how to use WSAD to create an XML application and become familiar with some of WSAD's XML tools is by example.

> **ON THE WEB:** To follow along with the style sheets example, download the code for this chapter from the companion site. Save it to a location that you can easily access. The download consists of an XML file, two XSL files, a Java servlet source file, and one HTML file.

Using stylesheets

This example takes you through how to use stylesheets on a server. First you create a new Web project called `GridProject`, and then you create a simple HTML page called `ListOptions.html` that gives two choices for displaying data. Next you create an XML file, `citygrid.xml`, and two stylesheets: `addresslist.xsl` and `subdivision.xsl`, each of which displays XML data differently. You do not use an XML Schema for this example. You also create the `ListServlet` servlet that acts as the controller during a transformation. Finally, you run the application in the WebSphere test environment by following these steps:

1. Start WebSphere Studio Application Developer.
2. Create a new Web Project. Choose File ⇨ New ⇨Project. Highlight Web, and select Web Project. Click Next. This opens the Create a Web Project screen where you can specify the name, location, and EAR project.

3. Enter **GridProject** as the project's name. Leave the default location check box checked. Enter **GridEAR** as the enterprise application project name. The context root is filled in automatically and should be the same as the project name, `GridProject`. Click Finish. Figure 18-2 shows the Create a Web Project screen with these entries.

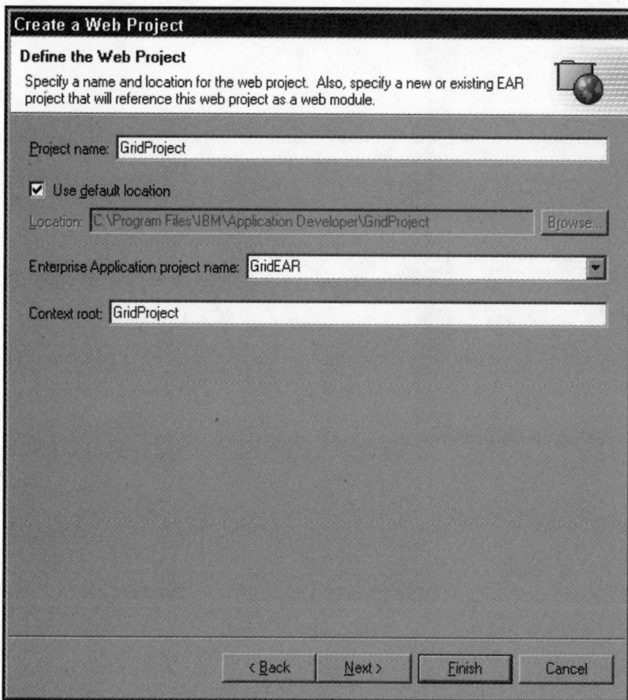

Figure 18-2: The Create a Web Project screen is the first screen that is shown when creating a new Web project. Here, the name of the project, Enterprise Application Project Name, and Context Root are specified.

4. The GridProject is created. In the Navigator window on the left side of the workbench, you see two new entries: GridProject and GridEAR. Take the time to expand the GridProject folder. Notice that several subfolders have been created for you automatically. Figure 18-3 shows the structure partially expanded. You add files to this structure as you continue with the example.

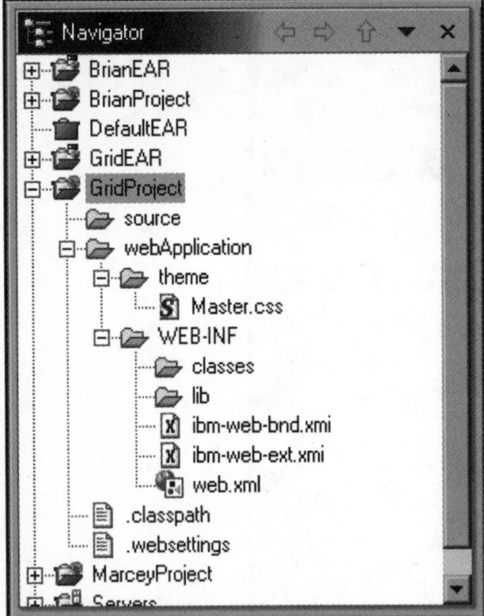

Figure 18-3: This is the initial structure of the GridProject before you create the HTML, XSL, and XML files.

5. Next, right-click the `webApplication` folder. Choose New ⇨ HTML file. Name the file **ListOptions.html** and be sure that it is created in the `webApplication` folder. Figure 18-4 shows the Create an HTML File screen. Click Finish. You have just created the HTML file that will be used to choose a listing option.

NOTE: If you create a file in the wrong folder, you can later cut and paste it to the appropriate location.

6. Copy and paste the contents of the `ListOptions.html` file that you downloaded into the one that you just created. Save the file.

TIP: To open files for cutting and pasting outside of WSAD, right-click the file, choose Open with, and select Wordpad. From there, you can copy and paste contents into files within WSAD.

7. Next, you create a folder to hold the XML and XSL files. Right-click the `WEB-INF` folder, which is located under the `webApplication` folder, and choose New⇨Folder. Name the folder **xml** and click Finish. You can name this folder whatever you want; however the servlet that you create later specifies the xml folder as the location of the XML and XSL documents.

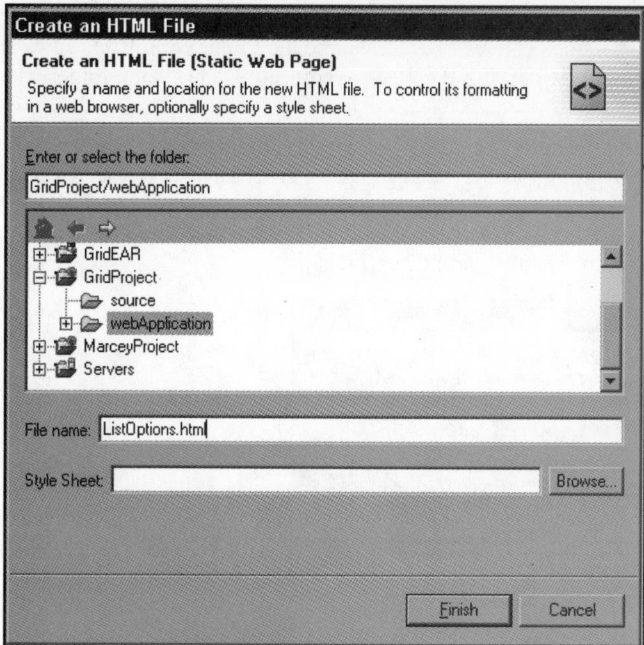

Figure 18-4: The Create an HTML File screen is where you specify the name and location of the new file and choose a style sheet if desired.

8. Right-click the xml folder and choose New ⇨ Other; highlight XML, and select XML File. Click the Next button. Choose Create an XML File from Scratch, and click Next.
9. Name the file **citygrid.xml** and click Finish. Highlight `citygrid.xml` to edit it. Copy and paste the contents of the `citygrid.xml` file that you downloaded into the file you just created. This file contains the data that will be used in the City Grid application.
10. Right-click the xml folder again and choose New ⇨ Other; highlight XML, and select XSL. Click Next and name the file **addresslist.xsl**. Copy and paste the contents provided into this new file. This stylesheet lists addresses and lot numbers from the XML file.
11. Create another XSL file in the xml folder. Name it **subdivisionlist.xsl** and paste in the provided content. This stylesheet lists subdivisions and block numbers from the XML file.

12. Next, you create some folders for your Java servlet. Right-clock the source directory beneath the GridProject. Choose New ⇨Folder. Name the folder **com.** Right-click the `com` folder, and create a folder beneath it called **mycompany**. This is the folder where the Java servlet class file goes.

13. Now you create the servlet. Right-click the `mycompany` folder and choose New ⇨ Servlet. Enter **com.mycompany** as the package name. Enter **ListServlet** as the servlet name. Leave the remaining settings unchanged and click Finish. Figure 18-5 shows the Create the Servlet Class screen. Click Next. Leave the Add to web.xml check box checked and all other settings as they are. Click Finish.

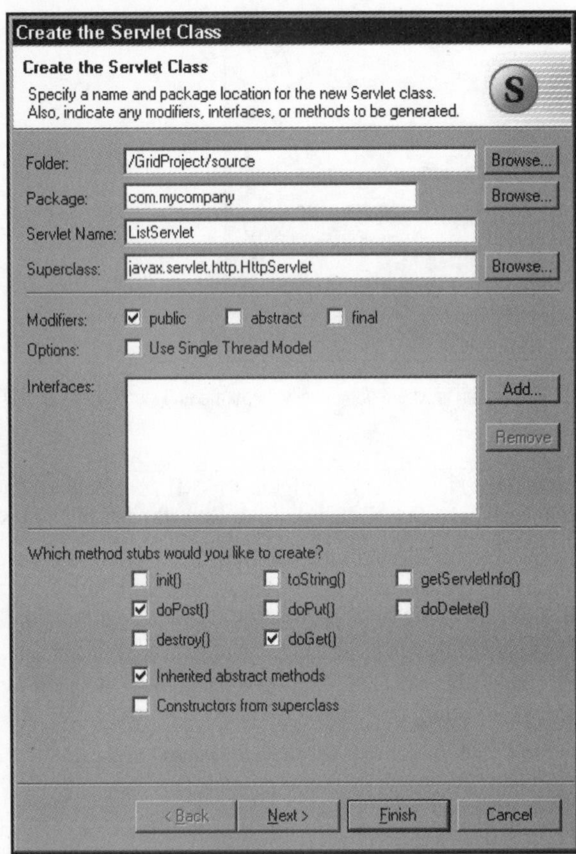

Figure 18-5: You specify the name and package location of the new servlet class on the Create the Servlet Class screen.

14. Edit `ListServlet.java` by copying and pasting the contents from the downloaded code into it. Save the servlet. Errors indicating that classes were not found may appear. (These are addressed after you update the classpath.)

15. At this point, all resources have been created. Your project should look like that shown in Figure 18-6. You still need to make a few minor changes before you can run the application.

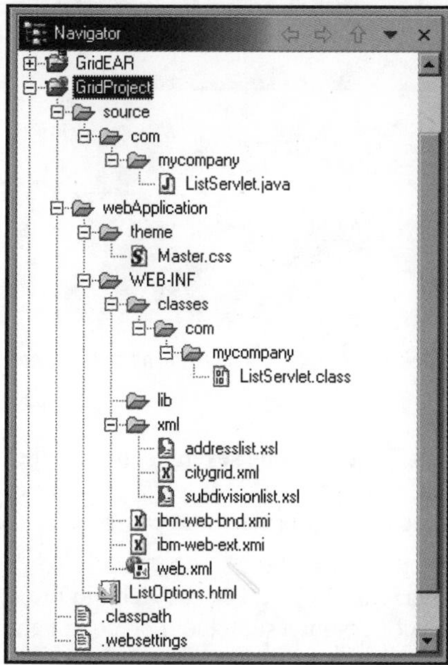

Figure 18-6: The complete structure for the GridProject is shown here, including the Servlet, XSL files, and XML file that were created.

16. Directly under the GridProject, is a file called `.classpath`. Double-click it to open it and add the following two lines directly above the closing `</classpath>` tag:

```
<classpathentry kind="var" path="WAS_XERCES"/>
<classpathentry kind="var" path="WAS_XALAN"/>
```

These two entries tell the application server where to find `xalan.jar` and `xerces.jar`, which are required resources for using XSLT. Save the `.classpath` file.

17. The `web.xml` file is where you define both the project's default pages (welcome pages) and the servlet's alias. Expand the `WEB-INF` folder and double-click `web.xml` to edit it. Select the Servlets tab, if necessary. Click the Add button and select ListServlet. You see that the servlet class is already filled in for you as `com.mycompany.ListServlet`. Enter **ListServlet** as the display name. (This is the servlet's alias, or in other words what you refer to in the HTML file.) Under the URL mapping section, the only entry should be `/servlet/*`. This is why you specify `action="servlet/ListServlet"` in the HTML form. It is a common way of noting that a servlet is being called upon a form's submission. Figure 18-7 shows these entries.

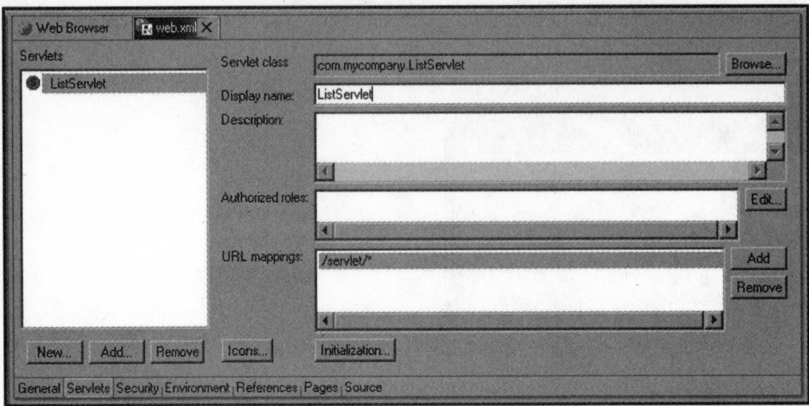

Figure 18-7: This screen shows the servlet set up in the web.xml file. It is here that a servlet's display name and class name are associated.

18. Also in the `web.xml` file, select the Pages tab. There may be several entries in the Welcome Pages window. Remove all of them, and add the HTML page you created, `ListOptions.html`. This is the default page for your project. Save `web.xml` and close it.
19. Return to the Navigator window and right-click GridProject. Choose Rebuild Project. This operation saves and rebuilds all the project's resources, including recompilation of any modified Java source and loading of properties.
20. Now you're ready to test the XML application! Right-click `ListOptions.html` and choose Run on Server. This starts the WebSphere test environment. After some delay, you should see the HTML page displayed. Figure 18-8 shows the page displayed in WSAD's Web browser window. Select the first radio button (List by Address) to view the data by address. Your results should look like those in Figure 18-9.

If you encounter exceptions when you submit the form, especially those indicating that the ListServlet cannot be found, double check GridProject's `web.xml` file. Be sure you have entered the ListServlet URL mapping (as shown in Step 17), and that you have the proper directory structure for the servlet (as in Step 12). If the ListServlet does not compile at all, be sure you have made the two entries in the `.classpath` file as shown in Step 16.

After you have the application functioning, try changing some of the XPath expressions in the XSL files to display different data or add additional templates for multiple tables. You may want to create brand-new XSL files and add additional radio buttons to `ListChoice.html` and update the ListServlet to account for different listing options.

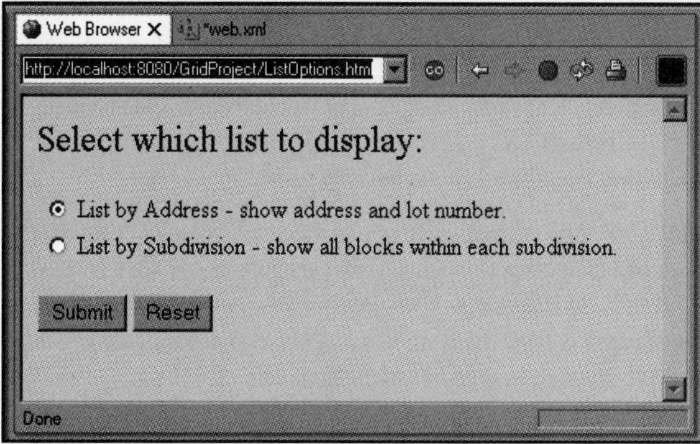

Figure 18-8: ListOptions.html is displayed in the WebSphere Test Environment.

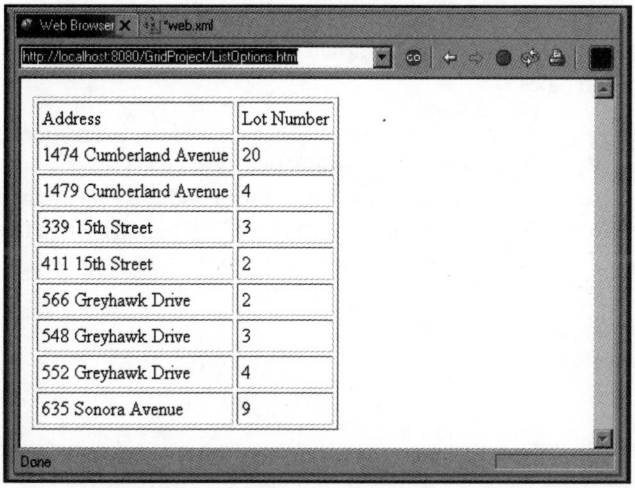

Address	Lot Number
1474 Cumberland Avenue	20
1479 Cumberland Avenue	4
339 15th Street	3
411 15th Street	2
566 Greyhawk Drive	2
548 Greyhawk Drive	3
552 Greyhawk Drive	4
635 Sonora Avenue	9

Figure 18-9: Data is displayed in a table after transformation using the addresslist.xsl stylesheet.

The City Grid example only scratches the surface of the XML tools that are provided with WSAD. You should work through several of the samples that are provided with WSAD and learn how to take advantage of all its features.

Summary

This chapter focused on development using XSL and XSLT. You learned that XML is a powerful technology that is used to describe and structure data, and you were presented with several examples of XML files that illustrated their hierarchal structure.

You learned the history behind XML and how it evolved from earlier technologies like SGML and HTML. XML has the advantage of being able to describe any data; and because it has a standardized format, you are assured that XML parsers correctly handle its content. XML is a flexible way to store and describe data that is subject to updates, and an example was given in the context of parsing a text file used to store data within an application.

The family of XML technologies, which includes DTDs, XPath, and XML Schemas, was introduced. You saw an example of an XML Schema, which is used to validate the contents of an XML document.

Next, stylesheets were introduced. XSLT is used to transform an XML document into other text-based documents, including XML and HTML. You learned the benefits of using XSLT over other dynamic Web page technologies.

Finally, the different pieces were brought together in an example that showed the interaction between XML, XSLT, and XPath. You created a Web application that used an HTML file to launch a servlet that interacted with the XSLT processor and XML parser and used a particular stylesheet to transform the contents of an XML file to one of two HTML outputs. Through this example, you saw how XML and XSLT are powerful and extendible tools for developing data-driven applications.

Chapter 19
Developing Web Services

In This Chapter

- Revisiting Web services components and operations
- Installing the SOAP samples on WebSphere
- Installing the Web Services Toolkit
- Installing a private UDDI registry
- Coding using the Apache SOAP ToolKit
- Generating WSDL descriptions with WSAD

Up to this point, you have been doing a lot of development with WebSphere Studio Application Developer. In this chapter, you finish up the application development part of the book by learning about the creation of Web services.

In Chapter 3, you learned about Web services. You also were introduced to Simple Object Access Protocol (SOAP), Web Services Description Language (WSDL), and Universal Description and Discovery Integration (UDDI).

In this chapter, you continue to delve deeper into the details of Web services. You install the Web Services Toolkit and implement a private UDDI registry as well as use WSAD to create, deploy, and test Web services.

As you know, SOAP, WSDL, and UDDI complement each other, but you can use them to develop and deploy them separately. For instance, you can publicize your business entity in a UDDI registry without needing a Web service implementation. In this chapter, you start by using the Web services protocols individually and after you have a clear understanding, you seamlessly integrate the three into a sample application.

Exploring Web Services

Figure 19-1 shows the three components of Web services (requestors, providers, and brokers). In Figure 19-1, the enabling technologies are placed by the components. After you see the tooling required by each component, you can gain a better understanding of how they integrate in a platform-neutral way.

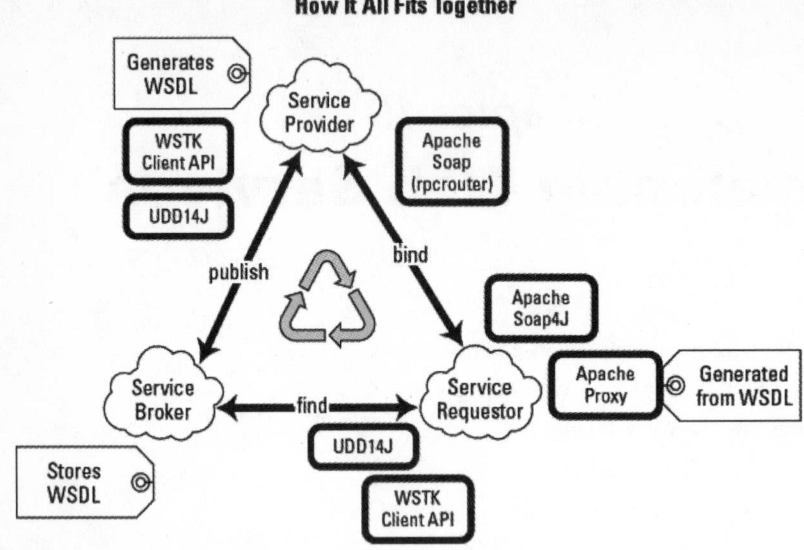

Figure 19-1: Web services' components.

In Chapter 3 it was stated "Web services are self-contained modular business applications that have open, Internet-oriented, standard-based interfaces." You now see how this is done.

Understanding the components of Web services

Web services are deployed on the Web by service providers (see the top of the triangle). The functions provided by the Web service are described using WSDL. The same service providers publish deployed services on the Web through brokers or partnerships.

A *service broker* helps *service providers* and *service requestors* locate each other. A service requestor uses the UDDI API to ask the service broker about the services it needs. When the service broker returns the search results, the service requestor can use those results to bind to a particular service. The following sections describe the roles of the individual components.

Understanding the role of the service broker

The service broker (also known as service registry) is responsible for making the Web service interface and implementation access information available to any potential service requestor. The Web services' method of implementing a service registry is using UDDI. Alternatively, the simplest form of service discovery is to request a copy of the service description from the service provider. After receiving the request, the service provider can simply e-mail the service description as an attachment or provide it to the service requestor on a transferable media, such as a disk. Although this type of service discovery is simple, it is not very efficient because it requires prior knowledge of the Web service, as well as the contact information for the service provider.

What would be useful is a distributed service discovery method that provides references to service descriptions at the service provider's point-of-offering. The Web Services Inspection Language (WSIL) provides this by specifying how to inspect a Web site for available Web services.

Understanding the role of the service requestor

The service requestor locates entries in the service registry using various find operations and then binds to the service provider to invoke one of its Web services. You might say that services are *discovered* and *invoked* by service requestors.

The service requestor is the business, corporation, or institution that requires a particular function and has the responsibility for discovering and invoking a service. It may utilize the services of a broker to find the service.

Understanding the role of the service provider

Services are *implemented* and *published* by service providers. The service provider creates a Web service and publishes its interface and access information to the service registry. From a business perspective, the service provider owns the service. You might also consider it as the platform that provides access to the service. The flow of information shown in Figure 19-1 can be summarized as follows:

- Web service descriptions can be created and published by service providers.
- Web services can be categorized and located by specific service brokers.
- Web services can be discovered and called by service requestors.

Understanding how Web services operate

So now you know what Web services are, but just what do they do? In the Web services model each component has responsibilities for various operations. The operations are publish, bind, and find:

- *Publish* involves service providers promoting their services to a registry (publishing) or removing entries from the registry (unpublishing). In a situation where a service provider utilizes a service broker, the service provider contacts the service broker to publish or unpublish a service.
- *Bind* takes place between the service requestor and the service provider. In the bind operation the service requestor invokes or initiates an interaction with the service at runtime using the binding details in the service description to find, contact, and invoke the service.
- During the *find* operation, service requestors and service brokers in tandem perform the find operation. Find operations entail searching for a service directly or searching a registry for a type of service desired.

Understanding the development strategies of Web services

You can use three strategies when developing Web services:

- The *bottom-up* scenario is for enterprise developers who are working to migrate their existing applications to the Web services architecture. In this case, you take a Java class and publish it using the Web services tools.
- The *top-down* scenario starts with an already existing Web services interface description and the work consists of creating application functionality that supports the interface. Just as with a Java interface, you need to create a Java class that implements the interface.
- The *meet-in-the-middle* scenario is a combination of the bottom-up and top-down scenarios. Here you have an interface you need to meet and an existing application that you need to set up to comply with the Web service. Here, you have both an existing Web services interface and existing application code (Java class), and you need to use them both to create your Web service.

The development lifecycle takes you through one or all these steps:

- *Discovery:* You need to find a service and support the necessary interface.
- *Create or transform:* You either create your own service or transform your application to comply with a discovered interface.
- *Build:* The build phase of the lifecycle includes development and testing of the Web service implementation, the definition of the service interface description, and the definition of the service implementation description. Web service implementations can be provided by creating new Web services, transforming existing applications into Web services, and composing new Web services from other Web services and applications.
- *Deploy:* The deploy phase includes the publishing of the service interface and service implementation definition to a service requestor or service registry. You also have to deploy of the executables for the Web service into WebSphere.
- *Test:* You need to test your service. You can use a private UDDI registry if you are publishing your service.
- *Develop:* During this phase, you create an application that uses a Web service, and you generate the appropriate interfaces and implementations.

Installing the IBM Web Services Tools

In this section, you install some of the necessary tools you need to develop Web services. You install the SOAP examples that come with WebSphere 4.03 and the Web Services ToolKit (WSTK) from IBM AlphaWorks. Some of the products are in a preview or beta state. With the emerging technologies still in flux, some of the products work only with WebSphere Application Server Single Server Edition. You work with the products that run on WebSphere Application Server Advanced Edition (AE).

The goal of this section is to introduce you to the technologies and run some simple samples to give you an idea of what is possible with these tools. Starting off, you install the SOAP samples that come with WebSphere Application Server. This is your introduction to the capabilities of SOAP.

Moving on, you install the Web Services ToolKit (WSTK) from AlphaWorks. The WSTK contains some of the latest Web services technology previews. After it is installed, you have the opportunity to create a private Universal Description and Discovery Integration (UDDI) registry on WebSphere.

From that point on, you have the necessary tools to try a few simple Web services routines to gain a better understanding of the power of Web services. Let's get started.

Understanding the tools

The tools that come with WebSphere and the WSTK that you learn about in this chapter are as follows:

- *SOAP*: W3C Version 1.1 and the Apache SOAP version 2.2, which is used as the platform-neutral transport mechanism.
- *AXIS (SOAP 3.0):* The next generation of Apache SOAP, which implements SAX processing of XML documents.
- *WSDL*: Web Services Description Language Version 1.1 which is the way to describe Web services' invocation and location.
- *WSDL4J:* IBM's Web Services Description Language open-source implementation for Java development of WSDL.
- *WSIL:* The Web Services Inspection Language is a new specification that provides a simple service discovery method. You can now use either the WS-Inspection service or UDDI for service discovery.
- *UDDI:* Universal Description, Discovery Integration Version 1 provides a registry to lookup businesses and services.
- *UDDI4J:* IBM's Universal Description, Discovery Integration open-source implementation for Java development of UDDI.

You utilize these tools throughout this chapter. Many other previews come with the WSTK. If you are interested in some of the other previews, see the `StartHere.htm` file in the `<WSTK_HOME>` directory.

Installing the SOAP examples on WebSphere Application Server (AE)

WebSphere 4.0 comes with a set of SOAP examples. You can find those examples under the `<was_home>/installableApps`. Each of these installable applications is contained in the J2EE standard of EAR files. You install a few EAR files in this chapter using the

Administrative Console. You start here by installing the SOAP examples. Figure 19-2 shows how you install an enterprise application.

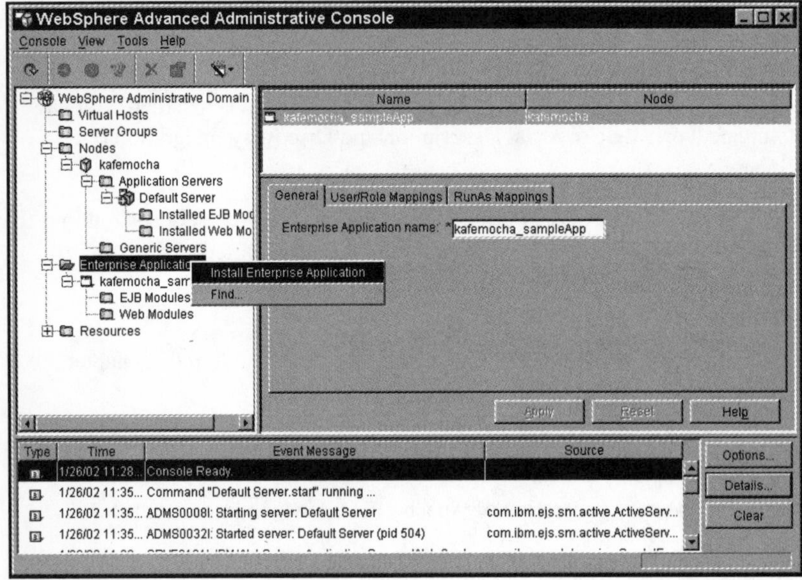

Figure 19-2: You begin installing an enterprise application in the Administrative Console.

1. Click Install⇨Install Enterprise Application. The wizard prompts you to select the EAR file to install. You can click the Browse button to navigate to the directory where you have an EAR file. In this case, navigate to the `<was_home>/installableApps` folder.

NOTE: To keep the number of screen shots to a minimum, some of the wizard screens are described in text.

2. You see a number of EAR files under the `installableApps` folder. Select the `soapsamples.ear` file.
3. The next eight wizard screens are shown in the following list. You click Next for all these screens. You are finally presented with the Completion screen, with the node and EAR file installed, as shown in Figure 19-3:
   - Mapping Users to Roles
   - Mapping EJB RunAs Roles to Users
   - Binding Enterprise Beans to JNDI Names
   - Mapping EJB References to Enterprise Beans
   - Mapping Resource References to Resources
   - Specifying the Default Datasource for EJB Modules

- Specifying Data Sources for Individual CMP Beans
- Selecting Virtual Hosts for Web Modules
- Selecting Application Servers

> **NOTE**: You must select a server if more than the default application server has been defined.

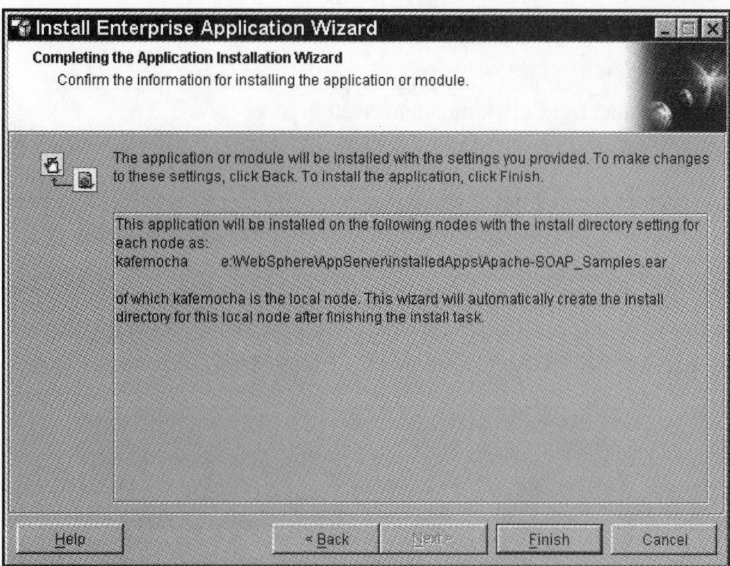

Figure 19-3: When you click Finish, the EAR files is expanded into the installedApps directory with the EAR file name used as the folder name.

4. You are asked to regenerate the code. Click Yes.
5. The Deploy dialog box opens. Accept the defaults and the install should be completed successfully.

Finally, you should ensure that the SOAP Server Manager client is enabled. To do so, find a file called `soap.xml` located in the `<was_home>\installedApps\Apache-SOAP_soapsamples.ear\soap.war` directory. Listing 19-1 shows the `soap.xml` file. You change the `SOAPInterfaceEnabled` value to `true`.

Listing 19-1: Setting the SOAPInterfaceEnable to True in the soap.xml file Enables the SOAP Service Manager Client

```
<!-- Sample Apache SOAP Server Configuration File -->

<soapServer>
  <!-- This section defines the same thing you get if you don't -->
  <!-- specify anything at all - aka the default                -->
```

Listing 19-1 ***(Continued)***

```
  <configManager
    value="com.ibm.soap.server.XMLDrivenConfigManager"/>
    <serviceManager>
      <option name="SOAPInterfaceEnabled" value="true" />
    </serviceManager>
</soapServer>
```

You are now ready to run a SOAP sample:

1. Start the Apache-SOAP_Samples Enterprise Application by selecting it in the Administrative Console, right-clicking, and selecting Start.
2. Start the Default Server by selecting it, right-clicking, and selecting Start.
3. In a command prompt window navigate to <was_home>\installedApps\Apache-SOAP_Samples.ear\ClientCode\nt_bat and type the following line:

```
EJBAdderSample localhost:9080
```

Figure 19-4 shows the expected results. By entering this code, you successfully call a Web service running an EJB on WebSphere that returns the simple answer to an algorithm.

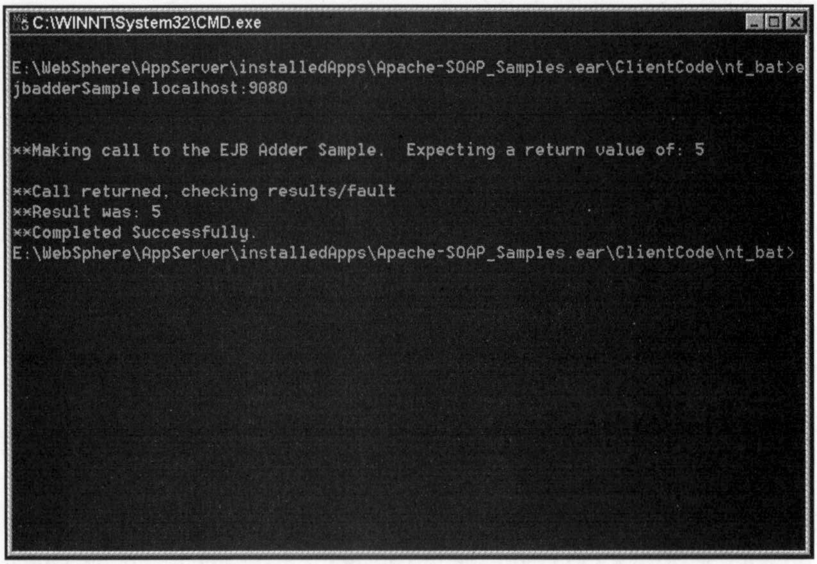

```
C:\WINNT\System32\CMD.exe

E:\WebSphere\AppServer\installedApps\Apache-SOAP_Samples.ear\ClientCode\nt_bat>e
jbadderSample localhost:9080


**Making call to the EJB Adder Sample.  Expecting a return value of: 5

**Call returned, checking results/fault
**Result was: 5
**Completed Successfully.
E:\WebSphere\AppServer\installedApps\Apache-SOAP_Samples.ear\ClientCode\nt_bat>
```

Figure 19-4: The SOAP example EJBAdderSample calls a remote procedure call (ejbadder) that receives two integer parameters and adds them together.

The `EJBAdderSample` is a simple SOAP example. You create your own SOAP application in the section titled, "Using WebSphere Studio Application Developer to Create a Web Services Component," but first you need to install some of the tooling necessary to develop your own application.

Installing the IBM Web Services ToolKit

IBM's Web Services ToolKit (WSTK) is a collection of preview technologies that enable you to start experimenting with Web services. You need to install the ToolKit to run the next few exercises.

> **ON THE WEB**: You need to download a copy of the Web Services ToolKit from `www.alphaworks.ibm.com/tech/webservicestoolkit`.

You should also verify that you have the appropriate prerequisites to run the exercises. You need the following:

- IBM Web Services ToolKit version 3.1
- Windows 2000 (with Service Pack 2 or higher) or Linux
- JDK 1.3 or higher
- Internet Explorer 5.0 (or higher) or Netscape 4.5 (or higher)

After you download and unpack the file containing the ToolKit, start the setup program. In the following steps if a screen is not provided in the text, accept the defaults and click Next.

1. When presented with the WSTK Installation Splash screen, click Next. If you met all the prerequisites, you should receive a screen that shows JDK 1.3.1 as your installed JDK. This value is set to `JAVA_HOME` by the installer.
2. You follow the wizard through three screens (Installation Notes, Licensing Agreement, and Directory Name). You should note where you installed the product because you execute several programs within that folder. Accept the licensing and continue.
3. Figure 19-5 shows the Configuration tool. Select WebSphere 4.0 and update the server location to `<was_home>`. Click Next.
4. You can ignore the ConfigureServices and Configure WS-Inspection tabs for now. If you have a proxy server, you have to configure a proxy/socks host using the Configure Proxies tab.
5. On the Configure UDDI screen, you should change the UDDI registry to Other UDDI Registry, as shown in Figure 19-6. The URLs, userid, and password are defaulted for you. Click Finish.
6. Messages notify you of your current status. When prompted to stop the Web server, use either the Start⇨Programs⇨IBM HTTP Server⇨Stop HTTP Server, or use the Services page in the Control panel to stop the service. After you stop it, you need to restart it.
7. You are returned to the Welcome screen. Click Next and you are done.

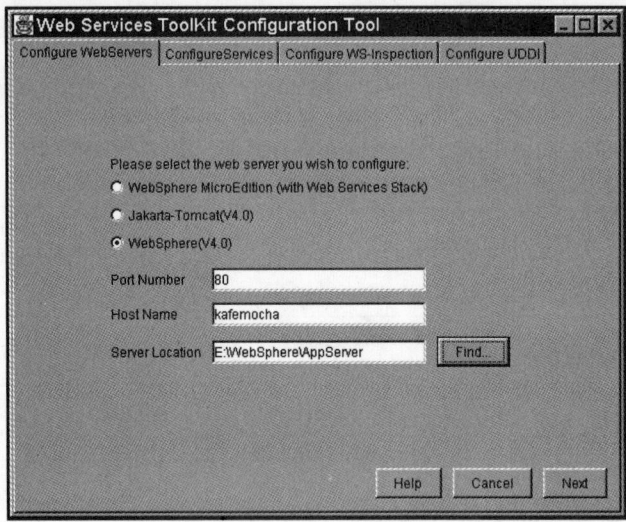

Figure 19-5: You set up WSTK to run on WebSphere 4.0, but you could also configure it to run on Tomcat.

NOTE: Loading the WSTK takes a few minutes and requires about 90 MB of disk space.

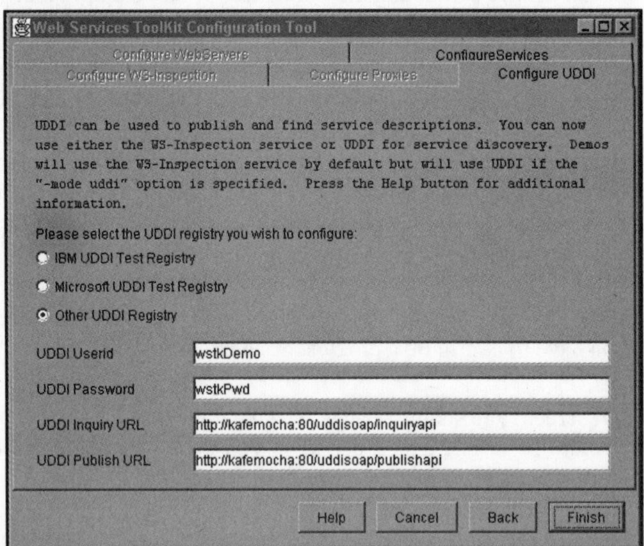

Figure 19-6: When configuring UDDI, you can choose from three registries. The first two are the IBM UDDI Test registry and the Microsoft Test registry; the other option is to point to your own registry.

You have successfully installed the Web Services ToolKit. Run some demos after you complete installing the Private UDDI registry.

Preparing to install a Private UDDI

In your WSTK installation, you elected to utilize a private UDDI registry. In the following section, you install the IBM WebSphere UDDI registry. With the IBM WebSphere UDDI registry, Web services developers can publish and test their internal e-business applications in a secure, private environment. The WebSphere UDDI level used in this book implements Version 2 of the UDDI specifications. The IBM WebSphere UDDI registry assumes that the following products are already installed on the user's system:

- DB2 Enterprise Edition 7.2 FP5
- A Web server, such as IBM HTTP Server (IHS) 1.3.19, Internet Information Server (IIS) 5.0, or any other Web server supported by WebSphere Application Server
- WebSphere Application Server Advanced Edition (AE) v4.0.3 or WebSphere Application Server Advanced Edition – Developer Only Option (AEd) v4.0.3
- A browser, such as Internet Explorer v5.5 or later or Netscape Navigator 6.1 or later

> **NOTE**: Internet Explorer is more effective for use with the UDDI User console.

You install the beta version of the IBM WebSphere UDDI registry. The beta runs on the following platforms:

- Windows 2000 Server 2000 SP1 or higher
- Windows NT Server 4.0 SP 6a or higher

You must download `IBMWebSphereUDDI_1.1_nt.zip` from the download site and unzip this file into a temporary directory

> **NOTE**: To download the file browse to `http://www7b.boulder.ibm.com/wsdd/downloads/UDDIregistry.html`.

Installing the IBM WebSphere UDDI registry

In this section, you install components directly to the WebSphere Application Server, so you need userids if you turned on WebSphere security. If you didn't turn on security, you don't need any userids other than a DB2 userid, the `db2admin` userid that you created during the WebSphere installation works.

You can determine whether you have JDBC at the 2.0 level by looking for the file `X:\Program Files\SQLLIB\java12\inuse`. The information contained with this files should be JDBC 2.0. With these prerequisites completed, run the `setup.exe` to start the installation.

> **NOTE**: The WebSphere Application Server is recycled during this install, so you should stop any other WebSphere work before running `setup.exe`.

Installation checks the environment for a couple of components. If you have DB2 installed, it verifies that it's at the right level. You need to have DB2 with FixPak 5 installed. You are prompted if the DB2 level is not correct. You have the choice to stop the install or continue. You should upgrade to the proper level of DB2. The installation also checks to see whether WebSphere is at the correct level. It is suggested that you always work with the proper level.

As the installation continues, you are prompted whenever you need to make a decision that affects the installation. You are presented with the following screens. Take the actions listed:

1. On the Licensing screen, accept and continue.
2. On the Default directory screen, accept the defaults or override. The folder is created if it doesn't exist.
3. For Custom or Typical install, select Custom. The Custom install enables you to select from the following components:
   - UDDI registry files
   - UDDI4J
   - InfoCenter
   - Sample files
   - Setup UDDI registry database

NOTE: The main purpose of the Custom Install is to enable you to install other components, such as the InfoCenter, the samples, or the UDDI4J package, on a separate machine from the UDDI registry files, as shown in Figure 19-7. Because some of these components are for development, you might want to install only UDDI registry files on your server. In this case, you should select all components.

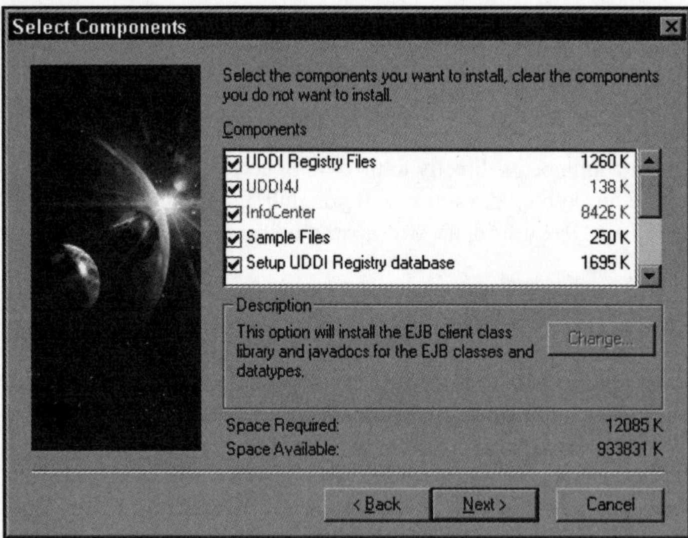

Figure 19-7: On this screen, you select the custom installation components. You also select all components.

4. If you are installing on top of a previous installation of the IBM WebSphere UDDI registry and want to preserve existing data in the registry, you can choose not to set up the registry database. However, be aware that the format of the registry data might have changed so that your old registry database might no longer be compatible.

> **NOTE:** Setting up the UDDI registry DB is essential if this is a new installation.

5. Continuing on with the installation, you are prompted to provide a DB2 userid and password. You should enter **db2admin** for userid and password. If the userid is not `db2admin` with a password of `db2admin`, you must remember to update the `uddi.properties` file in the Properties subdirectory of the WebSphere Application Server after the installation of the UDDI registry finishes.

The installation completes (after taking considerable time to copy files and configure the UDDI Registry in WebSphere) and information is logged in the `<UDDI-install-dir>\logs` directory. You find a new JDBC provider and data source named, `UDDI JDBC Driver` and `UDDI datasource`, respectively. You also find a new database called `UDDI20`.

> **NOTE**: The module visibility of your application server changes to Application, which is required by the UDDI Registry application.

After the install, you should install the UDDI registry EAR file (`<was_home>/installableApps/uddi.ear`). You use the same process for installing an enterprise application that you used for the SOAP Samples section, "Installing the Soap Examples on WebSphere Application Server (AE)."

> **NOTE**: If you attempt to start the Administrative Server and get errors, reboot to free port 9000, which could be in use.

To use the IBM WebSphere UDDI registry, you need to start the WebSphere Administrative Server (or stop and restart it if it is already running).

You can now run the installation verification programs. These are described in the InfoCenter, in a section titled, "Verifying the installation." (See the following section on accessing the InfoCenter for more information.) You can also find information in the InfoCenter about running the UDDI User console (GUI).

> **NOTE:** The documentation for the IBM WebSphere UDDI registry is provided via an online information center, or InfoCenter. To start the InfoCenter, you need to have installed the IBM WebSphere UDDI registry. You can then navigate to `<UDDI-install-dir>\infocenter and open index.html` with a supported browser. This launches the IBM WebSphere UDDI Registry InfoCenter.

Verifying the installation

After installation, you should verify that UDDI is working. After you start the Application server, go to a browser, and point the address to `http://localhost:9080/uddigui`. You see the Welcome screen for the UDDI registry, as shown in Figure 19-8.

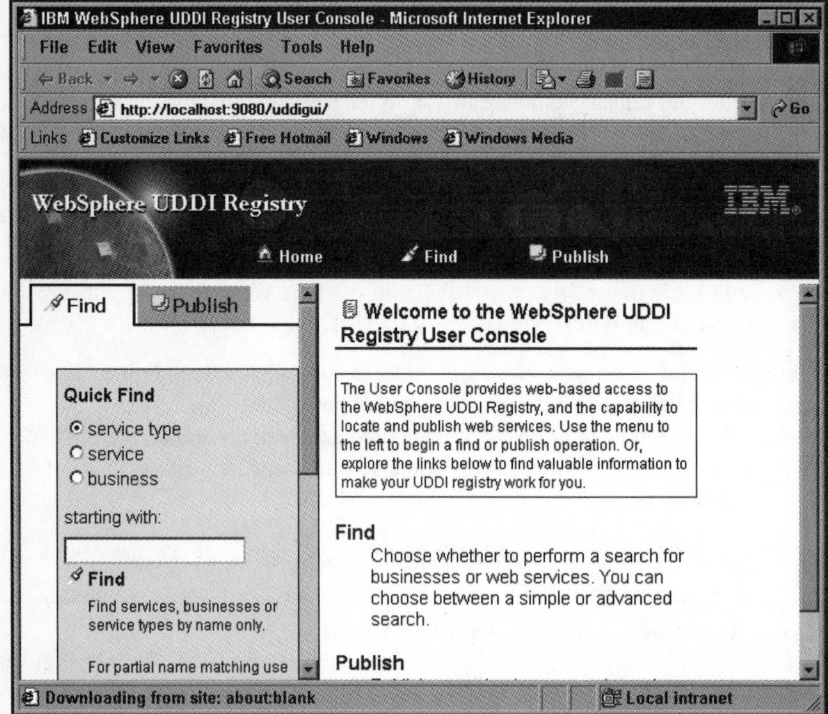

Figure 19-8: You can verify the installation by entering http://localhost:9080/uddigui. You should see the WebSphere UDDI Registry.

On the Welcome screen, you can find a published service or business. If you select the Find tab, select Service, enter a % in the starting with field, and then click Find, you see a list of all service types matching the wild card %, as seen in Figure 19-9.

To experiment with the registry, try adding a business:

1. Click the Publish tab.
2. Under Quick Publish, select the Business radio button.
3. Under Called, type **Commerce Solutions**.
4. Click Publish now.

> **NOTE:** These steps publish the business name only. It is left to you to experiment with using the Advanced Publishing. Advanced Publishing requires you to enter more specific data about the business.

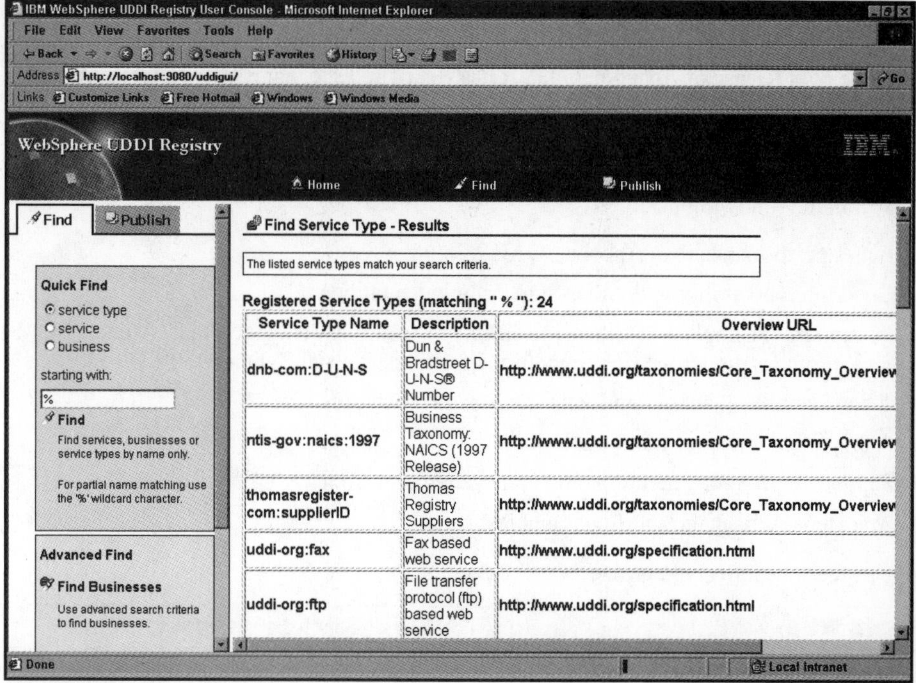

Figure 19-9: The Show all Service Types page displays a list of registered service that can be researched by an interested party.

The InfoCenter provides all the details about how to add a business or find a business within the registry. To view the InfoCenter use Windows Explorer to navigate to `x:\WebSphere\uddireg\infocenter.` Double-click `index.html`. This launches the IBM WebSphere UDDI Registry InfoCenter in your default browser.

Understanding the Apache SOAP ToolKit

As stated in the W3C SOAP 1.1 draft: "Soap is a lightweight protocol for exchange of information in a decentralized, distributed environment." With SOAP, standard issues, such as transport and packaging, have been addressed so that you, the developer, have a clear understanding of interface and concrete implementations. In this section, you are introduced to the implementation of SOAP-compliant applications.

Introducing AXIS: The next generation

AXIS is the next release of Apache SOAP. It is a Beta 1 release that is dated March 15, 2002. It is shipped along with the WSTK. Version 3.1 of the WSTK needs to be installed because prior versions of WSTK had problems with WebSphere 4.0. Such is the life of beta users. Some of the benefits you gain from using the AXIS release over the Apache SOAP 2.2 release are shown in the following list:

- Better performance than Apache SOAP 2.2.
- Good interoperability with other SOAP implementations.
- Its support of Simple API Extension (SAX) instead of Document Object Model (DOM). SAX provides, under the right conditions, better performance than DOM.
- A configurable chain of handlers for message processing.
- A pluggable transport framework.
- Support for WSDL generation and code generation from WSDL.
- An extensive package and functional test suite.

In spite of these benefits, you utilize SOAP 2.2 in the examples.

ON THE WEB: Visit `http://xml.apache.org/axis` for more information.

Administering SOAP

Installed with the SOAP samples is the XML-Soap Admin page, shown in Figure 19-10. You must ensure that you have the Default Server started and have started the `Apache_SOAP Samples` enterprise application. To access the Admin page, type **`http://localhost:9080/soapsamples/admin/index.html`**. This tool provides you with a way to list all the SOAP services registered with the application server as well as a way to start and stop services.

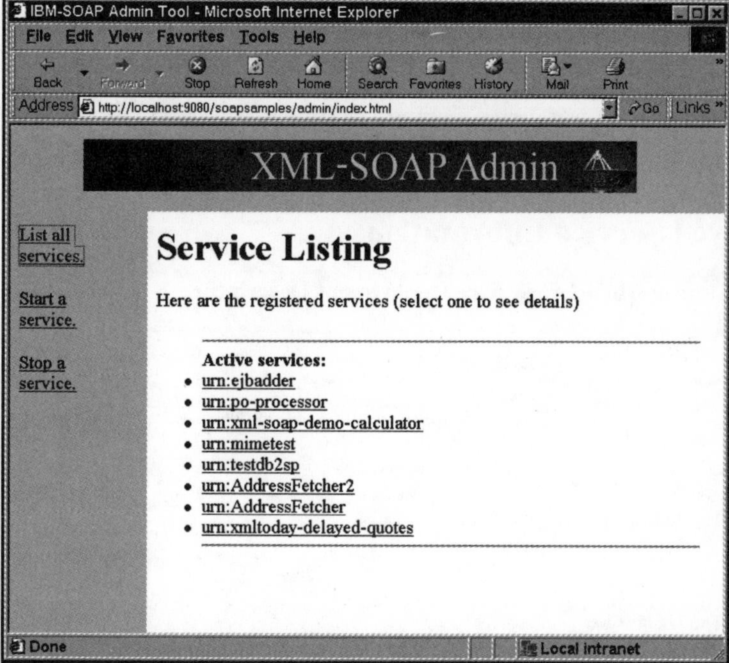

Figure 19-10: When you click the List all services link, you are presented with a page that shows theWeb services registered with SOAP.

In Figure 19-10, you see the registered active services. When you select an active registered service, you are presented with the SOAP deployment descriptor information. Click the urn:ejbadder link. Figure 19-11 shows the `ejbadder` service deployment descriptor.

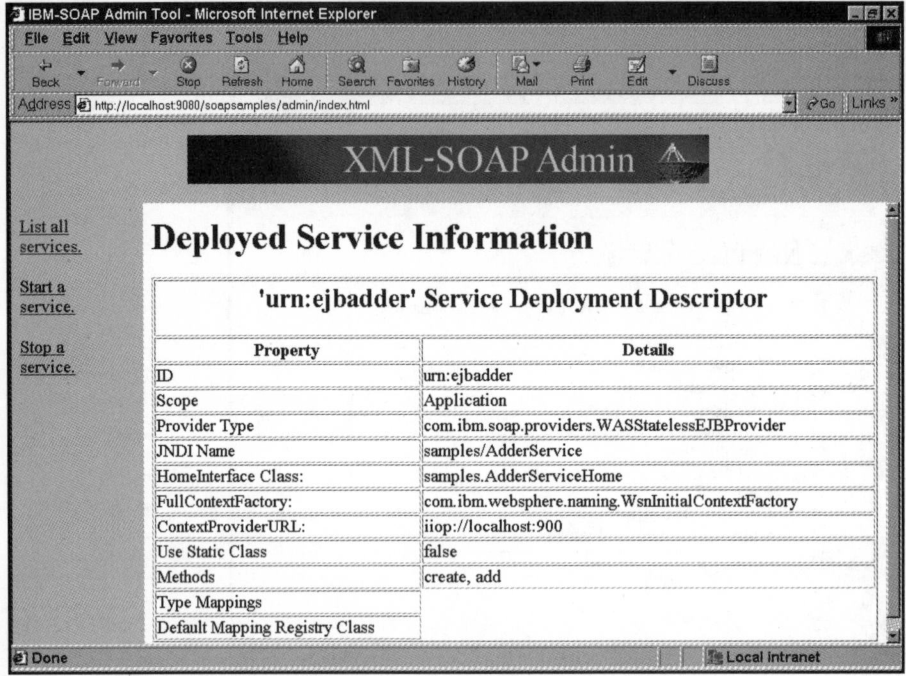

Figure 19-11: Showing details of a SOAP service descriptor.

In the section titled, "Installing the SOAP examples on WebSphere Application Server (AE)," you ran a simple EJBAdderSample program that added two numbers. The Web service accessed was the ejbadder service shown in Figure 19-11. You can see two methods that were exposed to developers wanting to interface with this Web service (`create` and `add`).

The information displayed comes from an XML document named `dds.xml`. This file contains the deployment descriptor for the Apache_SOAP samples. When you look at the `dds.xml` file, you see the code shown in Figure 19-12. If you compare the results from Figures 19-11 and 19-12, you see the same information displayed.

Now that you know how to display a service using the Administrative Console, you might be wondering what goes into creating a Web service.

> **NOTE**: If you receive a SOAP RPC Router error: `Sorry I don't speak via HTTP GET - you have to use HTTP POST to talk to me`, you need to update the `SOAP.XML` and change `SOAPInterfaceEnabled` value to `true`.

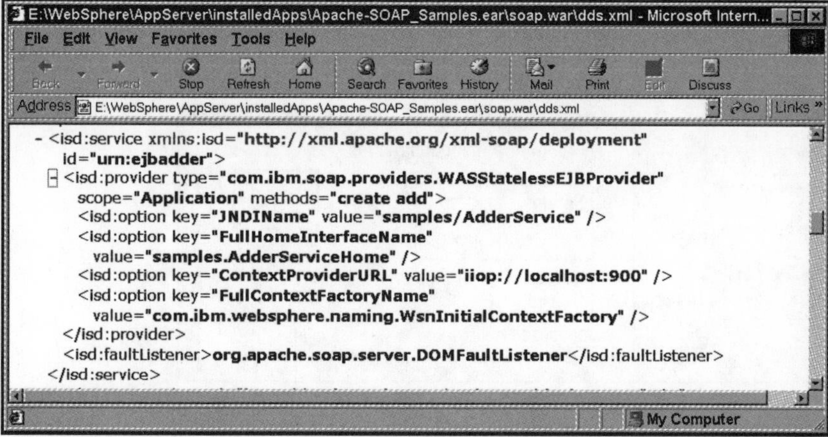

Figure 19-12: The deployment descriptor file (dds.xml) contains the descriptions of all the services in this application.

Understanding the development lifecycle

Probably the best way to fully understand the development cycle is to walk through an example. In this scenario, a service provider has developed a service that takes a Fahrenheit temperature as input and converts it to Celsius. A cruise line travel agent wants to utilize this service as a value-add for its customers. The interfaces were obtained from the service provider via e-mail.

Figure 19-13 shows the lifecycle of a SOAP application. Excluding the development of the user interface, the SOAP application is comprised of only three components: the Java object, the SOAP servlet for processing SOAP requests, and a SOAP client. SOAP manages the message interaction across the network. You learn about the underlying infrastructure before you actually look at code.

Because SOAP is transport independent, it can move messages in many ways. Most of the time, it uses the transport bindings for HTTP and uses the HTTP as the mechanism to pass the messages.

The SOAP messaging model fundamentally supports one-way messages, but sequences can be combined in a request/response manner. The model defines a message path for routing messages; and on the receiving end, the receiver looks at the message and processes it.

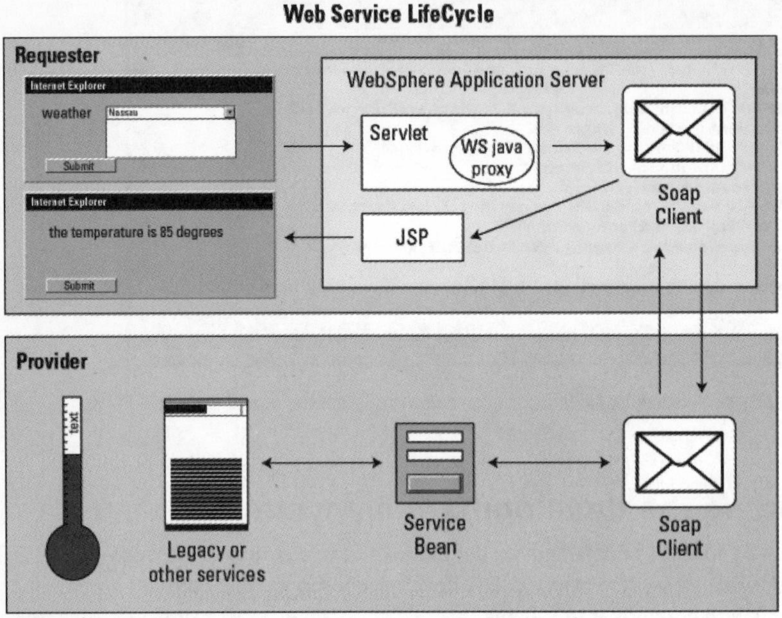

Web Service LifeCycle

Requester
Internet Explorer
weather Nassau
Submit
Internet Explorer
the temperature is 85 degrees
Submit
WebSphere Application Server
Servlet
WS java proxy
JSP
Soap Client
Provider
text
Legacy or other services
Service Bean
Soap Client

Figure 19-13: The development lifecycle begins with a servlet utilizing SOAP to transport the message over to the SOAP server. The service requested is processed and the results returned in a response displayed as a JSP.

Understanding the SOAP envelope

SOAP messages are wrapped in a XML SOAP envelope. You may have heard the saying "sending SOAP envelopes." The envelope consist of the following nodes:

```
<Envelope xmlns="http://schemas.xmlsop.org/soap/envelope/">
<Header>
 ...
</Header>
<Body>
 ...
</Body>
 ...
</Enveloper>
```

The root node must be `Envelope`. The header entries can contain no elements or several elements. The header has the following attributes:

- actor
- mustUnderstand
- encodingStyle

The body elements can contain no elements or several elements. It has only the `encodingStyle` attribute.

The specifications define one body entry that must be implemented: `Fault`. Otherwise you can define whatever you desire in the body. An example of `Fault` is as follows:

```
<SOAP-ENV:Fault>
 <faultcode>SOAP-ENV:Server</faultcode>
 <faultstring>Operation 'getConvert' is not supported.</faultstring>
 <faultactor>/ibm-soap/rpcrouter.jsp</faultactor>
</SOAP-ENV:Fault>
```

Using SOAP over HTTP

SOAP adds a header field called `SOAPAction`, which indicates the intent of the HTTP request, for example, `urn:webservices-workshop-convert`. The SOAP envelope is transported in the content of a post action. A HTTP response could contain a SOAP envelope. If a SOAP error occurs, you must send an HTTP 500 error and the SOAP envelope with the fault.

Understanding SOAP encoding

The specification defines a serialization mechanism that can be used to exchange instances of an application-defined data type. Serializers are Java class files that the Apache client and server use to serialize and deserialize complex types. SOAP is language independent, so you can use a data type scheme based on the XML Schema definitions, XSD, and some encoding rules for all data types. Encoding rules define a serialization mechanism that can be used to exchange instances of application-defined data types.

Using SOAP and remote procedure calls

Remote procedure calls (RPCs) are supported with SOAP. An RPC is a way to invoke operations/methods across a network, which gives you the opportunity to reuse your pre-existing operations using SOAP. What you need is the URI of the target object, the method names, and any parameters that need to be passed. The target object can also be a DB2 stored procedure. An envelope contained in an HTTP response delivers the RPC response. A sample of a SOAP envelope is shown in Listing 19-2.

Listing 19-2: A SOAP Envelope Contains the Information Expected by the Service

```
POST /spworkshop/servlet/rpcrouter HTTP/1.0
Host:localhost
Content-Type:text/xml;charset=utf-8
Content-Length:464
SOAPAction:"urn:webservices-spworkshop-convert"

<?xml version=' 1.0 ' encoding=' UTF-8 '?>
<SOAP-ENV:Envelope xmlns:SOAP-
ENV="http://schemas.xmlsoap.org/soap/envelope/"
     xmlns:xsi="http://www.w3.org/2001/XMLSchema-instance"
     xmlns:xsd="http://www.w3.org/2001/XMLSchema">
<SOAP-ENV:Body>
<ns1:convert x lns:ns1="urn:webservices-spworkshop-convert"
SOAP-ENV:encodingStyle="http://schemas.xmlsoap.org/soap/encoding/">
<degrees xsi:type="xsd:string">70 </degrees >
</ns1:convert >
</SOAP-ENV:Body>
</SOAP-ENV:Envelope>
```

Listing 19-2 contains a SOAPAction that specifies the target service and the particular method and parameters being implemented. `Convert` is the method that is called. It receives a string value of 70 for the parameter named `degrees`.

At this point, you have a good understanding of the underlying infrastructure. Now is a good time to look at some code snippets to gain a deeper understanding of how SOAP is coded.

Understanding client coding

The following are steps show you how to develop a SOAP client. Later in the chapter in the section titled "Using WebSphere Studio Application Developer to Create a Web Services Component," you create a SOAP client utilizing these steps. But first, it is important to understand the steps before you do any coding. Start by looking at some sample code. Listing 19-3 shows an example of SOAP client.

Listing 19-3: The TemperatureImplClient Represents the SOAP Client Code

```
package testpackage;
import org.apache.soap.*;
import org.apache.soap.rpc.*;
import java.net.*;
import java.util.*;
public class TemperatureImplClient {

 public static void main(String[] args) throws MalformedURLException,
SOAPException {

  Call call = new Call();
```

```
  call.setTargetObjectURI("urn:webservices-workshop-convert");

  call.setEncodingStyleURI
       ("http://schemas.xmlsoap.org/soap/encoding/");
  call.setMethodName("convert");

  Vector params = new Vector();
  Parameter degrees = new Parameter
         ("degrees", String.class, args[ 0] , null);
  params.addElement(degrees);
  call.setParams(params);

  Response resp = call.invoke(new
URL("http://localhost/spworkshop/servlet/rpcrouter"),
                       "urn:webservices-workshop-convert");

  if (resp.generatedFault()) {
   Fault fault = resp.getFault();
   throw new SOAPException(fault.getFaultCode(),
    fault.getFaultString());
  }
  Parameter retValue = resp.getReturnValue();
  System.out.println("Temperature in Celcius is "+retValue.getValue());
 }
}
```

Referring to Listing 19-3, the steps and implementation descriptions that follow describe the important code segments:

1. Create or obtain an interface description of the SOAP service. The interface should have methods with signatures that you want to publish. In Listing 19-3, the assumption is that you have obtained an interface.
2. If you are passing parameters that use complex objects, you need serializers/deserializer for each parameter. You are not using complex objects so there is no need for serializers or deserializers.
3. Create and register your mapping accordingly. The assumptions is that the `urn:webservices-workshop-convert` service has been registered with the server.
4. Add a `org.apache.soap.rpc.Call` instance. This is shown in Listing 19-3 in the following line:

   ```
   Call call = new Call();
   ```

5. Set the target URI with the `setTargetObjectURI()` method. This is shown in Listing 19-3 in the following line:

   ```
   call.setTargetObjectURI("urn:webservices-workshop-convert");
   ```

6. Set the method name using `setMethodName()`, shown in Listing 19-3 as follows:

   ```
   call.setMethodName("convert");
   ```

7. Create any Parameter objects necessary and add them using `setParams()`. Listing 19-3 shows the following:

```
  Vector params = new Vector();
  Parameter degrees = new Parameter("degrees", String.class,
rgs[ 0] ,
     null);
  params.addElement(degrees);
  call.setParams(params);
```

8. Set the `Response` object to the value returned when you execute the `invoke()` method.

```
Response resp = call.invoke(new
URL("http://localhost/spworkshop/servlet/rpcrouter"),
                    "urn:webservices-workshop-convert");
```

9. Check the response for an error; if an error is returned, use `getFault()`. This is shown in Listing 19-3 as follows:

```
if (resp.generatedFault()) {
   Fault fault = resp.getFault();
   throw new SOAPException(fault.getFaultCode(),
    fault.getFaultString());
  }
```

10. Otherwise, get the result or returned value using `getReturnValue()` and `getParams()`.

```
Parameter retValue = resp.getReturnValue();
  System.out.println("Temperature in Celcius is "+retValue.getValue());
```

As you can see, the steps are very straightforward. That was the client side. Now look at the server side.

Understanding service coding

You deploy your service to the SOAP server. The Java class in Listing 19-4 is the concrete implementation of a class named Temperature. The code exposes the conversion method that converts a temperature from Fahrenheit to Celsius. Notice there are no references to any SOAP implementation.

Listing 19-4: The TemperatureImpl of the Celsius Converter Deployed to a SOAP Server

```
package testpackage;

public class TemperatureImpl implements Temperature {
    public String convert(String degrees) {
         Float celsius = new Float(degrees);
         celsius = new Float((((celcius.floatValue()-32)*5)/9));
       return new Integer(Math.round(celcius.floatValue())).toString();
    }
}
```

Before you deploy, you need to develop a SOAP deployment descriptor (see Listing 19-5). In it, you describe the implementation of the service. There is a Unified Resource Name (URN) describing the service and methods that are exposed. A URN uniquely identifies the service to clients. The URN must be unique among all services deployed in a single SOAP server. A URN is encoded as a universal resource identifier (URI). In this case, the URN is `webservices-workshop-convert`, and the method is `convert()`.

Listing 19-5: The SOAP Deployment Descriptor

```
<?xml version="1.0" ?>
<isd:service xmlns:isd="http://xml.apache.org/xml-soap/deployment"
       id="urn:webservices-workshop-convert">
    <isd:provider type="java"
       scope="Application"
       methods="convert">
    <isd:java class="testpackage.TemperatureImpl" static="false" />
    </isd:provider>
<isd:faultListener>org.apache.soap.server.DOMFaultListener
</isd:faultListener>
</isd:service>
```

As you can see, it is easy to create the interfaces and implementations to enable an existing Java class for SOAP. In this case, you know all the components necessary to code the service. But what about someone who does not?

The deployment description identifies the service and class along with its exposed methods. What it doesn't provide is how another requestor can find and utilize your service. A client has no information about the interface of a service, the server URL, the URN, the methods, the types, and type mappings. That is where you need a better way to describe your service. WSDL serves that purpose.

Using WSDL to Describe Your Web Service

Web Services Definition Language (WSDL) is independent of SOAP. Its goal is to provide functional descriptions of the network-accessible services (IDL description, protocol, and deployment details). WSDL should provide all the required information about how to access the service programmatically in a standard platform-independent way.

WSDL provides functional descriptions of service offerings. It supports multiple service types (message oriented and procedural) and protocols (for example, HTTP and SOAP). Even though WSDL does not impose any particular choice, the dominant choice is XML Schema and SOAP (XML protocol). You can use WSDL two ways:

- As an IDL, it can be utilized in tooling to generate client stubs.
- When used as a language to standardize interface descriptions, it allows advertisement of services, dynamic discovery, and dynamic binding to a provider.

What you learn in this section is how WSDL descriptions provide the necessary definitions of messages, locations, and services between service requestor and the service provider.

Separating interface and implementation

WSDL provides a means of separating abstract descriptions from service interfaces. It also separates protocol bindings for the services that make them reusable. Finally, WSDL separates the deployment endpoints from the other two. Figure 19-14 shows the organization of a WSDL document.

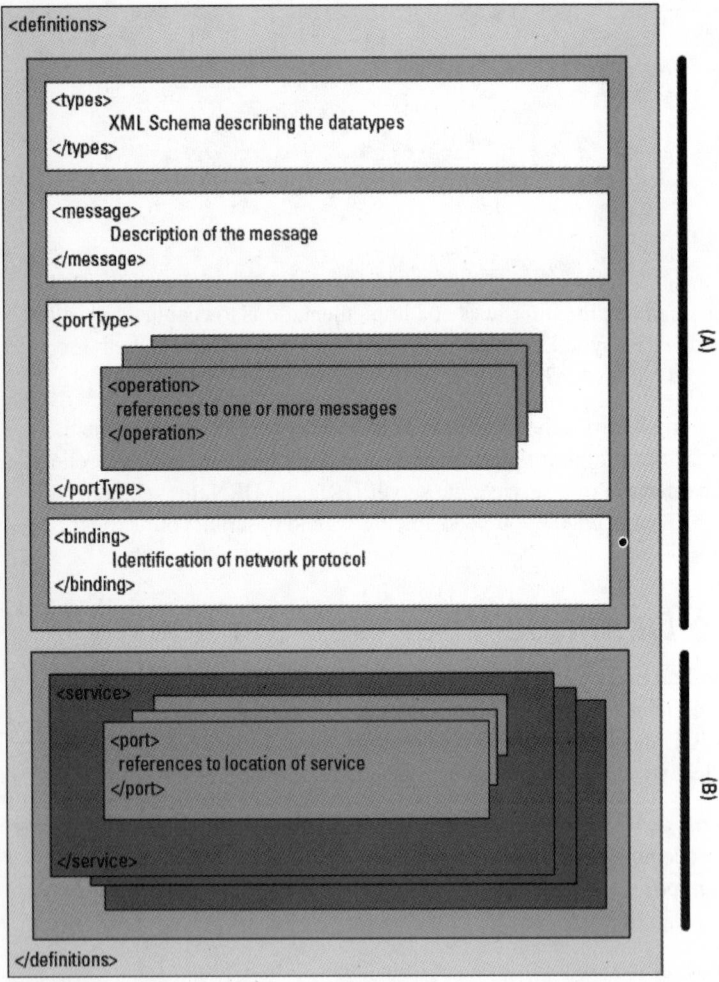

Figure 19-14: The WSDL definition is an XML document that describes the services, messages, locations, and bindings needed to program access to the service.

Every WSDL definition consists of an interface and a concrete implementation. In Figure 19-14, item (A) represents the sections that relate to the interface. The interface (reusable) definitions are data types, operations, port types, and bindings. The port definition is a concrete implementation pointing to a specific server deployment, which is shown as item (B) in Figure 19-14.

A best practice is to keep these two definitions divided into two WSDL files: one with everything but the port, and the other with the port only. The key benefit of this separation is that interfaces can be implemented on multiple machines referring to the same service.

Defining data types

Referring back to Figure 19-14, the `<types>` element encloses data type definitions that are relevant for the exchanged messages. As a service provider, you need to define the data types in XML generally using XML Schema for your services. There is no need for schemas if you are just using basic Java types. Listing 19-6 is a Java class, and Listing 19-7 is the associated XML Schema definition for that class.

Listing 19-6: The CruiseShip Java Class

```
public class CruiseShip {
    public String tonnage;
     public String name;
    // standard getters and setters
    ...
    public CruiseShip (String weight, String shipname) {
            tonnage = weight;
            name = shipname;
    }
}
```

This class results in the XML Schema shown in Listing 19-7. Note that the type of "string" is a Java string.

Listing 19-7: XML Schema Definition of CruiseShip

```
<types>
    <schema xmlns="http://www.w3.org/2001/XMLSchema"
targetNamespace="http://www.cruiseamerica.com/schemas/
   CruiseAmericaFinderRemoteInterface"
xmlns:xsd1="http://www.cruiseamerica.com/schemas/
   CruiseAmericaFinderRemoteInterface">
     <complexType name=testpackage.CruiseShip>
       <all>
       <element name="tonnage" type="string"/>
       <element name="name" type="string"/>
       </all>
     </complexType>
    </schema>
</types>
```

Defining messages, portTypes, operations, and bindings

After defining your data types, you need to describe your messages, portTypes, operations, and bindings, so that a service requestor can look at the WSDL and know how to interface with your service. Requestors use these specifications to map to your application.

A `<message>`, as shown in Figure 19-14, represents an interaction between service requestor and service provider. It represents an abstract definition of the data being transmitted. A message consists of logical parts, each of which is associated with a definition within some type system. You need to define two messages if you are utilizing an RPC call and are expecting results to be returned

From Figure 19-14, you can interpret that a `<portType>` is similar to a Java class and an `<operation>` is similar to a Java method. The `<portType>` specifies the name and operation (method name) and points to the input and output message. Within your schema, you can define multiple portTypes and within portType define multiple operations. Listing 19-8 shows an example of a `<portType>` that describes the `CruisePortType`. It has a single `<operation>`, named `GetLastDepartureDate` with an input and output message (`GetLastSailingRequest` and `GetLastSailingResponse`).

Listing 19-8: A Sample <portType> Definition

```
<portType name=' CruisePortType' >
  <operation name=' GetLastDepartureDate' >
        <input message=' tns:GetLastSailingRequest' />
        <output message=' tns:GetLastSailingResponse' />
  </operation>
</portType>
```

Now that there is an abstract definition of a `<portType>`, it needs to be specified in terms of real implementations. Figure 19-14 shows that the `<binding>` identifies the network protocol. A binding defines message format and protocol details for operations and messages defined by a particular portType. Another way to put it is that a `<binding>` specifies concrete protocol and data format specifications for the operations and messages defined by a particular `<portType>`. The bindings represent how the service is invoked. SOAP is the de facto standard.

> **NOTE**: A binding *must* specify exactly one protocol. A binding *must not* specify address information.

Listing 19-9 shows the concrete implementation of `<portType>` described in Listing 19-8. You can see how the operation names match up.

Listing 19-9: WSDL Binding

```
<binding name="CruisePortTypeBinding" type="tns:Cruise">
<soap:binding style="rpc"
transport="http://schemas.xmlsoap.org/soap/http"/>
<operation name="getLastDepartureDate">
```

```
<soap:operation soapAction="urn:Cruise" style="rpc"/>
<input>
<soap:body use="encoded"
encodingStyle="http://schemas.xmlsoap.org/soap/encoding/"/>
</input>
<output>
<soap:body use="encoded"
encodingStyle="http://schemas.xmlsoap.org/soap/encoding/"/>
</output>
</operation>
```

Defining ports

The port defines the installed endpoint of the service. Contrary to a portType, which is an abstract definition, a port defines an individual endpoint by specifying a single address for a binding. The port contains the URL where the SOAP `rpcrouter` servlet is running. You can define many services and within services many ports.

Any port in the implementation part must reference exactly one binding in the interface part. Listing 19-10 shows an example of port definitions.

Listing 19-10: Sample Port Definition

```
<service name="CruiseService">
<port name="CruisePort" binding="binding:CruisePortTypeBinding">
<soap:address
location="http://www.exch.com/soap/servlet/rpcrouter"/>
</port>
</service>
```

After you have specified the concrete endpoints, you are done. That was a lot of work. Luckily it was only reading the definitions and not typing them. The next section introduces some tooling that reduces the amount of entry required to set up WSDL documents.

Introducing tooling to make your life easier

Although it is rather straightforward to create the XML Schema, creating the schema is a tedious task. Luckily you have some tooling to make life a bit easier. When you installed the WSTK, you obtained access to two tools/utilities, which you can find in `<wskt_home>\bin`:

- *java2wsdl.bat*: The `java2wsdl` utility takes a classfile and outputs the XML Schema. `java2wsdl` performs the same function as a previously used utility called `wsdlgen`. In WSTK 3.1, `wsdlgen` was replaced with `java2wsdl`. Although `wsdlgen` is found in WSTK, it is now deprecated.
- *wsdl2java.bat*: `wsdl2java` takes a WSDL file and generates a skeleton implementation of the class.

`java2wsdl` is a utility that generates WSDL documents and SOAP deployment descriptors from existing Java classes. It works with JavaBeans, servlets, EJBs, or COM objects. The `java2wsdl` tool can generate serializers for complex data types. Serializers are Java class files that the Apache client and server use to serialize and deserialize complex types. The `wsdl2java` utility does the opposite of `java2wsdl`. It takes a WSDL file and generates the Java code.

NOTE: In WSTK 3.1, `wsdlgen` has been replaced with `java2wsdl` and `wsdl2java`.

The `wsdl2java` and `java2wsdl` utilities come with WSTK 3.1. As part of the AXIS toolset, these two utilities simplify the creation of WSDL documents and Java proxies. To run `wsdl2java`, you open a command prompt and issue the following:

```
java org.apache.axis.wsdl.Wsdl2java -s samples\addr\AddressBook.wsdl
-N urn:AddressGetter=samples.addr
```

The parameters and options are shown in Listing 19-11.

Listing 19-11: Using wsdl2java

```
Usage:  java org.apache.axis.wsdl.WSDL2Java [options] WSDL-URI
Options:
        -h, --help print this message and exit
        -v, --verbose print informational messages
        -s, --server-side emit server-side bindings for web service
        -S, --skeletonDeploy <argument>
            deploy skeleton (true) or implementation (false).
        -N, --NStoPkg <argument>=<value>
                mapping of namespace to package
        -f, --fileNStoPkg <argument>
            file of NStoPkg mappings (default NStoPkg.properties)
        -p, --package <argument>
            override all namespace to package mappings, use this
            package name instead
        -o, --output <argument> output directory for emitted files
        -d, --deployScope <argument> add scope to deploy.xml:
             "Application", "Request", "Session"
        -t, --testCase emit junit testcase class for web service
        -n, --noImports
            only generate code for the immediate WSDL document
        -a, --all
            generate code for all elements, even unreferenced ones
        -D, --Debug print debug information
        -T, --typeMappingVersion <argument> indicate 1.1 or 1.2.
            The default is 1.2 (SOAP 1.2 JAX-RPC compliant)
```

You don't utilize these tools in this chapter. If you want to learn more about `wsdl2java`, try the demo found in `<wstk_home>\services\demos\wsdl2java`.

> **TIP**: You can find out more about the demos for `wsdl2java` in `x:\wstk-3.1\services\demos\wsdl2java\README.htm`.

WSDL provides you with the tooling to describe services at a functional level. The use of tools, such as `wsdlgen`, `wsdl2java`, and `java2wsdl`, make the job of generating the WSDL document easier. For those who need to utilize WSDL programmatically, there is a Java API proposed to the JCP as JSP 110. WSTK 3.1 contains the WSDL API called `wsdl4j`.

> **NOTE**: The Java API for WSDL is found in `\wstk-3.1\wsdl4j\lib\wsdl4j.jar.`

Publishing, Finding, and Binding Your Services

Universal Description, Discovery, and Integration (UDDI) is a new standard for publishing and locating information about businesses and the services that they provide. You might think of UDDI as a form of advertising. Marketing managers are always looking for ways to get the word out about their products or services. On the other hand, scores of people are in search of good products and services that they cannot find easily. UDDI provides the opportunity for businesses to register their services in a common registry that is accessible by the Internet. UDDI is not limited to the Internet. You could implement a private UDDI registry on your company intranet to announce services provided by other departments. Then, a service requestor could access the UDDI registry (by browser) and search out services that fit various taxonomies and categories.

In this section, you learn more about Universal Description, Discovery, and Integration (UDDI), UDDI4J, and a new specification language: Web Services Inspection Language (WS-Inspections Language). With the three of these enablers you can publish, find, and bind to services available on the Net and within your organizations.

The approach in this section is to provide a basic understanding of the UDDI standard and then follow up with some coding snippets to solidify your knowledge. You begin with learning more about UDDI.

Understanding UDDI

UDDI creates a global, platform-independent, open framework to enable businesses to perform the following tasks:

- Locate (or discover) each other
- Define how they interact/cooperate over the Web
- Share information in a global registry

Currently, three UDDI operators, run by IBM, Microsoft, and HP, are available on the Web. These public UDDI registries are available for your company (or even your moonlighting company) to register services. Signing up for one automatically replicates to the others, so no matter which registry you access, your information is available.

> **NOTE**: Visit `www-3.ibm.com/services/uddi/` and follow the link to sign up for the IBM Test registry.

Publishing to a UDDI repository is fairly straightforward:

1. You register your business entity.
2. You register the WSDL interface.
3. Finally, you register the WSDL implementation description as a UDDI business service.

> **NOTE**: In the earlier section, "Separating interface and implementation," you learned to separate the WSDL file. In steps 2 and 3 of publishing to a UDDI repository, you register the WSDL files for consumption by others.

If you want to publish the fact that your moonlighting company specializes in WebSphere consulting, you can register your business. If you want to publish the fact that you have a Web service that identifies all the certified WebSphere 4.0 specialists and you want to enable others to implement the service, you can do that too.

So what are your choices for registries? From a developer's viewpoint, if you want to test a UDDI registry, you have two choices:

- The IBM Test Registry
- Private registry

You already installed the IBM Private registry. You can use that registry to test your publications. The IBM Test registry (which requires an Internet connection) is where you can learn more about how to use the interface to advertise your existence and service. Regardless of which direction you take, you still need to do the following to register:

- Get an ID to log on to the registry.
- Add a business.
- Add additional information about your business (contacts, locators, description, etc.).
- Categorize your business. The UDDI registries currently support five built-in categorization schemes: UDDITYPE, North American Industry Classification System (NAICS), Universal Standards Products and Service (UNSPSC and UNSPSC7), and Geographical taxonomy (GEO).

Each UDDI operator site has two endpoints: one for performing inquiry operations, and one for publish operations. You use these to perform the following activities:

- Find a business entity through its business key.
- Find a business entity using a wildcard (%).
- Find a business entity by categorization.
- Publishing/unpublish/change business entities.
- Publishing/unpublish/change business services and binding templates.

The endpoints of the IBM test are located at the following URLs:

- *Inquiry:* `www-3.ibm.com/services/uddi/testregistry/inquiryapi`
- *Publish*: `www-3.ibm.com/services/uddi/testregistry/protect/publishapi`.

UDDI4J enables you to access a UDDI registry via a UDDI proxy that implements all the various inquiry and publication operations. When you create a UDDI proxy, you can set its inquiry and publish URL values using `setInquireURL()` and `setPublishURL()`,respectively.

Getting information from UDDI

Earlier when you installed the Private UDDI registry, you added a Commerce Solutions business. If you did not, you may want to add one now. This section introduces some of the UDDI4J classes and methods. You inquire against the private UDDI registry using the `find_business()` method.

The `find_business()` method takes the name of a business, a qualifier, and a maximum result set size. A qualifier of `null` returns an unsorted list of businesses whose names begins with the specified value and a maximum result set size of 0 indicating that all results should be returned:

```
// find businesses whose name starts with "Commerce Solutions"
BusinessList bl = uddi.find_business( "Commerce Solutions", null, 0 );
```

The result set is a vector of `BusinessInfo` objects that contain information about each matching business, including the unique key that was allocated to each business during the registration process.

```
Vector businessInfoVector
= bl.getBusinessInfos().getBusinessInfoVector();
```

Listing 19-12 shows the complete client code. You use WebSphere Studio Application Developer to run some sample code to verify the information you stored in the UDDI registry earlier in the chapter. Follow these steps to run the example:

1. Create a shortcut on your windows desktop by right-clicking the desktop and selecting New⇨Shortcut.
2. Enter **"x:\Program Files\IBM\Application Developer\wsappdev.exe" -data "x:\code\uddi"** and click Next. (Note: x should be the drive letter you used to install WebSphere Studio Application Developer).
3. Name the shortcut **Chapter 19 UDDI**, and click Finish
4. Double-click your Chapter 19 UDDI shortcut.
5. Create a new Web project and name it **UddiTest**. Click Next.
6. Click Next past the Module Dependencies page.

7. On the Define Java Build Settings page, select the Libraries tab and click Add External Jars.

8. Select `soap.jar` and `uddi4j.jar` from `<was_home>/lib/`. Also add `mailapi.jar` from `x:wstk-3.1`. Click Finish.

9. Select File⇨Import and select File system. Click Next. Browse to the directory `x:\code\uddi`.

10. You can use UddiClient.java to cut and paste into WSAD to test or simply import it.. You can find `UddiClient.java` in `x:/Bible/chapter19/code/UddiClient.java`. Listing 19-12 shows the code.

Listing 19-12: UddiClient.java

```
import java.net.*;
import java.util.*;
import com.ibm.uddi.*;
import com.ibm.uddi.util.*;
import com.ibm.uddi.datatype.*;
import com.ibm.uddi.datatype.business.*;
import com.ibm.uddi.response.*;
import com.ibm.uddi.client.*;
public class UddiClient {

public static void main(String[] args) throws Exception {
 try {
 // create a UDDIproxy
 UDDIProxy uddi = new UDDIProxy();
 uddi.setInquiryURL("http://localhost:9080/uddisoap/inquiryapi");
 // use find_business to find "Commerce Solutions"
 BusinessList bl = uddi.find_business("Commerce Solutions", null, 0);
 Vector businessInfoVector =
  bl.getBusinessInfos().getBusinessInfoVector();
 // iterate vector and printout results
 for (int i = 0; i < businessInfoVector.size(); i++) {
  BusinessInfo bi = (BusinessInfo) businessInfoVector.elementAt(i);
  Vector descriptions = bi.getDescriptionVector();
  System.out.println("business name = " + bi.getNameString());
  System.out.println(" buskey = " + bi.getBusinessKey());
  for (int j = 0; j < descriptions.size(); j++) {
```

```
   Description description = (Description) descriptions.elementAt(j);
   System.out.println(" description = " + description.getText());
  }
  }
 } catch (UDDIException e) {
  DispositionReport report = e.getDispositionReport();
  if (report != null) {
   System.out.println(
   "UDDIException thrown faultCode:"
   + e.getFaultCode()+ "\n operator:"+ report.getOperator()
   + "\n errno:"      + report.getErrno()   + "\n errCode:"
   + report.getErrCode()+ "\n errInfoText:"
   + report.getErrInfoText());
  }
 }
}
}
```

11. Make sure you started the WebSphere Application Server and restarted the default server application server. You should have already installed the `UDDI.ear`.
12. From WebSphere Studio Application Developer, open up a `Java` perspective and highlight `UddiTest`; then click the Running Man icon. The results are shown in the WebSphere Studio Application Developer Administrative Console.

```
business name = commerce solutions
 buskey = 1F9A2C51-00D7-4B34-8A0D-320F331B1A76
```

Now you know how to access a UDDI Registry using UDDI4J. You can modify the code to include more business details. To do this, you simply utilize the `get_businessDetail()` method and pass in the keys of the business.

Making sense of UDDI

Now that you have experienced working with UDDI, the only thing left is to understand a little about what is under the covers and how it all fits. If you remember from Chapter 3, the UDDI specifications make use of tModels, business services, and binding templates. Figure 19-15 shows a graphic of the UDDI data types.

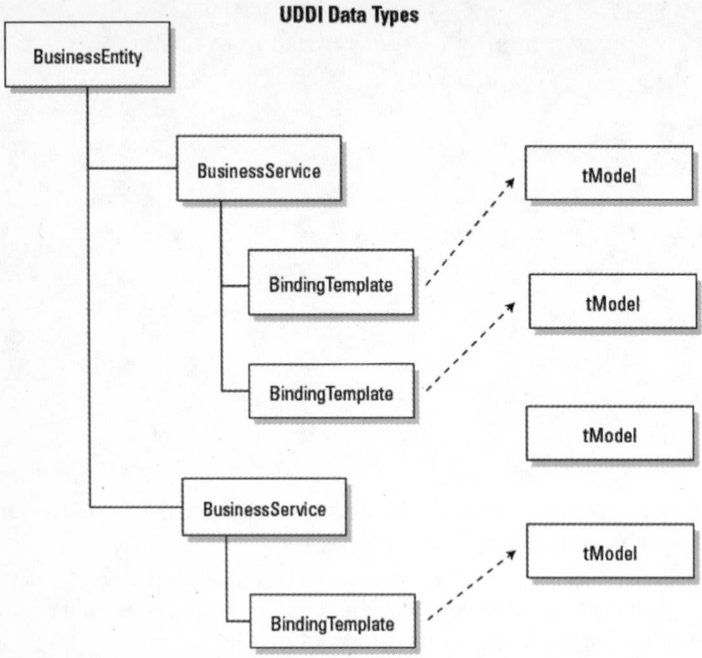

Figure 19-15: Businesses develop business services that they want published. UDDI provides the mechanism to organize the business into business services.

Understanding tModels

Although you can use tModels for a variety of descriptions, it might be best to start with tModels representing technical specifications. When a particular specification is registered with the UDDI repository as a tModel, it is assigned a unique key, which is then used in the description of service instances to indicate compliance with the specification. You saw the resulting keys in the UddiTestClient application you just completed. In that example the business key was

```
buskey = 1F9A2C51-00D7-4B34-8A0D-320F331B1A76
```

Services are represented in UDDI by the `businessService` data structure, and the details about how and where the service is accessed are provided by one or more nested `bindingTemplate` structures. A `bindingTemplate` specifies a network endpoint address (`accesspoint`) and a stack of tModels describing the service. The XML in Listing 19-13 represents the relationship between the `businessService`, `bindingTemplates`, and `tModelInstance`.

Listing 19-13: UDDI Business Service and Binding Templates

```
<businessService>
(...)
<bindingTemplates>
  <bindingTemplate>
    (...)
    <accessPoint urlType="http">
      http://www.whatever.com/</accessPoint>
    <tModelnstanceDetails>
      <tModelnstanceInfo tModelKey="...">
      </tModelnstanceInfo>
      (...)
    </tModelnstanceDetails>
    <overviewDoc>
    <overviewURL>http://localhost/wsdl/Cruise.wsdl</overviewURL>
    </overviewDoc>
  </bindingTemplate>
(...)
</bindingTemplates>
</businessService>
```

Creating UDDI Service Descriptions

So how does WSDL play in the population of the `businessServices`? In a nutshell, the process works as follows:

1. You create the WSDL service interface. Depending upon your company, you may define one or many service types and describe them with one or more service interfaces. It is those interfaces that are registered as UDDI tModels. Listing 19-13 shows an abbreviated excerpt from a UDDI registration. For other entities to utilize your service, they need to know where your WSDL file is located. With the UDDI registration, that information is provided by the service provider. The `<overviewDoc>` element points to the corresponding WSDL document. Listing 19-14 shows where to locate the WSDL file for the cruise service. The `<overviewURL>` element contains the pointer to the WSDL implementation file.

Listing 19-14: The <overviewURL> Element Provides the Location of the WSDL File

```
<overviewDoc>
  <overviewURL>http://localhost/wsdl/Cruise.wsdl</overviewURL>
</overviewDoc>
```

2. Next you build the services that adhere to the standard service definition. You do this by obtaining the tModel description and following the link (in the `<overviewURL>` element) to the corresponding WSDL document. Then you can use a tool, such as `wsdl2java` or WebSphere Studio Application Developer, to generate the interfaces.

3. The last step is to deploy and register the service in the UDDI repository. The preparation steps are as follows:
   - Using WebSphere Studio Application Developer, launch the IBM UDDI Explorer by selecting the WSDL file and clicking File⇨Export.
   - The Import wizard opens. Select UDDI and click Next. The UDDI Import wizard opens.
   - Click Finish. The IBM UDDI Explorer opens. You need to add the WebSphere UDDI registry. To add the registry to the IBM UDDI Explorer, in the UDDI Navigator pane, click the UDDI Main node.
4. In the Actions pane, type the Registry name: **WebSphere Test UDDI Registry** and the Inquiry URL (**`http://localhost:9080/uddisoap/inquiryapi`**). Click Go.
5. After it is added, select WebSphere Test UDDI registry in the Navigator window.
6. Log on to the registry by clicking the logon icon, which is a little man next to a lock. Enter in a publish URL and a userid and password. After you are logged on, you can find business entities, find business services, and find service interfaces.
7. Find your business entity (for example, Commerce Solutions).
8. Click Publish Service Interfaces and fill out the Web form to categorize and describe your service.

After it is implemented, you have a `bindingTemplate` for each service endpoint in which the network address is stored in the `accessPoint` element. Also a `tModelInstanceInfo` is created in the `bindingTemplate` for each tModel that is relevant to the service end point. You can also perform the opposite by finding a service and importing the WSDL file into WebSphere Studio Application Developer.

Understanding Web Services Inspection Language

The Web Services Inspection Language (sometimes referred as WS-Inspection or WSIL) is a new specification that provides a simple service-discovery method. In the prior sections, you had the opportunity to find services and learned how to published a service. For service discovery, you can use either the WS-Inspection service or UDDI for service discovery.

The WS-Inspection specification provides an XML format for inspecting a site for services and rules that govern how inspection-related information can be utilized. A WSIL document aggregates references to service description documents that have been created in any number of formats.

Another way of thinking about the need for WS-Inspection is by reviewing what WSDL and UDDI provide. WSDL describes services at a functional level. The UDDI schema goal is to provide a more business-centric perspective. The gap that exists between the two is the capability to tie together, at the point of offering, these various sources of information in a manner that is simple to create and use.

The WS-Inspection specification addresses the need by defining an XML grammar that integrates the references into a well-defined pattern of use. By achieving this, the WS-Inspection specification provides a means by which to inspect sites for service offerings.

It is easy to test the toolkit's implementation of WS-Inspection. No programming is necessary to advertise a service with WS-Inspection. To view the inspection document, start your Web application server and navigate your Web browser to where `localhost` indicates the appropriate server name and port for your environment:

```
http://localhost:9080/common/wsil/inspection.wsil
```

Figure 19-16 shows the output from the WS-Inspection. It shows the installed services on WebSphere.

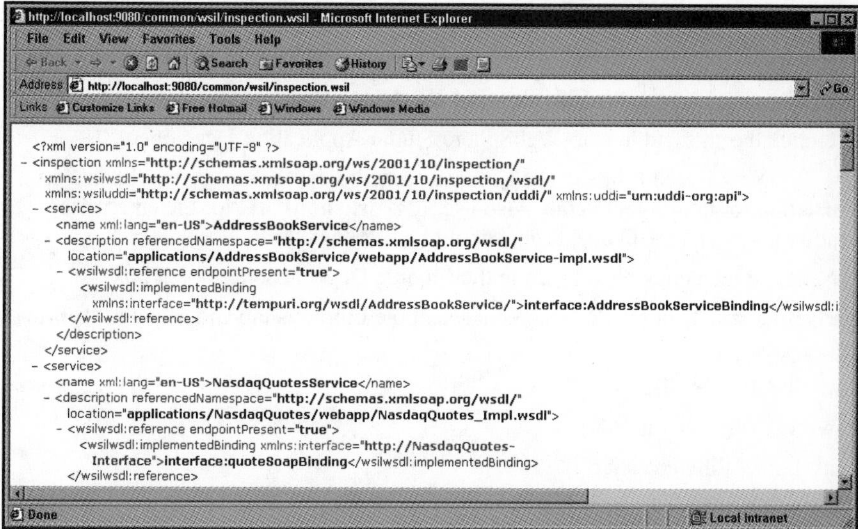

Figure 19-16: WS-Inspection XML output lists the services available in WebSphere.

As you can see in Figure 19-16, WS-Inspection provides an inspection document that you can use as input into your application. You do not use WS-Inspection in the exercises in this chapter, but you do see a demonstration of its use in the `addressbookdemo` at the end of the chapter.

Using WebSphere Studio Application Developer to Create a Web Services Component.

In this chapter, you actually develop a Web service using IBM WebSphere Application Developer (WSAD). Although you know about the wizards that come with WSAD, you develop a Web service without the services of the wizards.

Creating a Web Service Project

1. Create a new folder to contain your Web services workspace (for example, `x:\code\spworkshop`).
2. If you originally created a shortcut to WSAD, make a copy of that shortcut and update the properties for that shortcut. The shortcut target should be changed to add the following parameter: `-data "x:\code\spworkshop"` (for example, `"x:\Program Files\IBM\Application Developer\wsappdev.exe" -data "x:\code\spworkshop"`). This creates a shortcut to your source code.
3. Double-click the shortcut to start WebSphere Studio Application Developer.
4. Select File⇨New⇨Web Project. The Create a New Project Wizard opens. Enter **SPWorkshop** for the Project name. Also use **SPWorkshopEAR** for the enterprise application project name. Context root should be **SPWorkshop**.
5. Click Next and then click Next again in the Module Dependencies dialog box.
6. On the Define Java Build Settings screen, select the Libraries tab and select the following external JARs:
   - X:\wstk-3.1\lib\mailapi.jar
   - X:\wstk-3.1\lib\activation.jar
   - <was_home>\lib\xerces.jar
   - <was_home>\lib\soap.jar

> **NOTE**: You are selecting the `soap.jar` file instead of the `axis.jar` file. You could select the `axis.jar` file, but you need to ensure that the package names in your code reflect the AXIS packaging rather than the SOAP package names.

7. The Build output folder you use is `SPWorkshop/webApplication/WEB-INF/classes`. This is where the files will be stored. Click Finish to create the project.
8. To create a new Java package, click File⇨New⇨Other⇨Java, and select Java Package. Click Next.
9. The Folder name should be `/SPWorkshop/source`. Enter **testpackage** as the package name. Click Finish.

10. You create a Java class that converts Fahrenheit to Celsius. The `convert()` method takes a temperature (Fahrenheit) and returns the conversion. Simply subtract 32 degrees from the passed value and multiply the result by 5/9.You can highlight the test package and right-click selecting New⇨Other⇨Java and select Java Interface and click Next.
11. Your are creating an interface to ensure that users who use your service implement a `convert()` method. Name the interface **Temperature.** Click Finish.
12. The Temperature interface is presented in Edit mode. Add the `convert()` method declaration to the interface, as shown in Listing 19-15.

Listing 19-15: Adding the convert() Interface

```
package testpackage;
public interface Temperature {
 public String convert(String degrees);
}
```

13. You need to create a concrete implemention of Temperature. Create a class called TemperatureImpl using the context menu. Right-click and select New⇨Other⇨Java, select Java Class and click Next.
14. Enter **TemperatureImpl** as the class name. Click the Add button and type **Temperature**. You can then select the Temperature interface and click Add. Now click OK to close the dialog box. Ensure that you check Constructors from SuperClass and Inherit Abstract Methods when you create the class. Click Finish to generate the class.
15. When created, update the code as follows:

```
package testpackage;
public class TemperatureImpl implements Temperature {
 /**
  * @see Temperature#convert(String)
  */
    /**
     * Constructor for TemperatureImpl
     */
    public TemperatureImpl() {
        super();
    }
 public String convert(String degrees) {
 Float celsius = new Float(degrees);
        celsius = new Float((((celsius.floatValue()-32)*5)/9));
  return new Integer(Math.round(celsius.floatValue())).toString();
 }
}
```

NOTE: You might notice that there are no references to any SOAP implementations. The way you reference SOAP is through a deployment descriptor.

16. Create a new folder in `x:\code\spworkshop` called **exports**. Then create a file in `x:\code\spworkshop\exports` called **tempconvert-DD.xml** and add the following lines to `tempconvert-DD.xml`. You can also copy the file from your downloaded code folder `x:/Bible/chapter19/code` and place it in the `x:\code\spworkshop\exports` folder.

```
<?xml version="1.0" ?>
<isd:service xmlns:isd="http://xml.apache.org/xml-soap/deployment"
  id="urn:webservices-spworkshop-convert">
 <isd:provider type="java"
  scope="Application"
  methods="convert">
 <isd:java class="testpackage.TemperatureImpl" static="false" />
 </isd:provider>
<isd:faultListener>org.apache.soap.server.DOMFaultListener
</isd:faultListener>
</isd:service>
```

17. To deploy to WebSphere, you need to create the J2EE artifacts that are required the J2EE standards. You need to package your classes in a Web Archive (WAR) file and have the WAR file packaged in an Enterprise Archive (EAR) file.
18. To perform the steps with WebSphere Studio Application Developer, select File⇨Export⇨EAR file.
19. When presented with the EAR Export dialog box, enter the following information:
    - In the What Resources Do You Want Exported field, select `SPWorkshopEAR`.
    - In the Where Do You Want to Export Resources to field, enter **`x:\code\spworkshop\exports\spworkshop.ear`**.
    - Click Finish.
20. Verify that you have a copy of the `tempconvert-DD.xml` deployment descriptor file in `x:\code\spworkshop\exports` directory. You will use that file when you run the `SOAPEAREnabler` tool.

You are now ready to enable the EAR file for SOAP.

Updating the EAR file with SOAPEAREnabler

The EAR file you just created does not contain any of the required SOAP libraries. To enable any EAR file for use with SOAP, you need to run the `SOAPEAREnabler` tool that is provided with WSAD. `SOAPEAREnabler` merges your EAR file with the required SOAP libraries and deploys the selected service (convert) into the SOAP server.

1. Open a command window (Start⇨Run⇨`cmd.exe`), and navigate to the location where you exported the EAR file (`x:\code\spworkshop\exports`). Enter **soapearenabler**. You are asked a number of questions. The answers to the questions are:
    - Enter **spworkshop.ear** as the name of the EAR file.
    - For the number of services, enter **1**.

- For the filename of the SOAP deployment descriptor, enter **tempconvert-DD.xml.**
- Is this service an EJB? Enter **n** for No.
- How many jar files? Enter **0.**
- Should this service be secured? Enter **n** for No.
- The context root should be **/spworkshop**
- Install the Administrative Console? Enter **y** for Yes.

2. The process begins. Figure 19-17 shows a sample of the questions and answers.

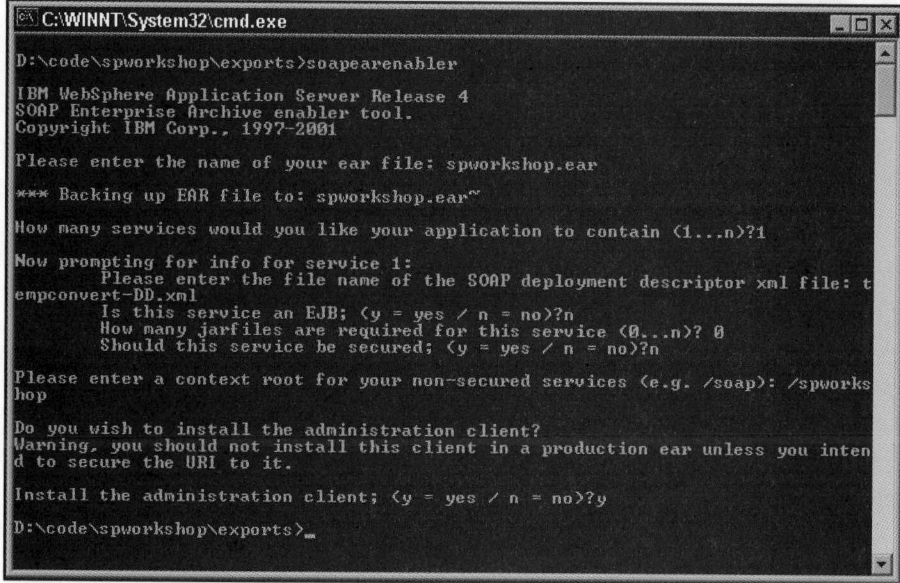

C:\WINNT\System32\cmd.exe
D:\code\spworkshop\exports>soapearenabler
IBM WebSphere Application Server Release 4
SOAP Enterprise Archive enabler tool.
Copyright IBM Corp., 1997-2001
Please enter the name of your ear file: spworkshop.ear
*** Backing up EAR file to: spworkshop.ear~
How many services would you like your application to contain (1...n)?1
Now prompting for info for service 1:
Please enter the file name of the SOAP deployment descriptor xml file: tempconvert-DD.xml
Is this service an EJB; (y = yes / n = no)?n
How many jarfiles are required for this service (0...n)? 0
Should this service be secured; (y = yes / n = no)?n
Please enter a context root for your non-secured services (e.g. /soap): /spworkshop
Do you wish to install the administration client?
Warning, you should not install this client in a production ear unless you intend to secure the URI to it.
Install the administration client; (y = yes / n = no)?y
D:\code\spworkshop\exports>_

Figure 19-17: When you run the SOAPEarEnabler tool, it modifies the EAR file to include the proper SOAP libraries.

3. Start the WebSphere Administrative server and Administrative Console if they are not already started. Follow the steps that you utilized earlier when you installed the SOAP examples. See "Installing the Soap Examples on WebSphere Application Server (AE)."
4. After the EAR file is installed, you can test your SOAP application by using Internet Explorer and entering **http://localhost:9080/spworkshop/admin/index.html**.
5. Select List all services to see a list of all registered services. Figure 19-18 shows your deployed service (`urn:webservices-spworkshop-convert`). You are now ready to create a client application to run your service.

Figure 19-18: Testing the SOAP deployment validates that the soap server is operating successfully.

Developing the SOAP client

Creating a client is straightforward. Start by either importing from `x:\Bible\Chapter19 TemperatureImplClient.java` into WebSphere Studio Application Developer, or create a new class called `TemperatureImplClient` and enter in the information in Listing 19-16.

1. If you choose not to import the code, right-click in the Navigator and select New⇨Other⇨Java and select Java Class and click Next.
   - Set the package name to **testpackage**.
   - Enter in the class name: **TemperatureImplClient**.
   - You should have a `main()` method generated to save you some typing. Click Finish.
2. After you define your class, you will be presented with TemperatureImplClient in the editor. You can choose to cut and paste the rest of the code from `x:\Bible\Chapter19 TemperatureImplClient.java` or type in the code found in Listing 19-16. If you choose to type it all, ensure that the `main()` method throws the required exceptions (`MalformedURLException` and `SOAPException`) and add the import statements.
3. The key to the entire class is the `Call` object. You create an instance of it and set the URI, `EncodingStyleURI` and necessary parameters. All the parameters are added to a vector and then set in the `Call` object using `setParams()`.
4. You initiate the `invoke()` method on the `Call` object and expect a return response. The response should contain the value from the service or a fault. The complete code is shown in Listing 19-16.

Listing 19-16: TemperatureImplClient.java Accesses Your SOAP Service

```
package testpackage;
import org.apache.soap.*;
import org.apache.soap.rpc.*;
import java.net.*;
import java.util.*;
public class TemperatureImplClient {

 public static void main(String[] args) throws MalformedURLException,
SOAPException {

 Call call = new Call();
 call.setTargetObjectURI("urn:webservices-spworkshop-convert");

 call.setEncodingStyleURI("http://schemas.xmlsoap.org/soap/encoding/");
 call.setMethodName("convert");

 Vector params = new Vector();
 Parameter degrees = new Parameter("degrees", String.class, args[0],
null);
 params.addElement(degrees);
 call.setParams(params);

 Response resp = call.invoke(new
URL("http://localhost:9080/spworkshop/servlet/rpcrouter"),
                          "urn:webservices-spworkshop-convert");

  if (resp.generatedFault()) {
  Fault fault = resp.getFault();
  throw new SOAPException(fault.getFaultCode(),
  fault.getFaultString());
 }
 Parameter retValue = resp.getReturnValue();
 System.out.println("Temperature in Celsius is "+retValue.getValue());
 }
}
```

After entering all of the code and saving, you are ready to run the example from WebSphere Studio Application Developer. Select the `TemperatureImplClient` class, and use the right mouse to update Properties. The Properties dialog box is shown in Figure 19-19.

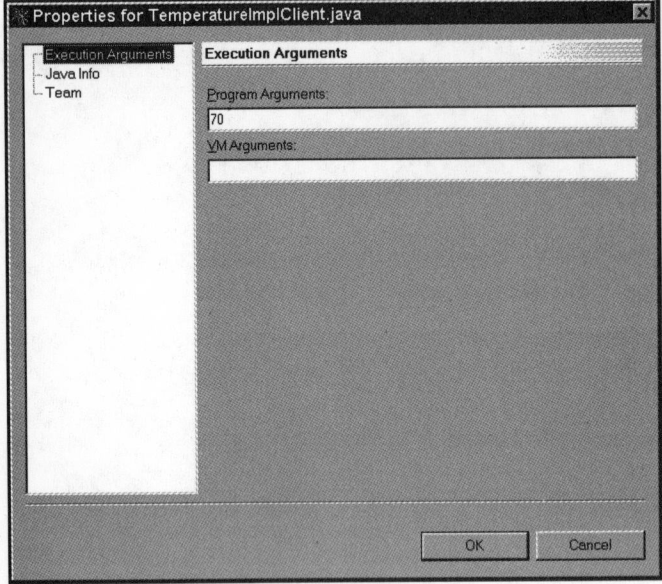

Figure 19-19: Setting program arguments.

In the Properties dialog box, you need to set the Fahrenheit temperature to pass to the service. Select Execution Arguments and set the Program Arguments value for the starting temperature to a value you like (example 70) and click OK. You are now ready to test. Follow these steps:

1. Ensure that WebSphere Application Server and the default application server are up and running. You are now ready to run the service.
2. If you are not in a Java Perspective, switch to a Java perspective using Perspective⇨Open⇨Java. Expand SPWorkshop, source, and testpackage. Select `TemperatureImplClient`.
3. Select the Running Man icon to start running the client. Choose to run it as a Java Application when prompted.

You are switched into the Debug perspective, and you see your answer in the console. Congratulations, you have a working Web service.

> **NOTE**: If you get a `ClassNotFound` error, you might have to update the Default Server module visibility to Application from Module.

TCPTunneling

Although your application is running, the results you receive might not be what you expected. One cool tool is the `TCPTunnelingGUI`. This tool shows you the header information from the HTTP request. Figure 19-20 shows the output from the `TemperatureImplClient`.

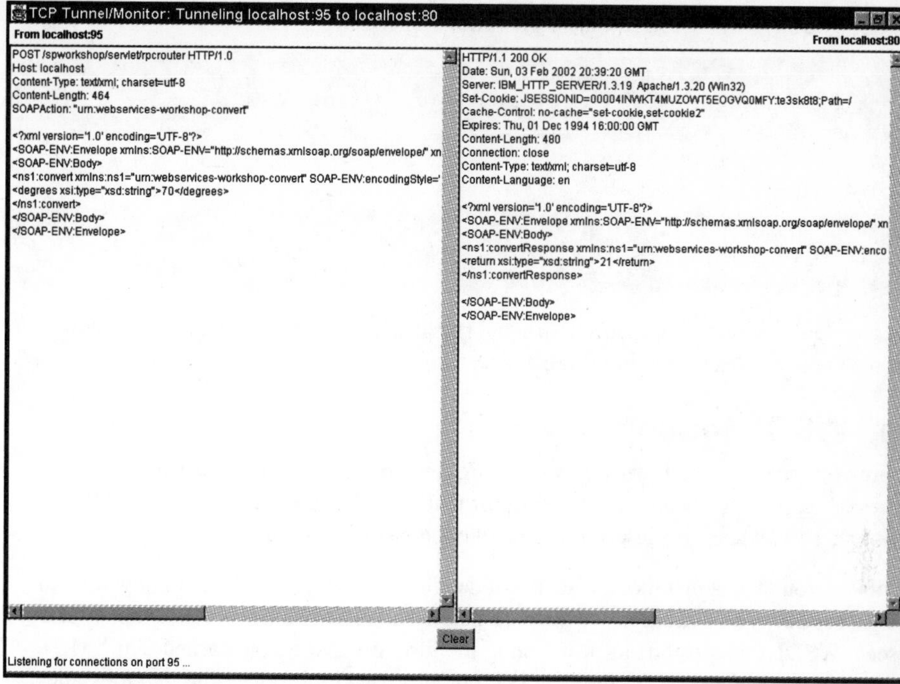

Figure 19-20: TCPTunnelGUI: The left side is the outgoing SOAP envelope. On the right side, is the incoming returned envelope.

`TCPTunnelGUI` is a swing application that runs from a command prompt. It listens to SOAP messages arriving at a specified TCP/IP port. This provides you with information as to how messages are being passed and returned to your program. To run `TCPTunnelGUI`, follow these steps:

1. From a command window, change directories to **<wstk_home>\bin** and run `wstkenv.bat`.
2. Set the classpath = **%wstk_CP%.**
3. Add the location of the `soap.jar` file to the classpath. You should find the file in `x:\wstk-3.1\WebSphere\lib`. Set the classpath by typing in the command window **set classpath=%classpath%;x:\wstk-3.1\WebSphere\lib\soap.jar**.
4. Enter **java org.apache.soap.util.net.TcpTunnelGui 95 localhost 9080**. The TCPTunnelGui should appear in a new window.

The 95 is the port number assigned to listen for SOAP messages. For this to work, you need to update `TemperatureImplClient`.

In `TemperatureImplClient`, update the following code:

```
Response resp = call.invoke(new
URL("http://localhost:9080/spworkshop/servlet/rpcrouter"),
"urn:webservices-spworkshop-convert");
```

to

```
Response resp = call.invoke(new
URL("http://localhost:95/spworkshop/servlet/rpcrouter"),
"urn:webservices-spworkshop-convert");
```

and recompile. Now start `TcpTunnelGui` and run `TemperatureImplClient` again. You should see the results as shown in Figure 19-20.

Using WSDL tooling

In the previous section, you learned how existing functions are implemented as SOAP interfaces. You created a deployment descriptor that describes the service. The SOAP `rpcrouter` servlet uses the descriptor to handle the incoming requests.

The problem you face is that the service is not detailed enough for a client to know how to invoke the service. The definitions of the parameters and return values are missing. WSDL to the rescue. WSDL contains this information in the form of XML. You learned that XML Schemas are used to describe the input and output data used by services and that messages, operations, and portTypes are well defined.

A bottom-up approach is in order. You use your Temperature service and expose it as a Web service using WSDL. To expose the Temperature service, you need to create a SOAP deployment descriptor and deploy the service in SOAP. You learned earlier that it's good to separate the interface and implementation definitions, so you need two WSDL documents. Finally, you need to publish the service to UDDI using your generated WSDL documents.

Running WSAD to generate the WSDL

Developers not using WSAD would use the WSTK tools (`wsdlgen`, `java2wsdl`, and `wsdl2java`) to develop bottom-up and top-down Web services. WSAD provides similar generation tooling by using the Web services wizards. You create a new Web services project with WSAD to demonstrate the ease of development with the wizards. When the exercise is completed, you will have performed a bottom-up implementation utilizing SOAP and WSDL.

Follow these steps:

1. Create a new folder to hold your files. Using the instructions in "Creating a Web Service Project," create another folder called **x:\code\spworkshop2** and adjust the shortcut to point WSAD to the new directory. Call your project **SPWorkshop2** and the enterprise project name **SPWorkshop2EAR**.
2. After you set up your project, switch to the `Java` perspective and create a new package called **testpackage**. After the package is created, select File⇨Import to import the same source files you created in SPWorkshop. You can find the Java files in folder `x:\code\spworkshop\SPWorkshop\source`.

NOTE: If you get errors you might have forgotten to add the external JAR files. Add `soap.jar`, `xerces.jar`, `activation.jar`, and `mailapi.jar`.

3. Select the `TemperatureImpl` class and select File⇨New⇨Web Services⇨Web Service. You should see the wizard screen shown in Figure 19-21.

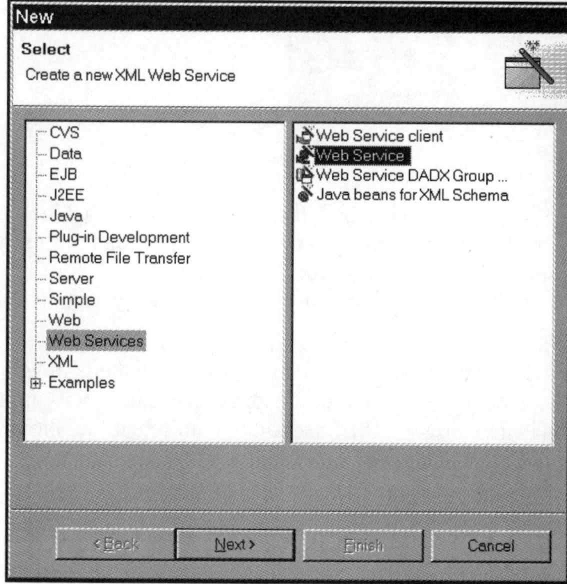

Figure 19-21: Creating a Web service.

4. When you click Next, you have the option of choosing how the wizard behaves. The wizard defaults shown in Figure 19-22 enable you to choose the full spectrum of Web services.

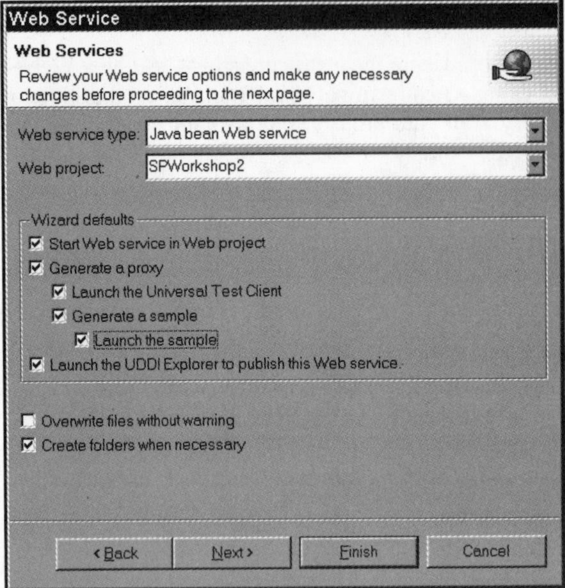

Figure 19-22: Web services options.

5. After clicking Next, you have the option of changing the JavaBean selected. Click Next to continue. On the Web Service JavaBean Identity screen, you have the opportunity to change some of the default values set for JavaBean identity, as shown in Figure 19-23. The Web Service URI should be changed in most cases to a more relevant name, but you can accept the default for now.
6. The Web Service JavaBean Methods page shows a summary of the methods in your bean. You see the `convert()` method displayed. In this page, you can specify input and output encoding as either SOAP encoding or XML encoding. You select the Show server (Java to XML) type mapping check box, and click Next to accept the defaults.
7. The next page is the Web Service Java to XML mappings page. Here you can verify your mappings and change them if necessary. You should accept the defaults and click Next.
8. The Web Service Binding Proxy Generation page is used for reviewing the bindings that you use when the Web service proxy is generated. The client proxy provides the remote procedure call interface to `TemperatureImpl`. The name of the client is `TemperatureImplProxy`. Select Show Mappings and click Next.

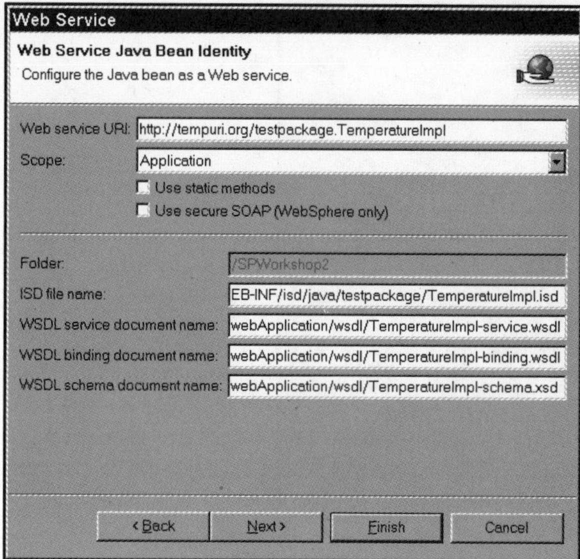

Figure 19-23: JavaBean identity.

9. The Web Service XML to Java Mappings page gives you the opportunity to review the client type mappings. Again, click Next.
10. In the Web Service SOAP Binding Mapping Configuration page, review your Web service SOAP binding mapping configuration. Click Next to accept the defaults.
11. In the Web Service Test Client page, ensure that the Launch the Test Client check box is selected. The test client is used to test the methods of your Web service. Click Next.
12. In the Web Service Sample Generation page of the wizard, ensure that both the Generate a Sample and the Launch the Sample check boxes are selected. The sample Web application demonstrates how to code a JSP in terms of the proxy file. The sample is generated into the `webApplication` folder of your Web project. Click Next to accept the defaults.
13. Before you reach the last step, you need to ensure that the WebSphere Administrative Server is stopped. Stop the Administrative Server using Windows Services.
14. The last step (shown in Figure 19-24) is to determine whether you want to launch the UDDI Explorer. If you select Launch the UDDI Explorer to publish the Web service, you have the opportunity to publish your Web service on the IBM test registry. Click Finish to complete the wizard.

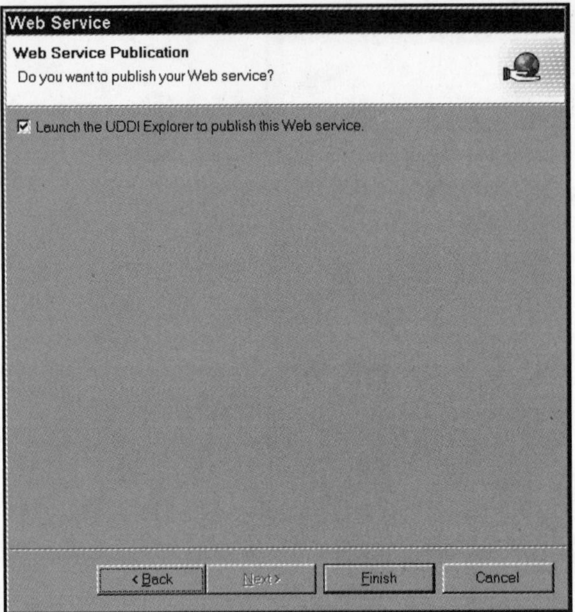

Figure 19-24: Launching the UDDI Explorer.

After some code generation and compilations, you are presented with the end results. Figure 19-25 shows the invocation of the test client that you specified earlier. You can see your exposed `convert` method, along with pages to provide input and display results. Also notice that your `Source code` folder and your `webApplication` folder have a few more entries. You might want to explore the WSDL folder and browse the `TemperatureImpl-binding.wsdl` file.

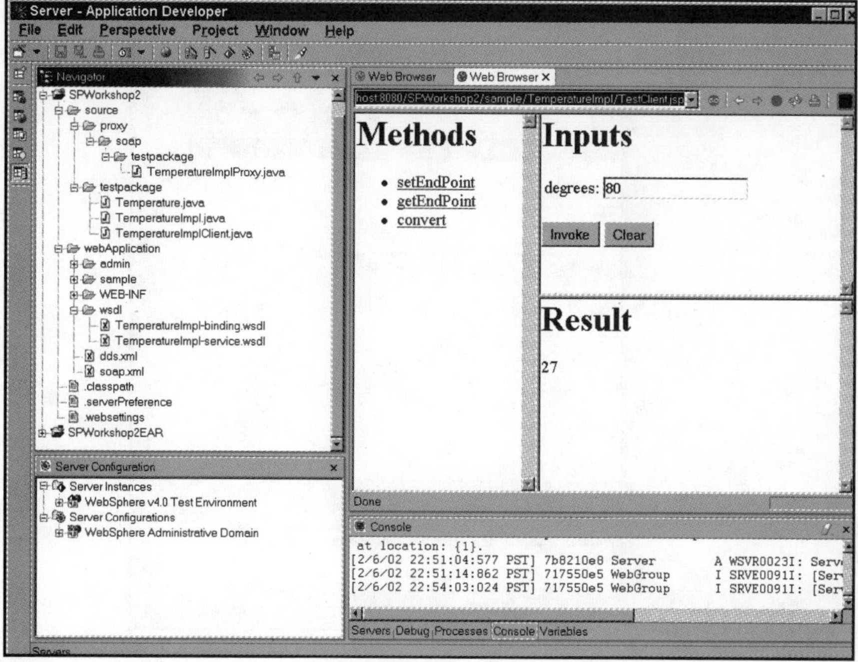

Figure 19-25: The TestClient.jsp is automatically created for you so you can test your Web service.

Another window that appears is the UDDI Explorer. The browser window shown in Figure 19-26 connects you to the IBM Test Registry on the Web. There you can register your service. You must first acquire a userid and password to work with the registry. After that, you can add and update your business entity, service, and contacts.

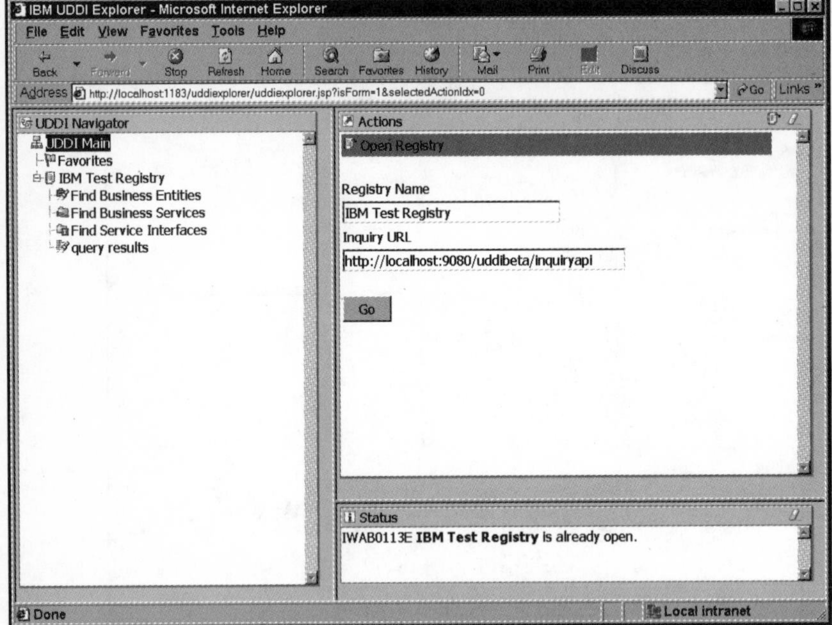

Figure 19-26: UDDI Explorer.

Congratulations. You have developed a Web service using WSAD that covers SOAP, WSDL, and UDDI publishing. Thanks to the wizard processing, you had to do very little to complete the development. This exercise also shows how standards within the three Web services initiatives have made it easier to interface them together.

Running the AddressBookSample demo

You have covered many of the Web services enablers. Previously, you ran one of the samples to show how WS-Integration fits within the overall architecture.

The Apache-SOAP samples that you installed have an application called the AddressBookSample. Ensure that the default server is started. Figure 19-27 shows the green arrow that signifies that the default server is running. You could also have selected the Ping icon to verify that the server is running.

Open a command prompt and change the directory as follows:

```
X:\wstk-3.1\services\demos\addressbook\client
```

Then enter the following command:

```
Addressbookdemo -mode wsil -role all -demo both
```

Listing 19-17 shows the results.

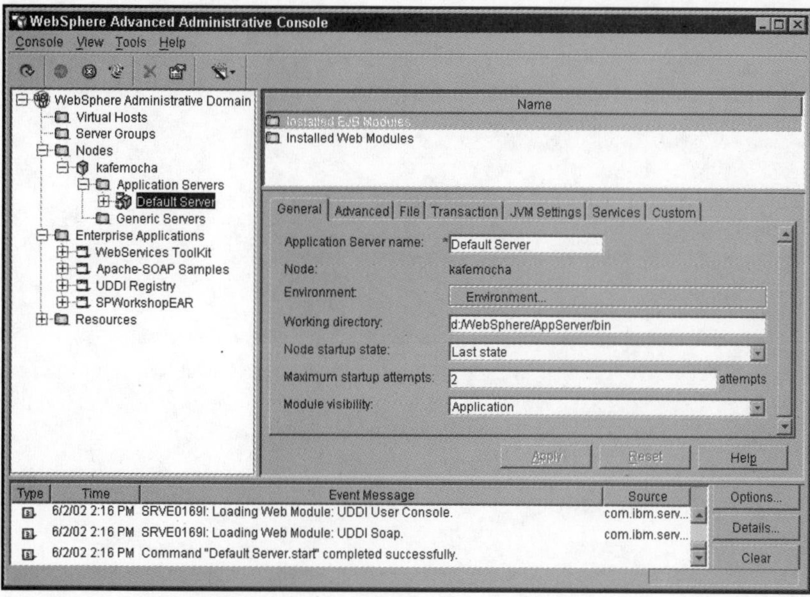

Figure 19-27: WebSphere Administrative Console.

Listing 19-17 Output from AddressBookDemo

```
D:\wstk-3.1\services\demos\addressbook\client>addressbookdemo  -mode wsil
-role all -demo both

==================================================
  ROLE: Service Provider
==================================================

[STEP 1] Deploy service implementation...
Deploying >> AddressBook_Service <<...
Service deployed.

==================================================
  ROLE: Service Requestor
==================================================

[STEP 1] WSIL based Find service implementation...
The following services were found:
Service name: AddressBook_Service

[STEP 2] WSIL based Bind [invoke] service implementation...
Invoking service >> AddressBook_Service <<...
Adding Linda...
Linda has been added.

Looking for Linda...
Found: 111 Main St.
Raleigh, NC 27513
(919) 334-8765

Storing 'sample_listings.xml'...
Stored listings

Getting all listings...
Found: <AddressBook>
      <Listing>
        <name>Dave Davis</name>
        <address>
          <streetNum>919</streetNum>
          <streetName>Baker Lane</streetName>
          <city>Sunnytown</city>
          <state>UT</state>
          <zip>43434</zip>
          <phoneNumber>
            <areaCode>789</areaCode>
            <exchange>654</exchange>
            <number>3210</number>
      </phoneNumber>
```

```
    </address>
  </Listing>
      <Listing>
        <name>Linda Smith</name>
        <address>
          <streetNum>111</streetNum>
          <streetName>Main St.</streetName>
          <city>Raleigh</city>
          <state>NC</state>
          <zip>27513</zip>
          <phoneNumber>
            <areaCode>919</areaCode>
            <exchange>334</exchange>
            <number>8765</number>
      </phoneNumber>
    </address>
  </Listing>
      <Listing>
        <name>Mary Smith</name>
        <address>
          <streetNum>888</streetNum>
          <streetName>Broadway</streetName>
          <city>Somewhere</city>
          <state>FL</state>
          <zip>87654</zip>
          <phoneNumber>
            <areaCode>222</areaCode>
            <exchange>333</exchange>
            <number>4444</number>
      </phoneNumber>
    </address>
  </Listing>
</AddressBook>

Removing Linda...
Removed Linda
Removing all...
Removed all
===============================================
  ROLE: Service Provider
===============================================
[STEP 1] Undeploy service implementation...
Undeploying >> AddressBook_Service <<...
Service was undeployed.

D:\wstk-3.1\services\demos\addressbook\client>
```

This demonstration actually shows you the full spectrum of Web services including the use of WSIL. You should review the sample code and supporting files (found in `x:\wstk-3.1\services\demos\addressbook\client`) to gain a better understanding of how all the components interact.

Summary

Web services are built around the concept of a service-oriented architecture. In a service-oriented architecture, services are created by entities referred to as service providers. The service providers would not make their services available if they didn't believe there was demand for these services. The demand is generated by service requestors. Service requestors seek out the services providers individually or through service brokers. Brokers, in turn, with service providers advertise the services so that service requestors have a standard way of looking up business entities and the services they provide.

Given this triangular relationship, it is important that you become familiar with how the interactions work and how standards play in its success. Perhaps the best way to learn about Web services is to install the tooling available to develop, deploy, and discover Web services.

IBM, being a leader in the Web services initiatives, has provided a toolkit named the Web Services ToolKit (WSTK). Found on AlphaWorks, this toolkit provides numerous technology previews that assist the developer in creating Web services. Now at version 3.1, the Web Services ToolKit provides Web services technologies, such as SOAP, WSDL, WSDL4J, AXIS, WSIL, UDDI4J, and WSFL. You installed the WSTK and ran some of the examples provided with the toolkit.

Understanding the different components is relatively easy. Built upon standards, such as HTTP and XML, Web services development is a matter of understanding the underlying infrastructure and meeting the specifications. As with any testing environment, you should begin by installing the products and ensuring that they are functioning. You learned how to install the WSTK and a private UDDI registry on WebSphere. After these are installed, you are in a position to create, test, and deploy Web services.

Early on, you learned that there are three approaches to developing Web services: top down, bottom up, and meet in the middle. Using the top-down approach, you are guided through the development process. You began with SOAP development and then learned about WSDL and WSIL. Eventually, the development process reaches deployment stage, so you learned how to deploy, test, and publish to a private UDDI registry and were introduced to terminology, such as business entities, templates, and tModels.

In the SOAP development process, you learned about tools, such as the `SOAPEarEnabler` and `TCPTunnelGui`. The chapter ended with the development of a Web service using WebSphere Studio Application Developer. Although this chapter only scratched the surface, you are aware of the process, tooling, and possibilities for your entry into Web services.

Part III

Systems Administration

Chapter 20
Configuring WebSphere Application Environments

Chapter 21
Configuring Session Management

Chapter 22
Using WebSphere's Application Packaging

Chapter 23
Configuring Security

Chapter 20

Configuring WebSphere Application Environments

In This Chapter

- ♦ Reviewing Web architecture
- ♦ Introducing the Administrative Server
- ♦ Introducing the Administrative Console
- ♦ Configuring resources
- ♦ Setting up JavaMail
- ♦ Setting up JMS

The previous chapters topics taught you about J2EE development using WebSphere Studio Application Developer. As you move into a new part of the book, the focus is on configuring and maintaining WebSphere Application Server 4.0.

In Chapter 2, you were given a whirlwind tour of the WebSphere Application server. Part of the discussion covered the Administrative Console. The details were kept to a minimum so that we could discuss them here. The format of the chapters in this section is as follows:

- ♦ Introduce the subject matter
- ♦ Provide descriptions of its importance
- ♦ Provide hands-on examples

In this chapter on configuring WebSphere, you become intimate with the WebSphere Administrative Console. You learn how to configure application servers and operate the WebSphere domain using the Administrative Console. The activities you must perform in order to configure application servers are discussed. You learn how to configure HTTP transports, Virtual hosts, JDBC providers, data sources, JavaMail, JMS, and J2C.

Because it has been a while since Chapter 2, in which you learned about the WebSphere architecture, a quick review is in order.

Reviewing WebSphere Architecture

Figure 2-1 in Chapter 2, WebSphere Application Architecture, showed the architecture of a single WebSphere domain. Being able to identify the components of a WebSphere domain is key to understanding how WebSphere works and can be configured.

Briefly, a WebSphere domain consists of a group of WebSphere application servers all utilizing the same administrative repository. The administrative repository is in the form of a relational database that can be one of the many supported by WebSphere. Throughout the book, we have been focusing on DB2 as that relational database.

CROSS-REFERENCE: Chapter 2 provides an excellent overview of WebSphere domains.

The key components of the WebSphere domain are as follows:

- *The Web server:* It communicates to the Administrative Server through a plug-in.
- *The embedded HTTP server:* Running on default port 9080, the embedded HTTP server is utilized to communicate requests to the Web and EJB containers components.
- *The Web container:* Contains Web components, such as servlets, JSPs, and resources.
- *The EJB container:*Responsible for Enterprise Beans and persistence to external databases.

Understanding the flow of request can help you understand the key points of configurations using the Administrative Server. If you do not remember the flow of a request, return to Chapter 2 for a more in-depth review.

Understanding the Administrative Server

Also in Chapter 2, you were first introduced to the Administrative Server. If you remember, the Administrative Server is composed of three services: the Location Service Daemon (LSD), the Bootstrap Naming Service (JNDI), and Security Services. The Administrative Server is responsible for runtime management, security, transaction coordination, and workload management.

CROSS-REFERENCE: For more information about the Administrative Server, see Chapter 2.

The Location Service Daemon (LSD) is used for persistent object references; its default port is 9000. The LSD processes requests to locate persistent object references and redirects clients to the appropriate application server. LSD listens at a fixed port (9000) and keeps track of the namespaces in use across a network.

When you launch the Administrative Console, it attempts to connect to 900. Port 900 is the port serviced by the Administrative Server to service requests for Java Native Directory Interface (JNDI) naming and security. JNDI provides a common interface that is used to access the various naming and directory services. Each object has a unique JNDI name by which other objects can identify and find it.

> **TIP**: The Administrative Server runs within its own JVM, separate from the JVM for each application server.

Using the Administrative Console

The Administrative Console is where you configure your WebSphere domains. The Administrative Console, shown in Figure 20-1, consists of multiple panes. The left pane shows the components you can configure. You can expand and collapse the tree to view child nodes within the tree. The right pane shows configurations already set and provides a way to navigate to sections where other configurations can be displayed or modified. The lower pane displays administrative events.

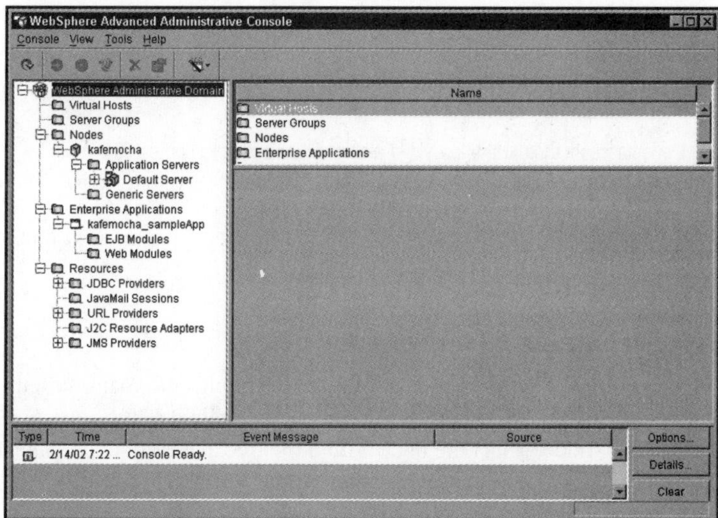

Figure 20-1: The Administrative Console is new with WebSphere 4.0 and provides a good interface for configuring WebSphere domains. You can launch the Administrative Console from anywhere on the network by using the adminclient.bat command.

The sections that follow walk you through the common configuration tasks implemented from the left pane of the Administrative Console.

Every administrator is responsible for several common tasks. These tasks range from starting and stopping servers, to reviewing history records, to determining who or what impacts the availability of a resource. Some of the common tasks can be accessed from the toolbar. Figure 20-2 shows the toolbar.

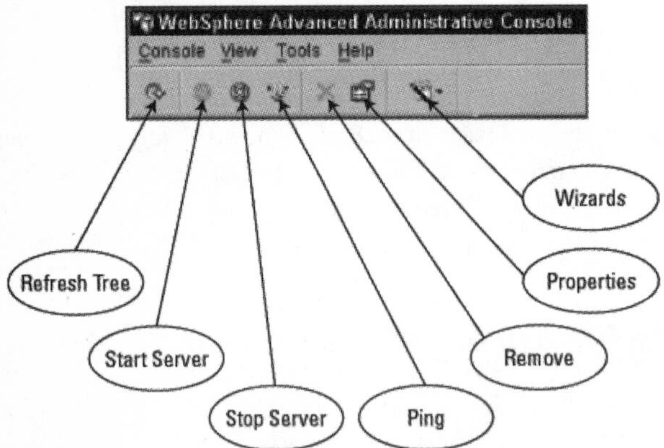

Figure 20-2: The Administrative Console has a toolbar that provides a single click action to some of the more common activities performed by an administrator.

The toolbar is attached to the Administrative Console. The toolbar items are enabled/disabled based on current status of the selected item.

Starting and stopping nodes

You may want to view nodes as individual machines within your WebSphere domain. When you start or stop a domain, you are basically starting or stopping the Administrative Server on that node. To invoke an action on a node, select the node within the tree and right-click. Select the Start or Stop option.

Creating application servers

You can create applications servers through XMLConfig and WebSphere Control Program (WSCP) as well as through the Administrative Console. In this section, you learn how to use the Administrative Console to create an application server.

Expand the node tree, select the node you are interested in, and expand it to show the Application Server node. Right-click Application Servers, and select New. Figure 20-3 shows an example of the Properties dialog box.

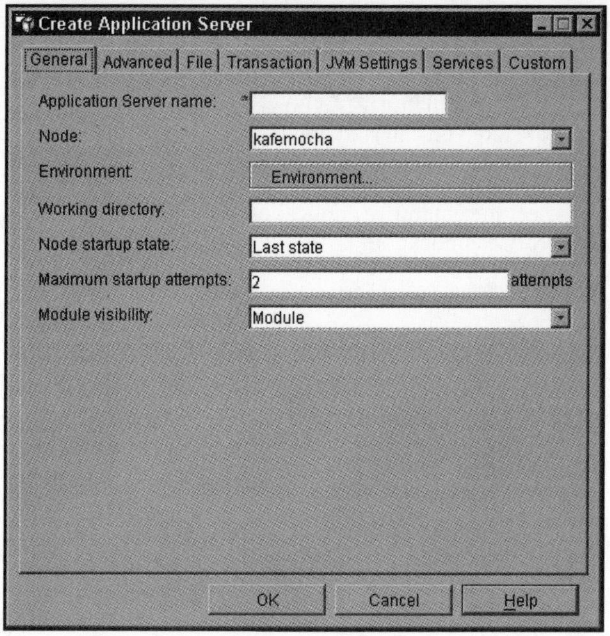

Figure 20-3: Creating an application server.

The key items you need to set are the application server name on the General tab and the unique standard out and standard error logs on the File tab.

> **NOTE**: WebSphere assigns a unique transport port with each new application server. You can verify that the port address is unique by selecting the Services tab and editing the Web Container properties. You find the unique port address under Transport.

You should create an application server and name it **AlmostFreeCruise**. You modify the transport later in this chapter in the section named, "Configuring the Web server plug-in."

Starting and stopping application servers

Application servers need to be started and stopped periodically, and there are three ways to do so:

- On the Administrative Console select the application server and right-click to display operations against the application server. Alternatively, you can select the application server and utilize the smart icons to start, stop, or restart the application server.
- You can use the WebSphere Control Program (WSCP).
- You can use XMLConfig.

> **CROSS-REFERENCE:** See Chapter 27 for an in-depth discussion of WSCP and Chapter 28 for a discussion of XMLConfig.

Starting and stopping enterprise applications

Enterprise applications are the J2EE programs and resources that are run on an application server. Enterprise applications are deployed with Enterprise archives (EAR). Enterprise applications can be started and stopped just like you can start application servers. Stopping or starting an enterprise application can be performed in three ways.

- On the Administrative Console, select the enterprise application and right-click to display operations against the enterprise application.
- Use WSCP.
- Use XMLConfig.

One way to determine whether the server is running is to ping the server. Pinging is not like TCP/IP `ping` command. Administrators can use the Ping feature to see whether certain application servers are running within the WebSphere domain. Select the Ping icon from the toolbar or select the application server, right-click, and select Ping. In either case, you receive a response message.

> **TIP**: If an application server hasn't yet been started, neither the Ping menu option nor the Ping icon on the toolbar are available.

Using the Regen WebSphere plug-in

Critical to the health of your WebSphere domain is the synchronization of changes to the WebSphere plug-in. Changes that you make that impact the plug-in are noted as warning messages in the Administrative Console. Unfortunately, it is the responsibility of the administrator to ensure that the plug-in gets regenerated and distributed to the proper Web server.

Using the Administrative Console, you can select the node that is impacted by the change and right-click that node. Select Regen WebSphere Plugin. The plug-in is generated, and it takes a manual step to copy the `plugin-cfg` file to the proper node. The plug-in is generated in `<was_home>\config`. You need to move the `plugin-cfg` file to the Web server.

> **TIP:** To find the location in which to place `plugin-cfg.xml`, look in the `httpd.conf` file and find the directive named `WebSpherePluginConfig`.

An alternative way to generate a plug-in is to use the command file `GenPluginCfg.bat`. You can find this file in `<was_home>\bin`.

Exporting and Importing XML configurations

At times, you should make a back-up copy of your administrative information. Within the Administrative Console, you find tools for exporting and importing configurations. These exports take the form of XML documents.

You can initiate an import or export by choosing the Console menu from the Administrative Console menu bar. The item names are Import from XML and Export to XML.

You can use these exported documents as a template for creating other WebSphere environments within your shop. You have to edit the document manually to ensure uniqueness in names. Alternatively, you might also want to save the information for disaster recovery.

> **NOTE**: Exports and import should not be thought of as backups of your administrative repository. You should ensure that you utilize proper database back-up measures to ensure the safety of your configurations.

Checking out deployment descriptors

One major difference between previous versions of WebSphere and WebSphere 4.0 is the capability to view the Web resources. In the past, Web resources were part of the Administrative Console, and you could navigate the tree to view information about servlets and EJBs. Version 4.0 gives you three places to view information about the J2EE module.

To view information about the details within the EAR, you must select the enterprise application and right-click to select the View Deployment Descriptor menu item. Figure 20-4 shows an example of that information.

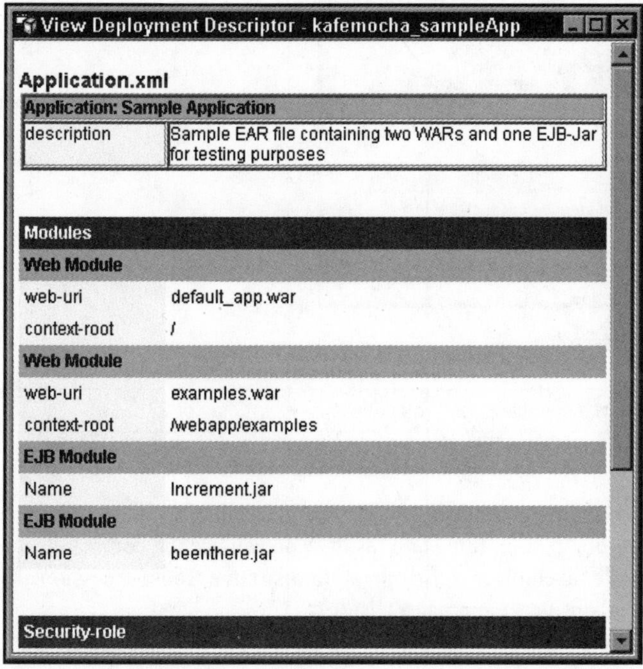

Figure 20-4: You can view information about the modules from within the application deployment descriptor.

To view detailed information about the EJBs, you select the enterprise application and expand it to reveal the EJB Module and Web Module nodes. Selecting a module produces a list of the resources contained within the module by name, server, and application. If you right-click a resource, you can view the details for that resource by choosing View Deployment Descriptor.

If you expand Web Modules and highlight one of the resources and view its deployment descriptor, you see something similar to Figure 20-5. The details shown in Figure 20-5 come from the `Web.xml` file that is contained within the WAR file.

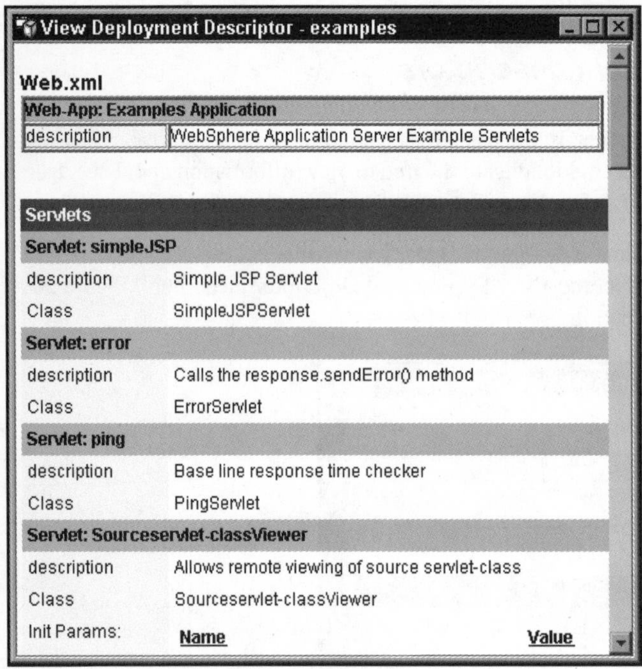

Figure 20-5: Web module deployment descriptor.

CROSS-REFERENCE: You learn more about deployment descriptors in Chapter 22.

Command History

The command history displays a window that lists WebSphere Application Server commands as well as each command's status, completion time, and result. You can use the command history to see what action may have taken place during an Administrative Console session. To see the command history, choose Console⇨Command History.

> **NOTE**: Activities invoked using WSCP or XMLConfig are not recorded in the command history of an Administrative Console session.

Running wizards

There always seem to be three ways of creating components within WebSphere's Administrative Console. The first is selecting the tree node and right-clicking to select from the pop-up menu items. The other is to use the Console⇨New item to select an option to create. The last way is using the wizards that walk you through the creation. The wizards are found under Console⇨Wizards. The Wizard menu gives you the following options:

- Install Enterprise Application
- Create Application Server
- Create Server Group
- Create Data Source
- Create JMS Resources
- Create J2C Connection Factory
- Create URL Resource
- Performance Tuner

The wizards are a good starting place if you are new to the WebSphere Administrative Console.

Configuring the Web Server Components

You should now be familiar with the basic flow and organization of a WebSphere domain. As you dive more deeply into the configurations of the individual components, having the background of the common tasks is important. In the following sections, you learn how to configure and customize components using the Administrative Console.

As mentioned earlier, the progression begins starting at the top of the tree pane in the WebSphere Administrative Console and works down.

Configuring the Web server plug-in

Figure 20-6 shows the browser accessing an HTTP server that has an application plug-in installed. A plug-in enables communication between the HTTP server and WebSphere Application Server.

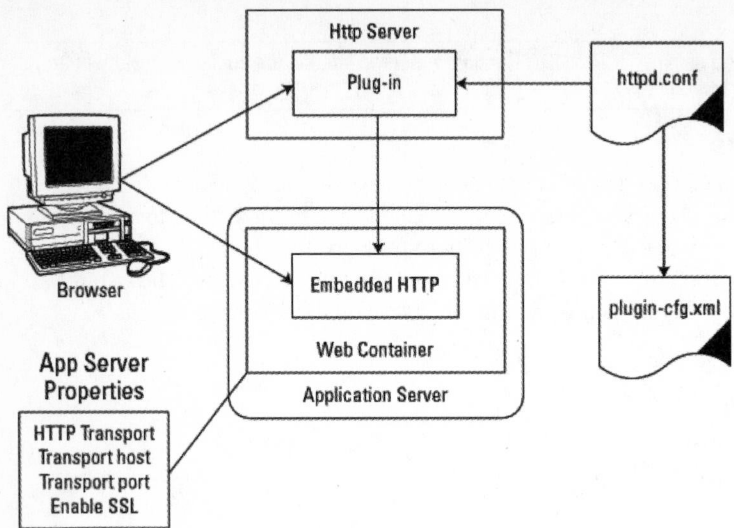

Figure 20-6: The lower-left corner shows the attributes that are taken into consideration.

Information is saved in the plug-in configuration file (`plugin-cfg.xml`). Depending upon your configuration, this file can be found in `<was_home>\config`. The reason that it may not be found in this location is that this file must be placed somewhere where the Web server can access it. Therefore, it can reside on the Web server machine or some other machine.

The location of the plug-in is best determined by looking at the `<HTTP_HOME>\conf\httpd.conf` file. The following code shows the directives at the bottom of the `HTTP.conf` file where the plug-in's location is specified. This is where the administrator can adjust the location in which the plug-in resides.

```
WebSpherePluginConfig d:\WebSphere\AppServer\config\plugin-cfg.xml
```

The directive in `httpd.conf` tells the Web server to load the plug-in and where to find the plug-in configuration. The `plugin-cfg` file tells the plug-in what to serve up and how to talk to the Web container. Figure 20-7 shows a `plugin-cfg file`.

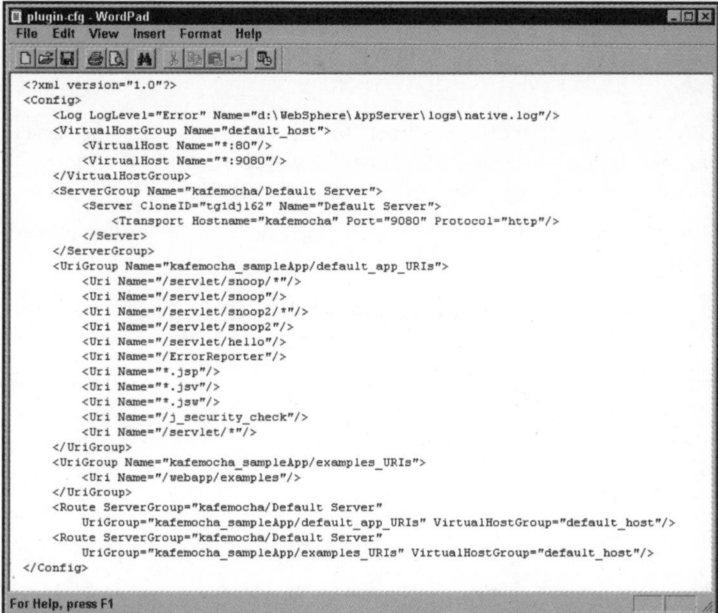


```
<?xml version="1.0"?>
<Config>
    <Log LogLevel="Error" Name="d:\WebSphere\AppServer\logs\native.log"/>
    <VirtualHostGroup Name="default_host">
        <VirtualHost Name="*:80"/>
        <VirtualHost Name="*:9080"/>
    </VirtualHostGroup>
    <ServerGroup Name="kafemocha/Default Server">
        <Server CloneID="tg1dj162" Name="Default Server">
            <Transport Hostname="kafemocha" Port="9080" Protocol="http"/>
        </Server>
    </ServerGroup>
    <UriGroup Name="kafemocha_sampleApp/default_app_URIs">
        <Uri Name="/servlet/snoop/*"/>
        <Uri Name="/servlet/snoop"/>
        <Uri Name="/servlet/snoop2/*"/>
        <Uri Name="/servlet/snoop2"/>
        <Uri Name="/servlet/hello"/>
        <Uri Name="/ErrorReporter"/>
        <Uri Name="*.jsp"/>
        <Uri Name="*.jsv"/>
        <Uri Name="*.jsw"/>
        <Uri Name="/j_security_check"/>
        <Uri Name="/servlet/*"/>
    </UriGroup>
    <UriGroup Name="kafemocha_sampleApp/examples_URIs">
        <Uri Name="/webapp/examples"/>
    </UriGroup>
    <Route ServerGroup="kafemocha/Default Server"
        UriGroup="kafemocha_sampleApp/default_app_URIs" VirtualHostGroup="default_host"/>
    <Route ServerGroup="kafemocha/Default Server"
        UriGroup="kafemocha_sampleApp/examples_URIs" VirtualHostGroup="default_host"/>
</Config>
```

Figure 20-7: The plugin-cfg.xml is where you specify the transport routing to WebSphere. The plug-in can be automatically regenerated by setting automatic generation to true.

When an HTTP request is made to the Web server for a WebSphere application URL, the plug-in looks at the routes defined in the plug-in configuration file. A *route* is basically a pointer to a description of criteria that uniquely identifies a location.

Routes can contain Virtual host groups and URI groups. If Virtual hosts are specified, the plug-in attempts to match host names and ports with defined virtual hosts. In the example in Figure 20-7, it points to `default_host`. As a default, if no other virtual host groups have been defined, the plug-in assumes that it matches all virtual hosts.

If URI groups are specified, similar processing occurs, but instead of host names and ports, the plug-in looks at URIs. If a match is found for both the URI and virtual host groups, the request is sent to the server group (`kafemocha/Default Server`) using either workload management or session affinity.

Figure 20-7 is a configuration running all components on the same node. If this were a domain with multiple servers within the server group, the plug-in would have to perform the following checks to route appropriately:

- *Checks for a session affinity:* Session affinity directs future requests to the same server. This checking is done through cookies or URL headers utilizing a session ID. More matching is done to ensure the request is sent to the proper clone.
- *Checks for load-balancing:* Load-balancing techniques distribute the request (provided session affinity isn't specified).

CROSS-REFERENCE: You can learn more about session affinity and load balancing in Chapter 24

Regenerating the plug-in

You need to regenerate the plug-in whenever you perform any of the following actions:

- Add a new URL
- Configure a new virtual host alias
- Change transport information
- Add a new application server
- Add new server groups/clones

Regenerating is a manual (but straightforward) task. To regenerate a plug-in, you simply right-click the node and select Regen WebSphere Plugin.

If you have the Administrative Console active, try regenerating the plug-in for your node. Figure 20-8 shows how you can set the system to regenerate the plug-in automatically. Select the particular application server (in this case the `Default Server`) and click the Custom tab.

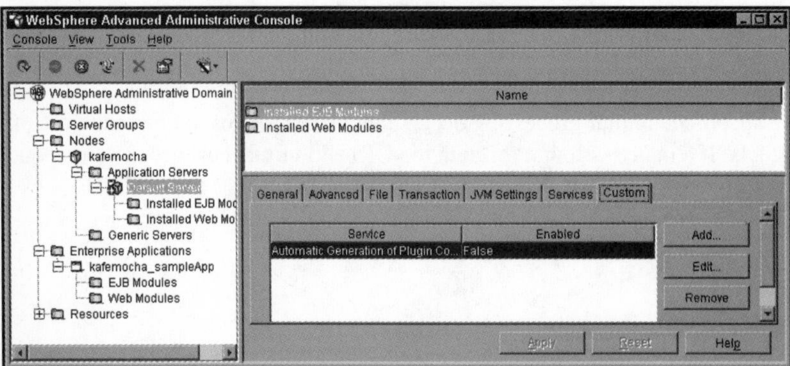

Figure 20-8: To regenerate a plug-in automatically, select the application server; click the Custom tab and click the Edit button to move to the next screen.

Click the Edit button and check the Enabled check box to change the Automatic Generation from False to True. You should switch back to False as it preferable to regenerate manually.

> **WARNING**: Setting Automatic Generation of the plug-in to True can cause performance problems because it regenerates after every change that affects transports, URLs, and Enterprise applications.

Installing the plug-in

Installing the plug-in is really not a big deal anymore. In prior versions, you had a group of files that needed to be deployed. Now you have to worry about deploying only a single file (`plugin-cfg`). How quickly the plug-in is ready depends upon the refresh interval and your topology.

> **NOTE**: The refresh interval is the time interval (in seconds) at which the plug-in should check the configuration file for modifications that have occurred since the last time the plug-in configuration was loaded.

The default refresh interval is 60 seconds. When you update the configuration and regenerate the plug-in, you no longer have to stop and start the Web server for the configuration to take effect.

Configuring virtual hosts

The term *virtual host* refers to the capability to maintain more than one server on a machine, as differentiated by its apparent hostname. A virtual host is a configuration enabling a single host machine to resemble multiple host machines, but is not associated with a particular node (machine).

Virtual hosts have logical names and a list of one or more aliases. An alias is a TCP/IP name and port number used to access a resource. The following list shows the default ports and aliases:

- 80 is the standard port address used by most external HTTP servers. (Port 80 is not secure.)
- 443 is the secure external HTTPS (SSL) port.
- 9080 is the unsecured embedded HTTP port.
- 9443 is the secure embedded HTTPS port.

Figure 20-9 shows the WebSphere Administrative Console with the default host alias for WebSphere's `default_host`. In the window, you can also see the port numbers associated.

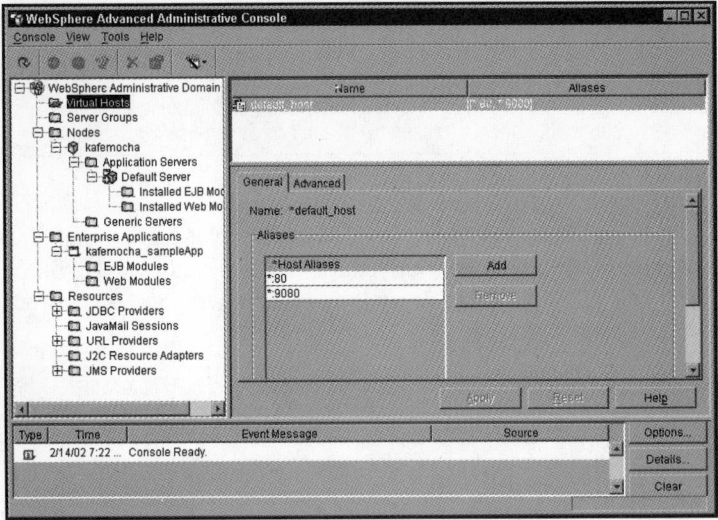

Figure 20-9: You can set up a new virtual hosts by right-clicking Virtual Hosts and selecting New. You then can assign the host aliases that apply to your new host. Here we are adding port 9080 to the default_host.

You can reuse the same servlet on multiple virtual host sites. Each has its own instances of the servlet, which are unaware of the other site's instances. Servlets on one virtual host do not share their context with the servlets on the other virtual host. To add a virtual host you have the same three options mentioned previously:

- Wizards
- Console⇨New⇨Virtual Host
- Right-click Virtual Host and select New

Use one of these methods and then enter the following information into the dialog box that is presented:

- *Name:* **AlmostFreeCruise.com**
- *Aliases:* Enter the aliases and include the port number. An IP address with port numbers is also allowed.
  - **AlmostFreeCruise.com:80**
  - **127.0.0.1:80**
  - **AlmostFreeCruise.com:9080**
  - **127.0.0.1:9080**
  - **CSICruise:80**
  - **AlmostFreeCruise.com:443**
  - **127.0.0.1:443**

When you have entered the aliases and returned to the Administrative Server, you should notice an audit message:

```
The administrative action just performed may invalidate the Web Server
plug-in configuration file. Use the Plug-in regen operation of the Node
to update this file.
```

You should regenerate the plug-in at this stage.

Understanding the transport options

A transport is the request queue between the WebSphere plug-in for Web servers and the Web container in which the Web modules of an application reside. It is considered a feature of the Web container. When a user at a Web browser requests an application, the request is passed to the Web server and then along the transport to the Web container. The HTTP transport properties are as follows:

- Transport host
- Transport port
- Tranport protocol (HTTP or HTTPS)

Transport properties include controls to perform the following tasks:

- Manage concurrent requests
- Enable secure connections between the Web server and WebSphere with SSL

To avoid port contention, the administrator must specify a unique port number for each application server (or clone) on a given machine.

Internal transport (the embedded HTTP server)

For applications in nonproduction environments, such as test or development environments, you can utilize the internal transport to process servlets and JSPs without the need of a Web server. The default port for the internal transport (embedded HTTP server) is port 9080.

When you are configuring for a production environment, you should not use the embedded HTTP server. Not only does it lack performance tuning, it is a security risk. For your own enjoyment, run the Snoop servlet using port 9080.

```
HTTP://localhost:9080/servlet/snoop
```

When you add a new application server, the system automatically creates a default transport port for you. It increases the last port address (9080) by one, so the next allocated port address is 9081. You should ensure that the range of ports is unique for your environment.

You have the ability to create a new transport. You might do this to provide additional control of your environment and/or implement a Secure Sockets Layer (SSL) between your Web server and the internal transport.

Non-SSL transport

Previously, you created a new application server named AlmostFreeCruise. The configuration automatically created a transport. In this section, you learn more about the properties you can configure within the transport:

1. Select the application server (`AlmostFreeCruise`) and select the Services tab. Next select the Web Container Service and Edit the properties. There should be a transport already defined. Depending on the number of application servers you created previously, your transport port number is somewhere above 9080. In this dialog box, four fields deserve some introduction:
   - *Maximum keep alives:* This field refers to persistent connections across all transports. With HTTP 1.1, you are able to keep alive several concurrent requests on the same wire. The default (25) is said to be 90 percent of the maximum number of threads in the Web Contain thread pool.
   - *Maximum requests per keep alive:* The maximum number of requests that can be processed on a single keep-alive connection. The default is 100 requests.
   - *Keep alive timeout:* The maximum time (in seconds) to wait for the next request on a keep-alive connection. The default is five seconds.
   - *I/O timeout:* The maximum time (in seconds) to wait when trying to read or write data during a request. The default is five seconds.
2. To add a new transport, click the Add button. You should be presented with the screen shown in Figure 20-10.

You can use this same screen to create an SSL-enabled transport. Checking Enable SSL enables a number of security-related fields. You add a non-SSL transport only.

The Transport host field is the host name or IP address of the machine on which the application server is running. The asterisk (*) is a placeholder until the plug-in is regenerated. When the plug-in's XML configuration file is regenerated, the asterisk is converted to the host name on which the application server is running. If the host name is not set to the asterisk, the value entered in this field is used as the target host by the plug-in.

The transport port is the TCP/IP port number that the plug-in uses when requests are sent to the application server. Be careful not to use a port that has already been taken.

Connection backlog is the maximum number of outstanding connect requests that the operating system buffers while it waits for the application server to accept the connections. If a client attempts to connect when this operating system buffer is full, the connect request is rejected. You should plan on setting this value to the number of concurrent connections that you want to allow. For now, accept the default. Keep in mind that a single client browser might need to open multiple concurrent connections. As with all connection-related applications, the higher the value the more memory is consumed.

If you have changed any of the fields, click OK and click Apply on the General tab to ensure the changes are not lost. Otherwise, just close the Properties dialog box. You must also regenerate the plug-in, and restart the application server.

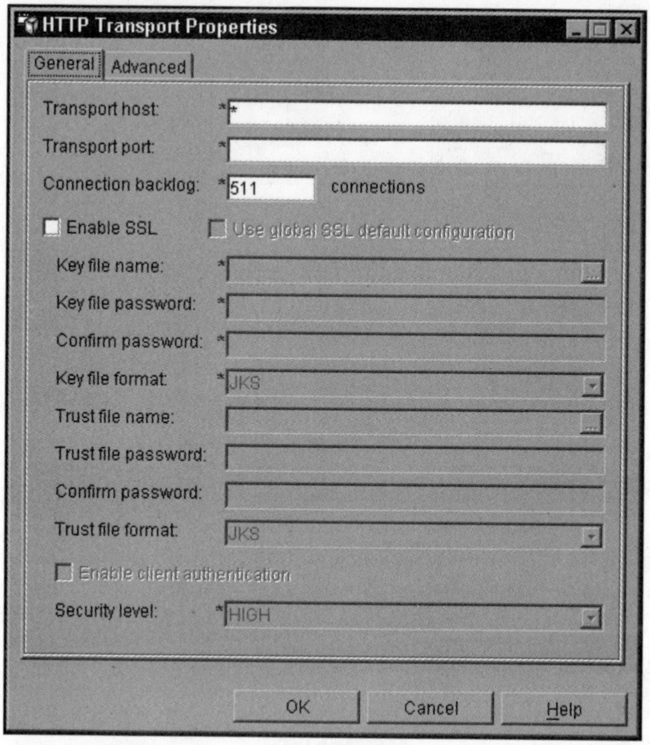

Figure 20-10: Adding a new transport sets up a new queue to process requests. When you add a transport, you need to regenerate the plug-in file.

Configuring Resources

This section covers the configuration of resources. Resource providers are a class of objects that provide resources needed by Java applications, and J2EE applications in particular. You might also think of them as services. Figure 20-11 shows how resources fit within the J2EE framework.

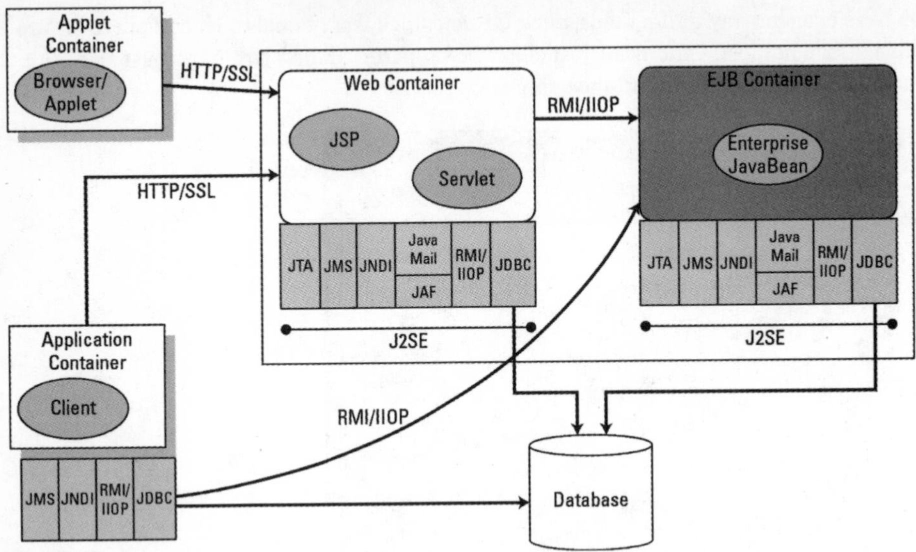

Figure 20-11: This graphic of the J2EE architecture shows how clients can access the Web and EJB containers within the application server. Notice the different protocols used to access the different containers.

Figure 20-11 shows JTA, JMS, JNDI, and other resources supporting the Web container, EJB container, and Application container. You learn about these resources in the following sections:

- JDBC providers build JDBC-compliant drivers to support their databases.
- JDBC datasources provide the reference to the JDBC providers' drivers.
- JavaMail enables the ability to send mail using SMTP or IMap.
- URL providers implement the functionality for a particular URL protocol.
- J2C is the technical preview that interfaces with adapters to EAI.
- JMS provides messaging support for products such as MQSeries.

Setting up JDBC connection pools

JDBC provides Java applications with middle-tier access to most database systems through Structured Query Language (SQL). When an application needs data, it acquires a JDBC connection through the JDBC provider's driver manager. Connections are expensive with regard to resource consumption. Making reusable connections available is beneficial.

Connection pooling is the maintenance of a group of database connections for reuse by applications on an application server. It is part of the JDBC 2.0 Optional Package API. Another part of the Optional Package API provides for the use of the Java Naming and Directory Interface (JNDI).

JNDI is independent of any specific directory-access protocol. It allows for easy deployment of new directory services and manipulation of Java instances by name. Naming services provide a name-to-object mapping.

Data sources enable you to define and configure specific connections to a relational database that supplies a JDBC provider library. Data sources provide support for the pooling of connections.

Each time a resource attempts to access a database, it must connect to that database. A database connection incurs overhead; it requires resources to create the connection, maintain it, and release it when it is no longer required. The overhead is particularly high for Web-based applications, because Web users connect and disconnect frequently.

Data sources provide support for pooling connections. Connection pooling spreads the connection overhead across several user requests, thereby conserving resources for future requests. Therefore, connection pooling can improve the response time of any application that requires connections, especially Web-based applications. To enable connection pooling you must first install a JDBC provider.

Creating a JDBC provider

JDBC provides vendor-independent database connectivity. It's a generic way to query and update relational tables and return the results into Java data types.

> **NOTE**: JDBC functionality is found in two Java packages: `java.sql` and `javax.sql`. The latter contains the connection pooling and transactional capabilities.

In this section, you add a new JDBC provider that supports connection pooling:

1. To begin, select the JDBC Providers node within the Administrative Console Tree view. Right-click the item and select New.
2. The JDBC Provider Properties dialog box opens. For the name, enter **CSICruiseDB2Driver**. Although not necessary, it is good practice to name your JDBC driver with the provider information. In this case, you are installing a DB2 driver.
3. Enter a description and then click the button with three dots. You see a list of valid classes to implement. Select com.ibm.db2.jdbc.DB2ConnectionPoolDataSource and click OK.
4. Now select the Nodes tab and click Install New. You see the Install Driver screen. It shows nodes that have been configured thus far. You should select the current node and click Specify Driver.
5. The Specify the Drivers screen opens. You need to specify the path to the provider's implementation file. In this case, you are utilizing the DB2 implementation. You should click Add Driver and use the File dialog box to locate your `db2java.zip` file. You can find `db2java.zip` in `<DB2_HOME>\java`. Select the file and click Set.

6. You return to the Install Driver screen. Click Install to continue. Returning to the JDBC providers screen, click OK to install. You should now see your new JDBC provider displayed as shown in Figure 20-12.

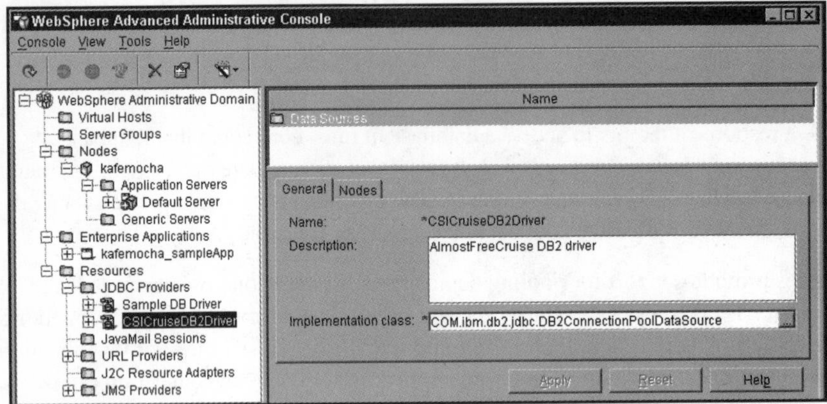

Figure 20-12: You are working with datas sources. You have set up the provider, but you still need to identify the database characteristics.

Creating a data source

Data sources enable you to define and configure specific connections to a relational database that supplies a JDBC provider library. Because your data source is still undefined, you need to create one:

1. To create a new data source, expand CSICruiseDB2Driver, select Data Source, and right-click to select New.

1. The Data Source Properties dialog box opens. You enter the following:
   - *Name:* **CSICruiseDataSource**
   - *JNDI name:* **jdbc/csicruise**
   - *Description:* **AlmostFreeCruise Data Source**

NOTE: In the next section, it is assumed that you have already installed the CRUISE database.

2. Under the Custom Properties, provide the following information:
   - Database name: **CRUISE**
   - User: **db2admin**
   - Password: **db2admin**

3. Click Test Connection. If you have the CRUISE database installed, your test connection should succeed.

> **NOTE**: Within your code, if you utilize the `getConnection(userid, password)` method passing in userid and password, the userid and password established in the data source are overridden.

4. Next you move to the Connection Pooling tab. You need to determine the following:
   - *Minimum pool size:* This is self explanatory (default 1).
   - *Maximum pool size:* Choose At initial allocation to get X connections (default 10).
   - *Connection timeout:* This is the length of time you want the client to wait before getting an error message (default 180).
   - *Idle timeout:* After X seconds, shrink the pool if unused connections are never used (default 1800).
   - *Orphan timeout:* If your programmer forgets to close the connection, wait X seconds, remove the connection, and create a new one (default 1800).
   - *Statement cache size:* If you want to keep your prepared statements cached, you can set the number to keep so you don't have to redo the access path (default 100).
5. Accepting the defaults is fine for now. Click OK and you have successfully added a data source.

Enabling JavaMail

If you need to interface e-mail and messaging with Java, you can use JavaMail, a set of APIs that implement functionality of a mail system. With JavaMail, you have the capability (in Java) to create technology-based mail and messaging. However, you are limited to providing general mail facilities for reading and sending mail.

The Java Activation Framework (JAF) is required in order to use JavaMail. You need JAF to deal with complex data types, such as Mime types. J2EE promises platform-independent applications, and JavaMail is no exception. A JavaMail program uses a resource factory reference to obtain a JavaMail session. A *resource factory* is a Java object that uses JNDI to access the resources in a program's deployed environment.

Service providers implement specific protocols, shown in the following list, that you can plug in to WebSphere:

- Simple Mail Transfer Protocol (SMTP) is a transport protocol for sending mail.
- Post Office Protocol 3 (POP3) is the standard protocol for receiving mail.
- Internet Message Access Protocol (IMAP) is an alternative protocol to POP3.

Figure 20-13 shows the relationship between the service providers and the Java components.

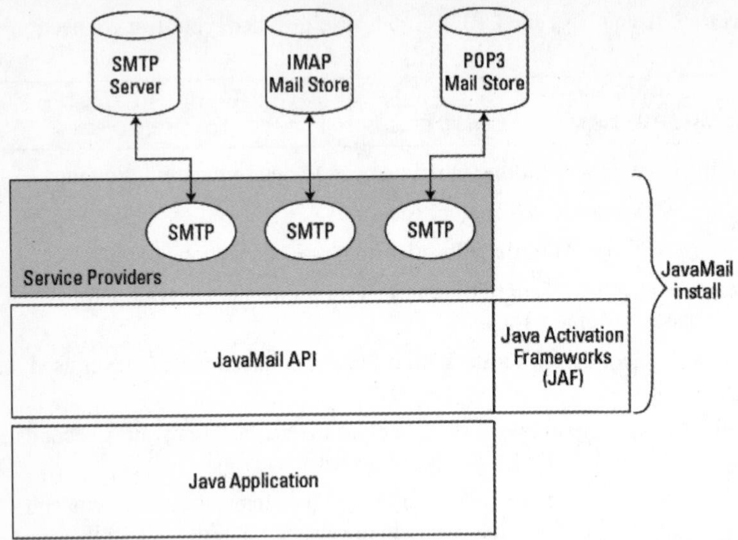

Figure 20-13: JavaMail relationships are comprised of services providers, the JavaMail API, and JAF.

With the exception of POP3, all the components shown in Figure 20-13 are shipped as part of WebSphere Application Server using the following packages:

- `mail.jar` contains JavaMail APIs, the SMTP service provider, and the IMAP service provider.
- `activation.jar` contains the JavaBeans Activation Framework (part of the Java Activation Framework).

WebSphere Application Server's implementation of JavaMail does not provide mail servers. Configuration of mail servers must be handled separately.

> **NOTE**: Only the SMTP and IMAP service providers are shipped with WebSphere Application Server. To use other protocols, install the appropriate service providers for those protocols.

In this section, you learn the initial set up for the JavaMail resource on WebSphere. Figure 20-14 shows a JavaMail session configuration for `cruiseMail`.

1. To setup `cruiseMail`, you right-click JavaMail Session, and select New. The JavaMail Session Properties dialog box opens.
2. You can enter some information, taking for granted that certain mail servers exist. You enter a name and, if required, a JNDI binding path and description.
   - The protocol for outgoing mail by default is SMTP.
   - The mail originator should be the value of the Reply to field in mail messages.
   - The username might not be required unless your mail provider requires it. For example, a userid and password could be required as an antispamming mechanism, in case someone infiltrates your mail server.

3. Enter the following properties into the Advanced tab fields:
   - *Enable Store:* Check to enable JavaMail sessions.
   - *Protocol:* This is where you set the configuration for the mail store access. The protocol shown is the only protocol supported (IMAP).
   - *Host:* The server to which to connect when reading mail. This property combines with the mail store user ID and password to represent a valid mail account. For example, if the mail account is `csi@commercesolutions.com`, type **commercesolutions.com**.
   - *Username:* The user ID to use when connecting to the mail store host. This property combines with the mail store user ID and password to represent a valid mail account. For example, if the mail account is `csi@commercesolutions.com`, enter **csi**.
   - *Password / Confirm password:* Enter the password to use when connecting to the mail store host. This property combines with the mail store user ID and password to represent a valid mail account. For example, if the mail account is `csi@commercesolutions.com`, enter the password corresponding to csi.

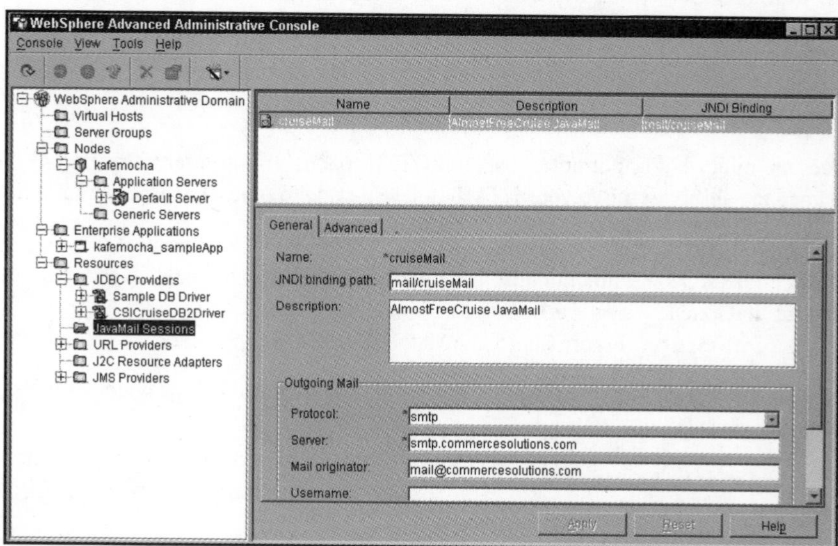

Figure 20-14: Setting up JavaMail enables you to send mail using SMTP and IMAP.

> **NOTE**: When you configure your mail servers, use fully qualified Internet host names.

Understanding URL providers

A default URL provider is included in the initial product configuration. It utilizes the URL support provided by the JDK. Any URL resources with protocols supported by the JDK, such as HTTP, FTP, and FILE, can use the default URL provider. A Uniform Resource Locator (URL) is an identifier that locates a service to a specific Web server and port. URLs have the following format:

- *Protocol:* The default is HTTP. Others are File Transfer Protocol (FTP), Local File (FILE), and Network News Transfer Protocol (NNTP).
- *Port:* Optional entry. If omitted, the default is 80 for HTTP. FTP uses 21, and SSL uses 443.
- *Host and identifiers:* The host must be a valid TCP/IP address or domain naming service (DNS). The identifiers are not so specific. They could name a file/servlet on the server and/or contain parameters for the particular task.

A URL and Uniform Resource Identifier (URI) are both identifiers. The slight differences are illustrated in the following list:

- *URL:* `http://www.commercesolutions.com/servlet/snoop`
- *URI:* `/servlet/snoop`

The differences are minor but important to JSP and HTML pages. If you refer to the partial address, you keep the ability to move your HTML and JSP code to other machines and not tie it to a single machine.

A URL provider implements the functionality for a particular URL protocol, such as HTTP. It is a pair of classes that extend `java.net.URLStreamHandler` and `java.net.URLConnection`. Figure 20-15 shows the default URL provider.

Creating your own URL is beyond the scope of this book. The default URL provider handles all the protocols supported by the JDK.

> **NOTE**: See the InfoCenter for more information on URL Providers.

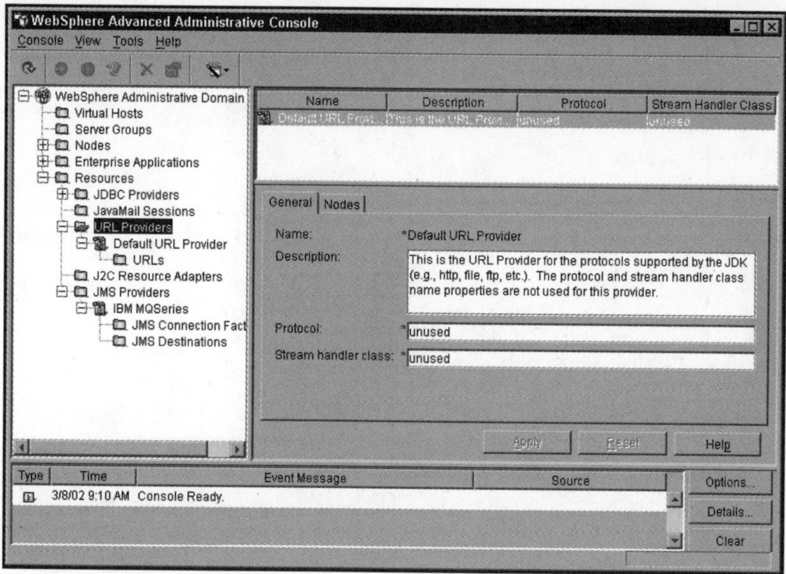

Figure 20-15: Setting up URLproviders enables you to specify protocols, such as HTTP, FTP, and FILE.

Setting up JMS

Support for Java Messaging Services (JMS) is one of the many features supported by WebSphere Application Server 4.0. JMS supports the development of message-based applications in the Java programming language, allowing for the asynchronous exchange of data and events throughout an enterprise.

TIP: J2EE 1.3 Message Beans allow loosely coupled, reliable, asynchronous interaction among J2EE components.

JMS provides a set of APIs that define a common set of messaging concepts and programming strategies that are supported by JMS technology-compliant messaging systems.

NOTE: The JMS APIs define interfaces for message services but do not define an implementation.

Understanding JMS providers

A JMS vendor provides an implementation of the `JMS` API on a JMS client application. MQSeries is considered a JMS provider. The following section shows you how to install MQSeries JMS support in WebSphere Application Server 4.0. If you don't have access to MQSeries or are using a different JMS provider, feel free to skip the section "Setting up JMS MQ support."

Setting up JMS MQ Support

The following products are assumed to be installed and functional on your server:

- WebSphere Application Server, Advanced Edition 4.0 (full, single server, or development server)
- WebSphere MQ 5.1 or 5.2

In addition, you need to download two support packages from the IBM Web site. Install both support packages before continuing:

- *MA88:* MQSeries classes for Java and MQSeries classes for JMS
- *MA0C:* MQSeries – Publish/Subscribe

JMSAdmin is an application for creating JMS administered objects. It creates connection factories and queues, to name a few, and binds them into a JNDI namespace.

> **NOTE:** `<MQ_JAVA>` represents the directory where MQ JMS support is located, for example: `d:\Program files\IBM\mqseries\java`.

For consistency, this example uses `%MQ_JAVA_INSTALL_PATH%` to represent the directory in which you have installed the MQ JMS support. You can launch the JMSAdmin application by call `JMSAdmin.bat`. This file is located in `<MQ_JAVA>/bin` and uses a configuration file in the same directory named `JMSAdmin.config`. You need to update this file as follows:

```
INITIAL_CONTEXT_FACTORY=com.ibm.ejs.ns.jndi.CNInitialContextFactory
PROVIDER_URL=iiop://localhost:900
```

Updating is accomplished by removing the comment (#) directives. Be sure to comment out the defaulted line. Modify the `JMSAdmin.bat` file to add the flag `-Dserver.root=%WAS_HOME%` to the command-line parameters passed into the JMSAdmin. All standalone Java applications that communicate with WebSphere Application Server 4.0 need to have this flag specified as a command-line argument. Listing 20-1 shows how the file should look:

Listing 20-1: Modifying JMSAdmin.bat to Accomplish Updating

```
rem -----------------------------------------------
rem  IBM MQSeries JMS Admin Tool Execution Script
rem
rem  Note that the properties passed to the java
rem  program are defaults, and should be edited
rem  to suit your installation if necessary
rem -----------------------------------------------
cls
java -DMQJMS_LOG_DIR="%MQ_JAVA_INSTALL_PATH%"\log
-DQJMS_TRACE_DIR="%MQ_JAVA_INSTALL_PATH%"\trace
-DMQJMS_INSTALL_PATH="%MQ_JAVA_INSTALL_PATH%"
-Dserver.root=%WAS_HOME% com.ibm.mq.jms.admin.JMSAdmin %1 %2 %3 %4 %5
```

Set up your PATH and CLASSPATH so that all the appropriate Java, WebSphere, and MQ classes are available to the JMSAdmin application. You can create a setupMQenv.bat file or update the following environment variables, as shown in Listing 20-2, to ensure the JMSAdmin starts correctly:

Listing 20-2: Sample setupMQEnv.bat

```
@echo off
set WAS_HOME=c:\Websphere\appserver
set MQ_JAVA=c:\program files\ibm\mqseries\java
set JAVA_HOME=%WAS_HOME%\java\bin
set MQ=%MQ%;%MQ_JAVA%\lib
set MQ=%MQ%;%MQ_JAVA%\lib\com.ibm.mq.jar
set MQ=%MQ%;%MQ_JAVA%\lib\com.ibm.mqjms.jar
set MQ=%MQ%;%MQ_JAVA%\lib\jms.jar
@rem LDAP
set MQ=%MQ%;%MQ_JAVA%\lib\ldap.jar
@rem File system for JNDI
set MQ=%MQ%;%MQ_JAVA%\lib\fscontext.jar
set MQ=%MQ%;%MQ_JAVA%\lib\providerutil.jar
@rem needed to use WebSphere name service for JNDI
set WebSphereClassPath=%WAS_HOME%\lib\ns.jar
set CLASSPATH=%MQ%;%WebSphereClassPath%;%CLASSPATH%
set PATH=%JAVA_HOME%;%MQ_JAVA%\lib;%PATH%;
```

You should change the drive letter (c:) to match your installation. Run setupMQEnv.bat or set the environment variables, and you are ready to run JMSAdmin. You start JMSAdmin as follows:

```
JMSAdmin -t -cfg JMSAdmin.config
```

You should set up your JMS connection factory and the MQ Queues you will be using and then bind them to the WebSphere JNDI name space. After starting JMSAdmin, you should see an InitCtx> prompt. Enter the following:

```
InitCtx> define  QCF (QCF)
InitCtx> define Q (Q1) QUEUE (SYSTEM.DEFAULT.LOCAL.QUEUE)
```

Run a display to see the output, by typing **display ctx** at the InitCtx prompt. You see a lot of information. Contained within the output, you should see the following lines:

```
...
a QCF com.ibm.mq.jms.MQQueueConnectionFactory
...
a Q1 com.ibm.mq.jms.MQQueue
...
InitCtx>
```

Your information is now set up, and you are ready to go to the Administrative Console to set up the JMS Provider properties.

1. Start the Administrative Console and navigate to the JMS Providers item.
2. Right-click JMS Providers and click Properties. You should see the JMS Provider Properties screen as shown in Figure 20-16.

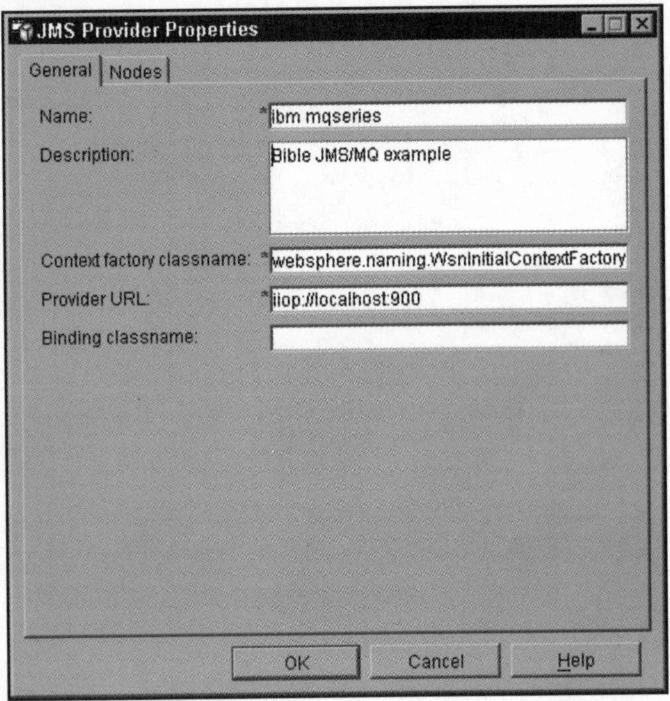

Figure 20-16: You need to install a new JMS provider to support products such as MQSeries.

3. Enter **IBM MQseries** in the Name field
4. Enter **Bible JMS/MQ example** in the Description field.

5. In the Context Factory Classname, enter **com.ibm.websphere.naming.WsnInitialContextFactory**.
6. In the Provider URL field, enter **iiop://localhost**.
7. Switch to the Node tab and click Install New. You see your node in the Install Driver screen. Click the Specify Driver button, and select the drivers as follows in Figure 20-17.

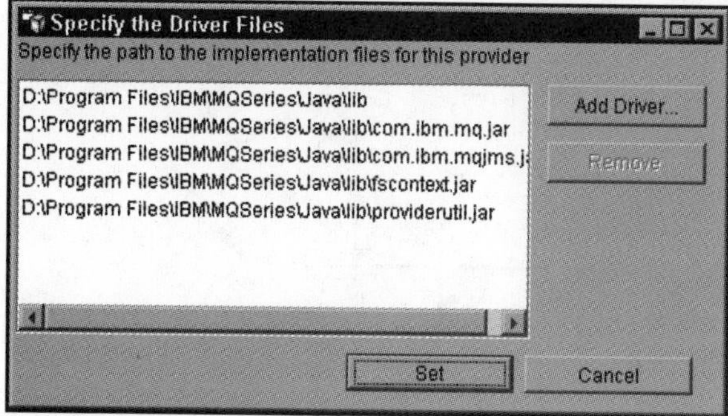

Figure 20-17: Specifying drivers.

8. Click Add Drivers, navigate to <MQ_JAVA>, and select the drivers listed in Figure 20-17.
9. When done click Set, and then click Install.
10. Now you need to set up a connection factory. Enter the following information:
    - *Name:* sample/QCF
    - *External JNDI path:* QCF
    - *Description:* Sample Connection Factory
11. You define the queues in a similar fashion. In this case, you use the JMS Destinations folder. Highlight the JMS Destinations, and right-click to select New. Enter the following information:
    - *Name:* sample/Q1
    - External JNDI path: **Q1**
12. Click OK and do the same for Queue 2. Figure 20-18 shows a graphic of how the queues are accessed via JMS.

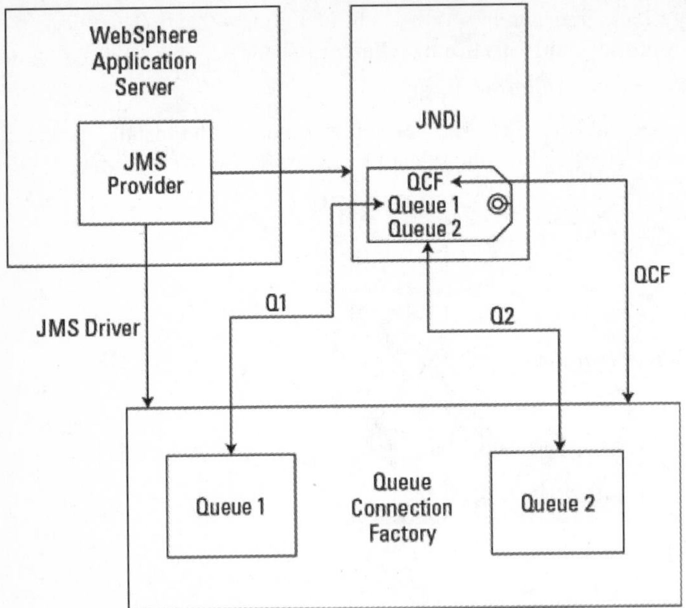

Figure 20-18: JMS utilizes JNDI to access queues created by the Connection Factory.

Listing 20-3 shows a JSP scriptlet that performs a lookup, creates a connection factory, and sends a funny message to Q1.

Listing 20-3: JSP Snippet

```
<%
//get JNDI context
javax.naming.InitialContext ctx =new javax.naming.InitialContext();
//access the JNDI environment
javax.naming.Context env =
(javax.naming.Context)ctx.lookup("java:comp/env");
//create/instantiate a queue factory
javax.jms.QueueConnectionFactory qcf =
(javax.jms.QueueConnectionFactory)env.lookup("QCF");
//get connection
javax.jms.QueueConnection qc =qcf.createQueueConnection();
//we need a session
javax.jms.QueueSession qSession =
qc.createQueueSession(false,javax.jms.Session.AUTO_ACKNOWLEDGE);
//fetch queue
javax.jms.Queue q =(javax.jms.Queue)env.lookup("Q1");
//use a queue sender and send a funny message
javax.jms.QueueSender sender =qSession.createSender(q);
sender.send(qSession.createTextMessage("A message in a bottle!"));
sender.close();
%>
```

You can put this code into your own JSP and package it within a Web module. Using the Application Assembly Tool (AAT), you then associate the naming and generate an Enterprise Archive (EAR) file and deploy it to WebSphere.

> **CROSS-REFERENCE:** The Application Assembly Tool is presented in Chapter 22.

Perform the following steps to process your Web module through AAT:

1. Start up AAT.
2. In the Web Modules folder, select the Resource References folder.
3. Right-click New to define a new resource.
4. When the window opens, enter the following information:
   - Name: **QCF**
   - Type: **javax.jms.QueueConnectionFactory**
5. Define the other resources (Q1, Q2) using the type of `javax.jms.Queue.`

You are now ready to install your EAR file in WebSphere. Use the Install Wizard to install your enterprise application. When you reach the Mapping Resource References to Resources page map, enter your references as follows:

- *Resource Reference:* **QCF**
- *JNDI Name:* **jms/sample/QCF**
- *Resource Reference:* **Q1**
- *JNDI Name:* **jms/sample/Q1**

Start your application and test it. You now have the capability to communicate with WebSphere MQ through JMS.

Introducing J2C

The Java Connector Architecture (JCA) is a standard way to connect heterogeneous enterprise information systems. Enterprise Information Systems (EIS) vendors provide functionality for the enterprise-like enterprise-resource planning (ERP), human-resource planning (HR), and supply-chain management (SCM). Companies such as PeopleSoft, SAP, and I2 are these types of providers.

> **NOTE**: The JCA is no longer bundled as a technology preview as it was in version 4. It is now implemented in WebSphere Version 5.

WebSphere Advanced Edition (AE) includes a beta form of the JCA implementation referred as J2C (Java to Connector). J2C provides a J2EE-compliant way for Java applications to interact with nonrelational back-end systems, such as CICS and IMS and EIS vendors

If you are familiar with Java Database Connectivity (JDBC), you already know that JDBC allows Java programs to connect to a variety of database products through the use of common interfaces. In JDBC, you fetch results by performing the following tasks:

- Set up the driver manager that is specific to each vendor.
- Establish a connection.
- Formulate your request.
- Execute your request.
- Receive a results set.

With J2C you perform a similar set of tasks:

- Set up a resource adapter.
- Get a connection.
- Set up the call.
- Execute the call.
- Receive a results set.

The J2EE connector architecture enables an EIS vendor to provide a standard resource adapter for its EIS. A resource adapter is a system-level software driver used by WebSphere or an application client to connect to an EIS. By plugging into WebSphere, the resource adapter collaborates with the server to provide the underlying mechanisms, the transactions, security, and connection-pooling mechanisms.

The resource adapter plugs into WebSphere, providing connectivity among the EIS, WebSphere, and the enterprise application. An EIS vendor needs to provide just one standard resource adapter that has the capability to plug in to any application server that supports the J2EE connector architecture.

A J2C resource adapter represents a library that supports connections from an application to a nonrelational back-end system. That is, a J2C adapter supports connections to an enterprise information system (EIS) resource. Figure 20-19 shows an architectural view of J2C in WebSphere.

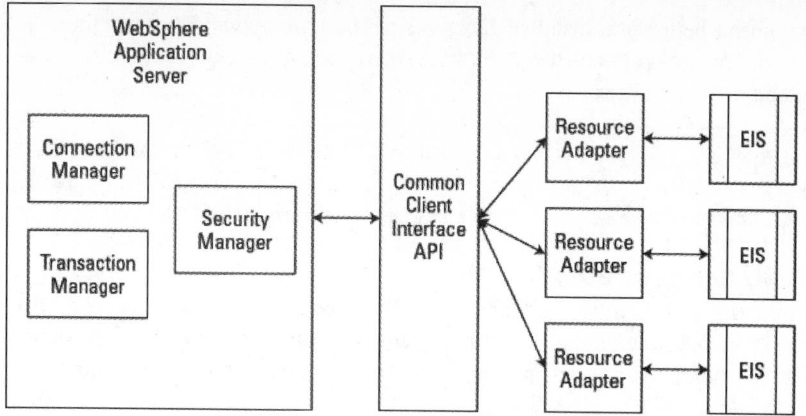

Figure 20-19: J2C utilizes a set of common client Application Programming Interfaces (API) to connect to resource adapters that can interface to your existing EIS systems.

Understanding Resource Adapter Archive (RAR)

Resource adapters are packaged with a Resource Adapter Archive (RAR) file. An RAR file can contain the following:

- EIS-supplied resource adapter implementation code in the form of JAR files or other executables, such as DLLs
- Utility classes
- Static documents, such as HTML files, images, and sound
- Connector Architecture (J2C) common client interfaces, such as `cci.jar`

Setting up J2C

J2C comes with WebSphere Advance Edition as an installation add-on. If you have not installed the connectors, you can download them from the IBM site. This section depends upon having EIS connectors with resource adapters; therefore, it only describes the fields without actually walking you through a real example.

> **CROSS-REFERENCE**: The connector architecture is available from IBM at `http://www7b.boulder.ibm.com/wsdd/downloads/jca.html`.

To install the technology, perform the following tasks:

- Stop all WebSphere processes, including the Administrative Server and Web server.
- Run the Connector Architecture installation batch file found on the CD rom, `x:\NT\connector directory: InstallJ2C.bat.`

If you don't remember whether you installed J2C, you can find out by verifying that the `<was_home>\lib` directory contains the `j2c.jar`, `jca.jar`, `eablib.jar`, `recjava.jar`, and `ccf.jar` files.

> **TIP**: If you did not install the J2C preview during your upgrade to WebSphere 4.02, you have to install the preview manually. You must unjar the the `J2Cinstaller.jar` file on the CD by issuing the `Java -jar J2Cinstaller.jar -target <was_home> -skipver` command.

Configuring J2C resource adapters

To create a new J2C resource adapter, right-click J2C Resource Adapters and select New from the pop-up menu. To update an existing J2C resource adapter, right-click the required adapter, and select Properties from the pop-up menu. Fill in information for the following options:

- *Name:* Administrative name for the resource adapter
- *Description:* Optional description of the resource adapter for your administrative records
- *Archive file name:* Path to the Resource Adapter Archive (RAR) file for the resource adapter.

Use the [...] button to access a window for selecting .RAR files based on a selected node. You then select the Connections tab. Custom connection properties are specific to the given J2C adapter. The information displayed includes the following:

- *Name:* TraceLevel
- *Description:* TraceLevel
- *Data type: (*example: `java.lang.Integer`)
- *Value of property:* 1

The Advanced tab shows the specifics of the Vendor's properties. These are specific to the adapter provided by the vendor. The final tab is the Node tab. You need to install a driver on each node where the J2C resource adapter is used. The values used are as follows:

- *Node:* The administrative node on which the J2C resource adapter is installed. You have to click Install New to create a new entry.
- *Classpath:* The path to the Java file containing the implementation classes for the J2C resource adapter.

Configuring J2C connection factories

Now that you have created a resource adapter, you need to create a new J2C connection factory. Right-click the resource factory and select New. The properties of J2C connection factories are as follows:

- *Name:* The administrative name for the J2C connection factory.
- *JNDI binding path:* The JNDI binding path is the location in the namespace at which to bind the J2C resource definition. The default value for this property is the value of the Name property prefixed with `eis/`, such as `eis/connectionName`.

- *Description:* Optional description of the J2C connection factory for your administrative records.
- *J2C Resource Adapter:* The J2C resource adapter on which this J2C connection factory is based.

The advanced properties of J2C connection factories are as follows:

- *Connection Timeout:* Time in milliseconds to abort if maximum or minimum connections are reached.
- *Maximum Connections:* Maximum number of connections that can be manufactured by the ManagedConnectionFactory. If set to 0, it grows indefinitely.
- *Minimum Connections:* The minimum number of connections to manage. The Java garbage collector does not discard any connections if the minimum is reached.
- *Reap Time:* Number of seconds before the next garbage collection pass.
- *Unused Timeout:* Number of milliseconds before an unused connection is released back to the pool.
- *Pool Name:* Name used by the pool manager to group connections created by multiple ManagedConnectionFactories.
- *Subpool Name:* Name of the pool manager to group connections created by multiple ManagedConnectionFactories within an individual pool.

Summary

An architectural view provides a basis for understanding the configuration points within WebSphere. The architectural components consist of the Web server, the plug-in, an embedded HTTP server (also known as a transport), and the containers within WebSphere Application Server (the Web container and EJB container).

An Administrative Server is composed of three components:

- The LSD (location service deamon) is used for persistent object references, finding objects.
- The bootstrap naming services handles JNDI naming.
- Security is also managed by the bootstrap.

An Administrative Server runs in its own JVM.

The Administrative Console is a remote Graphical User Interface (GUI). It provides you with the tooling necessary to configure WebSphere Application Server. Some of the common tasks are as follows:

- *From the toolbar:* Start server, stop server, properties, wizard utilization.
- *From the console:* Start nodes, create application servers, start/stop application servers, and regenerate plug-ins.

As a means of backing up and configuring other servers, you can utilize import/export XML. Deployment descriptors describe resources in XML and are the new J2EE way of declaring resources. You can view deployment descriptors to see which configurations are set up within a Web container and/or EJB container.

Wizards provide a guided way to create components. You can install applications, application servers, server groups, data sources, JMS resources, J2C connection factories, and URL resources.

After an architectural overview and walk around the block, you learned about configuration. You were introduced to `plugin-cfg.xml` and learned that it is a configuration file read by the Web server. It provides URL information, so the Web server can determine where to route a request. Stored in an XML file, the plug-in should be generated after any change to a transport that includes adding URLs, clones, virtual hosts, ports, and application servers. Default generation is accomplished by adjusting a parameter. This is not the recommended method, as it inflicts changes quite often.

Virtual host configuration maps aliases to a single Web server, making it seem like more than one system. Virtual hosts use as default ports 80, 9080, 443, and 9443.

Transports are keys to plug in mechanics. The internal transport runs on 9080. You shouldn't run this in production. The internal transport lacks the capabilities of the Web server but can be utilized as a way of quickly testing applications.

Resource configuration is possible for JDBC providers, data sources, JavaMail, URL providers, J2C, and JMS. JDBC connection pooling provides the necessary mechanism to allow multiple users access to a single source of data without causing severe degradation in performance. You begin by installing a driver and assigning a data source name. You can configure the data source to achieve maximum performance with minimal overhead.

JavaMail has been implemented to handle simple mail activities. It requires the Java Activation Framework (JAF). It supports IMAP, SMTP, and POP3. POP3 is not provided as part of the deliverable.

A URL provider is a configuration that specifies the type of services a URL provides. The default URL provider supports HTTP, FTP, NNTP, and FILE.

JMS provides messaging support to WebSphere Application Server. Backed by MQ, JMS can provide messages and publish/subscribe capabilities. JMS is based on queues that you create to route messages.

J2C is designed similarly to JDBC. It provides a common way of implementing EIS systems. It utilizes RAR files (resource adapters) to interface with the end point EIS. This technology preview will be fully implemented in version 1.3 of the J2EE specification.

Chapter 21
Configuring Session Management

In This Chapter

- Understanding session management
- Introducing workload management
- Setting up a session management tutorial
- Introducing session security
- Improving performance of session management
- Understanding and running traces

This chapter discusses the topic of session management. This chapter could be considered a tuning chapter, because session management has a lot to do with workload. You learned a little about sessions in Chapter 11. You learned that a Web application needs a mechanism to hold the state information of the user over a period of time. That mechanism is a session.

As you dive deeper into the machinery that creates and manages sessions, you become familiar with the ways sessions can impact the overall system performance. You also learn a little about some of the workload-management capabilities of WebSphere Application Server. Workload management is covered in the tuning chapter (Chapter 24) but it is an important aspect of session management and, therefore, is introduced here.

This chapter introduces session management as it pertains to the WebSphere Application Server. Session management is one of the critical workload-management features that must be implemented to ensure that state is maintained between sessions. Because session management goes hand in hand with workload management, this chapter also discusses workload management. You do a tutorial showing how to set up session management in WebSphere, and you learn some of the tuning parameters that you can adjust with session management.

Understanding HTTP Session Management

A Web application needs a mechanism to hold the state information of the user over a period of time. HTTP alone does not recognize or maintain state information for a user; each user request is treated as an independent entity. To help solve this problem, the Java Servlet 2.2 specification provides a mechanism for Servlet applications to maintain state for a user.

With that new capability, it became important to continue to maintain state in environments that supported clustering and workload-management schemes. WebSphere Application Server has a session manager that is part of the Web container. The session manager is responsible for managing HTTP sessions, providing storage for session data, allocating session IDs, and tracking the session ID associated with each client request. This is done through the use of cookies, URL rewriting, or SSL ID techniques.

You can configure session manager to maintain session-related information in memory so that it is shared with other application servers on the same machine or persisted in a database so that all application server machines can share the information.

Figure 21-1 shows the process of obtaining a session from the session manager.

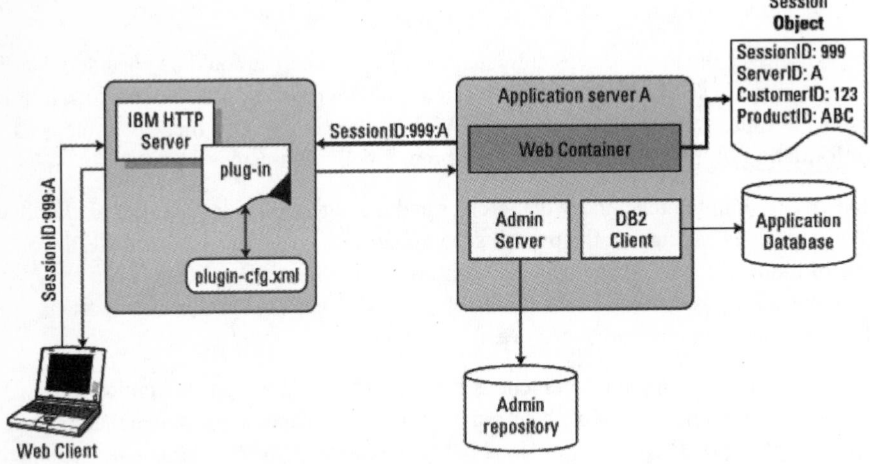

Figure 21-1: Session-management provides the capability to maintain state information between requests.

Figure 21-1 shows a browser accessing a Web application. The Web server receives the request and routes it through the plug-in. In this simple case, where there is no clustering or workload management, the plug-in passes the request on to the only Web container identified. The session manager generates a session ID and stores the information and returns the ID to the browser with one of three methods (cookies, URL encoded, or SSL ID).

On subsequent requests, the session ID is passed back to the Web container, and the servlet can access specific state information to perform its activities.

Understanding sessions

A *session* is a series of requests to a servlet, originating from the same user and the same browser. Sessions allow servlets running in a Web container to keep track of individual users. Figure 21-1 shows the classic shopping-cart example. A servlet, which supports multiple threads, processes each request from multiple users. It is important that the servlet not mistake requests from User A and process them for User B. Sessions help the servlet identify which user information to process.

A servlet identifies users by their unique session IDs. As shown previously, the session ID arrives with each request. If the user's browser is cookie-enabled, the session ID can be stored as a cookie. Two alternatives to using cookies are first, URL rewriting where the session ID is appended to the URL of the servlet or JavaServer Page, or second, using requests over HTTPS (SSL) to use the SSL information as a unique identifier.

The `javax.servlet.http.HttpSession` interface described in the Servlet API specification provides the mechanism to perform these actions.

NOTE: The session manager allows for session scoping only within the same Web application.

Only servlets in the same Web application can access the data associated with a particular session. Multiple requests from the same browser, each specifying a unique Web application, result in multiple sessions with a shared session ID. Any of the sessions that share a session ID can be invalidated without affecting the other sessions.

A session timeout can be configured for each Web application. A Web application timeout value of 0 (the default value) means that the global timeout value from the session manager is used.

Using Cookies for session management

Netscape defines a cookie as, "a general mechanism that server-side connections (such as CGI scripts) can use to store and retrieve information on the client side of the connection."

Utilizing the Cookie API is a common way for Web developers to handle session tracking. Cookies can store the unique session ID on the client machine on the first request; on subsequent requests, your servlet can access the cookie to identify the user uniquely.

You learn how to configure WebSphere to utilize cookies for session management in the "Persisting sessions" section later in this chapter.

Using URL rewriting for session management

With URL rewriting, every application's specific URL must be dynamically generated to include the unique identifier for tracking. The data is appended to the end of the URL string. Because of the limitation of URL lengths, usually only a unique user ID (session ID) is passed. For URL rewriting, you must supply a servlet or JSP file as an entry point to the application. You must also use either the `encodeURL()` or `encodeRedirectURL()` method. You cannot use plain HTML, because every link must use URL encoding.

Using SSL tracking for session management

SSL tracking uses the session ID obtained during the establishment of a SSL-encrypted session. SSL is established between the Web server and the browser only. SSL tracking is supported in only the IBM HTTP and iPlanet Web servers. In workload-management environments, you must use URL rewriting or cookies along with SSL tracking to maintain session affinity.

Introducing Workload Management

WebSphere Application Server Advanced Edition provides a wonderful foundation for extending your system and growing your business. It provides an extremely scalable, high-performance environment that satisfies all your business service levels.

Workload management (WLM) is the process of spreading multiple requests for work across multiple application servers and machines. WLM is really a procedure for improving performance, scalability, and reliability of an application.

This section introduces you to the concept of workload management (also known as clustering) and how session affinity can assist with unexpected failover. You learn that with WebSphere Application Server you can achieve balance between application servers, hardware, performance, and availability. Let's begin with the graphic in Figure 21-2.

Figure 21-2 shows a network dispatcher (perhaps the WebSphere Edge server) spraying IP requests to multiple Web servers. The network dispatcher may have specialized caching or intelligent load balancing.

From the plug-in to the application servers, requests can be distributed to multiple Web containers as shown in the figure. The containers can be contained within one machine or multiple machines.

Not shown are EJB requests. These requests can be shared across multiple EJB containers and can come from not only servlets, but also from Java clients and other EJBs.

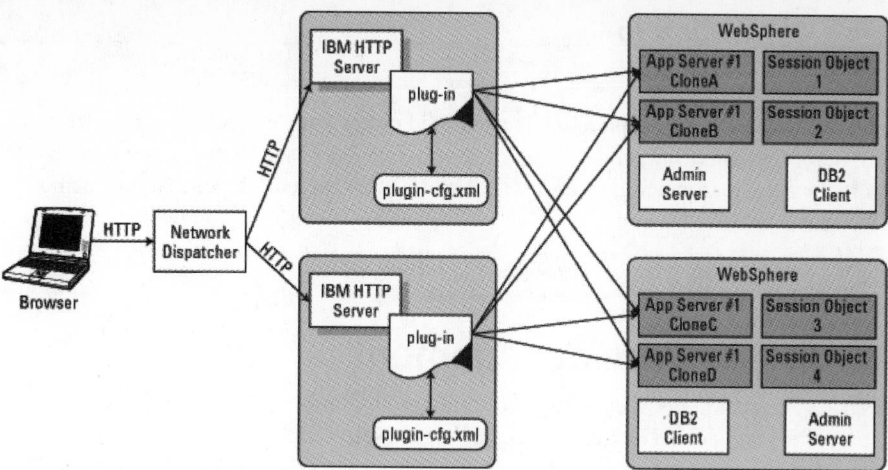

Figure 21-2: This depicts an architectural drawing of a typical workload-management spread.

Understanding clustering

Whenever you have multiple application server instances sharing a common pool of sessions, it is known as a *session cluster*. The session cluster binds the session to one or more application servers' Java virtual machines (JVMs). These JVMs all share the same common HTTP session table.

Session clustering is your fail-over protection. In the event of a system failure in your clustered environment, your session data is preserved. Clustering also provides the advantage of load balancing.

Understanding server affinity

The Servlet 2.2 specification specifies that multiple requests for a session cannot coexist in multiple JVMs. Having all requests for a particular session directed to the same JVM in the cluster is called *session affinity*.

Implemented by the WebSphere plug-in, session affinity ensures that if one of the servers in the cluster fails, it is possible for the request to be rerouted to another server in the cluster. As the new server receives the request, it can pick up the session information from the common repository.

The Web application must reside on all servers within the server group. A server group is a logical representation of a server. It has all the characteristics of its original server but doesn't provide services for handling requests.

NOTE: A server group is not a JVM. It is more of a convenience.

Regardless of whether a Web application is replicated on multiple machines (versus created as a server group), session affinity must ensure that only one JVM is used at a given time. In the case of a replicated environment versus a server group environment, the virtual host name is identical on each server.

CROSS-REFERENCE: Workload management is covered in more depth in Chapter 24.

Setting Up Session Management

You set up sessions using the WebSphere Administrative Console. The Session Manager Service properties are located on the Services tab of the selected Application server. Figure 21-3 shows the Administrative Console opened to the Services tab for the default server.

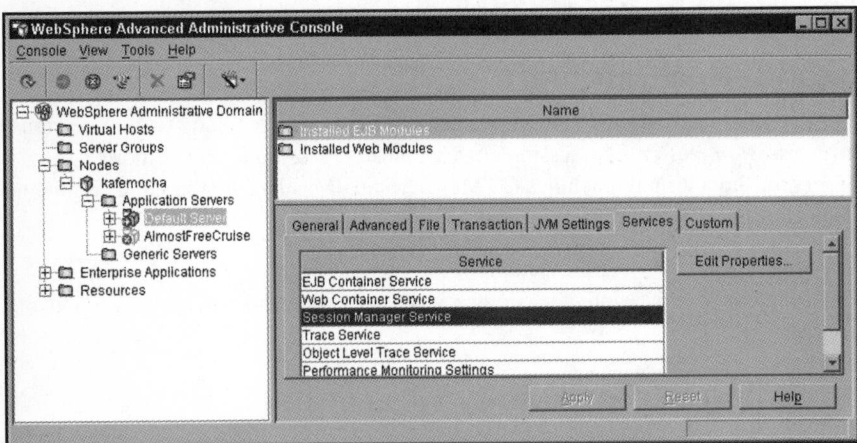

Figure 21-3: You set Service properties on the Session Manager Services tab.

Within the Administrative Console, you can perform the following tasks:

- Specify which session-tracking mechanism to use to pass the session ID between the browser and the servlet
- Specify whether to persist session data in a database
- Establish the persistent sessions characteristics

For example, say you want your application to have fail-over support. You are concerned with one server going down and losing valuable customers because of the outage. You have decided to persist your session information to prepare for future additions of a network sprayer and additional clustered servers.

In the next sections, you walk through the steps to activate the session manager to support your needs. Ensure that you have the Administrative Server started and make sure the AlmostFreeCruise application server is running.

CROSS-REFERENCE: See Chapter 20 for details about how to set up the AlmostFreeCruise application server, if you have not already done so.

Persisting sessions

By default WebSphere manages session in memory. You need to select a tracking method as your session-tracking mechanism. To begin the process, select the AlmostFreeCruise server and then the Services tab. Scroll down the services and select Session Manager Service. Click Edit Properties to display the Session Manager Service.

After you select Edit Properties, you are presented with a dialog box similar to Figure 21-4. You can choose from the three tracking-mechanism options:

- Enable SSL ID tracking
- Enable cookies
- Enable URL rewriting

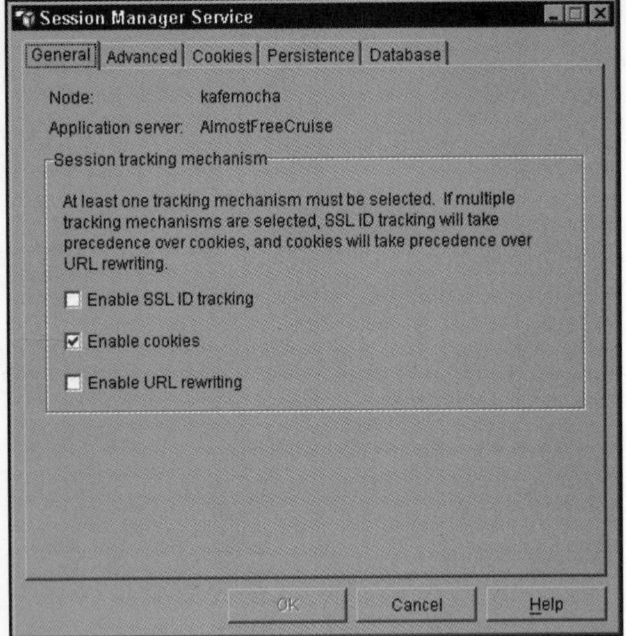

Figure 21-4: You begin enabling session management on the General tab of the Session Manager.

Enable cookies is enabled by default. You must select at least one option, but multiple selections are possible. SSL ID tracking is supported in only IBM HTTP and iPlanet Web servers. In workload-management environments, you must use URL rewriting or cookies along with SSL tracking to maintain session affinity.

You select Enable URL rewriting to ensure that browsers with cookies turned off are not excluded. This means you must add some additional code to your servlets and JSPs.

You should leave Enable Cookies checked, as this is the easiest to implement. Click the Advanced tab to set advanced Session Manager settings, shown in Figure 21-5.

On the Advanced tab you are able to perform the following tasks:

- *Set the maximum in-memory session count:* This number specifies the maximum number of sessions to maintain in memory. For in-memory sessions, this value specifies the number of sessions in the base session table.
- *Allow Overflow:* Use the Allow Overflow property to specify whether to limit sessions to this number for the entire session manager or allow additional sessions to be stored in secondary tables.
- *Integrate with WebSphere security:* When security integration is enabled, the session manager associates the identity of users with their HTTP sessions.

> **NOTE**: Enabling the Integrate with WebSphere security option could cause authorization failures if you have a Web application that has form login authentication and local operating system authentication.

- *Enable protocol switch rewriting:* Enable this field if you have a situation in which you are switching URLs to point from a HTTP to HTTPS URL and you want the system to switch automatically. This is only affected if you have selected Enable URL rewriting.
- *Invalidation timeout:* This setting specifies how long a session is allowed to go unused before it is considered invalid. If you set the timeout, the value must be at least two minutes, specified in minutes. When setting Web module deployment descriptors, this value is the default value for session timeout.

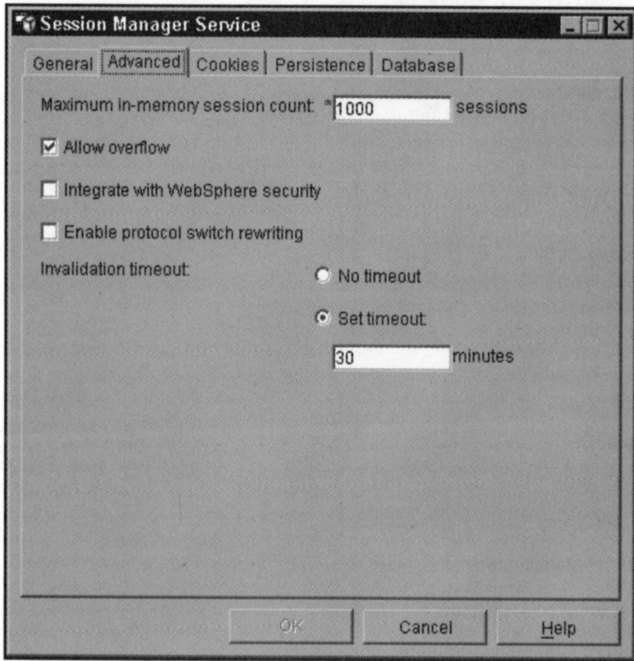

Figure 21-5: You set timeout values on the Advanced tab.

In this case, 30 minutes seems like a long time, so change the value to **20** minutes and reduce the session count to **750**.

Understanding overflows

When you use session persistence, you get to specify how many objects are kept in memory. This is specified in the Maximum in-memory session count (shown in Figure 21-5). If the maximum is achieved and a new request for a session is submitted, an overflow condition has occurred. If overflow is enabled, it allows the session to exceed the maximum.

A lot depends on your comfort level with the types of users using your system. If you believe that the people utilizing your system are legitimate users, you can allow overflow to ensure that every user gets a session. You might also decide that your site is subject to Denial of Service (DoS) attacks and choose not to allow additional sessions to be created.

The bottom line is that this is an administrator's decision. Click the Cookies tab to continue.

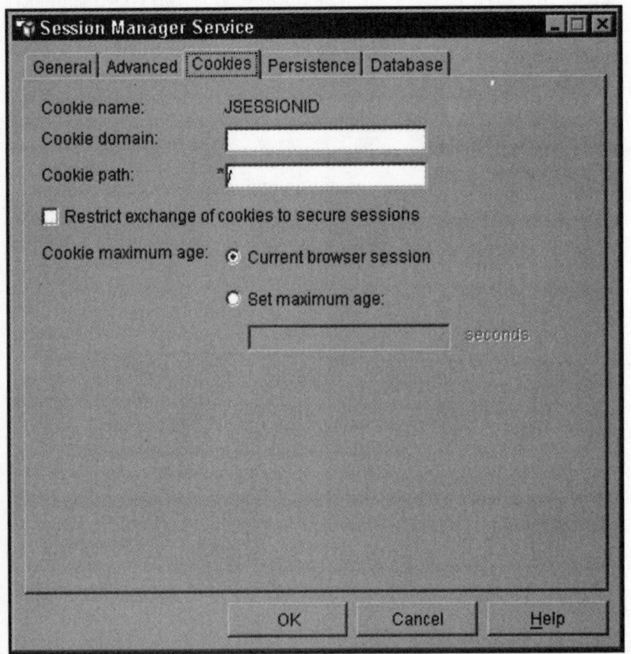

Figure 21-6: On the Cookies tab, you can set parameters for cookie use.

Figure 21-6 shows the cookie parameters that you can set. The following list provides a description of each setting:

- *Cookie name:* Per the Servlet 2.2 specification, the cookie is always named `JSESSIONID`.
- *Cookie domain:* Specify a particular domain if you want to restrict cookies so that they can be sent to only certain hosts. The default (blank) means there are no restrictions.
- *Cookie path:* Fill out this field if you want cookies restricted to certain URLs on the server. If you specify the root directory, the cookie is sent no matter which path on the given server is accessed.

- *Restrict exchange of cookies to secure sessions:* This setting restricts cookies to the SSL (HTTPS) session.
- *Cookie Max Age:* This setting specifies that the cookie lives only as long as the current browser session, or to a maximum age. If you choose the maximum age option, specify the age in seconds.

You can accept the defaults in the Cookies tab. Before setting persistence, it is necessary to do some setup work. To persist you need a database, a Java Database Connectivity (JDBC) provider, and the Java Naming and Directory Interface (JNDI) name.

Setting up persistence sessions

First and foremost, you need a database to store your session information. You should create a new database to hold this information instead of using an existing database. Using an existing database might reduce the performance because of additional overhead and locking.

To create a new DB2 database follow these instructions:

1. Open a DB2 command window using Start⇨Programs⇨IBM DB2⇨Command Window.
2. Enter the command **db2 create db session**.

If you are using multiple nodes and a multicloned environment, some additional steps are required. Follow these steps only if your environment is set up as stated.

1. If the node has not been catalogued, open a DB2 command window (see Step 1) and enter the command **db2 catalog tcpip node <node_name> remote <remote_hostname> server <service_name>**.

   In this command, the following is true:

   - Node_name is a descriptive name identifying the sessiondb database (for example, `SessionNode`).
   - Remote_host_name is the hostname that contains the session database (for example, `SessionHost`).
   - `Service_name` is a port number (defaulted to 50000).

2. Catalog the database at that node using the command **db2 catalog db session** as the session at node `SessionNode.`
3. Verify that you can connect to this database. Type the command **db2 connect to db session as user <userid> using <password>**.

You have now completed the database definition. You can close the DB2 command window. Next, you need to create a JDBC provider and a datasource. Figure 21-7 shows the Administrative Console open to the JDBC Providers Properties dialog box.

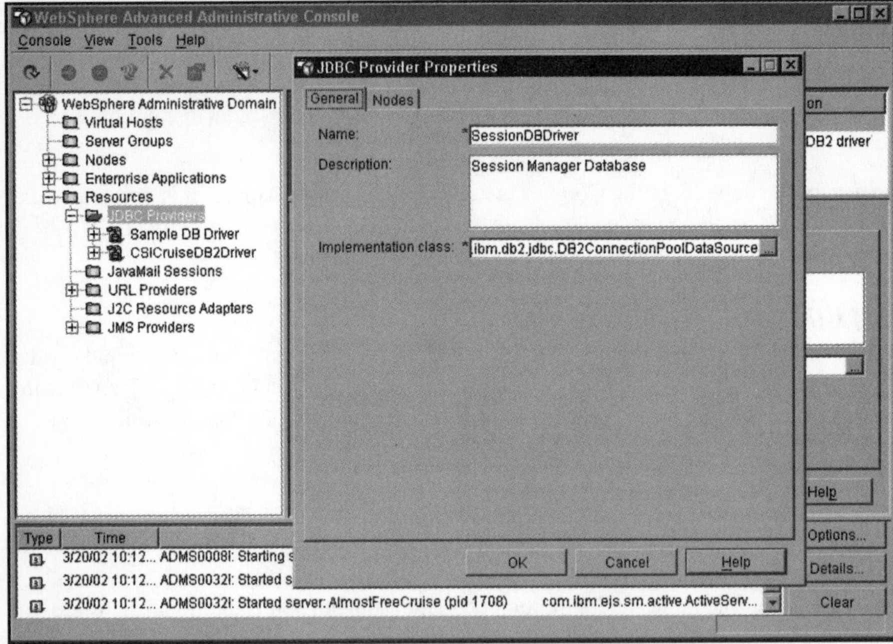

Figure 21-7: In the JDBC Provider properties window, you set the JDBC provider and a datasource.

To create a JDBC provider and a datasource, follow these steps:

1. Create a new JDBC Provider by right-clicking JDBC Providers in the left pane of the Administrative Console and clicking New.
2. Enter **SessionDBDriver** in the name field box.
3. Enter **Session Manager Database** in the Descriptions field.
4. Finally select `com.ibm.jdbc.DB2ConnectionPoolDataSource` in the Implementation class drop-down list.
5. Click the Nodes tab, and then click Install New.
6. Select your node and click Specify Driver.
7. Click Add Driver, and click the Browse buttton and locate and select <db2_home>/java/db2java.zip.
8. Click Set and on the next screen click Install.
9. When you return, click Apply.
10. The next step is to create the datasource. Open the new SessionDBDriver and right-click Data Sources. Select New. Figure 21-8 shows the information you should plug in to create the new datasource.

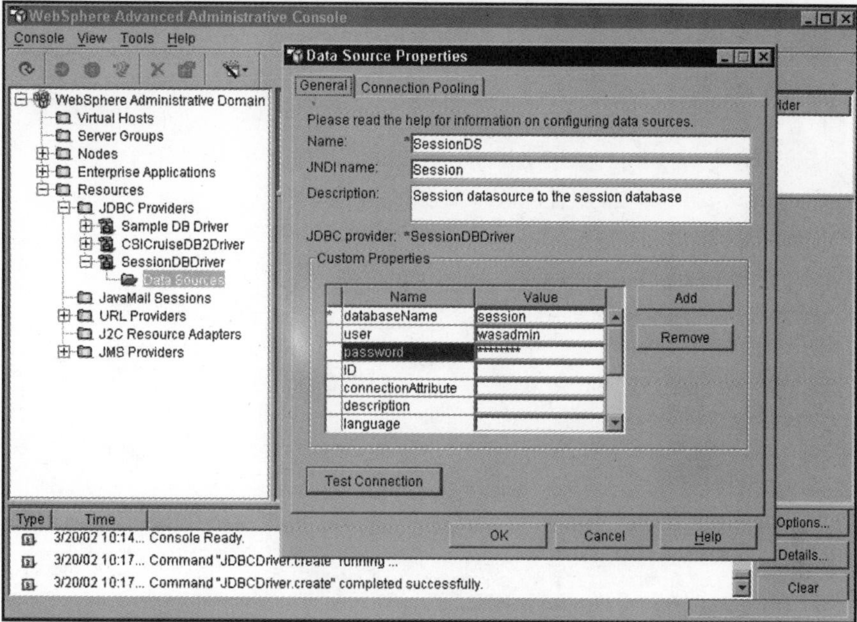

Figure 21-8: Creating the datasource for the session database.

11. Enter **SessionDS** into the Name field and **Session** into the JNDI name field.
12. Enter **Session datasource to the session database** in the Description field.
13. In the Custom Properties field, enter the database name, `session`, into the value field.
14. Enter **wasadmin** as the user and password (if that is what you set as a password). Click Add.
15. Click the Connection Pooling tab and accept the defaults.
16. Click Test Connection to verify that you keyed in the proper database name and credentials. You should get confirmation.
17. Click OK and you should see a message indicating that the datasource was successfully created.

You are now ready to complete configuring the session manager for persistent sessions.

18. Return to the Session Manager Properties by selecting the AlmostFreeCruise Application server, and then select the Services tab. Edit the properties and navigate to the Persistence tab, shown in Figure 21-9.

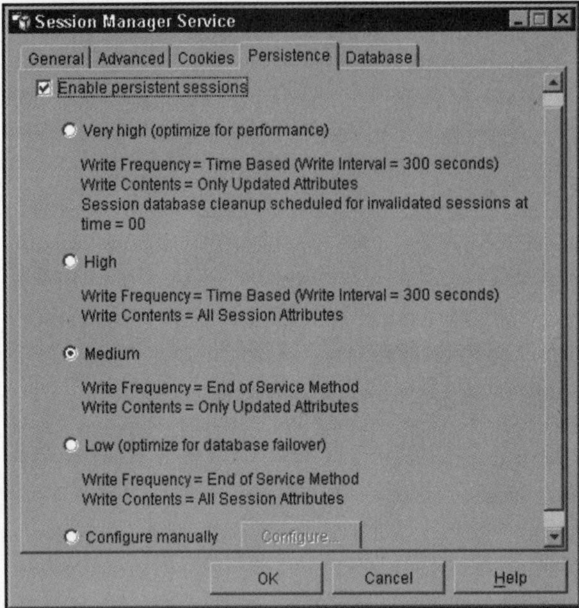

Figure 21-9: You can configure persistent session by choosing the Persistence tab and enabling persistent session. Then you can choose the performance options.

19. Check the Enable the Persistent Sessions check box. This action enables the other radio buttons, so you can configure for optimal performance. You can select one of the four preset options or select Configure manually and click Configure. Medium is set as the default. Medium writes at the end of service methods and performs only updates. If you select to configure manually, you need to know the following information:
    - Write frequency
    - Write contents
    - Database cleanup scheduling
20. For this example, accept the default, Medium. Select the Database tab to fill in the relevant database information. Figure 21-10 shows the Database tab with the information already filled in.

This Database tab of the Session Manager Properties dialog box has the following key fields:

- *Data source:* In this drop-down list, select the datasource you just created.
- *DB2 row size:* This is the tablespace page size configured for the `sessions` table. The default is 4K. Updating to a larger size could improve performance. If you change the row size to another number, you must also enter a tablespace name.

- *Use multirow sessions:* Here you determine whether to place each instance of application data in a separate row in the database, allowing larger amounts of data to be stored for each session. This can yield better performance in certain usage scenarios. If using multirow schema is not enabled, instances of application data can be placed in the same row. Leave it unchecked.

Update the information as follows:

1. Select SessionDS from the Datasource drop-down list.
2. Enter **wasadmin** as the user and password (if that is what you set as a password).
3. Confirm the password by typing it in again.
4. Set the DB row size to **4**.
5. Click OK to save your changes.

You have now configured session persistence. Restart the application server to invoke the configuration changes.

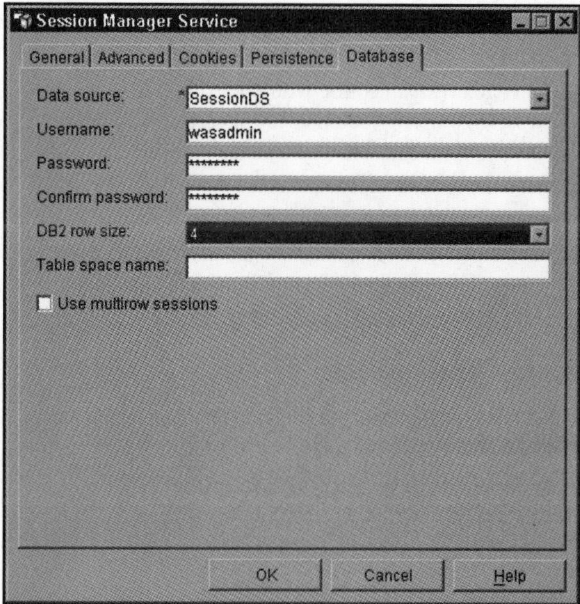

Figure 21-10: Database configuration for Session Manager.

Enabling single/multirow support

The default setting for WebSphere Application Server session management is for single row access. A single session maps to a single row in the database table used to hold sessions. With this setup, your sessions are limited to the amount of application data that can be stored into them. The maximum size for session data in a single row setting is 2 megabytes. WebSphere Application Server supports the use of a multirow schema option in which each piece of application-specific data is stored in a separate row of the database. This option enables you to store as much data as your database can handle.

You use single row for the following reasons:

- You can read or write all values with just one record read/write.
- This option takes up less space in a database because you are guaranteed that each session is only one record long.

You use multirow for the following reasons:

- The application can store an unlimited amount of data. (It is limited only by size of database and 2 MB per record limit.)
- The application can read individual fields instead of the whole record. When larger amounts of data are stored in the session, but only small amounts are specifically accessed during a given servlet's processing of an HTTP request, multirow sessions can improve performance by avoiding unneeded Java object serialization.

Configuring persistence manually

Configuring for persistence offers a manual configuration option. Under Session Manager Service on the Persistence tab (see Figure 21-9), if you select the Configure Manually radio button and click Configure…, you can set the following parameters manually:

- *Write Frequency*: This is when the session will be written to the database.
  - If you specify end of servlet service, a session is written to the database after the servlet completes execution.
  - If you specify manual update, programmatic sync on the IBMSession object is required in order to write the session data to the database.
  - If you specify time-based, session data is written to the database based on the specified Write Interval value
- *Write Contents:* This setting determines whether only updated attributes should be written to the database. Otherwise, all the session attributes are written to the database, even if they have not changed.
  - If you specify updated attributes, only the updated attributes are written to the database.
  - If you specify all session attributes, all attributes are written to the database.

- *Database cleanup scheduling:* Enables the scheduled process for cleaning up the invalidated `HttpSessions` from the `session` database. You enable this option to reduce the number of database updates that are required to keep the `HttpSessions` alive.

> **NOTE**: When manual configuration is not enabled, the invalidator process runs every few minutes to remove invalidated `HttpSessions`. When this option is enabled, this setting specifies the two hours of a day in which the invalidator process cleans up the invalidated persistent sessions in the database. Specify the times at which there will be less activity in the session database.

Setting up manual updates

You basically use manual configuration when you want better control. You can gain even more control by selecting the Manual update option of Write Frequency. This mode allows the application to decide when a session should be stored persistently. The only time the session manager persists is when it receives a request to sync information. The `sync()` method contained in the `IBMSession` class is the trigger to persist the data.

If the servlet or JSP terminates without invoking the `sync()` method, the session manager saves the contents of the session object into the session cache. This presupposes that caching is active. Cached sessions do not update the modified session data in the session database. That happens at predetermined intervals.

Web developers use this interface to reduce unnecessary writes to the session database and, thereby, to improve overall application performance.

> **NOTE**: All servlets in the Web application server must perform their own session management when using manual mode.

Setting up time-based writes to the session database

Using time-based writes is a new feature of WebSphere V4.0. Time-based writes write session data to the database every *n* seconds. The value of *n* is called the write interval. You use time-based writes to improve performance.

WebSphere adherence to the J2EE specification requires the following:

- The session can be accessed by only a single Web application.
- The session must prohibit concurrent access to a `HttpSession` from separate Web applications but allow concurrent access within a JVM.

WebSphere, thereby, guarantees session affinity, which means session information doesn't have to be written each time under normal conditions. It still is important for fail-over conditions.

Time-based writes base everything upon the last access time of the `HttpSession`. If you configure the system to persist the session at the end of a servlet or JSP, any time you access the session, the access time is updated and the session is persisted. That's a lot of I/O.

Now if you turn on time-based writes, the updates are deferred and performed all at once. Only the latest change to the access time is written. You can see the importance of time-based writes.

Understanding Session Security

You can turn on session security in WebSphere Application Server to maintain security of individual sessions. When enabled, the session manager checks the user ID of the HTTP request against the user ID of the session kept by WebSphere.

When the developer codes the `request.getSession()` method, a check is performed to validate the user.

> **NOTE**: WebSphere throws a `com.ibm.websphere.servlet.session.UnauthorizedSessionRequestException` exception if the security check fails.

After a successful authentication, the session data is returned to the program. An unauthenticated identity is set to `anonymous`.

Session management security has the following rules:

- Sessions in unsecured pages are treated as accesses by the anonymous user.
- The default user for unsecured pages that have sessions is anonymous user.
- Sessions in secured pages are treated as accesses by the authenticated user.
- Sessions created in secured pages are created under the identity of the authenticated user. They can only be accessed in other secured pages by the same user. To protect these sessions from use by unauthorized users, they cannot be accessed from an insecure page, that is, do not mix access to secure and insecure pages.
- Security integration in the session manager is not supported in HTTP form-based login unless Lightweight Third-Party Authentication (LTPA) is used.

Squeezing Out Performance

You have learned about some potential areas that could impact performance. As mentioned earlier, tuning performance is all about balance. This section provides some pointers to things you can tweak to get a little more horsepower out of your system. In general, you might want to start with some of the obvious areas, which are covered in depth in the following sections:

- Memory
- Caching
- Reduced I/O
- Connection pooling
- Creating more servers

- Shrinking object size
- Cleaning up session
- Using multirow persistence

Managing memory

WebSphere default heap size is 256 MB. You can increase this value to get more memory from the system. You should factor in the potential of growing too large. If the heap size is too big, it may impact garbage collection that would impact the system.

Managing Session cache size

By default, the session cache holds 1000 session objects. You might consider lowering the number. A lower number requires less memory. This option is counter-productive if sessions aren't in cache and you need to access them from the session's database.

Using the overflow option allows an unlimited amount of sessions, but again it's a balance against potential malicious attacks. To limit the cache size to the number specified in the session manager, you should turn off overflow and use session persistence.

Reducing I/O

Session persistence is governed by the last access time of the `HttpSession`. A JSP or servlet call to `request.getSession()` causes an update to the last access time. When persistent session management is set, the change writes the last access to the database. This obviously leads to a lot of I/O, if you have set the `End_Of_Servlet_Service` write frequency. Because it's based on the `request.getSession()` method, even a simple read of the session information causes a write.

> **NOTE**: JSPs access the session object each time they are executed.

As a developer, you could help the situation by following a few simple rules:

- Store only the minimum amount of data required in `HttpSession`.
- Utilize a property file, hash table, or some other technique rather than storing entire objects in the session object.
- JSPs that do not need to access the session object should use `<%@page session="false"%>` to remove unnecessary calls to update access time.
- Use time-based write frequency mode. This greatly reduces the amount of I/O. Using this mode, all the outstanding updates for a Web application are written out periodically based on the configured write interval.
- Use the Specify session database cleanup schedule for invalidated sessions option in the Manual Configuration Dialog box.

Configuring the session database connection pool

Database connections are expensive. Having connection pools helps reduce the overhead of acquiring a new connection for each database call. The datasource within WebSphere, by default, opens a pool of no more than 10 connections. This equates to a maximum of 10 concurrent accesses to the session database.

If your site is high volume, having so few connections might result in queuing. Datasource queuing can impact the overall performance of the Web application. This again refers to balance. You want the session manager to be balanced between the wait times for a client needing a connection. The optimal condition is when there are fewer connections than the number of clients.

Bigger is not necessarily better. As mentioned before, connections are expensive. Having a large pool of connections reduces memory and adds overhead. Licensing can have an impact on what you can do with database connectivity.

You might also try playing around with manual updating, time-based write frequencies, and multirow persistence to reduce I/O. Anything to reduce I/O always has a good effect on the overall system performance. Remember though, you are using I/O to survive failovers.

Adding application server clones

WebSphere provides you the capability to create more instances to balance the load between JVMs and/or additional servers. Clustering and increasing CPU and memory achieve satisfactory results. Again, your mileage may vary.

CROSS-REFERENCE: Chapter 24 discusses clones in detail.

Reducing session object size

You should always beware of session packrats, developers who need a bit of information and decide to toss it in the session as a quick way to create state. Often, these objects hang around forever. Developers should strive to keep things simple and small. Derive, if possible, and remove unnecessary and/or obsolete objects from the session.

From an architectural viewpoint, consider whether it's better to access data from a database or from the session. Consider the ramifications of persistent sessions. WebSphere must serialize all objects in the session so it can persist them to the database. That's a lot of overhead for each write. If you find this type of coding in your applications, refactor to reduce the impact.

Cleaning up unneeded sessions

As a reminder, if the users no longer need the session object because they completed their work, the session becomes an excellent candidate for invalidation. Invalidating a session removes it from the session cache, as well as from the session database.

CROSS-REFERENCE: Chapter 11 discusses the process for cleaning up unneeded session objects.

Doing the math

Large session objects are evil (in some instances). If the site uses session caching, large sessions reduce the memory available in the WebSphere instance for other tasks, such as application execution.

Try doing the math to calculate your memory utilization and make adjustments. For example, say the AlmostFreeCruise application stores 1 MB of information per user session object (ships, cabins, tours, and so on). If 100 would-be cruise-maniacs arrive over the course of 30 minutes, and you assume the session timeout remains at the defaulted 30 minutes, the application server instance must allocate 100 MB just to accommodate the newly arrived users in the session cache: 1 MB per user session * 100 users = 100 MB.

Here are some ways that increased memory can be alleviated:

- Shrink the size of the session object.
- Shrink the size of the session cache.
- Add additional application server instances.
- Clean up unneeded sessions.
- Buy or increase the memory available.
- Set the session to timeout earlier.

Changing session timeout intervals

By default, each user receives a 30-minute interval between requests before the session manager invalidates the user's session. You should consider evaluating your normal customer to determine timeframes that are acceptable. Don't adjust it too low or you will hear from your users (or your company will go belly up). You should consider peak loads during various times in the day.

Using multirow persistent session management

Multirow persistence provides granularity to the persisted session data that improves access to the database by utilizing a cache. As information is requested, instead of bringing the entire contents of the session back, you get the value you requested. That value is stored in cache, and subsequent requests for the same value are found in cache, thereby reducing database I/O.

Multirow session support provides a good compromise for Web applications requiring larger sessions. However, single-row persistent session management remains the best choice for Web applications with small session objects. Single-row persistent session management requires less storage in the database and fewer database interactions to retrieve a session's contents, because all the values in the session are written or read in one operation. This keeps the session object's memory footprint small, as well as reduces the network traffic between WebSphere and the persistent session database.

Summary

Session management provides the glue between the stateless HTTP environment and your application-state information. Because HTTP is stateless, the Servlet 2.2 specification provides a means to maintain state using a Java class called `HttpSession`.

Prior to the `HttpSession`, you basically had two ways of passing information between pages: Cookies and URL rewriting. Both of these session-management solutions exist today. Cookies are stored on local machines; whereas URL rewriting is performed by appending session information to the end of the URL.

WebSphere implements session management by assigning a session ID that adheres to the Servlet 2.2 specification. There is another aspect of the specification that is implemented in WebSphere: A session can only be accessed by one Web application. So two separate Web applications cannot access the same session.

Saving session information on a single server is not as complex as saving it within an environment that requires scalability and fail-over support. To accommodate those requirements WebSphere provides a foundation for workload management.

Workload management provides a scalable, high-performance environment that satisfies all your business service levels. Through the use of session clustering, you can distribute work throughout your domain.

To improve performance and ensure session integrity, a concept called server affinity was implemented. Server affinity ensures that session information is available on the machine you first collaborated with.

This chapter took these concepts and applied them to an example, so you walked through the configuration of session management. As each configuration page was presented, configuration parameters were described in detail.

After the example, manually configuring session management was presented. You can select manual configuration as you configure session management. Manual configuration gives you the best opportunity to tune your system. For example, you can take advantage of time-based writes (an optimization technique for writing to the database). The last major section reviewed the options you have to squeeze out some performance.

Chapter 22

Using WebSphere's Application Packaging

In This Chapter

- Understanding J2EE deployment
- Understanding deployment descriptors
- Understanding EJB and Web modules

Using the Application Assembly Tool (AAT), WebSphere 4.0 is fully compliant with the J2EE specifications. The changes to WebSphere packaging and deployment from prior versions are all for the better. In this chapter, you become familiar with the application packaging supported by WebSphere 4.0.

The J2EE platform specifications provide the implementation framework to ensure portability of your applications. Understanding the J2EE packaging is the best way to learn how to use WebSphere implementation of application packaging. *Application packaging* is the process of assembling reusable components into new applications. It's very similar to making a salad. You put in some romaine lettuce, throw in Parmesan cheese, mix a little raw egg and add the anchovies and *voila*! Caesar salad. Each of these items can stand on its own merits, but together they create a new experience. It's the same with J2EE components. You assemble Web archives (WAR), Java archives (JAR), and Enterprise archives (EAR) and describe them with deployment descriptors so you have a new enterprise application.

One of the benefits of developing J2EE applications is for its reusable components and its capability to deliver distributed objects. In this chapter, you learn about the terminology of J2EE packaging. You learn how to take one or more components and assemble them into a deliverable enterprise application package. You use the WebSphere console to implement the enterprise application and customize it. You are introduced to some new tooling to assist you in assembling applications created by some other vendor or department.

All of the things you do in this chapter, in WebSphere terminology, make up the process known as application assembly. When you finish this chapter, you should be able to assemble an application for a specific environment and deploy it on WebSphere. There is a lot to cover so let's begin with J2EE packaging.

Understanding J2EE Packaging and Deployment

Understanding the J2EE packaging guidelines is critical to the overall understanding of J2EE and WebSphere's implementation. Perhaps a good way to learn is to follow the *who, what, when, where, and how* methodology.

You need to know who will be organizing the packaging and who will be deploying the applications. The *who* are the roles specified in J2EE. The *what* are the J2EE modules and deployment descriptors that are defined by a developer or tool. The *when* happens after the application is ready for packaging. The *where* happens on assembly machines. The deployment tools describe *how* it can be accomplished in WebSphere. In the following sections, these questions will be answered.

The starting point is really the understanding what you are packaging. A J2EE application is packaged as an Enterprise Archive (EAR) file. An EAR file is a Java Archive (JAR) file that includes a deployment descriptor. Other than that, it's just a JAR file with an `.ear` extension. An EAR file is a portable application to any J2EE-compliant server.

> **TIP**: Think of an archive (.EAR, WAR or JAR) as a Zip file. You can view any archive with WinZip.

A J2EE application EAR contains one or more J2EE modules and a deployment descriptor. A *deployment descriptor* is an XML-based text file that has elements describing how to assemble and deploy the application unit into a specific environment, such as WebSphere Application Server.

Creating a J2EE application is a two-phase process. In the first phase, you develop J2EE application components such as EJBs, Web, and Client modules. These components are packaged in EJB jar files (JAR) and Web archives (WAR). So you may have an enterprise application (the AlmostFreeCruise application) that utilizes HTML, servlets and Java Server Pages (JSP) for display and session, and entity Enterprise JavaBeans that perform cruise line logic and access cruise line and ship data. In this example, you have a WAR file for the HTML, servlets and Java Server Pages (JSP), and a JAR file to contain the EJB components.

In the second phase, you assemble the WAR and JAR archives to create an enterprise archive (EAR).

As you get more sophisticated, the packaging can contain one or many units, which you can organize by functionality or organization. It is important to ensure that the packaging is as independent as possible so you can reuse it. Therefore, you can bundle various packages to formulate a larger customized system. For example, if you decide to offer airfare quotes on your Web site, you could add the EJBs and supporting Web components along with your cruise application. Figure 22-1 shows the J2EE packaging components.

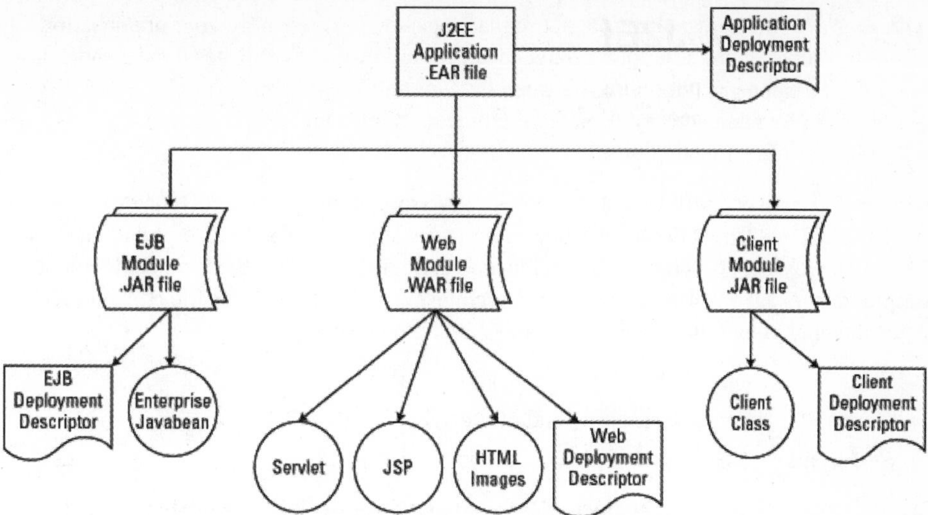

Figure 22-1: The J2EE assembly package contains three types of modules: EJB, Web, and Client.

In Figure 22-1, you see the four deployment descriptors:

- The application deployment descriptors maps WAR files and JAR files to Web modules and EJJB modules respectively, as well as security role information.
- The EJB deployment descriptor maps JNDI names references, resources, interfaces, EJB fields, and security roles to EJBs.
- The Web deployment descriptor contains servlet names, mappings, error pages, and form-based configuration.
- The client deployment descriptor maps JNDI names and references to EJBs.

A deployment descriptor is an XML text file with elements that describe how to assemble and deploy the group into an environment. The elements contained within the file consist of tags and values in the following format:

```
<tag>value</tag>
```

The descriptors specify structural information, such as the components in a JAR files and their relationship to one another. Descriptors also describe how the JAR file can be composed into a deployable unit.

CROSS-REFERENCE: You learn more about deployment descriptors in Chapter 16.

To create or assemble an application, a designated person or role within your organization modifies the deployment descriptors for each J2EE module and establishes the dependencies between the components within and between the EJB and Web archives (`JAR` and `WAR`). This is a predeployment activity. You learn more about roles in the next section (Understanding J2EE roles).

A relationship exists between each deployment descriptor and type of archive (WAR or JAR). The EJB, Web, and Client deployment descriptors are all included with an archive. The EJB and client deployment descriptors are included in JAR files; whereas the Web deployment descriptor is packaged in a Web application archive (WAR) file. A WAR file contains Web components including other resources, such as the following:

- Static Web resources (HTML, images, and so on)
- Client-side Java classes (applets and utilities)
- Server-side utilities (database beans, shopping carts)

A WAR file has a specific hierarchy as described in the Servlet 2.2 specifications. The top level includes the document root. The document root is where JSP pages and other Web resources, including the client-side classes and archives, are stored.

Within the structure of the document root is the `WEB-INF folder/directory`. The following files and directories are contained within the `WEB-INF` folder:

- *web.xml:* The Web application deployment descriptor
- *Tag library descriptor files:* An XML document that describes a tag library that defines a reusable module for JSPs
- *Classes:* A directory that contains servlets, utility classes, and JavaBeans
- *Lib:* A directory that contains JAR files, which contain tag libraries and server-side classes.

Package directories can be created under either the `WEB-INF/classes` or document root directories.

Returning to Figure 22-1, if you were the person responsible for organizing the delivered package, your responsibility would be to ensure that the descriptions of the EJB in the WAR file match those described within the EJB JAR file.

When you are ready to assemble the components into a deployable EAR file, you would have a designated person (the deployer) package all three types of modules, if they exist, along with the application deployment descriptor. You would most likely use an assembly tool, such as the Application Assembly Tool (AAT), to create the EAR file. At this point the EAR file is ready for deployment to any J2EE-compliant server.

Understanding J2EE roles

In the previous section, you learned that assembly of the components is the responsibility of someone or a group of people. These people represent the *who* information. You read about various persons or roles having the responsibility of packaging and assembling modules. The J2EE blueprints specifies the technology and the following roles to create, manage, and deploy applications:

- *Application component provider:* The people or companies in this role develop enterprise beans, HTML, and JSP pages, and their associated helper classes. They supply the structural information in the deployment descriptors (home and remote interfaces, persistence mechanisms, implementation classes of Enterprise JavaBeans, and so on).
- *Application assembler:* The person functioning in this role takes individual components and assembles them into a complete application. He or she might create components for launching JSP pages, design error pages, and establish security constraints and URL namespaces.
- *Deployer:* This person should be extremely knowledgeable about the particular target environments. Using tools, such as Application Assembly Tool (AAT), the deployer installs components onto WebSphere. The primary responsibilities are installation and configuration. This person is also responsible for mapping the security roles to the user accounts and groups.
- *Administrator:* People acting in the Administrator role are reponsible for configuration and administration of WebSphere. They are also responsible for administration of the network infrastructure in which the J2EE application runs.
- *Tool provider:* The person fulfilling this role provides tools for development and packaging of application components. WebSphere Studio Application Developer is a good example of such a provider.

Understanding deployment descriptors

As mentioned previously, a deployment descriptor is an XML-based text file with elements that describe how to assemble and deploy the unit into a specific environment. What that means is you describe the internal structure of a resource that provides details about the deployment. The deployment descriptors will be used in WebSphere to map characteristics of the installed application to the services rendered by the application server. For instance, when you create a deployment descriptor that describes the Snoop Servlet, the WebSphere administrator knows which application server it belongs to and which parameters it can accept.

Listing 22-1 shows an example of a Web deployment descriptor with the Snoop servlet.

Listing 22-1: Web Deployment Descriptor with a Snoop Servlet

```
<?xml version="1.0" encoding="UTF-8"?>
<!DOCTYPE web-app PUBLIC "-//Sun Microsystems, Inc.//DTD Web Application
2.2//EN" "http://java.sun.com/j2ee/dtds/web-app_2_2.dtd" >
   <web-app id="WebApp_1">
      <display-name>Default Application</display-name>
      <description>WebSphere&apos;s Default Application
       Example</description>
      <servlet id="Servlet_1">
         <servlet-name>snoop</servlet-name>
         <description>snoop servlet</description>
         <servlet-class>SnoopServlet</servlet-class>
         <init-param id="InitParam_1">
            <param-name>param1</param-name>
            <param-value>test-value1</param-value>
         </init-param>
         <init-param id="InitParam_2">
            <param-name>param2</param-name>
            <param-value>test-value2</param-value>
         </init-param>
      </servlet>
      <servlet id="Servlet_2">
         <servlet-name>hello</servlet-name>
         <description>hello servlet</description>
         <servlet-class>HelloWorldServlet</servlet-class>
      </servlet>
...
```

The XML grammar consists of a tag and a value expressed in the following syntax:

```
<tag>value</tag>
```

The example in Listing 22-1 shows the Web deployment descriptor for the sample application that comes with WebSphere. Tools, such as WebSphere Studio Application Developer, automatically generate deployment descriptors, so much of the typing is actually managed for you. Deployment descriptor elements contain behavioral information about components not included directly in code. Their purpose is to tell the (role) deployer how to deploy an application.

Deployment descriptors specify two types of information:

- Structurally, deployment descriptors describe the components in the JAR file. They describe the relationships with other components and external dependencies. An application assembler or deployer who modifies any of the information provided by the application component provider is at risk of breaking the application. Environment entries and resource requirements are part of structural information.

- Assembly information describes how contents of a JAR file can be packaged into a deployable unit. Although not required, assembly information can be described. Assembly information can be changed without breaking the functionality of the contents, although doing so might alter the behavior of the assembled application.

You should always use a tool to verify the compliance of the contents of EAR, WAR, and JAR files. The Application Assembly Tool provides a tool that runs a verification check on any of the archive files.

Understanding WebSphere J2EE compliance

For WebSphere to become J2EE-compliant, WebSphere needs to comply with the specifications for the deployment of the three types of modules (EJB, Web, and Client). Previous versions of WebSphere were not compliant. Version 4.0 is the first J2EE-compliant version put out by IBM.

For each Enterprise JavaBean, WebSphere has to perform the following tasks:

1. Generate and compile the stubs and skeletons for the enterprise bean.
2. Set up the security environment to host the enterprise bean according to its deployment descriptor. This is needed so that the access to the methods of the enterprise bean can be regulated according to the security policy of the application.
3. Set up the transaction environment for the enterprise bean according to its deployment descriptor. This is needed so that the calls to the methods of the enterprise bean happen in the correct transaction context.
4. Register the enterprise bean, its environment properties, and its resource references in the Java Naming and Directory Interface (JNDI) namespace.
5. Create database tables for enterprise beans that use container-managed persistence.

For each Web component, WebSphere has to perform the following tasks:

1. Transfer the contents of the Web component underneath the document root of the server. Because there can be more than one J2EE application installed, the server may install each under a specific directory.
2. Initialize the security environment of the application.
3. Register environment properties, resource references, and EJB references in the JNDI namespace.
4. Set up the environment for the Web application. For example, WebSphere performs the alias mappings and configures the servlet context parameters.
5. Precompile JSPs as specified in the deployment descriptor.

The tool used to deploy an application client and the mechanism used to install the application client are not specified by the J2EE specification. Therefore, implementations by vendors may vary.

Using WebSphere deployment tooling

WebSphere provides three deployment tools. WebSphere Studio Application Developer has the capability to deploy to the WebSphere Test environment as well as remote application servers. The other two tools are the Application Assembly Tool and EJBDeploy. These tools are both found in the `<was_home>\bin` folder and named `assembly.bat` and `ejbdeploy.bat`, respectively.

Having a deployment tool built within WebSphere Studio Application Developer gives speed and agility in development. A developer's needs are different from the needs of the deployer. A developer needs quick turnaround to build, deploy, and test, along with the ability to debug.

If you take a closer look at the J2EE specifications, there is some ambiguity (or flexibility) regarding how certain runtime requirements are implemented. Some examples provide mapping to security roles or JNDI lookup names as well as transaction isolation levels. IBM chose to go the route of XML to implement the necessary bindings required for the runtime environment. The following section examines how IBM implemented the bindings.

Understanding IBM bindings

A certain amount of information must be available to each container along with the application code and deployment descriptor for proper runtime support of an application. This information is usually related to bindings of the application in a vendor-specific or environment-specific setting. Following is a partial list of information that the deployer must know to bind the application:

- A JNDI name for each enterprise bean's home interface
- A mapping of security roles of the application to user and group names
- JNDI lookup names and account information for all databases

J2EE vendors have their own implementation to resolve the listed information. WebSphere 4.0 does it using IBM bindings. The IBM bindings associate local names with EJB and resource references in the global JNDI namespace. A resource reference is a "logical" name to the home of an EJB. You can use the IBM Application Assembly Tool (AAT) to make associations when you define the EJB and resource references. After the associations are made, they are automatically stored in one of three files:

- `ibm-web-jar-bnd.xmi`
  - Which binds EJB references to the EJB JNDI name
  - Which binds resource references to its JNDI name
- `ibm-ejb-jar-bnd.xmi`
  - Which binds EJB to JNDI name
  - Which binds EJB reference to its JNDI name
  - Which binds resource references to its JNDI name

- `ibm-application-bnd.xmi`
  - Which binds security roles to users and groups

Understanding IBM extensions

Not everything is covered by the J2EE specifications. The following are left up to the vendor to implement:

- Transaction isolations attributes that define how transactions are isolated from one another.
- Web Application reloading that defines where the servlet gets reloaded.
- File serving and servlet invoking by classname, which are specialized implementations that allow file serving without configuration steps and invocation of servlets by classname.

These are handled by WebSphere with what IBM calls IBM extensions. You use the AAT to configure these extensions, which are then stored in one of the following files depending on the type of extension:

- `ibm-ejb-ext.xmi` specifies attributes, such as run-as mode for methods, transaction isolation levels, bean cache, and local transaction.
- `ibm-web-ext.xmi` specifies attributes, such as reload interval, default error page, file serving enabled, and directory browsing enabled.
- `ibm-application-ext.xmi` specifies the type of modules and extensions for WebSphere specific implementations.

Understanding more about IBM extensions

You learned a little bit about how IBM extensions implement specifications not included in J2EE. There are a couple of topics that deserve a little more discussion.

EJB caching

The Enterprise JavaBeans specification defines three EJB caching options: options A, B, or C. The EJB container processes the EJB requests based on these options. EJB caching is set at the bean level and is stored in the IBM extensions deployment descriptor. The caching options are discussed in the following list:

- Option A assumes you have exclusive access to the data. Between transactions nothing can modify the information. This includes other Java applications and/or the same entity bean running in a different container/server. Given that, Option A cannot be set when you are running in a clustered environment. Option A utilizes memory cache. When you commit a transaction, the entity bean updates the data and keeps the instance cached in memory. Option A is good if you have lots of memory and do not plan to utilize workload management.
- Option B, which is new with WebSphere 4.0, is used if you plan to share access to the database. This means data could change between transactions. When you set Option B,

you are always synchronizing back to the database at the beginning of the transaction. Option B is good if you plan on clustering servers, and you need the latest information from the database.

- Option C (the default) is similar to B. It assumes shared access to the database but differs from options A or B in that it returns the entity bean back to the pool at the end of the transaction. Caching Option C has the best memory usage at the expense of a larger number of method calls.

Beginning with WebSphere Application Server 4.0, you have to use the AAT to set EJB caching. The setting is found on the IBM Extensions window of an entity EJB, in the Bean Cache category. You must combine the Activate at and Load at options to set the EJB caching option to A, B, or C. This setting, shown in the following list, is saved in the IBM extensions deployment descriptor, `ibm-ejb-jar-ext.xmi` file:

- To activate Option A, you must set `Activate At` to `Once` and `Load At` to `Activation`.
- To activate Option B, you must set `Activate At` to `Once` and `Load At` to `Transaction`.
- Option C is the default where `Activate At` is set to `Transaction` and `Load At` is set to `Transaction`.

You can find these setting in the AAT under EJB Modules⇨Entity Beans under the IBM Extension tab.

Using the FileServing servlet

The FileServing servlet is used when you want to serve up HTML pages from the Application server. The servlet can handle any resource that is stored in the WAR file. There might be a performance impact if you use the FileServing servlet. One problem with using the FileServing Servlet is its lack of customization options. A Web server has better caching capabilities.

One benefit to using the FileServing servlet is that it keeps the content (static and dynamic) together in a single deployable unit. Another benefit is security. Static pages can be protected using WebSphere security.

Using the Invoker servlet

The Invoker servlet can be used to invoke servlets by class name. You might want to rethink using the Invoker servlet in production environments, as it is a potential security risk. Do you want outsiders knowing your Java class name? Even an insider could maliciously modify the class to introduce unwanted behavior. You may want to use the Invoker servlet as a development aid to test servlets.

Using the Application Assembly Tool (AAT)

The Application Assembly Tool (AAT) is a utility you use to assist the J2EE provider or J2EE deployer with the generation of J2EE-compliant deployment descriptors and binding attributes. You learn how to create an enterprise application, EJB modules, Web modules, and Client modules using the Application Assembly Tool (AAT). The details behind the creation of the modules are discussed to further your understanding of how it all fits together.

Figure 22-2 shows a graphic that depicts the components that are assembled into a J2EE application EAR file using AAT.

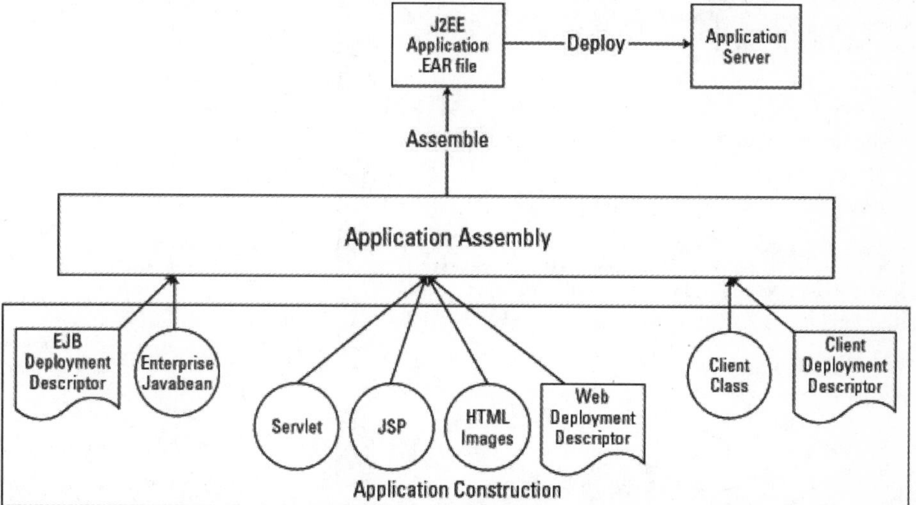

Figure 22-2: The application-assembly process uses EJB, JAR, WAR, and client JARs. There is a deployment descriptor for each module.

You can perform the following tasks with AAT:

- Create/edit J2EE modules
  - EJB modules (EJB JAR files)
  - Web modules (WAR files) servlets, JSPs, Web resources
  - Application clients (JAR files)
- Create/edit J2EE applications (EAR files)
- Modify deployment descriptors
- Modify binding information
- Modify IBM extension attributes

You can start the AAT in one of three ways:

- Run `<was_home>\bin\assembly.bat`.
- Open the Administrative Console and use Tools⇨Application Assembly Tool.
- Click Start⇨Programs⇨IBM WebSphere⇨Application Server V4.0AE ⇨Application Assembly Tool.

You do not have to have the Administrative Server running to launch AAT. Figure 22-3 shows the Welcome screen in AAT. As you can see, you can create applications, EJB modules, Web modules, and application clients.

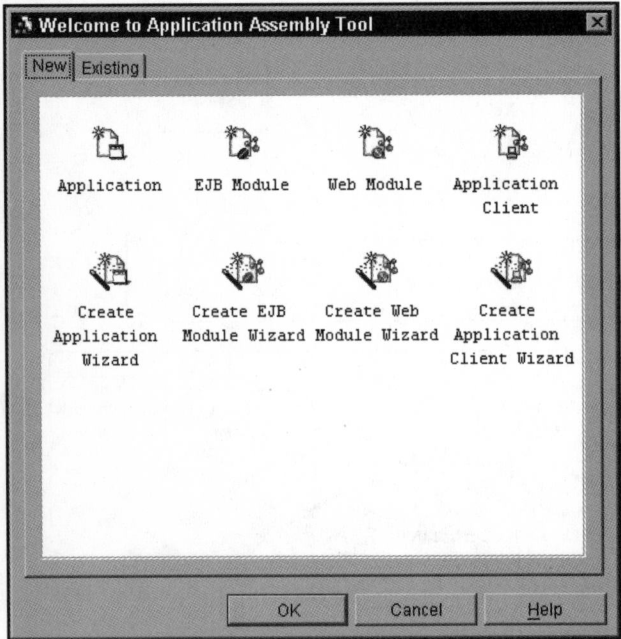

Figure 22-3: The Application Assembly Tool has four wizards to help you generate the application modules.

You can also see in Figure 22-3 that AAT provides the following wizards:

- Enterprise Application Wizard
- EJB Module Wizard
- Web Module Wizard
- Application Client Wizard

The Welcome screen offers you one way to start the wizards provided by AAT. An additional option for launching the wizards is to use File⇨Wizards, as shown in Figure 22-4. (First click Cancel if you still have the Welcome screen open.)

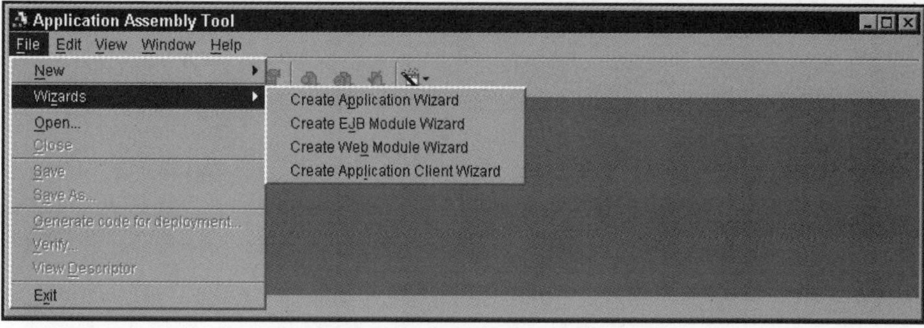

Figure 22-4: You can start the wizards by using the Start menu or through the welcome screen.

Using the Application Wizard

The Application Wizard walks you through the steps needed to capture the appropriate information to create an enterprise application. Using this wizard, you perform the following tasks:

- Specify the display name and EAR filename.
- Define application icons.
- Add EJB modules as JAR files.
- Add Web modules as WAR files.
- Add application clients as JAR files.
- Define security roles for the entire enterprise.

Using the EJB Module Wizard

The EJB Module Wizard walks you through the steps necessary to capture information about EJBs that formulate an EJB module. The wizard requires you to perform the following tasks:

- Specify the containing application (EAR file) and the JAR file for the module.
- Specify the files that comprise the module.
- Add the Enterprise JavaBeans and specify the type of bean (session, Bean-managed persistence (BMP), or Container-managed persistence (CMP).
- Add security roles.
- Add method permissions.
- Add transaction isolation levels for the bean's methods (which is part of the J2EE 1.3 specification).

Using the Web Module Wizard

The Web Module Wizard walks you through the steps necessary to capture information about JSPs, servlets, and Web resources that formulate a Web module. You can perform the following tasks:

- Specify the containing application (EAR file) and context root.
- Add resource, class or JAR files.
- Add JSP files and servlets.
- Add security roles.
- Map URLs to servlets.
- Add resource references to EJB homes.
- Add context parameters.
- Add EJB references.

Using the Application Client Wizard

The Application Client Wizard walks you through the steps necessary to capture information about the application client. Using the wizard, you perform the following tasks:

- Specify the containing application (EAR file) and the JAR file.
- Specify files that are included with the application.
- Specify the classpath and main class used by the application client.
- Add any icons.
- Add EJB references.
- Add resource references.

Exploring enterprise applications

The previous sections discussed what is specified when you create Web modules, EJB modules, Client modules, and the enterprise applications. In this section, you learn more about the dirty details of what gets installed.

Figure 22-5 shows an example of an enterprise application. In this example, you see the sample application that comes with WebSphere 4.0. You can browse to this sample application by choosing File⇨ Open, browsing to `<was_home>/installedApps/sampleApp.ear`, and clicking Open.

In Figure 22-5 on the left side, you can see the three types of J2EE deployments displayed (EJB modules, Web modules, and Application clients). Because the Application client is void of a (+) sign, there are no application clients defined.

> **NOTE**: You may want to follow along by opening the `sampleApps.ear` file.

Review the `<was_home>/installedApps/sampleApp.ear/META-INF` folder to see the files shown in Figure 22-6.

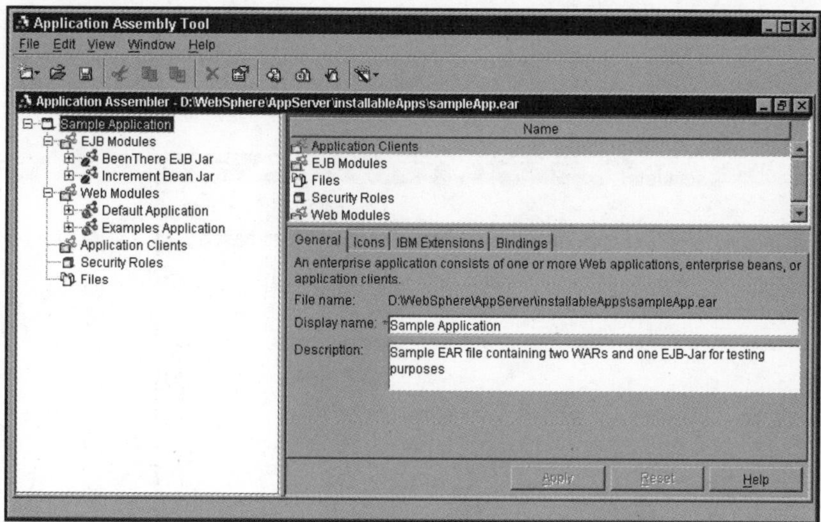

Figure 22-5: The Application Assembly Tool is divided by application. Within each application, you can specify EJB modules, Web modules, Application clients, and security roles.

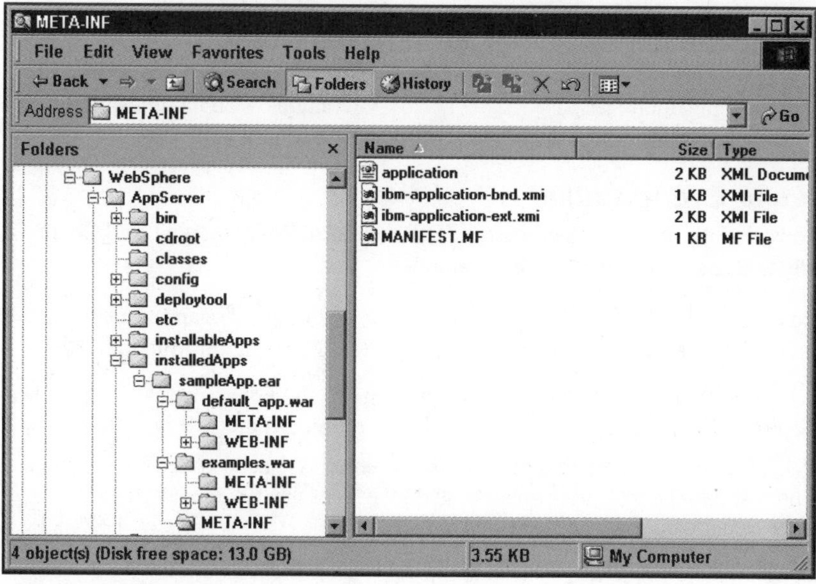

Figure 22-6: Deployment descriptors for sampleApp.ear.

The one thing you may notice is that an EAR file, originally deployed as an archive file (Zip), is expanded when it's actually deployed in WebSphere. By expanding automatically, it sets up WebSphere for what is called hot deploy.

The application deployment descriptor (`application.xml`) contains the descriptions of the WAR and JAR files included in this application. Figure 22-7 shows the application deployment descriptor.

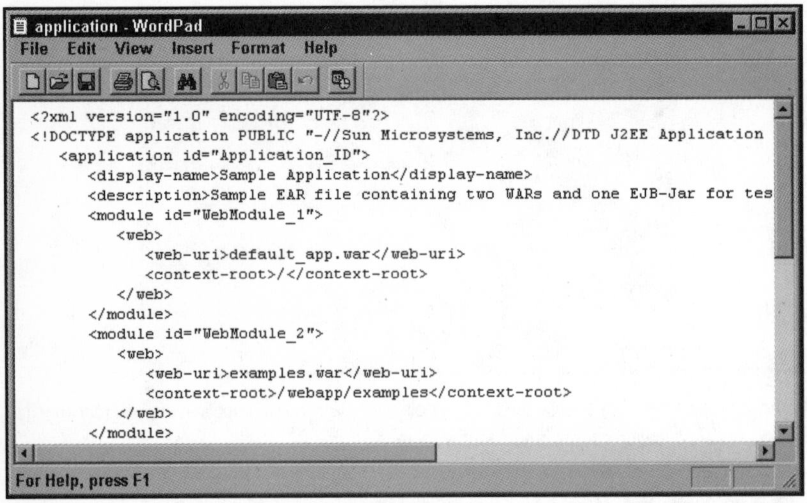

```
<?xml version="1.0" encoding="UTF-8"?>
<!DOCTYPE application PUBLIC "-//Sun Microsystems, Inc.//DTD J2EE Application
   <application id="Application_ID">
      <display-name>Sample Application</display-name>
      <description>Sample EAR file containing two WARs and one EJB-Jar for tes
      <module id="WebModule_1">
         <web>
            <web-uri>default_app.war</web-uri>
            <context-root>/</context-root>
         </web>
      </module>
      <module id="WebModule_2">
         <web>
            <web-uri>examples.war</web-uri>
            <context-root>/webapp/examples</context-root>
         </web>
      </module>
```

Figure 22-7: In the application deployment descriptor, you set the context root for the application.

You can see that the application `Sample Application` contains Web modules found in `default_app.war` and `examples.war`. Each has a unique context root.

Understanding EJB modules

Figure 22-6 shows that the application consists of EJB modules, Web modules, and Client modules. Figure 22-8 shows an expanded EJB module.

An EJB module is the smallest deployable and usable unit of enterprise beans. An EJB module is packaged and deployed as an EJB JAR file. It contains the following information:

- Java class files for the enterprise beans and their remote and home interfaces. If the bean is an entity bean, its primary key class must also be present in the EJB module.
- Any non-J2EE Java classes and interfaces that the enterprise bean code depends upon. This includes super-classes and the classes and interfaces used as method parameters, results, and exceptions.
- An EJB deployment descriptor that provides both the structural and application assembly information for the enterprise beans in the EJB module.

An EJB JAR file differs from a standard JAR file by the inclusion of a meta-file that is the deployment descriptor. The deployment descriptor in WebSphere 4.0 is different from deployment descriptors in previous versions, in that previous versions did not include a deployment descriptor for each EJB.

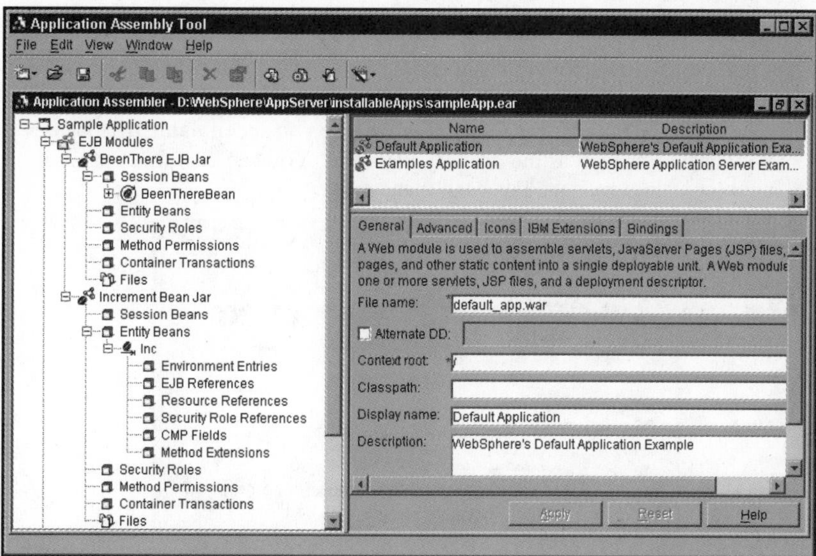

Figure 22-8: An EJB module definition requires several settings, such as a resource reference.

In Figure 22-8, a number of settings need to be set. Those settings are described next.

- Environment entries define variables used to customize the business logic of an application at runtime. If you code utilizing these externalized values, it makes changes to application code unnecessary.
- An EJB reference is a logical name used to locate the home interface of an EJB. At deployment time, the EJB reference is bound to the EJB's home in the target environment. If a session bean needs to access any EJB, all assembly properties for the EJB reference, such as name, home interface, remote interface, and JNDI binding, need to be provided.
- A resource reference declares a logical name used to locate a connection factory object.
- A security role reference specifies the name of a security role reference used in the application code.
- Extensions beyond the J2EE specification, such as transaction isolation and security identity, are stored as method extensions in the `ibm-ejb-jar-ext.xmi` file.
- Security roles specify the name of a security role. Security roles group operations that a principal is permitted to perform.

CROSS-REFERENCE: See Chapter 23 for more information on principals.

- A method permission is a mapping between one or more security roles and one or more methods that a member of the role can invoke.
- Container transactions specify the transaction attributes.
- Files contain the standard 1.1 EJB files and standard deployment descriptors.

Figure 22-9 shows a specific EJB under the General tab where you specify an EJB's home interface and remote interface as well as the primary key class. You can also find out what type of EJB is defined (container managed or bean managed).

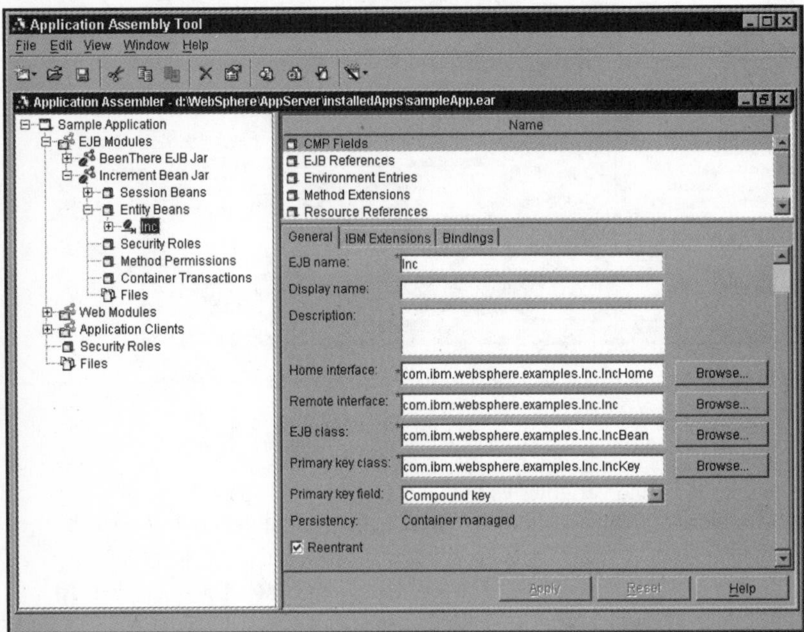

Figure 22-9: The General tab shows the EJB interface entries.

In Figure 22-9, you see the EJB Modules General tab as well as the IBM Extensions and Bindings tabs. Extensions are additions to the standard J2EE deployment descriptors. They enable the use of enterprise extensions, older systems, or behaviors not defined by the specification. Some setting categories under this tab include the following:

- Bean Cache is where you control how the cache is activated.
- Local Transactions specifies when a local transaction begins and ends.
- Concurrency Control specifies how to control concurrent access to databases.

Binding information is used by the container to locate external resources and EJBs required by a module or application. On the Binding tab you find the following fields:

- JNDI name specifies the Java Naming and Directory Interface (JNDI) name of the bean's home interface. This is the name under which the enterprise bean's home interface is registered
- Datasource details specifies the JNDI name for the bean's data source.

The output from each of the tabs goes to a specific file:

- General tab information goes to the EJB deployment descriptor.
- IBM extensions are written to `ibm-ejb-ext.xmi`.
- Bindings are written to `ibm-ejb-bnd.xmi`.

Understanding Web modules

Web modules group servlets, JSP pages, HTML, and images. They are packaged into a WAR file. The WAR file format does not conform to all the requirements of the JAR format because the classes in a WAR file are not usually loadable by a classloader if the JAR is added to a classpath.

Just like the EJB module, Web modules enable you to set environment variables, EJB references, security roles, and the like. Figure 22-10 shows an expanded Web module.

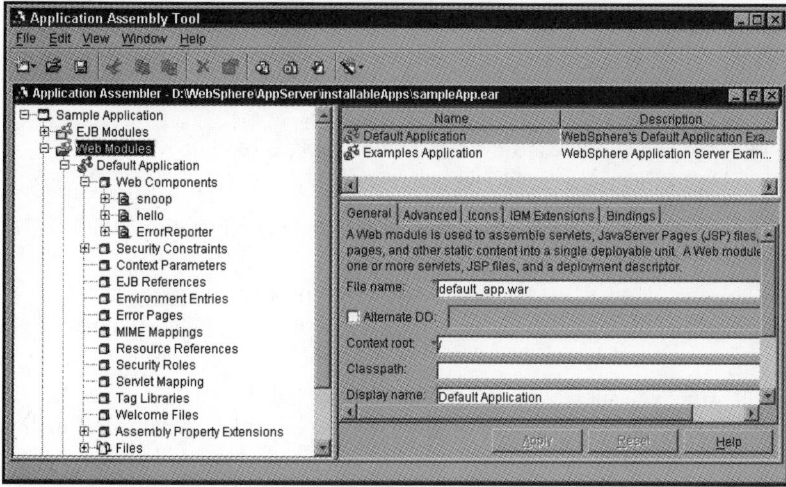

Figure 22-10: A Web module is where you set environment variables.

Servlet mapping is a linking between a client request and a servlet. You use this to specify the Uniform Resource Locator (URL) pattern of the mapping. Of particular importance is the Security Constraints item. Security constraints declare how Web content is protected. The properties shown in Figure 22-11 associate security constraints with one or more resources.

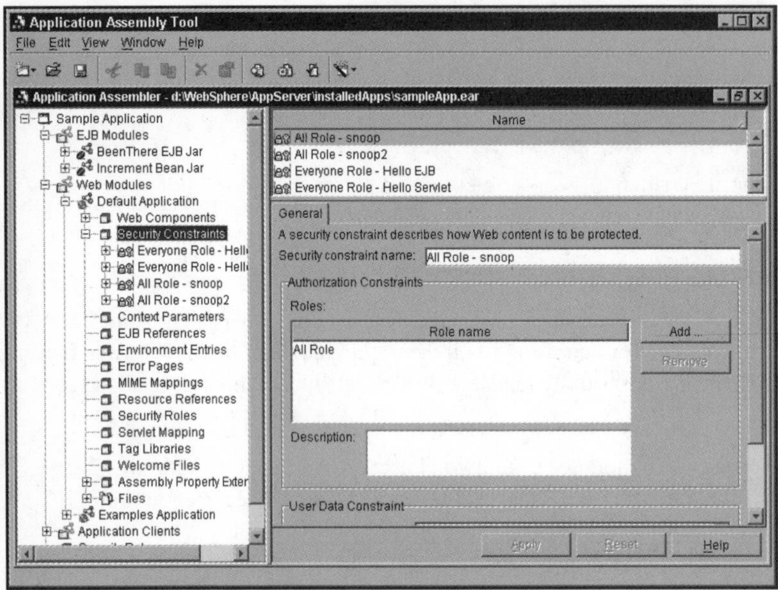

Figure 22-11: Here security constraints are associated.

The design of the Web Module window is similar to that of the EJB Module window. In addition to the General tab, it includes the following tabs:

- *Advanced:* Here you specify session configuration and login authorization configurations.
- *Icons:* These properties specify the location of JPEG or GIF files used as icons to represent the component in a GUI. The resolutions are 16x16 for small and 32x32 for large.
- *IBM Extensions:* Here you specify reloading information and other behavior not provided by J2EE specifications. File serving, serving servlets by classname and default error page are specified here.
- *Bindings:* Here you specify references to the external resources and enterprise beans required by a module.

The output from each of the tabs goes to a specific file:

- General tab information goes to the Web deployment descriptor (`web.xml`).
- Advanced and Icons tabs information also goes to the Web deployment descriptor.
- IBM extensions are written to `ibm-web-jar-ext.xmi`.
- Bindings are written to `ibm-web-jar-bnd.xmi`.

Understanding application client modules

Application client modules are packaged in JAR files with a `JAR` extension. Application client modules contain the following information:

- Java classes that implement the client
- An application client deployment descriptor

A J2EE application client differs from a standard Java program because it utilizes the JNDI name space to access resources. Having the resource information separate from the program makes the program more portable. The output from each of the tabs goes to a specific file:

- General tab information goes to the client deployment descriptor.
- Icons tab also goes to the deployment descriptor.

Exploring other AAT options

Within AAT, you have a couple more options. You can use the File menu to select Generate code for deployment, and you can perform a verification check to generate the code and verify the deployment descriptor prior to deployment.

Generating code (EJBDeploy)

Selecting this option enables you to performs the following tasks:

- Generate and compile container implementation classes.
- Process the implementation classes by using the RMIC compiler, which generates the client-side stub and server-side skeletons needed for remote method invocation (RMI).
- Validate the JAR file and display error messages if there are any J2EE specification violations within the JAR file. Verifying archive files is important for successful generation of deployment code for the application.
- For CMP entity beans, generate persistence code.
- Insert the files back into the JAR file.

Some special processing is performed for CMP entity beans. If the JAR file contains a map and schema document, that schema is used in the generation. If the JAR file does not contain a map and schema document, AAT uses a top-down mapping to generate the following files:

- `META-INF\Table.ddl`
- `META-INF\map.mapxmi`
- `META-INF\Schema\schema.rdbxmi`

Because the database table does not exist, someone who knows how to create a relation database, for instance, a database administrator (DBA), must create the database table manually.

> **NOTE**: You can find `ejbdeploy.bat` in `<was_home>\bin`.

Performing a verification check

AAT can run a verification check on any archive file. The check determines the deployment descriptor properties and references contain valid values. For EAR files it checks for the following conditions:

- EJB references: The target EJB must exist.
- Security roles must exist.
- Security roles must be unique.
- Each module in the deployment descriptor must exist.

For WAR files it checks for the following conditions:

- EJB references: The target EJB must exist.
- Security roles must exist.
- Security roles must be unique.
- Each module in the deployment descriptor must exist.
- The files, icons, servlets, and error and welcome pages listed in the deployment descriptor must be in the archive.

For EJB JAR files, it checks for the following conditions:

- All EJB references in the deployment descriptor must exist.
- Signatures for the EJB home, remote, and implementations must be compliant with J2EE 1.1 specifications.

Using EARExpander

The EARExpander expands EAR files into the format required by the Application server at runtime. EARExpander can also compress the format to an EAR file. EARExpander is found in `<was_home>/bin`. The command is executed as follows:

```
java com.ibm.websphere.install.commands.EARExpander -ear
        -expandDir -operation [ expansionFlags]
```

`expansionFlags` indicate whether you want every JAR file expanded, or just WAR files contained within the EAR file. The default is all.

To expand, use `-operation expand`, and to collapse, use `-operation collapse`.

Creating Your Own J2EE Application

The best way to learn about the application-assembly process is to look at an example. If you haven't downloaded the chapter code, please do so at this time.

You use the WAR file from AlmostFreeCruise in Application Assembly Tool to learn about how to assemble an EAR file.

Start by starting the Application Assembly Tool from one of the three methods:

- From the Programs menu
- From within the Administrative Console
- From the command line (`assembly.bat`)

Running an example application assembly

After starting the Application Assembly Tool, select the Create Application Wizard icon. You should be presented with the Create Application Display Names screen. That screen is shown in Figure 22-12.

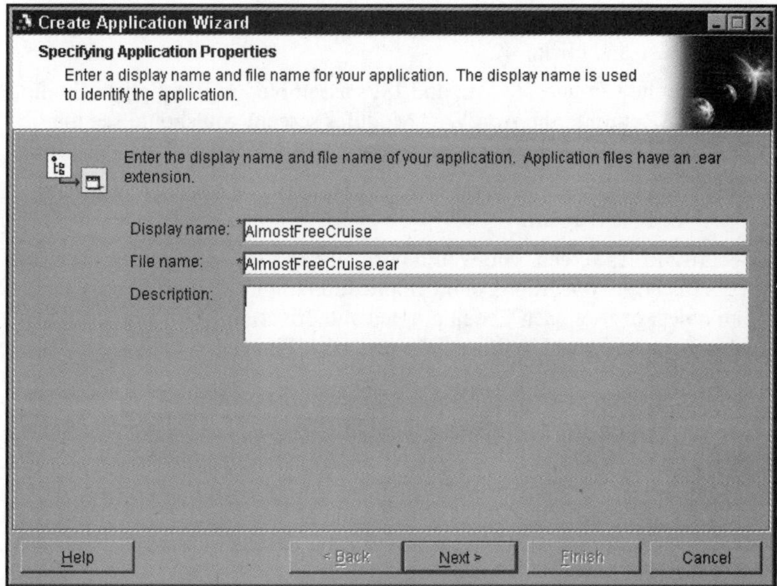

Figure 22-12: You begin the application assembly process in the Display Name screen.

To create your application, follow these steps:

1. Enter **AlmostFreeCruise** into the Display name text box and the enter same for the EAR file. You can enter a description if you want and click Next.

NOTE: Normally, you would specify files (other than J2EE modules) that your application needs by clicking Add. Some files that you might add are library files, icon files. and utilities. Because this is a simple example, you won't be adding any supplemental files. The same holds true with choosing application icons. Normally, you would click Browse and select the file that contains your application icons.

2. If there is an EJB JAR file to add, you would select it using the Adding EJB Modules window. Again click Next to continue.
3. On the Adding Web Modules screen, select Add. You need to add a WAR file, so browse to the directory where you placed the chapter code files. After you select the WAR file `CSICruiseWAR`, you are asked to enter the context root as shown in Figure 22-13.

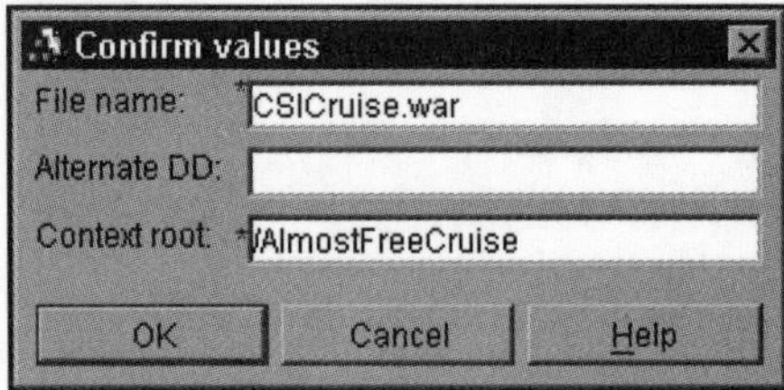

Figure 22-13: Enter the context root and then confim the values.

4. Enter **/AlmostFreeCruise** and click OK.
5. The WAR file contains the servlets, HTML, and JSPs assembled in WebSphere Studio Application Developer. Return to the Add Web Modules screen; you should see the `CSICruise` WAR file displayed, as shown in Figure 22-14.
6. Click Next to continue to the Client Module screen. You won't be adding any Client modules so you can click Next again.
7. In the Adding Security Roles screen, you would normally specify security roles for your application. Access to certain operations in the application might be granted only to certain roles. If an object or user hasn't been granted authorization, you cannot run those operations. For this exercise, you skip this screen and click Finish.

You are returned to the Application Assembly Tool main screen. Expand the Web Modules to expose `CSICruise`. If you expand Web Modules and highlight `CSICruise`, you should see a screen like Figure 22-15.

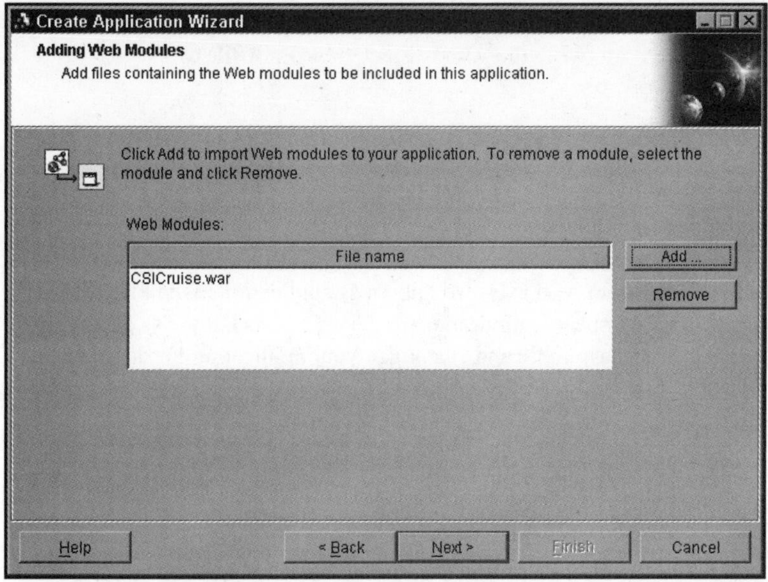

Figure 22-14: The WAR file you added to the application appears in the Add Web Modules screen.

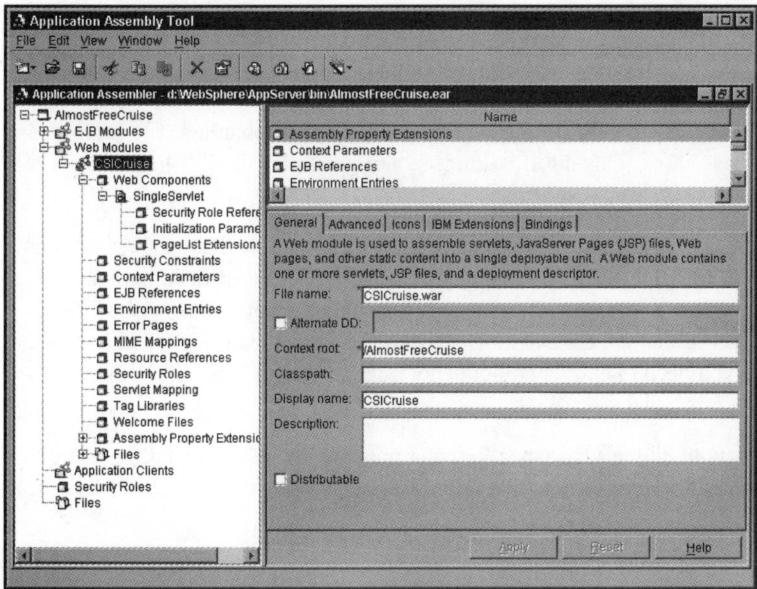

Figure 22-15: Completed assembly of CSICruise appears in the AAT main screen.

By default the .EAR file is saved in `<was_home>/bin`. For this tutorial, you should use choose File⇨Save As to write the AlmostFreeCruise.EAR file to `<was_home>\installableApps`.

Congratulations! You have successfully assembled an application.

Summary

This chapter focused on application assembly. Assembling components into modules is called packaging. In WebSphere terminology, this is also known as application assembly. Whenever you assemble an application for a specific environment, the process is known as deployment. With WebSphere, you are able to assemble and customize your application for deployments that are J2EE-compliant.

J2EE not only specifies technical aspects but also specifies roles. The roles are based on responsibilities. The J2EE role types are application component provider, application assembler, deployer, administrator, and tool provider

As applications are packaged, the application component provider helps specify the applications by creating deployment descriptors. A deployment descriptor is an XML-based text file with elements that describe how to assemble and deploy the unit into a specific environment. A certain amount of information must be available to each container along with the application code and deployment descriptor for proper runtime support of an application. WebSphere makes this information available in what is called IBM Bindings. The binding files are XML files that accompany the Enterprise Archive (EAR) file.

WebSphere also provides extensions that support Web application reloading, file serving, and servlet invoking by class name. This information is stored in another XML file that is also included in the EAR.

Given the amount of detail and the burden of creating XML files to describe the deployment, the Application Assembly Tool (AAT) that comes with WebSphere is utilized to make life easier. AAT provides wizards to help you create and assemble the enterprise application. It enables you to generate/deploy the code to an application server as well as expand and collapse EAR files if you need to extract components from within an EAR file. You can also run a verify utility to ensure that your XML files are complete.

With AAT you learn about all the J2EE-specified components that make up a deployable unit. The chapter concluded with a simple example to walk you through the Application Assembler Tool.

Chapter 23
Configuring Security

In This Chapter

- Understanding WebSphere security
- Applying WebSphere security with a sample
- Applying programmatic security
- Using LDAP as a repository

The topic of WebSphere Application Server security could easily be a book in itself, so there is no attempt to make any claims that this chapter is *everything* you will ever need to know. Instead this chapter tries to give you a basic working knowledge of the types of security available to the WebSphere Application Server 4.02 server. For example, this chapter demonstrates basic authentication in the example (username and password). However by reading this chapter, you should be able, with little trouble, to extend that example to certificate-based authentication.

Introducing Key Security-Related Definitions

Prior to jumping into WebSphere security, it important to understand a few key concepts in J2EE security that will be used throughout the chapter:

- *Principal:* The identity given to an authenticated user. In J2EE, it is represented by the object `java.security.Principal`. You can think of principals as being synonymous with the users of the system. However in Java, the principal is only identified after authentication has occurred. In Java, a principal may be assigned a role, or assigned to a group that, in turn, is assigned a role.
- *Credential:* The information that describes the security attributes of the principal. Examples would be Kerberos, LTPA (Lightweight Third Party Authentication), or even a Java-based object.
- *Roles:* Roles are business patterns of responsibility in which security can be applied. For example John Smith works in human resources as a benefits administrator. So he is assigned two roles — `Employee` and `BenefitsAdministrator` — which have certain privileges within the application deployed within WebSphere Application Server.
- *Groups:* Groups are logical grouping of users. In J2EE, a group can be assigned one or many roles. Groups often get confused with roles, and at times, they may look the same. However they are different concepts and defined differently.

- *Authentication:* This is the process of ensuring that the principals are who they say they are. Typically this is done by username and password. However, certificates and other means can be used as well.
- *Authorization:* The access rights a principal has or doesn't have after authentication takes place.

Understanding Security in WebSphere Application Server and J2EE

Security is a relative term because it can mean many things to so many people. When discussing WebSphere security, it is important to understand that it fits in as *part* of a larger security environment that is intrinsic to the J2EE. The following list helps illustrate how WebSphere security fits in as part of a larger security environment:

- WebSphere Application Server based artifacts (JSPs, servlets, EJBs) can be built on WebSphere Application Server security.
- WebSphere Application Server security is built on J2EE security.
- J2EE security is build on Common Object Request Broker Architecture (CORBA) security.
- CORBA security is built on Java 2 security.
- Java 2 security is built on the JVM 1.3.
- JVM 1.3 is built on your local OS security.

Although this chapter specifies WebSphere Application Server security and mainly addresses the first two bullets in the previous list, you, by default, attain the additional layers and their related security components as well.

You have two principal ways to achieve security within J2EE and WebSphere Application Server as per the specification:

- You can use role-based security defined in XML-based deployment descriptors that get deployed with an EAR file. This conforms to the J2EE specification; whereas, in previous version of WebSphere application server, this was a serialized file. The deployment descriptors define how a user belongs to a group that is assigned one or many roles. However, you can assign a user to a role directly if you want. In the case of EJBs, methods can be assigned to roles as well. The sample that follows illustrates these relationships a bit better.
- You can implement security programmatically within an API. The primary functionality you can achieve using this is attaining a principal (an authenticated user) and determining whether the current principal is within a given role that you have defined at deployment time.

Understanding Java authentication and authorization service

For those who love Java this begs the obvious question, "Why can't I just use JAAS?" Even though WebSphere Application Server supports JDK 1.3 as an optional package in WebSphere Application Server 4.02, the Java Authentication and Authorization Service (JAAS) specification is not fully supported yet for the WebSphere Application server. There is a caveat in stating this. Although the WebSphere Application server does not support the implementation of the standard for security, you can develop in WebSphere Application Developer (WSAD) in the JDK 1.3 standard and run the JAAS API against a Single Sign-On (SSO) tool that supports the API. For example, if you were to use policy director — an SSO product from Tivoli — you could implement JAAS on the WebSphere Application server because the API would run against the Policy Director security application and not the WebSphere Application server security.

The other components relating to security in JDK 1.3 are supported. You can still implement Java Cryptography (JDK 1.3 JCE) and Java Secure Sockets (JSSE) per the JDK 1.3 specification. However JAAS is not *quite* available if you want to apply it to WebSphere Application Server security

Understanding authentication and authorization

WebSphere Application Server supports the following authentication types:

- *Basic:* Basic username and password via pop-up box.
- *Digest:* Basic username and password with credentials encrypted.
- *Form:* HTML, Java ServerPages (JSP) and so on. (`<FORM>` submission of credentials to a servlet).
- *Certificate:* User presents a certificate as part of, or as the entirety of the credential.

> **NOTE:** These authentication types are defined in the `web.xml` deployment descriptors located in WSAD on the Security tab.

Using the authentication types in the previous list, the following path is what WebSphere Application Server applies for authorization. This generalization depends upon specific implementation; however the basic user path is the same:

1. WebSphere Application Server determines whether the Web-based artifact (JSP, servlet, and so on) is protected via the deployment descriptors.
2. Assuming it is, the WebSphere Application server tries to identify the principal. If it cannot (in other words, the user has not authenticated), the WebSphere Application server asks the principal for a login name, password certificate, and so on, based upon the authentication model set up in WebSphere Application Server.

3. After authentication, WebSphere Application Server performs an authorization check to ensure that the authenticated principal is authorized for at least one of roles that has been assigned access to the Web-based artifact.
4. If the principal has the role that is authorized for the Web-based artifact, the user is allowed to access that resource. Otherwise an error 403 is returned (not authorized).

Securing a sample in WSAD

There is no better way to learn something than to do it. So this sample walks you through the steps required to develop a J2EE application and secure it through the local OS user repository. You walk through the screens that secure a JSP, servlet, and EJB method so you can see how and where to apply security from development in WSAD to production in WebSphere Application Server.

> **NOTE:** Folders and files throughout this example can be found on the J2EE perspective Navigation tab.

WebSphere Application Server-based security in WSAD for development is heavily based on the OS you are developing. Therefore, some local OS preparation of users and groups is necessary to get the sample to execute. This example illustrates Windows 2000, but you might have to adjust your settings for the different flavors of Windows, Linux, and so on.

To start developing under WSAD with security, you need to perform a couple of operations. First, ensure that you are logged in as administrator or have administrative rights to the workstation you are working on. Next ensure that the effective policy settings under Windows Local Security Settings⇨Local Security Policies-⇨User Rights Assignment in the Administrative Console are set to the following:

- Access this computer from network
- Act as part of OS
- Create page file
- Log on as batch
- Log on as service
- Log on locally
- Manage auditing and security log
- Take ownership

> **NOTE**: If you are part of a domain, the rights given by your domain controller might supersede your rights on your local machine. If this is the case, talk to you system administrator about how to get these privileges via the domain.

In the User Administration console of Windows, follow these steps:

1. Add a user called **wasadm** with administration rights to your development machine. Give the password of **password** and set the password to never expire.

2. Add a user called **testUser** and give a password of **password**. Set the password to never expire. This user is the principal in the sample. This user does not have to be an administrator; however he or she should have all the privileges outlined previously.
3. Add a group called **employees** and add **testUser** to it.

You might be asking why you are adding all these users and groups. Although it might not be totally clear now, creating these users and groups takes care of the following:

- Set up a user, wasadm, that can run the local version of WebSphere Application Server under WSAD. This user, in a sense, is the local administrator of WebSphere Application Server.
- You create a group called `employees`, which has testUser as a member for OS authentication, so that later when you create the role of `employee` in the J2EE deployment descriptors, `testUser` has access as a member of the OS group `employees`.

Now that you have taken care of the housekeeping, you are now ready to begin applying WebSphere security to an application.

Developing security in WSAD

After setting up your local OS, you next have to create an application where you will apply WebSphere security. You start by creating a new enterprise application project in WSAD called **SecurityTest.**

1. You can perform this by navigating to the J2EE perspective and selecting File⇨New⇨Enterprise Application Project, which opens the Enterprise Application Wizard. Name the project **SecurityTest**, and leave the Web, EJB, and application client projects in their default naming constructs.
2. Next you need to add a WebSphere Application Server 4 server instance called **SecurityTestServer**. You can perform this by opening the Server perspective and selecting File⇨New⇨Server Instance and Configuration. Name the server **SecurityTestServer** and select WebSphere v4.0 test environment as the server.
3. Lastly, select the configuration and add the SecurityTest project to it. The result of these steps gives you a basic shell of a J2EE project in which security is applied.

After the server configuration has been defined and the SecurityTest project is added to it, you modify the server configuration:

- In the `server-cfg.xml` file on the Security tab (see Figure 23-1), check the Enable security box and type **wasadm** for Server ID and **password** for password.
- On the General tab, ensure that the Enable Administration Client box is checked. You are going to use this later in configuration.

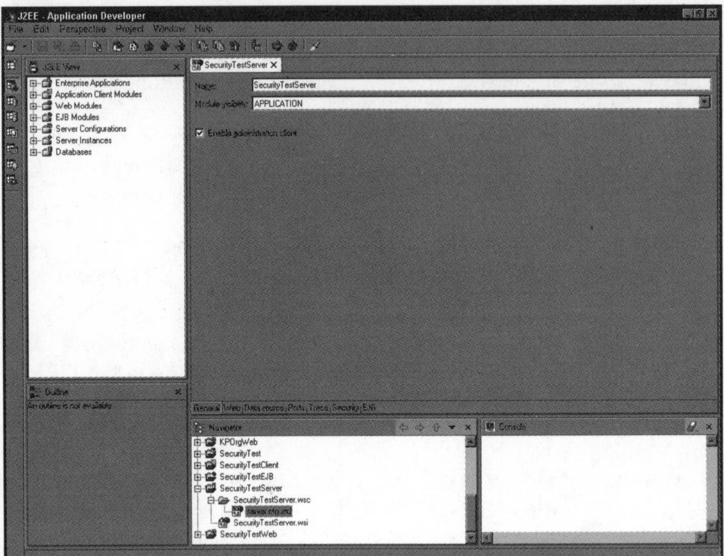

Figure 23-1: The General Tab of the Server Configuration file is used for enabling and disabling the administration client.

What would any sample be without the infamous "Hello World" sample servlet that most of us are familiar with? "Hello World" has already been used elsewhere in this book; however, this specific example is going to be used differently with WebSphere security. Start by creating a servlet in a package called **com.test.security.servlet.SecurityServlet** under the source folder in the SecurityTestWeb project of the application that looks like Listing 23-1.

Listing 23-1: Hello World

```
package com.test.security.servlet;

import javax.servlet.http.HttpServlet;
import javax.servlet.http.HttpServlet;
import javax.servlet.http.HttpServletRequest;
import javax.servlet.http.HttpServletResponse;
import javax.servlet.ServletOutputStream;
import javax.servlet.ServletException;

public class SecurityServlet extends HttpServlet {

 public void doGet(
  javax.servlet.http.HttpServletRequest request,
  javax.servlet.http.HttpServletResponse response)
  throws javax.servlet.ServletException, java.io.IOException {
```

```
    ServletOutputStream out = response.getOutputStream();

    out.println("<html>");
    out.println("<head><title>Hello World!</title></head>");
    out.println("<body>");
    out.println("<h1>Hello World!</h1>");
    out.println("</body>");
    out.println("</html>");
    out.flush();
    out.close();
  }
}
```

Assuming that you did not change any of the defaults when creating this servlet, you should be able to start the server and get Hello World to come up with the following URL:

```
http://localhost:8080/SecurityTestWeb/SecurityServlet
```

The results of getting this to work won't be very exciting. However the main objective isn't to get the Hello World servlet up and running. The objective is to get it to run with Local OS security turned on. You can verify that this occurs by looking at the console after the server is started. If when inspecting the console you notice your server does not start correctly and you get an error related to a Local OS authentication failure, retrace the previous steps that refer to local OS privileges for wasadm. Alternatively, the username and password might be incorrect on the Security tab of `server-cfg.xml`.

Creating the sample pages

Now that you have local OS security up and running on a WSAD server instance, it's time to work on developing form-based authentication. As described earlier, in form-based authentication, you are protecting Web-based artifacts with a username and password. If principals try to access the secured asset, they are redirected via the Application server to a login screen where they authenticate on the WebSphere Application server. After users are authenticated, WebSphere Application Server enables them to get to the protected resource. If the user is not authorized for accessing the resource, a 403 error — unauthorized access — should be displayed.

After login occurs, you can allow the user to log out using a button or link. For this example, you are going to need to create five JSPs in your SecurityTestWeb container:

- *Login.jsp:* For entering login name and password. This is the form for the form-based authentication.
- *Logout.jsp:* For logging off the Application server. After the principal authenticates, the user needs a way to log out of the server, so that the server can release resources and contexts. This form performs that operation.
- *Secure.jsp:* A sample JSP that is secured using roles. This page acts in your example as the protected Web-based artifact.

- *Error.jsp:* The standard error page if something goes wrong and the system throws an error.
- *Error403.jsp:* A Not Authorized screen. If the principal tries to access the protected asset and is authenticated but not authorized, this is the screen that is displayed.

Creating login.jsp

This is the form that is displayed when a user, who has not been authenticated, tries to access a resource that is protected by WebSphere Application Server. It can also be accessed for the typical login link, if you want authorization to occur prior to navigating to a secured asset. For form-based authentication, the WebSphere Application Server 4.0 server has predefined some authentication-level functionality for you. You see this in the source code for login.jsp shown in Listing 23-2.

Listing 23-2: Source Code for login.jsp

```
<!DOCTYPE HTML PUBLIC "-//W3C//DTD HTML 4.01 Transitional//EN">
<html>
<META HTTP-EQUIV = "Pragma" CONTENT="no-cache">
<META name="GENERATOR" content="IBM WebSphere Studio">
<title>Security Test Login Page </title>
<body>
<h2>Security Test Login Page </h2>
<FORM METHOD=POST ACTION="j_security_check">
<p>
<font size="2">  <B> Please Enter login and password: </B></font> <BR>
<B> Login</B>  <input type="text" size="20" name="j_username"><BR>
<B> Password </B>  <input type="password" size="20" name="j_password">
<BR>
<input type="submit" name="login" value="Login">
</p>
</form>
</body>
</html>
```

There is nothing exciting about this somewhat simple code. However, some special parameters are worth noting.

- The login name must be `j_username`.
- The password field name must be `j_password`.
- The post action must be `j_security_check`.

When this form is submitted, WebSphere Application Server recognizes the uniqueness of the submission parameters and executes a WebSphere Application Server authentication servlet located in the Web container. When the user is authorized, the container redirects the user to the secured resource he or she was trying to access; in this example, that is `secure.jsp`. If the user is not authorized, the server throws error 403, which is displayed by your `error403.jsp`.

Creating logout.jsp

`Logout.jsp` is not particularly complex either. However, it too has some special fields that are specific to WebSphere Application Server, as shown in Listing 23-3.

Listing 23-3: Creating logout.jsp

```
<!DOCTYPE HTML PUBLIC "-//W3C//DTD HTML 4.01 Transitional//EN">
<html>
<META HTTP-EQUIV = "Pragma" CONTENT="no-cache">
<META name="GENERATOR" content="IBM WebSphere Studio">
<title>Security Test Logout Page </title>
<body>
<h2>Security Test Sample Form Logout</h2>
<FORM METHOD=POST ACTION="ibm_security_logout" NAME="logout">
<p>
<BR>
<font size="2">  <B>Press to logout!: </B><BR>
</font>
<input type="submit" name="logout" value="Logout">
<INPUT TYPE="HIDDEN" name="logoutExitPage" VALUE="/login.jsp">
</p>
</form>
</body>
</html>
```

The form action `ibm_security_logout` is required so that WebSphere Application Server can intercept the submission and perform a logout from the Application server and free the resources allocated to the user. The hidden field `logoutExitPage` is also required and lets WebSphere Application Server know where to direct the user after a successful logout has occurred. In this example, you return to `login.jsp`, but you could put any page you want here, such as `successfullogut.jsp` or a home page of some sort.

Creating error.jsp, error403.jsp, and secure.jsp

`Secure.jsp` is the page that you protect in this example; you can put any text you want in this JSP. The other two modules, `error.jsp` and `error403.jsp`, give a better display when their respective errors occur. Other than this, there is nothing particular worth noting in the code of these modules. You can place any error messages you like in the modules.

Adding the XML Descriptors

Now that you have created all the JSP resources you need, the next step is to create deployment descriptors to specify to WebSphere Application Server how the security is going to be applied. Deployment descriptors are the mechanism for doing this. *Deployment descriptors* are XML files that are usually contained as part of an EAR file prior to deploying to the Application server. Security gets applied in accordance to the J2EE specification in these files.

WSAD gives you a nice graphical interface for creating deployment descriptors. When referring to these files, you can reach this interface by right-clicking on the XML file and selecting Open With⇨<*file*>.xml Editor. Not everyone likes to use the graphical tools and wizard. So those of you who love VI, Notepad, and UltraEdit can modify the XML file directly in the text editor of your choice. That is essentially what the WSAD interface does for you behind the scenes. In practice, you might find the interface helps you avoid programmatic errors and typos.

Under the SecurityTestWeb project under the WEB-INF folder, you find the `web.xml` file, which is where security deployment descriptors for Web-based artifacts are defined. Edit this using the WSAD XML Editor as shown in Figure 23-2.

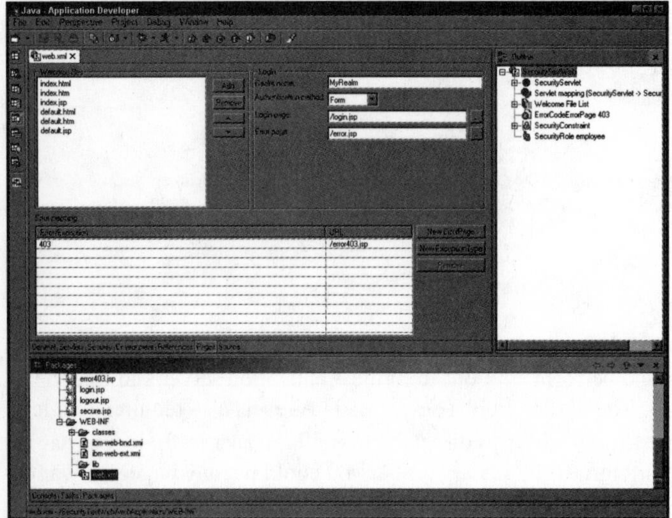

Figure 23-2: Use the Pages tab of web.xml to identify the authentication method and error handling.

Modify `web.xml` as described in the following list:

1. Realm name is a name specific to HTTP basic authorization and is defined on the server. This name can be anything you want, but it is specific to this server instance. For this example, type **MyRealm**.
2. In the Page name box, select `login.jsp` from the list.
3. In the Error page box, select `error.jsp` from the list.
4. This example uses form-based authentication, so select that from the Authentication Method list. Form-based authentication is by far the most popular and widely used. However, it is important to note if you are using authentication other than form-based authentication; this is where you would define that to WebSphere Application Server.

5. In the Error/Exception box, define the error code 403 for unauthorized access and identify the form to be displayed when this occurs. You can also define other error codes (for example, page not found). For this example, define the one related to unauthorized access. Select `error403.jsp` and place error code **403** as the error number.

Next you have to navigate to the Security tab of `web.xml` (shown in Figure 23-3) where you perform the following steps:

1. In the Security Roles text box, enter **employee** and a short description. This is the role that you are going to map to your Local OS group that you defined earlier.
2. In the Web Resource Location box, you need to define how you want security to apply to a particular resource. In this example, you are going to call your resource **WebResourceCollectionSecurity**, and you are going to protect the `get` and `post` HTTP methods by checking them. Do this by clicking the Add button and selecting these methods. Finally, add the URL **secure.jsp** because this is the resource pattern you want to protect. By doing this, you are forcing the user to be authenticated prior to reaching `secure.jsp`.
3. Click the Add button next to security roles. Then enter the role of **employee** and a short description. This action adds this role as a security constraint and *enforces* the security.
4. Leave User Data Constraints set at None. If you want to configure communication between the client and server with transport guarantees or transport security applied (such as SSL), this is where you would turn this on.
5. Save the file.

There was a lot to do in `web.xml`, and it comprises a majority of what is needed for deployment descriptors. After this is implemented, look at the `web.xml` code in a text editor or view the source by clicking the Source tab. The results should look like Listing 23-4.

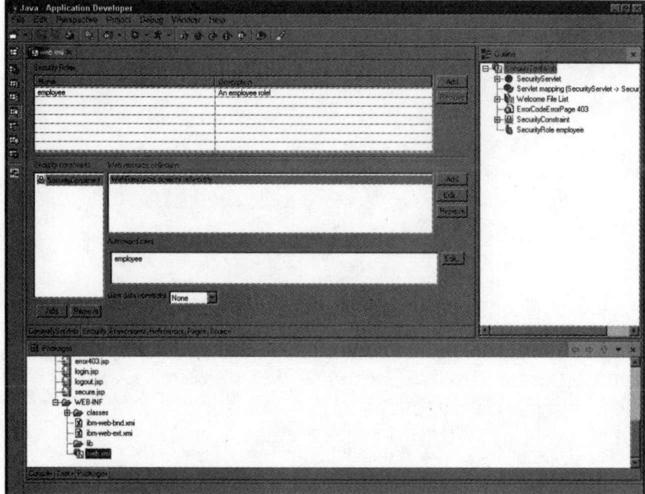

Figure 23-3: The Security tab of web.xml is used primarily to define security constraints for roles.

Listing 23-4: Viewing web.xml Results

```
<?xml version="1.0" encoding="UTF-8"?>
<!DOCTYPE web-app PUBLIC "-//Sun Microsystems, Inc.//DTD Web Application 2.2//EN"
"http://java.sun.com/j2ee/dtds/web-app_2_2.dtd">
<web-app id="WebApp">
 <display-name>SecurityTestWeb</display-name>
 <servlet>
  <servlet-name>SecurityServlet</servlet-name>
  <display-name>SecurityServlet</display-name>
  <servlet-class>com.test.security.servlet.SecurityServlet</servlet-class>
  <security-role-ref>
   <role-name>employee</role-name>
   <role-link>employee</role-link>
  </security-role-ref>
 </servlet>
 <servlet-mapping>
  <servlet-name>SecurityServlet</servlet-name>
  <url-pattern>SecurityServlet</url-pattern>
 </servlet-mapping>
 <welcome-file-list>
  <welcome-file>index.html</welcome-file>
  <welcome-file>index.htm</welcome-file>
  <welcome-file>index.jsp</welcome-file>
  <welcome-file>default.html</welcome-file>
  <welcome-file>default.htm</welcome-file>
  <welcome-file>default.jsp</welcome-file>
 </welcome-file-list>
 <error-page>
  <error-code>403</error-code>
  <location>/error403.jsp</location>
 </error-page>
 <security-constraint>
  <web-resource-collection>
   <web-resource-name>WebResourceLocationForSecuirty</web-resource-name>
   <description>Secure.jsp resource loaction</description>
   <url-pattern>/secure.jsp</url-pattern>
   <url-pattern>/SecurityServlet</url-pattern>
   <http-method>
   GET</http-method>
   <http-method>
   POST</http-method>
  </web-resource-collection>
  <auth-constraint>
   <description>Role Description here</description>
   <role-name>employee</role-name>
  </auth-constraint>
 </security-constraint>
 <login-config>
```

```
<auth-method>FORM</auth-method>
<realm-name>MyRealm</realm-name>
<form-login-config>
 <form-login-page>/login.jsp</form-login-page>
 <form-error-page>/error.jsp</form-error-page>
</form-login-config>
</login-config>
<security-role>
 <description>An employee role!</description>
 <role-name>employee</role-name>
 </security-role>
</web-app>
```

Notice that behind the GUI interface, XML-based descriptors are implemented. Now that you have defined the security for the Web-based resources, you have to let the application know about the roles that you want to define. To do this, you need to edit the `application.xml` file located in the `SecurityTest/Meta_INF` folder (see Figure 23-4).

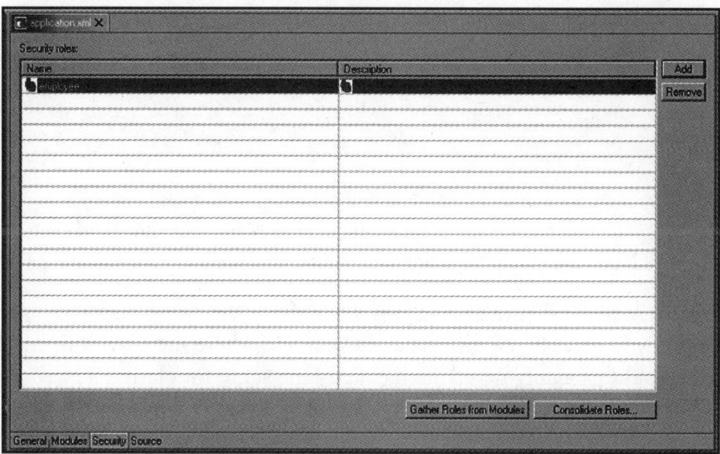

Figure 23-4: The Security tab of application.xml is used to define security roles.

To edit the `application.xml` file, follow these steps:

1. Navigate to the Security tab.
2. On the Security tab, you add the roles that the application has available to it. When you click Gather Roles from Modules button on the bottom, the editor should be able to pull in the employee role that you defined in the `web.xml`. You could also have added the role prior to editing the `web.xml` file, but doing this after tends to cut down on mistakes and ensures you defined the roles in the application correctly. If it is not there, be sure to add it.
3. Save this file. The completed `application.xml` file should look something like Listing 23-5:

Listing 23-5: application.xml File Illustrating Role-Based Security

```
<?xml version="1.0" encoding="UTF-8"?>
<!DOCTYPE application PUBLIC "-//Sun Microsystems, Inc.//DTD J2EE
Application 1.2//EN"
"http://java.sun.com/j2ee/dtds/application_1_2.dtd">
<application id="Application_ID">
 <display-name>SecurityTest</display-name>
 <module id="JavaClientModule_1">
  <java>SecurityTestClient.jar</java>
 </module>
 <module id="EjbModule_1">
  <ejb>SecurityTestEJB.jar</ejb>
 </module>
 <module id="WebModule_1">
  <web>
   <web-uri>SecurityTestWeb.war</web-uri>
   <context-root>SecurityTestWeb</context-root></web>
 </module>
 <security-role id="SecurityRole_1">
  <description>An employee role!</description>
  <role-name>employee</role-name>
 </security-role>
</application>
```

The last descriptor you have to modify for this example is the `ibm-application-bnd.xmi` file, located in the `SecurityTest->META-INF` directory. This is the file that binds the OS descriptions of roles with the J2EE roles you have defined in the application (see Figure 23-5).

This example purposely names the J2EE role `employee` and defines the groups created on the local OS `employees` so that you can see the difference in how and where they are defined. In a real implementation, you would probably name them exactly the same for clarity. The following list describes each field and how to populate it for the sample:

- *Security Roles:* These are the roles defined in the WebSphere Application Server J2EE environment. Here you need to define it as as **employee**.
- *Groups:* This is where you define the names of the groups in your user store. For you that is the Local OS user group called **employees**.
- *Users:* Here you can add OS specific users who have rights and authorities under WebSphere Application Server security. We are not populating any individual rights here, just group rights.
- *Bind the Role to:* This is the scope to which you want the permission to apply. In this example, you only want it to apply to users and groups, so check that option.

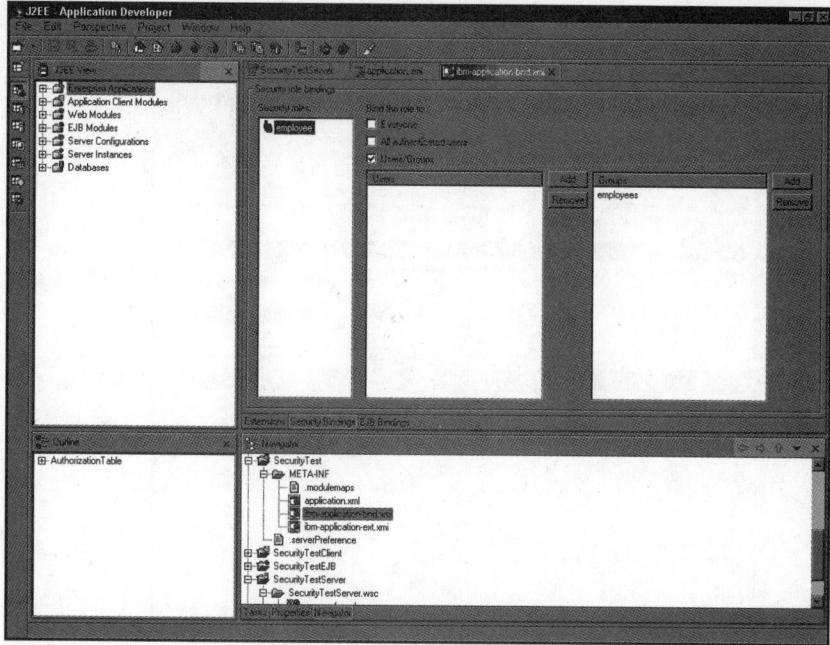

Figure 23-5: Security Binding tab of ibm-application-bnd.xmi illustrating the operating system to role bindings.

Finally, you are almost ready to test your application. The only issue is that the single-server edition of WSAD might not know about the specific `server-config.xml` created in the SecurityTest project. This appears to be an anomaly in WSAD. (It should know about it.) But just in case, you can confirm as follows (see Figure 23-6):

1. Start your Web server under WSAD.
2. Type **http://localhost:9090/admin** to get to the WAS Adminstrative console.
3. Enter **wasadm** and **password** to log into the server.
4. Click the Configuration button at the top of the screen.
5. Go to Open Configuration file and verify that the path is to your local `server-cfg.xml` file. If you used the default installation, it should look something like the following (verify in your path in your OS):

```
C:\Program Files\IBM\Application
Developer\SecurityTestServer\SecurityTestServer.wsc\server-cfg.xml
```

6. Click the Save button, and confirm the file save.

NOTE: Remember clicking the Enable Administration Client box on `server-cfg.xml`? It allows the administration of WebSphere Application Server (in the WSAD environment single server edition) through a Web interface. You clicked that so that you could perform the following.

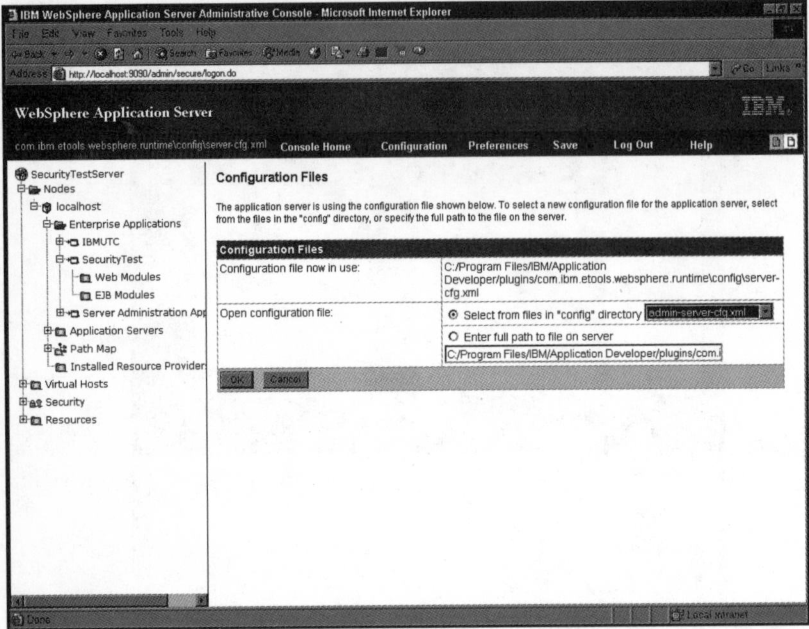

Figure 23-6: The Administrative Console shows where to modify the path to the server-cfg.xml file.

> **NOTE**: If you want to see or configure your roles via this console you can. Navigate on the left tree to Node⇨LOCALHOST⇨Enterprise Applications⇨SecurityTest. Here you see your roles and have the ability to change them. This last step is sort of a gotcha when developing with WebSphere Application Server security on in WSAD. For production deployment, you would not have to perform this step.

Testing what you have done so far

Ensure that your server instance has been restarted and the changes to the WebSphere Application Server Administrative Console have been made. You are now ready to test! Type in the URL for the `secure.jsp` page you protected with WebSphere Application Server security:

```
http://localhost:8080/SecurityTestWeb/secure.jsp
```

WebSphere Application Server should recognize this as a secured resource and take you to the `login.jsp` page.

At the login screen, if you type **testUser** and **password** for the login and password, WebSphere Application Server authenticates you and takes you to the `secure.jsp` page. Remember `testUser` is a member of the group `employees` that you created on the local OS.

If you typed a valid username other than a member of `employees`, for example, wasadm, and the password, you should get the `error403.jsp` screen. When the login is successful, type in the URL:

```
http://localhost:8080/SecurityTestWeb/logout.jsp
```

This URL enables you to log out and let WebSphere Application Server clear all the resources and context allocated to the authorized principal.

Adding Servlet Security

These steps are cumbersome at first, but after you perform them once, adding additional resources is pretty easy. You can now see how easy it is to secure the HelloWorld servlet you created earlier.

1. Go back to the `web.xml` document in the SecurityTestWeb-⇨WebApplication⇨`WEB-INF` directory. On the Servlet tab, add the role of `employee` by clicking the Add button and checking `employee`.
2. On the Security tab ensure that the URL pattern for `/SecurityServlet` is applied.
3. Save your changes
4. Restart the server and check your Administrative Console again to ensure that the proper `server-cfg.xml` file is being used as you did before.
5. Now try and access HelloWorld by typing the folowing:

   ```
   http://localhost:8080/SecurityTestWeb/SecurityServlet
   ```

The HelloWorld servlet (called SecurityServlet in this example) is now secure, as you can tell because it brings up the login screen forcing you to authenticate first.

Adding EJB Security

It is just as simple to add security to an Enterprise JavaBean (EJB). The difference is that you can secure EJBs down to the method level. This is a finer grained security than the security you get with servlets or JSPs where it is all or nothing.

Start by creating a stateless EJB called **Test**, not a very exciting name but this is just a sample. You can create this EJB by highlighting the **SecurityTestEJB** project in the J2EE perspective and selecting the Create an Enterprise Bean button on the top of the screen. Name the Bean **Test**, and place it in the package name of your choice. Normally, you would create methods in your EJB. However, because our goal is to show you how to secure an EJB method, you are going to protect the `create()` method of the EJB lifecycle, which you get by default when you create the EJB. You could create a bunch of methods and secure them, but the principle is the same no matter which method is secured:

1. Edit the `ejb-jar.xml` and navigate to the Security tab located in the SecurtyTestEJB module⇨ejbModule⇨`META-INF` folder of your project (see Figure 23-7).

2. In the Security Roles box, add the role of `employee` because that is the group you use to secure the `create()` method.
3. In the Method permissions box, you define the EJB method signature and interface you want to protect. You can select Home or Remote Interfaces and the methods that apply, respectively. For this example, select Test as the EJB, `create()` as the method, and Home as the interface to protect.

CROSS-REFERENCE: For more information about creating an EJB, refer to Chapter 13.

Any code that now executes the Test EJB and calls the `create()` method on the home interface has to be authenticated and authorized as an `employee` role prior to executing.

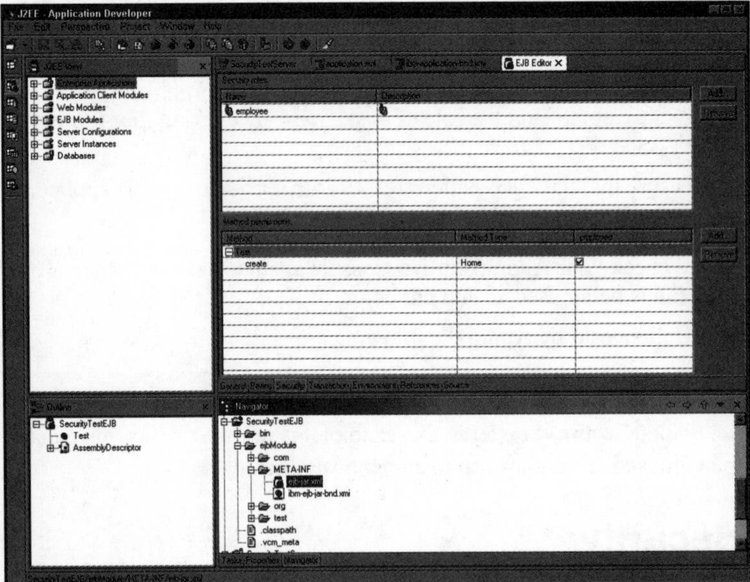

Figure 23-7: Security tab of the ejb-jar.xml that illustrates where to place security on an EJB method.

Moving Beyond Role-Based Security: Programmatic Security

Up to this point, only role-based security in WebSphere Application Server 4 has been discussed. This is wonderful security if all you need is front door role-based access to a servlet or EJB. However sometimes role-based security isn't enough to get the finer-grained authorization that is required. Quite often, you need the capability to secure artifacts and resources beyond checking the role of an authenticated user. This is where programmatic security comes into play.

Programmatically, you use two primary areas to identify who the authenticated principal is and to make authorization decisions: servlets and EJBs.

Understanding programmtic security in servlets

In a servlet, you can obtain the principal from the `HTTPServletRequest` object given by the service method and perform operations based upon it (see Listing 23-6).

Listing 23-6: Obtaining A Principal in a Servlet and Making Programmatic Decisions

```
...
public void doGet(
 javax.servlet.http.HttpServletRequest request,
 javax.servlet.http.HttpServletResponse response)
 throws javax.servlet.ServletException, java.io.IOException {

 //get the Pricipal
 java.security.Principal authUser = request.getUserPrincipal();

 //get the users login name
 String authUserName = authUser.getName();

 //lookup via JNDI to LDAP for other user attributes
 //assumes a connection pooling utility is in place for LDAP
 LDAPConnectionManager connMgr = LDAPConnectionManager.getInstance();
 DirContect con = connMgr.getConnection());

 Attributes matchAttrs = new BasicAttributes(true);
 matchAttrs.put(new BasicAttribute("cn", cn));

 // Search for objects that have those matching attributes
 NamingEnumeration answer =
  con.search("ou=HumanResources,o=YourCompany,c=US", matchAttrs);

 SearchResult sr = (SearchResult) answer.next();
 Attributes attr = sr.getAttributes();
 String state = attr.get("state").get().toString();

 //allow access if Pricipal lives in California otherwise send
them to not allowed screen

if (state == "CA") {
  response.sendRedirect("/SomeCaliforniaScreen.JSP);
 } else {
  response.sendRedirect("/NotAllowedScreen.JSP);
 }
...
```

> **NOTE**: If the principal has not been authenticated, the `getName()` method returns `anonymous`. This can be useful in your program in several areas, such as determining whether the user has authenticated or not.

In this example, the principal is attained from the request object and identified. A subsequent call is made thereafter against the LDAP server to see to which state the principal belongs. If the state is California, the user is allowed to proceed, otherwise the user is directed to a Not Allowed screen. This was a state lookup example, but you can use whatever additional security requirements you want: age, state, and so on.

Within a servlet, you can also ask which roles the authenticated principal belongs to. Although the majority of these situations can be handled with WebSphere Application Server security, in certain situations checking roles programmatically becomes useful. Listing 23-7 shows an example.

Listing 23-7: Obtaining a Role in a Servlet and Making Programmatic Decisions.

```
...
public void doGet(
 javax.servlet.http.HttpServletRequest request,
 javax.servlet.http.HttpServletResponse response)
 throws javax.servlet.ServletException, java.io.IOException {

//If principal is manager and in HR then they can administer benefits,
otherwise only let them update a profile
 if ((request.isUserInRole("ManagerRole")) &&
  request.isUserInRole("HumanResourcesRole")){
response.sendRedirect("/EmployeeAdministrationScreen.JSP);
 } else {
  response.sendRedirect("/EmployeeUpdateProfileScreen.JSP);
 }
...
```

In this example, the code inspects the request object for a two specific roles: `ManagerRole` and `HumanResourcesRole`. If the principal belongs to both roles, the user is forwarded to one screen; otherwise the user is directed to another. This action enables you to make decisions in your code based upon the roles you have set up in the WebSphere Application Server deployment descriptors.

Understanding programmtic security in EJBs

Enterprise JavaBeans for programmatic authorization in WebSphere Application Server behave similarly to servlets with some minor exceptions. The primary difference is in the way you attain the principal and roles, which is achieved by interrogating the `java.ejb.EJBContext` interface. Listing 23-8 is an example in which the principal is attained within an EJB method.

Listing 23-8: Obtaining a Principal in an EJB and Making Programmatic Decisions

```
...
public void getLoginName(EJBContect ctx){
 //Go and get the user name that was Authenticated under WAS

  //get the Pricipal
  java.security.Principal authUser = ctx.getCallerPrincipal();

  //get the users login name
  String authUserName = authUser.getName();
...
```

> **NOTE**: an important thing to notice if you use J2EE-based security is that the `EJBContext.getCallerIdentity()` method is deprecated. Hence migrating code might have to be refactored.

As with Listing 23-6, you could extend this for decisions in a manner similar to that shown in the servlet. Attaining role-based information programmatically follows the servlet pattern as well. The example in Listing 23-9 illustrates how.

Listing 23-9: Obtaining a Role in a EJB and Making Programmatic Decisions

```
...
public boolean isFinance(EJBContect ctx) {

//Look at the context and see if the user is in Finance
if (ctx.isCallerInRole("FinanceRole")) {
 return true;
} else {
 return false;
}
```

Using the Application Assembly Tool

Chapter 22 is devoted to the Application Assembly Tool (AAT). So there won't be great deal of explanation of this tool here. However, some valuable points, related to security and how it is translated from WSAD to this tool are worth noting.

What has been discussed thus far assumes that the Java developer in WSAD is going to be creating and modifying the security portion of the deployment descriptors and then exporting them in the EAR to be deployed to a production WebSphere Application Server server. Although this works fine, not all organizations are set up to work in this manner. Your organization might have one developer write the business-related code and then designate another a person who is not a Java developer to be responsible for deployment to test and production environments. If this is the case, you probably want to use the AAT for applying security.

The beauty of the J2EE-based security is that it is external to the business logic. You can apply authorization decisions based on roles entirely through deployment descriptors. The AAT, shown in Figure 23-8, facilitates this. It really is nothing different from what you have done so far in WSAD, so this section highlights the main points in relation to the sample SecurityTest.

If you export the SecurityTest project as an EAR and then open it in the AAT application, notice the deployment descriptors are already applied throughout the AAT environment. So as you can see, if you want to, you can apply the security via the descriptors directly in AAT. This illustrates that there is not necessarily a need to apply security in WSAD; the same functionality can be achieved in the AAT.

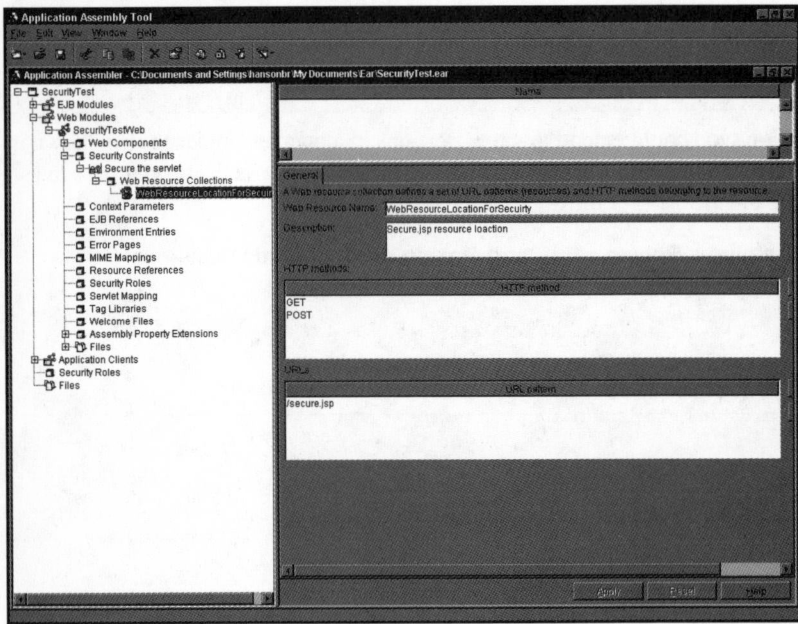

Figure 23-8: Application Assembly Tool illustrating security deployment descriptors.

Look at the following areas to see how the deployment descriptors relate to your SecurityTest sample are shown in the AAT. You can see how you can modify the deployment descriptors in the two different user interfaces:

1. Select Web Modules⇨Web Resource Collections to find the `get()` and `post()` methods that you applied in WSAD against `secure.jsp`. Notice that it is found under the name you gave it: `WebResourceLocationForSecurity`. The entry that you see in AAT was mostly configured on the Security tab of the `web.xml` in WSAD.
2. Under Security Roles in AAT, you find where you configured the J2EE roles and mapped them to the Local OS role in the SecurityTest example. Under the Bindings tab, you find the group name.

3. Click EJB Modules to find the Test EJB that you created. If you examine the Method Extensions that are on the AAT tree, you will notice the method `create()` on the home interface has security applied. You also see security roles defined for `employee` again here.

This explanation, by no means, gives you a comprehensive understanding of AAT. However, note that you *can* perform the same operations with this tool as you performed in WSAD.

Using an LDAP User Repository

Deploying the SecurityTest EAR file with the deployment descriptors included you are able to apply security in the example through the local OS on the server. All you have to do is create the testUser, wasadm users, and the employees groups on a Windows 2000 server instead of on your local workstation. Then start up the Application server and security gets applied through the local OS. Although this is functional, it isn't always practical. Normally, your user repository exists elsewhere, usually in an LDAP or RDBMS. In this case, you have to tell the WebSphere Application server to point to another source besides the local operating system for user names and groups.

> **NOTE:** The following only works in the AE version of WebSphere Application Server

WebSphere Application Server supports three types of user repositories for security mappings:

- Local OS, which has been discussed thus far
- LDAP (Lightweight Directory Access Protocol)
- Custom, usually RDBMS or something similar

To illustrate the ease of migrating from your example, look at LDAP because that seems to be the industry trend. In this example, you populate IBM Secureway LDAP 3.2 with the same information that you entered through the local OS user manager. The reason you perform this task is so that later WebSphere Application Server can use the LDAP as the user repository for authentication and authorization instead of the local OS.

Although you can use any LDAP-compliant product, IBM makes Secureway and WebSphere Application Server; therefore, IBM can use the default LDAP schema right out of the box, including an IBM auxiliary object, ePerson, which includes userid and password. For simplicity, this example takes advantage of that out-of-the-box ease of configuration. In doing so, the example points out areas in which you would change attributes for your particular LDAP schema.

> **NOTE:** This is not a book on Secureway 3.2 or LDAP, so this example does not include the complete step-by-step installation or configuration. Instead it concentrates on the LDAP V3 generic schema and how to configure WebSphere Application Server to LDAP. The same principles apply no matter what LDAP-compliant product you use.

The following steps give you a simple configuration for a simple population of the SecureWay version 3.2 LDAP:

1. Install the Secureway 3.2 on an available server with the administrator of the LDAP server login set to **cn=root and password** as the password.
2. Add the suffix of **o=YourCompany, c=US**.
3. Add the organizational unit of **ou=YourOrganization**.
4. Add the user **wasadm** with the password of **password**. The distinguished name is **cn=wasadm,ou=YourOrganization,o=yourcompany,c=us**.
5. Add the user **testUser** with the password **password**. The distinguished name is **cn=wasadm,ou=YourOrganization,o=yourcompany,c=us**.
6. Add a group called **employees** and add the distinguished name of **testUser** to the multivalued attribute member of the group to make `testUser` a part of the group (or role in J2EE) `employees`.

After you complete these steps, you should have a schema that exports (LDIF format) similar to that shown in Listing 23-10:

Listing 23-10: LDIF Export of the Sample LDAP Directory

```
...
dn: cn=employees, ou=YourOrganization, o=YourCompany, c=US
objectclass: top
objectclass: groupOfNames
description: The group that identifies employees
member: CN=NULL
cn: employees
member: cn=testUser,ou=YourOrganization,o=yourcompany,c=us

dn: cn=wasadm,ou=YourOrganization,o=yourcompany,c=us
objectclass: inetOrgPerson
objectclass: organizationalPerson
objectclass: person
objectclass: top
objectclass: ePerson
userpassword: {iMASK}>1dBNQvLRsA4YAx+jEIECdvE7a3dSKbgZlWqDZdP5+rypmv4NiphWslCh
 sxjNDbph6skc+ia8+bu8dhpkOfec+KYp7PEdxWmBzSz3azIbK0QW+brPLcwkBLUbRvXQI2WrJcli
 yCzserFhJ41BwHISvGN6BcxcOsARMx<
sn: wasadmLastName
cn: wasadm
uid: wasadm

dn: cn=testUser,ou=YourOrganization,o=yourcompany,c=us
objectclass: inetOrgPerson
objectclass: ePerson
objectclass: person
objectclass: organizationalPerson
objectclass: top
```

Listing 23-10 ***(Continued)***

```
userpassword: {iMASK}>1CboSSS3XKs9ws9VZmLaewODkqMr3gkq3146b/bUY6um31FwZuHmfBrz
 /4XSZ1P/9hic8by683wqdfsWNBq86Kp1jjPZ3iNMEAMCW+xDGAxzKtuYPrg6Rg0I9w7fDDz1Kj/1
 TmuBdorMxWBmOTTmSH5Qsq+ZVoyZVX<
sn: testUserLastName
cn: testUser
uid: testUser

dn: o=YourCompany, c=US
objectclass: top
objectclass: organization
o: YourCompany

dn: ou=YourOrganization, o=YourCompany, c=US
ou: YourOrganization
objectclass: organizationalUnit
objectclass: top
...
```

Next, you have to configure WebSphere Application Server to user the LDAP user repository that you just created instead of the local OS. To do this, you have to start the WebSphere Application Server Administration Server services and go to the Administrative Console. Open the Security Center and configure the following (see Figure 23-9).

1. On the General tab, ensure that the Enable Security box is checked. (Note: You also find SSL configuration here. This chapter does not cover this; however, for reference you may want to note where it is). The *timeout* is the length of time (in seconds) after which the user security information is refreshed. You want this balanced as a part of performance tuning, but for now leave it as the default.

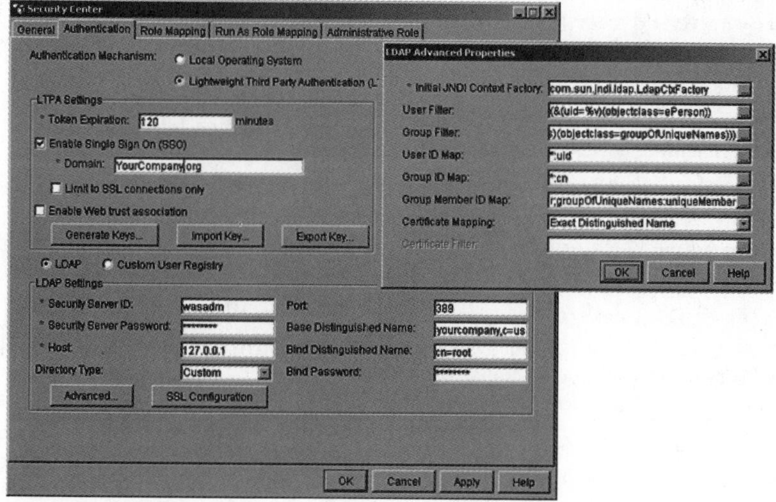

Figure 23-9: WebSphere AE security center illustrating LDAP configuration.

2. On the Authentication tab, apply the following settings:

    - *Local OS/LTPA:* Click the radio button for Lightweight Third Party Authentication (LTPA). LTPA is a credential that can be used for authentication and authorization by WebSphere Application Server and other products (Domino, Policy Director, and so on). If you want to keep using the local OS as the user repository, you leave this on local OS.
    - *Token Expiration:* This is the timeout (in minutes) that users' authentication credentials wait before the user's session is expeired and logged out. As a general rule, this should be equal to or less than the session timeout variable.
    - *SSO:* Click Enable Single-Sign On and enter the domain for the server you are using: YourCompany.com for example. This setting allows the LTPA nonpersistent cookie to be visible only on that domain and allows more than one application on the WebSphere Application server to use the defined security. In other words, another application can use the authorized principal after it is logged on. If you want it visible via only SSL (and you have configured SSL), you can click Limit to SSL Connections Only to let the credential be passed via SSL.
    - *Web Trust Authentication:* This example did not use Web trust authentication, but this option enables you to perform authentication from another third-party service, such as an SSO product.
    - *LDAP:* Select LDAP for the type of user repository. If you have an RDBMS, select Custom here instead.
    - *Security Server ID:* It does little good to provide security for the application if you do not secure the server's Admnistrative console. This setting for that purpose is the ID of the user. Enter **wasadm** or the distinguished name for wasadm in this field. The next time you enter the Administrative Console (after restarting the service), this ID and password are required to get to the console.
    - *Security Server Password:* Enter **password**. This is the corresponding password for wasadm that you entered on the LDAP.
    - *Host:* This is the IP address or domain name for the LDAP server. Enter the domain for wherever you have installed your LDAP instance. In this example, it happens to be the local machine, so **127.0.0.1** is entered.
    - *Directory Type:* In this example, you are going to select Secureway as your directory type. However, if you are using a different LDAP server, enter the appropriate response. Active Directory, Domino, Netscape, and Secureway are supported right out of the box.
    - *Port:* Most LDAP servers run on port 389, so that is specified here for the example. If left blank, port 389 is assumed. This may be different if you are running SSL to the LDAP server or running on a unusual port.

- *Base Distinguished Name:* You have to let the LDAP server know where to start looking for users in out LDAP directory. In this example, `ou=YourOrganization,o=yourcompany,c=us` is this base name. If you state this, WebSphere Application Server knows to look for users (testUser) with the distinguished name of `cn=testUser, ou=YourOrganization,o=yourcompany,c=us`.
- *Bind Distinguished Name:* The LDAP server needs its own authorization as well; in LDAP this is called binding. The administration name you gave was the default, `cn=root`, as per the previous instructions, so this is what you enter. If no name is given, the WebSphere Application server attempts anonymous access.
- *Bind Password:* To bind `cn=root` to the LDAP server, you must enter **password** as the password.

You now have to configure WebSphere Application Server to look at groups as you defined them in LDAP. Although this can be a bit tricky, WebSphere Application Server has done some of the work for you. If on the Authentication tab you selected Active Directory, when you click the Advanced tab, you see the default schema objects `sAMAccountName` and `user` that are searched when authentication or authorization under WebSphere Application Server occurs. In the same manner, the respective schema objects are populated when you select Netscape, Domino, or Secureway. If you modified the way users and groups are defined in these schemas, you have to change the corresponding mappings on the Advanced tab. If not, you can leave them as the default. In this example, you are using the Secureway directory and the schema objects `ePerson` and `groupOfUniqueNames`.

By clicking the Advanced button of LDAP settings on the Authentication tab, apply the following settings (see Figure 23-9):

- *Initial JNDI context factory:* This is the classname that WebSphere Application Server uses to access the LDAP directory. Usually the default `com.sun.jndi.ldap.LdapCtxFactory` is sufficient. However, if you want to use another class, you can expose it to the WebSphere Application server and declare it here.
- *User Filter:* The user filter is how WebSphere Application Server is going to look for users in the LDAP directory. The default object, `ePerson`, is being searched for with the attribute of `uid`. If you modified the schema or want WebSphere Application Server to look for users in another manner, you can perform that task here. For example, you can have it look for the `cn` attribute on the `person` object. For this example, leave it as the default.
- *Group Filter:* You use the group filter to specify to WebSphere Application Server how to look for the groups that translate into roles in J2EE. When you choose Secureway, the object `groupOfUniqueNames` is the default and `cn` is the attribute to search. When you configured the Secureway LDAP previously, you created the group `employees` and added the distinguished name `cn=testUser, ou=YourOrganization, o=YourCompany`, and `c=US` as a member of that group. So in the search filter, the Secureway LDAP searches the group `employees` for a user with the common name that matched the principal name. You only have one member: `testUser`.

- *User and Group ID Map:* These are the short-name return values from LDAP that WebSphere Application Server uses for comparing security credentials. Again the defaults are okay in this instance: `uid` for users and `cn` for groups.
- *Certificate Mapping:* Select Exact distinguished name because that is what you want to match. However, if you want to map to a filter, change this to Certificate filter and enter the appropriate filter in the Certificate Filter field.
- *Certificate Filter:* The example does not use this field; however, if you want to perform LDAP-to-certificate mapping, specify the LDAP attribute on the left and the Certificate attribute on the right, for example, `uid=$(dn)`.

Finally you have to change to the role mapping to recognize the new format that you have entered. Go to the Administrative Console⇨Enterprise Applications⇨User/Role Mappings to see the roles and groups once again. To perform role mapping, follow these steps:

1. Select the employee role.
2. Check Select user/groups.
3. Place and asterisks(*) in the Search field and click the Search button.
4. Add **testUser** as a user and **employee** to the group. Notice that these are the fully qualified distinguished names. It picked these up from the LDAP configurations you set previously.

That is it! Restart the server and test the AE server by trying to access the `secure.jsp` page. You should have the same results you got when you tried to access the local OS.

Understanding How Security Works

Now that you have seen a practical implementation of the WebSphere Application Server security services, it is probably good to know how it all works together. This section contains a mile-high view of the different components that WebSphere Application Server is using to support security within the Application server. This is by no means a complete description, but it is good to have a basic understanding of which components interact with each other (see Figure 23-10). In brief, the components have the following responsibilities:

- *WebSphere Application Server Security Administration and Security Services:* The WebSphere Application Server Security Administration and Securities Services component is responsible for authentication, authorization, and delegation. The diagram illustrates the Web collaborator and EJB collaborator making calls on behalf of their respective containers for authentication and authorization services. The WebSphere Application Server Security Services executes those calls on the collaborators' behalf. It might use the local OS, as in the first example for the user repository, an LDAP, as in the modified example, or finally a custom registry. Delegation was mentioned briefly in terms of allowing the third party, such as an SSO product, to perform security decisions on behalf of WebSphere Application Server.

- *Security Collaborators:* There are two types of security collaborators: Web and EJB. They are primarily responsible for making sure all the parameters that you stated in deployment descriptors (`web.xml`, `ibm-application-bnd.xmi`, and so on) are imposed through the security services. This includes authentication, authorization, and security logging on the Web collaborator; and authorization, and run-as permissions on the EJB collaborator.
- *EAR Module:* The EAR module contains the respective deployment descriptors for the Web container and EJB containers and contains the policies and rules that are to be enforced by the EJB and Web collaborators. As you have seen, these can define roles and permission to Web artifacts and/or EJB methods.

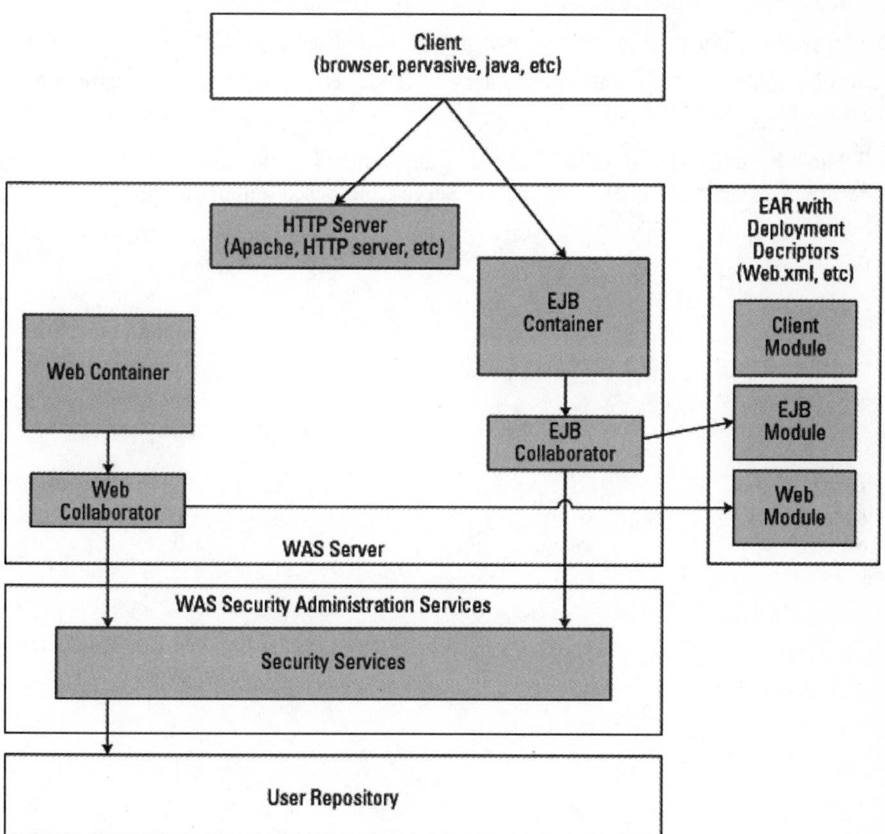

Figure 23-10: WebSphere Application Server security components.

Summary

In the SecurityTest example, you saw the main security functionality WebSphere offers. You performed the following actions:

- Created users and groups in the local OS and users and roles in an LDAP directory
- Created a login and logout screen to check credentials on WebSphere Application Server; created error screens when a user was not authorized
- Modified the deployment descriptors through the WSAD interface to add security attributes.
- Identified where to modify security descriptors in the AAT tool
- Secured the Administrative Console using a username and password
- Deployed the application in the AE environment and tested it in WSAD evironment
- Identified points of configuration for other LDAP servers, certificate authorization, SSL configuration, and SSO integration

You should now be able to expand this example to develop and deploy an application securing the J2EE artifacts using WebSphere Application Server role-based authorization and authentication.

Part IV

Managing WebSphere

Chapter 24
Workload Management and Optimization

Chapter 25
Using the Resource Analyzer

Chapter 26
Troubleshooting WebSphere

Chapter 27
Using the WebSphere Control Program

Chapter 28
Managing WebSphere with XMLConfig

Chapter 24

Workload Management and Optimization

In This Chapter

- Introducing workload management
- Introducing server groups and clones
- Optimizing WebSphere
- Using performance monitoring tools

Up to this point, much of the material covered applied directly to WebSphere Application Server Advanced Edition (AE), Advanced Edition for Developers (AEd), and Advanced Edition for Single Servers (AEs). This chapter discusses workload management (WLM). *Workload management* is the process of spreading requests for work among the resources that can perform the work. It's a procedure for improving the performance, scalability, and reliability of an application.

Workload management is only supported in the Advanced Edition (AE). If you are working only with the Single Server edition, you can browse this chapter to gain a better understanding of workload-management issues and perhaps pick up a tip or two about tuning. Those of you running Advanced Edition, learn all about the types of workload management, how to setup workload management in various environments, and finally how to measure and tune your system to balance your corporate service-level agreements.

Understanding Scaling and Workload Management

Figure 24-1 shows a high-level view of the components that make up the WebSphere domain. If this were a simple testing environment, you could have all these components on a single machine. As you look at Figure 24-1 and relate it to a fully operational production environment, what concerns should you have about scalability? How would you ensure maximum performance while maintaining 24-7 operations? These are questions that need to be considered early on in the process of developing your environment.

You need to consider your needs in the following areas:

- Security
- Performance
- Throughput
- Availability
- Maintainability
- Session state

To satisfy these requirements your application server needs to be scalable and have built-in workload management. Workload management is the process of spreading requests for work among the resources that can perform the work. It's a procedure for improving performance, scalability, and reliability of an application. Additionally, workload management provides the capability of balancing the work while providing failover support. *Failover* is a term used to describe a situation in which a fatal error — caused either by software or hardware — causes a machine to be rendered inoperable. *Failover support* is the means by which an alternative or backup machine is available to take on additional workload if a machine experiences a failure.

The bottom line is that workload management is your means for improving performance and reliability.

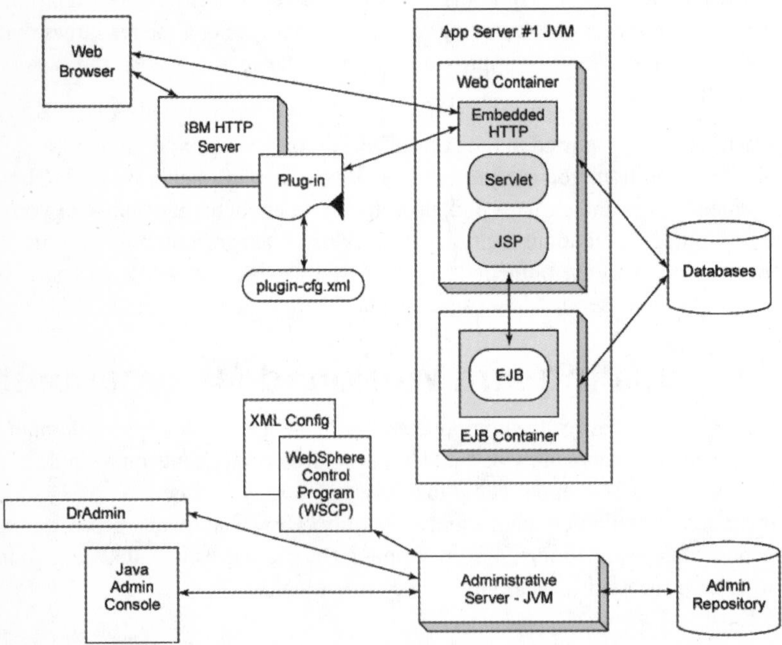

Figure 24-1: Interaction with Web servers, relational databases, and Java applications show how complex application server environments can be.

Refer to Figure 24-1 and determine the decision points that impact your decisions about scalability. You might consider impacts to the following components:

- Web servers
- Application server
- Network security
- Servers
- Firewalls (not shown in figure)
- Business object servers (not shown in figure)
- Database server

All these have impact on your workload service levels. You should work with your business partners to understand the characteristics and potential of your application. What is your appetite for new business? What risks are you willing to take? Are there seasonal conditions that could cause your application to be overrun by requests? Will slow responses frustrate your customers? You might consider categorizing your site's characteristics as follows:

- High volume, dynamic, transactional, fast growth
- High percentage of user-specific responses
- High percentage of cross-session information
- High volume of dynamic searches
- High transaction complexity
- High transaction volume peaks
- High data volatility
- High number of unique items
- High number of page views
- High percentage of secure pages
- High security

So, depending on your needs, you could implement any of the following solutions:

- Use better faster machines
- Cluster servers
- Segregate into specialized servers, for example, edge server security servers, and so on
- Segment workload
- Utilize batch processing
- Utilize caching techniques

WebSphere Application Server gives you the capability to satisfy all these concerns. In the next section, you learn about WebSphere's workload-management capabilities and set up workload management on a single node.

Understanding server groups and clones

The mechanisms that WebSphere Application Server provides to aid workload management are server groups and clones. A *server group* is a non-JVM convenience for creating additional copies of an application server and its contents. You might think of the server group as a logical representation of a server. It has the same structure and attributes but doesn't serve requests. From an administration point of view, server groups make it easier to administer multiple application servers as one logical server.

A *clone* is an application server modeled from the server group template. It runs on a particular node and takes its properties from the server group. Clones are identical, so any one of them can serve requests with the same results.

When clones are created from a server group, the server group becomes the manager of the clones. Any change made to the server group is immediately propagated to the clones. Workload management is automatically enabled when a server group and clones are created.

> **NOTE**: The easiest way to establish workload management is to build the application server, test your application, create a server group, and create clones. Your mileage may vary because workload management encompasses many factors, and creating server groups and clones is but one option.

If you were to update properties on a clone directly, it might cause the clone to become disassociated with the server group. When this occurs, the clone no longer takes part in workload management. Starting the server group starts all the clones within the server group, but you can start clones individually.

Understanding types of workload management

Just where does workload management occur? WebSphere supports basically three types of workload management. Figure 24-2 shows a configuration that identifies the three types of workload-managed components (IP sprayers, servlet, and EJB workload management). IP sprayers ensure that you obtain good distribution of your HTTP requests

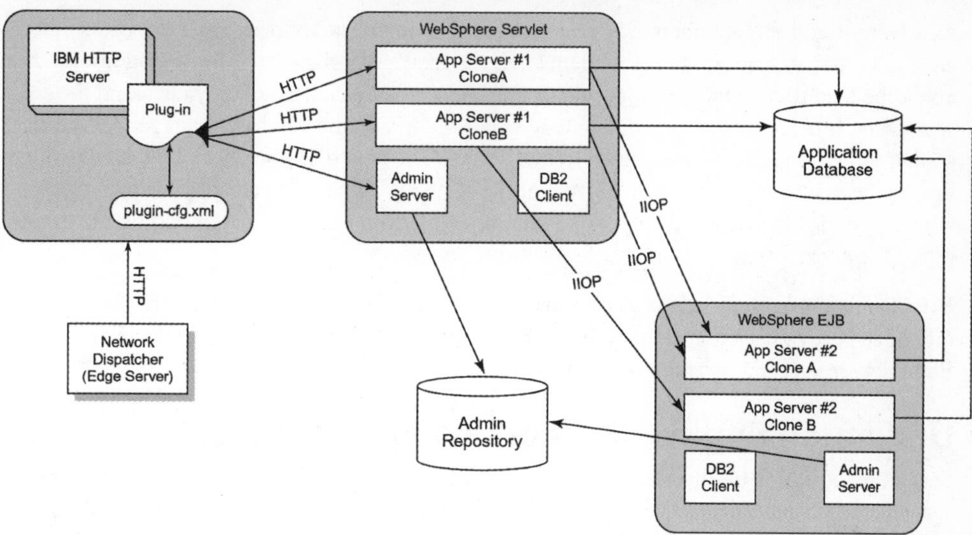

Figure 24-2: Workload management is not restricted to the application server. You can implement IP sprayers (Network Dispatcher) to distribute requests to multiple Web servers. After the request reaches the application server, the processing can be distributed to multiple Web containers and EJB containers.

Understanding Web server load management

HTTP requests can be shared across multiple HTTP servers. This requires the use of an IP sprayer. An IP sprayer takes incoming requests and distributes them among a group of HTTP servers. All this is done outside of WebSphere Application Server.

IP sprayers come in two forms: hardware and software. Network Dispatcher is a software-oriented IP sprayer that comes with the WebSphere Edge Server. Network Dispatcher applies intelligent load balancing. This balancing can be provided for HTTP, HTTPS (SSL), FTP, NNTP, IMAP, POP3, SMTP, and Telnet.

> **ON THE WEB:** See `www.ibm.com/software/webservers/edgeserver/library.html` for more information about the WebSphere Edge Server.

One feature of the WebSphere Edge Server that you might find interesting is the concept of advisors. *Advisors* are lightweight clients that run inside the dispatcher, providing information about the load of a given server. Advisors are like watch dogs, periodically checking the status of servers. If the advisor reports an outage, a port matrix is updated by a manager component so that future requests are not routed to that server. The next periodic check by the advisor can update the matrix to signify a new status of the server. You can also create your own custom advisors to enable load balancing based on unique platform and application requirements and report the status of the WebSphere Application Server.

You do not configure the Edge Server in this book, but if some of the characteristics mentioned previously suggest the use of an IP sprayer, you should check out the WebSphere Edge Server Web site for more information.

Understanding servlet workload management

Servlet requests can be shared across multiple Web containers. You should segregate your servlet loads to prevent failover and ensure balanced loads. You might also separate the HTTP server from the Web container to add an additional firewall between the Web server and application server. Figure 24-2 shows the servlet Web container on a separate node from the HTTP server.

The WebSphere plug-in to the HTTP server is responsible for the distribution of the servlet requests. You can configure WebSphere to have the Web containers on a single or on multiple machines. When you specify multiple Web containers, you must specify how to distribute the requests. With servlet requests, you can specify either of the following:

- Random
- Round robin (which is the default)

For predictable distribution, you should utilize Round Robin, which is the default. With Random it is possible to return to the same server with another request, but both should distribute equally.

> **TIP:** The default configuration parameter for servlet load balancing is named LoadBalance. You can find this parameter in the `plugin-cfg.xml` file. The default is set to Round Robin.

After you complete the configuration changes, you must always regenerate the plug-ins and redistribute them. When requests are submitted, the plug-in distributes the requests as specified and all log information is written to the `<was_home>\logs\activity.log` file per node.

You might want to consider the impact of having too many Web containers on a single machine, especially if you are also housing the administrative database. Too much contention among the processes could slow performance and possibly result in a single point of failure.

> **NOTE**: In almost all cases, the repository database should reside on a separate machine. That machine should support a high-availability solution to ensure that the database does not become a source of a single point of failure.

Understanding EJB workload management

Enterprise JavaBean (EJB) requests can also be shared across EJB containers. The protocol for passing request information is handled by HTTP for Web containers; however, EJBs utilize the Internet Inter-Orb Protocol (IIOP). The clients can be servlets, JavaServer Pages (JSPs), or other EJBs. Figure 24-2 shows the EJB container separated from the Web container.

Consider whether you should have the Web container in a separate node from the EJB container. Although each of the application servers will run its own JVM and its own thread pool, this might actually hinder performance. By placing the Web container and EJB container in the same application server, you gain performance because of the preferred local calls to the containers. Otherwise, you need to communicate through IIOP to the other application server, and IIOP is slower than preferred local calls to the containers.

So what does workload management manage for EJB? The workload-management service provides load balancing for the following types of enterprise beans:

- Entity or session beans' homes
- Entity bean instances
- Instances of stateless session beans

Understanding how EJB workload management works

To participate in WLM for EJBs, your client code needs to be enabled with the WLM stub code. In prior editions, you needed to specify that you want your EJBs to participate in WLM. With version 4.0, the cloning process automatically enables WLM for the cloned EJBs. A WLM client runtime is enabled as an Object Request Broker (ORB) plug-in that directs request to EJB clones. Following is the order of execution:

1. A client request utilizes the ORB to access the EJBs. The request can come from a standalone client, a servlet, or other EJBs.
2. The EJB request is passed through the ORB.
3. The ORB requires a reference to a clone from a server. This reference is called the Interoperable Object Reference (IOR). The WLM plug-in provides the IOR.
4. The WLM plug-in checks to see if it recognizes the IOR by checking whether the context of the transaction is the same.
5. If the WLM plug-in doesn't recognize the IOR, it contacts the Administrative Server to get the server group information. From there, the WLM plug-in extrapolates information about the server group.
6. Finally, the ORB directs the request to the appropriate clone.

Changes to the server group are passed to the clones. The clients get updated at the next request. When the client sends in the request, the version number of its server group is also sent. The version known as an epoch number is used to determine whether the server group information it has is stale. A comparison is done and, if the epoch numbers don't agree, new information about the server group is returned.

Understanding session beans

Stateless session beans have little impact on WLM. By definition, stateless session beans carry no state; therefore, there are no concerns about where the EJB was obtained. Stateful session beans are a little different. WebSphere Application Server currently supports the cloning of stateful session bean home objects among multiple application servers. But it does not support the cloning of a specific instance of a stateful session bean. In this situation, the same application server must be accessed.

Understanding entity beans

Entity beans are more transaction oriented. When requested by a client, an entity bean is instantiated in a container. This instance is utilized for all subsequent accesses for the duration of the transaction. The capability to hold on to the transaction is achieved through the context. The container needs to maintain state information only within the context of that transaction.

> **NOTE**: Workload management can be used only if option C caching is enabled in the container.

In Chapter 22, you learned that the Enterprise JavaBeans' specification defines three EJB caching options: A, B, or C. The EJB container processes the EJB requests based on these options. EJB caching is set at the bean level and is stored in the IBM extensions deployment descriptor.

In between transactions, the entity bean could be cached. This is where the caching option settings are important. Because you want your data refreshed at the start of each transaction, options B and C are compatible with WLM.

Understanding work-management selection policy

WebSphere manages the distribution of work through the work-management selection policy. Similar to the servlet policy, the EJB work-management selection policy supports the following settings:

- *Random:* Clones are selected are on a random basis from the defined server group.
- *Round Robin:* Clones are selected in a serial fashion, from A to B to C within the defined server group.
- *Random Prefer Local and Round Robin Prefer Local:* These options operate similarly to Random and Round Robin. The major difference is that Prefer Local attempts to optimize access to the local machine versus utilizing IIOP to access remote clones.

Setting Up Server Groups

Cloning is an advanced technique for improving the performance and efficiency of WebSphere Application Server. The utilization of server groups and clones makes WebSphere a highly efficient and reliable environment. In this section, you learn how to set up a server group and gain a better understanding of how to configure server groups.

As you might recall, a server group is a non-JVM convenience for creating additional copies of an application server and its contents. When you create a server group, the server being copied is referred to as the original. Copies of the original are clones.

When the administrator creates a new server group, information about the group is stored in the administrative repository, which is a database. Following are some of the attributes that are stored in the EJSADMIN.SERVERGROUP_TABLE database table:

- Name
- Number of clones
- Start time

Although it's good to know some of the internal structure of the database repository, you should not attempt to manipulate the information without the use of the Administrative Console, XMLConfig, or the WebSphere Control Program (WSCP).

In this section, you learn about the steps necessary to create a server group, but you do not actually create one here. You run a sample exercise later in this chapter that utilizes the AlmostFreeCruise application.

You should already have installed an application and have configured it appropriately. You should test your application to ensure that it is working properly. If you are satisfied with the results of your test, you can proceed with cloning your application. Creating a server group is very simple. Simply follow these steps:

1. From the Administrative Console, expand the Nodes item and continue expanding until you reach the application server you want to model.
2. Right-click the application server and select Create Server Group.
3. Update the Property sheet to designate a name for the group and set other properties as desired.
4. Click OK to create the server group.

> **NOTE**: When you configure an application server and then create a server group from it, the original application server is transformed from an application server into a clone. This is known as creating the "first clone."

You now have a server group that all clones inherit. Your server group is stored in the administrative repository and is now available to make clones on any node within the WebSphere domain.

Creating Clones

A clone is an application server modeled from the server group template. When you create a server group from an existing application, that application server becomes your first clone. You create additional clones, depending upon your workload-management strategy. The way in which you implement your cloning strategy should be based on the following factors:

- Security requirements
- Performance
- Throughput
- Availability
- Maintainability

Figure 24-3 shows one example of how clones can be distributed. In Figure 24-3, there are four machines within your WebSphere domain. Two machines are handling workload distributed by the network dispatcher (IP sprayer), and these two machines are routing requests to two other nodes (WebSphere Node 1 and WebSphere Node 2).

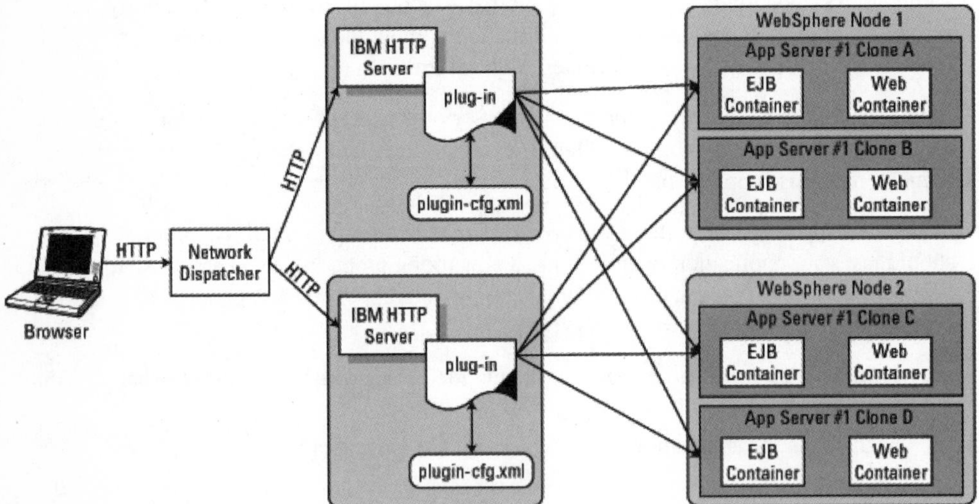

Figure 24-3: Vertical and horizontal cloning are the two methods of Workload management supported by WebSphere.

Both WebSphere nodes contain a cloned application server. WebSphere Node 1 is running App Server #1 in two JVMs. Clones A and B are co-located in WebSphere Node 1. When the same clone is located on the same node, this is called *vertical cloning*.

Also notice in Figure 24-3 that the same application server is implemented. Clones C and D are running on WebSphere Node 2. When the same clones are distributed throughout the domain on individual machines, this is known as *horizontal cloning*.

Understanding vertical cloning

The JVM limits it use to a single processor. This means some systems' CPUs are not fully utilized, especially on multiprocessor machines. Vertical cloning addresses this limitation.

Vertical cloning instantiates multiple copies of the application server group on the same node. Vertical cloning enables you to instantiate multiple copies of the JVM to run your application server clones, which enables you to take advantage of machines with multiple processors and machines with significant amounts of memory. Given this fact, the workload manager can now distribute the workload based on idle or under-utilized servers.

Figure 24-4 shows a single WebSphere node supporting two clones of the same application server. As mentioned earlier, creating a server group automatically enables the plug-in for Round Robin workload management. Requests for a particular application sever can be routed to a free or under-utilized clone. If one of the clones fails for whatever reason, another is available to handle the request.

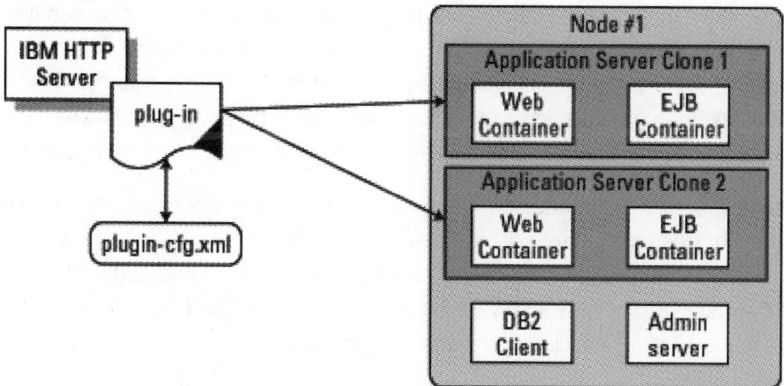

Figure 24-4: In this example of vertical workload management, a single WebSphere node supports two clones of the same application server.

Although this is an effective means for improving availability and response times, you should also consider the potential points of failure. In an environment, such as the one shown in Figure 24-4, you could experience points of failure at the following locations:

- The single HTTP server
- The single WebSphere node

A failure at either of these two entry points could render your system unavailable. Other bottlenecks to consider would be limited memory, single processor, and the WebSphere repository.

> **CROSS-REFERENCE**: Chapters 27 and 28 discuss using WSCP and XMLConfig as alternative ways of creating clones.

The simplest way to create a vertical clone is to use the Administrative Console wizards and run the Create Server Group Wizard. This wizard enables you to perform the following:

- Select an application server to use as the server group template.
- Associate a name for the server group.
- Select a workload-management selection policy (Round Robin, Random, and so on.).
- Enable various services within the group.

When you utilize the wizard, the outcome is a new server group with the original application server becoming the first clone and a new clone. You create a vertical clone in the sample exercise later in this chapter (see "Creating a Vertical Clone for AlmostFreeCruise").

Understanding horizontal cloning

The horizontal cloning process instantiates multiple copies of an application server on separate physical machines. It is similar to vertical cloning, but instead of adding additional JVMs, it distributes the application to separate physical machines. In horizontal cloning, you increase your ability to route requests, take advantage of more hardware, and improve your points of failure by adding additional physical machines to act as backups in the event of a node failure.

Figure 24-5 shows an example of a horizontal implementation, which differs from some of the others you have looked at. In this case, a network dispatcher (such as the Edge Server) is spraying requests to two separate machines that have both the HTTP server and application server co-located on the same piece of hardware. The application server has been cloned and distributed to the individual nodes. The clones are named Clone A and Clone B.

Figure 24-5 also shows the administrative repository. The server group information is shared throughout the WebSphere domain using this repository. So conceivably, you could add more nodes to expand your environment to increase throughput and reduce failover. This type of environment is appropriate for environments with smaller, less powerful machines.

Creating a horizontal clone can be accomplished only if you have more than one WebSphere node. When you create a horizontal clone, you need to specify the node on which to install the clone.

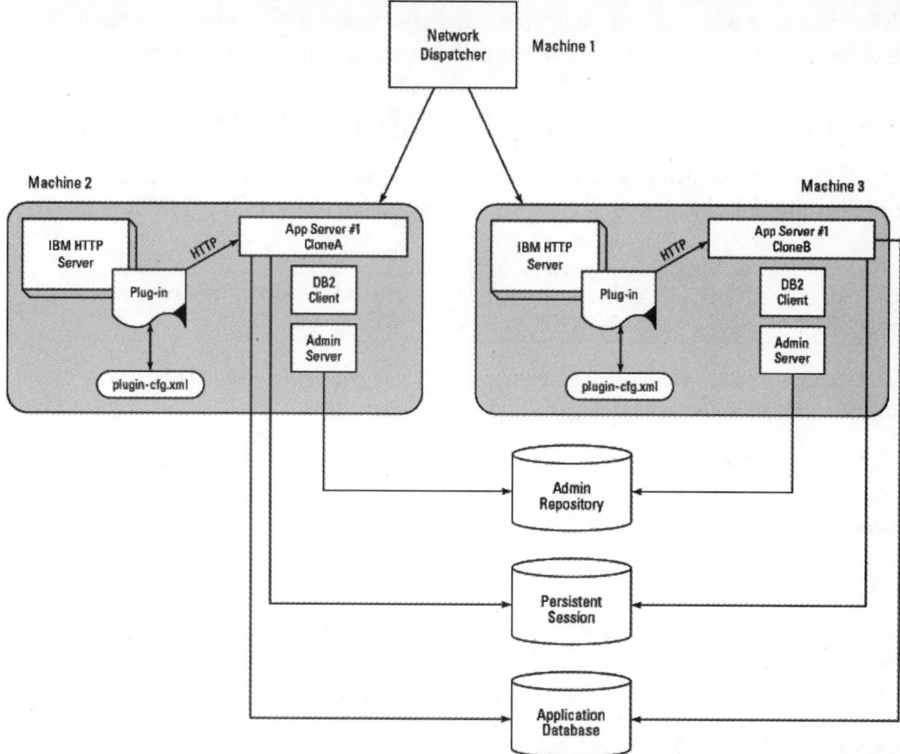

Figure 24-5: Horizontal scaling is a great way to utilize less expensive hardware to distribute workload. Here, two machines share a common administrative repository; within this repository,the configuration of clones is persisted.

If you remember, when you create a server group, the modeled application server becomes the first clone. That clone resides on the node where the original application server existed. To create a node using the same image as your server group, follow these steps:

1. Select the server group from within the Administrative Console.
2. Right-click and select New⇨Clone.
3. Provide an informative name for the new clone.
4. Select the node within the WebSphere domain on which to install the clone.
5. Click OK to create the clone.
6. Verify the clone has unique transport numbers by selecting the clone and selecting the Services tab. Edit the properties on the Web Container Service and ensure the transport settings are unique. If not update them so they are unique.
7. When completed, regenerate the plug-in.
8. Start the server group.

You should test your with application to verify that your application is routing properly. You learn how to use the showCfg application to verify transport ports in the next section.

Creating a Vertical Clone for AlmostFreeCruise

In this section, you actually create a server group and clone for the AlmostFreeCruise. If you haven't started the Administrative Server and Administrative Console, do so prior to this exercise.

> **CROSS-REFERENCE**: In Chapter 20, you should have created the AlmostFreeCruise application server. If AlmostFreeCruise was not implemented, refer to Chapter 20.

You create a server group from an existing application. If you remember, the best way to implement workload management is to follow these steps:

- Create an application server
- Test the application
- Create the server group
- Create additional clones

You use the wizards to create the server group and original clone. Figure 24-6 shows the list of wizards available. Be sure to stop the AlmostFreeCruise server prior to creating a server group. Click the Wizards button and select Create Server Group.

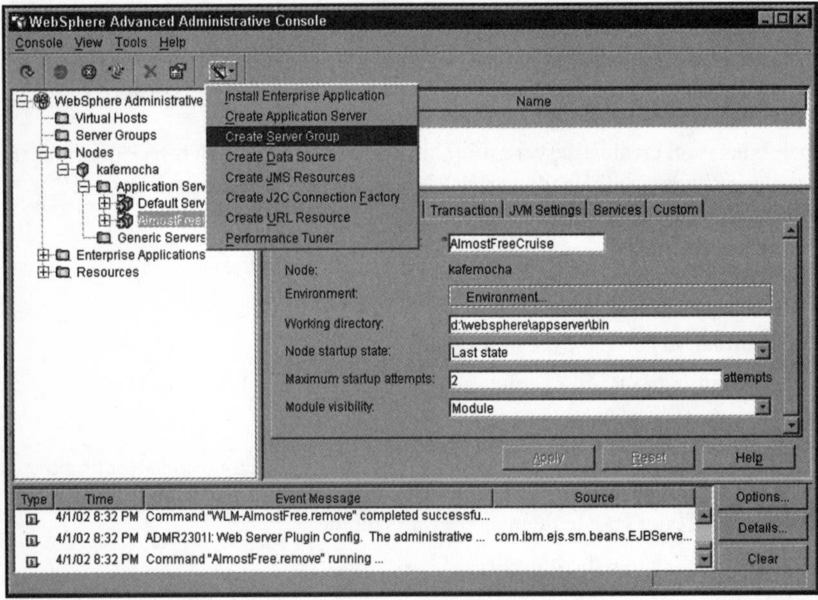

Figure 24-6: The wizard process makes it easy to create the server group.

Figure 24-7 shows the Server Group Properties screen. You should perform the following steps:

1. Check the Create Server Group based on an existing application server check box.
2. Select AlmostFreeCruise from the drop-down list.
3. Enter **AlmostFreeGroup** as the server group name.
4. Choose Round Robin Prefer Local as the workload-management selection policy.

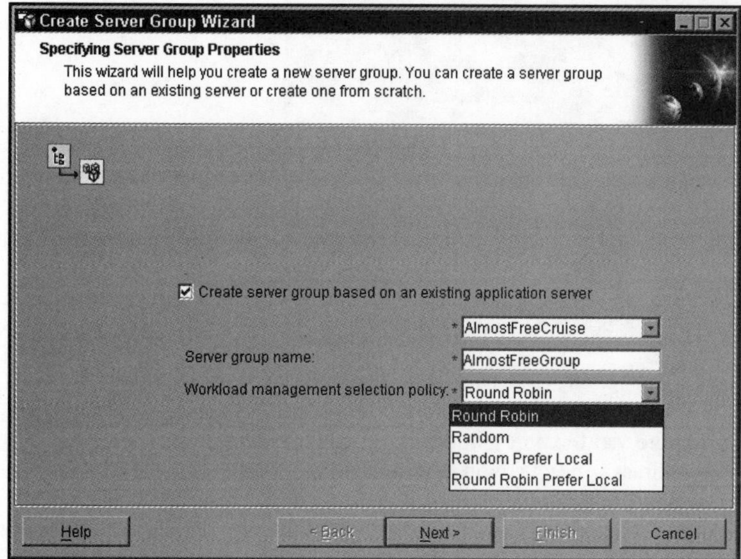

Figure 24-7: When you choose Round Robin as your workload-management selection policy, you are basically asking the workload manager to rotate the request through all the available clones, preferably on the local machine.

5. Click Next to go to the next panel. Depending upon your situation, you might or might not need to edit any services. For purposes of illustrating how WebSphere automatically increments the port number, you should do the following:
   - Select the Web Container Service.
   - Click Edit Service Properties.
6. You are presented with the Web Container Service dialog box. Click the Transport tab to review the Transport Settings (see Figure 24-8). The port address is incremented by one. You do not need to do anything with these settings. If you want to put in your own custom port address, this is where you do it. Click Cancel to continue.

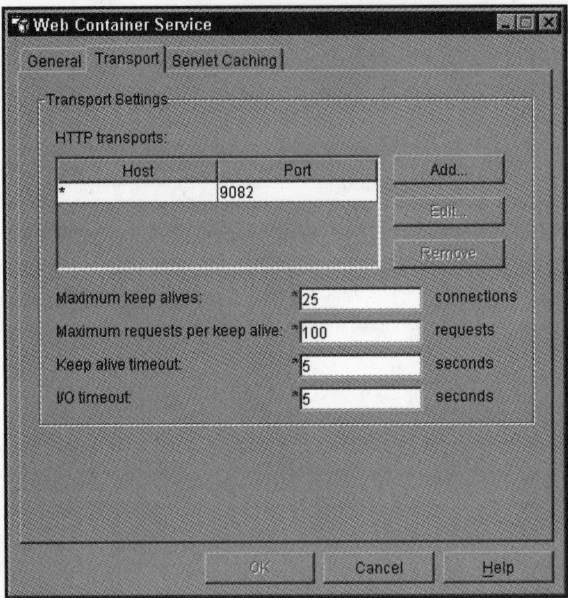

Figure 24-8: On the Transport tab, verify the HTTP transport ports and make adjustments for tuning.

You should also note that the port number might differ from the value in Figure 24-8. As long as the port address is unique, you are fine.

7. Click Next to continue to the Creating Application Servers as Clones panel. Figure 24-9 shows where you can create application servers that will act as clones in the server group.

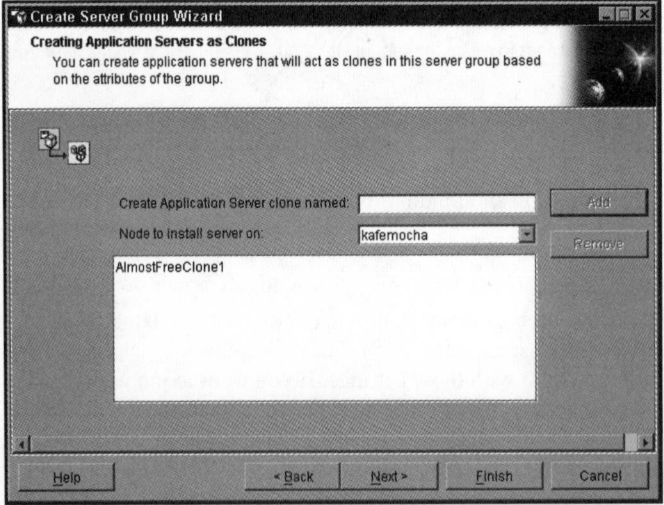

Figure 24-9: Creating a new clone with the Admnistrative Console Wizard is easy.

8. Enter **AlmostFreeClone1** in the Create Application Server clone named field. Leave the node as the defaulted node name. This should be your machine name.
9. Press the Add button to add the clone. Click Next to go to the Completing the Create Server Group Wizard.
10. Confirm your settings and click Finish. You get a confirmation dialog box informing you that the process was completed. Figure 24-10 shows the end results of all your effort.

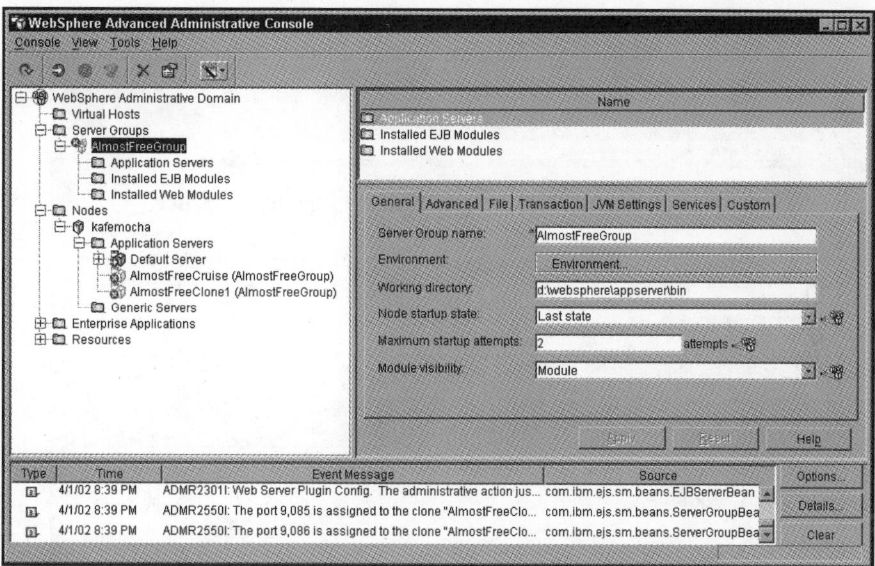

Figure 24-10: When you create a new server group from an existing application, you see your original application server as a clone and any newly created clones.

11. Click your node (the machine name of your workstation), and select Regen Webserver plug-in.
12. Start the AlmostFreeGroup server group that, in turn, starts the application servers.

You have successfully created a server group and your first vertically cloned environment.

Now that you have created a functioning workload-management environment, you might like to see it working. The best way to show you how it works is to run a demonstration.

NOTE: Make sure you have the Administrative Console running as well as the server group `AlmostFreeGroup`.

The `showCfg` servlet is included with the examples that come with WebSphere. It is a simple servlet that reports information about the WebSphere Web configuration. You use it to verify that workload management is actually taking place. Figure 24-11 shows the output from the `showCfg` servlet.

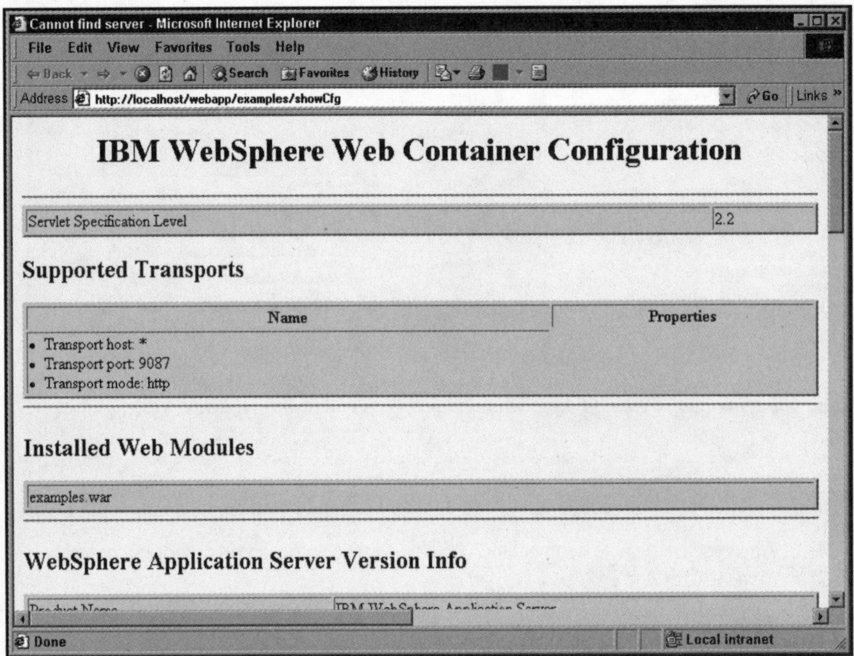

Figure 24-11: The showCfg servlet provides information about the Web container configuration.

The `showCfg` servlet is installed by default with the Default Server. It shows a lot of information about the configuration of WebSphere. Before you start the example, it would be best to perform some clean up. Start Internet Explorer 5.5 and select Tools⇨Internet Options. When the screen appears, select the Delete Files button to clear out all the old cached files. Removing the cached files ensures that your pages are refreshed from the server. You are now ready to enter in the URL:

```
http://localhost/webapp/examples/showCfg
```

You see a screen similar to Figure 24-11. Take note of the transport port number. Refresh the browser using the Refresh icon. If everything is working properly, you should see a new transport port being used. As you might guess, the clones are working in a round-robin fashion. Continue to refresh the screen to get a feel for it.

Now go to the Administrative Console and stop AlmostFreeClone1. When it is stopped, continue with your refreshing of the browser. Do you notice the change?

There you have it – workload management in action. In the next section, you can learn about creating horizontal clones. If you do not have a fully networked system with at least one additional machine, you will not be able to run the example. If that is the case, you can skip or quickly browse the rest of chapter.

Creating Horizontal Clones

To create horizontal clones, you need to be connected to a network with more than one node. Horizontal cloning is the process of copying application servers to additional machines to spread the work out and provide for failover support. In this section, you continue to extend the AlmostFreeGroup to another node. To create a horizontal clone, you need to have another machine with WebSphere Application Server installed.

There are a few things that need to be set up in order to have horizontal clones. First you must have multiple machines, and second, you must have defined a WebSphere domain. A WebSphere domain is a group of servers all sharing a common administrative repository. In all the examples so far, you have been limited to a single server domain.

Figure 24-12 shows the target environment you create. It shows two nodes (ABC and XYZ) that were previously individual WebSphere domains. You modify Node XYZ to point to the administrative repository for Node ABC and then add a clone from the server group created on Node ABC. From this point forward, ABC is referred to as the primary node, and XYZ as the secondary node.

You need to perform some adjustments to your setup. You learned about installation in Chapter 4. That chapter included a short discussion on setting up a DB2 client. When you set up a DB2 client, you are able to connect to a remote database. In this case, you want to uncouple your local database repository and use the DB2 client to point to the repository associated with the primary node, thereby creating a single WebSphere domain between the two machines.

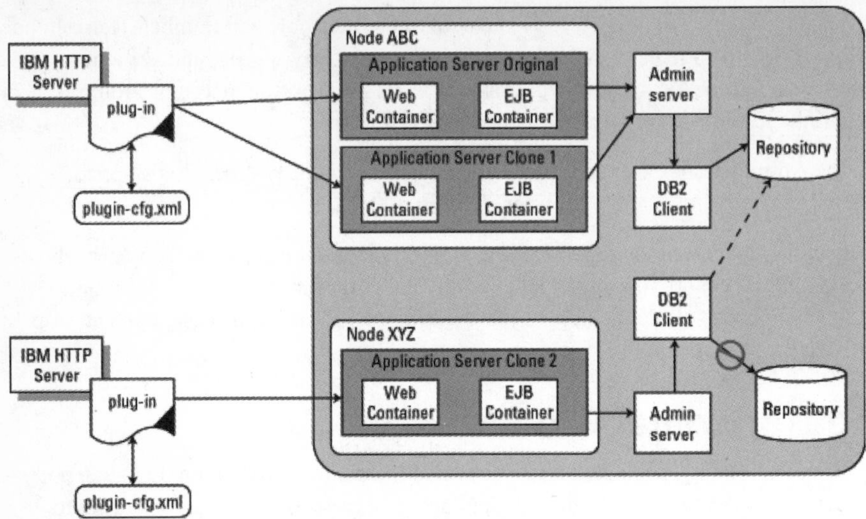

Figure 24-12: Changing from two WebSphere servers into one domain.

Manually configuring the DB2 client

An alternative way to configure a DB2 client (different from the way described in Chapter 4) is to use the Client Configuration Assistant that is bundled with DB2. This wizard approach simplifies the steps necessary to configure the DB2 client to point to other servers. The following steps assume that you have named your WAS repository as WAS40 on both your WebSphere servers. You eliminate the use of the secondary node's repository (as shown previously in Figure 24-12) and point to the primary node's repository. Follow these steps on your secondary node:

1. Open the DB2 Client Configuration Assistant using Start⇨Programs⇨IBM DB2⇨Client Configuration Assistant.
2. Next you inform the system where the remote database is located and provide it with an alias name. When the Client Configuration Assistant window opens, click Add to start the Database Wizard.
3. Click the Manually Configure a Connection to a Database radio button, and click Next.
4. On the Protocol tab, select TCP/IP and click Next.
5. In the TCP/IP tab enter the IP address of the primary node into the host name field.

TIP: You can determine the IP address in Windows by typing **ipconfig** in a command window.

6. Type **50000** as the port number, noting that this is the default implementation. Your implementation might be different. You might have to check the value of the DB2 connection port in the Services file under `x:\WINNT\System32\drivers\etc\services`.

7. Click Next.
8. On the Database tab, enter the database name **WAS40**, and set the alias name to WAS40REM (for remote WAS40).

> **NOTE**: DB2 database names are limited to eight characters.

9. Add a comment line if you want and click Finish.
10. You are given the option to test the connection. You should test the connection by clicking Test Connection.
11. In the dialog box that appears, enter a valid user and password for the database. Depending upon how you configured the database on the primary node, you might want to try db2admin as the userid and db2admin as the password. Click OK.
12. If all works well, you should receive the Connection Test Was Successful message.

You perform these steps for all other databases that you want to share when you are creating WebSphere domains.

Helping WebSphere find the shared repository

Your second WebSphere Application Server needs to find the `WAS40` database when you start it. All the application servers need to know what the shared repository is called. You help set that up by creating the alias in the Client Configuration Assistant.

To inform the second WebSphere Application Server of the database name, you need to update the configuration file on the second WebSphere Application Server machine.

1. Using WordPad, open the `admin.config` file found in `<was_home>\bin`. Figure 24-13 shows an example.

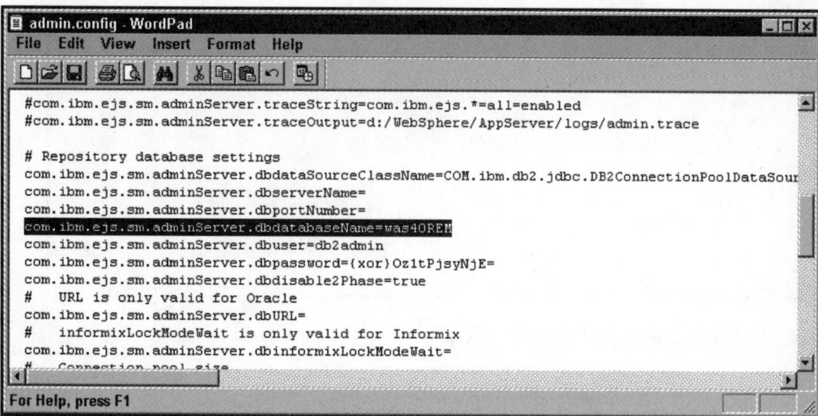

Figure 24-13: Updating admin.config for cloning.

2. You need to update two lines within this file. The first, as shown in Figure 24-13, is the `com.ibm.ejs.sm.adminServer.dbdatabaseName` property. Change the value from `WAS40` to **WAS40REM**.
3. Next, find the `install.initial.config` line. The value associated with this line is normally set to `false`. Set this value to `true`. The only time it is set to `true` is if you want the default server to be created. Normally, this is done at install time and is the default setting. Save the file and start the Administrative Server. This establishes the process of referencing the database WAS40REM. After the install is successful, the property is automatically set to `false`. You might be wondering why you are resetting the default server. When you first installed the application, the default server was automatically installed and configured in the repository. Because you are changing the repository, you need to reestablish default server using the new repository.

TIP: If you have been running the samples within the book without a network, you may have set the loopback adapter. Having the loopback adapter running while on a network might cause some conflicts. To disable the loopback adapter, you can add a line to the `admin.config` file. Add a line and enter as follows: `com.ibm.CORBA.LocalHost=<IP address>`, where `<IP address>` is the IP address of the primary node.

4. You should start the WebSphere Application Server on the secondary node. If it is already running, stop it and then restart it. Start the Administrative Console and you should see something similar to Figure 24-14.

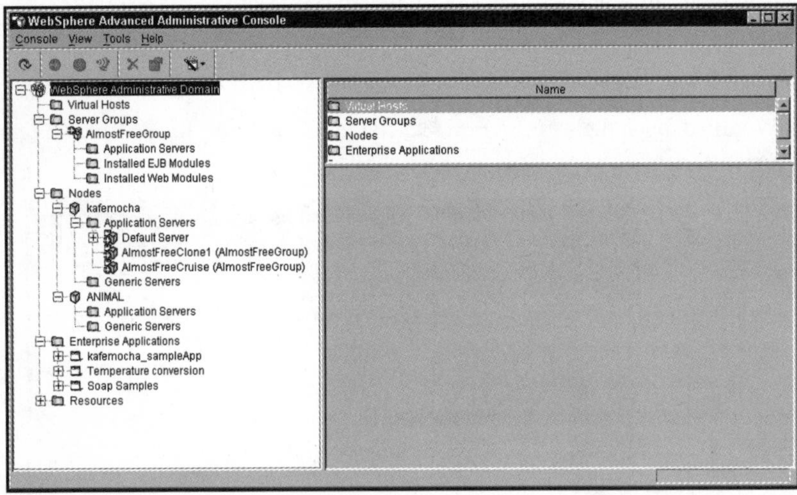

Figure 24-14: The running Administrative Console shows you the secondary node.

Figure 24-14 shows the AlmostFreeGroup server group and two nodes (kafemocha and Animal). Kafemocha was the primary node, and Animal is the secondary node. These two nodes now represent your WebSphere domain.

Creating the horizontal clone on the secondary node

You are now ready to create another clone but this time on the secondary node. The process is similar to the process you used to create your first clone. The difference is that you are selecting the node on which to install the clone. Perform the following steps:

1. Select the AlmostFreeGroup Server group, right-click, and select New⇨Clone. The Create Clone dialog box opens (see Figure 24-15)
2. Type **AlmostFreeClone2** into the name field.

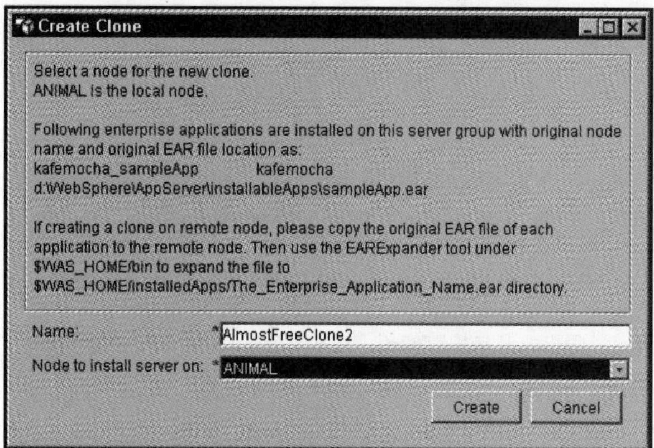

Figure 24-15: Creating a horizontal clone.

3. In the Node to install server on field, select the node that you utilized as your secondary node. In Figure 24-15, it is shown as the Animal node. Your case should be different.
4. Click Create.

> **NOTE**: Because you are creating a clone on a remote node, you need to copy the original EAR file of the application to the other node. Use the EARExpander tool to expand the file into the `installedApps` folder.

That's all it takes. Figure 24-16 shows that you have two nodes with clones of AlmostFreeCruise running on each node.

Remember that anytime you update any of the transports, you need to regenerate the WebSphere plug-in. You should now regenerate the plug-in for both nodes.

1. For each node right-click and select Regen WebServer Plugin.
2. When you see in the console that the regeneration was completed, start the server group. Don't forget to copy the EAR file to the new server and expand it into the `installedApps` folder.

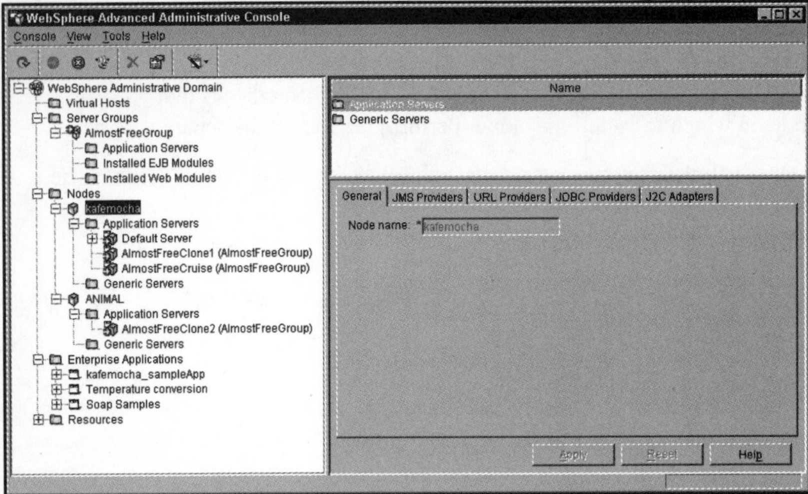

Figure 24-16: Horizontal clone. Your new clone should have a new transport port number established.

Try testing the horizontal cloning by running the `showCfg` servlet. Perform the same steps that you performed in the "Running a workload-management environment" section.

Figure 24-17 shows the `showCfg` servlet with a new transport port. In this case, it is port 9087. In your case, it might be something different. As you refresh the browser, you see the transport port changing in round-robin fashion between the vertical and horizontal clones.

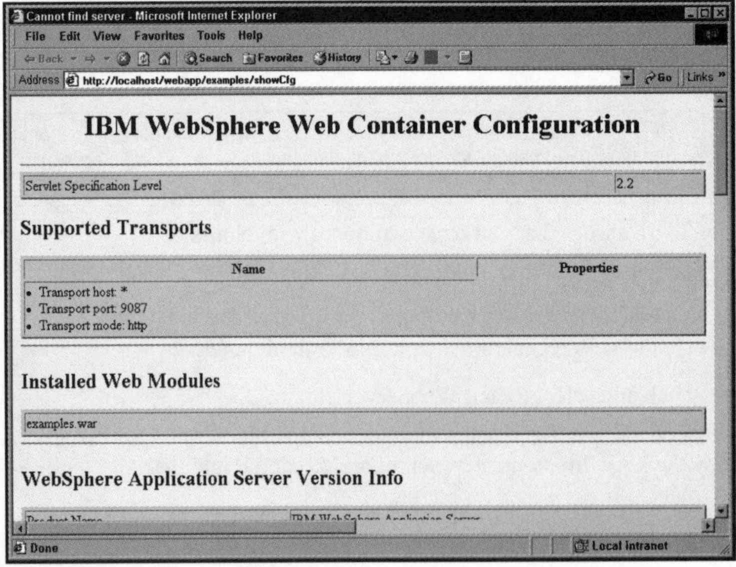

Figure 24-17: When you run showCfg again, you see your new transport port.

Installing JDBC drivers on secondary nodes

Applications that utilize additional resources, such as JDBC drivers, need to be installed on the secondary node. In the previous example, there was no need for a JDBC driver, but most of your applications are likely to need one.

To install a JDBC driver on a secondary node, follow these steps:

1. In the Administrative Console expand the Resources tree and JDBC Providers and select the JDBC driver you want to change.
2. In the Property sheet that displays on the right, select Nodes, and Click Install New.
3. On the subsequent screen, select the node on which you want to install the driver (a secondary node). There should be one or more nodes displayed.
4. In the Install Driver window, click the Specify Drive button.
5. In the Specify the Driver Files dialog box, click Add Driver. The File Browser dialog box opens. Select the appropriate driver. If you are using DB2, find the `db2java.zip` file located in `<db2_home>\sqllib\java`.
6. Click the Set button to add the driver
7. Click Install to install the driver.
8. In the Nodes property sheet, click Apply to apply the changes.

Remember that cloning provides you with a powerful way to increase performance and improve scalability as well as a way to provide failover support to your environment.

Understanding the WebSphere 4.0 Optimizations

Prior to this discussion on how to optimize WebSphere, you should be aware of the changes made to WebSphere 4.0 over WebSphere 3.5.3 to improve performance and scalability. There are four reasons why WebSphere outperforms the competition:

- Workload management for scalability
- Excellent throughput resulting from caching and pooling
- EJB optimizations
- Capability to take advantage of multiple CPUs

Workload management in WebSphere takes advantage of a new high-speed HTTP transport between Web server and Application server. The new transport replaces the previous Open Servlet Engine (OSE) transport, which was slower.

Another improvement takes advantage of an optimized Object Request Broker (ORB) that can be routed through RMI/IIOP from client applications and server applications, as well as WebSphere Application Server to WebSphere Application Server.

The other workload-management improvement was done in conjunction with the Edge Server. The Edge Server takes advantage of advisors that advise about which application server is ready to receive requests. In version 4.0, the advisor was implemented as a WebSphere servlet. To further extend the advisor, the advisor was made customizable so that you can adjust the criterion that specifies an application server available for work.

From a caching and pooling perspective, WebSphere was able to improve throughput by removing unnecessary communication to the next tier through the use of caches. If managed properly, having caches removes the cost of creating new objects (EJBs) and resources (database connections). Some improvements were also achieved when IBM rewrote the prepared statement cache. A prepared statement is a pre-compiled SQL statement that is stored in a prepared statement object. When cached and associated with a database connection, the cached statement improves performance..

Another improvement in the pooling of resources is the capability to set a maximum thread size for ORBs. This parameter specifies the maximum number of connections allowed to EJBs.

The EJB 1.1 specification states that method calls are to be pass-by-value, meaning that for every remote method call, the parameters are copied onto the stack before the call is made. Local refers to situations in which the EJB client and the EJB container are in the same JVM. In such cases, you can take advantage of using local references to EJBs created in the EJB container. This reduces the overhead of making calls over the network to access EJBs. For example, you can have a servlet calling, and EJB and/or an EJB calling another EJB in the same JVM.

TIP: To set pass-by-reference select the application server Services tab; select Advanced, and check pass-by-reference. You must stop and restart the application server.

The CMP-OPT tool is available on DeveloperWorks and as an e-fix with version 4.0.2 of WebSphere. The CMP-OPT tool performs the following tasks:

- Suggests performance-sensitive settings on EJBs based on usage
- Scans EARs and JARs
- Checks mutability of EJB parameters and results
- Suggest access intent of read-only, update

NOTE: The URL for WebSphere support and e-fixes is `www-4.ibm.com/software/webservers/appserv/support.html`.

Last but not least, WebSphere code was written to be symmetrical-multiprocessor (SMP) aware, so it can take advantage of having multiple processors running on a single machine.

Understanding IBM WebSphere Edge Server

The discussion so far has been centered on the WebSphere Application Server. There are opportunities to improve performance outside of WebSphere that can significantly improve throughput and performance. One such opportunity is the WebSphere Edge Server.

The WebSphere Edge Server v2 is Web-based software that addresses the scalability, reliability, and performance needs of enterprise applications in both local and distributed environments. It provides functions that improve caching and load balancing, which complement WebSphere Application Server's workload management. The following list contains some features of WebSphere Edge Server:

- **Delayering:** Taking an application program and decomposing into smaller modules, so you move parts of it closer to the "edge" of the network. Personalization is a good example of its use. This type of offloading improves performance by reducing network traffic.
- **Caching and filtering:** The caching proxy server is a server that provides highly scalable caching and filtering functions used in receiving requests and serving URLs.
- **Load balancing:** Network Dispatcher is a server that is able to dynamically monitor and balance TCP servers and applications in real time.
- **Content distribution:** The Content Distribution component is an infrastructure that you use to distribute static, dynamic, and multimedia Web content, along with application components to production servers, rehosting servers, and Edge Server caches throughout the network.
- **Application offloading:** Moves some of the presentation-logic and business-logic processing to the edge of the network. It enables the Edge Server to perform page composition from cached and rehosted fragments and Web objects.

WebSphere Edge Server functions in corporate, robust, leading-edge caching and load balancing that together compensate for the inherent weakness of the Internet in supporting critical business applications and expectations.

Understanding dynamic caching

Caching is key to the performance optimizations in WebSphere version 4. With today's Web sites displaying a myriad of dynamic content caching, a page is not the same as it once was. Dynamic caching has been supported since version 3.5.3 of WebSphere Application Server. Dynamic caching adds intelligence to the Application server, so servlets and JSPs can be analyzed and designated as cacheable. If a servlet or JSP gets cached, subsequent requests can be referenced out of cache versus traversing through the backend systems.

The request/response traffic looks like the diagram in Figure 24-18. Without a cache, the process would normally flow into the application server accessing the servlets or JSPs, which in turn, access other systems and/or database servers.

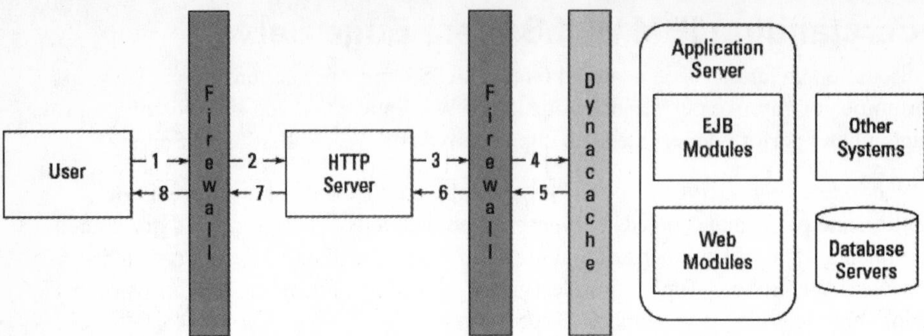

Figure 24-18: Utilizing a caching mechanism, request/response traffic flows as shown here.

Using WebSphere Edge Server's dynamic caching proxy server

Figure 24-18 shows one way to improve performance by using caching. But you can see that it does hop a number of times before it hits the cache. Implementing a separate external caching proxy server can reduce the communication overhead. A proxy server acts on the user's behalf and attempts to service the request. If the request is found in cache, the proxy returns its copy.

You can configure a separate external caching proxy server to sit in front of the HTTP server, at the edge of the network and closer to your users. This is an example of a reverse proxy. You can set up several of these boxes, which can share external caches among themselves. This enables you to cache and return dynamic data in a fashion similar to that illustrated in Figure 24-19. The WebSphere Edge Server provides this capability through an Edge Server Caching Proxy component.

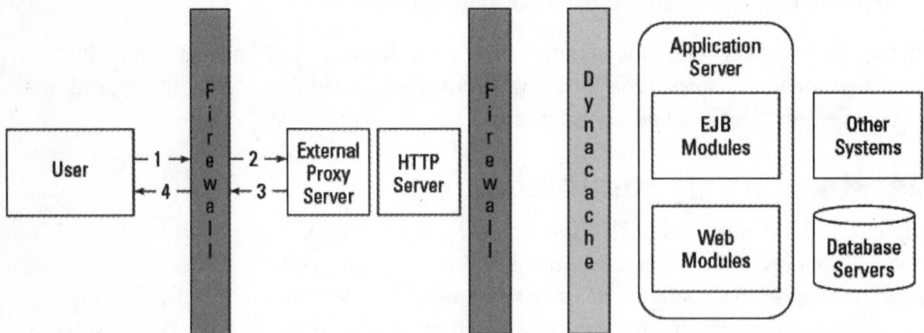

Figure 24-19: Implement the WebSphere Edge Server with a reverse proxy server to improve response time.

NOTE: The external caching server was formerly called Web Traffic Express (WTE).

The Edge Server provides you the capability to offload the dynamic caching work, as well as to use critical memory and CPU cycles from the application server. It puts the data even closer to the user.

The Edge Server also has the Network Dispatcher component that allows IP spraying (load balancing) between Web servers. The simplified graphic does not show interaction between the external caching proxy server and the application server and how they verify pages in the cache. An invalid page in this scenario causes the application server to notify the Edge Server, which then invalidates its own copy. There are two approaches to using a proxy server:

- A reverse proxy, shown in Figure 24-19, where you use the host name for the proxy server in the URL for the Web application. The proxy intercepts the request and makes a decision about whether to serve up the page from its cache or defer to the actual server that hosts the application.
- A forward proxy, where the request goes to the Web/Application server first, and from there a decision is made about whether to defer the request to the external caching proxy server.

Understanding how dynamic caching works in WebSphere

Servlets and JSPs are cacheable. In WebSphere 4.0, you can have the Web container check to determine whether the request can be served from cache before executing the target servlet.

You can designate servlets for caching by using their class names or by URIs. In cases where multiple URI aliases can result in the same servlet being executed, all those URIs must be designated in the configuration if you are using URIs to designate cacheable servlets. Listing 24-1 shows a sample of setting up a servlet for caching. Do not confuse this `<servlet>` entry with the entries you make in `web.xml`. This entry is inserted into a `servletcache.xml` document. You learn all about the `servletcache.xml` document in the section titled, "Enabling dynamic caching for WebSphere."

Listing 24-1: Setting Up a Servlet for Caching in servletcache.xml

```
<servlet>
   <timeout seconds="0" />
   <servletimpl class="SnoopServlet.class" />
   <externalcache id="afpa" />
</servlet>
```

The following list describes the rules used to determine whether the servlet is used from cache:

- Servlet is designated as a cached servlet
- Results are in cache
- Cache is valid

If all these are true, the cached version is returned. If not, the servlet is executed and the results are placed into the cache.

Enabling dynamic caching for WebSphere

You already learned about the WebSphere Edge Server's external caching. But using the WebSphere Edge Server requires that you purchase the WebSphere Edge Server product. You do have at your disposal another dynamic caching capability: The IBM HTTP Server for Windows NT/2000 contains a high-speed cache referred to as the Fast Response Cache Accelerator (FRCA), or Cache Accelerator. WebSphere Application Server's fragment cache can use IBM HTTP Server as an external cache with appropriate configuration. To enable dynamic caching, you update two XML configuration files:

- *dynacache.xml:* Toggles dynamic caching on/off based on its presence in the properties directory. It has parameters to control the size of the cache and to register any external caches to be used, such as IBM Edge Server dynamic caching proxy.
- *servletcache.xml:* Servletcache is where you specify which servlets to cache. You can specify the following in this file:
  - Servlets that are to be cached by class names or by URIs. (You must include all URIs that invoke this servlet.)
  - Time-out values, priorities, and whether each servlet is to be served from an external cache.
  - Which parameters, attributes, or session values to consider when creating the cache entry IDs for each servlet.
  - Which servlet *not* to cache, by using the `<invalidateonly/>` tag.

The following steps describe how to set up the Cache Accelerator, but are for discussion purposes only. You do not actually need to run the instructions. After you install the WebSphere Application Server and IBM HTTP Server for Windows NT, you can do the following to enable the Cache Accelerator:

1. Configure caching on the Web server by locating the `httpd.conf` configuration file, and adding the following two lines at the end of the file:

```
LoadModule afpaplugin_module x:<was_home>\bin\afpaplugin.dll
AfpaPluginHost 127.0.0.1:9081
```

2. Stop and restart your HTTP server.
3. Create an external cache group on the application server. For each application server that uses the Cache Accelerator, define an external cache group named `afpa`. Add a member to that group with an adapter bean name of `com.ibm.servlet.dynacache.Afpa`. For the address, enter the assigned port number from the Web server's `httpd.conf` file. Listing 24-2 shows the `dyncache.sample.xml` file located at `<was_home>\properties\dynacache.sample.xml`.

Listing 24-2: dynacache.sample.xml

```
<?xml version="1.0"?>
<!DOCTYPE cacheUnit SYSTEM "dynacache.dtd">

<cacheUnit>
  <cache size="1000" priority="1" />
<!--
This is an example of how to control an external cache with WebSphere.
If your deployment does not use this feature (as of 2/2001 there are no
external caches that work with websphere) then you may remove this
commented out section.

<externalCacheGroups>
 <group id="afpa" >
  <member address="9081"
   adapterBeanName="com.ibm.servlet.dynacache.Afpa"/>
</group>
</externalCacheGroups>
-->
</cacheUnit>
```

4. Configure a cache policy using external cache. You can refer to `<was_home>\properties\servletcache.sample.xml` as a sample to test.

> **CROSS-REFERENCE**: See the InfoCenter section 6.6.0.16.2 for more information about cache policies.

You can test your configuration by doing the following:

- Change folders to the `<was_home>\properties` directory.
- Copy the `servletcache.sample.xml` file to `servletcache.xml`.
- Update the first entry with the following definitions to enable the external high speed cache:

```
<servlet>
   <timeout seconds="0" />
   <servletimpl class="SnoopServlet.class" />
   <externalcache id="afpa" />
</servlet>
```

Start your WebSphere Application Server and the default application server. Test your changes using the `Snoop` servlet sample for external caching. You should point your browser to `http://<yourhost>/servlet/SnoopServlet` where <yourhost> is the machine's host name for your server.

The first request for `Snoop` servlet results in the response being loaded in the high-speed cache, and subsequent requests are served directly from the cache, which significantly enhances performance.

Using WebSphere Edge Server's external cache

The previous section showed how to take advantage of caching using the Fast Response Cache Accelerator, or Cache Accelerator. If you have decided to purchase the Edge Server to take advantage of its features, you have already done most of the work and only need to update two files to specify the use of the Edge Server. You configure `dynacache.xml` as follows:

```
<externalCacheGroups>
 <group id="WTE-EDGE-1" type="shared">
 <member address="yourhost"
  adapterBeanName="com.ibm.wte.WteAdapter"/>
</group>
</externalCacheGroups>
```

You can use `dynachache.sample.xml` as an example, copying it to `dynachache.xml` and making these changes. Then, modify your `servletcache.xml` file as follows:

```
<servlet>
 <timeout seconds="0" />
 <metadatagenerator class="com.ibm.wte.WteMetaDataGeneratorImpl" />
 <externalcache id="WTE-EDGE-1" />
 <path uri="/SnoopServlet.class" />
</servlet>
```

ON THE WEB: Refer to the WebSphere Edge Server documentation for more information: `www.ibm.com/software/webservers/edgeserver`.

Understanding Optimization Methodology

Up to this point in this chapter, you have learned about workload management and how to create server groups and clones. You also learned about some caching options available with WebSphere and its family of products. In this section, you are introduced to some ways to discover, optimize, and tune your WebSphere Application Server.

Often when an application is implemented in testing for the first time, some performance issues arise. It is important to have an optimization methodology established prior to reaching this point. An optimization methodology includes establishing an application profile, ensuring that you have adequate testing environments, and having a team of knowledgeable specialists in the areas of network topology, Web servers, security, application development, and WebSphere administration.

NOTE: A wealth of information about tuning is found in section 9 of the WebSphere InfoCenter.

You probably already know that a WebSphere domain is more than an application server. It might have network dispatchers, one or many HTTP servers, one or many application servers, multiple databases, and transaction messaging. Determining where performance is being impacted requires some thoughtful investigation.

You can be pretty certain that any Web Application Server performance problems will occur in one of three areas:

- The hardware capacity and settings
- The operating system (OS) settings
- The Web Application Server settings

Other than the memory requirements specified in Chapter 4, this book does not discuss hardware capacity or settings. It's probably not a surprise to anyone that one of the simplest ways to solve performance problems is to increase memory and processors. Exceptions to this involve problems with database throughput and network bandwidth, but in these cases you have options. You learn about those options in the next section.

Other considerations are your network topology and network card settings. You want to run network cards and network switches full-duplex. Running half-duplex decreases performance. Verify that the network speed can accommodate the required throughput. Make sure that 100MB is in use on 10/100 Ethernet networks. Details like these are why it is important to have a performance team that incorporates all areas of technology.

> **TIP**: A good memory rule of thumb is to allocate 512 MB per application server on Win2000/NT and 768MB per application server on UNIX.

Understanding Optimization Issues

In the previous section, you learned that performance problems can occur because of the hardware configuration, the operating system settings, or your Web application server. So where should you begin if you encounter a problem? You basically have six decision points in the architecture that affect performance:

- Your application
- The operating system
- The Web server
- The JVM
- The application server
- The database

Your application could be a source of performance problems. Tuning your application is left up to you. In addition, there are many books on Java performance that can help you optimize your application.

The operating system settings are also something that is specific to your environment. Most likely someone in your organization is a specialist on your particular operation environment. This book does not discuss specific operating-system tuning parameters.

The rest of this section focuses on the last four decision points: the Web server, the JVM, the application server, and the database.

Optimizing from the outside in

Perhaps the best approach is one in which you can utilize existing optimization techniques and parameters to improve performances. Taking an outside-in approach starting from the HTTP server and continuing to work your way down to the application server is the suggested approach. Figure 24-20 shows a graphic suggesting the order of optimization.

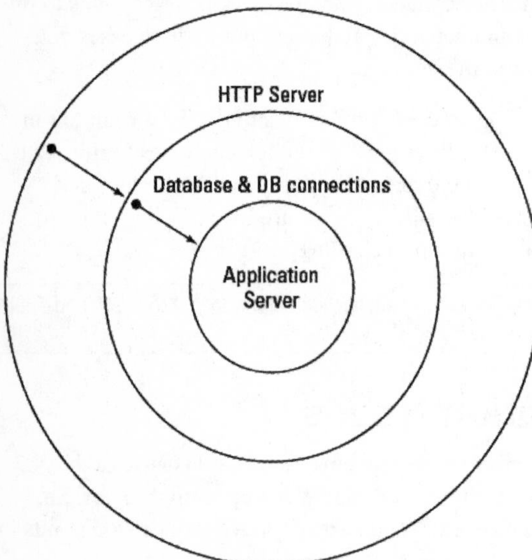

Figure 24-20: Checking performance from the outside in.

Figure 24-20 suggests starting with the HTTP server as your first decision point for optimization. After you have configured your HTTP server for optimal performance, you can investigate the next level (database and DB connections) and continue on until you finally reach the application server and JVM settings.

Optimizing HTTP server settings

WebSphere supports various HTTP servers. In this section, the discussion focuses on IBM HTTP Server, which is really just the Apache Web server with added support for SSL.

You have already learned that dynamic caching can improve response time, assuming that you actually remove the HTTP server from the same node as the application server. From an overall standpoint, separating your HTTP server from your application server is a good thing. By separating the HTTP server, you can add additional firewall support to improve security. Also depending upon your application, you can add additional HTTP servers to balance loads and reduce point-of-failure issues.

In addition to adding HTTP servers, you can install and configure a Network Dispatcher and incorporate the IP Sprayer to your environment. Some of the HTTP Server configuration (`httpd.conf`) parameters that impact performance are as follows:

- *MaxClients:* Limits the total number of simultaneous HTTP requests that the IBM HTTP Server (IHS) can serve. Because IHS uses one child server process for each HTTP request, this limits the number of child server processes that are able to run simultaneously. The default value is 150, and maximum value is 2048. The value of this directive can significantly impact your application performance, particularly if it is too high, so bigger is not necessarily better. Never increase if the CPU is at 100 percent. Try testing the application with the `MaxClients` setting at 40 or 60 and monitor its performance.
- *MinSpareServers (default 5), MaxSpareServers (default 10), and StartServers (default 5):* These three settings can also affect the performance of your application. For optimum performance, specify the same value for the `MaxSpareServers` and the `StartServers` parameters. As with `MaxClients`, bigger is not necessarily better. Specifying like values reduces the CPU usage for creating and destroying HTTPD processes. It pre-allocates and maintains the specified number of processes so that new processes are created and destroyed as the load approaches the specified number of processes (based on `MinSpareServers`).

You should initially start with `MaxClients` set to 50 and set `MaxSpareServers` and `StartServers` with the same value.

Optimizing the database

This section points out areas where performance improvements can result from database tuning. For a more in-depth study on database tuning, you should refer to one of the many books on database design and performance tuning.

CROSS-REFERENCE: For DB2 tuning, refer to the DB2 System Monitor Guide and Reference.

Tuning buffer pools

The database buffer pool is one tuning parameter where you can increase your cache hits. You should investigate adjusting the `DB2 BUFFPAGE` to optimize the buffer pool size.

Tuning database logs

Database logs impact performance in that they are another hit to the disk. With DB2, you adjust the `LOGBUFSZ` to obtain an optimal size.

Tuning database indexes

When designing and developing your own databases, indexes provide one of the best performance improvements. One area to investigate is your custom finder methods. You should add indexes to avoid full table scans for any of your custom finder methods.

Determining optimal location

The location of you database is extremely important. Databases generally require vast amounts of memory for buffer pools and the database engine. You should consider utilizing a separate server for the WebSphere repository and other databases.

Tuning the session persistence database

Using a strategy similar to the one for locating the WebSphere repository database, you configure a separate database for the session database when utilizing session persistence. You should also configure and tune separate data sources for session management.

Using prepared-statement caching

A prepared statement is a pre-compiled SQL statement that is stored in a prepared statement object. This object can then be used to efficiently execute the given SQL statement multiple times. Prepared-statement caching is a connection-pooling mechanism that can improve session database response times. There is a cache of previously prepared statements available on a connection. When a new database request using a prepared statement is issued on a connection, the cached prepared statement is returned if one exists. To calculate the size of cache, you can use the following formula:

```
Size = (total number of prepare statements) * min (number of concurrent
users, connection pool size)
```

You can set this parameter by using opening the Administrative Console and clicking Resources ⇨JDBC Providers⇨My Database Driver⇨Data Sources⇨Connection Pooling ⇨Statement cache size.

Tuning connection pooling

Each data source controls a set of database connections known as a connection pool. When accessing any database, the initial database connection is an expensive operation. WebSphere Application Server supports JDBC 2.0 Standard Extension APIs to provide support for connection pooling and connection reuse.

When you created data sources, you might have noticed that the default is 10 connections. The minimum is 1. The maximum size (10) can be viewed as the number of concurrent accesses to the database.

> **NOTE**: If you are using clones, one data source pool exists for each clone. This is important when configuring the database server maximum connections.

For best performance, having a large number of connections might not be appropriate. You should balance the number of connections versus the number of seconds you want a user to wait for a connection. Releasing connections promptly and keeping the number of connections small are both best practices. You may even consider making the minimum equal to the maximum. In addition, you can also run utilities, such Reorgchk and Runstats, to optimize the database access.

Tuning the JVM

The JVM offers several tuning parameters that can affect the performance of WebSphere Application Servers (which are primarily Java applications), as well as the performance of your own applications. In this section, you learn about the key JVM performance influencers and the parameters that adjust them:

- *JIT:* The Just In Time (JIT) compiler has been known to significantly affect performance. The JIT compiler is enabled as the default and should always be enabled.
- *Heap size:* Setting the heap size can also have an impact on performance. The heap is where all the new objects are allocated. The heap-size settings are used to set the maximum and the initial and maximum heap sizes for the JVM. Strive to increase the Java heap until the heap can no longer reside in memory. When it can no longer reside in memory, it is swapped to the disk. This disk IO reduces performance dramatically. Therefore, the maximum heap size needs to be low enough to contain the heap within physical memory. As a starting point, try a maximum heap of 128MB on a smaller machine (1GB of physical memory or less, 256MB for systems with 2GB memory), and 512MB for larger systems. You can use the JVM settings tab of the application server to set the following:
  - Initial Java heap size
  - Maximum Java heap size

> **TIP**: Keep in mind that you might be sharing memory with other JVMs and other applications. It's best to use a smaller heap on machines without a lot of physical memory

- *Garbage collection:* This is the process of cleaning up unused objects allocated within the Java Virtual Machine. The default behavior is to run with garbage collection on. In most cases, you want to run with class garbage collection turned on. To modify the setting for garbage collection, use the command-line property of the application server you configure in the administrative domain to set the JVM parameters:
  - In the Administrative Console, click the application server you are tuning.
  - Click the Services tab.
  - On the Advanced tab, click JVM Settings.
  - In Command Line Arguments, enter **-Xnoclassgc**.

Starting Java Virtual Machine Profiler Interface

Java Virtual Machine Profiler Interface (JVMPI) is a profiling tool that enables the collection of information, such as data about garbage collection or JVMs that run the application server.

JVMPI exchanges information between the JVM and an in-process profiler agent. The JVM notifies the profiler agent of various events, such as heap allocations and thread starts. In turn, the profiler agent can activate or deactivate specific event notifications, based on the needs of the profiler.

JVMPI supports partial profiling by enabling the user to choose which types of profiling information is to be collected and to select certain subsets of the time during which the JVM is active. JVMPI moderately increases the performance impact.

The JVM Profiler interface provides internal runtime performance data about the following resources:

- Garbage collector
- Number of garbage collection calls
- Average time in milliseconds between garbage collection calls
- Average duration in milliseconds of a garbage collection call monitor
- Number of times that a thread waits for a lock
- Average time that a thread waits for a lock object
- Number of objects allocated
- Number of objects freed from heap
- Number of objects moved in heap thread
- Number of threads started
- Number of threads terminated

You can start JVMPI for any application server. To start JVMPI you perform the following steps:

1. Select an application server from the Administrative Console.
2. Right-click the application server, and select Properties from the context menu.
3. In the window that appears, click the JVM Settings tab and click the Advanced Setting button.
4. The Advanced JVM Settings window opens.
5. In the Command line arguments field, type -**XrunpmiJvmpiProfiler**.
6. Click OK to close the Advanced JVM Settings window, and click OK again to close the Application Server Properties window.
7. Click Apply to apply the changes. You must then start or restart the application server.

> **NOTE**: To disable JVMPI, simply remove the JVM command-line argument.

Optimizing the Application Server

Up to this point you have been learning how optimize the individual components. The WebSphere Application Server process also has several parameters influencing application performance. Each application server in your WebSphere Application Server product comprises an enterprise bean container and a Web container.

Use the WebSphere Application Server Administrative Console to configure and tune applications, Web containers, enterprise bean containers, application servers, and nodes in your administrative domain. The following sections discuss the various parameters and how to set them.

Setting Web container maximum thread size

With WebSphere 4.0, communication between the Web server and the Web container requires the use of communication threads. Use the maximum thread size parameter to specify the number of connections to use for the communications channel between the Web server and a Web container. Each connection represents a request for a servlet. The following steps show you how to configure the maximum thread size:

1. In the Administrative Console, select the application server you are tuning and click the Services tab.
2. Click Web Container Service and click Edit Properties.
3. In the Web Container Service window, click the General tab.
4. Specify the value in the Maximum Thread Size field.
5. Click Apply after returning to the Web Container Service window to ensure that the changes are saved.
6. Stop and restart the application server.

Setting the URL invocation cache

The invocation cache holds information for mapping request URLs to servlet resources. A cache of the requested size is created for each thread/process. The number of threads/processes is determined by the Web container maximum thread size setting.

The size of the cache can be specified for the application server along with other JDK parameters by performing the following steps:

1. In the Administrative Console, click the application server you are tuning.
2. Click the JVM Setting tab.
3. On the same panel, click Add in the System Properties section.

4. Add the name **DinvocationCacheSize** and a value of **50**.
5. Click Apply to ensure that the changes are saved.
6. Stop and restart the application server.

Deploying parameters for Web applications

You learned that you could create multiple application servers to balance the workload and improve performance. For each Web application you deploy, you can set parameters that affect performance.

Through the Reload Interval and Reloading Enabled servlets, WebSphere Application Server offers an auto-reload capability. The default automatically reloads servlets in the Web application when the class files change.

The Reload Interval and Reloading Enabled servlets can be set for your application by using the Application Assembler from the Administrative Console. When creating a new Web module, you can configure these parameters by selecting the IBM extensions and performing the following steps:

1. Uncheck the Reloading Enabled box.
2. Update the Reload Interval field.

Optimizing the EJB container

You can optimize the EJB container in a number of areas:

- *Object Request Broker thread pool size:* This item represents the size of the thread pool. To change these settings, start in the Administrative Console, and click the appropriate application server. Click the Services tab. Select Object Request Broker and then Edit Properties. The thread pool size is on the General Properties panel.
- *Cache settings:* To determine a rough approximation of the cache absolute limit, multiply the number of enterprise beans active in any given transaction by the total number of concurrent transactions expected. Then add the number of active session bean instances. To change these settings, select the application server on which you want to make changes. Edit the EJB container service properties for the application server you are tuning.
- *Deployment descriptors:* When creating deployment descriptors for your entity beans, pay close attention to the beans' functions, and define your descriptors accordingly. When it is appropriate for the requirements of an application, set an entity bean's method to read-only in the deployment descriptor. For each enterprise bean, the commit options are configured using the Activate at and Load at settings:
    - Commit Option A
    - Commit Option B
    - Commit Option C

CROSS-REFERENCE: See Chapter 22 for more information on EJB caching.

- *Security:* When security is enabled, performance can be degraded between 10 and 20 percent. Therefore, it is practical to disable security when you do not need it.

NOTE: Security is a global setting.

- *ORB:* Several settings are available for controlling internal ORB processing. Use these to improve application performance in the case of applications containing enterprise beans.

Setting pass-by-value versus pass-by-reference (NoLocalCopies)

The EJB 1.1 specification states that method calls are pass-by-value. Pass-by-value means that for every remote method call, the parameters are copied onto the stack before the call is made. This can be expensive. It is possible to specify pass-by-reference, which passes the original object reference without making a copy of the object.

To set up pass-by-reference, set these parameters:

1. Select the application server you want to update and then use the Services tab and click Edit Properties.
2. Click the Advanced tab.
3. Check the Pass by Reference and click OK.
4. Click Apply to save the changes.
5. Stop and restart the application server.

Introducing Introscope

One tool that takes advantage of the Performance Monitoring Infrastructure (PMI) is Introscope by Wily Technology. Introscope is a Java Web application management solution. You can monitor performance of any Java Web application in real-time whether it is in testing or production. Figure 24-21 shows a WebSphere Performance dashboard that you can configure using Introscope.

Most likely you don't have a copy of Introscope, so you can skip to the next section or continue reading about what Introscope can do. Introscope is made up of several components. The base product performs typical application and OS-level performance monitoring. Following are some of the monitored components:

- Monitor critical WebSphere resources
  - Servlet threads pool
  - JDBC connections pool
  - HTTP sessions

- Manage system resources
  - CPU utilization
  - GC heap usage
  - Sockets input/output bandwidth
  - File input/output rate
  - JDBC query/update performance
- Fine-tune application performance
  - Optimal WebSphere configuration
  - EJBs, servlets, JSPs, and more
- Seamless integration with Introscope
  - Zero development effort
  - Inherits Introscope features, such as Blame, Dashboard views, Alerts and Historical Reporting

Figure 24-22 shows Introscope displaying information about JDBC connections.

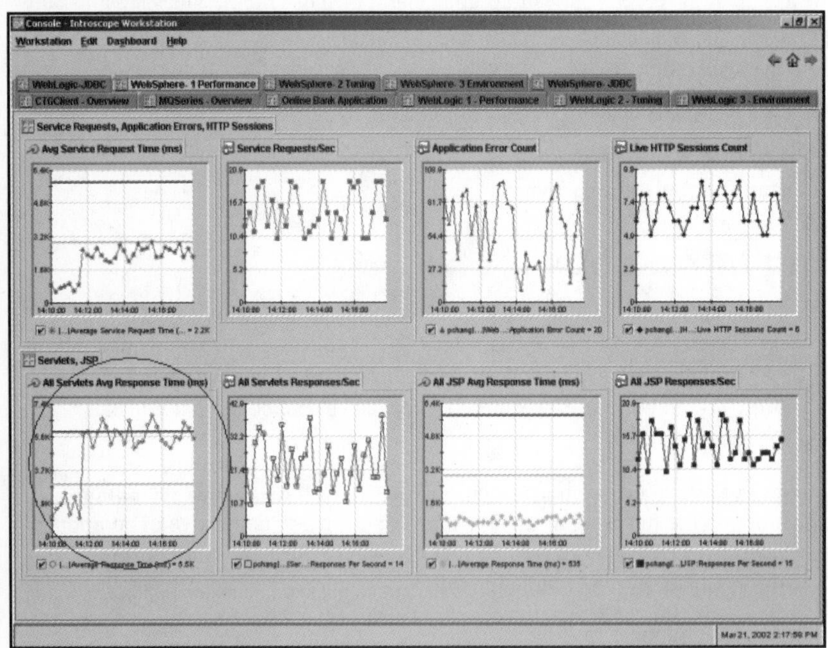

Figure courtesy of Wily Technology.

Figure 24-21: With Introscope, you can measure performance on a number of components. The circled area show the average response time for all servlets.

> **ON THE WEB**: Visit `www.wilytech.com` for more information about Introscope.

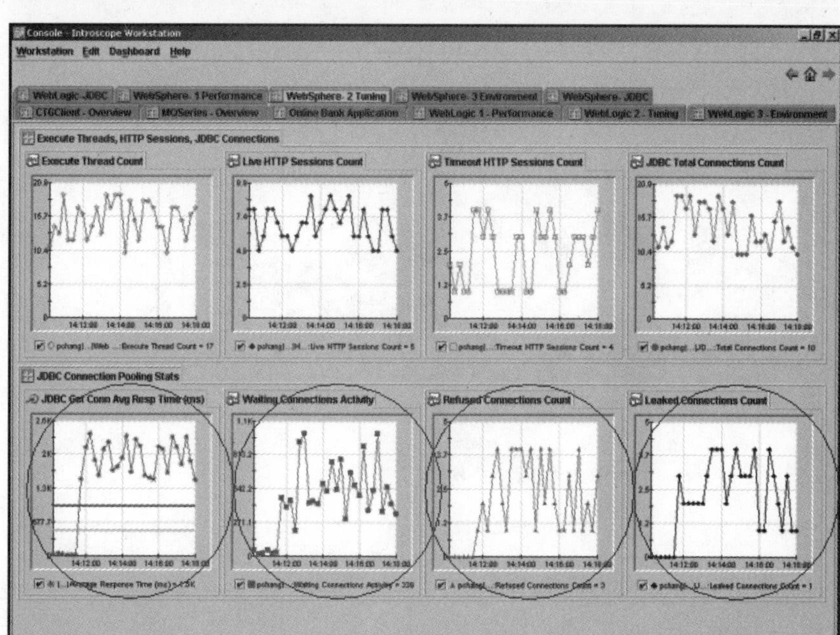

Figure courtesy of Wily Technology.

Figure 24-22: JDBC monitoring with Introscope. The circled areas are showing the impact of JDBC and its connection pool.

As the graphs show, response time increases as users wait for a connection. This might dictate a configuration change in the number of connections. Introscope enables customers to pinpoint and eliminate performance bottlenecks whether inside the application, the application server, or anywhere in any of the connected back-end systems. Introscope helps you to ensure high performance and availability of your mission-critical Web applications.

Introducing Panorama

Another product similar to Introscope is Altaworks Panorama. Built on top of J2EE, Panorama manages key performance indicators of real-time, distributed applications and infrastructure. Similar to Introscope, Panorama monitors live transactions in a production environment. Taking as little as 3 percent of the CPU, Panorama attempts to get to the root of a problem. Figure 24-23 shows how Panorama key features.

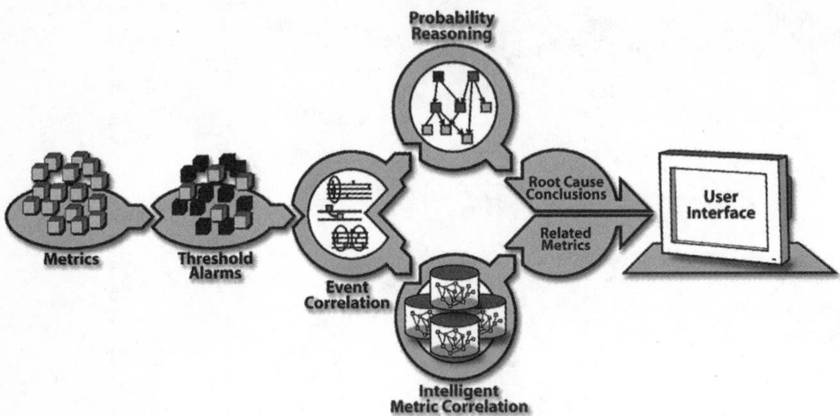

Figure courtesy of Altaworks Corporation.

Figure 24-23: Panorama is unique in that it uses probability reasoning to diagnose the root cause of the problem.

Perhaps the most unique feature of Panorama is its use of probability reasoning to analyze situations and provide a root cause of the problem. So instead of looking at metrics and determining what the problem might be, Panorama provides a probable cause. This feature provides the novice and experienced administrations with probable causes and helps take the guess work out of problem-solving, complex topologies. Panorama supports the following metrics:

- Servlets
  - Individual average and maximum response time
  - Requests started per second
  - Requests completed per second
  - Exceptions per second
- EJBs
  - Individual average and maximum response time
  - Requests started per second
  - Requests completed per second

- Exceptions per second
- Activiation
- Passivation

♦ JDBC

- Database response time
- Connections opened per second
- Connections closed per second
- Database requests started per second
- Database requests completed per second

♦ JNDI

- Average lookup response time
- Enumerations started per second
- Enumerations completed per second
- Average enumerations response time
- Updates started per second
- Updates completed per second
- Lookups completed per second

With these features, the benefits to your business are realized by promoting customer satisfaction, saving troubleshooting time to resolve problems, and establishing baselines for transaction performance.

> **ON THE WEB**: Visit `www.altaworks.com` for more information about Panorama.

Summary

Achieving optimal performance for your application is possible with WebSphere Application Server 4.0. Although it is achievable, it is not possible without some good investigative research. To utilize some of the built-in features of WebSphere to be able to manage workload and prevent failover, you need to be able to understand your environment and come to grips with your requirements for performance and service.

Understanding these requirements enables you to take advantage of alternative topologies and server group and clones. A server group is a template of an application server that gives the administrator the ability to manage a group of application servers. The template application can be cloned and distributed vertically or horizontally. When implementing vertical cloning, you create additional clones within the same machine. Operating as separate JVMs, vertical cloning provides you with better performance and some failover support.

When using horizontal cloning, you distribute the application server to many nodes within the same WebSphere domain. You achieve added protection against a loss of a server when you utilize horizontal cloning.

The Administrative Console provides wizards that enable you to create server groups and clones easily. This chapter stepped you through a tutorial in which you created a vertical clone and another tutorial in which you set up a horizontal clone.

Although server groups and clones provide some performance improvements, you can improve performance by optimizing many other settings. By taking an outside-in approach you can begin looking for performance improvements on the products closer to the user and work your way towards the final optimization of the application server.

WebSphere Edge Server provides caching and proxy services to improve the processing of servlets that can be cached. It reduces the number of hops a request must make to provide the proper response. With the proper configurations of two XML files, you can identify servlets that are cacheable.

This chapter finished with discussions on optimizing the application server components (Web Container, EJB Container, JVM, and database.)

Chapter 25
Using the Resource Analyzer

In This Chapter

- Introducing the Resource Analyzer
- Tracking Web resources and enterprise beans
- Running a Resource Analyzer example

This chapter introduces you to one tool that enables you to monitor the performance of the WebSphere Application Server. That tool is the Resource Analyzer.

You learn about the features of the Resource Analyzer, how data is collected, how you select the performance data to monitor and analyze, and how to save it so you can execute the analyzer offline to investigate problems without impacting response times.

Introducing the Resource Analyzer

The Resource Analyzer is a standalone performance monitor for WebSphere Application Server version 4.0 Advanced Edition (AE). The Resource Analyzer provides performance information on WebSphere resources and runtime by periodically polling the Administrative Server. Data is collected continuously and is retrieved as needed from within the Resource Analyzer.

You can specify the level of data collected by using the Resource Analyzer or the WebSphere Advanced Administrative Console. You view the data through the analyzer's graphical user interface from a stored log file.

Analyzer provides a wide range of performance data for two kinds of resources:

- WebSphere resources (for example, Enterprise JavaBeans (EJB) and servlets)
- Runtime resources (for example, Java Virtual Machine (JVM) memory, application server-thread pools, and database-connection pools)

You can accomplish the following things with the Resource Analyzer:

- View performance data in real time
- Record performance information into a log file
- Monitor and estimate the load on application servers and the average wait time for clients.
- View historical performance data from the log file
- View information captured in a chart
- Perform a comparison evaluation for a single resource to a group of resources on a single node

Data collection and online reporting affects the performance of your distributed applications. You can collect the information at specified intervals, but this is not by default. You must specify the details of information you want captured for each resource you want to monitor. Information detail is segregated by high-impact and low-impact data. The selection of the type of data collected has a direct impact on performance.

Performance data includes statistical data, such as the response time for each method invocation of an EJB, and load data, such as the average size of a database-connection pool.

Figure 25-1 shows an overview of the Resource Analyzer.

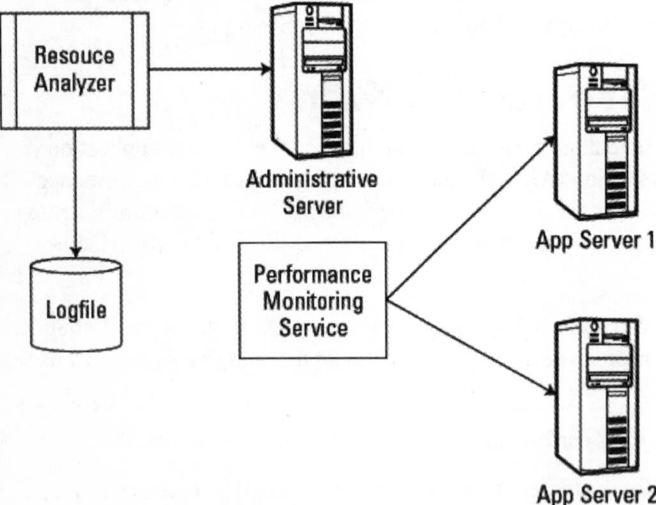

Figure 25-1: The Resource Analyzer has the capability to gather information from application servers using the Performance Monitoring service. It outputs information to a log file for future reference.

Figure 25-1 shows that the Resource Analyzer is a standalone product that accesses the Administrative Server to gather information on application servers. In this case two application servers are available for monitoring.

The data is gathered using the Performance Monitoring Infrastructure (PMI) Application Programming Interface (API). The PMI APIs provide you with the capability to develop your own performance-monitoring tools.

Understanding tracking

You can ask the analyzer to collect and report performance data on the following resources:

- *Java Runtime:* Reports memory used by a process as reported by the JVM — for example, the total memory available and/or the amount of free memory for the JVM.
- *Database connection pools:* Gathers the average size of the connection pool (number of connections), the average wait time for a connection to be granted, and the average time the connection was in use.
- *EJBs:* Reports the average number of active beans and the average number of methods being processed concurrently. You would use this to understand the lifecycle impacts on your EJBs.
- *EJB methods:* Reports the number of times a method is called and the average response time for the method.
- *Enterprise bean object pools:* Monitors the size and usage of a bean's cache object, reporting information such as the number of calls attempting to retrieve an object from a pool, or the number of times an object is found available in the pool.
- *Transactions:* Reports transaction information for the container — for instance, the average number of active transactions, the average duration of transactions, and the average number of methods per transaction.
- *Web Applications:* Captures and reports information about a specific server. Examples include the average number of concurrent requests for a servlet, the amount of time it takes for a servlet to perform a request, the number of loaded servlets in a Web application, and the average number of concurrently active HTTP sessions.

Understanding performance data organization

The Resource Analyzer organizes performance data in a hierarchy of groups. A *group* is a set of statistics, or counters, associated with a particular resource. The hierarchy has the following objects:

- *Node:* Represents a physical machine
- *Server:* Represents a server that provides functionality over a network
- *Module:* Represents one or more resource catagories (EJB, connection pools, JVM, and so on)

- *Method:* A software operation within a Java class
- *Servlet:* A Java program that provides dynamic capabilities to a Web server.
- *Counter:* A data type used to hold performance data

No performance data is gathered on the node or the server; they serve only as ways to organize the data. Perhaps the best way to learn more is to actually run the Resource Analyzer and gather some information.

Starting the Resource Analyzer

There are three ways you can start the Resource Analyzer:

- From the Administrative Console
- From the Program Start menu
- From the command line

Most of the Resource Analyzer's features require that the Administrative Server be running. You should ensure that you have started the Administrative Server.

Starting from the Administrative Console

If you do not have the Administrative Console running, start it now.

You can start the Resource Analyzer by selecting Tools⇨Resource Analyzer from the action bar, as shown in Figure 25-2.

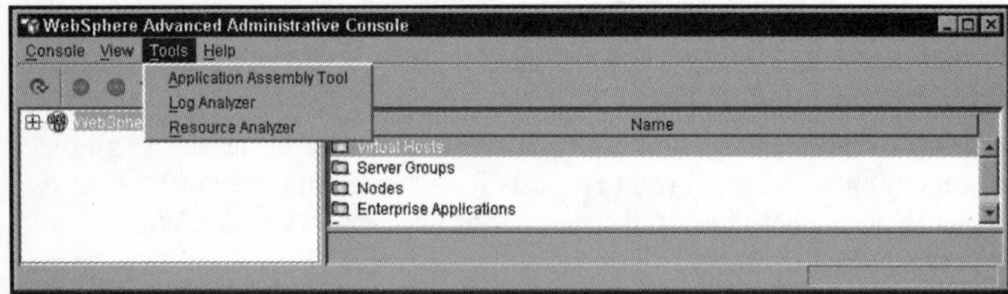

Figure 25-2: The Tools menu offers the Resource Analyzer, Log Analyzer. and Application Assembly Tool.

Selecting this option launches the Resource Analyzer in a separate window. To begin monitoring, you should ensure that the application servers are started.

Starting from the Start Programs menu

You can start the Resource Analyzer from the Start menu. As with any other menu installed on Win2000 you simply select Start⇨Programs⇨IBM WebSphere⇨Application Server V4.0 AE⇨Resource Analyzer.

Starting the Resource Analyzer with this method assumes that the Administrative Server is started. If it is not started, you can start it by clicking Start⇨Programs⇨IBM WebSphere⇨Application Server V4.0 AE⇨Start Admin Server.

Starting from the command prompt

The final way to invoke the Resource Analyzer is from the command prompt. The batch file used to start the Resource Analyzer is `ra.bat`. The file is found in `<WAS_HOME>/bin`.

When you start a command prompt, you need to pass the Resource Analyzer the host name and port address or the system defaults to a host name of localhost and port 900. Using this method, as well as the others previously mentioned, launches the Resource Analyzer in a separate window.

> **NOTE**: You can start the Resource Analyzer without having the Administrative Server started if you just want to replay log files

If you start the Resource Analyzer using either the Start Program option or the command line, you might encounter the following warning message:

```
PMON3002W: The WebSphere admin server is not running. Please start the
admin server if you want to use the Resource Analyzer to display current
data. The server is not required for replaying log files.
```

This warning message lets you know that the Resource Analyzer could not find the Administrative Server running. You do not need to have it running if you are replaying previously captured information. Selecting OK enables you to continue with the Resource Analyzer. If you want to do more than replay log files, close the Resource Analyzer, start the Administrative Server, and then restart the Resource Analyzer.

If all has gone well, you should be presented with the Resource Analyzer console.

Understanding the Resource Analyzer Console

Figure 25-3 shows the Resource Analyzer console. The look and feel of this window is similar to the Administrative Console. To the left is the Resource Selection pane. The Data Monitoring pane is to the right, and the Counter Selection pane is on the bottom right.

The node (`kafemocha`) is highlighted with a green arrow to signify that the node is running and available A red X beside the AlmostFreeCruise server means that the node (or server in this case) is stopped.

The following icon colors indicate whether data is being collected for a resource:

- *Blue:* Data is being collected.
- *Red:* Data is not being collected.

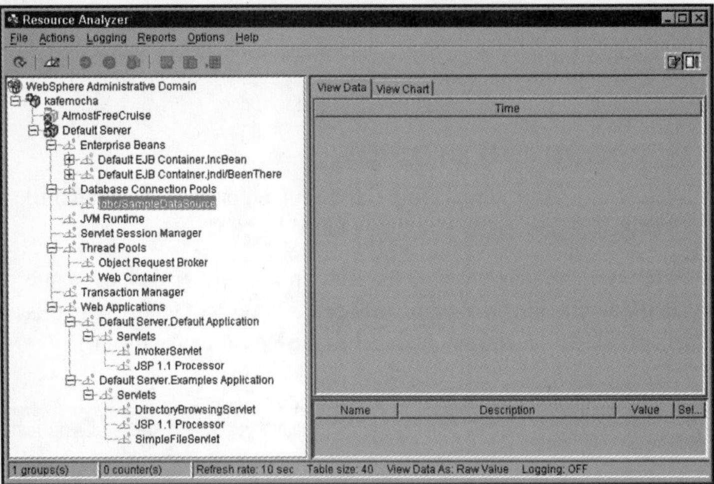

Figure 25-3: Use the Resource Selection pane to select resources to analyze within the Resource Analyzer console.

Using the Resource Selection pane

In Figure 25-3 on the Resource Selection pane, you see the node (`kafemocha`). This first level of the hierarchy contains the nodes within the WebSphere domain. In this case, you are working locally, so there is only one node.

Beneath the node are two application servers (`AlmostFreeCruise` and `Default Server`). Below each application server, all the resources are listed. You can expand and collapse the resources to display the information.

If you drill down the Web Application branch, you can see various application modules installed. Drilling down further, you can see the servlets contained within these modules.

When you click an individual bean or container instance that is being monitored, the corresponding counters are displayed in the Data Monitoring pane. Different counters are displayed depending upon type.

Using the Data Monitoring pane

The Data Monitoring pane, shown on the right side in Figure 25-4, contains two panels:

- Data Display panel (top right)
- Counter Selection panel (bottom right)

These two panels show details from the Snoop servlet. The Snoop servlet only shows up in the Resource Selection pane after you run the Snoop servlet in the browser.

> **TIP**: To see a servlet display in the Resource Selection pane, you need to run the servlet.

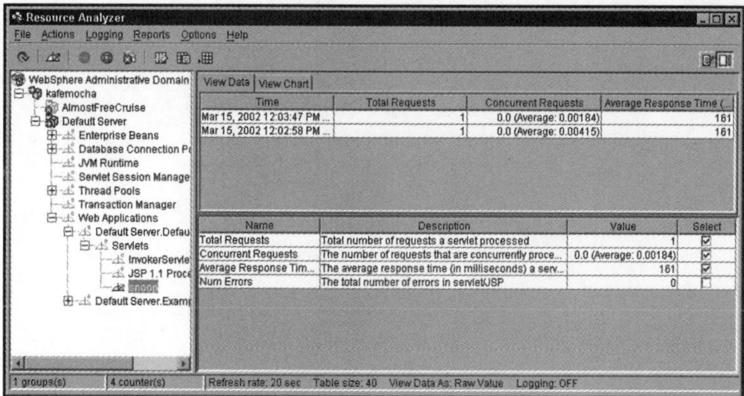

Figure 25-4: After selecting a servlet to monitor, the data display gathers statistics about the servlet. Here you see the Snoop servlet statistics in the Data Monitoring pane.

The Counter Selection pane shows the counters available for selection from the Resource Selection pane. In this case, it's the Snoop servlet. After you select a counter, the statistics gathered from the counter are displayed in the Data Display pane (top right in Figure 25-4). You can view the Data Display pane in either a table or chart view. You switch the views by selecting the appropriate tabs.

If multiple resources are selected, the Data Monitoring pane displays a single data sheet for viewing summary information. The data sheet groups similar resources. For instance, if you select seven servlets instead of just the Snoop servlet, the data panel shows a table of counters for all the servlets.

Understanding instrumentation levels

The last bit of introductory material is the instrumentation level. The instrumentation level determines which counters are available to be collected. Depending upon the level, this is where performance might be impacted. Counters with a low rating have little performance impact, but counters with high values can significantly impact performance.

You use the Performance Monitoring Settings dialog box to set the instrumentation levels. (See Figure 25-5.) You can access this dialog box from either the Resource Analyzer console or the WebSphere Administrative Console.

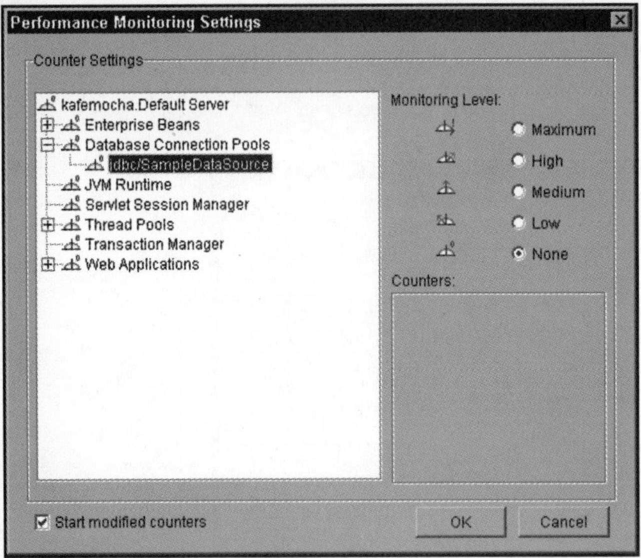

Figure 25-5: You can choose which resources to monitor by using the Performance Monitoring Settings panel. The Performance Monitoring settings can be adjusted to four levels from Maximum to Low, or you can choose None.

To access the settings from the Resource Analyzer, simply right-click the resource and choose Monitoring Settings. To access the settings from the Administrative Console, right-click the resource you are interested in from the resource topology tree and select the Services tab. Highlight Performance Monitoring Settings and select Edit Properties.

NOTE: The information set for the instrumentation level is stored in the administrative repository.

The monitor levels are shown on the right. When you select a resource and apply a level, the level is applied recursively to all elements below the selected resource. Maximum makes all counters available and increases granularity. A monitoring level of Low sets only counters that have low impact. You have your choice of Maximum, High, Medium, Low, or None.

Setting a level at a root element means each child can have a level equal to or lower than the setting set in the parent. Using Figure 25-5 as an example, if the Database Connection Pools element is set to Medium, the `jdbc/SampleDataSource` element can be set to Medium or Low, but never Maximum or High.

Running an Example

Perhaps the best way to learn is with an example. In this section, you utilize the Snoop servlet as the resource to monitor. Start by ensuring that the Administrative Server is running. After the server starts, start the Administrative Console. When the console is running perform the following steps:

1. Expand Nodes and select your node.
2. Expand Application Servers and select Default Server. Information about the Default Server displays on the right side. Select the Services tab. Figure 25-6 shows a graphic of these steps.

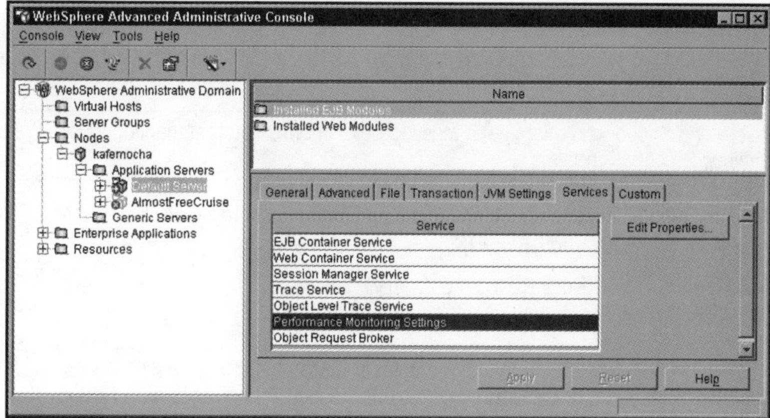

Figure 25-6: To select the Performance monitoring settings, you need to select an application server and choose Services to configure the resources to monitor.

3. Click the Edit Properties button.
4. Check the Enable Performance Counter Monitoring check box.
5. Select the Performance counter in Counter settings if it is not already selected. You perform these steps to enable performance monitoring on WebSphere Application Server.
6. Click OK and Apply to apply the changes and store the information in the administrative repository
7. Now you start the Resource Analyzer from the Administrative Console, by selecting Tools⇨Resource Analyzer.
8. When the Resource Analyzer is started, expand the node and expand Default Server.
9. You collect data on the Snoop servlet in this example. Because collecting data impacts performance, be careful which level you choose. You should open a browser and enter the following to launch the Snoop servlet:

```
http://localhost:9080/servlet/snoop
```

Information begins being collected after you set the monitoring for the Default Server. To set the monitoring levels with the Resource Analyzer, right-click the Default Server and select Monitoring Settings. The monitoring settings enable you to specify how much detail to collect.

The Performance Monitoring Settings dialog box opens. So far you haven't set monitoring levels for any resource under Default Server. Close the Performance Monitoring Settings dialog box and then perform the following steps:

1. Expand the node.
2. Expand Default Server.
3. Expand Web Applications.
4. Expand Default Server.Default Application.
5. Expand Servlets and select Snoop. (If you do not see the Snoop servlet, highlight the node, right-click, and select Refresh. Keep in mind that you may not see Snoop until after it runs.)

NOTE: Upon selecting Snoop, you might get a message that informs you that monitoring is not enabled. Select Yes and check Do not ask again.

6. Figure 25-7 shows the Performance Monitoring Settings dialog box. Set the Monitoring Level from None to High and click OK.

   You should be returned to the Resource Analyzer console. You are now ready to start gathering reporting data.

7. In the left pane of the Resource Analyzer console, select the Snoop servlet again. Right-click and select Start (if it is not already started). In a few seconds, data begins showing up on the Data Monitoring panes. Figure 25-8 shows the results.
8. On the Options menu, try changing the Refresh Rate to 5 seconds. Select Options⇨Set Refresh Rate. In the dialog box that opens, change the number to **5** and click OK.

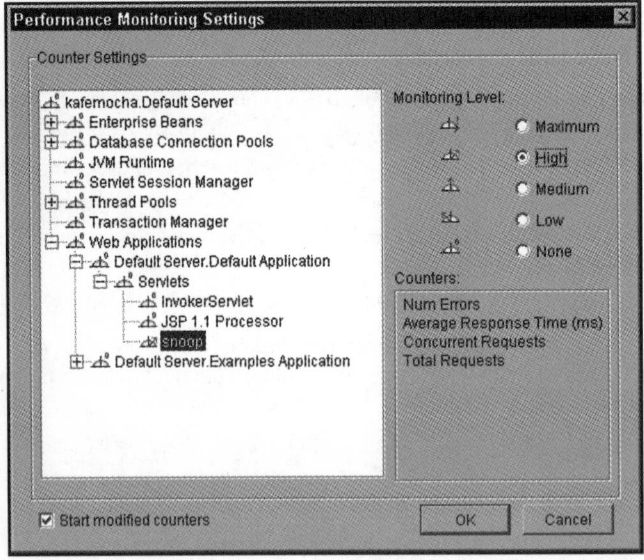

Figure 25-7: When you select a particular servlet ,you can adjust the monitoring level.

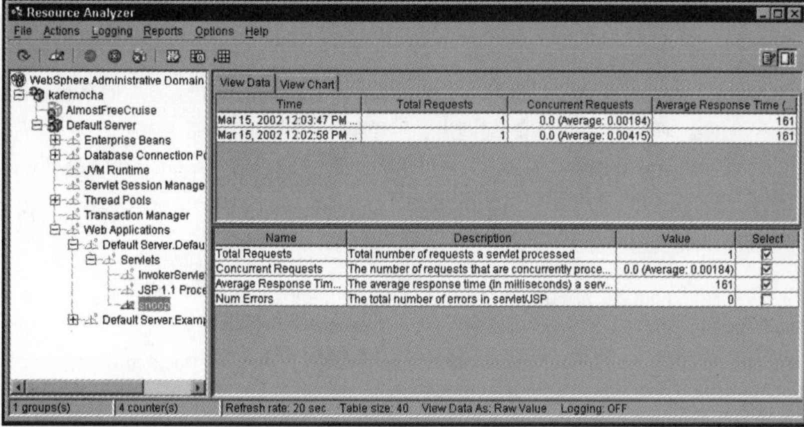

Figure 25-8: Results are displayed in the View Data panel

In Figure 25-8, you can see that the information shows zero requests. Try using the Refresh button on your browser to reload Snoop multiple times. Now take a look at the data and see the results. If you want to remove the data shown, right-click Snoop, and select Clear Values.

Logging and replaying data

The final feature you need to understand is how to log and replay the log file. You might want to replay a log file to ensure that performance is not impacted for long periods of time as you investigate performance and resource issues.

1. To beginning logging, you simply select Logging On in the Resource Analyzer console. A Save dialog box asks where you want to put the log file. Log files end with the extension of `.LRA`. You should enter a filename, for example `RALogExample` and click OK.
2. The next step is to provide some logging information. Try rerunning the Snoop servlet again. If you reload it multiple times, it should provide you with enough information to play with.

> **TIP**: Logfiles have an extension of .LRA and are stored in `<was_home>\logs`.

After refreshing the servlet a number of times in the browser, turn off logging by selecting Logging Off. Close the Resource Analyzer and answer Yes if any questions are displayed.

To Replay the log file, start the Resource Analyzer from the command prompt. You don't need to have the Administrative Server running to run the Resource Analyzer for replaying logs:

1. To start the Resource Analyzer, type **ra** in a Windows command prompt. When the Resource Analyzer is started, open the log using File⇨Open Log File.
2. Navigate to where you saved your log file; select it, and click Open. You see three buttons that govern the actions on the log file:
   - Play
   - Stop
   - Rewind
3. Expand the Node (your machine), Default Server, Web Applications and Default Server.Default Application. Then expand Servlets and select snoop.
4. Click Play. The events are replayed every 10 seconds. Let it run for a couple of passes and then click Stop. Try setting the replay speed to another number. Select Options⇨Play Speed, and set it to 20x. This replays the log 20 times faster. Click Play again and watch the results.

That covers the major components of the Resource Analyzer. Try to monitor some other objects on your own.

Summary

The Resource Analyzer is a tool you can use to monitor the activity on WebSphere Application Server. It runs at specified intervals and captures information related to the resources you have selected.

You might use the Resource Analyzer to check performance on JVMs, database connections, EJBs, and so on. You can place all the information that you collect in log files for future reference. Log files end with an extension of .LRA and are found in `<was_home>\logs`.

The Resource Analyzer contains a hierarchy of objects that begin with a node. Other components within the hierarchy are servers, modules, methods, servlets and counters.

You can start the Resource Analyzer in three ways: from the Administrative Console, from the command line, and from the Start menu.

After you learned what the Resource Analyzer does, you were walked through some examples that illustrated the features that the Resource Analyzer provides.

Chapter 26
Troubleshooting WebSphere

In This Chapter

- ♦ Understanding the types of error logs
- ♦ Using logs to resolve problems
- ♦ Using the Administrative Console to spot high-level problems
- ♦ Using Log Analyzer
- ♦ Using the distribute debugger and object-level trace
- ♦ Understanding and running traces
- ♦ Stepping through the troubleshooting process

In this chapter, you are reacquainted with your old adversary Murphy's Law: If anything can go wrong, it will. Just when you think you have everything under control, up pops Murphy and problems appear. Battling your old nemesis is not as difficult as it was before. You have an arsenal of tools to help you find where the problem is occurring and stop the uprising. In this chapter, you learn about those tools and how to infiltrate the source and neutralize Murphy. You learn about the following tools:

- ♦ Logs that help you identify and find the source of a problem, such as the administrative logs (activity.log and tracefile)
- ♦ Tools like Log Analyzer and Trace facility
- ♦ Error messages that point out problems

You engage Murphy head on. Your campaign may be hard fought, but you shall persevere. As they said in the1970's television show *The Six Million Dollar Man*, "We have the tools and the technology. . . ."

As you work your way through this chapter, you are first introduced to the logs that help you identify the problem. There are logs for the Web server, the Administrative Server, individual Application servers, and database logs. You learn about each of these and how they relate. You will also become more familiar with the Administrative Console and how error messages are presented. You learn how to filter some of the error messages so you don't become overwhelmed by messages.

Finally, you are introduced to Log Analyzer and Trace facilities, and you actually perform the steps necessary to utilize the tools.

Determining Problems

Murphy has struck. He has covertly undermined your WebSphere environment into a sea of console messages, stack traces, and useless error messages. Even though the blitzkrieg seems daunting, you are resilient, and this chapter helps you outflank Murphy with your superior knowledge and WebSphere's superior tooling.

Your arsenal of tools is comprised of a number of devices that enable you to observe the symptoms and diagnose the problem. For instance, you have at your disposal a set of log files that output installation results, error conditions and warnings, and Java stack traces and messages. You also have at your disposal the means to start up and/or adjust the output by fine-tuning the underpinnings of the WebSphere Administrative Server and application servers. You have the following error informants at your disposal:

- Logs
- Console messages
- Pop-up messages
- Trace

You have the following investigative espionage tools to ferret out the offending incidents:

- Log Analyzer
- Distributed Debugger and OLT
- Trace facility

You can add the following additional tools to add to your quiver:

- Java Database Connectivity testing tool (JDBCtest)
- Java Naming and Directory Interface (JNDI) namespace tool (DumpNameSpace)

You should become familiar with the tools at your disposal prior to starting your investigative expedition.

Introducing logs

Logs are your first line of defense against problems. WebSphere provides many logs that give you information about progress, status, and problems. This section discusses logs and the information they possess. Table 26-1 lists, by component, the logs available to you.

Table 26-1: WebSphere's Informational Logs

Log Name	***Log Source***
Wasdb2.log	CreateDB.bat
Wssetup.log	Setup.exe
Access.log	IBM HTTP Server
Error.log	IBM HTTP Server
Native.log	Plug-in
Adminserver-stderr.log	Administrative Server
tracefile	Administrative Server
Activity.log	Administrative Server
Stderr.log	Application Server
Stdout.log	Application Server
Default-server-stderr.log	Default Application Server
Default-server-stdout.log	Default Application Server

You can see in Table 26-1 that there are a number of categories of log files. You have logs from the supporting products (HTTP Server and DB2), and logs that provide administrative information, as well as logs that contain information from the applications (application servers) you have written.

Because the logs are acting as agents on your behalf, you can have them output more information to help you pinpoint a problem. You can adjust the level of the output by updating the logging property file. The logging property file is found in `<was home>\properties`. Several properties are specified in the logging property file. Each property is documented. The one you should adjust is `com.ibm.ws.ras.MessageFilterLevel`. Following is a list of the valid values:

- *Audit (default):* Use this value to cause all messages to be logged.
- *Error:* Use this value to report severity errors. Severe errors represent abnormally terminated errors that have occurred within a process. Neither audit nor warning messages are reported.
- *Warning:* Use this value to report both severity errors or warnings. Warnings indicate a problem has occurred and should be corrected. With Warnings, Audit messages are not logged

As you are learning WebSphere, you may want to maintain the default of Audit, but as you become more proficient with WebSphere, you might want to change the settings to either Warning or Error.

Understanding installation logs

Installation problems always seem to be a mystery. If you are new to WebSphere and are installing it for the first time, errors that crop up are always baffling. You don't know where to go to research the error, and you don't know the cause. In Chapter 4, you learn how to install WebSphere. What you learn there could reduce potential installation errors. If you haven't read Chapter 4, you may want to read it before you install.

Having errors out of the box may be unfortunate especially for a novice, but this section helps you find the confidence to resolve such errors. You begin by leaning about two logs that are associated with installation — `wssetup.log` and `wasdb2.log`:

- *wssetup.log:* This log is created during processing of `setup.exe`. As with most log files, `wssetup.log` is found in `<was home>\logs`. You refer to this log file if you receive errors during the installation or have problems starting the Administrative Server. Wssetup provides information pertaining to the following:
  - Hardware configuration
  - Software prerequisites present (IBM HTTP Server, DB2, and so on)
  - Configuration of the Administrative Server
- *wasdb2.log:* You may recall from Chapter 4, that the WAS40 database is created when you restart your system. When the `createDB2.bat` file runs, the Administrative database is created and configured. Listing 26-1 shows the contents of the `wasdb2.log` file. Your investigation might lead to this file when you are having problems starting the Administrative Server.

Listing 26-1: wasdb2.log Showing DB2 Commands and Resulting Output

```
db2start
SQL1026N  The database manager is already active.

CREATE DATABASE was40
DB20000I  The CREATE DATABASE command completed successfully.

UPDATE DB CFG FOR was40 USING APPLHEAPSZ 256
DB20000I  The UPDATE DATABASE CONFIGURATION command completed
successfully.
DB21026I  For most configuration parameters, all applications must
disconnect from this database before the changes become effective.
```

To determine whether a problem is database related, you have to utilize some of the other logs to get a clearer picture.

Understanding Administrative Server logs

Installation problems can prevent you from starting the Administrative Server, but other conditions can also cause problems.

The Administrative Server maintains three logs to help you monitor progress and errors:

- _adminserverFatalError.log
- tracefile
- adminserver-stderr.log

The adminserverFatalError log is one of the first places to look for errors with the Administrative Server. Sometimes, you might hear it referred to as the Serious Error log. Listing 26-2 shows an example of a fatal database error that prevents the Administrative Server from starting. You can view these logs using your favorite editor.

Listing 26-2: A Database Error Contained within adminserverFatalError.log

```
[02.02.13 21:14:19:146 PST] 15afa2f9 DBMgr F SMTL0026E: Failure to
create a data source: COM.ibm.db2.jdbc.DB2Exception: [IBM][CLI Driver]
SQL1032N  No start database manager command was issued.  SQLSTATE=57019
 at
COM.ibm.db2.jdbc.app.SQLExceptionGenerator.throw_SQLException(SQLExcepti
onGenerator.java:174)
 at
COM.ibm.db2.jdbc.app.SQLExceptionGenerator.check_return_code(SQLExceptio
nGenerator.java:431)
 at COM.ibm.db2.jdbc.app.DB2Connection.connect(DB2Connection.java:445)
 at COM.ibm.db2.jdbc.app.DB2Connection.<init>(DB2Connection.java:354)
 at
COM.ibm.db2.jdbc.app.DB2ReusableConnection.<init>(DB2ReusableConnection.
java:66)
 at
COM.ibm.db2.jdbc.DB2PooledConnection.getConnection(DB2PooledConnection.j
ava:183)
```

When a serious error occurs, WebSphere creates the serious error file with the following naming format:

```
<server_process_name>FatalError<ts>.log
```

`<server_process_name>` is the name of the server process that encountered the fatal error, and `<ts>` is a timestamp when the fatal error occurred. You can find this file located in the `<was_home>\logs` folder.

Do you want to know how the Administrative Server starts and stops? The tracefile logs the startup and shutdown of the Administrative Server. Listing 26-3 shows an example of a tracefile. It is one of the best places to find out where the problem is happening, because it shows the events that precede the error. You can find this file located in the `<was_home>\logs` folder. View it with WordPad.

Listing 26-3: tracefile Showing a Database Error When the Database Server Is Inadvertently Shut Down

```
[2/27/02 6:01:45:426 PST] 15807281 EJBEngine I WSVR0037I: Starting EJB
jar: Tasks
[2/27/02 6:01:54:479 PST] 15807281 Server A WSVR0023I: Server
__adminServer open for e-business
[2/27/02 6:01:57:123 PST] 7b613286 ActiveServerP A ADMS0008I: Starting
server: Default Server
[2/27/02 6:01:57:463 PST] 7b613286 ActiveServerP A ADMS0032I: Started
server: Default Server (pid 1960)
[2/27/02 6:10:06:777 PST] 3ba33289 StaleConnecti A CONM7007I: Mapping
the following SQLException, with ErrorCode -1,224 and SQLState 40003, to
a StaleConnectionException: COM.ibm.db2.jdbc.DB2Exception: [IBM][CLI
Driver][DB2/NT] SQL1224N  A database agent could not be started to
service a request, or was terminated as a result of a database system
shutdown or a force command.  SQLSTATE=55032
```

Standard errors contain Java exception stack traces. If errors occur during startup, there is a good chance they will be logged in the `adminserver-stderr.log`. As with all logs in the administrative category, you can find this file located in the `<was_home>\logs` folder.

Understanding application server logs

All application servers you define enable you to define the name and location of a standard output and standard error log. When you set the location of these logs, WebSphere ensures that these files are created for you. The default_server that ships with WebSphere is always set up to output its logs to `default_server_stdout.log` and `default_server_stderr.log`.

The `default_server_stdout log`, shown in Figure 26-1, is found in `<was_home>\logs`. The information provided in the standard output log is the same information that is displayed in the Administrative Console. The key phrase that you are always looking for when you start the server is `Open for e-business`. If you see that message, you know you have started the server successfully. If you get anything other that the `Open for e-business`, such as a stack trace, you know you have some troubleshooting ahead. Now you have to read through the stack trace to see if you can determine the cause of the error.

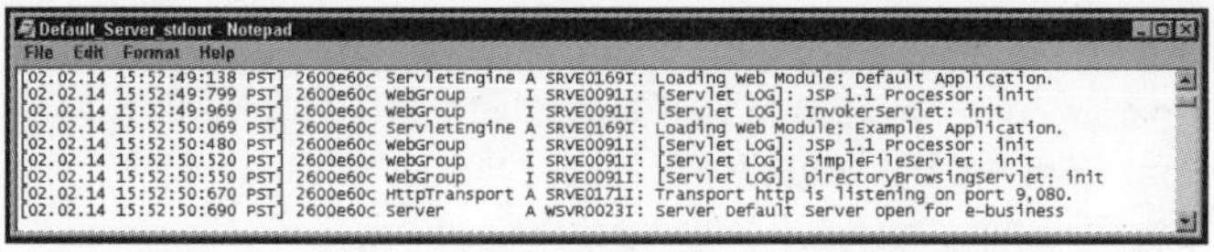

Figure 26-1: The last line of the output from default_servers_stdout shows that the server is open for e-business

You may not be able to see the "open for e-business" line in Figure 26-1. It looks like:

```
[ 02.02.14 15:52:50:690 PST] 2600e60c Server          A WSVR0023I: Server
Default Server open for e-business
```

The `<was_home>\logs\default_server_stderr log` file contains logging information about failures within the Java components running under the Application server. It contains exceptions thrown by the applications running under the default_server. Usually these are in the form of Java stack traces. Listing 26-4 shows a sample of RMI exception that was recorded in the `default_server_stderr.log` file.

Listing 26-4: A Sample Exception and Stack Trace

```
java.rmi.MarshalException: CORBA COMM_FAILURE 1 No; nested exception is:
 org.omg.CORBA.COMM_FAILURE:   minor code: 1  completed: No
org.omg.CORBA.COMM_FAILURE:   minor code: 1  completed: No
 at com.ibm.CORBA.iiop.ConnectionTable.get(ConnectionTable.java:629)
 at com.ibm.CORBA.iiop.ConnectionTable.get(ConnectionTable.java:412)
 at com.ibm.CORBA.iiop.GIOPImpl.locate(GIOPImpl.java:164)
 at com.ibm.CORBA.iiop.ClientDelegate.createRequest(ClientDelegate.java:1099)
 at com.ibm.CORBA.iiop.ClientDelegate.request(ClientDelegate.java:1728)
 at org.omg.CORBA.portable.ObjectImpl._request(ObjectImpl.java:237)
 at com.ibm.ejs.jts.tranLog._tranLogWire_Stub.retrieve(_tranLogWire_Stub.java:82)
 at com.ibm.ejs.jts.tranLog.tranLogTran.recover(tranLogTran.java:218)
 at com.ibm.ejs.jts.jts.Jts.init(Jts.java:129)
 at com.ibm.ws.runtime.Server.initializeTran(Server.java:1548)
 at com.ibm.ws.runtime.Server.initializeRuntime0(Server.java:941)
 at com.ibm.ejs.sm.server.ManagedServer.initializeRuntime0(ManagedServer.java:407)
 at com.ibm.ws.runtime.Server.initializeRuntime(Server.java:882)
 at com.ibm.ejs.sm.server.ManagedServer.main(ManagedServer.java:168)
 at java.lang.reflect.Method.invoke(Native Method)
 at com.ibm.ws.bootstrap.WSLauncher.main(WSLauncher.java:158)
```

When you create your own application servers, you have to provide the location and filenames of the standard output and standard error logs. These logs operate in the same fashion as the default_server standard output and standard error logs. As an aid to debugging your application, you can utilize Java println statements to output information directly to the two logs (although in Chapter 8, this practice is frowned upon). Here is a snippet of code that would print out in the standard output log:

```
System.out.println("Did Murphy log on? User=" + req.getRemoteUser());
```

Understanding IBM HTTP Server Logs

Because the Web server is a separate component, it makes sense that it would have its own logs. The two logs that are output from the IBM HTTP Server are `access.log`, and `error.log`. These two logs are found in `<http_home>\logs`.

The `access.log` file provides information about the HTTP request and the response returned by the Web server. It is defined by a `CustomLog` that outputs information based on a `LogFormat` directive. List 26-5 shows an example of a series of requests and responses.

List 26-5: Request Information Found in the access.log File

```
169.254.25.129 - - [13/Feb/2002:21:11:41 -0800] "GET / HTTP/1.1" 200 7017
169.254.25.129 - - [13/Feb/2002:21:11:44 -0800] "GET /whole.jpg HTTP/1.1"
200 85708
169.254.25.129 - - [13/Feb/2002:21:11:46 -0800] "GET /Configure.jpg
HTTP/1.1" 200 104497
169.254.25.129 - - [13/Feb/2002:21:11:48 -0800] "GET /website.jpg HTTP/1.1"
200 90165
```

In Listing 26-5, the format of the `CustomLog` directive is as follows:

```
LogFormat "%h %l %u %t \"%r\" %>s %b" common
```

This format follows the Common Log Format (CLF), which is expected by off-the-shelf log analyzers. If you want to use one of them, you should leave this directive alone.

The `error.log` file logs any errors that the HTTP server encounters. It is created by the `ErrorLog` directive. The ErrorLog directive is a default directive that is implemented when you install the IBM HTTP Server. Both of these logs are directives found in the `<IBM_HTTP_HOME>\conf\httpd.conf` file.

Also notice an `adminAccess.log` and `adminError.log` in the `<IBM_HTTP_Home>\logs` folder. The IBM HTTP Administration service outputs these logs, which provide the same logging services as the access and error logs.

Understanding plug-in logs

The plug-in provides the interface from the Web server to the application servers. Transport information (for example virtual host names and port numbers) is contained within the plug-in's configuration file (`plugin-cfg.xml`). The transport information should match what is created on the Administration server. If the plug-in does not, for some reason, find the same transport information it expects from the application server, errors can result.

The `native.log` is found in `<was_home>\logs`. The log contains error and informational messages generated by the Web server plug-in. The log shows information about the startup and changes applied to the server (such as start, stop, and restart). You can change the `native.log` name by updating the `plugin-cfg.xml` file as follows:

```
<Log LogLevel="Error" Name="d:\WebSphere\AppServer\logs\webserv1.log"/>
```

You might change the name of the log to correspond with the HTTP server name that is utilizing this plug-in. You can also change the location of the log.

You can set the log level to `Trace`, `Warn`, or `Error`. The previously shown directive showed the log level set to `Error`. If you want to set it to `Trace`, you simply change `Error` to `Trace`. You have to be careful whenever you set the `LogLevel` to `Trace`. Tracing impacts performance and generates a large log file.

Understanding the Administrative Console

The Administrative Console (shown in Figure 26-2) is another place where you can see problems being presented. On the bottom of the Administrative Console are the console messages. Whenever the Administrative Console is started, console messages begin appearing, providing you with statuses and error messages. The Administrative Console is an important starting point when checking for errors.

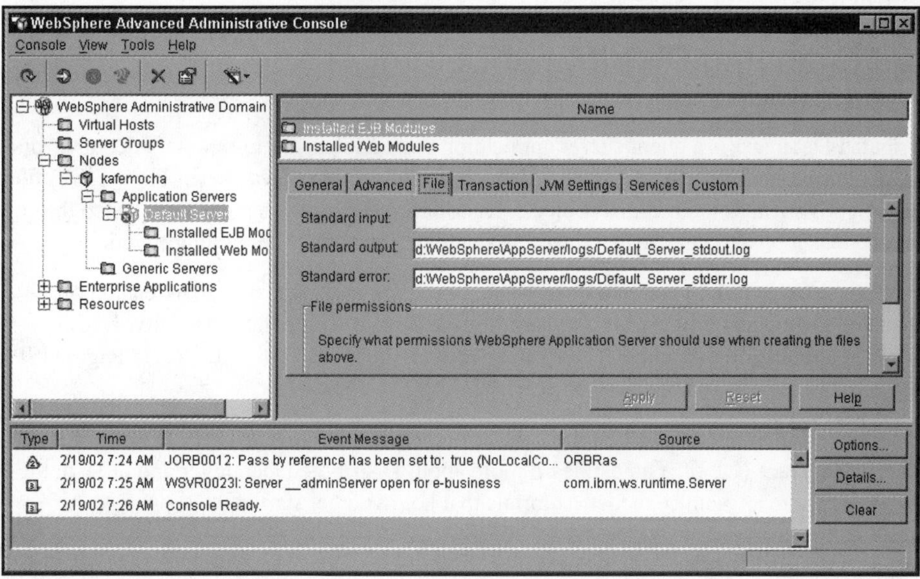

Figure 26-2: The Administrative Console displays error messages in the lower frame.

Messages displayed within the console are divided into three categories:

- Audit messages describe important (nonfatal) messages.
- Severe errors represent abnormally terminated errors that have occurred within a process. Events in this category are recorded into the trace buffer and dumped to the tracefile.
- Warnings indicate a problem has occurred and should be corrected.

The console also periodically displays an error window. In these cases, you can click the Details button to view Java stack traces.

Understanding Log Analyzer

Log Analyzer is a tool, included with WebSphere 4.0, which looks at error conditions in the Activity log. It then attempts to decipher and diagnose the problems and provide some possible solutions.

> **TIP**: To adjust the level of detail, you collect, change the `logging.properties` file found in `<was_home>\properties`. Update the property `com.ibm.ws.ras.MessageFilterLevel` to `Error`, `warning`, or `audit`.

Log Analyzer performs its diagnosis through an XML file called the Symptom database, which includes suggestions, fixes, and alternative places to find information. This file is located in `<was_home>\properties\logbr\symptoms`.

Understanding Distributed Debugger and Object-Level Trace

Distributed Debugger is a client/server application that enables you to remotely debug errors in your Java programs. With the debugger, you can debug servlets, Java Server Pages (JSP) files, Enterprise JavaBeans, and business objects. Distributed Debugger enables you to step through source code, set breakpoints, inspect variables, and perform other debugging functions.

Object Level Trace (OLT) is a remote application tracing facility that is an extension of Distributed Debugger. You use OLT to monitor the flow among components involved in distributed application execution. The components can be servlets or Java Server Pages (JSP), Enterprise JavaBeans, and business objects.

During the installation process, you have the option of installing Distributed Debugger and Object Level Trace (OLT). You can learn more about Distributed Debugger and OLT in the InfoCenter. There are some excellent tutorials that help you get started.

> **CROSS-REFERENCE**: The HitCount tutorial, found in the InfoCenter, is an excellent reference on how to use the Distributed Debugger and OLT.

Using traces

Traces are ways to get additional information from the IBM code base. Traces enable you to get under the covers of the actual operational aspects of WebSphere. Trace operations are disabled due to the volume of information they produce and their negative impact on the system overhead. Therefore, you need to enable Trace. Depending upon the particular problem you are trying to trace, you may want to start Trace prior to starting the Administrative Server or during execution of an application server.

You can enable Trace at two levels:

- Administration server
- Application server

> **NOTE**: Actually there is a third level. That is the Administrative Console, but it should only be used with the assistance of IBM support.

When you start a trace, you are asking for additional information from the executing Administrative Server code. The code is organized in components, so you can select different components to trace. An example might be `HTTP_Transport`. You could set trace specifications to provide information on all trace options. Trace specifications provide the capability to have trace inform you when the execution thread performs:

- An entry or exit from a component
- Events within the code that the developer believes are important to note
- Debugging information that the developer inserted

You can mix and match the trace types to get the level of trace output that you desire or choose All to have them all.

All this is available from the Administrative Console by selecting the application server and then selecting the Services tab. You select Trace Service from the services available for the application server and click Edit Properties. You then specify the trace specification and choose the method of output. The output can be sent to the standard error target `<was_home>\logs\default_server_stderr`, the standard output log `<was_home>\logs\default_server_stdout`, the ring buffer, or to a file of your choice.

The ring buffer is a circular memory buffer. Because of the volume of information that is returned, writing to a file increases the performance degradation. Placing information in the ring buffer enables you to select when you want to dump the information to a file. After you perform your trace on the component of the application server, you can then dump the ring buffer to a file for later review.

You can also set trace in a trace string within the `<was_home>\bin\admin.config` file. You utilize this strategy if the Administrative Server experiences problems starting.

Understanding JNDI namespace

Distributed computing environments often employ naming and directory services to obtain shared components and resources. Naming and directory services associate names with locations, services, information, and resources. The association of the names to objects is called the Java Naming and Directory Interface (JNDI) namespace.

Naming services provide name-to-object mappings. Directory services provide information about objects and the search tools required to locate those objects. There are many naming and directory service implementations, and the interfaces to them vary.

To help verify that the services are properly associated, you can use the DumpNameSpace utility that shows the JNDI directory contents. DumpNameSpace is a way to ensure correct associations to named objects, such as data sources and EJBs. You can redirect the output to a file for future inspection as well as dump a specific JNDI namespace. The DumpNameSpace utility is found in `<was_home>\bin`. Use the following syntax to invoke it:

```
<was_home>\bin\DumpNameSpace.bat
 [-host bootstrap_host_name (defaults to localhost)]
 [-port bootstrap_port_number (defaults to 900)]
 [-startAt subcontext/in/the/tree]
  [-factory com.ibm.websphere.naming.WsnInitialContextFactory]
 [-root [ tree | host | legacy ]]
 [-format [ jndi | ins ] (default jndi)
 [-report [ short | long ]] (default short)
 [-traceString "some.package.name.to.trace.*=all=enabled"
```

The default output goes to the file `DumpNameSpaceTrace.out`.

Troubleshooting: First Steps

Finding the problem in a complex environment might seem to be a formidable task, but when you systematically demarcate the components, isolating the vermin is not that difficult. And therein lies the secret. With the logging, tracing, and debugging tools to which you have previously been introduced, you can start breaking down the components into a set of steps to verify.

Revisiting WebSphere topology

Keeping with our e-business espionage theme, your mission, "should you choose to accept it," is to locate the problem using all the tools at your disposal. Your first step is to perform some reconnaissance to understand the landscape and climate within which you are working. Figure 26-3 shows the internal Web architecture and log file clues to solve your problem.

Figure 26-3 can be storyboarded as follows:

1. The scenario begins with a browser sending a URL request to the HTTP Server for a resource (for example a servlet, Java Server Page (JSP) or HTML page). The WebSphere Application Server plug-in interrogates the URL, and based on the cross-reference between the `<was_home>\config\plugin-cfg` and the URL, the request is dispatched to the proper resource. For the sake of the scenario, it's a servlet.

2. Servlets might already be loaded based on a previous request, but if the servlet is not loaded, it is dynamically loaded by the classloader. The servlet lifecycle is started and the `init()` method is invoked. The `doGet()` or `doPost()` methods then execute, and application-specific methods are called to perform business logic.
3. If Enterprise JavaBeans are utilized, a `create` is performed on the home interface and a JNDI lookup is performed. The Web container instantiates the enterprise bean. If the bean is an entity bean, datasources and JDBC drivers locate the database URL. The datasource uses a connection from the connection pool managed by WebSphere.
4. Method calls through the remote interface are executed by the Enterprise JavaBeans. Data persistence is performed with SQL and results are provided in the form of data beans or mediators. The servlet forwards control to a Java Server Page (JSP) to respond to the request.
5. Finally, a JSP generates the proper HTML that is returned through the plug-in and back to the browser.

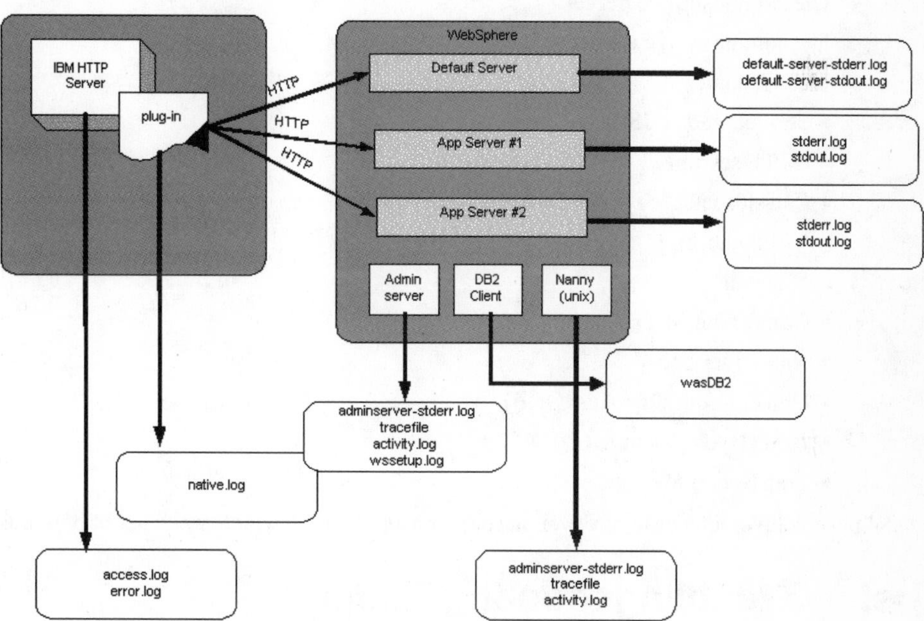

Figure 26-3: Understanding the Web architecture helps you recognize which steps to take to resolve a variety of problems.

Now that you are familiar with the routine, you should begin extrapolating where the problems could occur and where your verification points are.

Understanding problem categories

Figure 26-3 shows the components that integrate to form a cohesive unit, and the scenario presented discusses the flow through the system. All that makes one assumption: The components are actually working to begin with. Here are some of the problems you might encounter:

- Installation and configuration errors.
- The Administrative Server does not start.
- An application server won't start.
- You cannot access servlet, JSP, or HTML files from a browser.
- Error messages are popping up or being displayed in the console

So where are some of the points of failure? You may have problems with the following:

- The Administrative Server
- The administrative client
- Web container
  - Servlets and/or JSPs
  - HTTP session
  - Classloaders
  - Virtual hosting
- EJB container
  - Connection Manager
  - Named services
  - Object Request Broker (ORB)
  - Java Development Kit (JDK)
  - Transaction Manager

With so many points of failure, you need to consult the tools you learned about previously.

Using Troublingshooting Tools

When you receive an error or failure, you need to utilize the tools in your bag of tricks. The tools provide some assistance to ascertain the type of problem based on the type of error or message presented. Receiving an error might require you to take the following actions:

- Investigate messages that show important events.
- Review Java stack traces.
- Review log files.

- Run Log Analyzer to diagnose problems from the activity log.
- Run a trace to understand better which components are failing.

You may see these errors in the following formats:

- Pop-up error message
- Console messages
- Log-file entries
- Nonfunctioning components

Configuring console messages

One of the first places to get an idea about a problem is the Administrative Console. The console's Event pane provides you with a ten-thousand–foot view of errors occurring in the system.

> **CROSS-REFERENCE**: Console messages are described in the earlier section "Understanding the Administrative Console."Refer to that section for descriptions of types of events displayed in the console.

To adjust the type of events displayed in the console's Event pane, click the Options button in the Event pane to display the Event Viewer Options dialog box (see Figure 26-4).

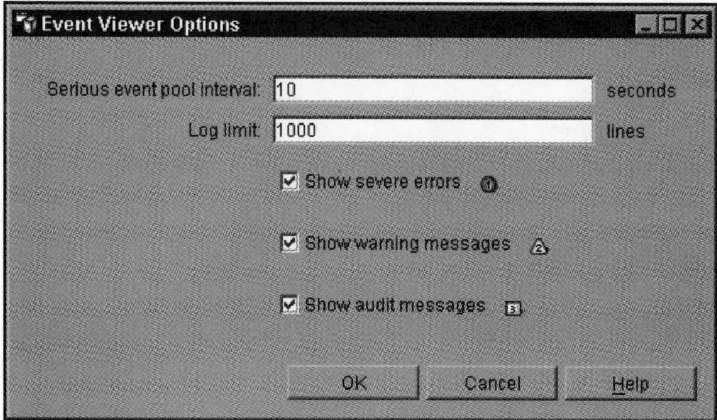

Figure 26-4: Change the log size or the messages being displayed from the Event Viewer Options dialog box.

As shown in Figure 26-4, you can set the log size limit and the message types being displayed. Color-coded message types provide visual feedback on the type of message being displayed in the Event Viewer as small colored icons. Severe errors are shown as the number 1 surrounded by a red circle. Warning messages are shown as the number 2 in a yellow triangle, and finally audit messages are shown as the number 3 within a green square.

The Log limit value directly reflects the number of rows stored in the `EJSADMIN.SE_TABLE` found in the WebSphere database repository. The rows stored are the most recent serious events. Changing the value increases/decreases the number of rows stored.

Deciphering error pop-up windows

Pop-up error windows appear when the Administrative Console is unable start or utilize a component. Figure 26-5 shows an example of a pop-up error.

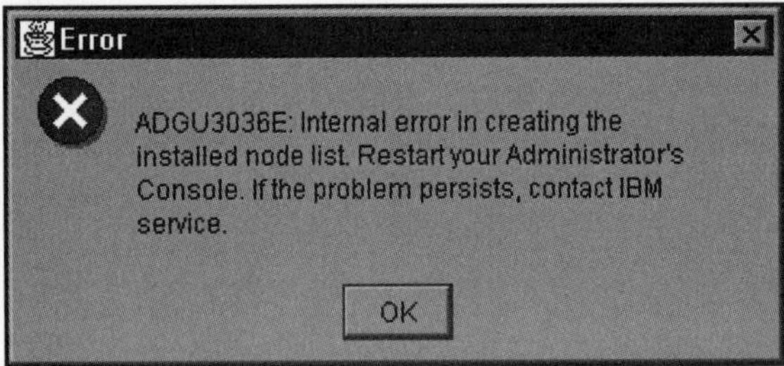
Error
ADGU3036E: Internal error in creating the installed node list. Restart your Administrator's Console. If the problem persists, contact IBM service.
OK

Figure 26-5: The Administrative Console displays this error message when the connection to the WebSphere repository is lost.

When you see an error message like the one in Figure 26-5, one of the first places to look is in the log files to see what additional information might be available.

Reviewing log files

The error shown in Figure 26.5 creates a lot of activity within WebSphere. In addition to the pop-up error message, information is persisted in the `activity.log` and the tracefile located within the `<was_home>\logs` folder. The Event Viewer also is filled with information pertaining to the error, as shown in Figure 26-6.

Type	Time	Event Message	Source
	2/27/02 6:03 AM	Console Ready.	
	2/27/02 6:10 AM	CONM7007I: Mapping the following SQLException, with ErrorCode -1...	com.ibm.ejs.cm.portability.StaleConnec...
	2/27/02 6:10 AM	CONM7007I: Mapping the following SQLException, with ErrorCode -1...	com.ibm.ejs.cm.portability.StaleConnec...
	2/27/02 6:10 AM	CONM7007I: Mapping the following SQLException, with ErrorCode -1...	com.ibm.ejs.cm.portability.StaleConnec...
	2/27/02 6:10 AM	SMTL0010W: Exception on database query (read by primary key):	com.ibm.ejs.sm.util.db.DBMgr
	2/27/02 6:10 AM	CNTR0019E: Non-application exception occurred while processing ...	com.ibm.ejs.container.util.ExceptionUtil
	2/27/02 6:10 AM	CNTR0019E: Non-application exception occurred while processing ...	com.ibm.ejs.container.util.ExceptionUtil
	2/27/02 6:10 AM	CNTR0019E: Non-application exception occurred while processing ...	com.ibm.ejs.container.util.ExceptionUtil
	2/27/02 6:10 AM	CNTR0019E: Non-application exception occurred while processing ...	com.ibm.ejs.container.util.ExceptionUtil

Options...
Details...
Clear

Figure 26-6: The Event Viewer displays all three types of events (Audit, Warning, and Errors).

The Event Viewer messages provide an error message code. The first four characters of the code contain the event ID. Table 26-2 shows the list of WebSphere message IDs.

Table 26-2: WebSphere Message IDs

Acronym	*Component*
AATL	Application assembly tool
ADGU	Administrative GUI
ADMR	Administrative repository
ADMT	Administrative tasks
ADMS	Administrative Server
ALRM	Alarm
CHKJ	IBM validation tool
CHKW	WebSphere server validation
CNTR	EJB container
CONM	Connection Manager
DBMN	Database Manager
DRSW	Data replication service
DYNA	Cache Management
INST	Install
J2CA	J2EE connector
JORB	IBM Java ORB
JSAS	Security Association service
JSPG	JavaServer Pages
LTXT	Localizable text
MSGS	Messaging
MIGR	WebSphere migration tools
NMSV	JNDI - name services
PLGN	Web server plug-ins and native code
PMON	Performance Monitor
SECJ	WebSphere security
SESN	Session and user profiles
SMTL	WebSphere systems-management utilities
SRVE	Servlet engine

Table 26-2 *(Continued)*

Acronym	*Component*
TRAS	Tracing component
WCMD	WebSphere systems-management commands
WINT	Request interceptors
WOBA	WebSphere object adapter
WPRS	WebSphere persistence
WSCL	Client
WSCP	WSCP command line
WSVR	WebSphere server runtime
WTRN	WebSphere transactions
WTSK	WebSphere systems-management tasks
WWLM	EJB workLoad management
XMLC	XML configuration

What follows is sample message format taken from Figure 26-6 showing the Administrative Console's Event pane.

```
2/27/02 6:10 AM  SMTL0010W Exception on database query (read by primary
key); com.ibm.ejs.sm.util.db.DBMgr
```

The format of the message is as follows:

- Type (color coded as a yellow triangle)
- Date and time (`2/27/02  6:10 AM`)
- Error Message identifier (`SMTL0010`)
- Event code (`Warning=W`)
- Text message (Exception on database query read by primary key)
- Source (`com.ibm.ejs.sm.util.db.DBMgr`)

TIP: To find the messages and a brief description of the error, check in the InfoCenter under Section 8.2.

The tracefile shows many errors similar to Listing 26-6.

Listing 26-6: Tracefile Log Entry

```
[2/27/02 6:10:06:727 PST] 44da7285 StaleConnecti A CONM7007I: Mapping
the following SQLException, with ErrorCode -1,224 and SQLState 40003, to
a StaleConnectionException: COM.ibm.db2.jdbc.DB2Exception: [IBM][CLI
Driver][DB2/NT] SQL1224N A database agent could not be started to
service a request, or was terminated as a result of a database system
shutdown or a force command. SQLSTATE=55032
```

The types of message you see in the tracefile vary considerably. You might see database errors like the example shown in Listing 26-6. The Administrative Server needs to regenerate plug-in information. The best way to see the different types of errors is to actually look at the file.

WebSphere Application Server supports various trace formats as well as log formats. A properties file enables you to specify how you want the information presented. If you search the `<was_home>\properties` folder for a file named `logging.properties`, you come across a property called `com.ibm.ws.ras.TraceFormat`. You can set the log information to display in the following formats:

- *Basic* generates limited information. Basic information shows timestamp, thread ID, and component.
- *Advanced* adds more information to the basic presentation. For instance, it might add the name of the process running in the Administrative Server.
- *Loganalyzer* generates a trace output that can be interpreted by Log Analyzer. The output from this option is hefty.

Listing 26-6 uses the basic format. The format is demarcated as follows:

- *Timestamp:* `[2/27/02 6:10:06:727 PST]`
- *Thread ID:* `44da7285`
- *Component short name:* `StaleConnecti`
- *Level:* A Audit, W Warning, X Error, E Event, D Debug, T Terminate, F Fatal, and I Informational.
- *Two addition levels:* The levels > and < are the entry and exit of a method used for debugging.
- *Message:* `CONM7007I: Mapping the following SQLException, with ErrorCode -1,224 and SQLState 40003, to a StaleConnectionException: COM.ibm.db2.jdbc.DB2Exception: [IBM][CLI Driver][DB2/NT] SQL1224N A database agent could not be started to service a request, or was terminated as a result of a database system shutdown or a force command. SQLSTATE=55032`

This example demonstrates how the events recorded in the console provide you with the first level of information. Tracefile drills down even closer to the error by providing SQL error codes and a better description of the problem. To resolve the problem, use the information that Log Analyzer outputs to the Activity log to test the symptoms against known problems.

Performing educated prognostication

Can you prognosticate the solution to problems encountered in WebSphere? With an understanding of the WebSphere topology and the tools presented so far, you should be able to find solutions to most problems you encounter. The earlier section "Revisiting WebSphere topology," walked you through the round-trip steps associated with accessing an e-business application. Table 26-3 shows some areas of failure and what to check to isolate the problem.

Table 26-3: Problem Isolation

Verification Scenario	*Points of Failure/Actions*
Installation of WebSphere	Installation problems could occur with improper installation of supporting components (DB2, HTTP server, JDK, and JDBC drivers) ♦ You should check the installation log files (`wssetup.log` and `wasdb2.log`)
The browser sends a request to the HTTP Server for a servlet that must reside in the application server not the Web server. The WebSphere Application Server plug-in interrogates the URL and based on cross-reference between `<was_home>\config\plugin-cfg` and the URL, the request is dispatched to the proper servlet.	Web servers could be separated from the application server. If you can't reach a resource on the Application server, you need to determine whether the plug-in is incorrect or your Web server is improperly configured. One way to eliminate the Web server is to attempt to access the resource using the embedded Web server (port 9080). ♦ Various configuration changes affect the `plugin-cfg` file. If changes have occurred that impact transport layers and URLs, ensure that the plug-in is updated properly. Console warnings are also provided when changes impact the plug-in. ♦ Check `native.log`, Administrative Console, Application Server status and event logs. Verify that the WebSphere ports are utilized by only WebSphere (ports 900, 9000).

Verification Scenario	***Points of Failure/Actions***
Servlets may already be loaded based on a previous request, but if the servlet is not loaded, it is dynamically loaded by the classloader. The Servlet lifecycle is started and the `init()` method is invoked. The `doGet()` or `doPost()` method is then executed and application-specific methods are called to perform business logic.	This scenario impacts the Web container. Failure to load a servlet could be caused by an inactive Application server, improper configuration in the deployment descriptor, or an out-of-sync plug-in. ♦ Check the Administrative Console, Application server status, Application server standard out/error and event logs. ♦ Servlets are Java classes. Verify that your servlets are included in the application classpath.
If Enterprise JavaBeans are utilized, a `create` is performed on the home interface, and a JNDI lookup is performed. The Web container instantiates the enterprise bean. If the bean is an entity bean, data sources and JDBC drivers are used to locate the database URL. The data source uses a connection from the connection pool managed by WebSphere.	Utilizing EJBs adds additional points of failure. The container accesses datasources, the JDBC driver, and databases and is possibly configured separately from the Web container. ♦ Failures to access an EJB should be checked by running DumpNameSpace, and reviewing Administrative Console errors, tracefile, and application server logs. ♦ Use the verify process in the Administrative Console to verify signatures and availability of classfiles in the EJB jar.

If you cannot isolate the problem using the tools in Table 26-2, you should consider using the Trace facility.

Running traces

Tracing is useful as a supplementary tool to the logging tools and console messages you have accessed. The Application server has built-in tracing that sends messages to the log for analysis. You must manually activate traces. You can do so at three places:

- Application server
- Administrative Server
- Administrative Console (using DrAdmin), which is used mainly by IBM Support

Setting up an Application server trace

To start a trace on a running application, from the Administrative Console select the Application server you want to trace. Figure 26-7 shows the default server as the selected Application server to trace. In the Administrative Console, click the Services tab; select Trace Service, and click the Edit Properties button.

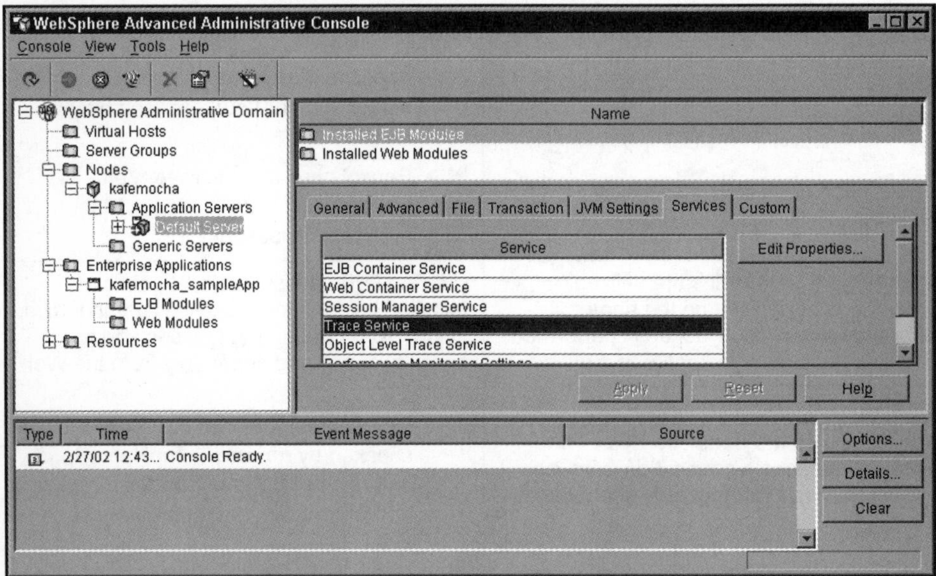

Figure 26-7: Use the Administrative Console Services tab to set up a trace.

When you click Edit Properties, you are presented with a Trace dialog box where you can select the components or groups to trace. Figure 26-8 shows an example of selecting the HTTP_Transport group. The package name is highlighted. Right-click to select the level of tracing. You can also enter a dump filename, and when you are ready, you can flush out the ring buffer to an external file.

The ring buffer is where the trace information is kept. It is actually stored in memory, so the server isn't constantly writing to a file. Depending upon your selection, some events output more information than others, so it is a good practice to set the ring buffer size based on the amount of output you want to capture. If you reach that limit, the information is dropped off on a first-in–first-out basis.

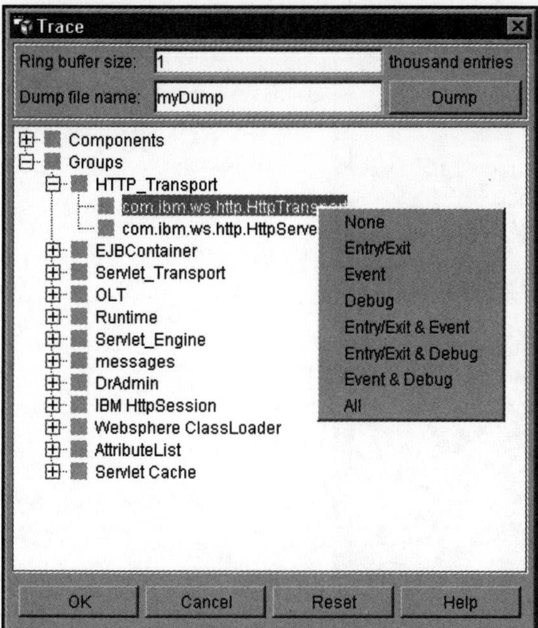

Figure 26-8: You choose a component you want to trace from within the Groups menu. Using the context menu, you can select the trace specification that provides you with the information you are seeking.

Selecting events changes the gray boxes into color-coded icons. Each color represents what you selected. The trace coding colors are as follows:

- *Gray:* Nothing selected
- *Blue:* Entry/Exit (exit and entry points into the package)
- *Yellow:* Event selected (specialized events within the code are fired)
- *Red:* Debug selected (debug code embedded with the code is fired)

You either see a single color or a combination of colors based on your selection. Click OK to see the trace string specification. You also have the opportunity to change the output file from the ring buffer to the standard error, standard output, or a file that you specify, as shown in Figure 26-9.

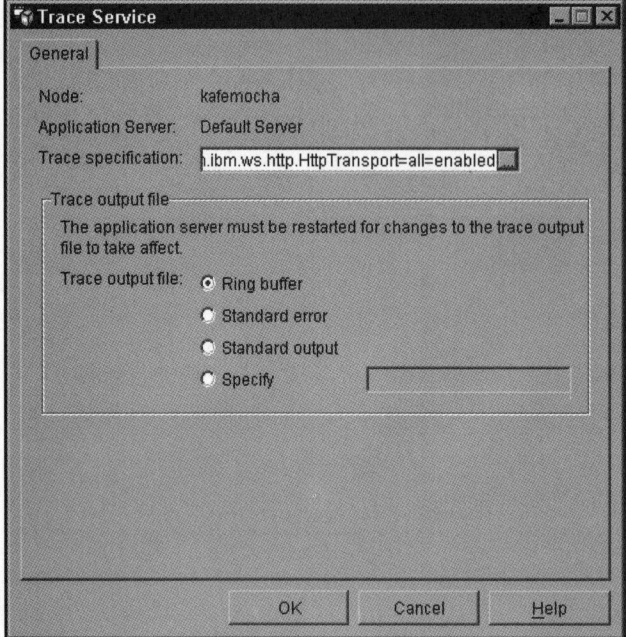

Figure 26-9: Clicking and selecting the Trace specification generates the proper specification for the tracing facility. You have the option of deciding where to send the output. The ring buffer is the suggested method.

Click OK and click Apply to set the changes. If you make changes to the trace output file, you need to shut down and restart the application server.

When you complete your tracing, return to the Services tab and edit the properties again. Your selections should be there from before. Type a dump filename and click Dump. Your information is dumped to the file. An example is shown in Figure 26-10.

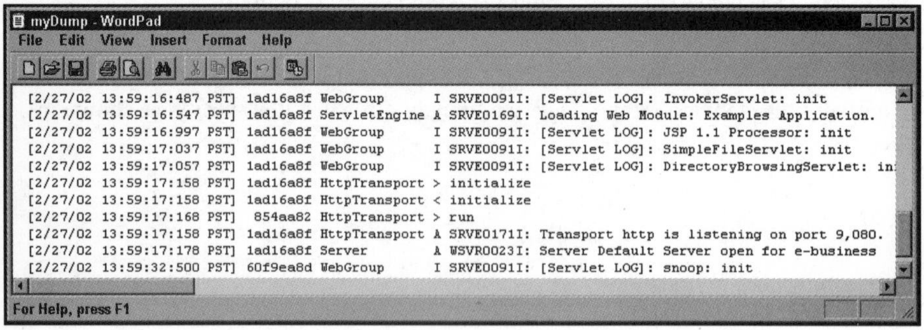

myDump - WordPad

File Edit View Insert Format Help

```
[2/27/02 13:59:16:487 PST] 1ad16a8f WebGroup      I SRVE0091I: [Servlet LOG]: InvokerServlet: init
[2/27/02 13:59:16:547 PST] 1ad16a8f ServletEngine A SRVE0169I: Loading Web Module: Examples Application.
[2/27/02 13:59:16:997 PST] 1ad16a8f WebGroup      I SRVE0091I: [Servlet LOG]: JSP 1.1 Processor: init
[2/27/02 13:59:17:037 PST] 1ad16a8f WebGroup      I SRVE0091I: [Servlet LOG]: SimpleFileServlet: init
[2/27/02 13:59:17:057 PST] 1ad16a8f WebGroup      I SRVE0091I: [Servlet LOG]: DirectoryBrowsingServlet: in
[2/27/02 13:59:17:158 PST] 1ad16a8f HttpTransport > initialize
[2/27/02 13:59:17:158 PST] 1ad16a8f HttpTransport < initialize
[2/27/02 13:59:17:168 PST]  854aa82 HttpTransport > run
[2/27/02 13:59:17:158 PST] 1ad16a8f HttpTransport A SRVE0171I: Transport http is listening on port 9,080.
[2/27/02 13:59:17:178 PST] 1ad16a8f Server        A WSVR0023I: Server Default Server open for e-business
[2/27/02 13:59:32:500 PST] 60f9ea8d WebGroup      I SRVE0091I: [Servlet LOG]: snoop: init
```

For Help, press F1

Figure 26-10: You can see in the ring buffer dump how the trace inserts its information.

Figure 26-10 shows that the trace output for `HttpTransport` is identified in the dump. Three lines in particular show some tracing:

```
[2/27/02 13:59:17:158 PST] 1ad16a8f HttpTransport > initialize
[2/27/02 13:59:17:158 PST] 1ad16a8f HttpTransport < initialize
[2/27/02 13:59:17:168 PST] 854aa82 HttpTransport > run
```

The log entry shows the entry (>) and exit (<) from the `initialize()` method and the entry into the `run()` method. This means that you know that the initialize process was completed and that you are now in the run process.

Tracing the Admininstrative server

You can also trace the Administrative Server. You might do this sort of trace if the Application server does not start, in which case you could trace several different components.

The procedures are similar to the application server tracing, but in this case, you select the packages to trace by selecting the node on the Administrative Server tree. Then, you right-click, and select Trace. You see a different dialog box with different selections to trace than you did before. Figure 26-11 shows an example.

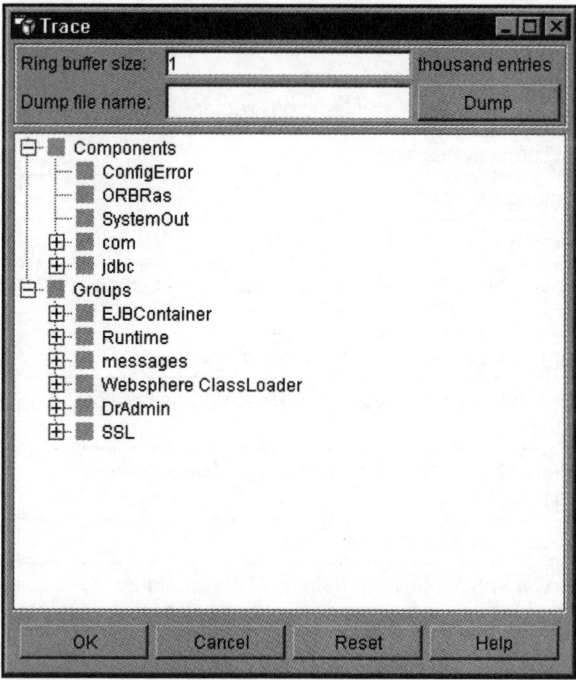

Figure 26-11: In an Administrative trace, the procedures for selecting and collecting data are the same as those used in an application server trace.

Formatting trace specifications strings

You may have noticed the cryptic trace specifications displayed in some of the windows shown in the preceding figures. The terse nature of these strings may confuse those new to WebSphere tracing, but after you understand their meanings, they're fairly straightforward. The trace specification format is as follows:

```
<component>=<type>=[ enabled | disabled]
```

The component is a package name, and the type is either entry/exit, event, debug, or all. An example trace could be `com.ibm.ejs.sm.*=all=enabled`. This string represents tracing of all events for all classes in the `com.ibm.ejs.sm` package. Table 26-4 provides a list of the packages and what they do in WebSphere.

Table 26-4: WebSphere Package Names

Package	Component/Service
com.ibm.ejs.com	Connection pooling manager, data sources
com.ibm.ejs.container	EJB container – TransactionRolledBackException
com.ibm.ejs.csi	Container Services Interface – Transaction attribute
com.ibm.ejs.jts	Java Transaction Service
com.ibm.ejs.ns	Naming service, Java Naming Directory Interface
com.ibm.ejs.persistence	EJB persistence layer
com.ibm.ejs.ras	Logging services
com.ibm.ejs.security	Security manager, security content
com.ibm.ejs.sm.active.	Active objects of Administrative Server – starting server
com.ibm.ejs.sm.beans	Administrative Server repository objects
com.ibm.ejs.sm.client	Administrative Console – client-side administrative problems
com.ibm.ejs.sm.server	Administrative Server process – application server process
com.ibm.ejs.sm.util	Utilities like the Nanny service
com.ibm.servlet	Servlet engine, Java plug-in, HTTP transport
com.ibm.WebSphere	Data source factory, JNDI context factory
com.ibm.ws	Classloader, HTTP transports, workload management

You can use this string format in some of the configuration files to initiate tracing prior to the Administrative Server startup. You learn about that in the following section.

Tracing Administrative Server startup

If you are having problems starting the Administrative Server, you might want to run a trace to get some information about the problems that are occurring. The `admin.config` configuration file, found in `<was_home>\bin`, contains lines within it that can turn on tracing. By default, they are commented. If you uncomment them and start the Administrative Server, the output trace file is written to the location specified in the `Admin.config`. You should adjust the output locations as appropriate for your configuration.

Listing 26-7 shows actual trace settings in the `admin.config` file. You can uncomment those lines to start tracing everything in the Administrative Server. The number sign (#) is a comment line. Removing the number sign (#), saving the file, and restarting the Administrative Server initiates the trace. The third line in Listing 26-7, when uncommented, sends the output to the `admin.trace` file.

Listing 26-7: Trace Settings within the admin.config File

```
# Trace settings
#com.ibm.ejs.sm.adminServer.traceString=com.ibm.ejs.*=all=enabled
#com.ibm.ejs.sm.adminServer.traceOutput=d:/WebSphere/AppServer/logs/admin.trace
```

> **TIP**: Be aware that the default is to trace everything in the `admin.config` default setting for trace. Be prepared for a lot of output.

As an example, try making the changes to the `admin.config` file to start tracing the start of the Administrative Server. Remove the comments for the trace settings and save the file. If you already have the Administrative Server started, you must stop and restart it. When the Administrative Server starts, open the `admin.trace` file found in `<was_home>\logs\`. Listing 26-8 displays some of the output from your trace.

Listing 26-8: Output of a Trace in admin.config

```
Current trace specification = com.ibm.ejs.*=all=enabled
************* End Display Current Environment *************
[ 5/5/02 11:42:33:455 PDT] 4da5bdc6 NLS            > NLS, messages/en_US
[ 5/5/02 11:42:33:465 PDT] 4da5bdc6 NLS            < NLS
[ 5/5/02 11:42:33:475 PDT] 4da5bdc6 Server         U Version : 4.0.2
[ 5/5/02 11:42:33:485 PDT] 4da5bdc6 Server         U Edition: Advanced
Edition for Multiplatforms
[ 5/5/02 11:42:33:485 PDT] 4da5bdc6 Server         U Build date: Tue Dec
18 00:00:00 PST 2001
[ 5/5/02 11:42:33:485 PDT] 4da5bdc6 Server         U Build number:
a0150.05
[ 5/5/02 11:42:33:606 PDT] 4da5bdc6 LocationServi > initServer 9000
[ 5/5/02 11:42:33:606 PDT] 4da5bdc6 LocationServi > initClient 9000
[ 5/5/02 11:42:33:606 PDT] 4da5bdc6 LocationServi > <init>     9000
```

First, you should see the current trace specification. It matches what was set in the `admin.config` file. You also see some entries and exits into the National Language Support (NLS) method. At the bottom of the listing is the initialization of the Location Server Daemon (LSD). 9000 is the default port address for the LSD. Don't forget to turn off tracing, or you will be unpleasantly surprised at the performance.

> **TIP**: When starting the IBM WS AdminServer from the Services window sometimes you get a cryptic error message like `Error 10`. This usually is caused by a database error. If you need to re-establish the administrative database, make the following modifications to the existing lines in the `<was_home>\bin\admin.config`:
>
> ```
> install.initial.config=false
> com.ibm.ejs.sm.adminServer.initializeDb=true
> #Create AdminServer database tables
> com.ibm.ejs.sm.adminServer.createTables=true
> ```
>
> When you start the Admininistrative server, it re-creates the basic installation database for you.

Using Log Analyzer

In this section, you learn how to operate Log Analyzer, which reads error conditions in the Activity log and can provide some guidance as to how to correct the error. You learn about the ways to start the Log Analyzer and how to read the output. Again this section uses a simple example to demonstrate the use of the facility.

Lets begin with a scenario that you will attempt to use the Log Analyzer to resolve. The exercise shows that the Symptoms database provides the information necessary to solve the problem. Here is your scenario: You have the Administration server running on your server. You have started and stopped the default server. You pretend that you are completely unaware of this fact. Perform these steps to prepare the scenario.

1. Start the Administrative Server.
2. Start the Administrative Console. Expand Nodes and your node. Expand Application Servers and select Default Server. Start and stop the default server.
3. Open a DB2 Command window, and type **db2 force applications all**.
4. Pressing Enter forces all DB2 applications to stop running. Your goal now is to use Log Analyzer to investigate for potential errors.

You can start Log Analyzer in three ways:

- Using a Command window and typing **`<was_home>\bin\waslogbr.bat`**
- Using the Start⇨Programs⇨IBM WebSphere⇨Application Server V4.0 AE⇨Log Analyzer
- From the Administrative Console under the Tools menu.

Start Log Analyzer from any of the mentioned options. Log Analyzer comes up with absolutely nothing in any of the panes. You need to load the `<was_home>\logs\activity.log` file, by selecting File⇨Open and finding the `activity.log` file. Select it and click OK.

Figure 26-12 shows a sample Log Analyzer. You use this sample to describe the layout of the screen and the specific color-coding. The Log Analyzer screen you have on your machine will display completely different records.

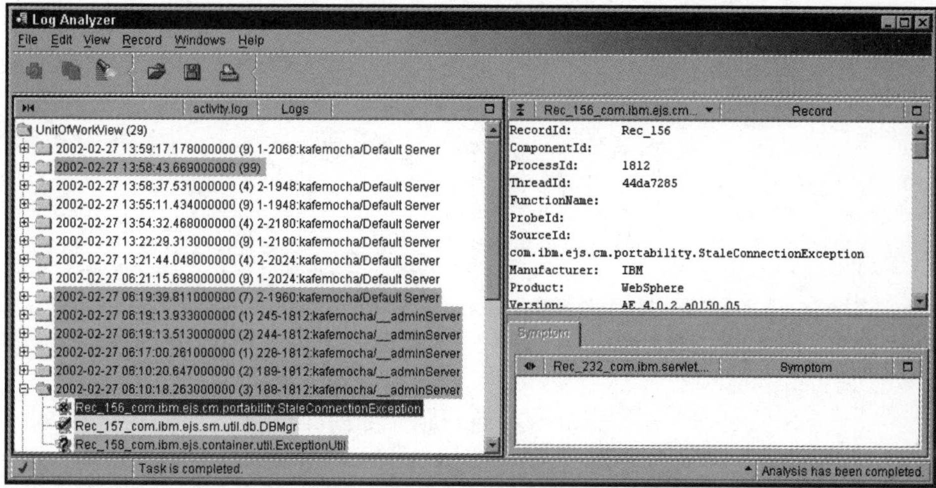

Figure 26-12: The Log Analyzer is divided into three panes.

In Figure 26-12, the left pane represents the errors recorded in the `activity.log` file. The upper-right pane (Record pane) shows the details about the selected record in the UnitOfWorkView pane, and the Analysis pane (bottom right) shows the Symptoms database information for the particular selected record, if one is available.

> **CROSS-REFERENCE**: The Symptom database can be downloaded from `ftp://ftp.software.ibm.com/software/websphere/info/tools/loganalyzer/symptoms/adv/symptomdb.xml`. You should place the `symptomdb.xml` file in the `<was_home>\properties\logbr\symptoms\adv` directory on your workstation.

Operating Log Analyzer is relatively easy. Ordered by units of work, each unit of work is comprised of a series of records. Records are color coded to signify error state. Look at your Log Analyzer. Do you see any different colors displayed in the UnitOfWorkView? These colors have meaning. They represent the severity of the error. The colors also change if you have selected items.

Unselected log entries have the following background colors:

- *Pink:* A severity 1 (Error) error.
- *Yellow:* A severity 2 (Warning) error.
- *White:* A severity 3 (Audit) error.

Selected log entries the following background colors:

- *Red:* A severity 1(Error) error.
- *Green:* A severity 2 (Warning) error.
- *Blue:* A severity 3 (Audit) error.

TIP: You can change the colors to suit your taste by using the Preferences option under the File menu.

In the scenario did you find any color-coded records? Try expanding any pink Units of Work to see what sort of records are shown. To see whether the symptom database has any information about the particular record, highlight the record, right-click, and select Analyze. Analyze retrieves and displays additional documentation on known errors and error messages in the Analysis pane. Depending on whether the symptom database has any records an icon appears. The following icons can be displayed:

- The check mark indicates that the entry has some analysis information in one or more pages in the Analysis pane.
- The plus indicates that the entry has some analysis information that surfaced prior to this record. You may want to look at the log entry prior to this one when diagnosing problems.
- The question mark indicates that the entry has either a severity 1 (Error) or 2 (Warning) error, but no additional analysis information is available for it.
- The cross indicates that the entry has a severity 3 (Audit) error, and it has no analysis information.

At this point, you are left to investigate the rest of the records. Eventually you will find the records that describe the problem as a DB2 problem.

Summary

Murphy's law has a way of catching up with you, and this chapter introduced you to some of the tooling available to investigate problems. WebSphere has a number of investigative tools and information logs to assist with your troubleshooting. Starting with the Administrative Console, you can gain a high-level idea of what problems are occurring. From this high level, you can be informed about severe errors, audit messages, and warning messages.

But the console is not enough. When errors strike, you can turn to the many log files available to help you decipher the clues. For installation errors, you can turn to the `wssetup.log` and the `wasdb2.log`. These two logs provide the status of the initial setup of WebSphere and DB2.

Tracefile is the first log you go to for problems with the Administrative Server. You find information, such as server configuration and Java stack traces, for exceptions that were thrown. You also find similar information in the standard error and standard output logs from the Administrative Server and application servers.

If problems are caused by the HTTP Server, you can check the `native.log` file and look for problems. The native log provides information on the health of the WebSphere plug-in.

You learned about the many logs that are output from the many components of WebSphere. The understanding of the topology is critical in your investigative process.

When logs are not enough and you need to get more detailed information, you can turn to traces. WebSphere provides a robust tracing facility. You can trace the entire Administrative Server or individual Java packages. The trace specifications can be set to output existing debug traces, as well as traces that identify which methods are actually being run.

You can run traces from the console or at the start of the Administrative Server. Normally you wouldn't want to keep Trace running very long, because it is resource intensive.

If the trace cannot provide enough information, and you are looking for some expert advice, turn to Log Analyzer. Log Analyzer reads an activity log file that contains records of the errors, warnings, and audits produced. The `activity.log` file is produced from the Administrative Server. The log can be used in conjunction with a downloadable symptoms table. By selecting color-coded records, you can sometimes find matching answers to the symptoms you are experiencing.

With the use of messages, traces, logs, and Log Analyzer, you have the means to solve most problems.

Chapter 27

Using the WebSphere Control Program

In This Chapter

- ♦ Introducing wscp
- ♦ Understanding Tcl
- ♦ Launching wscp
- ♦ Writing wscp scripts
- ♦ Migrating wscp scripts

This chapter discusses the WebSphere Control Program (wscp), a command-line client alternative to the Administrative Console for performing server administration and configuration tasks. This chapter contains a WebSphere Control Program (wscp) overview that describes how the wscp relates to the Administrative Console. It briefly discusses the benefits and shortcomings of wscp. The overview section also lists the object types and services that wscp can support.

A section about understanding Tcl covers the basic syntax of the underlying scripting language. Then you move on to learn how to launch WebSphere Control Program. This section describes how to use wscp in command-line and interactive modes, how to run Tcl scripts, and how to access the help facility.

The next section covers writing and using wscp scripts, providing you with the basics of creating a script. You step through a more complicated script to deploy the sample application provided with the WebSphere installation.

"Using the WscpCommand interface" covers how to execute wscp commands from within a Java application by using the WscpCommand class. The section on migrating scripts from version 3.5.x to version 4.0 talks about some of the changes you need to be aware of if you have scripts from a prior version you want to use.

Introducing WebSphere Control Program (wscp)

WSCP was first introduced in WebSphere Version 3.5. Readers already familiar with this facility might want to skip ahead to the section "Migrating scripts from 3.5 to 4.0." Using wscp, you can administer almost all the resources available to the console in a command-line or interactive interface. One additional item to note is that wscp is not supported in the Advanced Single Server Edition.

WCSP is based on the Java Command Language (Jacl), which is a 100 percent Java implementation of Tcl (tool command language). Tcl is a portable command language with full programming-language functionality (procedures, variables, conditional logic, and so on). This chapter covers only Tcl, because Jacl does not add any syntactical differences and all documentation available to you talks about Tcl. This section contains the following subsections:

- Understanding the Administrative Console and wscp
- Understanding the benefits of using wscp
- Understanding the limitations of using wscp
- Understanding supported object types

Understanding the Administrative Console and wscp

The Administrative Server manages a domain by maintaining a repository of contents and activities. The repository provides a central location and access point for descriptive data about the applications that are deployed to the domain.

All administration of the domain is accomplished by manipulating the objects in the repository. Every object in the repository represents a resource in the domain. As an example, an application server would have an application server object in the repository.

The Administrative Console and the wscp can both be used to administer the domain's resources. Both modify the repository. Both have access to system and task status information. Actions performed in one are reflected in the other. The Administrative Console provides a graphical user interface, and wscp uses a command line interface or scripts.

Choosing one or the other is a matter of preference. You might choose to use wscp instead of the Administrative Console for several reasons. You might have developed scripts under WebSphere 3.5 and want to take advantage of the scripts already developed. You might prefer to use the command-line interface rather than bringing up the console. Lastly, you might want to automate repetitive tasks that take several steps in the console.

Understanding the benefits of using wscp

The wscp interface provides a command-line tool for administering the domain repository. With wscp, you can use Tcl to automate administrative tasks by creating scripts (for example, create a script to start and stop applications as a group, something you can't do with the Administrative Console). You can write a Tcl script to create a full environment or (as illustrated later) deploy an application. Lastly, you can execute UNIX or Windows NT commands from within a wscp script or while in interactive mode.

Understanding the limitations of using wscp

You might have the impression by now that you can do anything with wscp that you can do with the Administrative Console. Unfortunately, there are some differences:

- As mentioned earlier, actions performed in one interface are reflected in the other. However, new configurations or changes made with wscp do not automatically reflect in the Administrative Console. To see changes in the console, you must poll the repository for changes by selecting the subtree of interest and using the Refresh button The same holds true in reverse. Changes or additions to the console do not automatically reflect in the wscp (interactive session). You must issue a wscp list command for the instance's object type or exit the sessions and start a new one for the changes to be seen. It is easiest to use just one tool at a time, and not both at the same time. Although this last statement might seem obvious, there are some who prefer to have all tools readily at hand.
- All administrative tasks that you can perform through the Administrative Console you can also perform with wscp, except some high-level tasks requiring wizards, such as creating an application, and security. These items require the use of wscp scripts.

Understanding supported object types

As mentioned previously, every resource is represented by an object in the repository. Each object has attributes (referred to as properties in the console). Object types are like classes, defining what a particular object will "look" like. Instances of these objects (specific objects) are the repository representations of domain resources.

You use the wscp interface to manipulate objects in the repository by performing operations on the selected objects. The wscp supports the following objects:

- ApplicationServer
- Context
- DataSource
- Domain
- DrAdmin

- EnterpriseApp
- GenericServer
- Help
- J2CConnectionFactory
- J2CresourceAdapter
- JDCDriver
- JMSConnectionFactory
- JMSDestination
- JMSProvider
- MailSession
- Module
- Node
- PmiService
- Remote
- SecurityConfig
- SecurityRoleAssignment
- ServerGroup
- URL
- URLProvider
- VirtualHost
- XMLConfig

You must provide certain attributes for each object type. The wscp provides default values for the other attributes that can be overridden.

Understanding Tcl

Tcl is a scripting language that was developed by John Ousterhout. Both Tcl and Jacl are available from Active State (`http://tcl.activestate.com`). Tcl and Jacl are open source and follow the guidelines of the GNU Open Source License agreement. Jacl is a pure Java implementation of Tcl; however, you should note that the same syntax is used for both. Jacl has the added advantage of being platform independent and provides the capability to access Java methods.

For a scripting language, Tcl has a simple syntax. A Tcl command is formed by words separated by white space. The first word is the name of the command, and the remaining words are arguments to the command:

```
cmd arg arg arg
```

The dollar sign (`$`) substitutes the value of a variable. In this example, the variable name is `foo`:

```
$foo
```

Square brackets execute a nested command. For example, if you want to pass the result of one command as the argument to another, you use this syntax. In this example, the nested command is `clock` and the argument is `seconds`, which gives the current time in seconds:

```
[ clock seconds]
```

Double quotation marks group words as a single argument to a command. Dollar signs and square brackets are interpreted inside double quotation mark:

```
"some stuff"
```

Curly braces also group words into a single argument. In this case, however, elements within the braces are not interpreted:

```
{ some stuff}
```

The backslash (\) is used to quote special characters. For example, `\n` generates a new line. The backslash is also used to turn off the special meanings of the dollar sign, quotation marks, square brackets, and curly braces:

```
\
```

The following Tcl command prints the current time. It uses three Tcl commands: `set`, `clock`, and `puts`. The `set` command creates the variable `myseconds`. The `clock` command retrieves the current time in seconds. The `puts` command prints the text, and the `clock` command is used again to format the seconds into date and time:

```
set myseconds [ clock seconds]
puts "The time is [ clock format $myseconds] "
```

Note that you do not use `$` when assigning to a variable. You use `$` only when you want the value. The `myseconds` variable isn't needed in the previous example. You could print the current time with one command:

```
puts "The time is [ clock format [ clock seconds] ] "
```

The Tcl syntax is used to guide the Tcl parser through three steps: argument grouping, result substitution, and command dispatch.

- *Argument grouping:* Tcl needs to determine how to organize the arguments to the commands. In the simplest case, white space separates arguments. As stated earlier, the quotation marks and braces syntax is used to group multiple words into one argument. In the previous example, double quotation marks group a single argument to the `puts` command.

- *Result substitution:* After the arguments are grouped, Tcl performs string substitutions. Put simply, it replaces `$foo` with the value of the variable `foo`, and it replaces bracketed commands with their results. It is crucial that substitutions are done after grouping. This sequence ensures that unusual values do not complicate the structure of commands.
- *Command dispatch:* After substitution, Tcl uses the command name, such as `puts`, as a key into a dispatch table. It calls the C procedure identified in the table, and the C procedure implements the command. You can also write command procedures in Tcl. There are simple conventions about argument passing and handling errors.

Here is a more complex example of a Tcl command that uses a `while` loop:

```
set i 0
while {$i < 10} {
    puts "$i squared = [expr $i*$i]"
    incr i
}
```

In this example, curly braces are used to group arguments without doing any substitutions. The Tcl parser knows nothing special about the `while` command. It treats it like any other command. It is the implementation of the `while` command that knows the first argument is an expression, and the second argument exists of more Tcl commands. The braces group two arguments: the Boolean expression that controls the loop, and the commands in the loop body.

You also see two math expressions: the Boolean comparison and multiplication. The `while` command automatically evaluates its first argument as an expression. In other cases, you must explicitly use the `expr` command to perform math evaluation. The following example uses conditional logic to determine a factorial:

```
proc fac {x} {
    if {$x < 0} {
        error "Invalid argument $x: must be a positive integer"
    } elseif {$x <= 1} {
        return 1
    } else {
        return [expr $x * [fac [expr $x-1]]]
    }
}
```

Note the use of nested commands on the return line.

> **ON THE WEB:** For more information on Tcl, check out the Tcldeveloper Web site at `www.scriptics.com`.

Launching wscp

Now that you have an understanding of Tcl basics, you are ready to begin using wscp, which you launch from the command line on Windows platforms by running the following code:

```
<WAS_HOME>\bin\wscp.bat
```

On UNIX platforms, you launch by running the following code:

```
<WAS_HOME>/bin/wscp.sh
```

You will probably want to add the `<WAS_HOME>\bin` directory to your path environmental variable to avoid the extra typing. Remember, the Administrative Server must be running prior to starting wscp.

Understanding the basic syntax

The syntax for the wscp command is as follows:

```
wscp [-h] [-c command] -f file] [-p file] [-x extension] [-- options]
```

Following are the command-line options and arguments:

- `-h` displays usage information.
- `-c` command evaluates the specified Tcl command.
- `-f file` evaluates the specified file of Tcl commands.
- `-p file` evaluates the specified properties file.
- `-x extension` loads the specified Tcl extension class.
- `-- options` sets Tcl `argc` and `argv` variables as specified.

You can get this information on syntax by entering **`wscp -h`** at the command prompt.

The general format of all wscp actions is as follows:

```
<object-type> <action> [name] [options]
```

- `object-type` is the name of an object type.
- `action` is the action to be performed.
- `name` is the name of the object instance.
- `options` varies by action.

Some objects and options require additional fields in the command:

- `value` for options that require a value.
- `attribute` available for some objects.
- `attribute_list` provides a list of valid attributes for selected object type and action.

You can see how to get a list of available objects later in the section, "Getting help for objects."

NOTE: Commands in wscp are case sensitive; be sure to check the online references to determine which form to use.

Referring to objects

You refer to objects with the following syntax:

```
/<object_type>:<name>/
```

You refer to an application server with the following syntax:

```
{ /Node:localhost/ApplicationServer:Default_Server/}
```

You see examples of both of these in the section, “Writing and using wscp scripts.”

Using the command shell

What you have seen so far can be executed from the command line. If no `-c`, `-f`, or `-h` option is specified with the wscp command, the interactive shell is started. Interactive mode is indicated by the command prompt changing from `c:\`, for example, to `wscp>`.

The wscp tool executes commands you enter and returns the results in the shell. To leave the shell, use the `exit` command:

```
wscp>exit
```

In an interactive session, you can break the line of a wscp command after a left brace (`{`) or after typing a backslash (`\`). A question mark (`?`) prompt is displayed, and you can continue typing the command.

Executing wscp scripts

Scripts can be executed from the command line or from the interactive shell. From the command line you specify the `-f` option and the name of the executable file that contains the script. So, for example, the following command

```
wscp -f testScript.tcl
```

executes the script in the `testScript.tcl` file.

To execute the same script from the interactive session, you must first use the Tcl `source` command followed by the source filename without extensions:

```
wscp> source showStatus.tcl
wscp> showStatus
```

Invoking the wscp properties file

When you invoke the wscp tool, it reads a Java properties file you specify with the `-p` option on the command line:

```
wscp -p myProperties
```

The properties file can be used to automatically load settings for various properties, amending or replacing system properties that are already defined. If you don’t specify a properties file, wscp looks for `<USERPROFILE>\.wscprc` to use as properties file, where

`<USERPROFILE>` is the value of the Java property `user.home`. If that file does not exist (and it won't unless you create it), you get the default properties for `hostName=localhost` and `hostPort=900`. Although you can get by with the defaults, it is good practice to explicitly define the properties for your environment. Listing 27-1 is an example of my base properties file.

Listing 27-1: Sample Properties File

```
#
# hostName is used for com.ibm.CORBA.BootstrapHost
#
wscp.hostName=was.local.com
#
# hostPort is used for com.ibm.CORBA.BootstrapPort
#
wscp.hostPort=900
#
```

Connecting to remote nodes

When you start wscp, you are normally connected to the local Administrative Server. You can change this by changing the `wscp.hostName` property in the properties file to identify a different host. When you do this, you also need to change the `wscp.hostPort` property to point to a port other than 900 (the default for the local port). Listing 27-2 is the base properties file from Listing 27-1, changed for a remote connection.

Listing 27-2: Properties File Specifying a Remote Node

```
#
# hostName is used for com.ibm.CORBA.BootstrapHost
#
# wscp.hostName=was.local.com
wscp.hostName=wasdev.remote.com
#
# hostPort is used for com.ibm.CORBA.BootstrapPort
#
#wscp.hostPort=900
wscp.hostPort=800
#
```

Accessing online help

Getting help in the wscp shell is pretty straightforward; simply enter **Help** at the `wscp>` prompt or specify Help as a command:

```
c:\wscp -c Help
```

The output from either form of the command gives you the first-level help for the subsystem as illustrated in Figure 27-1.

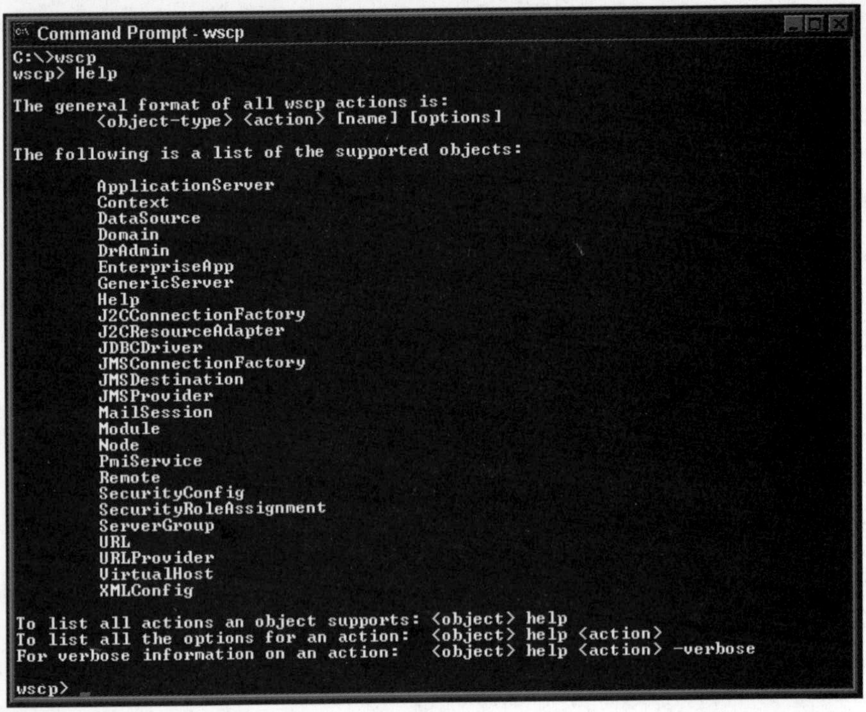

```
Command Prompt - wscp
C:\>wscp
wscp> Help

The general format of all wscp actions is:
        <object-type> <action> [name] [options]

The following is a list of the supported objects:

        ApplicationServer
        Context
        DataSource
        Domain
        DrAdmin
        EnterpriseApp
        GenericServer
        Help
        J2CConnectionFactory
        J2CResourceAdapter
        JDBCDriver
        JMSConnectionFactory
        JMSDestination
        JMSProvider
        MailSession
        Module
        Node
        PmiService
        Remote
        SecurityConfig
        SecurityRoleAssignment
        ServerGroup
        URL
        URLProvider
        VirtualHost
        XMLConfig

To list all actions an object supports: <object> help
To list all the options for an action:  <object> help <action>
For verbose information on an action:   <object> help <action> -verbose

wscp> _
```

Figure 27-1: Result of entering Help at the wscp> prompt.

NOTE: To get help on an object you specify, use help not Help; the shell is case sensitive.

Getting help for objects

You use the help action to get general syntax, to list all options for a given option, and even to get detailed information about the options by using the `-verbose` option with an action. Not all actions have additional detail to display.

For example, if you want to find all the available actions for the `ApplicationServer` object, enter the following command:

```
wscp>ApplicationServer help
```

The results of this command are shown in Figure 27-2.

You probably already noticed that using `Help` and `help` give you only information on wscp help. If you enter **?** at the wscp prompt, you get a list of all the Tcl commands supported.

```
Command Prompt - wscp
wscp> ApplicationServer help
WSCP0000I: The following actions are available for ApplicationServer

attributes          Display the attributes of the object
containment         Display the containment hierarchy for the object
create              Create the specified object
defaults            Display attribute defaults
help                Display this help message
list                Display all the instances of this type
modify              Modify the attributes of the specified object
operations          List all the actions available on the object type
remove              Remove the specified object
show                Display the attributes of specified object
showall             Display all attributes of specified object
start               Start the specified object
stop                Stop the specified object

wscp>
```

Figure 27-2: ApplicationServer help shows you the available actions for this object.

Getting a list of objects

To display all the instances of a particular type of object, you need to use the `list` command. To find out the syntax of the `list` subcommand, specify help as follows:

```
wscp> ApplicationServer help list -verbose
```

Figure 27-3 shows the results of this command. Here the use of the `-verbose` modifier shows the definitions for the available options to add to the command.

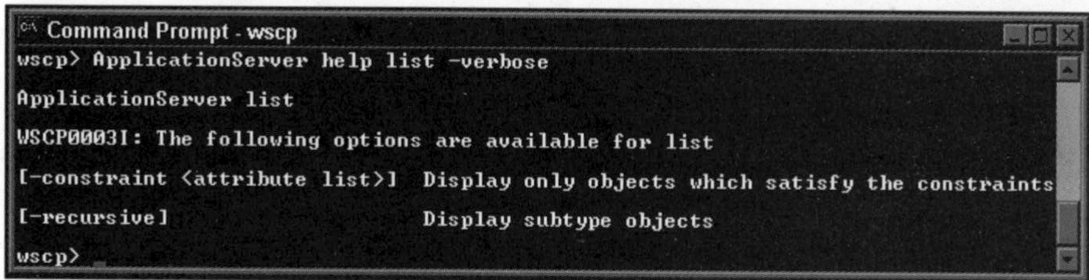

```
Command Prompt - wscp
wscp> ApplicationServer help list -verbose

ApplicationServer list

WSCP0003I: The following options are available for list

[-constraint <attribute list>]  Display only objects which satisfy the constraints

[-recursive]                    Display subtype objects

wscp>
```

Figure 27-3: Detail on options for list action.

You can also use the `-recursive` option to list all instances of object subtypes. For example, `JDBCDriver list -recursive` is used to list subtypes for the `JDBCDriver` object. Figure 27-4 shows the results.

```
Command Prompt - wscp
wscp> JDBCDriver list -recursive
{/JDBCDriver:Sample DB Driver/} {/JDBCDriver:Sample DB Driver/DataSource:SampleDat
aSource/} {/JDBCDriver:Sample DB Driver/DataSource:sample/} {/JDBCDriver:Sample DB
 Driver/DataSource:PetStoreDatasource/}
wscp>
```

Figure 27-4: JDBCDriver list with –recursive option.

You can refine your listing by specifying the `-constraint` option. Code in the following example lists only the data sources whose `DatabaseName` is `PETSDB`:

```
wscp> DataSource list -constraint {{DatabaseName PETSDB}} -recursive
```

Figure 27-5 shows the results of using the `-constraint` option.

```
Command Prompt - wscp
wscp> DataSource list -constraint {{DatabaseName PETSDB}} -recursive
{/JDBCDriver:Sample DB Driver/DataSource:PetStoreDatasource/}
wscp>
```

Figure 27-5: DataSource list with constraints applied.

Understanding error and status handling

The wscp shell supports error handling with the `errorCode` and `errorInfo` variables. When a wscp command is successful, it returns a result or an empty string. When these commands are run from the shell (`wscp>`), the results are displayed in the shell. If a wscp command fails, it raises a TclException, which stops the execution of the enclosing procedure, unless you use the Tcl `catch` command.

When wscp catches an exception, it appends the stack trace to the `errorInfo` variable. This variable can be viewed from within the shell using either of the following commands:

```
wscp>puts $errorInfo
wscp>set errorInfo
```

When wscp commands are executed, the Tcl variable `errorCode` is set. An error is represented by a nonzero return value. The `errorCode` variable is an integer. The static method `statusToString` of `com.ibm.ejs.sm.ejscp.WscpStatus` can be used to translate an `errorCode` value. The following is an example of a Tcl procedure that translates an `errorCode` value:

```
proc statusToString {{status -1}} {
global errorCode
if {$status == -1 && $errorCode != "NONE"} {set status $errorCode}
java::call com.ibm.ejs.sm.ejscp.WscpStatus statusToString $status
```

Notice how, in this script, the call to the Java method, `statusToString`, is made from within the Tcl script.

Writing and using wscp scripts

You can use scripts for a number of things. Mostly you will want to use scripts to automate tasks or make some of the more common tasks easier to handle. For example, you can create a script that enables you to get the status for all servers in the domain (see the `showStatus` script in the next section). Without a script, it would be necessary to issue the status command individually for each server. You can also write a simple script to create a complete environment.

Creating a wscp script

You create a script with the editor of your choice and save it with an extension of `.tcl`. This section walks you through an example that displays the value for the `Name` and `CurrentState` attributes of all application servers on a domain. Listing 27.3 shows you the script.

Listing 27-3: Sample wscp Script

```
proc showStatus {} {
puts stdout "\nStatus of servers in the domain:\n"

foreach ejbserver [ApplicationServer list] {
puts [ApplicationServer show $ejbserver -attribute {Name CurrentState}]
}
}
showStatus
```

In the first line, you declare a procedure named `showStatus`. This procedure has no arguments, hence the empty curly braces { }. Next you write a line to `stdout` to print a report title. Then you create a loop that looks at every `ejbserver` defined (using `[ApplicationServer list]` to list them all and prints out the `Name` and `CurrentState` using the `puts` command. Finally, you add a line to execute the procedure you just created:

You don't need to add this final line unless you run the script from the command line with the `-f` option, but it doesn't hurt to add it. It gives you more flexibility.

Running a wscp script

To execute the script you wrote in the preceding section from the command line, enter the following command:

```
wscp -f showStatus.tcl
```

Alternatively, you can start WebSphere Control Program and run the following command:

```
wscp>source showStatus.tcl
```

If you left out the `showStatus` line at the end of the `showStatus.tcl` file, you need to execute the script after loading it by running the following line:

```
wscp>showStatus
```

You need to remember that the `source` command is valid only for an active wscp shell session. If you exit the shell, you need to rerun any source commands. If you consistently run a series of scripts or procedures, you might find it more convenient to create a script that loads all scripts with a single command.

The following steps cover a more complicated script that is used to load the sample application provided with WebSphere. The complete script can be seen in Listing 27-4.

Listing 27-4: Script to Install sampleApp

```
set mynode xxxxxxxx
set instdir c:/WebSphere/AppServer/installableApps/
set earfile sampleApp.ear
set sname "Default Server"
set jdbcdrivername "Sample DB Driver"
set datasourcename SampleDataSource1
set vhostname "default_host"
set db2implclass Com.ibm.db2.jdbc.DB2ConnectionPoolDataSource
set db2zipfile "c:/Program Files/SQLLIB/java/db2java.zip"
set dbname WAS
set dbuser db2admin
set dbpassword db2admin
set implclassattr [ list ImplClass $db2implclass]
set descriptionattr [ list Description "Sample JDBC Driver build by
wscp"]
set attributelist [ list $implclassattr $descriptionattr]

JDBCDriver create /JDBCDriver:$jdbcdrivername/ -attribute $attributelist
JDBCDriver install /JDBCDriver:$jdbcdrivername/ -node /Node:$mynode/ -
jarFile $db2zipfile

set databasenameattr [ list DatabaseName $dbname]
set defaultuserattr [ list DefaultUser $dbuser]
set defaultpasswordattr [ list DefaultPassword $dbpassword]
set descriptionattr [ list Description "Sample DataSource build by wscp"]
set attributelist [ list $databasenameattr $defaultuserattr
$defaultpasswordattr $descriptionattr]

DataSource create
/JDBCDriver:$jdbcdrivername/DataSource:$datasourcename/ -attribute
$attributelist

EnterpriseApp install /Node:$mynode/ $instdir$earfile -defappserver
/Node:${ mynode} /ApplicationServer:${ sname} /
```

The next several steps break down the script and detail what each section does. Note that this script was written with the condition that the JDBCDriver has not already been created and installed and that the data source has not been previously created. It also assumes that you not have already installed the sample application (sampleApp).

1. First you set the variables you need later in the script, as shown in the following:

```
set mynode xxxxxxxx
set instdir c:/WebSphere/AppServer/installableApps/
set earfile sampleApp.ear
set sname "Default Server"
set jdbcdrivername "Sample DB Driver"
set datasourcename SampleDataSource1
set vhostname "default_host"
set db2implclass Com.ibm.db2.jdbc.DB2ConnectionPoolDataSource
set db2zipfile "c:/Program Files/SQLLIB/java/db2java.zip"
set dbname WAS
set dbuser xxxxxxxx
set dbpassword xxxxxxxx
```

2. You need to change the values for variables `mynode`, `instdir`, `db2zipfile`, `dbuser`, and `dbpassword` to match your configuration. An easy way to find your node name for the `mynode` variable is to issue the command `Node list`.

   The next section creates the JDBCDriver. If the driver was already installed, you get an error indicating that a driver with that name has already been installed:

```
set implclassattr [ list ImplClass $db2implclass]
set descriptionattr [ list Description "Sample JDBC Driver build by wscp"]
set attributelist [ list $implclassattr $descriptionattr]

JDBCDriver create JDBCDriver:${ jdbcdrivername} -attribute $attributelist
```

   In Figure 27-6, you can see how the `JDBCDriver create` statement matches with the syntax:

```
Command Prompt - wscp
wscp> JDBCDriver help create
JDBCDriver create <name> [-attribute <attribute list>]
wscp>
```

   Figure 27-6: JDBCDriver help create.

   Note the use of the `$attributelist` variable to chain attributes and make the `create` statement easier to read. Now that you have created the driver, you need to install it. Figure 27-7 shows you the syntax.

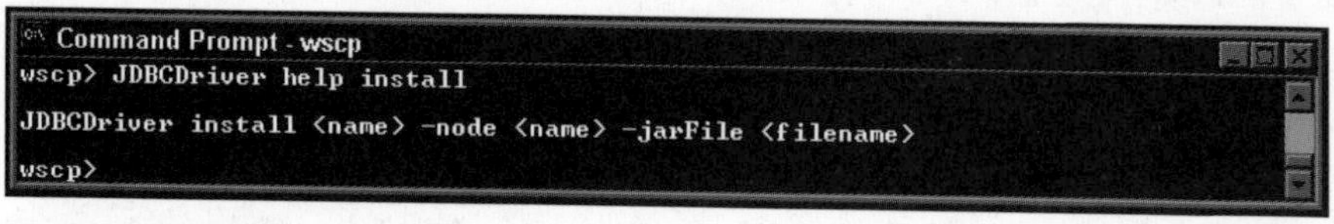

```
Command Prompt - wscp
wscp> JDBCDriver help install
JDBCDriver install <name> -node <name> -jarFile <filename>
wscp>
```

   Figure 27-7: JDBCDriver help install.

3. Enter code the line using your variables:

```
JDBCDriver install /JDBCDriver:$jdbcdrivername/ -node /Node:$mynode/
-jarFile $db2zipfile
```

4. Set the variables and create the data source:

```
set databasenameattr [ list DatabaseName $dbname]
set defaultuserattr [ list DefaultUser $dbuser]
set defaultpasswordattr [ list DefaultPassword $dbpassword]
set descriptionattr [ list Description "Sample DataSource build by wscp"]
set attributelist [ list $databasenameattr $defaultuserattr
$defaultpasswordattr $descriptionattr]

DataSource create
/JDBCDriver:${ jdbcdrivername} /DataSource:${ datasourcename} / -attribute
$attributelist
```

By now, you know how to check the syntax. Note that, due to margin settings used here, the data source appears to be on multiple lines. In your editor, you will want this on a single line. Note the use of the curly braces {} in the fully qualified name

```
/JDBCDriver:${ jdbcdrivername} /DataSource:${ datasourcename} /
```

They keep the parser from treating the rest of the object as part of the variable.

5. Next you create the virtual host:

```
set aliaslist [ list *:80 *:9080]
set aliasattr [ list AliasList $aliaslist]
set attributelist [ list $aliasattr]

VirtualHost create /VirtualHost:$vhostname/ -attribute $attributelist
```

6. Finally, you install the application:

```
EnterpriseApp install /Node:$mynode/ $instdir$earfile -defappserver
/Node:${ mynode} /ApplicationServer:${ sname} /
```

7. Now save the script and execute it in the shell following the directions given in the subsection "Executing wscp scripts."

Using the WscpCommand interface

wscp is built on Jacl, which means that you should be able to execute wscp commands from within a Java program.

You use the `com.ibm.ejs.sm.ejscp.wscpcommand.WscpCommand` interface to embed wscp operations in a Java application. You link the to the interface with the `wscp.jar` file located in `<WAS_HOME>\lib\`.

Using WscpCommand Constructors

There are two constructors provided with the `WscpCommand` interface:

- `WscpCommand(String node, String port)`
  - `node` indicates the name of the WebSphere Application Server node on which the wscp operation is executed (such as `localhost`).
  - `port` indicates the port number of the Administrative Server
- `WscpCommand()`

The default values for this constructor are `localhost` for node and 900 for port (the default port number of the Administrative Server).

Using WscpCommand public methods

There are two public methods in the WscpCommand interface: `WscpResult evalCommand(String command)` and `String getErrorInfo()`.

The `WscpResult evalCommand(String command)` method evaluates a wscp operation and returns the results. Use the same syntax as you would for interactive or scripted wscp operations.

The results of the `evalCommand` method are encoded in a `com.ibm.ejs.sm.wscpcommand.WscpResult` object. Table 27-1 lists the methods this object can use to evaluate the returned value.

Table 27-1: WscpResult Methods

Method	*Description*
toString	Returns a string representation of the results of the wscp operation.
success	Returns a Boolean value indicating whether the wscp operation was successful.
listToVector	If the expected result of the wscp operation is a list; use this method to return a vector containing the list elements.
attribPairsToVector	If the expected result of the wscp operation is a list of attribute-value pairs, use this method to return a vector containing the list. Each element of the vector is an attribute-value pair.
attribPairsToHashTable	If the expected result of the wscp operation is a set of attribute-value pairs, use this method to return a hash table containing the values keyed on the attributes.

The method `String getErrorInfo()` returns the status of an `evalCommand` method whose results are returned in a `WscpResult` object:

- If the wscp operation specified in the `evalCommand` executes successfully, the `getErrorInfo` method returns an empty string.
- If the wscp operation does not execute successfully, the `getErrorInfo` method returns the exception information that was received from wscp. `getErrorInfo` does not receive any information, it merely reports the contents of the variable that was set by the error code.

The following is an example of how to use the `evalCommand` and `getErrorInfo` methods:

```
String cmd = "ApplicationServer list";
WscpResult results = wscpCommand.evalCommand(cmd);
if (!results.success()) {
      System.out.println("Command failed; exception information: " +
                             results.getErrorInfo());
}
```

Using qualified names

Another difference between the Administrative Console and wscp is the use of qualified names. The console uses simple names, such as AppServer and EJBSource, (it concatenates the names under the covers). The wscp requires fully qualified names. *Fully qualified names* are representations of the object hierarchy in the repository. Fully qualified names have the following form:

```
/objectType:objectInstance/
```

For example, if the application server named sampleApp runs on node named kafemocha, the fully qualified name found in the repository would be: `/Node:kafemocha/ApplicationServer:sampleApp/`.

`WscpQualifiedName` is a utility class that is part of the `WscpCommand` interface. This class enables you to manipulate fully qualified wscp object names.

`WscpQualifiedName(fullyqualifiedname)` is the constructor for the `WscpQualifiedName` method where `fullyqualifiedname` is the fully qualified wscp name of an object. Table 27-2 shows the methods available for the `WscpQualifiedName` class.

Table 27-2: WscpQualifiedName Methods

Method	*Description*
getName	Gets the object name at the specified containment level
getObject	Gets the object type at the specified containment level
toString	Returns a string representation of the object name
numberOfLevels	Returns the number of containment levels

The `WscpQualifiedName` class contains the following constants, which define the containment levels at which various components are named:

- ENTERPRISE_APPLICATION
- DATASOURCE
- JDBC_DRIVER
- NODE
- SERVER_GROUP
- VIRTUAL_HOST
- APPLICATION_SERVER
- GENERIC_SERVER
- WEB_RESOURCE
- WEB_APPLICATION
- MODULE
- JMS_PROVIDER
- JMS_CONNECTION_FACTORY
- JMS_LISTENER
- J2C_CONNECTOR
- MAIL_SESSION
- URL
- URL_PROVIDER

The following example shows how this class can be used:

```
String name = "{ /Node:MyNode/ApplicationServer:MyAppServer/} "
WscpQualifiedName qName = new WscpQualifiedName(name);
qName.numberOfLevels();          // returns 2
qName.getObject(2);              // returns "Application Server"
qName.getName(2);               // returns "MyAppServer"
qName.getName(WscpQualifiedName.APPLICATION_SERVER)  // returns "MyAppServer"
```

Migrating scripts from version 3.5.x to version 4.0

You might have scripts already developed in 3.5.x that you want to use with version 4.0. You need to consider a number of changes. This section exposes the most common ones. For additional detail, you should refer to the WebSphere InfoCenter. It is probably a good idea to test all 3.5.x scripts before migrating them to your 4.0 production environment.

Discontinued objects

If you went through the Help section that shows you how to obtain a list of available objects, you probably noticed some of the following to be missing:

- EJBContainer
- EnterpriseBean
- Servlet
- ServletEngine
- ServletRedirector
- SessionManager
- UserProfile
- WebApplication
- WebResource

These objects have all been removed.

Renamed objects

The following objects were renamed in version 4.0:

- EnterpriseApplication is renamed `EnterpriseApp`.
- Model is renamed `ServerGroup`

Same name, new syntax

In 4.0, DataSource has a new syntax. Refer to the online Help for detailed information on the syntax for DataSource.

New objects

The following objects are new in WebSphere 4.0. Each of these objects is available for use in a Tcl script. For detailed information on each of these items, refer to the online help using the command `<object> help` from the `wscp>` prompt:

- Enterprise Information Systems (EIS) connectivity
  - *J2CConnectionFactory :* A set of connection configuration values that are used by the J2C connection poolmanager to specify how applications connect to a backend system.
  - *J2CresourceAdapter:* A module that enables connections to a specific back-end system.
- Java Message Service (JMS)
  - *JMSConnectionFactory:* A client uses a JMS connection factory object to connect to the messaging system.
  - *JMSDestination:* A client uses a JMS destination object to specify the target of the messages it sends or the source of the messages it receives.
  - *JMSProvider:* A JMS provider implements the JMS messaging interfaces.
- J2EE modules
  - Module
- URL
  - *URL:* Enables you to create an instance of a URL.
  - *URLProvider:* Enables you to create an instance of a URL provider.
- Performance data
  - *PmiService:* Enables you to get performance information and perform functions like enabling and disabling tracing.
- Security
  - *SecurityConfig:* Enables you to enable and disable WebSphere security on a global basis.
  - *SecurityRoleAssignment:* Enables you to manage security roles for J2EE applications.

Summary

This chapter has given you a brief exposure to wscp. A full treatment of this powerful tool could make a book in itself. You are encouraged to checkout the WebSphere InfoCenter for a complete treatment of this subject area.

You began with an overview of wscp. You learned about its origins and how it relates to the Administrative Console. You read about its advantages and saw that there are limitations. You learned how wscp is a valid alternative to using the console and how it gives you the capability to create scripts for repetitive tasks or to access status on multiple objects, which would take several steps in the console.

You learned a little bit about Tcl, the foundation for wscp. You learned syntax and, perhaps, you tried some of the simple examples yourself. You were shown how Tcl is a full-featured language that includes advanced features, such as conditional logic and nested processing. You are encouraged to check out the references in the Tcl section to learn more about this powerful scripting language.

You learned next about the extensions that enable you to use Tcl to gain access to objects in the WebSphere repository. You learned how to start an interactive wscp session and how to write Tcl scripts that run from the command prompt using the `-f` operator. You also learned how to use the `Help` and help keywords to get more information on what is available for each object and the syntax to get the information. You also learned that you can use `?` to get general Tcl command help.

You stepped through a sample script that can be used to install one of the WebSphere sample applications. Remember, that the script provided assumes that you don't have the Sample DB Driver installed or default_host set as the virtual host.

You then moved on to the Java interface to wscp – `WscpCommand`. In this, section you learned about the methods that give you programmatic access to the same commands you use from the wscp prompt.

Lastly, you stepped through the changes to WebSphere 4.0 that are accessible from the wscp interface. Be sure to check out the references, and you will see that you can do anything with commands and script in wscp, including starting and stopping servers and applications. Creating applications, removing applications, and modifying parameters in existing applications are all actions you can perform.

Chapter 28
Managing WebSphere with XMLConfig

In This Chapter

- Understanding XMLConfig
- Using XMLConfig
- Managing changes using XMLConfig

In Chapter 27, you learned about the WebSphere Control Program (wscp). With wscp, you can automate and perform many of the repetitive tasks for which the WebSphere administrator is responsible. Another tool that can simplify management of WebSphere domains is XMLConfig.

In this chapter, you learn how to create utilities that use XMLConfig to simplify some of the tasks that normally take too long to handle using the Administrative Console. For instance, starting and stopping the application server can be done with a single command-line execution.

Given the name, XMLConfig, you can probably guess that XMLConfig has something to do with Extensible Markup Language (XML). You are right, XML has a lot to do with it. You get a quick overview of XML to get you started followed by the basics of the XMLConfig structure. You learn about objects and actions that are used in XMLConfig.

The chapter ends with a series of XMLConfig examples showing how to start and stop applications servers, update configurations without the use of the Administrative Console, and create server groups and clones that make workload-management administration easier. You can perform all these actions as you work through the examples in the chapter. So let's get started with XMLConfig.

> **NOTE**: A new scripting interface call WSADMIN will be replacing XMLConfig, the WebSphere Control Program (wscp), and SEAppInstall. It is written in the JACL scripting language.

Introducing XMLConfig

XMLConfig was first introduced with WebSphere 3.02. It significantly enhances the administrator's ability to back up, deploy, and inquire into the WebSphere repository. With XMLConfig, you can transform repetitive steps into simple scripts to manage environments effectively.

WebSphere Application Server stores your configuration information in a relational database management system (DBMS). The benefit of having a relational DBMS, such as DB2, as your shared repository is that it provides the following:

- Concurrent access
- Query capabilities
- Distributed access

All these capabilities have to be developed if a database doesn't provide them.

Persistence and accessibility needs are satisfied by storing configuration information in a database. Additions and updates to this information are conveniently done through the Administrative Console GUI. However, this interface is limited to a task-by-task approach.

> **NOTE**: XMLConfig uses XML documents as input parameters. Within these documents are the actions that instruct XMLConfig which administration activity to execute.

Determining when to use XMLConfig

The Administrative Console is perfect for interactive processing. Using the console, you can perform the following activities:

- Configure enterprise applications
- Review configurations
- Run an interactive export or import

Some activities are implemented less gracefully than others. For example, to perform a backup, you must first export the configurations and then perform some necessary steps to ensure that archival information is saved. You might also want to perform these steps while not attached to a user interface. Another activity that is not easily completed via the Administrative Console is replicating one configuration among multiple machines. Having to enter the same configuration in both your testing environments and your production environment is cumbersome. XMLConfig and wscp fill the gap between the user interface and command driven (and often unattended) activities.

Both administrative tools, the Administrative Console and XMLConfig, are similar because they help you administer resources in the administrative repository. The similarities continue in that both the console and XMLConfig enable you to perform WebSphere administration from any node in the environment.

The Administrative Console uses a graphical user interface (GUI), whereas XMLConfig uses commands and XML documents. The biggest difference is the number of changes that you can make. XMLConfig can execute many changes from a single command, whereas the Administrative Console changes only one thing at a time.

Understanding the role of XMLConfig

XMLConfig is a command-line tool that can modify, extract, or import configuration data. The changes to the configuration are held in XML documents that instruct XMLConfig what changes or commands need to be executed. XMLConfig can perform most of the same tasks as the interactive Administrative Console. Any changes done through XMLConfig are actual changes to the administrative repository.

With XMLConfig, you can export and import repository information from one Administrative Server repository to another. In WebSphere domains with multiple machines, this capability can reduce the possibility of errors and can streamline processes. An example would be moving configuration information defined in a WebSphere system-testing environment over to a quality-assurance testing environment.

XMLConfig bridges the gap left by the Administrative Console by enabling you to perform multiple administrative tasks with a single command. It supports the import and export of configuration data to and from the administrative repository. Figure 28-1 shows an architectural portrait.

Another major benefit to using XMLConfig is its use of Extensible Markup Language (XML). XML is the de facto standard in document information. XMLConfig takes full advantage of XML Document Type Definitions (DTD) to ensure information is properly represented. A DTD is a series of definitions for element types, attributes, entities, and notations. Now that's a mouthful. A simplified explanation would be to think of it as document style guide. If your document doesn't conform to the style guide, your document will be rejected. By having a document that has a DTD (style guide) that enforces the rules, you can be guaranteed that the document is system independent.

As you move to the next sections, you learn more about XML and how XMLConfig utilizes XML to provide data to the administrative and configuration commands. You learn which XML tags are used to map WebSphere resources or objects, how action attributes direct the type of action to perform, and how names identify the specific resource.

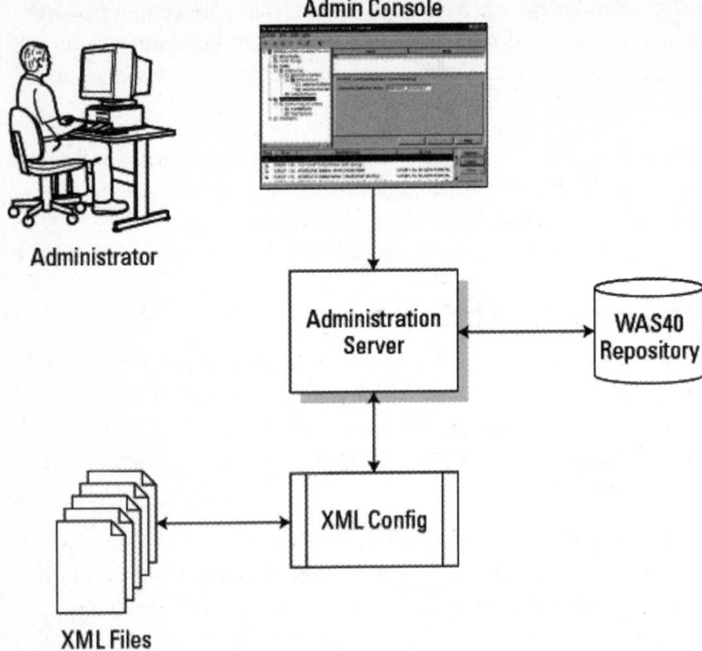

Figure 28-1: XMLConfig architectural overview.

Introducing XML basics

The XML framework for defining documents plays an important role in many of today's heterogeneous implementations. Its capability to describe the structure and content of documents has led to increased interoperability. Without XML, XMLConfig's capability to work across platforms, this wouldn't be as easy. As mentioned in the previous section, DTDs provide the validating structure to ensure the XML document is set up properly. With XMLConfig, you need to create XML documents that are validated against a DTD. These documents provide the instructions and commands to XMLConfig that will be applied to WebSphere. The following sections look a little deeper into DTDs.

Understanding the structure of Document Type Definition (DTD)

XML is all about structure, a hierarchical structure to be precise. Within this structure, elements provide a starting and ending point. Contained within the element is the data that the element represents.

XML contains element tags that identify content by utilizing start and end tags. Start and end tags follow a specific format. A start tag `<start>` must always have a closing end tag `</start>`. Tags can contain other tag pairs representing sub-elements (children). This parental behavior or structure is defined in the Document Type Definition (DTD). In addition to the parental structure, DTDs define the grammatical content and structure of an XML document by listing all the tags that can be used in an XML document. You might think of it as a laundry list of all the elements you can have within a document and the rules on how the document can be structured.

DTDs orchestrate the structure of XML documents by defining XML subcomponents of XML elements. The number of times an XML subcomponent can be repeated can be governed by the DTD. An example might be in order. By now you should know that a WebSphere Administrative Server contains a number of resources. It might have the following defined:

- Virtual hosts
- Database drivers
- Nodes
    - Application server

All these resources are contained with a WebSphere Administrative Server. Notice how the application server falls beneath Nodes in the previous list. An application server resides on a node (machine).

The DTD defines the general format and identifies valid values for XML elements. Listing 28-1 shows an abbreviated version of XML exported from the administrative repository. Many of the elements have been removed, but you get the idea.

Listing 28-1: Abbreviated Version of XML from the Administrative Repository

```
<?xml version="1.0"?>
<!DOCTYPE websphere-sa-config SYSTEM
"file:///$XMLConfigDTDLocation$$dsep$xmlconfig.dtd" >
<websphere-sa-config>
   <virtual-host action="update" name="default_host">
    ...
    </virtual-host>
   <jdbc-driver action="update" name="Sample DB Driver">
    ...
   </jdbc-driver>
   <node action="update" name="kafemocha">
     <application-server action="update" name="Default Server">
      <stdout>e:\WebSphere\AppServer/logs/ stdout.log</stdout>
      <stderr>e:\WebSphere\AppServer/logs/ stderr.log</stderr>
      <web-container>
         ...
      </web-container>
     </application-server>
   </node>
    ...
</WebSphere-sa-config>
```

As shown in Listing 28-1, the first line always is the XML version, and the second line is documentation type and location of DTD. Notice how the indenting helps show how certain elements can contain other elements. For instance, in Listing 28-1 you see that `<application-server>` contains `<stdout>`, `<stderr>`, and `<web-container>` elements. This powerful relationship enables you to select (or find) a particular element and affect changes upon its nested elements.

Not all of the elements are shown in Listing 28-1. Normally, you would see the following:

- Virtual hosts
- Java Database Connectivity (JDBC) driver
- Machine node information
- Application server
  - Web container
  - Transport and session management information
- Security configuration
- Enterprise application
- Enterprise archive (EAR) file name
- Role bindings
- Enterprise JavaBeans (EJB) modules
- Web modules

The grammar in Listing 28-1 shows is a hierarchy similar to the Administrative Console tree view shown in Figure 28-2.

Because of XML's hierarchical structure, XML documents work well with the tree structure. In Figure 28-2, a node has a name (`Kafemocha`) and contains the Application server, `Default Server`. If you compare the tree view with the DTD, you can see that the elements in the tree view identically match the elements within the XMLConfig document shown in Listing 28-1.

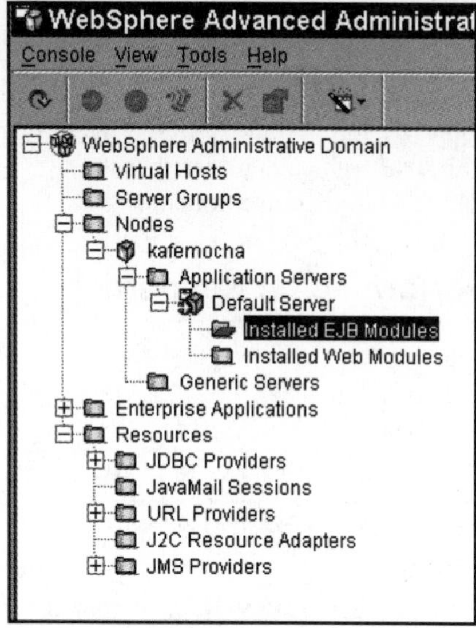

Figure 28-2: The Administrative Console tree view can be represented within an XML document and managed by XMLConfig.

Using objects, actions, and names in XML

In Listing 28-1, you might have noticed the attributes of some of the elements. Each element refers to a WebSphere resource or WebSphere `object`. A resource/object has `name` and can have some actions associated with it. Because the creators of the XMLConfig wanted it to perform actions on objects, they created the DTD to allow the addition of attributes such as `action` with valid values of `update`, `delete`, `locate`, `create`, and a few more.

The XML document has only the elements you decide to put into the document. If you enter some elements that cannot be validated, the document cannot be processed, and you will get errors returned. You then have to compare the DTD with the XML document to determine what rule you broke. What follows is a well-formed object from an XML document.

```
<application-server action="update" name="Default Server">
</application-server>
```

In the preceding object, the object type is `application-server`. The action is `update`, and the name is `Default Server`. The object type identifies the WebSphere object type. Although it is `application-server`, in this case, it could have been `virtual-host`. Both are valid objects. The `action` specifies the action to perform on the resource. The `name` uniquely identifies the resource to which the action is applied. Table 28-1 describes the supported actions that you could apply to your WebSphere administrative domain.

Table 28-1: Actions That Can Be Performed on Resources

Supported Actions in XMLconfig	***Action Results***
start	Starts the specified resource.
stop	Stops the specified resource.
restart	Restarts the specified resource. Valid only for machine notes and servlets.
stopforrestart	Stops the resource and preserves its state. On restart the state is restored. StopforRestart is only valid with machine nodes.
enable	Enables the resource for user requests. Valid for servlets only.
disable	Makes resources unavailable. Valid for servlets only.
locate	Locates the specified resource, establishes a path to child resources, and establishes the partial export and import actions.
create	Adds a resource, but if the resource already exists, it defaults to update. You must provide all required attributes on an create.
delete	Removes the resource. *Warning*: All children of the object will be removed.
update	Updates the resource. If resource does not exist it defaults to create. For update you need to provide only attributes to be updated.
export	Exports the resource configuration and all associated children. This applies only to partial exports.
ping	Determines whether the resource is active. Note: This functions similar to the TCPIP ping command.
createclone	Creates a clone.
associateclone	Associates a clone with a server group.
disassociateclone	Disassociates a clone from a server group.

The actions listed in Table 28-1 can be used in conjunction with administrative command. Of course, you must use them in the right context; otherwise, validation errors stop the process. For instance with the `application-server` object, you can use only the following actions:

- create
- update
- delete
- locate
- export
- start
- stop
- ping
- createclone
- associateclone
- disassociateclone

If you are unsure about which actions are applicable to an object, review the DTD found under `<was_home>/bin/xmlconfig.dtd`.

> **NOTE**: Do not assume that using the `update` action will default to a `create` action if the object does not exist. Unless all required attributes are provided for the create, the action fails.

Understanding XMLConfig Basics

Up to this point, you have learned about XMLConfig architecture. In this and following sections, you actually begin working with XMLConfig. You learn how to start XMLConfig with the command file. You also learn a little about the command file itself, what files it calls, and what parameters it can receive. The configuration changes you make start out as simple commands and then become more sophisticated. At that point, you learn how to substitute values within the XML document so you can override defaults.

In the following sections, you begin running examples of basic XMLConfig functionality. Keep in mind that XMLConfig commands are case-sensitive. This case sensitivity applies to names of objects as well. It all begins with the XMLConfig command.

Running XMLConfig

As mentioned in the previous section, XMLConfig is a Java application that takes in as a parameter an XML document, which provides the type of object to configure, the name of the object, the action taken, and the updated values. You start XMLConfig via a command file named `x:\WebSphere\AppServer\bin\xmlconfig.bat`.

Looking under the covers, you find that XMLConfig is actually a Java program. All the features you learn about XMLConfig are all contained in the Java class `com.ibm.websphere.xmlconfig.XMLconfig.class`. For all you Java programmers out there, this means you can use the XMLConfig class to create your own custom administration. Some useful applications that you can write using the XMLConfig Application Programming Interface (API) might perform automatic deployment or migration, or report configurations.

CROSS-REFERENCE: The XMLConfig API documentation can be found at this address: `www-4.ibm.com/software/webservers/appserv/doc/v40/ae/apidocs`.

When you call `XMLConfig.bat,` you must pass it the Administrative Server's `adminNodeName` where the Administrative Server is located. The `adminNodeName` is the host name of the machine. XMLConfig needs this information to know which WebSphere domain you are updating. You also supply additional arguments and a XML document that contains the configuration information. XMLConfig can be invoked from a command line by running: the following:

```
<was_home>\bin\XMLConfig -adminNodeName <nodename> <argument parameters>
```

Listing 28-2 shows the command file `XMLConfig.bat`, which runs the XMLConfig Java application. It is important to note the call to `setupCmdLine.bat`. This call sets up important environment variables used with XMLConfig.

Listing 28-2: The Internal Workings of the XMLConfig.bat File

```
@echo off
setlocal
call "%~dp0setupCmdLine.bat"
%JAVA_HOME%\bin\java %CLIENTSAS% -Dserver.root=%WAS_HOME%
-Dws.ext.dirs=%WAS_EXT_DIRS% -classpath %WAS_CLASSPATH%
com.ibm.ws.bootstrap.WSLauncher com.ibm.websphere.xmlconfig.XMLConfig %*
endlocal
```

The command file basically sets up needed environment variables that point to properties files necessary for XMLConfig to work properly. Because you know that XMLConfig is a Java application, you need to ensure the classpath points to the proper root. Within the line that starts the Java application, the classpath argument is set to `%WAS_CLASSPATH%`. The command accepts the default classpath. Listing 28-3 shows the environment variables declared in `setupCmdLine.bat`. The environment variables basically tell XMLConfig where to find all the important files it needs.

Listing 28-3: Environment Variables Are Set in SetupCmdLine.bat

```
SET COMPUTERNAME=KAFEMOCHA
SET WAS_HOME=e:\WebSphere\AppServer
SET JAVA_HOME=e:\WebSphere\AppServer\java
```

```
SET ITP_LOC=e:\WebSphere\AppServer\deploytool\itp
SET DBDRIVER_JARS=E:\PROGRA~1\SQLLIB\java\db2java.zip
SET DBDRIVER_PATH=E:\PROGRA~1\SQLLIB\java
SET CLIENTSAS=
-Dcom.ibm.CORBA.ConfigURL=file:/e:/WebSphere/AppServer/properties/
sas.client.props
SET WSCPCLIENTSAS=
-Dcom.ibm.CORBA.ConfigURL=file:/e:/WebSphere/AppServer/propert
ies/sas.client.props
SET SERVERSAS=
-Dcom.ibm.CORBA.ConfigURL=file:/e:/WebSphere/AppServer/properties/
sas.server.props
SET WAS_EXT_DIRS=
%JAVA_HOME%\lib;%WAS_HOME%\classes;%WAS_HOME%\lib;%WAS_HOME%\li
b\ext;%WAS_HOME%\web\help;%DBDRIVER_JARS%
SET WAS_CLASSPATH=%WAS_HOME%\properties;%WAS_HOME%\lib\bootstrap.jar
SET QUALIFYNAMES=-qualifyHomeName
```

The XMLConfig command syntax is as follows:

```
XMLConfig -adminNodeName <nodename> <argument parameters>
```

The `adminNodeName` is a required element. You specify the node name, because XMLConfig can be run from any node within the WebSphere domain. `adminNodeName` points to the node that contains the administrative repository, as shown in the following example:

```
XMLConfig -adminNodeName myMachine -export myOutputXMLtarget
```

This command queries the configuration on the Administrative Server machine, `myMachine`, and outputs (in XML) the configuration setting to a file called `myOutputXMLtarget`. This is about as basic as you get. So what can you do with `myOutputXMLtarget`? You can use it to create a report. To do so, you would have to write a Java application that parsed the output into a more readable format for the user. Other than that, you could cut and paste sections of the file for inclusion in new XML files that you are creating.

Now look at some of the other optional parameters. The optional parameters are shown in the following example.

```
XMLConfig.bat
{[ (-import <xml data file>)||
(-export <xml output file>[ -partial <xml data file>] )]
-adminNodeName <primary node name>
[ -nameServiceHost <host name>[  -nameServicePort <port number>]]
[ -traceString <trace spec>[ -traceFile <file name>]]
[ -generatePluginCfg <true || false>.]
[ -substitute <"key1=value1 [ ;key2=value2;[ ...]] ">]}
```

This snippet is actually the help output when you type in XMLConfig without any parameters passed. Minimally, you need to provide the `-adminNodeName` with a primary node name and either a valid `-import` or `-export` argument with a valid XML file. Table 28-2 lists the arguments for XMLConfig and their descriptions.

Table 28-2: Arguments Passed to XMLConfig

Argument	*Description*
-adminNodeName	Required argument that specifies the node containing the Administrative Server. This must match the node name of your configuration.
-import <xml file>	Uses an XML file and imports into the administrative repository. The XML tags are executed based on the action within each tag.
-export <xml file>	An exported XML file specified by the user to utilize for the export processing.
-partial <xml file>	An XML file specified by the user to utilize for the partial processing.
-nameServiceHost <host> -nameServicePort <port number>	Specifies the host name of the machine that contains the naming service and the assigned port number. Default is 900.
-traceString <trace spec> -traceFile <file name>	Specifies the trace specification and the output file of the trace log.
-substitute <"key1=value;...">	Provides the capability to substitute values in the XML document using name-value pairs. Separators between pairs are semicolons(;).
-generatePluginCfg	Set to True to regenerate the plug-in configuration file.

Each invocation of XMLConfig requires either an export or import parameter to provide an output results document or serve as an input processing XML document. You learn the syntax next.

NOTE: In next few sections, you learn how to use the optional arguments in XMLConfig commands. As you go through these sections, `<your node>`, `<export file name>`, `<filter file name>`, and `<import file name>` should be substituted with your personal preferences for your machine name and the appropriate filenames. You can find the XML documents under the downloaded code folder x:\Bible\Chapter28

Exporting information

When you export information from the repository, you have two choices. You can perform a full export or a partial export. A full export takes the entire administrative repository and outputs an XML document. You use a filtering mechanism to accomplish a partial export. This method has the best results, because a full export is not really useful as a tool to administer WebSphere domains. You can use the full export as a means of backing up the setting within a domain and, with a little programming assistance, provide a nice little report using the XML file as input.

Filters can be used to export a single object (such as an Application Server) that you want copied in another WebSphere domain. By using the action `locate` within your XML document, you can locate the AlmostFreeCruise Server application and export all its settings to an XML file. You could then take that over to your new WebSphere domain and use XMLConfig to import the AlmostFreeCruise Server.

Performing a full export

A full export generates an XML document that describes the configuration of the entire administrative domain. The syntax is as follows:

```
XMLConfig -adminNodeName <node name> -export <export file name>
```

Performing a partial export

A partial export generates an XML document with only specific administrative resources. You accomplish a partial export by providing an additional XML file that specifies the filter to be applied to the export. When you set up a partial export, you need to utilize the action `locate`. You use the `locate` action to search within the repository database to find a particular name of a node. After it is found, you can specify that it export the default server setting. Look at the XML command line syntax and at the XML document that would export the default server. The syntax is as follows:

```
XMLConfig -adminNodeName <node name> -export <export file name>
-partial <filter file name>
```

Upon execution, XMLConfig accesses the administrative repository using the filter file to locate the specified value. It exports the XML into the export filename. Listing 28-4 shows a sample filter file.

Listing 28-4: The partialExport.xml File Exporting the Default Server

```
<?xml version="1.0"?>
<!DOCTYPE websphere-sa-config SYSTEM
"file:///$XMLConfigDTDLocation$$dsep$xmlconfig.dtd" >
<websphere-sa-config>
  <node action="locate" name="<your node>">
  <application-server action="export" name="Default
   Server">
  </application-server>
  </node>
</websphere-sa-config>
```

In the XML document in Listing 28-4, you see the standard first two lines that identify the XML version and DTD that you are using. You should notice that the actual DTD file has a funny-looking name:

```
$XMLConfigDTDLocation$$dsep$xmlconfig.dtd.
```

The information between the ($) signs is used to substitute the location of the DTD and the path separator. You need to do this for portability between different operating systems (Windows and UNIX).

The DTD also requires that the first element is `<WebSphere-sa-config>`, so between this element are the actions to be taken with this file. To explain the XML in English, the meaning is: "Find me the node called 'your node' within the repository database." Within that node there is an application server defined: `Default Server`. Export all information about the default server (in XML format) into the export file passed in as a parameter to XMLConfig. After changing <your node> in partialExport.xml to the node of your workstation, use the following command to perform a partial export of the application server:

```
XMLConfig -export <export file name> -partial partialExport.xml
    -adminNodeName <your node>
```

Importing information

The import feature reads an XML document that adds, modifies, or removes administrative resources. This XML document can replace the administrative repository contents completely or partially. In the previous section, you learned about exporting the Application Server named Default Server. You can now import the Default Server Application Server into another WebSphere administrative repository, as well as importing any resource that you have previously exported using XMLConfig. Importing essentially relieves you of typing in new configurations and also keeps the configurations consistent. The import syntax is as follows:

```
XMLConfig -adminNodeName <node name> -import <import file name>
```

Depending upon the XML input contained within the import file, you can perform a number of configuration changes. The changes can be updates, additions, or deletions of specified resources. The nature of the changes you implement is determined by the `action` attribute for the particular elements.

> **NOTE**: When using the downloaded from the web code, please replace x: with the appropriate drive letter for your system.

Next, you view some examples of imports using various actions. You need to modify <your node> to match your particular machine name. In the "Performing substitution" section, you learn about using the `-substitution` option of XMLConfig. The substitution makes it possible to pass in a node name (and other variable substitution) rather than update it manually.

Creating resources

Listing 28-5 shows the XML code to update your administrative repository with a new application server. You first create the `createAppServer.xml` file with the actions desired, and then you run the XMLConfig command file to process the update.

Listing 28-5: Using createAppServer.xml to Update to a New Application Server

```
<?xml version="1.0"?>
<!DOCTYPE websphere-sa-config SYSTEM
"file:///$XMLConfigDTDLocation$$dsep$xmlconfig.dtd">
<websphere-sa-config>
<node action="locate" name="<your node>">
  <application-server action="create" name="cruiseamerica server">
       <stdout>x:\WebSphere\AppServer\cruiselogs\stdout.log</stdout>
<stderr>x:\WebSphere\AppServer\cruiselogs\stderr.log</stderr>
 <jvm-config>
  <initial-heap-size>128</initial-heap-size>
  <max-heap-size>256</max-heap-size>
 </jvm-config>
 </application-server>
</node>
</websphere-sa-config>
```

In Listing 28-5, you see two types of actions (`locate` and `create`). The first action is in the `Node` element. The `locate` action locates your node and `create` creates a new application server called `cruiseamerica  server`.

After updating `createAppServer.xml` and replacing `<your  node>` with your machine name, you can run the following command to create the application server:

```
XMLConfig -import createAppServer.xml -adminNodeName <your node>
```

Updating a resource

Listing 28-6 shows the XML code for modifying the working directory of the application server. You first create the `updateAppServer.xml` file with the actions desired, and then you run the XMLConfig command file to process the update.

Listing 28-6: Modifying the Application's Working Directory with updateAppServer.xml

```
<?xml version="1.0"?>
<!DOCTYPE websphere-sa-config SYSTEM
                "file:///$XMLConfigDTDLocation$$dsep$xmlconfig.dtd">
<websphere-sa-config>
<node action="locate" name="<your node>">
   <application-server action="update" "name="cruiseamerica server">
   <working-directory>x:\WebSphere\AppServer\cruiselogs\workdir
     </working-directory>
   </application-server>
</node>
</websphere-sa-config>
```

Note that in Listing 28-6, the action is now `update`. The particular node needing an update is the `working-directory` node.

After updating `updateAppServer.xml` and replacing `<your node>` with your machine name, you can run the following command to update the Application Server:

```
XMLConfig -import updateAppServer.xml -adminNodeName <your node>
```

Deleting a resource

You have experienced creating and updating an application server. The only thing left to do is to remove one. The process is the same as the `create` and `update` actions. You first update the `deleteAppServer.xml` file with the `delete` action. You accomplish that by using the `action="delete"` attribute, as shown in Listing 28-7, and then you run the XMLConfig command file to process the update.

Listing 28-7: Using deleteAppServer.xml to Remove an Application Server

```
<?xml version="1.0"?>
<!DOCTYPE websphere-sa-config SYSTEM
"file:///$XMLConfigDTDLocation$$dsep$xmlconfig.dtd">
<websphere-sa-config>
<node action="locate" name="<your node>">
  <application-server action="delete" "name="cruiseamerica server">
  </application-server>
</node>
</websphere-sa-config>
```

In Listing 28-7, you still need to use the `locate` action to find your node. After you find it, you remove `cruiseamerica server` by performing the `delete` action.

After updating `deleteAppServer.xml` and replacing `<your node>` with your machine name, you can run the following command to create the application server:

```
XMLConfig -import deleteAppServer.xml -adminNodeName <your node>
```

Backing up and restoring the administrative repository

Saving your repository configuration is one task you need to incorporate into your system-management strategy. Backing up using XMLConfig should not take the place of utilizing a relational database backup. The reason you need the XMLConfig export is to provide the capability of utilizing the exported configuration and modifying it for other machines. Use the following command to back up the administrative repository:

```
XMLConfig -export yourBackupAdminServer.xml -adminNodeName <your node>
```

In this particular case, `yourBackupAdminServer.xml` is an exported XML file. There really is no difference between this command and the command you learned in the section named, "Performing a full export."

You can restore the complete configuration to the repository by using the exported file, but you must carefully review the action attributes to ensure you are performing the action correctly. Use the following command to restore the administrative repository:

```
XMLConfig -import yourBackupAdminServer.xml -adminNodeName <your node>
```

Starting and stopping Application servers

Probably the task you will perform most often is the starting and stopping of the application servers. Rather than using the Administrative Console to start or stop the application server, you can use XMLConfig to do it. The XML in Listing 28-8 shows how to set up the XML to perform the start action.

Listing 28-8: Setting Up appsvr-start.xml to start an Application Server

```
<?xml version="1.0"?>
<!DOCTYPE websphere-sa-config SYSTEM
"file:///$XMLConfigDTDLocation$$dsep$xmlconfig.dtd" >
  <websphere-sa-config>
  <node name="<your node>" action="locate">
  <application-server name="Default Server"
    action="start">
  </application-server>
  </node>
  </websphere-sa-config>
```

Use the following command to start the application server:

```
XMLConfig -import appsvr-start.xml -adminNodeName <your node>
```

To stop the server, you need another XML file that has a `stop` action. Listing 28-9 shows the `appsvr-stop.xml` file.

Listing 28-9: The appsvr-stop.xml File Used to Stop an Application Server

```
<?xml version="1.0"?>
<!DOCTYPE websphere-sa-config SYSTEM
"file:///$XMLConfigDTDLocation$$dsep$xmlconfig.dtd" >
 <websphere-sa-config>
  <node name="your node" action="locate">
  <application-server name="Default Server" action="stop">
  </application-server>
  </node>
 </websphere-sa-config>
```

After updating `appsvr-stop.xml` and replacing `<your node>` with your machine name, you can run the following command to stop the Application Server:

```
XMLConfig -import appsvr-stop.xml -adminNodeName <your node>
```

The `appsvr-start` and `appsvr-stop` files are handy to use to stop and start application servers, but you can probably guess that using substitution variables could reduce the number of files from two to one. You learn how to make those updates in the next section.

Management Activities

In this section, you learn more about utilizing XMLConfig to manage your environments. You learn about the value of substitutions and how they apply to changing configurations. This section also includes examples of how to configure application servers, JDBC drivers, data sources, and so on using XMLConfig.

Performing substitutions

You may have noticed in the `appsvr-start` and `appsvr-stop` that the XML was very similar. Wouldn't it be great if you could just substitute start and stop somehow and not have to maintain two separate files? Well you can do just that with substitutions. WebSphere provides the following generic substitution variables to assist with platform independence:

- *$server_root$:* Shows the WebSphere server installation root directory
- *$psep$:* Functions as a path separator
- *$dsep$:* Functions as a directory separator

You already have seen substitutions of variable in XML files you have been utilizing in this chapter. In the `<!DOCTYP>` tag shown in the examples, you should have seen the following:

```
<!DOCTYPE websphere-sa-config SYSTEM
"file:///$XMLConfigDTDLocation$$dsep$xmlconfig.dtd" >
```

The `<!DOCTYPE>` tag is utilizing the generic substitution variables to ensure portability between operation systems. In this case, you are substituting path information and directory separators. You don't need to do anything with `<!DOCTYPE>`, but it should clarify what this unique element is doing.

You can create your own substitution variables. Substitution variables provide you with a way to set placeholders in the XML configuration files, so you can substitute values in their place. Listing 28-10 shows a start XML file updated to accept substitution variables for `$node-name$`, `$server-name$`, and `$action$`.

Listing 28-10: The appsvr-startstop.xml Used to Start and Stop an Application Server

```
<?xml version="1.0"?>
<!DOCTYPE websphere-sa-config SYSTEM
"file:///$XMLConfigDTDLocation$$dsep$xmlconfig.dtd" >
       <websphere-sa-config>
         <node name="$node-name$" action="locate">
           <application-server name="$server-name$"
             action="$action$">
           </application-server>
         </node>
       </websphere-sa-config>
```

By substituting placeholders for node name, server name, and server action, you can issue the substitution variables command, as shown in Listing 28-11.

Listing 28-11: Using Substitution Variables

```
xmlconfig -adminNodeName kafemocha -import c:\sample-xml\
appsvr-startstop.xml -substitute "node-name=kafemocha;
server-name=Default Server;action=start"
```

You can use this XML file to not only start any application server but also stop the application server. From this point on, each XML file shown utilizes substitution variables to allow for more flexibility.

Making configuration changes

In addition to starting and stopping application servers, you use XMLConfig for making configuration changes. As administrator, you will be adding new application servers, updating providers and data sources, and performing workload management activities. XMLConfig provides you the tooling to perform these steps at a level that enables you to reuse scripts repeatedly.

Adding application servers

Listing 28-12 is an export listing of the SPWorkshopEAR enterprise application. Even if you used the Administrative Console to install the enterprise application previously, by developing an XML file, you can modify the changes or support multiple changes with a single call.

Listing 28-12: Export Listing for enterpriseApp.xml

```
<?xml version="1.0"?>
<!DOCTYPE websphere-sa-config SYSTEM
"file:///$XMLConfigDTDLocation$$dsep$xmlconfig.dtd" >
<websphere-sa-config>
<enterprise-application action="create" name="SPWorkshopEAR">
  <source-node>kafemocha</source-node>
  <ear-file-name>E:\spworkshop\ear\spworkshop.ear</ear-file-name>
  <enterprise-app-install-info>
    <node-name>kafemocha</node-name>
    <ear-install-directory>
      e:\WebSphere\AppServer\installedApps\SPWorkshopEAR.ear
    </ear-install-directory>
  </enterprise-app-install-info>
  <application-binding>
  <authorization-table/>
  <run-as-map/>
  </application-binding>
  <web-module name="SPWorkshop">
    <war-file>SPWorkshop.war</war-file>
    <context-root>SPWorkshop</context-root>
    <module-install-info>
    <application-server-full-name>
       /NodeHome:kafemocha/EJBServerHome:Default Server/
    </application-server-full-name>
    </module-install-info>
    <web-module-binding>
       <virtual-host-name>default_host</virtual-host-name>
    </web-module-binding>
  </web-module>
  <web-module name="Apache-SOAP">
    <war-file>soap.war</war-file>
    <context-root>/balance</context-root>
    <module-install-info>
       <application-server-full-name>
          /NodeHome:kafemocha/EJBServerHome:Default Server/
      </application-server-full-name>
    </module-install-info>
       <web-module-binding>
           <virtual-host-name>default_host</virtual-host-name>
       </web-module-binding>
  <web-module>
</enterprise-application>
</websphere-sa-config>
```

Using this methodology makes it simple to replicate environments. For example, you might have a quality-assurance program that requires the configurations to be the same in multiple environments. Having XMLConfig perform the activities ensures that the configurations are the same.

Updating JDBC drivers

JDBC drivers were actually renamed Providers in WAS40. Unfortunately, the grammar didn't change to reflect the naming change. You still have to refer to Providers as `jdbc-driver`. Listing 28-13 shows the XML for updating the Provider (JDBC driver). If you look at Figure 28-2, you can see that JDBC drivers or resources not associated with a particular node, which is why you do not see the update happening to a particular node. In this case, it's just applying the change to the Administrative Server.

Listing 28-13: Updating the Provider with provider.xml

```
<?xml version="1.0"?>
<!DOCTYPE websphere-sa-config SYSTEM
"file:///$XMLConfigDTDLocation$$dsep$xmlconfig.dtd" >
<websphere-sa-config>
  <jdbc-driver name="$name$" action="update">
 <description>This is the Sample DB Driver</description>
  </jdbc-driver>
</websphere-sa-config>
```

After updating the provider information, you can run the following command to update the Administrative Server:

```
XMLConfig -import provider.xml -substitute "name=Sample DB Driver" -
adminNodeName kafemocha
```

Updating data sources

List 28-14 shows the XML to update the SampleDataSource that comes with WebSphere. This listing uses three substituted attributes to make the command more flexible: `$name$`, `$db-name$`, and `$jndi$`.

Listing 28-14: Updating Data Sources with datasource.xml

```
<?xml version="1.0"?>
<!DOCTYPE websphere-sa-config SYSTEM
"file:///$XMLConfigDTDLocation$$dsep$xmlconfig.dtd" >
<websphere-sa-config>
<jdbc-driver action="locate" name="Sample DB Driver">
  <data-source name="$name$" action="update">
    <database-name>$db-name$</database-name>
    <jndi-name>$jndi$</jndi-name>
    <minimum-pool-size>1</minimum-pool-size>
    <maximum-pool-size>10</maximum-pool-size>
    <connection-timeout>180</connection-timeout>
    <idle-timeout>1800</idle-timeout>
    <orphan-timeout>1800</orphan-timeout>
```

Listing 28-14 *(Continued)*

```
  </data-source>
</jdbc-driver>
</websphere-sa-config>
```

After creating the XML file, use the following command to update the data sources:

```
XMLConfig -import x:\sample-xml\datasource.xml -substitute "db-
name=WAS40;name=SampleDataSource;jndi=jdbc/SampleDataSource" -
adminNodeName kafemocha
```

Changing Vhosts

The `virtualhost.xml` in Listing 28-15 has been shortened due to the size of the mime-table list of mime types. Use the following XML to add the SSL port alias to `default_host`. In this case, you are updating the virtual host so it knows that ports 80, 443, and 9080 are valid aliases for this host.

Listing 28-15: Using virtualhost.xml to Add the SSL Port Alias

```
<?xml version="1.0"?>
<!DOCTYPE websphere-sa-config SYSTEM
"file:///$XMLConfigDTDLocation$$dsep$xmlconfig.dtd" >
<websphere-sa-config>
<virtual-host action="update" name="$name$">
        <mime-table>
            <mime type="application/vnd.lotus-wordpro">
                <ext>lwp</ext>
                <ext>sam</ext>
            </mime>
            ...
        </mime-table>
        <alias-list>
            <alias>*:80</alias>
            <alias>*:443</alias>
            <alias>*:9080</alias>
        </alias-list>
    </virtual-host>
</websphere-sa-config>
```

After you create the XML file in Listing 28-15, you use the following command to update the virtual host:

```
XMLConfig -import virtualhost.xml -substitute "name=default_host" -
adminNodeName kafemocha
```

Deploying domains

The flexibility of XMLConfig and the capability to perform multiple commands makes working within a WebSphere domain easy. You can now export a source configuration and, with a little effort, and create substitute variables to make deployment standardized and process-oriented.

Implementing server groups and cloning

One area in which using XMLConfig increases your efficiency is the process of creating server groups. A *server group* is a template for creating additional, nearly identical, copies of an application server and its contents. In Listing 28-16, you see a scaled-down version of the creation of a server group called `CruiseServerGroup`. It actually creates two clones (`CruiseAmerica01` and `CruiseAmerica02`). Clones are application servers based on the server group template. The clones inherit the server group's attributes.

Listing 28-16: Creating a Server Group

```
<?xml version="1.0"?>
<!DOCTYPE websphere-sa-config SYSTEM
"file:///$XMLConfigDTDLocation$$dsep$xmlconfig.dtd" >
<websphere-sa-config>
...
<server-group action="create" name="CruiseServerGroup">
<server-group-attributes>
...
<module-visibility>1</module-visibility>
<web-container>
...
<session-manager>
...
<write-contents>0</write-contents>
<write-frequency>0</write-frequency>
<write-interval>0</write-interval>
...
<persistent-sessions>true</persistent-sessions>
<data-source name="cruiseDS">
<default-user></default-user>
<default-password></default-password>
</data-source>
...
</session-manager>
</web-container>
<orb-config>
...
</orb-config>
<custom-service-config-list>
...
</custom-service-config-list>
</server-group-attributes>
<clone name="CruiseAmerica01">
<parent-node>$node$</parent-node>
</clone>
```

Listing 28-16 *(Continued)*

```
<clone name="CruiseAmerica02">
<parent-node>$node$</parent-node>
</clone>
</server-group>
</websphere-sa-config>
```

Two attributes that don't have Administrative Console counterparts are `associateclone` and `disassociateclone`. They were listed in Table 28-1, but we haven't used them. You use these attributes if you want to perform some change that you don't want spread out to the clones.

Regenerating the HTTP Server plug-in

The HTTP Server plug-in is a component that handles all communication between the HTTP Server and WebSphere Application Server. The plug-in enables you to locate the HTTP Server and WebSphere Application Server on different systems. Whenever you update the configuration with new transport properties, you need to regenerate the plug-in. The plug-in configuration `<was_home>/config/plugin-cfg` is an XML file that is regenerated upon demand. XMLConfig supports the automation of the regeneration. Use the following command to regenerate the plug-in:

```
XMLConfig -import enterpriseApp.xml -adminNodeName kafemocha
-generatePluginCfg true
```

With the regeneration of plug-in information, you can create a set of XMLConfig commands that update transport information and then call another XMLConfig command that regenerates the plug-in and restarts the server.

Summary

In this chapter, you learned about how to use XMLConfig to improve your ability to configure systems anywhere in your WebSphere domain. XMLConfig gives you an alternative to utilizing the Administrative Console to configure resources.

You learned that XML plays an important role in XMLConfig. When you create scripts to make administrative life easier, you need to create XML configuration files that are fed to the XMLConfig processing.

Each XML file contains the directives for the specified configuration changes. The names and actions can be given placeholder names and substituted with each call, resulting in improved flexibility. Some of the actions you can perform are `locate`, `create`, `delete`, and `update`. You can create substitution variables to provide the capability to dynamically pass in specified names to locate, create, delete, or update.

In this chapter, you were also provided working examples of how to start and stop an application server, how to add an application server, and much more.

Index

A

AAT (Application Assembly Tool), 8, 445
  Application Client Wizard, 612
  application deployment, 609-610
  Application Wizard, 611
  EARExpander, 620
  EJB Module Wizard, 611
  generating code, 619-620
  running, 621-624
  security, 645-647
  verfiying archive files, 620
  Web Module Wizard, 612
access beans
  Almost Free Cruise, 397-399
  design, 454
ACID qualities of transactions, 163, 407, 418
actions, XMLConfig, 776-777
addCookie( ) method, 294
AddressBook, WSAD, 534-538
addresses, ports, 91
Admin Console
  application servers
    creating, 544-545
    starting and stopping, 545
  command history, 548
  compared to wscp (WebSphere Control Program), 748
  compared to XMLConfig, 770-771
  connection port, 543
  exporting/importing configurations, 546-548
  nodes, starting and stopping, 544
  panes, 543
  plug-ins, synchronizing, 546
  Resource Analyzer, launching, 706
  Security Center, 649-652
  toolbar, 544
  troubleshooting, 723-724
    configuring messages, 729-730
  Web server plug-in
    configuring, 549-552
    configuring virtual hosts, 553-555
    installing, 553
    internal transport, 555
    locating, 550
    non-SSL transport, 556-557
    refresh interval, 553
    regenerating, 552-553
    transport options, 555
  wizards, 549
Admin Server, 27-28, 542
  logs, troubleshooting and, 719-720
  starting and stopping, 544
  startup, troubleshooting, 741-742
  traces, activating, 739
  WAP installation, 115-118
admin.conf file, WAP installation, 114-115
administration
  XMLConfig, 770
    actions, 776-777
    adding application servers, 787-789
    backing up administrative repositiry, 785
    changing virtual hosts, 790
    compared to Admin Console, 770-771

creating resources, 783
deleting resources, 784-785
deploying domains, 790-792
exporting information, 781-782
importing information, 782-783
regenerating plug-in, 792
running, 777-780
server groups and cloning, 791-792
starting and stopping application servers, 785-786
substitution variables, 786-787
updating data sources, 789
updating JDBC drivers, 789
updating resources, 784

administration of WAS, 44-45
admin.config file, 48
Administrative Console, 45-47
administrative repository, 45

administration repository location, 89-90
administrator (J2EE role), 603
adminNodeName (XMLConfig), 779
advisors (Edge Server), 662
AE (Advanced Edition), 10-11, 13
administration repository, location, 89-90
hardware requirements, 80
SOAP, installation, 485-489
software requirements, 80

AEd (Advanced Edition Developer Only), 13
AEd (Advanced Edition for development), 10
AEs (Advanced Edition Single Server), 10
aliases
setup, 101
virtual hosts, 553

Almost Free Cruise, 175
access beans, 397-399
beans, integrating, 401-405
CMP entity beans, 380
data sources, 385-387
databases, 377-378
deployment descriptor, 429
EJB creation, 378-379
EJB Extension Editor, 380-384
EJB relationships, 415-417
EJB-RDB mapping, 379-380
finder, custom, 394-397
JSPs, 348-351
server instance setup, 384
session beans, 392-393
updating, 399-400
session support, 319-321
tables, 377-378
Test Client, 387-392
transactions, setting, 423-425
vertical cloning, 670

Apache SOAP 2.2, 66-68
Apache SOAP toolkit, 495
administration, 496-498
AXIS, 496
client coding, 502-504
development lifecycle, 499-502
HTTP and, 501
RPCs, 501
SOAP encoding, 501
SOAP envelopes, 500
service coding, 504-505

APIs (Application Program Interfaces), 259
Cookie, 292-293
J2EE, 19
RequestDispatcher, 281
Servlet API, 259, 263-264
ServletContext, 281

application assembler (J2EE role), 603

application assembly, 427. *See* also deployment
application client modules, 619
Application Client Wizard, 612
application component provider (J2EE role), 603
application data, sessions, 306-307
application deployment, AAT
  EARExpander, 620
  generating code, 619-620
  verfiying archive files, 620
application development, XML
  development tools, 471-472
  WSAD and, 471-472
application layering, 166-168
  design patterns, 167-168
  services, 167
  strict layering, 166
application models, Web application models, 325-327
  EJB application model, 326
  J2EE, 327
  JDBC, 326
  scalable application model, 326
application packaging, 599
  assembly, 621-624
  deployment tools, 606
    EJB caching, 607-608
    FileServing servlet, 608
    IBM bindings, 606-607
    IBM extensions, 607
    Invoker servlet, 608
  enterprise applications, 612-614
    application client modules, 619
    EJB modules, 614-617
    Web modules, 617-619
  J2EE, 600
    deployment, 601-605
    roles, 603
application server
  performance optimization, 695-697
  WAS topology, 172
Application Server Security Administration and Security Services, 652
application servers
  adding, XMLConfig, 787-789
  authentication, types of, 627
  authorization, types of, 627
  clones
    adding, 596
    creating, 666-667
  creating
    Admin Console, 544-545
    XMLConfig, 783
  deleting, XMLConfig, 784-785
  enterprise applications, starting and stopping, 546
  logs, troubleshooting and, 720-721
  starting and stopping, 545
    XMLConfig, 785-786
  traces, activating, 736-739
  updating, XMLConfig, 784
  WAS topology, 173
application topology, 172-175
Application Wizard, 611
applications
  assembling, 621-624
  deploying, AAT, 609-612
  e-business application framework (IBM), 156-158
  enterprise
    packaging, 612-619
    starting and stopping, 546

enterprise applications, 33-34
J2EE, creation phases, 600
resources
configuring, 557-558
data sources, creating, 560-561
JavaMail, enabling, 561-563
JDBC connection pools, 558-559
JDBC providers, creating, 559-560
JMS (Java Messaging Services), 565
JMS MQ support, 566-571
URL providers, 564
sample applications, 120-121
WAS topology, 173
Web applications, architecture, 6
WSAD development
additional forms, 633
deployment descriptors, 633-640
form-based authentication, 631-632
login.jsp form, 632
logout.jsp form, 633
security, 628-629
security testing, 629-631
testing, 640-641
architecture
transactions, 420-422
WAS, 24-41
admin server, 27-28
clones, 38-39
EJB modules, 34
enterprise applications, 34
HTTP server, 29-31
JVMs, 33
nodes, 28
plug-ins, 29-31
resources, 37
server groups, 38-39
server organization, 35-36
topology, 39-43
virtual hosts, 31-32
WAR files, 35
Web services, 55-57
WebSphere, 542
argument grouping (Tcl), 751
arguments, XMLConfig, 780
ASPs (Active Server Pages), 323
assembly-descriptor element, 437-438
associateclone action (XMLConfig), 776
associations, EJB-RDB mapping tool, 408
Atomic, ACID properties, 418
attributes
cookies, 293-294
requests, getting/setting, 273
transactions, 421-422
audit messages, virtual hosts, 555
authentication, 626
application servers, types of, 627
form-based
additional forms, 633
login.jsp form, 632
logout.jsp form, 633
WSAD application development, 631-632
Java, 627
principals, 625
authorization, 626
application servers, types of, 627
Java, 627
automatic builds, WSAD, 217
AXIS, 485-496

B

B2B (Business-to-Business), 51
B2C (Business-to-Consumer), 51

back-end systems, connecting, 571-572
bean class, EJBs, 362
bean-managed persistence, entity beans, 369
beans. See EJBs
best practices, EJBs, 447-458
design, 448-450
development, 453-454
Java, 451-452
binding
IBM, application packaging, 606-607
Web services, 59, 483
WSDL, 508
bindingTemplate data type, 64
BMP (bean-managed persistence), 361
bottom-up development, Web services, 484
browsers, integrated, WSSD and, 179
BSF (Bean Scripting Framework), 67, 337
buffer pools (databases), tuning, 691
build phase, Web services development, 484
businessEntity data type, 63
businesses, Web services benefits, 54
businessService data type, 63
buttom-up mapping, 409

C

caches
EJB, IBM extensions, 607-608
external, Edge Server, 688
session management, 595
SQL prepared statements, 692
cachesLEJB containers, 696
caching
dynamic, 683
Edge Server proxy server, 684-685
enabling, 686-687
principles of operation, 685
EJB homes, 453
initial context (EJB), 453
servlets and, 288
calling
JSPs from servlet, 340
servlets from a JSP, 338-340
CGI (Common Gateway Interface), 160, 259
programs, servlet comparison, 260-261
chaining, servlets, 291-292
classes
bean class, EJBs, 362
GenericServlet, 270
HttpServlet, 271-272
client coding, SOAP, 502-504
client/server solutions, WAP models, 171
clients, 158
advisors (Edge Server), 662
cookies, reading from, 294
DB2, configuring, 676-677
EJB, developing, 366-368
EJB Test Client, 387-392
fat clients, 158
SOAP, developing, 524-526
thin clients, 159-160
transactional clients, 419
client-side processing vs server-side processing, 158-159
clones, 38-39
creating, 666-667
configuring DB2 client, 676-677
horizontal, 675
installing JDBC drivers on secondary node, 681
locating shared repository, 677-678
secondary node, 679-680
horizontal cloning, 668-675

vertical cloning, 667-668
AlmostFreeCruise, 670
workload management, 660
XMLConfig, 791-792
clustering, 581
CMP (container-managed persistence), 361-365
entity beans, Almost Free Cruise, 380
coding practices, 451
collaboration, servlets, 290-291
colors, Log Analyzer, 744
com.ibm.WebSphere.servlet.session.IBMSession interface, 311-312
command dispatch (Tcl), 752
command history, Admin Console, 548
command prompt, Resource Analyzer, 707
commands
Tcl, syntax, 750-751
wscp, 754-753
XMLConfig syntax, 779
comments, JSP, 336-337
compliance, J2EE, 428
Composers and Converters, 408
compression, streams, 289
configuration
Admin Console, messages and troubleshooting, 729-730
application resources, 557-558
data sources, 560-561
JavaMail, 561-563
JDBC connection pools, 558-559
JDBC providers, 559-560
JMS (Java Messaging Services), 565
JMS MQ support, 566-571
cruiseMail, 562-563
exporting/importing with Admin Console, 546-548
horizontal clones
DB2 client, 676-677
installing JDBC drivers on secondary node, 681
locating shared repository, 677-678
secondary node, 679-680
HTTP server, 690-691
J2C (Java 2 Connector), 573-575
Security Center, 649-652
server groups, 665
Server perspective, 241-243
servers
Server perspective, 244-246
WSSD and, 179
session management, 582-593
virtual hosts, 553-555
Web server plug-in, 549-552
XMLConfig, usefulness of, 771
connection factories, configuring, 574-575
connection pool
JDBC, configuring, 558-559
Resource Analyzer, 705
sessions, 596
connection pooling, tuning, 692
Consistency, ACID properties, 418
console, Resource Analyzer, 707
Data Monitoring pane, 708-709
Resource Selection pane, 708
Console view, Java perspective (WSAD), 192
constructors
Cookie, 293
wscpCommand interface, 763
Container page, EJB Extension Editor, 380
container, EJBs, contract, 360
container-managed persistence, entity beans, 369

containers
EJBs, 364-366
J2EE development model, 327
WAS topology, 174
Content Assist, 233
controllers
MVC pattern, 165
servlets and, 282
Cookie API, 292-293
session tracking and, 300
Cookie constructor, 293
CookieCounterServlet, 294-297
cookies, 292-297
attributes, 293-294
creating, 293
reading from client, 294
response headers, 294
session management, 579
copy helper, access beans, 398
CORBA (Common Object Request Broker Architecture), 56
EJB architecture and, 357-358
IDL, 358
ORBs, 357
RPCs and, 161-162
Create a JSP File Wizard, 329
create action (XMLConfig), 776
createclone action (XMLConfig), 776
creation phase, Web services development, 484
credentials, 625
CRM (Customer Relation Management), 4
cruiseMail, configuration, 562-563
CSS (cascading style sheets), 229
CSS Designer, WSSD and, 178
CSS editor, 229
custom actions, JSP, 343-347
CVS (Concurrent Versions System), 139
installation, 140-141
overview, 150-151
CVSNT
installation, 141-143
WSAD setup, 144-146

D

data class access beans, EJB, 398
data management, 164-165
data sources
Almost Free Cruise, 385-387
configuring, 560-561
data transfer, HttpServletRequest object, 272-275
data types, WSDL, 507
Database Connection Wizard, 205-211
Database Web Page Wizard, 203-205
databases
installation, 90
tuning, 691-693
WSAD, Almost Free Cruise, 377-378
WSSD and, 179
DB2 7.2 installation, 102-108
DB2 client, configuring, 676-677
DB2 Universal Database, 18
debuggers, distributed debugger, 147
debugging, 73
testing and, 255-258
declarations, JSP, 335
declarative transaction management, 420, 437
decompression, streams, 289
decryption, input streams, 289
delete action (XMLConfig), 776
deployer (J2EE role), 603

deployment, 427
- AAT
  - EARExpander, 620
  - generating code, 619-620
  - verifying archive files, 620
- applications, AAT, 609-612
- domains, XMLConfig, 790-792
- EJBs, 428
- J2EE application packaging, 602
- J2EE compliance, 428-429
- tools, 74
- WSAD, 231-232

deployment descriptors
- EAR files, 429
- EJB containers, 696
- J2EE application packaging, 601-605
- overview, 429-438
- viewing, 547-548
- WSAD application development, security, 633-640
- XML and, 429-431
  - assembly-descriptor element, 437-438
  - document body, 432
  - document header, 431
  - enterprise beans, 432-433
  - environmental entries, 435-436
  - referencing beans, 435
  - resourcing references, 436

deployment phase, Web services development, 484

deployment tools, application packaging, 606
- EJB caching, 607-608
- FileServing servlet, 608
- IBM bindings, 606-607
- IBM extensions, 607
- Invoker servlet, 608

descriptors
- deployment, 232
- EJB security descriptors, 442-445
- JSP tag libraries, 345-347

design best practices
- proactive, 448, 449
- problems to avoid, 449, 450
- process considerations, 450

Design Gallery, WSSD and, 178

design patterns, 167, 168

destroy( ) method, 263
- HttpServlet class, 272

developer image files, WSAD, 135

development
- EJB best practices, 453-454
- execution and, 74
- Web services, 484

development lifecycle, SOAP, 499-502
- encoding, 501
- envelopes, 500
- HTTP and, 501
- RPCs, 501

development tools, 13-16, 128
- XML, 471-472

development-process wizards, 72-73

devlopment phase, Web services development, 484

directives, JSP, 334-335

directory tree, 49-50

dirty reads, transactions, 422

disable action (XMLConfig), 776

disassociateclone action (XMLConfig), 776

discovery phase, Web services development, 484

distributed data-management solutions, 165

distributed debugger, 147

Distributed Debugger, troubleshooting, 724

distributed logic objects, RPCs, implementation, 160-163
documentation, XMLConfig, 778
doDelete( ) method, 263
doGet( ) method, 263
  HttpServlet class, 271
doHead( ) method, 263
domains, 24-26
  Admin Console, 543-544
  deploying, XMLConfig, 790-792
  repository, administration, 748
  workload management considerations, 657-660
doPost( ) method, 263
  HttpServlet class, 271
doPut( ) method, 263
doTrace( ) method, 263
double quotes (, 180
DTD (Document Type Definition), 772-775
  XML, 429, 464
DTD editor, XML, 471
Durability, ACID properties, 418
dynamic caching, 683
  Edge Server proxy server, 684-685
  enabling, 686-687
  principles of operation, 685
dynamic content in JSPs, 333-338
dynamic Web pages, JSP and, 325

E

EAR (Enterprise Archive) files, 9
  deployment descriptors and, 429
  SOAPEAREnabler, 522-523
  WSAD and, 219-223
EAR module, security, 653
EARExpander (AAT), 620
e-business application framework (IBM), 156, 158
Eclipse, 128
Edge Server
  advisors, 662
  dynamic caching
    enabling, 686-687
    principles of operation, 685
    proxy server, 684-685
  external cache, 688
  features, 683
  IP sprayers, 661
editors
  DTD editor, XML, 471
  EJB Extension Editor, 380-384
  Enterprise Bean Java editor, 233
  RDB to XML maping editor, 472
  WSAD, 192-198
  XML editor, 471
  XML Schema Editor, 471
  XML to XML mapping editor, 472
  XSL Trace editor, 471
efficiency, servlets vs CGI programs, 261
EJB (Enterprise JavaBeans), 3, 354
  access beans, Almost Free Cruise, 397-399
  architecture, 356-359
    CORBA and, 356-358
    RMI, 356, 358-359
  bean class, 362
  best practices, 447-458
    development, 453-454
  BMP, 361
  caching, IBM extensions, 607-608
  characteristics, 360-361
  clients, developing, 366-368
  CMP, 361

containers, 364
contract, 360
services, 365-366
WAS topology, 174
creating, 380-387
Almost Free Cruise, 378-379
deployment, 428
entity beans, 368-370, 375
bean-managed persistence, 369
container-managed persistence, 369
lifecycle, 369
object-to-relational mapping, 370
primary key class, 362
homes, caching, 453
home interfaces, 362
integration, Almost Free Cruise, 401-405
meet-in-the-middle development, 413
method passing, 697
methods, read-only, 453
modules, 34, 378, 614-617
optimizing container, 696-697
overview, 353, 361-368
reasons for using, 354-355
relationships, 414-415
Almost Free Cruise, 415-417
many-to-many, 414
one-to-many, 414
one-to-one, 414
remote interfaces, 362
Resource Analyzer, 705
RPCs and, 161-162
security, 439
adding, 641-642
descriptors, 442-445
method-permission tag, 439-440
overloaded methods, 441
programmatic, 644-645
security-role declaration, 439
session beans, 371, 375
Almost Free Cruise, 392-393, 399-400
stateful, 372
stateful, lifecycle, 372-373
stateless, 371
stateless, lifecycle, 371-372
top-down development, 410-412
transactions, 420
WebSphere compliance with J2EE, 605
workload management, 663-664
XML documents, deployment descriptors, 432-433
EJB application model, 326
EJB Extension Editor, Almost Free Cruise, 380-384
EJB JAR files, 379
EJB Module Wizard, 611
EJB Test Client, Almost Free Cruise, 387-392
EJB to RDB Mapping Wizard, 408-409
ejbadder service deployment descriptor, 497
EJBDeploy (AAT), 619-620
EJBHome interface, 362
ejb-jar.xml file, 429
EJBObject interface, 362
EJB-RDB mapping tool, 408-417
elegance, servlets vs CGI programs, 261
elements, DTDs, 774
enable action (XMLConfig), 776
encryption, output streams, 289
Enterprise Application Project, 182
enterprise applications, 33-34
application packaging, 612-614
application client modules, 619
EJB modules, 614-617
Web modules, 617-619

Enterprise Bean Java editor, 233
EnterpriseBean interface, 362
entity beans, 368-370, 375
  bean-managed persistence, 369
  CMP entity beans, Almost Free Cruise, 380
  container-managed persistence, 369
  lifecycle, 369
  object-to-relational mapping, 370
  primary key class, 362
  stateless session beans, 453
  workload management, 664
environments, test environment
  planning, 151
  setup, 238-253
error handling, wscp, 758
error messages, 730
errors
  HTTP error codes, 102
  tracefiles and, 732
Event Viewer, troubleshooting and, 730-732
exceptions, 451
  IllegalArgumentException, 275
  IllegalStateException, 277
execution, 74
  wscp scripts, 754
explicit transaction management, 420
export action (XMLConfig), 776
exporting
  configurations, Admin Console, 546
  XMLConfig, 781-782
expressions, JSP, 337
extensibility/flexibility, servlets vs CGI programs, 261
Extensible Markup Language. *See* XML
Extensible Stylesheet Language Transformation mechanism. *See* XSLT
extensions (IBM)
  application packaging, 607
    EJB caching, 607-608
    FileServing servlet, 608
    Invoker servlet, 608
external cache, Edge Server, 688
external editors, WSAD, 192
  adding, 196
external services, 158

F

failover support, 658
fast view, WSAD, 198
fat clients, 158
fields, hidden, 301
file extensions, servers, 246
file handling, Java best practices, 452
file transfer, FTP, 232
file types, WSAD and, 194
files
  archive, verifying with AAT, 620
  deployment descriptors, 602
  directory tree, 49-50
  HTTP.conf, Web server plug-in location and, 550
  JMSAdmin.bat, updating, 566
  logging property, updating, 717
  logs, reviewing for troubleshooting, 730-734
  plugin-cfg.xml, 550
  setupMQEnv.bat, 567
  wscp, invoking properties file, 754-755

FileServing servlet (IBM extensions), 608
filters, servlets and, 291-292
find operations, Web services, 483
finders, Almost Free Cruise, 394-397
Finders page, EJB Extension Editor, 380
FixPak 4.0.3, WAP installation and, 84-86
flushBuffer( ) method, 277
folders, WEB-INF, 602
form-based authentication, security
  additional forms, 633
  login.jsp form, 632
  logout.jsp form, 633
  WSAD applications, 631-632
forward( ) method, 286
forwarding, redirection and, 286-288
FTP (File Transfer Protocol), 232, 299
full builds, WSAD, 216

G

Gallery view, Web perspective (WSAD), 191
garbage collection, JVM tuning, 693
GenericServlet class, 270
GEO (Geographical taxonomy), 512
getAttribute( ) method, 283, 306
getAttributeNames( ) method, 283
getBufferSize( ) method, 276
getContextPath( ) method, 275
getCookie( ) method, 294
getCreationTime( ) method, 303
getId( ) method, 303
getInitParameter( ) method, 283
getInitParameterNames( ) method, 283
getIntHeader( ) method, 275
getLastAccessedTime( ) method, 303
getMaxInactiveInterval( ) method, 303
getNamedDispatcher( ) method, 285
getParameterNames( ) method, 273
getParameterValues( ) method, 273
getPathInfo( ) method, 275
getRequestDispatcher( ) method, 284
getResource( ) method, 284
getResourceAsStream( ) method, 284
getServletInfo( ) method, HttpServlet class, 272
getServletPath( ) method, 275
getSession( ) method, 302
groups, 625

H

hardware, WSAD installation, 131
hardware requirements, AE, 80
heap memory, 451
heap size, JVM tuning, 693
Hello World
  JSP expressions, 329
  JSP scriptlet, 329
  JSPs in WSAD environment, 328-330
Hello World servlet source code, 265-266
help, wscp
  accessing online, 755
  for objects, 756
hidden fields, session tracking and, 301
Hierarchy view, Java (WSAD), 191
hit count servlet, 307-310
home interfaces, EJBs and, 362
horizontal cloning, 668-675
  creating clones, 675
    configuring DB2 client, 676-677
    installing JDBC drivers on secondary node, 681
    locating shared repository, 677-678
    secondary node, 679-680

hosts
filenames, WAP installation and, 89
virtual, changing with XMLConfig, 790
virtual hosts, 31-32
HTML (Hypertext Markup Language), 462
remote presentation and, 159
Studio Page Designer, 224-229
HTML entry form servlet source code, 268
HTTP
error codes, 102
SOAP and, 501
HTTP Server, 29-31
configuring, 690-691
logs, troubleshooting and, 722
HTTP.conf file, Web server plug-in location and, 550
HTTP/FTP imports, WSAD, 217-223
HTTPr, 65
HttpServlet class, 271-272
HttpServletRequest object, 260
data transfer and, 272-275
HttpServletResponse object, 260-266, 276-278
HttpSession object
HttpSessionBindingListener interface, 310-311
session management and, 302-311
Snoop servlet and, 303-306
state data access, 303
tracking user visits, 307-309
HttpSessionBindingListener interface, 310-311

I

I/O (input/output), sessions, 595
IBM HTTP Server, 17
installation, 95
IBM Test Registry, 512
IBM Web services tools, 484-495
ibm-ejb-jar-bnd.xmi source code, 382
IBMSession interface, 311-312
IDL (interface definition language), CORBA, 358
IIOP (Internet InterORB Protocol), 28, 161
IllegalArgumentException, 275
IllegalStateException, 277
Image Creator/Editor, WSSD and, 178
image files, WSAD installation, 135
implementation
messaging, 163
RPCs, 160-163
separating from interfaces, WSDL, 506-509
services, 483
implicit objects, JSP, 337-338
importing
configurations, Admin Console, 546
HTTP/FTP imports, WSAD, 217-223
XMLConfig, 782-783
include( ) method, 285
incremental builds, WSAD, 216
indexes, databases, 692
infopop, WSAD, 192
infrastructure services, 158
inheritance, EJB-RDB mapping tool, 408

Inheritance page, EJB Extension Editor, 380
init( ) method, 263, 271
initial context, caching (EJB development), 453
initial heap size, 451
inlining, coding and, 451
input streams, decryption, 289
installation
  CVS, 140-141
  CVSNT, 141-143
  databases, 90
  DB2 7.2, 102-108
  IBM HTTP Server, 95
  JDK, different versions, 147
  logs, troubleshooting and, 718
  SOAP on AE, 485-489
  UDDI, private, 491
  UDDI registry, 491-495
  WAP, 108-112
    admin.config file, 114-115
    Administration Server, 115-118
    common migration, 93-102
    host filenames, 89
    LDAP and, 91
    logs, 112-113
    plug-in regeneration, 118
    ports, 88-89
    sample applications, 120-121
    silent install, 123-125
    troubleshooting, 118-120
    verification, 112-113
    WebSphere, 92-93
    Win2000/NT platforms, 78-92
  WSAD, 133
    from CD-ROM, 133-135
    from developer image files, 135
    hardware, 131
    migrating from earlier versions, 136-137
    permissions, 128-130
    preparations, 131
    software, 131
    verification, 137-138
  WSTK, 489-490
instances, server instances, Almost Free Cruise, 384
instrumentation levels, Resource Analyzer, 709-710
integrated Web browser, WSSD and, 179
integration
  Almost Free Cruise beans, 401-405
  servlets vs CGI programs, 261
interaction techniques, servlets, 290-292
interactions, JSP, 338-341
interfaces
  com.ibm.WebSphere.servlet.session.IBMSession, 311-312
  EJBHome, 362
  EJBObject, 362
  EnterpriseBean, 362
  GenericServlet class, 270
  home, EJBs, 362
  HttpServlet, 271-272
  HttpSessionBindingListener, 310-311
  IBMSession, 311-312
  remote, EJBs, 362
  RequestDispatcher, 284-286
  separating from implementation, WSDL, 506-509
  ServletContext, 282-284
  SessionBean, 362
  SingleThreadModel, 264
  UnauthorizedSessionRequestException, 311

wscpCommand, 762
constructors, 763
public methods, 763-764
qualified names, 764-766
internal editors, WSAD, 192
internal transport, Web server plug-in, 555
Introscope, 697-699
invalidate( ) method, 303
Invoker servlet (IBM extensions), 608
invoking, JSPs from JSPs, 340-341
IP sprayers, 661
isCommitted( ) method, 277
isNew( ) method, 303
isolation levels, transactions, 422-423
isolation, ACID properties, 418

J

J2C (J2EEE Connection Architecture), 3
J2C (Java 2 Connector), 571-572
configuring, 573
connection factories, 574-575
resource adapters, 574
resource adapters, 573
J2EE (Java 2 Enterprise Edition)
APIs, 19
application packaging, 600
deployment, 602
deployment descriptors, 601-605
roles, 603
certification, 3, 9
components, 18-19
services, 19
Web application models and, 327
WebSphere compilance with, 605
J2EE compliance, 428-429
J2EE perspective, WSAD, 189-190
J2EE view, J2EE perspective (WSAD), 190
JAF (Java Activation Framework), 561
JAR files
deployment descriptors, 602
EJB JAR files, 379
WSAD and, 219-223
Java
best practices, 451-452
code testing, JREs, 234-236
methods, 233
resource factories, 561
security, authentication and authorization, 627
Java bean wrappers, EJB, 398
Java Integrated Development Environment, WSSD and, 178
Java perspective, WSAD, 191-192
Java runtime, Resource Analyzer, 705
Java Virtual Machine Profiler Interface. *See* JVMPI
java.io.Serializable interface, session management and, 302
java.lang.System class, servlet collaboration and, 290
java2wsdl.bat, 509-511
JavaBeans, WSSD and, 178
JavaMail, enabling, 561-563
javax.servlet package, 260-263
javax.servlet.http package, 260-263
JCA (J2EE Connector Architecture), 7
JCA (Java Connector Architecture), 571. *See also* J2C
JDBC (Java Database Connectivity), 326
connection pools, configuring, 558-559
drivers, updating with XMLConfig, 789
providers, configuring, 559-560

JDK (Java Development Kit), 127, 130
  installation, different versions, 147
  WSAD and, 139
JDK switching, WSSD and, 178
JIT (Just In Time) compiler, tuning, 693
JMS (Java Messaging Services), 3, 163
  configuring, 565-571
JMSAdmin.bat file, updating, 566
JNDI (Java Naming and Directory Interface), 366
  connection pools and, 558
  troubleshooting, 725-726
JNDI (Java Native Directory Interface), admin server and, 28
JRE (Java Runtime Environment), 130
  Java code testing, 234-236
JRE switching, WSSD and, 179
JSP (Java Server Pages), 3, 323
  Almost Free Cruise, 348-351
  calling from a servlet, 340
  comments, 336-337
  custom actions, 343-347
  declarations, 335
  directives, 334-335
    taglib, 343
  dynamic content in, 333-338
  dynamic Web pages and, 325
  expressions, 337
  implicit objects, 337-338
  interactions, 338-341
  invoking by URL, 338
  invoking from another JSP, 340-341
  MVC pattern and, 166
  running, 330-333
  scripting, 337
  scriptlets, 336
  servlets, calling from, 338-340
  specification differences, 347-348
  Studio Page Designer, 224-229
  syntax, 333-338
  tag libraries, descriptors, 345-347
  tags, 341-342
    tag handlers, 344-345
  WSAD environment and, 328-330
  XSLT and, 467
JTA (Java Transaction API), 420
JTS (Java Transaction Service), 420
JUnit, unit testing and, 169-170
JVM (Java Virtual Machine), 33
  horizontal cloning, 668-675
  tuning, 693
  vertical cloning, 667-668
  WAS topology, 173
JVMPI (Virtual Machine Profiler Interface), 694

L

large scale session management
  multirow access, 313
  overflows, 313
  persistent sessions, 312
layering applications, 166-168
layers, design and, 448
LDAP (Lightweight Directory Access Protocol)
  user repositories, security, 647-652
  WAP installation and, 91
lifecycle
  of a servlet, 264
  of entity beans, 369
  of stateful session beans, 372-373
  of stateless session beans, 371-372
  SOAP development lifecycle, 499-502

Link Manager, WSSD and, 179
Links view, Web perspective (WSAD), 191
load-balancing, 552
locate action (XMLConfig), 776
Location Service Daemon. See LSD, 542
locking, transactions, 422-423
Log Analyzer, 742-744
  troubleshooting, 724
logging property file, updating, 717
logs
  databases, tuning, 692
  installation verification, 112-113
  Resource Analyzer, 713-714
  reviewing for troubleshooting, 730-734
  troubleshooting
    Admin Server, 719-720
    application server, 720-721
    HTTP Server, 722
    installation, 718
    plug-in, 722-723
  types of, 716-718
loop termination, coding and, 451
LSD (Location Service Daemon), 28, 542

M

many-to-many relationships, EJBs, 414
mapping
  bottom-up, 409
  Composers and Converters, 408
  EJB-RDB mapping tool, 408-417
  meet-in-the middle, 409
  top-down, 409-410
  types, 408-409
maximum heap size, 451
meet-in-the-middle development
  EJBs, 413
  Web services, 484
  mapping, 409
memory
  cache size, management, sessions, 595
  garbage collection, JVM tuning, 693
  heap memory, 451
  heap size, JVM tuning, 693
  management, sessions, 595
  sessions, reducing overhead, 597
Merant SequeLink Server and Driver, 420
messages
  virutal hosts, 555
  WSDL, 508
messaging, implementation, 163
method-permission tag, 439, 440
methods
  addCookie( ), 294
  destroy( ), 263
    HttpServlet class, 272
  doDelete( ), 263
  doGet( ), 263
    HttpServlet class, 271
  doHead( ), 263
  doPost( ), 263
    HttpServlet class, 271
  doPut( ), 263
  doTrace( ), 263
  EJB
    marking as read-only, 453
    pass-by-reference, 453
    pass-by-value, 453
    Resource Analyzer, 705

flushBuffer( ), 277
forward( ), 286
getAttribute( ), 283, 306
getAttributeNames( ), 283
getBufferSize( ), 276
getContextPath( ), 275
getCookie( ), 294
getCreationTime( ), 303
getId( ), 303
getInitParameter( ), 283
getInitParameterNames( ), 283
getIntHeader( ), 275
getLastAccessedTime( ), 303
getMaxInactiveInterval( ), 303
getNamedDispatcher( ), 285
getParameterNames( ), 273
getParameterValues( ), 273
getPathInfo( ), 275
getRequestDispatcher( ), 284
getResource( ), 284
getResourceAsStream( ), 284
getServletInfo( ), HttpServlet class, 272
getSession( ), 302
include( ), 285
init( ), 263
  HttpServlet class, 271
invalidate( ), 303
isCommitted( ), 277
isNew( ), 303
Java, 233
overloaded, 441
removeAttribute( ), 283
reset( ), 277
sendError( ), 278
sendRedirect( ), 277, 286, 340
service( ), 263
  HttpServlet class, 271
ServletContext, 283
ServletPath( ), 275
setAttribute( ), 283, 306
setBufferSize( ), 277
setContentType( ), 278
setLocale( ), 278
setMaxInactiveInterval( ), 303
wscpCommand interface, 763-764

Methods page, EJB Extension Editor, 380
migration
  common migration, 93-102
  from WebSphere version, 92-93
  WSAD early versions, 136-137
models
  MVC pattern, 165
  WAP, 171
modules
  application client, 619
  EJBs, 614-617
  Web, 617-619
monitoring performance
  Introscope, 697-699
  Panorama, 699-701
  Resource Analyzer, 703-705
MTS (Microsoft's Transaction Server), 354
multirow access, session management, 313
MVC (Model View Controller), 282
  design and, 448
  pattern, 165-166
    JSPs (JavaServer Pages), 166

N

NAICS (North American Industry Classification System), 512

naming EJB containers, 366
Navigator view, J2EE (WSAD), 190
Network Dispatcher, 6
nodes, 28
  Admin Console
    creating application servers, 544
    starting and stopping, 544
  WAS topology, 172-174
  wscp, connecting to remote, 755
non-SSL transport, Web server plug-in, 556-557
no-output comments, JSP, 337
n-tier programming, WAP models, 171

O

object persistence, 359
objects
  distributed logic objects, RPC implementation, 160-163
  DTDs and, 775
  HttpServletRequest, 260
    data transfer and, 272-275
  HttpServletResponse, 260, 266, 276-278
  HttpSession object, session management and, 302-311
  referencing, wscp, 754
  sessions, reducing size, 596
  wscp (WebSphere Control Program), 749-750
    getting list of, 757-758
    help with, 756
object-to-relational mapping, entity beans, 370
OLT (Object Lvevl Trace), troubleshooting, 724
OMG (Object Management Group), transactions and, 420
one-to-many relationships, EJBs, 414
one-to-one relationships, EJBs, 414
online help, wscp, 755
operations, WSDL, 508
optimization
  application server, 695
    optimizing EJB container, 696-697
    passing methods (EJBs), 697
    setting application parameters, 696
    setting container thread size, 695
    setting URL invocation cache, 695-696
  issues, 689-690
    database tuning, 691-693
    HTTP server settings, 690-691
    JVM tuning, 693
    strategy, 690
  methodology, 688-689
  Web module, 456-458
ORB (Object Request Broker)
  CORBA, 357
  EJB containers, 697
OSE (Open Servlet Engine), 7, 29
OTS (Object Transaction Server), transactions and, 420
Outline view, WSAD
  J2EE perspective, 190
  Java perspective, 191
output comments, JSP, 336
output streams, encryption, 289
overflows (session management), 313, 585-587
overloaded methods, 441

P

packages
  javax.servlet, 260, 263
  javax.servlet.http, 260, 263
  list of, 740
Packages view, Java perspective (WSAD), 191
packaging, 427, 612. *See also* application assembly; application packaging
Page Designer, WSSD and, 178
Panorama, 699-701
parameters
  JVM tuning, 693
  servlet engine, WAS topology, 174
pass-by-reference methods, 453
pass-by-value methods, 453
path elements, requests, 275
patterns, design and, 448
PDF (Portable Document Format) files, 464
performance
  application server, 695
    optimizing EJB container, 696-697
    passing methods (EJBs), 697
    setting application parameters, 696
    setting container thread size, 695
    setting URL invocation cache, 695-696
  dynamic caching, 683
    Edge Server proxy server, 684-685
    enabling, 686-687
    principles of operation, 685
  Edge Server, external caches, 688
  monitoring
    Introscope, 697-699
    Panorama, 699-701
  optimization issues, 689-690
    database tuning, 691-693
    HTTP server settings, 690-691
    JVM tuning, 693
    strategy, 690
  optimization methodology, 688-689
  Resource Analyzer, 703-705
    console, 707
    Data Monitoring pane, 708-709
    data organization, 705
    instrumentation levels, 709-710
    launching, 706-707
    logging and replaying data, 713-714
    Resource Selection pane, 708
    running, 710-713
    supported resources, 705
  server groups, configuring, 665
  sessions, 594
    cache size, 595
    changing timeout intervals, 597
    configuring connection pool, 596
    invalidating, 596
    memory management, 595
    multirow, 597
    reducing I/O overhead, 595
    reducing memory overhead, 597
    reducing object size, 596
  workload management considerations, 658-660
permissions
  method-permission tag, 439-440
  WSAD installation, 128-130

persistence
  bean-managed, entity beans, 369
  container-managed, entity beans, 369
  EJB containers, 365
  object persistence, 359
persistent sessions, 312, 583-585
  creating, 587-591
  manual configuration, 592-593
  manual updates, 593
  time-based writes, 593-594
perspectives, Server perspective, server object management, 239-253
perspectives, WSAD, 188-192, 199-202
  customizing, 196-197
  J2EE perspective, 189-190
  Java perspective, 191-192
  Web perspective, 191
ping action (XMLConfig), 776
pinging servers, 546
planning, workload management considerations, 657-660
plug-in regeneration, WAP installation, 118
plugin-cfg.xml, 550
plug-ins, 29-31
  logs, troubleshooting and, 722-723
  regenerating, XMLConfig, 792
  synchronizing, 546
points of failure, 728
policies, workload management, 664
pop-up error messages, 730
portability, servlets vs CGI programs, 261
Portable Document Format (PDF) files, 464
ports
  addresses, 91
  Admin Console, 543
  application servers, verifying uniqueness, 545
  WAP installation, 88-89
  WSDL, 509
portTypes, WSDL, 508
post-condition processing, 289
PostScript files, XML and, 464
power, servlets vs CGI programs, 261
precondition processing, 289
preinstall checklist for WAP installation, 86-92
prepared statements (SQL), caching, 692
primary key class, EJBs entity beans, 362
principals, 625
Private registry, 512
private UDDI, installation, 491
proactive design practices, 448-449
proactive practices, Java, 451
process flow, servlets, 263-264
processing
  post-condition processing, 289
  precondition processing, 289
programmatic security
  EJBs, 644-645
  servlets, 643-644
proof-of-concept wizards, 203-214
properties, J2C connection factories, 574
properties file (wscp), invoking, 754-755
Properties view, J2EE perspective (WSAD), 190

protocols, stateless, 299
proxies, RPCs and, 161
proxy servers, Edge Server, 684-685
pserver, CVSNT installation and, 143
public methods, wscpCommand interface, 763-764
public modifiers, element, 234
publishing
- services, 483
- to UDDI repository, 512
- Web services, 59

publishing services, 483

Q–R

QoS (Quality of Service), Web services and, 57
qualified names, wscpCommand interface, 764-766

random workload management policy, 664
RAR (Resource Adapter Archive), 573
RDB to XML mapping editor, 472
Read Committed transactions, 422
Read Uncommitted transactions, 422
reading cookies from client, 294
Readme file, WAP installation and, 83-84
redirection, 286-288
refactoring, 233
- Web development and, 168-169

referencing objects, wscp, 754
refresh interval, Web server plug-in, 553
Regan WebShpere Plugin, 546
relational databases, EJB-RDB mapping, Almost Free Cruise, 379-380
relationships, EJBs, 414-415
- Almost Free Cruise, 415-417

Relationships page, EJB Extension Editor, 380
reliability, workload management considerations, 658-660
remote data-management solutions, 164-165
remote interfaces, EJBs and, 362
remote nodes, connecting to with wscp, 755
remote presentation, 159-160
removeAttribute( ) method, 283
Repeatable Read transactions, 422
repositories
- administrative, backing up, 785
- domains, administration of, 748
- exporting and importing information, 771

request.getCookies( ), 292
RequestDispatcher API, 273, 281, 284-286
requests
- attributes, getting/setting, 273
- path elements, 275

reset( ) method, 277
resource adapters, configuring, 574
Resource Analyzer, 703-705
- console, 707
  - Data Monitoring pane, 708-709
  - Resource Selection pane, 708
- instrumentation levels, 709-710
- launching, 706
  - from Admin Console, 706
  - from command prompt, 707
  - from Start Menu, 706
- logging and replaying data, 713-714
- performance data organization, 705
- running, 710-713
- supported resources, 705

resource factories, 561
resource manager, transactions, 419

resources
  configuring, 557-558
    data sources, 560-561
    enabling JavaMail, 561-563
    JDBC connection pools, 558-559
    JDBC providers, 559-560
    JMS (Java Messaging Services), 565
    JMS MQ support, 566-571
  creating, XMLConfig, 783
  deleting, XMLConfig, 784-785
  Resource Analyzer, 705
  updating, XMLConfig, 784
  URL providers, 564
  WAS, 37
  XMLConfig actions, 776-777
response headers, cookies, 294
response.addCookie( ), 292
responses, redirection, 286-288
responsibilities
  Web development, 156
  WSAD, 148-149
restart action (XMLConfig), 776
result substitution (Tcl), 752
rewriting URLs, session tracking and, 301-302
RMI (remote method invocation)
  EJB architecture and, 358-359
  Java best practices, 452
  RPCs, 161
  UID, 300
RMIC (Remote Method Invocation Compiler) Code, 383
roles, 625
  bean relationships, 414
  J2EE application packaging, 603
  Web development, 156
  WSAD, 148-149
root element, XML document, 431
round robin, workload management policy, 664
round robin servlet request distribution, 662
routes, 551
RPCs
  EJBs and, 162
  implementation, 160-163
  proxies and, 161
  SOAP and, 501
runtime environments
  project types, 239
  server instances, 238

S

safety, servlets vs CGI programs, 261
SAX (Simple API Extension), 496
scalability, workload management, 659
scalable application model, 326
Schemas, XML, 464
SCM (source control management), 139
SCM (Supply Chain Management), 4
scripting, JSP, 337
scriptlets, JSP, 336
scripts, wscp
  creating, 759
  executing, 754
  migrating from version 3.5.x, 766-767
  running, 759-762
SDLC (Software Development Life Cycle), 70-71
Search view, Java perspective (WSAD), 192
SearchBean methods, 399
searches
  text, WSSD and, 179
  XML, 464

security, 438
  AAT, 645-647
  concepts, 625
  EJB containers, 365, 697
  EJBs, 439
    adding to, 641-642
    descriptors, 442-445
    method-permission tag, 439-440
    overloaded methods, 441
    security-role declaration, 439
  Java, authentication and authorization, 627
  overview, 626
  programmatic
    EJBs, 644-645
    servlets, 643-644
  servlets, adding to, 641
  sessions, 594
  user repositories, LDAP, 647-652
  WebSphere components, responsibilities, 652-653
  WSAD application development, 628-629
    additional forms, 633
    deployment descriptors, 633-640
    form-based authentication, 631-632
    login.jsp form, 632
    logout.jsp form, 633
    testing, 629-641
Security Center, configuring, 649-652
security collaborators, 653
sendError( ) method, 278
sendRedirect( ) method, 277, 286, 340
serializable transactions, 422
serialization, Java best practices, 452
server affinity, 581
server groups, 38-39
  application server clones, creating, 666-667
  configuring, 665
  workload management, 660
  XMLConfig, 791-792
server instances, Server perspective, 241-243
server load management, 661-662
server objects, Server perspective, 239-253
Server perspective
  configuration, 241-243
  server configuration, 244-246
  server instances, 241-243
  server object management, 239-253
  server project creation, 241
server projects, Server perspective, 241
servers
  Admin, 542
    activating traces, 739
  admin server, 27-28
  application
    activating traces, 736-739
    adding with XMLConfig, 787-789
    creating with Admin Console, 544-545
    creating with XMLConfig, 783
    deleting with XMLConfig, 784-785
    logs, troubleshooting and, 720-721
    performance optimization, 695-697
    starting and stopping, 545
    starting and stopping enterprise applications, 546
    starting and stopping with XMLConfig, 785-786
    types of authentication, 627
    types of authorization, 627
    updating with XMLConfig, 784

configuration
Server perspective, 244-246
WSSD and, 179
Edge Server
dynamic caching, 685-687
external cache, 688
features, 683
file extensions, 246
instances, Almost Free Cruise, 384
pinging, 546
proxy, Edge Server dynamic caching, 684-685
Web application servers, 157
Web servers, supported, 87-88
service brokers, 58, 482
service coding, SOAP, 504-505
service descriptions, UDDI, 517-518
service providers, 59, 482-483
service registry, 58
service requestors, 59, 482-483
Web services, 59
service( ) method, 263
HttpServlet class, 271
services
application layering, 167
application layering and, 167
defining, 167
EJB containers, 365
naming, 366
persistence, 365
security, 365
transactions, 365
external services, 158
infrastructure services, 158
standardizing, 167
transaction services, 421
See also Web services
Servlet API, 259-264
RequestDispatcher, 281
ServletContext, 281
servlet engines, WAS topology, 172
parameters, 174
Servlet Wizard, 230-231
ServletContext API, 281
methods, 283
ServletContext interface, 282-284
ServletRequests, 263
ServletResponses, 263
servlets, 160, 262
caching and, 288
calling from JSP, 338-340
calling JSPs from, 340
CGI program comparison, 260-261
chaining, 291-292
collaboration, 290-291
controllers and, 282
Cookie API, 292-293
counter servlet source code, 267
FileServing, 608
filtering, 291-292
hit count servlet, 307-310
interaction techniques, 290-292
Invoker, 608
lifecycle, 264
multiple, WAP models, 171-172
process flow, 262-264
sample code, 265-270
security
adding, 641
programmatic, 643-644
sessions, 579
single, WAP models, 171-172

Snoop, 122
monitoring, 710-713
virtual hosts, 554
wizards, 178
workload management, 662
WSAD, 229-231
session affinity, 552
session beans, 371, 375
Almost Free Cruise, 392-393
updating, 399-400
stateful, 372-373
stateless, 371-372
workload management, 664
session clustering, 581
session management, 578-579
Almost Free Cruise application, 319-321
application server clones, adding, 596
configuring, 582-583
connection pool, 596
creating persistent sessions, 587-591
manual persistent session updates, 593
manual persistent sessions, 592-593
persisting sessions, 583-585
session overflows, 585-587
time-based writes, 593-594
cookies, 579
HttpSession object and, 302-311
java.io.Serializable interface and, 302
large scale
multirow access, 313
overflows, 313
persistent sessions, 312
overview, 300-312
performance, 594
cache size, 595
changing timeout intervals, 597
invalidating sessions, 596
memory management, 595
multirow persistence, 597
reducing I/O overhead, 595
reducing memory overhead, 597
reducing object size, 596
security, 594
single/multirow support, 592
Snoop servlet and, 303-306
SSL tracking, 580
URL rewriting, 580
Session Manager (WAS), 314-319
session objects, values, displaying, 304-305
session overfolws, 585-587
session persistence, database tuning, 692
session tracking
Cookie API, 300
hidden fields, 301
URL rewriting and, 301-302
SessionBean interface, 362
sessions, 299, 579
access, 303
application data use, 306-307
persistent, large scale session management, 312
setAttribute( ) method, 283, 306
setBufferSize( ) method, 277
setContentType( ) method, 278
setLocale( ) method, 278
setMaxInactiveInterval( ) method, 303

setupMQEnv.bat file, 567
SGML (Standard Generalized Markup Language), 461
silent install, 123-125
SimpleHTTPServlet source code, 269-270
SingleThreadModel interface, 264
Snoop servlet, 122
  HttpSession object, 303-306
  monitoring, 710-713
  session management, 303-306
SOA (Service-Oriented Architecture), 52
SOAP (Simple Object Access Protocol), 7, 20, 60-62, 485
  AE installation, 485-489
  Apache SOAP toolkit, 495
    administration, 496-498
    AXIS, 496
    client coding, 502-504
    development lifecycle, 499-502
    service coding, 504-505
  client coding, 502-504
  client development, 524-526
  development lifecycle, 499-502
    HTTP and, 501
    RPCs, 501
    SOAP encoding, 501
    SOAP envelopes, 500
  envelopes, 500
  service coding, 504-505
  Web services and, 56
SOAP Server Manager, 487
SOAPEAREnabler, 522-523
software
  IP sprayers, 661
  WSAD installation, 131
software requirements, AE (Application Server), 80
source code
  CookieCounterServlet, 294-297
  counter servlet, 267
  CruiseShip Java class, 507
  doGet( ) implementation, session object values display, 304-305
  ejb-jar.xml, 429
  Hello World servlet, 265-266
  HTML entry form servlet, 268
  ibm-ejb-jar-bnd.xmi, 382
  JSP scriptlet and JSP expressions in Hello World, 329
  servlet samples, 265-270
  SimpleHTTPServlet, 269-270
  TemperatureImplClient, SOAP client code, 502
  TemperatureImplClient.java, 525
  tracking user visits with HttpSession object, 307-309
  UddiClient.java, 514
  wsdl2Java, 510
  XML data descriptions, 463-464
  XML validations with schema document, 465-466
  XML, simple document, 460
source control managment. *See* SCM
specifications, XML, 464-466
SQL (Structured Query Language), prepared statements, 692
SSL (Secure Socket Layer), 8
SSL tracking, session management, 580
stacks, thread stacks, 451
start action (XMLConfig), 776
state data, access, 303
state information. *See* session management
stateful session beans, 372-373
stateless protocols, 299

stateless session beans, 371-372
stop action (XMLConfig), 776
stopforrestart action (XMLConfig), 776
streams
  compression, 289
  decompression, 289
String getErrorInfo( ) method, 764
string layering, applications, 166
string processing, 452
Studio Application Developer, 606
Studio Page Designer, 224-229
stylesheets, XML, 472-479
substitution variables, XMLConfig, 786-787
synchronization, plug-in, 546
syntax
  JSPs, 333-338
  Tcl commands, 750-751
  traces, 740-741
  wscp commands, 753-754
  XMLConfig, 779
system design, workload management considerations, 657-660
system requirements, WAP installation, Win2000/NT, 79-80

T

tables, WSAD, Almost Free Cruise, 377-378
tag libraries, JSP, 341-342
  descriptors, 345-347
taglib directive, 343
tags
  JSP, 341-342
    tag handlers, 344-345
  XML, 772
Tasks view
  J2EE perspective (WSAD), 190
  Java perspective (WSAD), 191
Tcl, command syntax, 750-751
TCPTunneling, WSAD and, 526-528
team repository, 139. *See also* SCM
team support, WSSD and, 179
test phase, Web services development, 484
testing
  debugging and, 255-258
  EJB Test Client, Almost Free Cruise, 387-392
  environment setup, 238-253
  environments, planning, 151
  security, WSAD applications, 629-631
  WSAD application development, security, 640-641
text searches, WSSD and, 179
thin clients, 159-160
thread stacks, 451
Thumbnail view, Web perspective (WSAD), 191
timeouts, sessions, 579
  changing intervals, 597
TM (Transaction Manager), 164
TM data type, 64
tModels, 516-517
Tomcat runtime environment, server instances, 238
tool provider (J2EE role), 603
toolbars, Admin Console, 544
tooling, 509-511
  WSDL, 528

tools
deployment, 74
development tools, 128
WSTK, 69
top-down development
EJBs, 410-412
Web services, 484
top-down mapping, 409-410
topology, 39-43
application topology, 172-175
troubleshooting and, 726-727
TP monitor (transaction processing monitor), 164
tracefiles, 732
traces
activating
Admin Ser
ver, 739
application servers, 736-739
Admin Server, troubleshooting startup, 741-742
syntax, 740-741
troubleshooting, 724-725
tracking sessions. *See* session tracking
transaction context, 419
transaction management, 417-418
declarative, 437
declarative transaction management, 420
explicit transaction management, 420
transaction manager, 419
transaction processing models, 163-164
transactional clients, 419
transactional objects, 419
transactions, 163-164, 407
ACID, 163, 407, 418
architecture, 420-422
attributes, 421-422
dirty reads, 422
EJB containers, 365
EJBs, 420
isolation levels, 422-423
JTA (Java Transaction API), 420
JTS, 420
locking, 422-423
Read Committed, 422
Read Uncommitted, 422
Repeatable Read, 422
Resource Analyzer, 705
serializable, 422
services, 421
setting, Almost Free Cruise, 423-425
two-phase commits, 419-420
units of work, 418
use, rationalizing (EJB development), 453
transform phase, Web services development, 484
transformations, XSLT, XPath and, 468-471
transport options, Web server plug-in, 555
troubleshooting
Admin Console, 723-724
configuring messages, 729-730
Admin Server, startup, 741-742
Distributed Debugger, 724
Event Viewer and, 730-732
installation, 118-120

isolating problems, 734-735
JNDI, 725-726
Log Analyzer, 724, 742-744
logs
Admin Server, 719-720
application server, 720-721
HTTP Server, 722
installation, 718
plug-in, 722-723
reviewing log files, 730-734
types of, 716-718
OLT (Object Level Trace), 724
pop-up error messages, 730
steps
problem categories, 728
topology and, 726-727
tools, 716, 728-729
trace syntax, 740-741
traces, 724-725
two-phase commits, transactions, 419-420

U

UDDI (Universal Description Discovery Integration), 20, 57, 62-64, 485
information gathering, 513-514
overview, 511-515
private, installation, 491
registry
installation, 491-493
installation, verification, 493-495
service brokers, 482
service descriptions, 517-518
tModels, 516-517
UDDI4J, 485
UIDs (unique IDs), 300
UML (Unified Modeling Language), design and, 449
UnauthorizedSessionRequestException interface, 311
unit test environments, WSSD and, 179
unit testing, JUnit and, 169-170
units of works, transactions, 418
UNSPSC (Universal Standards Products and Service), 512
update action (XMLConfig), 776
URL providers, 564
URL rewriting, session management, 580
URLs (Uniform Resource Locators)
JSPs, invoking, 338
rewriting, session tracking and, 301-302
user repositories, security, LDAP, 647-652
userids
characteristics, 82-83
creating, 81-82
WAP installation, Win2000/NT, 81-83
users
groups, 625
principals, 625

V

variable substitution, XMLConfig, 786-787
VCS (Version Control System), 127
verification, WSAD installation, 137-138
vertical cloning, 667-668
AlmostFreeCruise, 670
view bean model, 203

Viewers, Workbench, 186
views
  MVC pattern, 165
  WSAD, 187-188
    fast view, 198
virtual hosts, 31-32
  changing, XMLConfig, 790
  configuring, 553-555
  WAS topology, 173-174
VisualAge for Java, 14, 233

W

WAP
  installation, 108-112
    admin.config file, 114-115
    Administration Server, 115-118
    host filenames, 89
    logs, 112-113
    migrating from earlier WebSphere version, 92-93
    migrating, common migration, 93-102
    plug-in regeneration, 118
    ports, 88-89
    sample applications, 120-121
    silent install, 123-125
    troubleshooting, 118-120
    verification, 112-113
    Win2000/NT platforms, 78-92
  models, 171
WAP models
  n-tier programming, 171
  servlets, 171-172
WAR (Web Archive) files, 35
  deployment descriptors, 602
  WSAD and, 219-223
WAS (WebSphere Application Server)
  administration, 44-45
    admin.config file, 48
    Administrative Console, 45-47
    administrative repository, 45
  architecture, 24-41
    admin server, 27-28
    EJB modules, 34
    enterprise applications, 34
    HTTP server, 29-31
    JVMs, 33
    nodes, 28
    plug-ins, 29-31
    resources, 37
    server clones, 38-39
    server groups, 38-39
    server organization, 35-36
    topology, 39-43
    virtual hosts, 31-32
    WAR files, 35
  default server, 35
  development tools, 13-16
  EJB container, 36
  new features, 4.0 version, 7-9
  packaging for 4.0, 10
  runtime environment, server instances, 238
  Session Manager, 314-319
  supporting products, 17-20
  topology, 172-175
    EJB containers, 174
  version comparison, 9
WASD (WebSphere Studio Application Developer), 69-70
WCS (WebSphere Commerce Suite), 5
Web application archive packaging, WSSD and, 179

Web application models, 325-327
  EJB application model, 326
  J2EE, 327
  JDBC, 326
  scalable, 326
Web application servers, 157
Web applications
  architecture, 6
  Resource Analyzer, 705
  WAS topology, 173
Web components, WebSphere compliance with J2EE, 605
Web Container Service, 36
Web development
  e-business application framework, 156-158
  MVC pattern, 165-166
  refactoring, 168-169
  WSAD and, 199-202
Web development process, client-side processing vs server-side processing, 158-159
Web Module Wizard, 612
Web modules, 617-619
  optimization, 456-458
Web pages
  HTML, Studio Page Designer and, 224-229
  JSP, Studio Page Designer, 224-229
Web perspective, WSAD, 191
Web Project Wizard, 200-202
Web Seal, 18
Web server plug-in
  configuring, 549-555
  installing, 553
  internal transport, 555
  locating, 550
  non-SSL transport, 556-557
  refresh interval, 553
  regenerating, 552-553
  transport options, 555
Web servers supported, 87-88
Web services, 20
  architecture, 55-57
  benefits, 52-54
  binding, 59, 483
  components, 58-59, 482
  development, 484
  find operations, 483
  IBM tools, 484-495
  implementations, 59-64
  model overview, 57-65
  operations, 59
  overview, 481
  publishing, 59, 483
  QoS and, 57
  service brokers, 58, 482
  service providers, 59, 482-483
  service requestors, 59, 482-483
  SOAP and, 56, 60-62
  UDDI and, 62-64
  WSSD and, 178
  XML and, 56
Web-development process overview, 156-158
WEB-INF folder, application packaging, 602
WebSphere Studio Site Developer, 128
WebSphere
  advantages over competition, 681, 682
  architecture, 542
  overview, 3-13
  product descriptions, 5
WebSphere Edge Server, 6
WebSphere Studio, 14-15

WebSphere Studio Application Developer, 128
WebSphere Transcoding Publisher, 5
WES (WebSphere Everyplace), 5
Win2000/NT, WAP installation, 78-79
  FixPak 4.0.3, 84-86
  preinstall checklist, 86-92
  Readme file, 83-84
  system requirements, 79-80
  userids, 81-83
wizards
  Admin Console, 549
  Application, 611
  Application Client, 612
  Create a JSP File Wizard, 329
  Database Connection Wizard, 205-211
  Database Web Page Wizard, 203-205
  development-process, 72-73
  EJB Module, 611
  EJB to RDB Mapping Wizard, 408-409
  proof-of-concept wizards, 203-214
  Servlet, 230-231
  servlets, 178
  Web Module, 612
  Web Project Wizard, 200-202
WLM (workload management), 580-581
workbench, WSAD, 183-186
  options, 185
  persectives, 189
  perspectives, customizing, 196-197
  Viewers, 186
workload management
  EJBs, 663-664
    entity beans, 664
    session beans, 664
  planning considerations, 657-660
  policy, 664
  servlets, 662
  server groups and clones, 660
  server load, 661-662
  types, 660
workspace, WSAD, 180-182
  creating, 376-377
WPS (WebSphere Portal Server), 5
WSAD (WebSphere Application Developer), 15-16, 237, 520
  AddressBook sample demo, 534-538
  application development
    additional forms, 633
    deployment descriptors, 633-640
    form-based authentication, 631-632
    login.jsp form, 632
    logout.jsp form, 633
    security, 628-629
    security testing, 629-631
    testing, 640-641
  CSSs, 229
  CVSNT, setup for, 144-146
  data sources, Almost Free Cruise, 385-387
  databases, Almost Free Cruise, 377-378
  deployment, 231-232

EAR files, 219-223, 522-523
editors, 192,-198
EJB Extension Editor, Almost Free Cruise, 380-384
external editors, adding, 196
fast view, 198
file types, 194
HTTP/FTP imports, 217-223
infopop, 192
installation, 133
 from CD-ROM, 133-135
 from developer image files, 135
 hardware, 131
 migration from earlier versions, 136-137
 permissions, 128-130
 preparations, 131
 software, 131
 verification, 137-138
JAR files, 219-223
JDK and, 139
JSP development, 328-330
migrating from other versions, 136-137
perspectives, 188-202
 J2EE, 189-190
 Java, 191-192
 Web, 191
projects, 182-183, 199-202
 building, 215-217
 full builds, 216
 incremental builds, 216
responsibilities, 148-149
roles, 148-149
server instances, Almost Free Cruise, 384
service projects, creating, 520-522
servlets, 229-231
SOAP client development, 524-526
SOAPEAREnabler, 522-523
tables, Almost Free Cruise, 377-378
TCPTunneling, 526-528
testing, environment setup, 238-253
views, 187-188
WAR files, 219-223
Web development, 199-202
workbench, 183-186
 options, 185
 perspectives, 196-197
Workbench, Viewers, 186
workspace, 180-182
 creating, 376-377
WSDL generation, 528-534
WSSD comparison, 178-179
XML application development, 471-472
ZIP files, 219-223
wscp (WebSphere Control Program), 748
 admin server and, 28
 benefits, 749
 command shell, 754
 command syntax, 753-754
 compared to Admin Console, 748
 error handling, 758
 launching, 752
 limitations, 749
 object types, 749-750
 objects
  getting list of, 757-758
  help with, 756
 online help, accessing, 755

properties file, invoking, 754-755
remote nodes, connecting to, 755
scripts
creating, 759
executing, 754
migrating from version 3.5.x, 766-767
running, 759-762
wscpCommand interface, 762
constructors, 763
public methods, 763-764
qualified names, 764-766
WscpResult evalCommand( ) method, 763
WSDL (Web Services Definition Language), 20, 56, 56-60, 485, 505-509
data types, 507
file generation, 68
tooling, 528
WSAD to generate, 528-534
wsdl2java.bat, 509-511
WSDL4J, 485
WSFL (Web Services Flow Language), 65
WSIL (Web Services Inspection Language), 483-485, 518-519
WSSD (WebSphere Studio Site Developer), 16
CSS Designer, 178
databases and, 179
Design Gallery, 178
Image Creator/Editor and, 178
integrated Web browser and, 179
Java Integrated Development Environment, 178
JavaBeans, 178
JDK switching, 178
JRE switching, 179
Link Manager and, 179
Page Designer, 178
server configuration and, 179
team support and, 179
text searches and, 179
unit test environments and, 179
Web application archive packaging, 179
Web services and, 178
WSAD comparison, 178-179
XML, 178
WSTK (IBM Web Services Toolkit), 69, 484-485
installation, 489-490
WSXL (Web Services Experience Language), 65
WTE (Web Traffice Express), 6

X–Y–Z

XML (Extensible Markup Language), 33, 459
application development
development tools, 471-472
WSAD and, 471-472
deployment descriptors and, 429-431, 633
assembly-descriptor element, 437-438
document body, 432
document header, 431
enterprise beans, 432-433
environment entries, 435-436
referencing beans, 435
resourcing references, 436
DTD (Document Type Definition), 429, 464, 772-775
flexibility, 464
messaging, Web services and, 56

output formats, 464
overview, 459-466, 772
advantages of, 462-464
need for XML, 461-462
Schemas, 464
searches, 464
specifications, 464-466
stylesheets, 472-479
Web services model and, 64
WSSD and, 178
XPath, 465
XML (Extensible Markup Language) messaging
Web services and, 56
XML editor, 471
XML Schema Editor, 471
XMLConfig, 770
actions, 776-777
admin server and, 28
administrative respoitory, backing up, 785
application servers
adding, 787-789
starting and stopping, 785-786
arguments, 780
command syntax, 779
compared to Admin Console, 770-771
creating resources, 783
deleting resources, 784-785
documentation, 778
domains, deploying, 790-792
exporting information, 781-782
importing information, 782-783
JDBC
updating data sources, 789
updating drivers, 789
plug-in, regenerating, 792
running, 777-780
server groups and cloning, 791-792
substitution variables, 786-787
updating resources, 784
usefulness of, 771
virtual hosts, changing, 790
XMLto XML mapping editor, 472
XPath, 465
XSLT transformations, 468-471
XSL Trace editor, 471
XSLT
JSP and, 467
overview, 467
transformations, XPath and, 468-471
XSLT (Extensible StyleSheet Language Transformation) mechanism, 459

ZIP files, WSAD and, 219-223